Lecture Notes in Artificial Intelligence   1348

Subseries of Lecture Notes in Computer Science
Edited by J. G. Carbonell and J. Siekmann

Lecture Notes in Computer Science

Edited by G. Goos, J. Hartmanis and J. van Leeuwen

Springer
Berlin
Heidelberg
New York
Barcelona
Budapest
Hong Kong
London
Milan
Paris
Santa Clara
Singapore
Tokyo

Sam Steel Rachid Alami (Eds.)

Recent Advances in AI Planning

4th European Conference on Planning, ECP'97
Toulouse, France, September 24–26, 1997
Proceedings

Springer

Series Editors

Jaime G. Carbonell, Carnegie Mellon University, Pittsburgh, PA, USA
Jörg Siekmann, University of Saarland, Saarbrücken, Germany

Volume Editor

Sam Steel
University of Essex, Department of Computer Science
Wivenhoe Park, Colchester CO4 3SQ, UK
E-mail: sam@essex.ac.uk

Rachid Alami
LAAS/CNRS
7, Avenue du Colonel Roche, F-31077 Toulouse Cedex 4, France
E-mail: rachid@laas.fr

Cataloging-in-Publication Data applied for

Die Deutsche Bibliothek - CIP-Einheitsaufnahme

Recent advances in AI planning : 4th European conference ;
proceedings / ECP '97, Toulouse, France, September 24 - 26, 1997.
Sam Steel ; Rachid Alami (ed.). - Berlin ; Heidelberg ; New York ;
Barcelona ; Budapest ; Hong Kong ; London ; Milan ; Paris ; Santa
Clara ; Singapore ; Tokyo : Springer, 1997
  (Lecture notes in computer science ; Vol. 1348 : Lecture notes in
  artificial intelligence)
  ISBN 3-540-63912-8

CR Subject Classification (1991): I.2.8, I.2

ISSN 0302-9743
ISBN 3-540-63912-8 Springer-Verlag Berlin Heidelberg New York

© Springer-Verlag Berlin Heidelberg 1997
Printed in Germany

Typesetting: Camera ready by author
SPIN 10652689   06/3142 – 5 4 3 2 1 0   Printed on acid-free paper

Preface

ECP, the European Conference on Planning, grew from EWSP, the European Workshop on Planning. It is now the principal European meeting for planning in artificial intelligence. There were three previous meetings, EWSP '91 in St Augustin (Germany), EWSP '93 in Vadstena (Sweden), and EWSP '95 in Assisi (Italy). ECP '97 took place in Toulouse (France), hosted by LAAS (Laboratoire d'Analyse et d'Architecture des Systèmes). However, its appeal extends far wider than Europe: papers were submitted from Mexico to Korea. The range of topics is no narrower: almost all aspects of current artificial intelligence planning are represented among the 35 papers presented.

The conference was also very glad to hear from three invited speakers each with a great reputation in planning: Erik Sandewall, Tom Dean, and Malik Ghallab.

October 1997
Sam Steel
Rachid Alami

Organization

Programme Committee

Sam Steel (programme chairman)
Rachid Alami (local arrangements)

Sylvie Thiebaux	Christer Bäckström	Paolo Traverso
Joachim Hertzberg	Jana Koehler	Malik Ghallab
Eric Jacopin	Brian Drabble	Steve Hanks
Susanne Biundo	Mark Drummond	Louise Pryor
Ruth Aylett	Fahiem Bacchus	Alfredo Milani
Damian Lyons	Amedeo Cesta	Peter Haddawy
Dan Weld	Qiang Yang	Alessandro Saffiotti
Bernhard Nebel	Paul Scott	Maria Fox
John Bell	Robert Goldman	Gerry Kelleher
Murray Shanahan	Michael Beetz	Patrick Prosser
Philippe Morignot	Toby Walsh	Jon Spragg
Ian Gent	Claude Le Pape	

Reviewers

Werner Stephan	Angelo Oddi	T. Simeon
Felix Ingrand	Vu Ha	John Hallam
Philippe Baptiste	Marco Baioletti	Philip Kilby
Paul Shaw	Shlomo Zilberstein	Alessandro Cimatti
Luca Spalazzi	Massimo Benerecetti	Francesco Ricci
Paolo Bouquet	Marc Friedman	David E. Smith

ECP '97 benefited from the support and funding of

- The Région Midi-Pyrénées
- The Conseil Général de Haute Garonne
- The Mairie de Toulouse
- LAAS/CNRS
- The University of Essex

We are grateful to Mme Marie-Thérèse Ippolito (LAAS), Mme Jaqueline Som (LAAS) and Mme Sylvie Barrouquère (ADERMIP) for the organization of the conference.

Contents

Context Dependent Effects
in
Temporal Planning

Patrick Albers & Malik Ghallab

LAAS-CNRS
7, Av. Colonel Roche, 31077 Toulouse, France
email: {patrick,malik}@laas.fr

Abstract. A major problem in planning, as in most AI domains, is to find an adequate representation. In particular, there is the issue of which effects of an action should be specified unconditionally in its model and which can be stated conditionally with respect to the context. Indeed, most actions do have several different effects depending on the context in which they are executed.

In this paper, we propose an approach and different extensions in order to take into account context dependent effects into IxTeT, a temporal planner. Expressiveness requires a great flexibility of representation, but it may lead to a computational cost not compatible with a practically efficient planner. The proposed approach offers a slight extension in representation which enables to express conditional subtasks. Furthermore, empirical results show that this approach and the corresponding implementation provide also some efficiency benefits with respect to a domain description that details all unconditional action models.

Keywords: temporal planning, actions with context dependent effects

1 Introduction

In planning, a major difficulty is to find an appropriate representation of actions. In particular, the problem is to correctly describe all conditions and effects of an action. Classical planners based on STRIPS-like operators propose an approach where all changes must be specified explicitly. An action may have different effects depending on the context in which it is executed. Consider for example the motion of a robot; if one add the possibility of attaching a trailer to it, a model of the action *move* must consider the position of trailer and all the objects which are on it. Cases like *move without trailer*, *move with attached trailer*, *move with trailer and one object* represent different contexts of the *move* action. If we specify this problem in STRIPS-like operators, we must create as many *move* actions as contexts.

The first non-linear planner to take into account context dependent effects was SIPE [15]. It extends STRIPS representation using deduction operators, which are triggered at each planning step in order to complete the description of the plan. Pednault's Action Description Language (ADL) extends the classical representation [11][12]. Preconditions are partitioned into two sets: primary ones represent the usual preconditions of an action, and secondary ones define the contexts in which an action produces particular effects. The planner *Pedestal* was the first implementation of a linear planner using ADL [10]. It suffered however from a too large algorithmic complexity. The non-linear planner *UCPOP* handles a large subset of ADL; in particular it allows conditional effects [13]. UCPOP is a good compromise between efficiency and expressiveness. Indeed a rich representation is often a conflicting issue with efficiency considerations. One may limit the representation to keep a planner efficient.

This paper focuses on the extension of IxTeT a temporal planner. It proposes to generalize its representation in order to take into account context dependent effects. The following section summarizes the IxTeT planner. The proposed extension is explained in section 3. Finally, some experimental results showing the benefits of the approach are given.

2 IxTeT restricted representation

2.1 Representation

IxTeT is based on a reified logic formalism. It uses temporal and atemporal variables. The elementary primitive is the time-point [5]. IxTeT handles temporal symbolic constraints (precedence, simultaneity) and numeric constraints expressed by lower and upper bounds on the temporal distance between two points. A time-map manager maintains the consistency of the constraint network and answers queries about time-points.

Atemporal variables ranging over finite domains are managed in a variable constraint network. Propagated constraints are domain restrictions, equalities and inequalities between variable. Inequalities are propagated by a local path consistency algorithm.

The world is described by a set of multi-valued domain attributes, where each attribute is a functional term over atemporal variables. Two predicates are available in IxTeT. Predicate $event(att(x_1, ...) : (v_1, v_2), t)$ says that attribute $att(x_1, ...)$ changes its value instantaneously from v_1 to v_2 at time t. Predicate $hold(att(x_1, ...) : v, (t_1, t_2))$ asserts the persistence of the attribute $att(x_1, ...)$ to value v for $t : t_1 \leq t < t_2$. It is used in action models but also by the planner to manage causal links.

IxTeT manages resource predicates[8]. There are two types of resources: unsharable ones are single items with a unit capacity (e.g. a key), sharable resources (e.g. electricity) can be used simultaneously by different actions, not exceeding a total maximal capacity. Three operations are possible: $use(typ(r) : q, (t_1, t_2))$ borrows a part q of resource between time-points t_1 and t_2; $consume(typ(r) : q, t)$ and $produce(typ(r) : q, t)$ correspond to consuming and producing a quantity q of a resource at time t.

Planning operators in IxTeT are called tasks. Tasks are *deterministic* operators, without ramification effects. They are composed of: (1) a set of subtasks, (2) a set of events describing the changes of the world induced by the task, (3) a set of assertions (*hold*) to express conditions that should prevail during part of the task, (4) a set of resource uses, and (5) a set of constraints binding the different time-points and atemporal variables in the tasks. The possibility of using subtasks within tasks makes the description hierarchical, but without allowing recursion or other complex control structures. This hierarchy is a programming facility only. A compilation procedure expands subtasks into a flat set of tasks.

The example below describes a planning domain with few constants, attributes and tasks. It is a simple transportation problem with 3 robots, one trailer and several containers. The task *attach_trailer* makes one robot attach a trailer to another distinct robot. The task *put_on_trailer* consists of loading a container onto a trailer, the robot loading the container must not be the one eventually attached to the trailer.

```
constant ROBOTS      = { robot1, robot2, robot3 };
constant TRAILERS    = { trailer1};
constant CONTAINERS  = { container1, container2, container3, container4, container5,
container6, container7 };
constant ROOMS       = {Labroom1, Labroom2, Labroom3, Labroom4, Labroom5, Labroom6, RoomD4};

attribute is_attached(?trailer, ?robot)
   {?trailer in TRAILERS; ?robot in ROBOTS; ?value in {yes, no};}
attribute on_trailer(?container, ?trailer)
   {?container in CONTAINERS; ?trailer in TRAILERS; ?value in {yes,no};}

task  put_on_container(?robot, ?trailer, ?container) (start, end) {
  ?robot in ROBOTS; ?trailer in TRAILERS; ?container in CONTAINERS;
variable ?X in ROOMS;
  event( on_trailer(?container,?trailer): (no,yes), end);
  hold ( location(?robot): ?X, (start,end));
  hold ( location(?trailer): ?X, (start,end));
  hold ( location(?container):?X,(start,end));
  event( is_occupied(?robot): (no,yes), start);
  hold ( is_occupied(?robot): yes,(start,end))
  event( is_occupied(?robot): (yes,no), end;
  hold ( is_moving(?trailer): no, (start,end));
  hold ( is_attached(?trailer, ?robot): no, (start,end));
    (end - start) in [ 1:00; 2:00];  }

task attach_trailer(?robot,?robot2,?trailer) (start,end) {
  ?robot in ROBOTS; ?robot2 in ROBOTS; ?trailer in TRAILERS; ?robot2 != ?robot; variable ?X in ROOMS;
  event( is_attached(?trailer,?robot): (no,yes), end);
  hold ( location(?robot): ?X, (start,end))   ; event( is_moving(?trailer): (no,yes), start);
  hold ( location(?robot2): ?X,(start,end))   ; hold ( is_moving(?trailer): yes,(start,end));
  hold ( location(?trailer):?X,(start,end))   ; event( is_moving(?trailer): (yes,no), end);
  event( is_occupied(?robot):(no,yes), start) ; event( is_occupied(?robot2): (no,yes),start);
  hold ( is_occupied(?robot): yes,(start,end)); hold ( is_occupied(?robot2): yes,(start,end));
  event( is_occupied(?robot):(yes,no), end)   ; event( is_occupied(?robot2): (yes,no), end);
    (end - start) = 0:30; }
```

In IxTeT, preconditions and effects do not appear explicitly separated within a task, since the same event predicate can express both for its two values. The temporal representation enables to easily express the various things that hold before, what prevail during which part of the action, or that change as an effect of the action and when this change takes place along the duration of the action.

A simple analysis procedure of task models provides at compilation time the separation of preconditions from effects.

2.2 The planner

IxTₑT relies on the closed world hypothesis. The initial plan $\mathcal{P}_{init}$ describes the problem scenario, that is: (1) initial values for all instantiated attributes, (2) expected availability profile of resources, and (3) goals that must be achieved. The user has the possibility of describing a dynamic domain with contingent events [6], *i.e.* what is expected to happen in the world while the plan will be executed. This description is assumed to be complete; events on the same instantiated attribute should be totally ordered with compatible values.

Starting with the initial plan $\mathcal{P}_{init}$, the search incrementally constructs a solution by refining a partial plan through the insertion of tasks or variable constraints. IxTₑT is based on the classical notion of *causal links* [9][14], handled in our case by the *hold* predicate. The search control relies on an *extended least commitment* strategy according to a near admissible algorithm A_ϵ. IxTₑT also uses a dynamic hierarchy of domain attributes which guides the choice of flaws to be solved [4], a *flaw* being either an unexplained proposition, a threat or a resource conflict.

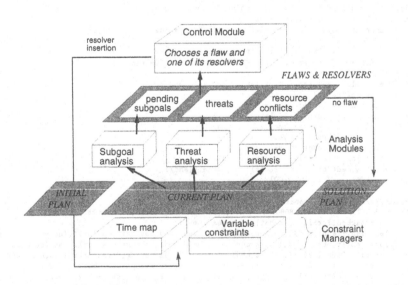

Fig. 1. the IxTₑT planner architecture

A partial plan $\mathcal{P}$ is a solution when all goals and sub-goals are satisfied, and there are no causal link or resource conflicts. The global IxTₑT architecture is presented in figure 1, and detailed in [6][8].

3 IxTeT with context dependent effects

The proposed extension remains within the usual assumptions of a closed world and deterministic actions. Contexts and corresponding conditional effects must be defined explicitly within a task model. A task may contain several conditional parts, each corresponding to a particular context, let call these *conditional subtasks*. When a task is added to a partial plan, it is not always possible to know if a context holds or not. Hence, all conditional parts of a new task remain hypothetical and need to be kept as such. Consequently, a partial plan is split into two different parts. The first one is composed of the unconditional propositions of the partial plan (*i.e.* events, assertions, resource uses and variable constraints). The second part corresponds to the hypothetical conditional subtasks of the partial plan.

Since the conditional parts of a partial plan are hypothetical, only non-conditional propositions (event and hold) can contribute to open subgoals. On the other hand, all effects of a partial plan, *i.e.* conditional or not, may be a threat to a causal link [9]. Similarly, resource analysis must handle all resource uses, conditional or not.

Managing context-dependent effects does not change the global architecture of IxTeT (figure 1). However, each analysis module needs be modified. Let us first present the representation and define partial plans with hypothetical conditional parts before explaining these modifications.

3.1 Conditional subtasks

A conditional subtask may contain all that can be expressed within a task. It has two field : **if** (*condition-field*) { *body-field* }

An element of the condition-field may be either an assertion (hold) or an atemporal constraint. An element of the body-field may contain any proposition. For example, the task below specifies additional effects for a robot motion attached to a trailer:

```
{task move(?robot,?from, ?to) (start, end)
  {?robot in ROBOTS; ?from in PLACES; ?to in PLACES; variable ?trailer in TRAILERS;
  event(location(?robot):(?from,Inway),start);
  hold (location(?robot): Inway, (start,end));
  event(location(?robot):(Inway,?to), end);

  if( hold(is_attached(?trailer,?robot): yes, (start,end))) {
     event(location(?trailer):(?from,Inway), start);
     hold (location(?trailer): Inway, (start,end));
     event(location(?trailer):(Inway,?to), end);      }
  ?from != ?to; (end - start) in [03:00, 5:00];    }}
```

Since in IxTeT preconditions are not explicitly separated from effects, the body-field a conditional subtask, relying on the same temporal representation, may also contain implicit preconditions. The condition-field enhances some preconditions in order to simplify programming. For example, in the task *move*, the conditional subtask has two preconditions: *is_attached(?trailer, ?robot) = yes* during the action, and *location(?trailer) = location(?robot)* before time *start*.

An effect in a conditional subtask may be unwanted in a plan. A solution to such a conflict is to make sure that the conditional subtask does not apply; *i.e.* one of its preconditions does not hold. Possible resolvers for such a conflict are *negations* of preconditions of a conditional subtask.

For that, let us focus on the conditions in the conditional-field, without taking into account other preconditions eventually in its body-field. This restriction limits the number of resolvers. The condition-field of a conditional subtask is composed of assertions and atemporal constraints. The negation of a constraint is its complement. The negation of an assertion: $hold(att(x_1, ..., x_n) : v, (t_1, t_2))$ states that this attribute takes another value during interval $[t_1, t_2[$. This is expressed by the assertion $hold(att(x_1, ..., x_2) : v', (t_3, t_4))$ with the constraints: $v \neq v'$, and $t_1 < t_3 < t_4 < t_2$.

Note that by restricting the set of resolvers to the condition-field only, we lose the search completeness. However, one may choose to specify all preconditions within the condition-field.

3.2 Partial plans with conditional subtasks

Let us assume here that a conditional subtask cannot contain other conditional subtasks. We'll handle later nested conditionals.

Let $\mathcal{P}$ be a partial plan: $\mathcal{P} = (EVT, HLD, RES, IF, CV, CT)$, where EVT is the set of event predicates, HLD the set of assertions, RES the set of resources, IF the set of elements in the condition-field of all conditional subtasks in $\mathcal{P}$, CV and CT represent the sets of constraints on atemporal and temporal variables respectively.

Each set EVT, HLD, USE, CV and CT is decomposed into two subsets: a set of conditional propositions (which come from a conditional subtask), noted with subscript cd, and a set of non-conditional propositions with subscript nc. The set IF is decomposed into two sets: the set IF_h contains assertions, and IF_v which contains atemporal constraints. A partial plan is then defined in the following way:

$$\mathcal{P} = ((EVT_{nc}, EVT_{cd}), (HLD_{nc}, HLD_{cd}), (RES_{nc}, RES_{cd}),$$
$$(IF_h, IF_v), (CV_{nc}, CV_{nc}), (CT_{nc}, CT_{cd}))$$

The conditional sets contain all conditional subtasks which are still hypothetical. In order to differentiate between these, an index is associated to the elements of a conditional subtask.

A conditional subtask in a partial plan may either:

1. have an effect which explains a subgoal. In this case, the conditional subtask may be needed, it can be transfered from the conditional sets to the non-conditional sets. In that case, all preconditions of this conditional subtask contribute to open subgoals.

2. have an effect which may be a threat to a causal link. A resolver for this flaw, *i.e.* the negation of one condition, is added to the partial plan. The conditional subtask is removed from the partial plan, since it cannot be later verified[1].

3. or none of the two preceding cases holds, the conditional subtask remains hypothetically in the plan.

Let $\mathcal{C} = (\overline{EVT}, \overline{HLD}, \overline{RES}, \overline{IF_h}, \overline{IF_v}, \overline{CV}, \overline{CT})$ be a conditional subtask of index i, where the sets $\overline{EVT}, \overline{HLD}, \overline{RES}, \overline{CV}, \overline{CT}$ specify the body-field of the conditional subtask; the sets $\overline{IF_h}$ and $\overline{IF_v}$ represent its condition-field. Formally these sets are:

$$\overline{EVT} = \{event | event \in EVT_{cd} \wedge index(event) = i\}$$
$$\overline{HLD} = \{hold | hold \in HLD_{cd} \wedge index(hold) = i\}$$
$$\overline{RES} = \{res | res \in RES_{cd} \wedge index(res) = i\}$$
$$\overline{IF_h} = \{hold | hold \in IF_h \wedge index(hold) = i\}$$
$$\overline{IF_v} = \{cv | cv \in IF_v \wedge index(cv) = i\}$$
$$\overline{CV} = \{cv | cv \in CV_{cd} \wedge index(cv) = i\}$$
$$\overline{CT} = \{ct | ct \in CT_{cd} \wedge index(ct) = i\}$$

The insertion of a conditional subtask $\mathcal{C}$ into a partial plan $\mathcal{P}$ (case 1 above) is performed as follows:

$$\mathcal{P} \oplus insertion(\mathcal{C}) =$$
$$((EVT_{nc} \cup \overline{EVT}, EVT_{cd} - \overline{EVT}), (HLD_{nc} \cup \overline{HLD} \cup \overline{IF_h}, HLD_{cd} - \overline{HLD}),$$
$$(RES_{nc} \cup \overline{RES}, RES_{cd} - \overline{RES}), (IF_h - \overline{IF_h}, IF_v - \overline{IF_v}),$$
$$(CV_{nc} \cup \overline{CV} \cup \overline{IF_v}, CV_{cd} - \overline{CV}), (CT_{nc} \cup \overline{CT} CT_{cd} - \overline{CT}))$$

The insertion of a resolver for a conflict with a conditional subtask $\mathcal{C}$ (case 2) corresponds to:

$$\mathcal{P} \oplus negation(\mathcal{C}) =$$
$$\bigvee_{hold \in \overline{IF_h}} ((EVT_{nc}, EVT_{cd} - \overline{EVT}), (HLD_{nc} \cup \{\neg(hold)\}, HLD_{cd} - \overline{HLD}),$$
$$(RES_{nc}, RES_{cd} - \overline{RES}), (IF_h - \overline{IF_h}, IF_v - \overline{IF_v}),$$
$$(CV_{nc}, CV_{cd} - \overline{CV}), (CT_{nc}, CT_{cd} - \overline{CT}))$$
$$\bigvee_{cv \in \overline{IF_v}} ((EVT_{nc}, EVT_{cd} - \overline{EVT}), (HLD_{nc}, HLD_{cd} - \overline{HLD}),$$
$$(RES_{nc}, RES_{cd} - \overline{RES}), (IF_h - \overline{IF_h}, IF_v - \overline{IF_v}),$$
$$(CV_{nc} \cup \{\neg(cv)\}, CV_{cd} - \overline{CV}), (CT_{nc}, CT_{cd} - \overline{CT}))$$

We remove the conditional subtask from the partial plan, and add the negation of one of its conditions. Note that the choice of a resolver and possible backtrack points are handled by the control module. Again, possible preconditions which are in the body-field of the conditional subtask are not taken into account.

3.3 Search control

Subgoal analysis Subgoals are expressed in IχT$_{E}$T by unexplained propositions. Explained propositions are events or assertions which are established by a causal

---

[1] Weld calls this *confrontation* [14].

link. In I×TℰT, establishers are naturally represented by events and causal links by assertions. To explain a proposition, the planner must find an event either already in the partial plan or in a task model that needs to be added to it.

Let $\mathcal{E}$ be an event which may establish an unexplained proposition P of partial plan $\mathcal{P}$. The procedure for handling P is the following:

1. If $\mathcal{E}$ belongs to $\mathcal{P}$ and is not conditional: add a causal link between $\mathcal{E}$ and P, and corresponding variable binding constraints
2. If $\mathcal{E}$ belongs to a conditional subtask C of $\mathcal{P}$: add the conditional subtask C which contains $\mathcal{E}$, and add a causal link between $\mathcal{E}$ and P.
3. If $\mathcal{E}$ belongs to a task to be added to $\mathcal{P}$ and C is not conditional: add a new instantiated task and a causal link between $\mathcal{E}$ and P.
4. If $\mathcal{E}$ belongs to a conditional subtask C of a task to be added: add the new instantiated task, the conditional subtask C, and a causal link between $\mathcal{E}$ and P.

Resolvers of types (2) and (4) have been added in I×TℰT in order to take into account conditional subtasks.

Threat analysis An assertion $\mathcal{H} : hold(att(x_1, ..., x_n) : v, (t_1, t_2))$ of a partial plan is threatened if an event $\mathcal{E} : event(att(x'_1, ..., x'_n) : (v'_1, v'_2), t')$ or an assertion $\mathcal{G} : hold(att(x_1", ..., x_n") : v", (t_1", t_2"))$ concerning the same attribute happens at overlapping intervals. Propositions $\mathcal{H}$, $\mathcal{G}$ or $\mathcal{E}$ may or may not belong to a conditional subtask.

A threat is a couple:

1. $< \mathcal{H}, \mathcal{G} >$ such that the partial plan does not contain one of those constraints: $\{(t_2" < t_1); (t_2 < t_1"); (x_1 \neq x_1"); ...; (x_n \neq x_n"); (x_1 = x_1" \wedge ... \wedge x_n = x_n" \wedge v = v")\}$, or
2. $< \mathcal{H}, \mathcal{E} >$ such that the partial plan does not contain one of those constraints: $\{(t' < t_1); (t_2 < t'_1); (x_1 \neq x_1"); ...; (x_n \neq x_n"); (t' = t_1 \wedge v'_2 = v); (t' = t_2 \wedge v'_1 = v)\}$.

For each possible threat, a disjunction of the above temporal and atemporal constraints is found. If the threatening proposition ($\mathcal{G}$ or $\mathcal{E}$) belongs to a conditional subtask, this subtask cannot stay hypothetical. We may either add it into the partial plan, together with one of the above constraints to avoid the threat, or we may remove it, but add the negation of one of its conditions.

Resource analysis There is a conflict for a type typ of resource with a maximal capacity Q, if there exists a set $U = \{u_1, ..., u_n\}$ with $u_i : use(typ() : q^i, (t_1^i, t_2^i))$, such that: (1) $\sum_{i=1}^{n} q_i > Q$, and (2) the partial plan does not contain one of the constraints $\{(t_2^i < t_1^j)\}_{(i \neq j)}$.

Each u_i may or may not belong to a conditional subtask.

Resolvers of a resource conflict consist of a disjunction of temporal constraints, variable inequalities if different resources of the same type are allowed, and if u_i belongs to a conditional subtask, the negations of its conditions. A resource conflict may also be solved by adding a task producing this resource, if possible.

Solution plan criterion A *flaw* being either an unexplained proposition, a threat or a resource conflict, a partial plan is a solution if and only if: (1) there are no flaws, (2) the temporal constraint network is consistent, and (3) the variable binding network is consistent.

A conditional subtask introduced by a task while planning may remain in the set of conditional subtasks according to the least commitment strategy, unless required for explaining a subgoal or solving a threat. However, a conditional subtask may be verified if all its preconditions are true in a final plan, *i.e.* all its conditions as well as all the preconditions which appear in its body do hold. In this case the conditional subtask must be included unconditionally in the plan. If we do not complete a plan in this way, it will remain consistent; but the predicted world states will not be correct: additional effects have to be added. Notice that the completion of a final plan with respect to its conditional subtasks that remains hypothetical, can be pursued during plan execution time. This can be helpful for monitoring purposes.

4 Illustration and results

4.1 A detailed example

As described in section 2.1, the chosen example concerns three robots, one trailer and seven containers. The trailer cannot be attached to two different robots. A robot cannot pick up or put on a container on a trailer, when the trailer is moving, or when the trailer is attached to this robot.

Initially the 3 robots, the trailer and all the containers are in *RoomD4*. Containers number 3, 4 and 5 are on the trailer. The goal is to keep *container3* in *RoomD4* during the totality of the plan; containers 1 and 2 must be in *LabRoom1*, and *containe4* in *LabRoom2*. The solution plan is presented in figure 2; the solution plan is found in 393 steps (number of developed partial plans) and with four backtracks.

Let us analyze an early partial plan where the goal *"container3 stays in RoomD4"* is satisfied by a causal link between this goal and the event in the initial situation; the goal *"container1 in LabRoom1"* is satisfied by an instantiated task *move* with the appropriate conditional subtask.

The subgoal analysis module could satisfy the goal *container2 in LabRoom1* in two ways: add the conditional subtask of the task *move*, or add a new instantiated task *move*. Adding a new instantiated task *move* satisfies as well the goal *container4 in Labroom2*. The threat analysis module detects that the conditional subtask of the task *move* in this partial plan, which concerns *container3*, threatens the previously established causal link. The only possible resolver for

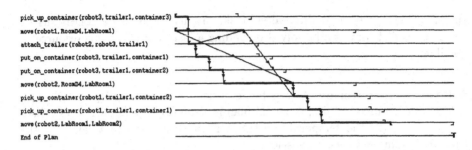

Fig. 2. Solution plan

this flaw is to insert the negation of this conditional subtask (*i.e. container*3 must not be on the trailer). There are other threats to temporal or atemporal constraints. The heuristically chosen flaw and resolver is the negation of the conditional subtask, because this flaw has just one resolver.

When a solution plan is found, the completion phase detects that the position of *container*5, which is on the trailer at the beginning of the plan, changes. We can see here that the completion is a necessary step; otherwise, the solution plan will not say that *container*5 has moved along with the trailer and the robot.

4.2 Some results

Several domains and many problems have been tested with similar results. In the multi-robots transportation domain for example, there are 129 different possible contexts for the *move* action, but only 8 conditional subtasks (one trailer and seven containers).

We tried to compare the system extended with conditional subtasks to the standard approach of IxTeT, *i.e.* without conditional subtasks. The task *move* must be rewritten differently as many times as there are contexts. Some representative results are presented below; the 4 examples correspond to different goals and initial situations:

	example 1	example 2	example 3	example 4
without conditional subtasks	35/0/15.1	86/0/67.8	492/5/408.6	415/4/522.4
with conditional subtasks	29/0/2.6	76/0/41.2	391/8/279.6	58/0/8.6

(number of developed partial plans / number of backtracks / time in seconds)

The results depend on the problem to be solved and the number of *move* tasks required. The threat module requires more time with conditional subtasks (about 80% more). Indeed, for each insertion of a task *move*, all contexts must be taken into account. However, without conditional subtasks the planner spends more time in the subgoal analysis; the average branching factor is larger.

Our experiments reports that generally IxTeT with context dependent effects is faster. But this does not always hold. It depends on the position of the solution in the search tree: the branching factor being smaller, there are fewer backtracks. This is may be a significant advantage. In particular, if there is no solution, planning with conditional subtasks takes less time. But there is an overhead, mainly due to the threat analysis module.

In order to estimate this overhead as a function of the number of conditional subtasks, we used the same simple domain varying the numbers of containers and hence the number of conditional subtasks; notice that this does not change the planning. The results are presented in the following table.

nb of containers	1	7	14	21	28	35	42	49
planning time in seconds	2	2.9	4.2	5	5.9	7.7	9.2	10.6

It seems that the increase in time depends linearly on the number of conditional subtasks.

5 Conclusion

Temporal planning with context dependent effects is interesting for two essential reasons: it improves the expressiveness of the representation and it reduces the branching factor. Altogether, it seems to have a benefit in efficiency, even if the complexity of the threat analysis module increases linearly with the number of conditional subtasks.

The fact of characterizing a context through a subset of preconditions in a conditional subtask may improve the efficiency of the search, but this is paid by a significant drawback: the loss of completeness of the planner. Again, a programming flexibility remains here which enables to overcome this drawback.

The case of nested conditionals is easily handled using partially ordered indexes, such that if $i < j$, then the conditional subtask i contains the subtask j. When a subtask j is added, all subtasks i, such that $i < j$, must be added too in a partial plan. When a conditional subtask j is removed, all subtasks i such as $j < i$ must be removed.

Finally, it is possible to reduce the number of conditional subtasks in a partial plan: when a precondition of a conditional subtask does not necessarily hold; *i.e.* its negation is in the partial plan, this subtask can be removed. According to our preliminary experiments, this reduces the time of the threat analysis module sufficiently to pay for the extra work involved to detect those situations.

References

1. D. Chapman. *Planning for Conjunctive goals*. Artificial Intelligence, vol. 32, pages 333–377, 1987.
2. G. Collins & L. Pryor, *Achieving the functionality of filter conditions in a partial order planner*. AAAI 92.
3. R.E.Fikes & N.J.Nilsson. *STRIPS: a new approach to the application of theorem proving to problem solving*. Artificial Intelligence, vol 2, pages 189–208, 1971.
4. F. Garcia & P. Laborie, *Hierarchisation of the search space in temporal planning*. 235–249, proceedings EWSP-95.

5. M. Ghallab & T. Vidal, *Focusing on the sub-graph for managing efficiently numerical temporal constraints.* In proceedings, FLAIRS-95.

6. M. Ghallab & H. Laruelle. *Representation and control in I_XT_ET, a temporal planner.* In proceedings AIPS-94, 61-67.

7. S. Kambhampati, C. Knoblock, Q. Yang. *Planning as rafinement search; a unified framework for evualuting tradeoffs in partial order planning.* Artifical Intelligence, 95, 167-238.

8. P. Laborie & M. Ghallab. *Planning with sharable resource constraints.* In proceedings IJCAI-95, 1643-1649

9. D. McAllester & D. Rosenblitt. *Systematic nonlinear planning.* In proceedings AAAI-91, pages 634-639, 1991.

10. D. McDermot, *regression planning.* International Journal of Intelligent Systems 6:357-416, 1991.

11. E. Pednault. *Synthesizing plans that contains actions with context-dependent effects.* Computational Intelligence, 4(4):356-372, 1988.

12. E. Pednault. *Generalizing non-linear planning to handle complex goals and actions with context-dependents effects.* Proceedings of the Twelfth International Joint Conference on Artificial Intelligence, july 1991.

13. J.S.Penberty & D. Weld. *UCPOP: a sound, complete, partial planner order planner for ADL.* Third International Conference of Knowledge Representation and Reasoning, 103–114, october 1992.

14. D. Weld *An introduction to least-commitment planning.* AI magazine, pages 27-61, Winter 1994

15. D.E. Wilkins, *Representation in a domain independent planner.* IJCAI 83

Information Gathering Plans
With Sensing Actions*

Naveen Ashish,[1] Craig A. Knoblock,[1] and Alon Levy[2]

[1] University of Southern California, Information Sciences Institute and Department
of Computer Science, 4676 Admiralty Way, Marina del Rey, CA 90292
[2] AT&T Labs, AI Principles Research Dept., 180 Park Avenue, Room A-283,
Florham Park, NJ 07932

Abstract. Information gathering agents can automate the task of retrieving and integrating data from a large number of diverse information
sources. The key issue in their performance is efficient query planning
that minimizes the number of information sources used to answer a query.
Previous work on query planning has considered generating information
gathering plans solely based on compile-time analysis of the query and
the models of the information sources. We argue that at compile-time
it may not be possible to generate an efficient plan for retrieving the
requested information because of the large number of possibly relevant
sources. We describe an approach that naturally extends query planning to use run-time information to optimize queries that involve many
sources. First, we describe an algorithm for generating a *discrimination
matrix*, which is a data structure that identifies the information that can
be sensed at run-time to optimize a query plan. Next, we describe how
the discrimination matrix is used to decide which of the possible run-time
sensing actions to perform. Finally, we demonstrate that this approach
yields significant savings (over 90% for some queries) in a real-world task.

1   Introduction

Information gathering agents are programs that answer queries using a large
number of diverse information sources (e.g., sources on the Internet, company-
wide databases). These information sources do not belong to the agent, instead
they are provided by autonomous sources, possibly for a fee. An information
agent does not maintain any real data, but only has *models* of the contents of
the available information sources. An agent has a domain model of its area of
expertise and a description of how the contents of an information source relate

* The first and second authors are supported in part by Rome Laboratory of the
Air Force Systems Command and the Advanced Research Projects Agency under
contract no. F30602-94-C-0210, and in part by the University of Southern California
Integrated Media Systems Center (IMSC) - a NSF Engineering Research Center.
The views and conclusions contained in this paper are the author's and should not
be interpreted as representing the official opinion or policy of DARPA, RL, IMSC,
AT&T Labs, or any person or agency connected with them.

to the classes in the domain model of the agent. User queries are posed using the domain model of the agent. Given a query, an agent serves as a mediator between the user and the information sources, by decomposing the query, sending requests to the appropriate information sources, and possibly processing the intermediate data. As such, the information agent frees the user from being aware of and sending queries directly to the information sources.

Several characteristics of this problem require us to develop solutions beyond those considered traditionally in knowledge and database systems. The main characteristic is that the number of information sources will be very large, and the agent has only the models of the sources in determining which ones are relevant to a given query. In addition, some information will reside redundantly in many sources, and access to any particular source will not always be possible (e.g., network failures) and may be expensive (either in time or in money).

To answer queries efficiently, an information agent must be able to determine precisely which information sources are relevant to a given query. Previous work on information agents (e.g.,(Knoblock and Levy 1995), SIMS (Arens et al. 1996, Knoblock et al. 1994), the Unix Softbot (Etzioni and Weld 1994), the Information Manifold (Levy et al. 1996), Occam (Kwok and Weld 1996)) has largely focused on determining relevant sources by analyzing the query and the models of the information sources. However, as the following example shows, it is not always possible to significantly prune the set of information sources without gathering some additional information that was not explicitly mentioned in the query. Suppose we are given a query asking for the phone number of John McCarthy:

$$\text{Person}(x) \wedge \text{Name}(x, \text{``JohnMcCarthy''}) \wedge \text{PhoneNumber}(x, number).$$

We have access to a large number of name server repositories that contain information about individuals, email addresses, phone numbers, etc. These repositories are usually organized by institution, but without any additional information about John McCarthy this query will require accessing every repository until the information is found. In some cases the query processor can add *new* subqueries into the query plan in order to obtain additional information to constrain the sources that need to be considered. For example, the query processor could issue the subquery Affiliation("John McCarthy",org) to the various professional organization databases to find his current affiliation. Using this information, the query processor can now go directly to the relevant name servers.

This example illustrates two points. First, we can obtain at run-time additional information about *individuals* or *classes* of individuals appearing in a query. The second point is that the information is obtained by *adding* discriminating queries to the original query. There are other kinds of information that can be obtained at run-time. We can obtain information about a *source* that enables us to refine our model of that source. Or, the fact that we found an individual in a *specific* source can be used later to find additional facts about this individual.

In this paper we focus on the problem of finding additional information about individuals or classes of individuals by adding discriminating queries, called *sens-*

ing actions, to the original query. We describe a novel approach to query planning that can exploit sensing actions to optimize information gathering plans. A key component of the approach is a data structure, the *discrimination matrix*, that enables the query planner to evaluate the utility of additional sensing actions. Informally, the discrimination matrix tells us how many information sources we may be able to prune if we perform a proposed sensing action, which allows us to estimate the cost of plans with additional sensing actions. We show how to build the discrimination matrix efficiently and how to use it in query planning. Finally, we present experimental results that demonstrate that this approach produces savings of over 90% in a real-world task.

2   The Domain Model and Source Models

An information agent has a representation of its domain of expertise, called the *domain model*, and a set of *source models*, i.e., descriptions of information sources. In our discussion, we use a KL-ONE type knowledge representation language. Such a language contains unary relations (called *concepts*) which represent classes of objects in the domain and binary relations (*roles*) which describe relationships between objects. In our discussion, *complex concepts* are built from primitive concepts using the following set of constructors: (A denotes a concept name, C and D represent complex concepts, and R denotes a role):

$$C, D \rightarrow A \mid$$
$$C \sqcap D \mid C \sqcup D \mid \text{(conjunction, disjunction)}$$
$$(R < a) \mid (R > a) \text{ (range constraints)}$$
$$(\geq n R) \mid (\leq n R) \text{ (role-filler cardinality restrictions)}$$
$$(\text{fills } R\ a) \text{ (filler restriction)}$$
$$(\text{oneOf } R\ \{a_1, \ldots, a_n\}) \text{ (restriction on fillers)}$$

As an example, the concept Person $\sqcap$ (fills occupation research) $\sqcap$ (oneOf affiliation {ISI, Stanford}) $\sqcap$ ($\geq$ 3 student) represents the set of people, whose occupation is research, affiliated with either ISI or Stanford, and having at least three students.

The agent also has models of the external sources. A description of a source has the form $(D_S, r_1^s, \ldots, r_n^s)$, meaning that S has instances of the concept D_S, and for these instances it contains role fillers of the roles $r_1^s, \ldots, r_n^s$. Note that S does not necessarily contain *all* instances of D_S or all the role fillers.

Figure 1 shows some information sources that could be used to answer queries about technical reports. The most recent source for Carnegie Mellon would be modeled as shown below. This source provides the authors, title, year, department and abstract for Carnegie Mellon technical reports since 1990.

((TechReport $\sqcap$ (fills affiliation "Carnegie Mellon") $\sqcap$ ($\geq$ year 1990)),authors, title, year, department, abstract)

Given a query, an information agent needs to determine which information sources are relevant. Previous work (Etzioni and Weld 1994, Arens et al. 1996, Levy et al. 1996) showed how to determine the relevant sources based on the

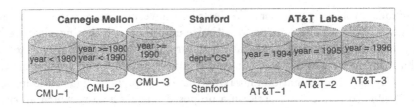

Fig. 1. Example technical report repositories.

query and the models of the information sources. As a simple example, suppose our query is TechReport(x) ∧ Author(x, "John McCarthy") ∧ Year(x,1996). The system can infer from the query that only three of the seven technical report repositories need to be considered since the other ones only contain reports from other years. Similarly, if the query was further specialized to include affiliation or department the set of possible sources could be pruned further. The remainder of this paper will describe techniques for performing this type of pruning at run time when relevant constraints are not explicitly specified in the query.

3 Building a Discrimination Matrix

Our approach to actively seeking information about objects involves considering query plans that contain one or more additional subqueries, called *discriminating queries*. Such queries have the form $R(\alpha, Y)$, where α is a constant and Y is the result of the discriminating query. The values obtained for Y will be used to prune the information sources considered for the subsequent subqueries in the query, because some sources will become irrelevant after obtaining new information about α.[3] Adding discriminating queries changes the cost of the query plan in two ways. First, it adds the cost of solving the additional subquery, and second, it enables us to prune the sets of the information sources relevant to subsequent subqueries. The key to evaluating the utility of the added queries, is to determine how the relevant set of information sources can be pruned when we obtain new information. The main challenge is to estimate which information sources will be pruned *without* actually knowing the values returned for $R(\alpha, Y)$.

Recall that each source S contains instances of a given class D_S, and fillers for some roles of those instances. Suppose we are searching for the fillers of role P of an individual a, and the query entails that a is a member of concept C. In this case, we will consider every information source S, such that $D_S \sqcap C$ is non-empty (i.e., is a satisfiable concept description), and such that S provides fillers for P. By obtaining the value b of the role filler R of a using a sensing action, we can further restrict the relevant sources to those for which $D_S \sqcap$ (fills $R\,b$)

---

[3] Discriminating queries are not treated exactly as ordinary ones. Specifically, if a discriminating query fails (i.e., no values are found for Y), then that only means that we could not obtain additional information, and therefore we need to consider the subsequent subqueries without pruning any of the sources relevant to them.

is non-empty. The discrimination matrix of a role R and class C tells us which information sources would be relevant if we *also* knew the value of the filler of R of the object a.

Formally, the discrimination matrix for a role R and class C provides two kinds of information. First, the matrix partitions the possible values of R into *regions*, such that two values of R in the same region will have the same set of relevant information sources. Second, for every region r, the discrimination matrix tells us which information sources contain instances of C, given that the value of R falls within r. Intuitively, a role R provides good *discrimination* if R partitions the set of relevant information sources evenly over many regions.

Consider the example of repositories for technical reports. Building the discrimination matrix for the role year and class TechReport yields the following regions and partition of information sources:

Region	relevant sources
< 1980	CMU-1, Stanford
[1980, 1990)	CMU-2, Stanford
[1990, 1994)	CMU-3, Stanford
[1994, 1994]	CMU-3, Stanford, AT&T-1
[1995, 1995]	CMU-3, Stanford, AT&T-2
[1996, 1996]	CMU-3, Stanford, AT&T-3
> 1996	CMU-3, Stanford

Therefore, if we know the year of the technical report for which we are searching, the number of relevant sources will be at most three, instead of seven.

Below we describe an algorithm for constructing the discrimination matrix. The discrimination matrix is persistent and is modified only when an information source is added or deleted. In particular, it is built at compile-time, based on the source descriptions, before answering any queries. We distinguish roles whose range values are numeric from those whose range is non-numeric. In what follows we describe an algorithm for creating a discrimination matrix for numeric roles that use constraints specified by the constructors $<$ and $>$ to partition the information sources. We then briefly sketch the algorithm for non-numeric roles, using the constructors fills and oneOf. We focus on the above constructors because these are the most likely to yield discrimination between sources.

3.1 Numeric Roles

We denote by $\mathcal{A}$ the set of constants that appear in constraints involving $<$, $\leq, >, \geq$ in the models of the information sources. The regions found by the discrimination matrix are the possible (open and closed) intervals involving two consecutive constants in $\mathcal{A} \cup \{\infty, -\infty\}$.

The algorithm, shown in Fig. 2, builds a vector $\mathcal{V}$ of triplets (a_i, S_i^+, S_i^-). The first element in every tuple in the vector a_i is a pair of the form (n_i, θ), where n_i is a number in the set $\mathcal{A} \cup \{-\infty, \infty\}$, and θ is either $=$ or $>$. S_i^+ are S_i^- are sets of information sources. The set S_i^+ are the information sources that *become* relevant when the value of R is greater than n_i if θ_i is $>$, and greater

18

procedure compute-numeric-matrix(S)
// S is a set of information sources
Begin with the vector $V = \{((-\infty, >), \emptyset, \emptyset), ((\infty, =), \emptyset, \emptyset)\}$.
for every source $S \in S$, **do:**
    Let D_S be the class description in the model of S.
    Let a_{low} be the largest number for which $D_S \models (R\,\theta\,a_{low})$, where $\theta \in \{>, \geq\}$.
    Let a_{high} be the smallest number for which $D_S \models (R\,\theta\,a_{high})$, where $\theta \in \{<, \leq\}$.
        if $D_S \models (R > a_{low})$ **then add-to-vector**(V, $((a_{low}, >), S, \emptyset)$).
            else add-to-vector(V, $((a_{low}, =), S, \emptyset)$).
        if $D_S \models (R < a_{high})$ **then add-to-vector**(V, $((a_{high}, =), \emptyset, S)$).
            else add-to-vector(V, $((a_{high}, >), \emptyset, S)$).
return V.

procedure add-to-vector(V, (a, S^+, S^-))
// V is a vector of the form $((a_1, S_1^+, S_1^-), \ldots, (a_n, S_n^+, S_n^-))$.
if a is the first argument in the i'th element of V **then**
    $S_i^+ = S_i^+ \cup S^+$.
    $S_i^- = S_i^- \cup S^-$.
else add (a, S^+, S^-) to V so that the first elements of each
        triplet are ordered as follows:
    $a_i = (n_i, \theta_i)$ comes before $a_j = (n_j, \theta_j)$ if $n_i < n_j$ or $n_i = n_j$,
        and θ_i is = and θ_j is >.

Fig. 2. Building a matrix for numeric roles.

or equal to n_i if θ_i is =. The set S_i^- are the information sources that *become* irrelevant when the value of R is n_i if θ_i is =, or become irrelevant when the value of R is greater than n_i, when θ_i is >.

The discrimination matrix is constructed from V as follows. Consider for example the region $[a_i, a_k)$, where $a_i, a_k \in A$. The sources in the partition of this region are those that appear in the set S_j^+ for an a_j that would come before $(a_i, >)$ in V, and do not appear in the set S_j^- for an a_j that would come before $(a_i, >)$ in V.

Example 1. Consider the technical report repositories. We begin with the vector

$\{((-\infty, >), \emptyset, \emptyset), ((\infty, =), \emptyset, \emptyset)\}$.

Inserting the first Carnegie Mellon repository will result in the vector:

$\{((-\infty, >), CMU_1, \emptyset), ((1980, =), \emptyset, CMU_1), ((\infty, =), \emptyset, \emptyset)\}$

Inserting the other Carnegie Mellon repositories will yield the vector:

$\{((-\infty, >)CMU_1, \emptyset), ((1980, =), CMU_2, CMU_1), ((1990, =), CMU_3, CMU_2), ((\infty, =), \emptyset, CMU_3)\}$.

Adding the Stanford repository only changes the first and last elements of the vector:

$\{((-\infty,>),\{CMU_1, Stanford\},\emptyset),\ ((1980,=),CMU_2,CMU_1),$
$((1990,=),CMU_3,CMU_2),\ ((\infty,=),\emptyset,\{CMU_3,Stanford\}))\}.$

Finally, adding the AT&T Labs repositories will yield the following vector:

$\{((-\infty,>),\{CMU_1, Stanford\},\emptyset),\ ((1980,=),CMU_2,CMU_1),$
$((1990,=),CMU_3,CMU_2),\ ((1994,=),ATT_1,\emptyset),\ ((1994,>),\emptyset,ATT_1),$
$((1995,=),ATT_2,\emptyset),\ ((1995,>),\emptyset,ATT_2),\ ((1996,=),ATT_3,\emptyset),$
$((1996,>),\emptyset,ATT_3),\ ((\infty,=),\emptyset,\{CMU_3,Stanford\}))\}.$

Inserting an information source into the matrix can be done in time $O(log(n))$ in the number of information sources, n. Therefore, the overall running time of the algorithm is $O(nlog(n))$. Since the determination of the regions of R requires that we sort the values in $\mathcal{A}$, it is clear that $O(nlog(n))$ is also a lower bound on the time to build the discrimination matrix.

3.2   Non-numeric Roles

In the algorithm for non-numeric roles we assume that the domain model entails that the role R can only have a *single* filler. In the case that R may have multiple fillers, the algorithm is the same, except that we ignore the fills constructor.[4] Suppose we have a constant a in our query, and we found that b is the filler of the role R of a. This can affect the relevance of an information source S in two ways. If the description of S says that it contains instances of the class D_S, then

1. If D_S entails (fills R a), then S will be relevant if and only if a $=$ b.
2. If D_S entails (oneOf R $\{a_1, \ldots, a_m\}$), then S will be relevant if and only if b $\in \{a_1, \ldots, a_m\}$.

Hence, if $\mathcal{A}$ is the set of constants that appear in fills and oneOf constraints in the models of the information sources, then the possible values of R can be classified into $|\mathcal{A}| + 1$ regions: one region for every value in $\mathcal{A}$ and one region for all values not mentioned in $\mathcal{A}$. Our algorithm creates a hierarchy of *labels*. Each label denotes a subset of the regions of R. With each label L, the algorithm associates a set of information sources $Sources(L)$. An information source S will be in $Sources(L)$ if the description of S entails that the value of R *must* be in one of the regions in L. Given a set of information sources $\mathcal{S}$, we use the discrimination matrix to partition them as follows. The set of information sources in the partition of a value r are those sources in $\mathcal{S}$ that appear in the set associated with *some* label that includes r. It should be noted that although the number of possible labels that can be generated is exponential in the number of constants in $\mathcal{A}$, the algorithm will only generate at most a number of labels as the number of information sources.

---

[4] The fills constructor is useful for discrimination only if we have an upper bound on the number of fillers of R.

4 Using the Discrimination Matrix

In the previous section we described how to perform the required preprocessing of a domain to identify the potentially useful discriminating queries. In this section we first describe the space of possible plans that include discriminating queries, and we then show how to use the discrimination matrix to evaluate the cost of plans.

4.1 Planning with Discriminating Queries

In the general framework described in this paper, a user issues a query in terms of the domain model and the system then determines how to efficiently retrieve the requested data. This requires selecting an appropriate set of sources to query, finding an efficient ordering of the queries, and determining what operations to perform on the data to produce the required result. Space does not permit a detailed review of these algorithms, but earlier work describes these algorithms in detail (Levy et al. 1996, Arens et al. 1996, Knoblock 1995).

We consider a new space of plans in which additional discriminating queries are considered whenever there is a corresponding entry in the precomputed discrimination matrix. This new space can include plans with single discriminating queries, multiple discriminating queries, and even recursive discriminating queries. The number of additional plans considered in the new space will be relatively modest, since there are likely to be very few roles that can provide good discrimination for a given subquery in the query. The roles that do not provide good discrimination can be eliminated from consideration early on (e.g., eye color will not provide good discrimination on phone numbers, even though it is a role of class **person** since people are rarely organized by eye color).

We can extend any algorithm for searching the original set of plans as follows. Given any plan P from the original space, we consider all plans in which one or more discriminating queries are added to P immediately prior to the subqueries for which they are used to discriminate. This process is repeated until there are no additional discriminating queries to consider. The query processor would then select from among the possible plans the one with the lowest estimated cost.

Consider the problem of planning queries to the CIA World Factbook. The Factbook is organized as a set of 267 Web pages, one for each country in the world, and contains information about each country's geography, population, government, etc. Queries about a specific country can be executed quickly, but queries that involve accessing large numbers of countries can take a long time because of the large number of pages that must be retrieved. Related information that can be used for discriminating queries is available in a variety of sources, such as the Yahoo Region Information, which provides data about the organization of countries into regions and the NATO Homepage, which provides a list of the current NATO countries.

Since all of the sources provide data about countries, the domain model contains the top-level class **Country** and subclasses that correspond to the individual sources. Each of the 267 countries is modeled as a separate class, each of which is

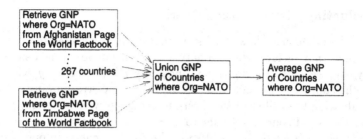

Fig. 3. Original plan without discriminating query.

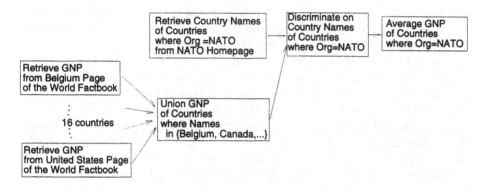

Fig. 4. Plan with a discriminating query.

a subclass of **Country** distinguished by the name of the country. There are also subclasses that correspond to different regions (i.e., Europe, Pacific Rim, etc.) and organizations (i.e., NATO, WHO, etc.). The user can ask queries about a single country, a subclass of countries, or all of the countries.

The use of discriminating queries in the Factbook can greatly reduce the number of sources that would need to be accessed. Without the use of discriminating queries, a plan for answering a query for the average GNP of all NATO countries will require accessing all 267 pages from the Factbook. Figure 3 shows the plan produced when the system cannot exploit discriminating queries. With the use of discriminating queries, the discrimination matrix would show that first determining the names of the required countries could greatly reduce the number of pages from the Factbook that would need to be retrieved.[5] Figure 4 shows this resulting plan, where the system first performs a sensing action to retrieve the names of all of the NATO countries. Then it uses this information to generate the subplan that only requires retrieving the 16 pages from the Factbook that correspond to the NATO countries.

---

[5] Note that this optimization cannot be performed with the standard database technique of moving a selection earlier because the name attribute is not requested in the original query.

4.2 Evaluating Discriminating Queries

In this section we describe how the discrimination matrix is used to estimate the cost of a plan that includes discriminating queries. Suppose g is a subquery in the query, and we added the discriminating query $R(\alpha, Y)$ before g, where α is a constant that appears in g and Y is the result of the discriminating query. The key to evaluating the utility of the discriminating query is to determine how it will affect the set of sources relevant to g. Suppose that the query entails that α is a member of class C (e.g., TechReport, Person, or Country in our examples). The discrimination matrix for R and C tells us which sources are relevant in each possible region of R. Suppose $\mathcal{I}_1^i, \ldots, \mathcal{I}_m^i$ is the partition given by the discrimination matrix. Since we do not know in *which* of the regions the answer to the discrimination query will be, we use the average case. If the combined cost of solving the discriminating query and the savings obtained for g are lower than the original cost of solving Q, then we will on average save some work.

In the example that requested the technical reports for "John McCarthy" there are several possible discriminations on technical reports. The query processor would consider discriminating the technical report repositories on year, organization, and both year and organization. Based on the cost and availability of this discriminating information and the amount of discrimination provided, the query processor would select the most promising plan.

The discrimination matrix can also be used to partition the sources given *multiple* discriminating queries about an object a. To determine the discrimination achieved by multiple discriminating queries, we simply take the cross products of the regions given by each query. For example, suppose the analysis of the query shows that there are six potentially relevant information sources, $\mathcal{S} = S_1, \ldots, S_6$, for retrieving the information for a query Q_i. We have two discrimination matrices, one for role R_1 and one for R_2, each having three regions. Suppose that for the role R_1 we obtain the partition $\{\{S_1, S_2\}, \{S_3, S_4, S_5\}, \{S_6\}\}$, and for R_2 the partition is $\{\{S_1\}, \{S_2, S_3\}, \{S_4, S_5, S_6\}\}$. Taking the cross products of these partitions to compute the discrimination that would be obtained by finding both R_1 and R_2, would yield nine regions, the non-empty ones being:[6]

$$\{S_1\}^{1,1}, \{S_2\}^{1,2}, \{S_3\}^{2,2}, \{S_4, S_5\}^{2,3}, \{S_6\}^{3,3}.$$

Note that the partitions for R_1 and R_2 mean that if the value for one of them is known, then at most three sources would be relevant. If both R_1 and R_2 are known, then at most two sources are relevant.

5   Experimental Results

This section presents empirical results to demonstrate that the use of sensing actions can significantly reduce the number of sources that must be accessed. To evaluate the use of sensing actions, we implemented the algorithms for building the discrimination matrix and extended the query planner developed by

---

[6] The superscripts denote the original regions from R_1 and R_2 respectively.

Table 1. Experimental results on CIA World Factbook queries.

Query	Time w/o sensing	Time w/ sensing	Percent Reduction
1. Find total defense expenditure of NATO countries	3793 sec.	287 sec.	92.4%
2. Find average GNP of all European countries	3823 sec.	518 sec.	86.5%
3. Find languages spoken in the Pacific Rim.	3710 sec.	289 sec.	92.2%
4. Find population of the United States.	14 sec.	NA	NA

Knoblock (1995) to generate sensing actions. We then applied the resulting system to the problem of retrieving data from the CIA World Factbook.

We wrote a small set of queries to demonstrate the usefulness of the discriminating queries in this domain. The system generates the discrimination matrix for this domain model in 0.067 seconds of CPU time on a Sun Sparc 20. Table 1 shows the time required for answering a small set of test queries both with and without sensing actions. In the first query, without sensing actions, the time required to answer the query is very high (more than an hour) as the system has to access information about each of the 267 countries to determine which countries are members of NATO. However with sensing actions, the planner decides to first fetch the names of all NATO countries (this is the sensing action) and then proceeds to fetch the defense expenditure of all the NATO countries. The agent needs to access information only about the 16 NATO member countries, which provides a significant reduction in execution time as the same query can now be answered in less than five minutes. A similar optimization is done in queries 2 and 3 where the sensing actions are to find the lists of European countries and countries in the Pacific Rim, respectively. In query 4, however, no sensing action is generated as the number of information sources to be accessed is already small (one source) in the plan without sensing actions. Thus an additional sensing action is not really expected to provide information that can further prune the number of sources to be accessed.

6 Related Work

Our work can be viewed as a form of semantic query optimization (SQO) (King 1981, Chakravarthy et al. 1990), where new subqueries are added to a query by analyzing the integrity constraints known about the data. In our context, the analogue of integrity constraints are the descriptions of the information sources. One key issue in SQO is determining when the additional subqueries that are introduced actually lead to better performance. A contribution of our work is to provide a method for evaluating the saving achieved by the new subqueries, by estimating the number of information sources that would be accessed. Our method relies on using the models of the information sources, which have no analogue in traditional databases.

The work on Softbots for Unix by Etzioni and Weld (1994) exploits the use of additional sensing actions to determine where to locate information. The sensing actions are in the context of a software agent that can manipulate the environment as well as gather information. However, the specific sensing goals are encoded as explicit preconditions of the planning operators. In this paper we present a more general information gathering framework for automatically inserting useful sensing goals.

This work is also related to a variety of work on sensing in planning. In terms of the taxonomy of different uses of sensing proposed by Olawsky and Gini (1990), our approach to sensing corresponds to deferring planning decisions that depend on sensor readings (i.e., the choice of which sources to query). Much of the work on sensing has focused on introducing sensing actions when there is insufficient knowledge about a problem to proceed (Olawsky and Gini 1990, Ambros-Ingerson 1987). In contrast, the discriminating queries exploit sensing for optimization. Finally, the previous work by both Knoblock (1995) and Levy (1996) presents more limited types of sensing for information gathering that exploit subqueries already in a query, but do not introduce new subqueries.

7 Limitations

There are two potential limitations to the use of discriminating queries in information gathering plans. First, the paper presented an approach to *automatically* obtaining the additional data from other sources, but there may not be another pre-existing source that can provide the required data. An alternative approach is to ask the user to provide the information about a query. This would provide an important user interface capability, where the system can effectively determine precisely what information is needed from the user in order to process a query efficiently. Another alternative is to use the techniques for building a discrimination matrix to precompile a set of discriminating data sources. The system can determine what information would be most useful by analyzing the model. This data can then be cached locally and updated as the sources change to provide more efficient access to the required data.

Second, the use of a discriminating query could result in a different answer from the one produced without the use of the discrimination. This would only happen if the data used for the discrimination is inconsistent with the original data. This is a general problem when integrating heterogeneous information sources. There are two ways to address this problem. First, any system that can retrieve data from multiple sources needs to make it clear where any given data actually came from so the user can assess the accuracy of the data. Second, if the integrity of the final answers is critical, then the system can perform off-line processing to verify that redundant sources contain consistent sets of data.

8 Conclusion

This paper provides an important capability for using sensing actions in query planning to efficiently locate information in a setting that involves a large number of sources. Such optimizations are critical in query planners for information gathering agents since the number of sources available can be quite large. We have argued for the need for exploiting information obtained at run-time and presented an approach that extends classical query planning to exploit run-time information through the use of sensing actions. We also presented an algorithm for building a discrimination matrix, which is used to determine which sensing actions can be used to optimize a plan, and described how existing query planners can exploit the discrimination matrix to insert sensing actions. In future work, we plan to explore approaches to automatically generate rich models of sources by analyzing the contents of sources, which will improve the likelihood of finding useful discriminating queries.

References

Jose Ambros-Ingerson. *IPEM: Integrated Planning, Execution, and Monitoring*. PhD thesis, Department of Computer Science, University of Essex, 1987.

Yigal Arens, Craig A. Knoblock, and Wei-Min Shen. Query reformulation for dynamic information integration. *Journal of Intelligent Information Systems, Special Issue on Intelligent Information Integration*, 6(2/3):99–130, 1996.

Upen S. Chakravarthy, John Grant, and Jack Minker. Logic-based approach to semantic query optimization. *ACM Transactions on Database Systems*, 15(2):162–207, 1990.

Oren Etzioni and Daniel S. Weld. A softbot-based interface to the Internet. *Communications of the ACM*, 37(7), 1994.

Jonathan Jay King. *Query Optimization by Semantic Reasoning*. PhD thesis, Stanford University, Department of Computer Science, 1981.

Craig A. Knoblock and Alon Levy, editors. *Information Gathering from Heterogeneous, Distributed Environments*, Technical Report SS-95-08, AAAI Press, Menlo Park, CA, 1995.

Craig A. Knoblock, Yigal Arens, and Chun-Nan Hsu. Cooperating agents for information retrieval. In *Proceedings of the Second International Conference on Cooperative Information Systems*, Toronto, Canada, 1994.

Craig A. Knoblock. Planning, executing, sensing, and replanning for information gathering. In *Proceedings of the Fourteenth International Joint Conference on Artificial Intelligence*, Montreal, Canada, 1995.

Chung T. Kwok and Daniel S. Weld. Planning to gather information. In *Proceedings of the Thirteenth National Conference on Artificial Intelligence*, Portland, OR, 1996.

Alon Y. Levy, Anand Rajaraman, and Joann J. Ordille. Query-answering algorithms for information agents. In *Proceedings of the Thirteenth National Conference on Artificial Intelligence*, Portland, OR, 1996.

Duane Olawsky and Maria Gini. Deferred planning and sensor use. In *Proceedings of the Workshop on Innovative Approaches to Planning, Scheduling and Control*, pages 166–174, San Diego, CA, 1990.

What Does a Planner Need to Know About Execution?

Ruth Aylett, Alex Coddington,
David Barnes, Rob Ghanea-Hercock
University of Salford

Abstract

This paper discusses how far the characteristics of the execution systems impact the planner which plans for them. It does this in the context of the MACTA project in which multiple cooperating mobile robots running a behavioural architecture are integrated with a Reflective Agent based on a computer running a symbolic planner, in this case UCPOP. The paper proposes some solutions but concludes that it is very difficult to produce a clean interface between a planner and its execution systems.

1. Introduction

This paper discusses the knowledge of execution agents and their capabilities needed by a planner which is creating plans for cooperative action by multiple autonomous robots. The context for this discussion is work on the MACTA architecture [Aylett et al 97] in which a conventional symbolic AI planner - currently UCPOP [Penberthy & Weld 92] - supervises a number of robots with a sub-symbolic behavioural architecture.

Execution is a major concern in mobile robot domains since the whole point of planning is to have the planned actions carried out in the real world. However real-world (that is, not simulated) robotic domains are inherently difficult. Firstly, complete information is out of the question, either for the planning or executing systems. Accurate knowledge of the current state of the domain can only be gathered via sensors and these are practically and theoretically limited in scope. Only the part of the domain within range can be perceived and even here sensor data is noisy and difficult to interpret. The construction of higher level models from raw data is fraught with problems of which not the least is the time and computational resource required, so that the pre-requisite for correct symbolic planning - the existence of an accurate and complete symbolic model - is usually far from being met.

Building an accurate model off-line with static, calibrated sensors is also problematic since no useful mobile robot domain is static in practice - changes outside the control of the robot itself are inevitable. For these reasons, many workers in mobile robotics have developed on-board reactive planning systems [Firby 89, Firby 94, Gat 92, Bonasso 93] which allow as many decisions as possible to be made at execution time. Others have followed Brooks [Brooks 86] in creating sub-symbolic behavioural architectures and this was the path taken at Salford where the novel multi-robot behavioural architecture the Behavioural Synthesis Architecture (BSA) was developed [Barnes 96] as discussed below.

Devolving intelligence to execution time produces systems that are less fragile and more responsive to a changing world but it does not remove the need for predictive planning. Decisions based on local knowledge may not achieve global goals at all or may only do so very inefficiently. This is not acceptable in industrial task-oriented domains. A predictive planner offers some guarantee that if the projected actions can be executed in the expected states, the desired goal will be reached. Moreover, the execution-level structures used by robots, whether RAPS [Firby 89, Firby 94], digital circuits [Rosenschein & Kaelbling 86] or behaviour packets as in the BSA, have to come from somewhere, and allowing a planner to generate them from high-level goals is more practical than hardwiring them in where robots must carry out many different tasks as in most industrial environments.

We argue that to successfully perform these functions the planning system must have knowledge of the capability of the execution systems for which it is planning. We will discuss this point in the context of the use of a standard AI planner for the multi-robot system mentioned above.

2.   Relationships Between Planning And Execution

Insofar as classical planning considered execution at all, it assumed a determining relationship between planner actions (or planner primitive actions in the case of hierarchical planning) and executed actions. Primitive planning actions for robots may each require a number of even lower level actuations well below the level one would wish to manipulate symbolically (because of real-time constraints and the need for numerical representations). An 'open gripper' action in a plan for a manipulator results in many actions at the level of motors and gears. Nevertheless in the classical approach there is still a causal one-to-many relationship between the planner action and the eventual actuations.

However this is not the only possible relationship between planned and executed actions, as much work in the last ten years or so has shown, for example [Agre & Chapman 87, Gat 92, Lyons & Hendrik 92]. One alternative is to see planner actions as *enabling* execution actuations [Gat 92]: a planner action constrains actuation but the latter is directly determined by sensor input, breaking the direct causal relationship between planner primitives and executed actuations. Such an enabling relationship makes it possible to use the behavioural approach - with its requirement for a tight connection between sensor inputs and actuator outputs - as an execution mechanism while still giving symbolic planning a powerful role. A further consequence is to raise the level of abstraction at which the planner operates since it need no longer be concerned with the world at the level of robot sensor input - the robot can deal with this itself.

There is also a temporal dimension to the relationships between planning and execution: plan-then-execute, or interleave; and if the latter then with what granularity? In robotics this dynamic relationship is constrained by whether symbolic planning is mounted on-board the robot or not. If on-board, there may be severe resource implications as noted above and the interaction of two systems working on such different time-scales, usually with different representations, must be very carefully managed [Aylett et al 91]. The existence of multiple cooperating robots each with their own on-board symbolic planner may also result in a high inter-robot communications overhead since problems of model inconsistency at the planner level then become significant.

On the other hand, if a planner is located off-board, the consequence of a determining relationship between planning and execution is to severely limit the autonomy of the robot and to create a potential communications bottleneck between the two systems. High-bandwidth communications with little or no error are required and this is an additional structuring constraint on the environment in which the robot operates (no radio frequency 'shadows' for instance). An enabling relationship requires less moment-to-moment interaction between planning and execution systems since it need not access sensor data and the robot does not require a planner primitive in order to act. Thus interleaving of planning and execution can operate at a much coarser granularity.

3.   The MACTA System

The original motivation for multi-robot work at Salford was to explore the idea that many small simple robots might be more successful at carrying out complex tasks than

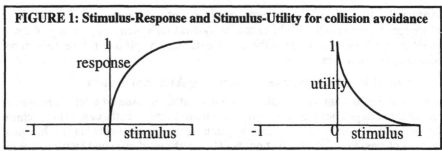

FIGURE 1: Stimulus-Response and Stimulus-Utility for collision avoidance

the traditional single more complicated one had turned out to be. A novel behavioural architecture (different from subsumption) was developed for this purpose.

3.1 The Behavioural Synthesis Architecture (BSA)

The basic unit of the BSA is the behaviour pattern. Each pattern is composed of two functions: a stimulus-response mapping, which for any sensory stimulus determines the motion response (either in terms of rotation or translation), and a stimulus-utility mapping, which for any sensory stimulus determines the importance of the motion response. Thus a collision avoidance behaviour pattern has a stimulus-response function which reduces translation as the distance sensor returns a stronger response (indicating an obstacle is close) together with a stimulus-utility function which gives a higher importance to this response as the obstacle gets closer. These can be seen in Figure 1. Note that both of these functions are non-symbolic in nature.

As is usual in a behavioural architecture, many behaviour patterns are concurrently active and thus conflict resolution is required. Unlike the subsumption architecture in which patterns are time-sliced, with only one pattern controlling the actuators at a given moment, the BSA synthesizes the responses of all active patterns as weighted by their current utility. Thus the emergent translation and rotation are a combination of all the weighted outcomes of the active patterns.

The BSA as so far described suffers from the same problem as any other behavioural architecture (and other reactive architectures): if all patterns are always active, then unwanted interactions often occur. An obvious example is the conflict between patterns producing collision avoidance and patterns producing docking for a mobile robot, or worse still, grasping, for a manipulator. The patterns that should be active at a particular

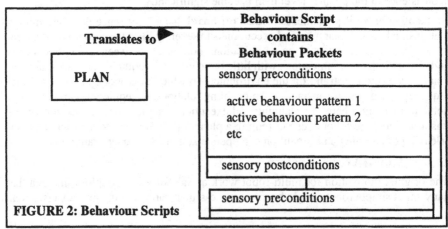

FIGURE 2: Behaviour Scripts

time are those required to carry out the current task; in other words the behavioural system needs to be able to use the subtask structure in order to avoid destructive conflicts. At Salford, this subtask structure is embodied in a construct called a Behaviour Script.

3.2 Behaviour Scripts

A Behaviour Script is made up of a sequence of behaviour packets. Each behaviour packet names a number of behaviour patterns which are to be active, and includes a sensory precondition for their activation and a sensory postcondition for their deactivation - see Figure 2. Thus a behaviour script is composed of a sequence of triplets: (<sensory precondition(s)><behaviour patterns><sensory postcondition(s)>).

Each behaviour packet within the script may be thought of as accomplishing a part of the overall task: thus a NAVIGATE-TO-BEACON packet contains a sensory precondition that the beacon is sensed, the behaviour patterns required to carry out the subtask (translate to beacon, rotate to beacon, and obstacle avoidance patterns), and the sensory postcondition that the robot is within the target distance of the beacon. If the robot is to dock at the beacon, the next packet would control this process, with its list of active behaviour patterns leaving out collision avoidance.

A behaviour script therefore uses the sub-task structure to create a series of contexts in which only relevant behaviour patterns are active. An individual behaviour packet could be expressed algorithmically as shown in Figure 3, where the SYNTHESIZE function represents the BSA process described in the previous section.

3.3 Cooperation

The MACTA project considered tasks in which several robots cooperated together. Real-world experiments involved two B12 platforms known as Fred and Ginger while simulated experiments involving larger numbers of robots were computer-based. In these experiments, the type of cooperation involved can be classified over two different dimensions: close-coupled versus loose-coupled and equal versus unequal.

Close-coupled cooperation occurs when two or more robots carry out a task in one linked physical system. This need not mean direct contact between the robots themselves: a number of experiments were carried out in cooperative object relocation where the robots were indirectly linked by the object they were carrying, much as a table would link two people transporting it. In loose-coupled cooperation, on the other hand, there is no physical linkage between the robots and cooperation relies on distance or other perceptual sensors only. An example here is one robot tracking another, for example training a camera on its partner's activities, as may be necessary in a hazardous environment where direct human observation is difficult.

Equal cooperation occurs where two robots cooperate to carry out the same task - say cooperative object relocation - with identical behaviours available to them. In this situation there is no leader or follower since both independently strive to move the object to the desired location. This might also be true in loose-coupled cooperation if robots

```
Figure 3 - Behaviour packet algorithm
if (sensory preconditions TRUE)
then
            while NOT (sensory postconditions)
            do
                        synthesise (active behaviour packets_
            endwhile
endif
```

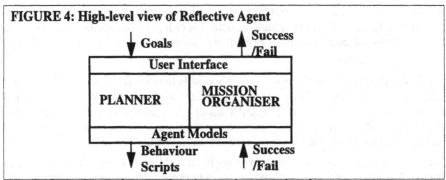

FIGURE 4: High-level view of Reflective Agent

move in formation to the same location, each possessing the same TRANSLATE-TO-BEACON and ROTATE-TO-BEACON behaviour patterns. If one robot broke down, this would not affect the ability of the other robots to continue.

While unequal cooperation looks much the same externally, only a subset of the robots has a complete set of behaviour patterns for the current subtask. Other robots 'help', that is, for instance, include behaviours which allow an object to be transported cooperatively without the patterns which allow movement to the desired location. The 'helping' robot would complete the task because it was able to follow its leading partner rather than because it had the ability to find the destination itself. In the same way, a loose-coupled formation of robots might include only one containing the TRANSLATE-TO-BEACON and ROTATE-TO-BEACON behaviour patterns while others merely followed it. In this case if the leading robot broke down, the other robots would not be able to proceed.

It is important to note that all of these forms of cooperation can be achieved as emergent behaviour: it is not necessary for robots to have explicit internal models of the process of cooperation or of each other [Aylett et al 96]. The synthesis mechanism of the BSA means that so long as appropriate behaviour patterns are provided (that is, the pairs of stimulus-response and stimulus-utility functions) for the appropriate sensors, cooperative activity is coordinated by adaption rather than by planning.

3.4 The Reflective Agent

Initially, behaviour scripts were hand-crafted. However the translation of an overall mission into a subtask structure is exactly what a planner does, and the BSA was therefore incorporated into a larger multi-agent architecture comprising multiple agents running the BSA (behavioural agents, or BAs), and a single Reflective Agent (or RA) including a predictive planning system [Aylett et al 97]. A high-level view of the RA architecture can be seen in Figure 4. The RA is responsible for transforming user goals into a partial order plan, using its Planner component, and then passing this to its Mission Organiser component which transforms it into an appropriate set of behaviour scripts (a *mission*). The Mission Organiser then sends the behaviour scripts to the robots chosen for the task. The robots carry out the mission autonomously, without further reference to the RA, until either the mission is complete and they can report a success or fail to the RA, or until any robot is involved in an unrecoverable error.

The work has always had an industrial focus, so that the typical organisational context envisaged was one in which a human operator was responsible for a team of behavioural agents - a supervisory hierarchy in which policy is decided centrally but execution details are handled by local initiative [Ephrati & Rosenschein 92]. This was the first reason for locating the planning capability in a single RA running on a work station which could interact in a straightforward way with such an operator.

Secondly, this approach is compatible with the enabling relationship between planning and execution adopted, allowing the behavioural components of the overall architecture to deal with all sensor input while the planner creates the context for its reactions. Where then does the model used in planning come from? It was decided that the planning model would be confined to an abstract a priori level and to those aspects of the world which were relatively unchanging. The dynamic aspects of the world would be confronted at execution time only.

This separation depends on the sub-task structure - at the level of primitive planning actions - referencing only the relatively stable aspects of the domain. This seems very plausible in the types of semi-structured industrial domains targeted by the project: within a factory for example, the basic internal layout is well-known to those working there precisely because this simplifies the execution of their plans. This separation of the world into abstract planning aspects and real-time execution aspects simplifies planning as already shown by work at Edinburgh [Malcolm&Smithers 90].

It is thus unnecessary to derive symbolic models directly from sensor data, an expensive and error-prone process as already noted. The subtask structure, in the form of a behaviour script, can be communicated to every robot involved in a cooperative task and execution can then proceed autonomously with a final success message allowing the planner to update its model with the logical consequences of the planned actions. A behaviour script can be encoded into a very small data structure since it only references patterns which are actually held within the robots. Thus only a low bandwidth connection is needed between the RA and BAs.

3.5 Implementing the Reflective Agent

In building the RA, it was decided to use a standard AI planner rather than constructing yet another from scratch. AI Planning Technology is sometimes said to be 'mature', in that it derives from work of the mid 1970s. Yet the planning community has devoted a considerable amount of effort to developing new theory, architectures and planning systems, and much less to examining the problems of applying existing planners to new domains. Using an existing planner brings into sharp focus the requirements at the planner level and tests the extent to which a planner can be considered 'general purpose' with respect to domains of application and particular execution agents.

Two demonstrator tasks in the MACTA domain were used to derive planner requirements. The first was an object interchange task, carried out in the environment of Figure 5. Robot1 collects an object from a beacon location and transports it to another location where the object is transferred to Robot2. Robot1 returns to its home station while Robot2 delivers the object. This can be expressed as the following set of goals:

`(AND(TRANSFERRED ?O ?R1 ?R2 AT BEAC2)(OBJECT-POSITION ?O AT BEAC3)(ROBOT-POSITION ?R1 AT BEAC4)(ROBOT-POSITION ?R2 AT BEAC5))`
This task was implemented all the way down to the execution level.

The second task was one of cooperative object relocation, in which an object is jointly carried by two robots to a destination at which Robot1 releases the object and tracks Robot2 while it docks and releases the object. This task was only modelled within the planner.

The overall planner requirements derived from these two tasks were as follows:
1. the need to allocate robots to actions;
2. concurrent execution of actions;

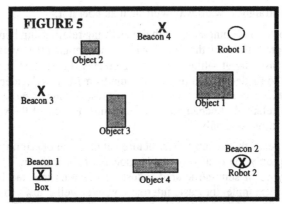

FIGURE 5

3. actions carried out by more than one agent (multi-robot actions);
4. actions with conditional effects (the effect of a robot releasing an object depends on how many robots were carrying it);
5. close-coupled cooperation;
6. loose-coupled cooperation;
7. intermediate goals (one robot tracks the other for part of the overall task).

After an evaluation of available planners [Coddington & Aylett 96], including PROD-IGY and NONLIN, UCPOP [Penberthy & Weld 92] was chosen. UCPOP is described by its authors as a clean Common Lisp implementation of an elegant algorithm for partial order planning with an expressive action representation. It has state-of-the-art facilities such as universal quantification, conditional effects, and domain axioms (inference rules). It is claimed that its simplicity and the efficiency of the implementation make it an excellent vehicle for further research on planning. However we argue that it has not been designed for research into the interaction between planning and execution.

4. Planning and Execution

We are now in a position to start answering the question posed above: what does a planner need to know about execution? Our investigations suggest that execution characteristics impact a number of different areas, which we summarize as: choice of planner primitive actions; modelling choices for individual actions; plan linearization; allocation of agents to tasks. Both the design process, in which the planner is adapted to a new domain, and the planning process itself are affected. The impact is particularly clear in the MACTA project because of its use of multiple cooperating execution agents, but may also be generalized, we argue, to other planner and execution systems.

4.1 Choice of Planner Primitives

An early design decision for any planner and any execution system is what actions to plan with, or for a hierarchical planner, what actions are the planner primitives. This determines what can be reasoned about in the planning domain and what must be left to execution systems and constitutes the primary interface between the two. In the MAC-TA system, it defines the actions, the unit of the plan constructed by UCPOP, and the basic mapping of each onto behaviour packets, the unit of the behaviour scripts.

We argue that a one-to-one mapping across this interface is highly desirable in order to support replanning at a later stage. For example, if a planner action NAVIGATE-AND-DOCK mapped to two behaviour packets - NAVIGATE-TO-BEACON and DOCK-WITH-BEACON - the planner would not be able to reason about a docking failure without also replanning the navigate. The actions chosen thus mirror the capabilities of the particular robots: for example, if, as in this case, their navigational abilities are limited to moving to the nearest beacon, any route planning becomes a planner problem.

This mapping is not only needed at the design stage. It must be carried out - in MACTA by the Mission Organiser - every time a plan is passed to execution agents. Thus it forms one part of the execution knowledge that must be explicitly represented. In MACTA this is held in a Behaviours Library as described in the next section, but any system with a planning-execution interface must maintain the equivalent.

The following actions were designed for the object interchange task described above: NAVIGATE, DOCK, ACQUIRE, RELEASE. The latter two, needed for object exchange, raised some interesting issues. In the first design a single TRANSFER action was created which involved both robots in its preconditions. However at the execution level, two different behaviour packets are needed, a RELEASE packet for one robot and an AC-QUIRE packet for the other. The translation mechanism could produce the two packets from the TRANSFER action, since it is possible to work out from the pre- and postconditions which robot is performing which role, but it was seen as undesirable to embed this type of domain knowledge in the translation mechanism.

In the solution adopted, the RELEASE action is modelled with preconditions:

        (ROBOT-POSITION ?ROBOT AT ?BEACON)
        (HOLDING ?ROBOT ?OBJECT)
and postconditions:
        (HOLDING ?ROBOT NOTHING)
        (OBJECT-POSITION ?OBJECT AT ?BEACON)
        (RELEASED ?OBJECT ?ROBOT AT ?BEACON)

The ACQUIRE action has preconditions:

        (ROBOT-POSITION ?ROBOT AT ?BEACON)
        (OBJECT-POSITION ?OBJECT AT ?BEACON)
        (HOLDING ?ROBOT NOTHING)
and postconditions:
        (:NOT (OBJECT-POSITION ?OBJECT AT ?BEACON))
        (HOLDING ?ROBOT ?OBJECT)
        (ACQUIRED ?OBJECT ?ROBOT AT ?BEACON)

These action definitions are identical with those used to acquire or release objects in fixed locations. For a transfer to occur, a RELEASE-ACQUIRE pair must be linked together, and a UCPOP domain axiom has to be used to achieve this:

(:AXIOM TRANSFER
:CONTEXT (:AND (RELEASED ?OBJ ?ROB1 ?REL ?REF)
        (ACQUIRED ?OBJ ?ROB2 ?REL ?REF))
:IMPLIES (TRANSFERRED ?OBJ ?ROB1 ?ROB2 ?REL ?REF))

This allows a RELEASE-ACQUIRE pair to meet the TRANSFERRED goal shown in section 3.5. The behaviour patterns in the packets generated from the mapping process deal with all the coordination issues at execution time.

4.2 Modelling Choices for Individual Actions

Cooperation between execution agents had a particular impact on the design of individual actions. It required multi-robot actions to be modelled and as a consequence of this, conditional effects. The second impact of execution characteristics was the difference between conditions at the planning and execution level which will also be discussed.

That many robots can carry an object in close-coupled cooperation suggests the need for multi-robot actions in which a variable number of agents execute an action. One could avoid this if say a TRANSPORT always required two robots, but different combinations of robots may in fact be capable of carrying out a given task: for example a ten ton load may be shifted by one ten-ton carrying robot or by two five-ton carrying robots. Separate actions for each possible combination would be very clumsy.

Here is how universal quantification was to model the effect of a set of robots X transporting an object ?o from location ?rel1 ?ref1 to ?rel2 ?ref2.

```
(:and (transported ?o ?rel1 ?ref1 ?rel2 ?ref2)
        (:forall (?x)
                (:when (:and (robot ?x)
                        (robot-position ?x ?rel1 ?ref1)
                        (holding ?x ?o))
                (:and (:not (robot-position ?x ?rel1 ?ref1))
                        (robot-position ?x ?rel2 ?ref2)))
```

An object ?o is transported when, for all x s.t x is a robot, x is holding ?o, x is at the initial location ?rel1 ?ref1 and moves to the destination location ?rel2 ?ref2.

The problem of one robot in a cooperative TRANSPORT releasing an object was solved using existential quantification and a conditional effect for the new RELEASE action:

```
(:and (:not (holding ?rob ?ob))
        (:when (:not (:exists
                (robot ?y)
                (:and (holding ?y ?ob) (:neq ?rob ?y))))
                (object-position ?ob ?rel ?ref)))))
```

The object ?o will be released at the location of a robot ?rob if there is no other robot ?y still holding it. Thus these general mechanisms were shown to be powerful enough to cope with the planning requirements even if the solution seems rather cumbersome.

Loose-coupled cooperation also raises specific issues which caused a lot of modelling difficulties. A typical example is one robot tracking another which is carrying out a specific task. Tracking is an example of an action which depends on successful sensing and which may also be dependent on the action being performed by the tracked robot. Thus an action ROBOT2 TRACK ROBOT1 actually involves a change in position for robot2 which is determined by the activity of robot1. We do not have space to discuss the issues in detail here, but a UCPOP axiom able to infer loose-coupledness proved essential to a solution. In other words, the planner had to have knowledge of loose-coupledness to plan correctly.

The second topic in this section concerns the significant difference between conditions at the planner level and the sensory conditions attached to a behaviour packet. This difference is general and exists for other planner-execution systems. In the case of planner actions, the pre- and postconditions produce a logically coherent structure for the plan guaranteeing that the given actions will allow the desired end-state to be reached from that given start-state. In the case of behaviour packets, pre- and postconditions control the subset of a robot's behaviour patterns active at a particular time. They can only relate to states of the world a robot is capable of sensing.

Thus for a single-robot RELEASE action, the planner action has a postcondition that the object is at the place it was released. For the robot, which has no conception of 'an object', the behaviour packet sensory postcondition is simply that the gripper is empty, since this is all that can be sensed. For this reason, even though a one-to-one mapping between planner actions and behaviour packets was adopted, behaviour packets have fewer pre- and postconditions in general than the action to which they correspond. We refer to the planner pre- and postconditions as *logical* conditions, and to the behaviour packet conditions as *transition* conditions.

Behaviour packets are stored in a library within the RA. They are small structures since the behaviour patterns they control exist only in the robots and are of no interest to the RA. Crucially, the packet sensory pre- and postconditions, the transition conditions, are represented in a symbolic form. Thus they form an execution model of the conditions in the world perceivable by execution agents. Again, we argue that any planner-execution system has to represent this knowledge, if only to successfully monitor execution.

4.3 Linearization

Standard planner linearization algorithms implicitly assume a single execution agent, as we see in the case of UCPOP. Thus linearization is another point at which knowledge of execution is required. Multiple execution agents usually result in concurrent execution and while a partially ordered plan is not formally equivalent to parallel execution, linearization can be modified to interpret the branches of a plan graph as concurrent activity *where the execution agents are specified for each action.* This allows accurate ordering information to be sent to each individual agent but requires them to have sufficient intelligence to organize the parallel aspects of execution in real-time.

The overall process of moving from UCPOP output to behaviour scripts in MACTA is shown in Figure 6. In order to insulate the Planner from the Mission Organiser components of the RA, a MACTA Plan Net Formalism (MPNF) was defined. Thus, if an alternative planner to UCPOP was used, it would not impact the implementation of the Mission Organiser. It also allows the separation of general issues in the mapping of planner actions to behaviour packets from the idiosyncrasies of UCPOP. We do not have space to describe MPNF in detail, but in fact it is a fairly standard STRIPS-like representation with the significant difference that it holds a specific slot in its action representation for the agent(s) executing it. This slot points to the relevant entry or entries in the Agents KB discussed below. We argue that any planner that supports multi-agent execution should explicitly represent the agent(s) needed to execute each action. Of course, if the planning community were able to agree on a suitable representation, then this could be used as a standard interface between planning and execution systems.

Figure 6 shows that two processes are involved in moving from plan to behaviour scripts: CONVERT which turns UCPOP output into MPNF, and TRANSLATE which maps MPNF into behaviour scripts. We said above that UCPOP was not designed for investigating the interaction between planning and execution: one reason for saying this is that the partial plan UCPOP builds is not easily accessible for passing on to execution systems, while its linearization - which assumes a single execution agent - is embedded in the generation of final output via print statements. The underlying data structures do not hold all the information about the partial plan in one place, and in particular do not instantiate all the variables, especially in expressions involving universal quantification, which we have shown above is necessary for the modelling of multi-robot actions.

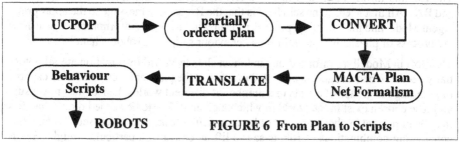

FIGURE 6 From Plan to Scripts

Having completed this essentially syntactic - and rather trying - conversion, the TRANS-LATE process maps MPNF onto a behaviour script for each robot involved in the mission as follows:

For each agent **a** in the MPNF Plan Net:

1. Determine which of the MPNF actions are to be executed by **a** and create the set of **a**-actions.

2. Using the temporal constraints of the MPNF Plan Net, linearize **a**-actions.

3. For each linearized element in **a**-actions, look in the behaviours slot of **a**'s model in the Agent Models (see next section) for an equivalent behaviour packet.

4. Form the chosen packets into a behaviour script.

5. Send to the agent.

Thus linearization has been extended to the multiple execution agent case.

4.4 Allocating Robots to Tasks

Any plan that is to be executed must have execution agents allocated to its actions as we have just seen. This might be seen as a separate scheduling task, carried out at linearization time, were it not that the allocation of execution resources interacts with the actions to be included during planning. For example, a plan which requires a robot to carry out a task such as docking or collecting an object from another robot, must also plan to get that robot to where the task is being carried out. If robots can also cooperate this issue becomes more acute, since as noted above, multi-robot actions may allow variable numbers of agents to be allocated to a particular action.

We argue that the knowledge of agents needed to allocate them to a task should be located in explicit models of the execution agents, which in the MACTA architecture are located in the Agent KB. This KB contains Agent Models, each as shown in Table 1.

Table 1: Agent Model

WORLD **INFORMATION**	Unique agent ID List of members of this Agent class World ID (e.g. real/simulator) Current Location (rel/ref pairs)
MODELLING **INFORMATION**	Available Behaviours (pointer to Behaviours Library) Capacities (non-behavioural - like lifting capacity) Status (e.g. ready, busy) Power level (e.g. high, recharging)
COMMS **INFORMATION**	Last contact time Message repertoire Comms routines (pointer to Comms library) Message buffers (in- and out-going)

The Comms Information slots in this table support communications between the RA and BAs. All that needs to be said here is that the RA sends a message to the appropriate Agent Model and the rest of the process is dealt with using this information. This is how the process of physically transmitting a behaviour script to a robot is handled.

The slots in Modelling Information, and most slots in World Information are all potentially needed when an agent is allocated to a task at the planner level. The RA is capable of planning for groups of agents in a number of different worlds, hence must make sure all those chosen exist in the world in which a given task is to be carried out. Capacities may be important in choosing a robot for a particular task, or as discussed above, when considering combinations of robots say to lift an object of a particular weight. Status and power-level are considered at the start of planning - a process not discussed in this paper establishes which robots are available for a task before planning starts.

The behaviour slot has already been mentioned in the previous section when the TRANSLATE process was described. Listing the available set of behaviour packets in the Agent Model has the important advantage of hiding some specialization of behaviour packets from the planner level. For example, a collection of robots may include some six-legged instances, and others which run on wheels. The NAVIGATE-TO-BEACON packet will contain different behaviour patterns for each type, but the TRANSLATE mechanism need not know this.

Our current proposal is not only to modify the classic planner action format to specify execution agent as in MPNF, but also to return to a concept which appeared in the original Script construct of [Schank & Abelson 77]. This is the idea of a Role, which provides an abstract description of the capabilities and behaviours needed to carry out an action or set of actions. In the MACTA system, this would correspond to an Agent Template, attached to a planner action, which could be mapped onto models in the Agent KB. In a hierarchical planner, this might only occur for primitive *executable* actions - where some reference to execution appears essential.

5. Discussion and Conclusions

The MACTA project has shown that it is possible to take a standard AI Planner - UCPOP - and interface it to an execution system consisting of multiple cooperating robots running a completely different behavioural architecture. This is an encouraging result. We have found that use of some of the more recent features in standard AI planning - notably universal and existential quantification, conditional effects and domain axioms - make it possible to model relatively unusual planning requirements, even if some of the solutions do not look very elegant and depend on the intelligence of the execution systems to produce the anticipated behaviour.

However in order to achieve this, much knowledge about the characteristics of the execution systems has had to be used at the planning level. The use of Agent Models has helped to insulate the planning process from some of the details, but many other aspects are embedded in the design process through choice of planner actions and design of pre- and postconditions. In particular, the different modes of cooperation discussed in 3.3 are difficult to model explicitly and the relationship between the capabilities of the agents, as held in the Agent Model, and the planner actions which they are able to execute also fails to appear explicitly, but is scattered in a selection of action preconditions. Our proposal for Roles would deal with this problem.

We note that execution issues are often not taken into account when planning systems are developed. As we have stated previously [Coddington & Aylett 96], most of UCPOP's examples leave entirely open who or what is actually going to execute the actions in the plan. Allocating agents to actions does not appear as a specific process since there is no privileged position for the execution agent in the planner action representation. We suggest that this lack of emphasis on execution is a problem, since it will often be true in real-world planning applications that the whole point of planning is to have the plans successfully executed as noted above.

We have proposed some answers of general use to our question 'What does a Planner need to know about execution?'. Agent Models, the Behaviours Library, and the explicit representation of execution agent in MPNF take us some of the way, and we expect that Roles will take us further. However other knowledge is still implicit in many of the modelling and design choices rather than declaratively stated and explicit. More work is needed in order to arrive at a situation where the relationship between planner and execution system can be completely defined cleanly and in a principled way.

6. References

Agre, P and Chapman, D. (1987). Pengi: An implementation of a theory of activity. Proceedings of the Sixth National Conference on Artificial Intelligence, AAAI 87 Morgan Kaufmann

Aylett, R.S. Fish, A.N. & Bartrum, S.R. (1991) HELP - a Hierarchical Execution-Led Planner for Robotic Domains. Proceedings, 1st European Workshop on Planning, EWSP '91, Springer-Verlag, 1991. pp1-12

Aylett, R.S; Coddington, A.M; Ghanea-Hercock, R.A. & Barnes, D.P. (1996) Communicating goals to behavioural agents - A hybrid approach. Proceedings, 3rd World Congress on Expert Systems, vol2, pp782-789, Seoul, Korea, Cognizant Corporation Ltd, 1996

Aylett, R.S. & Jones, S.D. (1996) Planner and Domain: Domain Configuration for a Task Planner. International Journal on Expert Systems Theory and Applications, v9 no2 pp279-318, JAI Press

Aylett, R.S; Coddington, A.M; Barnes.D.P. & Ghanea-Hercock, R.A. (1997) Supervising multiple cooperating mobile robots. Proceedings, 1st International Conference on Autonomous Agents, Marina Del Ray, Feb 1997

Barnes, D.P. (1996) A behaviour synthesis architecture for cooperant mobile robots. Advanced Robotics and Intelligetn Machines, eds J.O.Gray & D.G.Caldwell, IEE Control Engineering Series 51.295-314 1996

Bonasso, R.D. (1993) Integrating Reaction Plans and Layered Competences Through Synchronous Control *Robotica*, pp1225-1231

Brooks, R. (1986) A Robust Layered Control System for a Mobile Robot, *IEEE Journal of Robotics and Automation* RA-2(1) pp14-23

Coddington, A.M. & Aylett, R.S. (1996) Plan generation for multiple agents: an evaluation. Proceedings, 15th Workshop of the UK Planning & Scheduling SIG, vol 1, Liverpool John Moores University, Nov 1996

Ephrati,E. & Rosenschein, J.S. (1992) Constrained Intelligent Action: Planning Under the Influence of a Master Agent. *Proceedings, 10th National Conference on Artificial Intelligence, AAAI 92*, pp263-268.

Firby, R.J. (1989) Adaptive execution in complex dynamic worlds. Technical Report YALEU/CSD/RR no679, Computer Sceince Dept, Yale Univ.

Firby, R.J. (1994) Task networks for controlling continuous processes. Proceedings, 2nd International Conference on AI Planning Systems. pp49-54

Gat, E. (1992) Integrating Planning and Reacting in a Heterogeneous Asynchronous Architecture for Controlling Real-World Mobile Robots. Proceedings, 10th National Conference on Artificial Intelligence, AAAI-92, pp809-815

Lyons, D.M. & Hendriks, A.J. (1992) A Practical Approach to Integrating Reaction and deliberation. Artificial Intelligence Planning Systems: Proceedings of the 1st International Conference. Ed. James Hendler. pp 153-162. Morgan Kaufmann 1992.

Malcolm, C. & Smithers, T. (1990) Symbol grounding via a hybrid architecture in an autonomous assembly system. Robotics and Autonomous Systems, 6, pp123-44, 1990

Penberthy, J.C. & Weld, D. (1992) UCPOP: A sound, complete, partial-order planner for ADL. Proceedings, 3rd Int. Conf. on Priciples of Knowledge Representation and Reasoning, pp103-14, Oct 1992

Rosenschein, S. & Kaelbling, L. 91986) The synthesis of digital machines with provable epistemic properties. In: J.Y.Halpern (ed) Theoretical Aspects of Reasoning about Knowledge: proceedings of the 1986 Conference, pp83-98. Morgan-Kaufmann, 1986

Schank, R.C. & Abelson, R.P. (1977) Scripts, Plans, Goals and Understanding. Lawrence Erklbaum, 1977

Planning and Chemical Plant Operating Procedure Synthesis: a Case Study

Ruth Aylett, Gary Petley, Paul Chung, James Soutter, Andrew Rushton

ITI, Salford University, UK. email: R.S.Aylett@iti.salford.ac.uk

Abstract

Operating Procedure Synthesis (OPS) has been used to produce operating procedures for chemical plants. However, the application of AI planning to this domain has rarely been considered, and when it has the scope of the system used has limited it to solving 'toy' problems.

This paper describes a case study for the INTergrating OPerability (INT-OP) project at Salford and Loughborough that used a state-of-the-art least commitment planner with 'goals of prevention', called CEP (Chemical Engineering Planner), to produce procedures for a real-world chemical plant. A double effect evaporator test rig is the domain for the case study.

The development of the domain is discussed. Particular attention is paid to the domain modelling, which involved the description of the domain, development of operators/ safety restrictions, and the definition of the problem. There is then a presentation of the results, the lessons learned and the problems that remain.

1.0 Introduction

In this paper we discuss the application of AI Planning Technology to the domain of Operating Procedure Synthesis (OPS) for chemical process plants, considering in detail a particular case study, the Double Effect Evaporator (DEE) Test Rig. We argue that OPS is an important industrial application of AI Planning that not only has the potential to reduce the substantial time currently devoted to developing plant operating procedures manually, but also to support the consideration of operability problems at a much earlier stage in the plant life-cycle, therefore avoiding late changes to the design.

All industrial plants require an extensive set of operating procedures which define the steps required - for example - to start the plant up, to shut the plant down, to isolate pieces of equipment for maintenance or to deal with emergency situations. In older plants, all of these steps are carried out manually by human operators, but in highly automated modern plants these steps are embodied in the plant control system. It is clearly vital for reasons both of safety and efficiency that procedures are of a high quality. In the case of the chemical process industry, a multi-disciplinary commissioning team is normally responsible for defining sets of procedures, which takes of the order of two person-years of effort. If operability problems are uncovered during this work, then late changes to the design of the plant may result, in some cases while the plant is actually being constructed. These are the motivations for the development of computer-based tools to aid in the authoring of operating procedures.

OPS is a field of research that has largely been carried out in the chemical engineering domain [Rivas & Rudd 74; Ivanov et al 80; Fusillo & Powers 87; Foulkes et al 88; Lakshmann & Stephanopolous 88a,88b,90; Kinoshita et al 91; Aelion & Powers 91; Crookes & Macchietto 92], rather than in the AI Planning Community. Work has been carried out examining the links between planning and qualitative reasoning [Drabble 93], but using execution monitoring as a way of dealing with problems rather than handling them within the planning process itself. Yet there is an intuitively obvious relationship between an operating procedure and the output of a planning system. The steps in a procedure are actions to be carried out; the procedure is designed to take a plant from a start state to an end state; each step in the procedure must be carried out in the appropriate state and will result in a new state. Only Aelion and Powers [Aelion & Powers 91] of the works referenced above have seriously considered AI Planning technology (in this case a linear STRIPS type engine) and modern hierarchical and least-commitment techniques have not been applied. This has limited the scope of the systems developed to 'toy' plant domains. The case study discussed below is a larger and more complex problem than previously tackled by other researchers, representing a real plant, albeit one scaled down and simplified for teaching purposes.

1.1 The Chemical Engineering Planner (CEP)

The Chemical Engineering Planner (CEP) has been developed over the last four years, initially as a PhD project [Soutter 96] and in the last year as part of the EPSRC-funded INTergrating OPerability (INT-OP) project being carried out jointly between Loughborough and Salford Universities in the UK. CEP is being developed incrementally through case studies of increasing scope and complexity, and as the case study discussed in this paper shows, is already more capable than any of the systems referenced earlier. We will only summarise the structure of CEP in this paper.

In overview, CEP divides the tasks involved in OPS into three areas: planning using operators, the handling of safety considerations and valve sequencing. The first two of these three areas is handled by a state-of-the-art least-commitment planner [Penberthy & Weld 92], which uses the concept of 'goals of prevention' [Soutter & Chung 96] to prevent actions being incorporated into the operating procedure that will take a plant through any unsafe states.

Valve sequencing is dealt with as a special case. A characteristic of the opening and closing of valves in a chemical plant - actions required in order to produce flows of chemicals to specified vessels or other components - is that the effect of the primitive action at a particular valve is dependent on associated actions at other valves. However an assumption of the standard STRIPS representation of actions is that the effect of an action should be represented through its add-delete list - and should therefore always be the same. Valve operations violate this assumption.

Conditional operators - as in UCPOP [Penberthy & Weld 92] - represent one method of dealing with this problem, but the number and content of conditions required in the case of valves would depend on the configuration of the plant, and would be complex to specify, as well as specific to the particular plant under consideration. Therefore, valve sequencing is handled by a specialist module in CEP that uses an approach known in the OPS field as 'action synergy' [Foulkes et al 88]. Thus CEP can be seen as a general-purpose planner with domain-related specialist additions.

2.0 Double Effect Evaporator (DEE)

The case study discussed in this paper is based on a double effect evaporator test rig constructed in the Chemical Engineering department at Loughborough University. Although no longer used, the test rig was designed for teaching principles of plant operation to chemical engineering students. The layout of the test rig is shown in the

Fig. 1. Plant Diagram for Double Effect Evaporator Test Rig

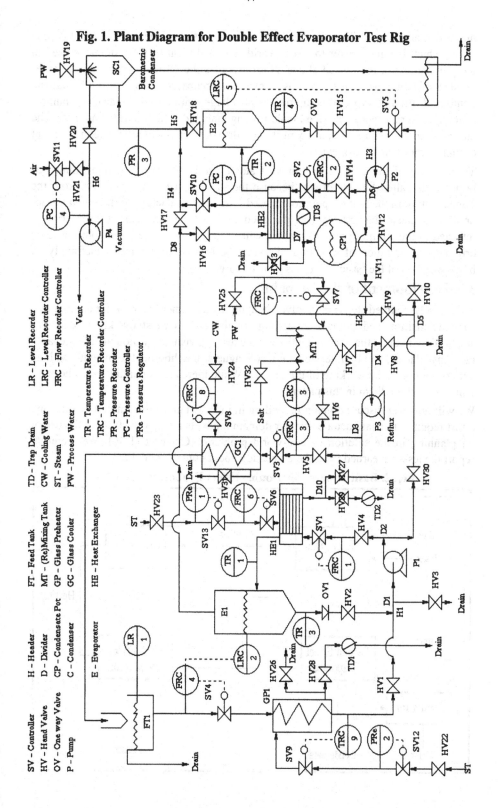

SV – Controller H – Header FT – Feed Tank TD – Trap Drain LR – Level Recorder

HV – Hand Valve D – Divider MT – (Re)Mixing Tank CW – Cooling Water LRC – Level Recorder Controller

OV – One way Valve CP – Condensate Pot GP – Glass Preheater ST – Steam FRC – Flow Recorder Controller

P – Pump C – Condenser GC – Glass Cooler PW – Process Water

E – Evaporator HE – Heat Exchanger TR – Temperature Recorder

TRC – Temperature Recorder Controller

PR – Pressure Recorder

PC – Pressure Controller

PRe – Pressure Regulator

plant diagram - fig. 1. This figure shows the complexity of the domain for this case study, which is much nearer to a real-world chemical plant than the domains used in the previous work referenced above. Not only does the DEE set-up contain a larger number of components than in most previous domains considered in OPS, but the number of different types of equipment is also large, with valves, controllers, pumps, heaters, coolers, evaporators, feed tank, mixing tank and a barometric condenser. The diagram shown is simplified; many protective devices which will intervene in the event of maloperation are not shown.

The purpose of the DEE is to remove water from a salt water solution (known as brine). It is called 'double effect' because the steam that is evaporated off from the brine solution in the first evaporation is used to supply the energy for the second evaporation. Because the test rig was designed for teaching, the concentrated brine is returned to the starting point and mixed with water to return the brine solution to its original concentration of salt, thus allowing the process to continue indefinitely. A block diagram of the basic process is shown in fig. 2.

3.0 Development of the Domain

Two closely-coupled steps are involved in applying a planner to a new domain: knowledge acquisition and domain modelling. In the DEE case-study, knowledge was acquired by reading the documentation on the test rig, visiting the double effect evaporator installation, and by interviewing a colleague at loughborough university with an understanding of the working of the test rig. While there are important issues here we will not touch on them in this paper.

We will however discuss domain modelling in more detail, as the amount of time and effort required to construct a particular domain model is a major obstacle to the use of AI planning in the solution of real-world problems [Chien et al 96]. We therefore report the lessons learned from the case study about domain modelling.

Fig. 2. Basic Process for Double Effect Evaporator Test Rig

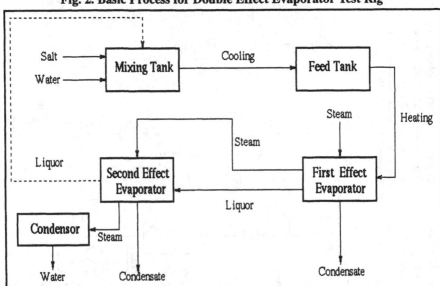

Fig. 3. DEE Component Hierarchy

```
Unit
  Inlet
      Heat Inlet
      Cool Inlet
  Outlet
      Drain
  Vessel
      Evaporator
      Barometric Condenser
      Feed Tank
      Condensate Pot
      Mixing Tank
  TempChanger
      Heater
          Heat Exchanger
              Heat ExchangerII
          Glass Preheater
      Cooler
          Glass Cooler
  Valve
      Solenoid
      Hand
      OneWay
      Controller
          Regulator
  Pump
      Vacuum
      Centrifugal
  Header
  Divider
  Trap Drain
```

Fig. 4. Example CEP Domain Description

frame(unit).

frame(vessel isa unit).

frame(feed_tank isa vessel, [
  propLinks info
  [
  arc([in, composition], 1, [out1, composition]),
  arc([in, composition], 1, [out2, composition])
  ]).

instance(FT1 isa feed_tank,
[
outports info [out1 is [FRC_4+LRC_2, in]],
outports info [out2 is [Output3, in]]
]).

3.1 Domain Modelling

After the knowledge acquisition, the information acquired must be transformed into a form that the planner CEP can understand and use. CEP requires the following:

- Domain description
- Safety restrictions
- Operators
- Domain problems

3.1.1 Domain description

A process plant can be described in terms of a hierarchy of components and the connections between them. The complete hierarchy for the components in the DEE domain is shown in fig. 3. CEP uses an implementation of such a hierarchical frame-based description developed during earlier work at Loughborough [Chung 93] - of which fig. 4. shows an example.

As the complexity of fig. 1. demonstrates, manual entry of the instances required for a particular plant is non-trivial: it is both very time-consuming and prone to error. An automatic system was therefore developed for producing the domain description. A popular drawing package, AutoCAD, has been adapted to provide the standard chemical engineering equipment symbols for the user. When a new piece of equipment is added to the plant diagram, a text box appears prompting the user to add the name and connections for it. Thus on completion of the drawing, the necessary information has been collected to allow the automatic creation of a file, in the form of the instance shown in fig. 4, that describes the plant to CEP.

3.2 Planning Operators

The next stage is to develop the planning operators used to produce the plan (the operating procedure). A CEP operator consists of a goal(s) that can be achieved when the precondition goal(s) for the operator are true - essentially the STRIPS representation. The CEP operator for operating a hand valve is shown in fig. 5.

Fig. 5. Hand Valve Operator　　　　**Fig. 6. Hierarchical Operator**

```
operator OperateHandValve
{
    aperture ?state1;
    aperture ?state2;
    hand ?h;

    ?state1 != ?state2;

    achieve
     * aperture of ?h is ?state2;
    using
     aperture of ?h is ?state1;
    end

    print (?n) [name of ?state2 is ?n; ]
                        ' valve ' ?h;
}
```

```
operator OperateSingleEffectPlant
{
    expand
        * state of DoubleEffectPlant
                        is single_effect;
    using
        state of Evaporator1 is started;
        state of MixingTank1 is started;
        state of Evaporator2 is stopped;
        state of HeatExchanger2 is started;
        state of SprayCondensor1 is started;
    end
}
```

The identifiers starting with '?' represent variables which will be instantiated with actual components when the operator is used: ?h with the particular hand valve, ?state1 with the initial state of the valve, ?state2 with the final state of the valve.

Operator development is another time-consuming part of domain development and one on which there is minimal guidance in the literature. The Task Formalism Guide [Tate 94] for use in constructing O-PLAN [Currie & Tate 91] domains is the only example so far discovered. Yet the correctness and efficiency of the planning process in a domain depends very heavily on operator definition. We therefore summarise the lessons of the DEE case study in the sections below.

Required Operators

The initial step is to establish the task requirements by producing a list of all the tasks to be carried out in the domain. For example, the DEE requires operating procedures to start the plant up as a single effect or double effect evaporator; to shut the plant down; to switch between the previous states; to isolate pieces of equipment for maintenance or to deal with emergency situations. Therefore, operators are required for the start-up and shutdown of each piece of equipment in the test rig.

Generality of Operators

One important issue concerns the generality of operators. The more generic the operators, the fewer the number required, and, even more important, the greater the scope for re-use. On the other hand operators must be specific enough in relation to the domain description to prevent vast amounts of search when instantiating pre and post-conditions [Aylett & Jones 96] and to capture appropriate differences in functionality. For example, in the DEE class hierarchy shown in fig. 3., an operator at the level of *vessel* would be too general since there are significant differences in functionality between, say, an evaporator and mixing tank, and instantiation would have to consider every vessel in a plant.

It was decided to limit the number of operators by using those generic to any piece of equipment of the same type, where type was defined as one of the leaves in the class hierarchy for the domain shown in fig. 3. Thus the DEE has over 30 hand valves, but only one operator is required to open and close these valves, see fig. 5. One might expect operators for particular types of equipment to occur in pairs: one for start-up and one for shutdown. While this generally proved to be the case, sometimes it was possible to combine both into one operator acting as a toggle between states - as in the case of valves, further reducing the number of operators that are necessary.

Library of Operators

A consequence of producing generic operators is the possibility this opens up of providing a good-quality library of operators for equipment commonly found in chemical plants, such as valves, pumps, heat exchangers etc. A suitably comprehensive library would standardise the design of operators by reducing the task to one of selection with possibly some scope for specialisation. Indeed, it is hard to see how CEP could be applied to new plants in an industrial context without such a library since one could not expect a target user such as a plant design engineer to design operators from scratch. The library of operators for CEP is being extended with each case study as new components are encountered and an interface for accessing the library of equipment operators is being designed. As we will see below, one criterion for evaluating the success of CEP in the case-study domain was the extent to which it proved possible to solve the required tasks with generic operators. A number of interesting issues arose which will be discussed later.

Hierarchical Structure of Operators

There is a substantial difference in granularity between the task requirement level (e.g. start-up plant in single-evaporator mode) and the primitive action level (e.g. open valve HV5) in OPS domains. This shows [Aylett & Jones 96] a clear need for hierarchical structure in all the operators in the model. The task of starting up the plant in single-evaporator mode is represented as a high level operator (fig. 6.) with an effect which expands into a set of goals satisfied by operators at the next level of expansion. These in turn may expand the effects further to a new level of operators. The result is a goal-hierarchy which represents the declarative structure of planning in the domain. The goal-hierarchy for the DEE domain can be seen in fig. 7., showing that the top-level goals for the system concern the state of the DEE system itself, expanding into the states of vessels and temperature changers, which may be started or stopped. These expand in turn into fill and flow goals, where each may be true or false - the goal of

Fig. 7. Goal Hierarchy

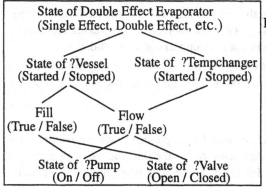

Fig. 8. Example Safety Restriction

```
restrictions
{
    prevent
        state of HE1 is started;
        state of GC1 is stopped;
    end
}
```

making a fill false is equivalent to emptying a vessel for example. At the lowest level, goals reduce to the states of valves and pumps. Thus there are two types of operator: expansion operators as shown in fig. 6., and primitive operators as for example in fig. 5. The latter include a print statement used to display the final operating procedure and use the keyword 'achieve' in place of the keyword 'expand'.

3.2.1 Safety restrictions

Safety is a particular concern in a chemical plant domain. A plan which moves the plant to an end-state is unacceptable if, for example, along the way explosive gases have been mixed with air. Safety restrictions in CEP are constraints that prevent unsafe situations from occurring during planning through the specification of incompatible states. Fig. 8. shows a safety restriction for the DEE that specifies that heat exchanger HE1 is not allowed to be started if the state of the glass cooler GC1 is stopped. The reason for this restriction is to prevent energy from entering the plant - because a heater is on - before there is a mechanism for energy to leave the plant - a cooler is on.

Safety restrictions allow issues of safety to be dealt with separately from the design of operators. An alternative is to add extra pre-conditions to operators specifying safe states for their use. Thus, the safety restriction of fig. 8. could be replaced by an operator for activating HE1 with a precondition that the glass cooler is on, though in general this may require both quantification and disjunction in the operator preconditions.

There are two arguments against this latter approach: firstly, this will not prevent the glass cooler being turned off at a later stage while the heat exchanger is still on. Secondly, the operator created is specific to the heat exchanger, HE1, and so it is not generic. For these reasons, we argue that restrictions should be used in preference to modified operators. In addition, the use of safety restrictions ensures that safety knowledge is represented in one place, where it can be assessed and checked against safety regulations, an important consideration for user acceptance in the industry. We will return to this issue in section 4 since it is an example of a general point: it appears that problematic aspects of a domain can often be dealt with by manipulating operators but that such solutions turn out in practice to be very much ad hoc.

While restrictions are a good way of separating out safety information, in practice they often turn out to be task dependent. In particular, restrictions for the start-up of a plant can make the shut-down impossible. For example, looking at glass cooler GC1 on fig. 1., and the associated valve HV5, a restriction (preventing HV5 open and GC1 off) stops the flow of brine into GC1 until on, which is desired on start-up of a plant, but on shutdown of the plant it is fine to let all the brine run back into the feed tank and then turn off the glass cooler without closing HV5. Therefore, separate files are required for the restrictions in the DEE domain, one for start-up and one for shut-down.

A library of safety restrictions is not thought to be worthwhile as they are much more domain specific than operators, but a record of the safety rules used in their construction must be maintained.

3.2.2 Domain problems

Finally, a definition of a problem in the domain for the planner to solve is required. The problem definition requires two domain states, one at the start and the other at the end of the problem. A domain state is described by the state of each component in the plant. From this CEP will produce a plan of actions that accomplish the change in the plant's operating conditions, if one exists for the given operators and restrictions. The AutoCAD tool used to provide the domain description also provides a method for defining the state of the equipment for a domain state, allowing the domain problem to be developed in parallel with the domain description.

4.0 Results and evaluation

CEP successfully produced operating procedures for the double effect evaporator. A single model of the domain allowed procedures to be created for the start-up, shutdown and to isolate pieces of equipment for maintenance.

The start-up procedure generated by CEP for the double effect evaporator contains 50 steps. The total number of operators used in planning was under 20. The time taken to generate the operating procedure was under a second on a Sparc 5. Moreover CEP proved capable of finding alternative procedures via backtracking at user request.

4.1 Comparison with previous systems

The planner CEP has been used to produce operating procedures using AI planning for a domain more complex than others previously attempted. The work of the early 80s [Ivanov et al 80, Kinoshita et al 81] using state-graphs limited sample problems to plants containing a handful of valves because of the number of states they generated: 20 valves each with 2 states produces 1,048,576 nodes in a state-graph. Other workers used larger plants [Rivas & Rudd 74] but only considered valves and not vessels. A real-world nuclear fuel processing plant was used [Crookes & Macchietto 92], but this work concentrated on optimising a hand-generated plan. CEP has successfully solved every sample problem reported in the OPS literature except for those requiring numerical calculations. We therefore argue that this case study demonstrates a big step in the state-of-the-art for OPS.

4.2 Quality of results

The procedures produced were evaluated by the same expert who had been used for the knowledge acquisition. He found the generated procedures adequate, in the sense that the start-up procedure could successfully start up the plant. This is an important result for a domain of this complexity and validates the overall approach of using AI Planning technology on this problem. However the generated procedures were in some ways naive - in that they were not always identical to those an expert would produce.

A major example of this concerned the use of the glass preheater (GP1 in the top-left of fig. 1.). It is possible to start up the plant without using this preheater, and accordingly CEP originally generated a procedure that did not use it. The reasons for using the preheater during start-up are: the temperature of the brine can be increased in stages - protecting the glass lined vessels, and the control of the temperature of the brine entering the first evaporator is easier with two heaters. An expert in operability, seeing that the design contained a glass preheater, would infer that it was there for the purpose of start-up and accordingly use it. This operability knowledge does not appear to be representable within the confines of planning operators and we are currently examining the issue in more detail.

Producing a start-up procedure which uses the glass preheater required the use of the restrictions mechanism discussed above. A restriction that flow cannot occur through the glass preheater, and therefore the rest of the plant, until the pre-heater is on, forces its use. While the restrictions mechanism provides a general capability which can be used for other issues than safety, its use in this way is an ad hoc solution, since it does not explicitly represent the operability knowledge being used but only the plant-specific consequences of applying it. We are exploring the possibility of dealing with such issues in a more generic way: For example the domain expert states 'start the *cold side* of the plant before the *hot side*' as a general Plant Operations heuristic, which could sensibly be encoded in a restriction.

A further quality issue concerns the glass cooler (GC1 in fig. 1.) in the test rig. The cooler is turned on by flowing cooling water through it at any time before there is a flow of brine into the cooler. Now, the smaller the time gap between turning on the cooler and the brine arriving, within the constraints of safety, the smaller the amount of cooling water wasted and the more economical the start-up of the operating procedure.This kind of optimization is not, we feel, well handled by a planner and suggests the need for an optimising back-end [Crookes & Macchietto 92].

4.3 Linking and ordering actions

An interesting issue arose from considering the linearization process in which the partially ordered output of CEP is turned into a sequence of operating instructions. An extract from a plan graph generated by CEP can be seen in fig. 9. and represents a plan fragment for the operation of a pump, showing that actions OperateValve-3, OperateValve-4 are partially ordered and thus can be taken in any order.

However, not all linearizations of a partial plan are equally acceptable. It may be the case that some actions which are ordered in the plan should be carried out one after another, without interpolation of other actions partially ordered with respect to them. For example, changing the operation of the plant from using one evaporator to using both requires the opening of one valve and the shutting of another at virtually the same time to create a flow of steam through the second heat exchanger. One would not wish other valve operations elsewhere in the plant along a different branch of the plan graph to be inserted into this sequence, though this linearization is formally possible. Currently, a plan graph representation is not sufficiently rich to represent this information.

An ad hoc solution to this problem can be arrived at by using an operator that achieves both actions and states in the plan 'open valve x and close valve y'. However, as

Fig. 9. Plan for Operating Pump

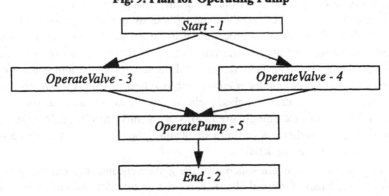

already discussed when safety restrictions were described above, this manipulation of the operators is not a general solution since it implicitly encodes the configuration of a particular plant into an operator which cannot then be easily included in the library of generic operators. We are considering the use of *short links* between actions that allow the links in the plan graph to carry the information that actions should be kept close together at linearization [Soutter et al 97].

The plan graph supports user interaction in the linearization process since it shows what actions can be moved in a particular linearization and which cannot. The re-ordering of actions may be desirable for two reasons in addition to the one just discussed. Firstly, grouping actions together for operating a certain piece of equipment makes the plan clearer. Secondly, a 'better' plan may be produced by taking the actions in a certain order. For example, if two valves have to be opened manually, then these actions should be together if they are geographically next to each other in the plant and other constraints do not prevent them from being adjacent actions

4.4 Valve sequencing problem

The development of the procedures in CEP required many different flows around the plant. CEP's valve sequencing component establishes a flow by closing all valves between the desired start and end of the flow and any other valves neighbouring these [Soutter & Chung 97]. Only the valves immediately on the flow path are then opened, leaving the surrounding valves closed [Foulkes et al 88]. This works for simple flows, but results in valves being closed which should in fact be open when a flow which branches is required in conjunction with a previously established flow. An example is the mixing tank recycle, where there is a flow from the mixing tank, through valve HV7, pump P3, valve HV6 and back to the mixing tank. The valve sequencing for CEP is being expanded to deal with such flows [Soutter et al 97], but an ad hoc solution was adopted for the DEE. This involved creating a non-generic operator for the mixing tank recycle, which specified the opening of HV7, HV6, and P3 to create the recycle.

4.5 Problems with generic operators

We argue that the extent to which operators are generic is a touchstone for the extent to which CEP has principled solutions to OPS problems. The use of safety restrictions and of a specialist valve sequencing component removes the need to solve particular problems by manipulating operators into a plant-specific form. Correspondingly, where valve sequencing is currently insufficient, the encoding of plant-specific information into an operator allows a temporary fix. The effect of such fixes can be limited by the use of hierarchical operators so that a top level generic operator is added to the library which expands into a plant specific lower level operator, allowing every component in the DEE to be included in the component library.

A more important issue concerns the extent to which real-world components in process plant are generic. For example, of the two heat exchanger in the DEE, one has an extra out port for the steam used to heat the material passing through the exchanger. In real plants, components are sourced from a variety of manufacturers and so there may be differences in the way each is constructed and operated. If this variation is empirically shown to be very large, a generic library of operators might be impossible. An obvious approach to this problem is to consider attaching the library of operators more firmly to the component hierarchy, with the use of object-oriented inheritance and specialisation mechanisms to control variation, and this is now being investigated.

5.0 Conclusions

A number of conclusions can be drawn from the DEE case study, some specific to the domain of Process Plant Operating Procedure Synthesis, and others of more general relevance to industrial applications of AI planning.

A positive conclusion is that the DEE case study validates the use of state-of-the-art AI planning techniques in OPS. As discussed above, this has made it possible to deal successfully with large and complex domains. A further case study has now started using a full-scale industrial plant belonging to one of the project's industrial collaborators.

This is not to overstate CEP's current capabilities - the DEE case study has made it clear that a number of improvements are needed: in the linearization process, in the valve sequencing component and in the incorporation of general operability knowledge. We argue that this indicates that though general-purpose hierarchical least-commitment planning algorithms are powerful, real domains also require domain-specific problem-solving along with a great deal of domain-specific knowledge. Hopefully, in the same way as work in knowledge-engineering methodologies has identified specific approaches to different types of diagnosis, work in a wider range of real-world planning domains will begin to establish abstract categories in such domains which will support a more principled approach to the choice of planning technologies for particular problems [Valente 95, Aylett & Jones 96, Soutter et al 97].

A number of knowledge engineering issues arose from the DEE case study. Firstly, the time and effort required to develop the domain was substantial, with about 20 person-days of effort involved in developing the operators alone (though a proportion of this was due to a learning curve which would be climbed quicker next time as a result of this experience). Development of tools to assist in domain development is, we believe, vital to the use of AI planning to solve real-world problems. The automatic generation of the domain description, as for CEP from AutoCad, is a step along this path, and the library of generic operators derived from the case study is an even more important one. Validation and verification tools such as those described in [Chien 96] are also important. A project which could produce a tool kit of (preferably planner-independent) domain development tools would do the whole community a major service.

The production of a library of generic operators in the DEE case study illuminated a particular problem. It is often possible to solve problems in a particular domain by ad hoc fixes, frequently in the planning operators. We discussed some of these in section 4 and remarked that a measure of CEP's ability in this domain lay in how many or few such fixes were required. As CEP's capabilities are increased, so it becomes possible to solve each problem in a more general and principled way. Thus the ability to produce a library of generic operators is not only an indispensable tool for domain development in the future, it is also, we argue, indirectly a measure of the adequacy of a planner.

OPS is a new area for AI Planning, but we suggest one of considerable promise. The DEE case study forms the basis for continuing work in the INT-OP project towards a system which can be used in a real-industrial environment to produce quality operating procedures earlier in the plant life-cycle with real savings in time and effort. This research illustrates the potential of AI planning in industrial applications.

6.0 Acknowledgements

This work was made possible through funding from the EPSRC grant: "Intergrating Operability into Plant Design", the ESRC, the SERC, BG plc, BP, Cogsys, ICI and Subs-IAD. Paul Chung is grateful to BG plc and The Royal Academy of Engineering for financial support through a Senior Research Fellowship.

7.0 References

Aelion, V. & Powers, G.J. (1991) A Unified Strategy for the Retrofit Synthesis of Flowsheet Structures for Attaining or Improving Operating Procedures. In: Computers and Chemical Engineering, vol. 15 no 5, pp349-360, Pergamon 1991.

Aylett, R.S. & Jones, S.D. (1996) Planner and Domain: Domain Configuration for a Task Planner. International Journal of Expert Systems v9 no2 pp279-318, JAI Press 1996.

Chien, S.A. (1996) Static and Completion Analysis for Planning Knowledge Base Development and Verification. Proceedings, 3rd International Conference on AI Planning Systems, pp53-61, AAAI Press, 1996.

Chien, S.A; Hill, R.W; Wang, X; Estlin, T; Fayyad, K.V. & Mortenson, H.B.(1996) Why Real-world Planning is Difficult: a Tale of Two Applications. In: New Directions in AI Planning, M.Ghallab & A.Milani, eds, IOS Press, Washington DC 1996 pp 287-298.

Chung, P.W.H. (1993) Qualitative Analysis of Process Plant Behaviour. Proceedings,Industrial and Engineering Applications of AI and Expert Systems,ed. P.W.H.Chung, G.Lovegrove & M.Ali, pp277-283 Gordon & Breach 1993.

Crooks, C.A. & Macchietto, S. (1992) A Combined MILP and Logic-Based Approach to the Synthesis of Operating Procedures for Batch Plants. Chem. Eng. Comm. 114, pp117-144.

Currie, K, & Tate, A. (1991) O-plan: the Open Planning Architecture. AI, 52:49-86, 1991.

Drabble, B. (1993) Excalibur: a program for planning and reasoning with processes. Artificial Intelligence, v62 no1, pp1-40, Elsevier 1993.

Foulkes, N.R.; Walton, M.J.; Andow, P.K. & Galluzo, M. (1988) Computer Aided Synthesis of Complex Pump and Valve Operations. Computers and Chem. Eng., 12 pp1035-1044.

Fusillo, R.H. & Powers, G.J. (1987) A Synthesis Method for Chemical Plant Operating Procedures. In: Computers in Chemical Engineering, vol 11 no 4, pp 369-382, Pergamon, 1987.

Ivanov, V.A.; Kafarov, V.V.; Perov, V.L. & Reznichenko, A.A. (1980) On Algorithmization of the Start-up of Chemical Productions. Engineering Cybernetics, 18, pp104-110.

Kinoshita, A.; Umeda, T & O'Shima, E. (1981) An Algorithm for Synthesis of Operational Sequences of Chemical Plants. 14th Symposium on Computerized Control and Operation of Chemical Plants, Vienna, Austria, 1981.

Lakshmanan, R. & Stephanopolous, G. (1988a) Synthesis of Operating Procedures for Complete Chemical Plants - 1. Hierarchical Structured Modelling for Nonlinear Planning In: Computers in Chemical Engineering, vol 12 no 9/10, pp985-1002, Pergamon 1988.

Lakshmanan, R. & Stephanopolous, G. (1988b) Synthesis of Operating Procedures for Complete Chemical Plants - 2. A Nonlinear Planning Methodology In: Computers in Chemical Engineering, vol 12 no 9/10, pp1003-1021, Pergamon 1988.

Lakshmanan, R. & Stephanopolous, G. (1990) Synthesis of Operating Procedures for Complete Chemical Plants - 3. Planning in the Presence of Qualitative Mixing Constraints In: Computers in Chemical Engineering, vol 14 no 3, pp301-317, Pergamon 1990.

Penberthy, J.S. & Weld, D.S. (1992) UCPOP: A Sound, Complete, Partial Order Planner for ADL. 3rd Int. Conf. on Knowledge Representation and Reasoning. Oct. 1992.

Rivas, J.R. & Rudd, D.F. (1974) Synthesis of Failure-Safe Operations. In: AIChE Journal, vol 20 no 2, pp 320-325, March 1974.

Soutter, J. (1996) An Integrated Architecture for Operating Procedure Synthesis. PhD thesis, Loughborough University, Loughborough LE11 3TU, UK.

Soutter, J. & Chung, P.W.H. (1996) Partial Order Planning with Goals of Prevention. proceedings, 15th Workshop of the UK Planning and Scheduling SIG, vol 2 pp300-311, John Moores University, Liverpool, UK.

Soutter, J. & Chung, P.W.H. (1997) Utilising Hybrid Problem Solving to Solve Operating Procedure Synthesis Problems, IChemE Research Event 97, vol2 pp793-796, Nottingham.

Tate, A. (1994) O-Plan2 Task Formalism Manual Ver 2.2. Internal Report of the AI Applications Institute, 1994, University of Edinburgh.

Valente, A. (1995) Knowledge-level Analysis of Planning Systems. ACM SIGART Bulletin Special Issue, 6(1), Jan 1995.

Task Planning and Partial Order Planning: A Domain Transformation Approach

M. Baioletti, S. Marcugini, A. Milani

Dipartimento di Matematica
Università di Perugia
Via Vanvitelli, 1
06100 Perugia, Italy
E-mail addresses: {marco,gino,milani}@dipmat.unipg.it
Fax number: +39-75-585-5024
Keywords: Partial Order Planning, Task Planning,
Domain Transformation, Expressivity.

Abstract In this paper [1] we introduce techniques of domain transformation for representing and managing task network goals in the framework of partial order planning. A task network planning model, extended to describe external events, is introduced. We prove that it is always possible to express a task network problem in terms of an equivalent problem stated in partial order planning formalism on an appropriate domain. A linear cost technique of domain transformation is described: a given task domain is compiled to generate an equivalent operator based domain which is then submitted to a nonlinear planner. This result shows how to reuse existing partial order planners for solving task network problems. This technique has been successfully demonstrated by the implementation of two TN planners based on domain tranformation for UCPOP and for GRAPHPLAN.

1 Introduction

In the last years many papers have dealt with Hierarchical Task Network (HTN) approach in AI planning ([15],[7],[5],[8],[6]). The success of this approach is due to its effectiveness from both the expressivity and computational sides.

The works of Yang [15], Erol et al.[5] [7] and Kambhampati [10] have extensively investigated semantics and complexity of this approach. They show that HTN is strictly more powerful than ordinary (STRIPS-like) planning. This result basically derives from the fact that the set of solution plans of an ordinary planning problem is a regular language, while the set of solution plans of HTN planning problems is a higher level language, (i.e. the solutions space can be expressed as intersection of context free languages).

HTN planning problems are described in terms of a task network, whose nodes are of three different types: *achieve*, *do* and *perform* tasks. A partial order relation is given on task nodes.

---

[1] This work has been partially supported under Italian National Research Council–C.N.R. "Strategie di controllo innovative per sistemi di Intelligenza Artificiale"

An *achieve* task can be seen as a generalization of user goals: the task is executed by achieving a given condition at a certain instant which is not necessarily the final situation.

A *do* task requires the execution of a given action at a certain instant.

A *perform* task allows hierarchical execution of subtasks by means of the *reduction methods*: each task of this type can be replaced by a task network, which can contain other perform tasks.

The last feature adds the possibility of giving a hierarchical partition to the solution space and most importantly it allows to define recursive plans, which generate a solution language qualitatively different, at a higher level, from PO planning. On the other hand the other features of HTN planning, such as the *do* tasks, are still interesting and have no direct equivalent in PO planning.

Typical examples of problems which cannot be directly modeled in STRIPS-like planners are problems in which the activity is more significant than the goal state, like problems with identical initial and final state (i.e. "making a round trip from Rome to Florence", "using the computer in the lab but leaving it in the same state it was found "); or problems requiring that some particular actions are to be executed in some specific order ("knock the door, then ring the bell, then knock the door again, then open"); or some specific intermediate states are to be achieved ("be in Florence, then be in Venice").

The main reason is the lack of an explicit notion of time in partial order (PO) planners, in which a problem goal is only described in terms of reaching a final state from some initial condition, without considering what happens in the other instants.

The results of HTN shows that an explicit time management (and the associated computational overhead) is not strictly necessary to model this class of problems.

In the following we restrict our study to a significant subset of HTN planning, that we call Task Network planning (TN), showing that problems in this formalism can be solved, by an appropriate domain transformation, within the partial order planning (PO) model. The same equivalence result is obtained when TN planning is extended to handle with *external events*. In this framework external events are meant as events which are known, at planning time, to happen in some intermediate instants. The planner is thus required to generate a solution plan which reaches the goals taking into account the external events. The management of external events is not usually included in most HTN planners in the literature.

2 PO Planning

A simple widely accepted Partial Order planning model (PO) is used as reference in the following.

A planning problem is a tuple $(\mathcal{I}, \mathcal{A}, \mathcal{G})$, where $\mathcal{I}$ is an initial state, $\mathcal{G}$ a set of conjunctive user goals, and $\mathcal{A}$ is the set of available action schemata.

Each action a of $\mathcal{A}$ is represented by a triple (v, p, e), where v, p, e respectively represent variables, preconditions end effects of action a.

A plan P is a triple $(\mathcal{S}, \mathcal{C}, \mathcal{O})$ where the elements of $\mathcal{S}$, the plan steps, are instances of actions in $\mathcal{A}$, $\mathcal{C}$ is a set of constraints (binding and auxiliary) and $\mathcal{O}$ is a partial order relation on $\mathcal{S}$.

P is a solution plan if it reaches the final goal $\mathcal{G}$ when executed in the initial state $\mathcal{I}$, assuming the classical semantics of PO planning model as, for example, that of UCPOP [14].

3 Task Network Planning

Our notation in the following will be partially similar to that one of [5], [7] and [10].

A Task Network planning model requires the user to describe intermediate goals G, execution goals S, external events I and a partial order O relation among $G \cup S \cup I$.

Intermediate goals

Intermediate goals, $G = (\text{achieve}(p_1), \ldots, \text{achieve}(p_m))$, represent goals which are required to be achieved in some intermediate state of the solution plan, temporally located between the initial and the final state. A partial order relation $\preceq$ can be defined on G and it states in which order the partial goals have to be achieved, i.e., $\text{achieve}(p_i) \preceq \text{achieve}(p_j)$ if and only if p_i has to be true in some instant preceding the instant in which p_j has to be true.

A typical case in which intermediate or "partial" goals are useful is when the user final goal is equal to the initial state, but it is also required a different intermediate state. In the **round trip** example, described in the introduction, the initial and final state are the same, (i.e. be_in(Florence)) while the intermediate state is different (i.e. be_in(Rome)).

Note that a classical PO planner would trivially (and uncorrectly) solve any given problem, where $\mathcal{I}$ and $\mathcal{G}$ coincide, by generating the empty plan.

Another useful case is when the goals to obtain are some result p and its negation $\neg p$, for example pick up an object (in order to observe it) and put it down. In this case the two goals taken(object) and ¬taken(object) would be in contradiction and clearly they cannot be expressed by a unique final goal.

Execution goals

Execution goals, $S = (\text{do}(\alpha_1), \ldots, \text{do}(\alpha_n))$, are some specific steps that have to be executed in some specific instants, in order to solve the task problem. In other words, it is required that any final solution plan contains the specific actions instantiation in S. Also for execution goals it is possible to specify a partial order relation $\preceq$ which holds on S, which is similar to that one defined on G. A typical example of task problem with intermediate actions is the buy_a_house problem

[10]. This problem requires that the solution space should be constrained to all those plans which reach the final goal (have(house)) using a specific intermediate action (buy(house)), thus avoiding to use other actions (like build(house)).

It is worth noting, as it is already shown in [10], that we cannot trivially exclude the build operator from the domain, because it could be used in other problems or, possibly, in the same solution plan.

External events

External events or *intermediate states*, $I = \{\text{happen}(q_1), \ldots, \text{happen}(q_t)\}$ represent partial situations which are known to happen during plan execution.

While intermediate goals are generalization of final goals, i.e. intermediate states which the planner has to obtain, *external events* are generalization of initial states, i.e. intermediate states which the planner has to take into account in order to find a solution plan. This feature represents an extension with respect to the HTN planning model.

The main application for external events is to model, in dynamical domains, some expected events whose effects cannot be modified by the planner actions. These intermediate partial states are generated by external events which are assumed, at planning time, unavoidable and fully expected, even if the instant in which the events will take place is not known, or it is only *qualitatively* known by means of a temporal partial order relation $\preceq$ defined on I. Consider, for instance, to have to take into account of astronomical events as day and night cicle, or events like "banks are closed", or simpler events like "Someone will close the door".

The task planner should handle in a special way the precedence constraints on I, in that every solution cannot add further constraints to those provided by user. Since external events are assumed to be out of the planner control, unordered external events have to remain unordered at planning time.

Task planning problem

A task planning problem is a tuple $(I, S, G, O, \mathcal{A})$ where $\mathcal{A}$ is defined as in PO and O is a partial order relation on $\mathcal{N} = I \cup S \cup G$. The pair $(\mathcal{N}, O)$ is also called a task network.

The elements of $\mathcal{N}$, called *nodes*, are partitioned in three different types, according to which subset (I, S, G) they belong:

- happen(q), which specifies the intermediate state q.
- do(α), which requires to execute α, a possibly instantiated action belonging to $\mathcal{A}$;
- achieve(p), which requires to achieve a condition p;

Since the initial state, let i_0, and the final goal, let g_∞, of the PO planning model are particular cases, respectively, of external events and intermediate goals, we can include i_0 as the first external state in I, and g_∞ as the last goal in G, without losing any expressivity power.

In our model however there is no constraint on the existence of an initial state: problems with empty initial state can exist but they could be solved only in some particular conditions (e.g. when actions with empty preconditions are available).

Note that O is defined on the whole $\mathcal{N}$, that is each node can be ordered with respect to any other node, also of different type.

Task Planning Plan

A plan $\mathcal{P}$ for a task planning problem $(I, S, G, O, \mathcal{A})$ is a tuple (S', C', O'), where

- S' is the set of plan steps to be executed (composed only with instances of actions in $\mathcal{A}$),
- C' is the set auxiliary and bindings constraints
- O' is a precedence relation defined on $S' \cup I$ such that $O' \cap (I \times I) = O \cap (I \times I)$.

The last condition specifies that no other precedence constraints can be added on the external events, because any new constraint on them would produce a solution plan which can be executed only in the case that those events happen in that order. A plan with this sort of constraints should be considered as a part of a conditional plan.

Task Planning Solution

A plan $P = (S', C', O')$ for a task planning problem $(I, S, G, O, \mathcal{A})$ is a solution plan if:

- it achieves the intermediate goals G,
- it performs the activity goals S,
- it is executable taking into account of the external events I,
- temporal constraints between tasks and external events are verified.

More formally, a plan P is a solution plan if for each possible completion $\bar{P} = (S', \bar{C}, \bar{O})$ of P (that is $\bar{O}$ is a complete temporal relation on $S' \cup I$ and $\bar{C}$ assigns to every variable present in the plan a domain object), the following conditions have to hold:

1. each step $s \in S'$ has to be executable in the state σ_s determined by the execution of the previous steps and by the external events happened before s;
2. S' must include S, the user activity tasks;
3. each intermediate goal g must be true in some state σ_g;
4. $\bar{O}$ must be consistent with O, i.e. for each user constraint $t_1 O t_2$, in which t_1 and t_2 are tasks or external events, σ_{t_1} must precede σ_{t_2} with respect to temporal relation among states induced by $\bar{O}$, where σ_{t_1} and σ_{t_2} denote respectively the states associated to t_1 and t_2.

Rules 1–4 provide a semantics for TN Planning.

4 TN Planning into PO Planning

In this section we investigate on the relationships between TN and PO planning showing how the constraints embedded in a task planning problem can be expressed in a PO domain. Our goal is to use existing PO planners as tools for generating TN solutions.

Since a special tool for handling of precedence constraints on external events would be necessary (and the planner could have no means to distinguish external events from the other actions), we will assume in the following that external events are totally ordered.

The basic idea is to add to the PO knowledge $(\mathcal{I}, \mathcal{A}, \mathcal{G})$ some dummy actions, facts and goals which will induce the required constraints.

We assume to be able to generate as many dummy symbols as we need, the new symbols are guaranteed to be unique and not present in the domain.

It is worth noticing that the use of dummy actions is not new to planning. A dummy initial and final action have been used by most planners to represent respectively the initial state and the user goals of the problem. The difference is that the we add dummy objects to the domain, instead of adding them to the plan under development.

We now describe some techniques for coding different kinds of constraint which will be used in compiling TN problems: action existence, intermediate goal, external events, use-once and ordering contraints.

In the following a given TN problem $(I, S, G, O, \mathcal{A})$ is assumed and a corresponding PO problem $(\mathcal{I}', \mathcal{A}', \mathcal{G}')$ is incrementally generated, starting with $\mathcal{I}' = \emptyset$, $\mathcal{A}' = \mathcal{A}$ and $\mathcal{G}' = \emptyset$.

Action existence constraints

If an action a_i, instance of operator op_a, is required to be in each solution plan, then a new operator op_{a_i} is added to the set $\mathcal{A}'$ of operators. op_{a_i} is a copy of a_i with a new dummy fact, occur_a_i in its effects, which represents the occurrence of action instance.

The dummy goal occur_a_i is also added to the set of goals $\mathcal{G}'$ to represent the fact that action existence is required. If some parameters of a_i are bound to constants then the corresponding codesignation constraint on op_{a_i} operator description is added.

This method can be used for encoding the execution goals.

Intermediate goals constraints

If the solution plan in the task network is required to satisfy an intermediate goal g_i, then a dummy operator op_{g_i} is added to the set $\mathcal{A}'$. op_{g_i} has preconditions g_i and a single dummy effect (occur_g_i). The goal occur_g_i is also added to the set of goals $\mathcal{G}'$. This dummy operator has not to be executed by the execution system. It is also required to add a use-once constraint (see below).

External events constraints

An intermediate external event $I_i =$ happen(q_i) is modeled in a PO problem by a dummy action op_{I_i}, representing the event that it is required to exist in any final plan of PO problem. The dummy action will have as effects the conditions q_i and empty preconditions (with the exception of possibly dummy facts needed to guarantee its uniqueness and other constraints).

Use-once constraints

If it is required that a given node t_i has to occur at most once in every solution plan, then the dummy fact use-once$\_t_i$ is added to the initial state $\mathcal{I}$, and the operator op_{t_i} is modified by adding the same dummy fact to the preconditions and its negation ¬use-once$\_t_i$ to the effects.

Note that the uniqueness of dummy precondition guarantees use-once$\_t_i$ that no other action instance will be added.

Precedence Constraints between Actions and States

If a precedence constraint between two nodes, say $t_i \preceq t_j$, is required then the operators op_{t_i} and op_{t_j} are modified as following: a new dummy fact (before$\_t_i\_t_j$) is added to the effects of op_{t_i} and to the preconditions of op_{t_j}.

Compacting the dummy items

For each node t_i represented in a task network the corresponding op_{t_i} is required to exist in the final plan, to be used only once, and to respect any precedence constraints stated in the goal network, therefore we should use several dummy conditions in its preconditions and effects.

It is possible to reduce the number of these dummy conditions by exploiting the fact that these constraints are needed at the same time. It is easy to see that the dummy facts (occur$\_t_i$), (use-once$\_t_i$), (before$\_t_i\_t_j$) can be merged in a unique dummy fact, say u_{t_i}, as shown in the example in the figure 1.

Theoretical results for TN planning

By iterating the application of domain transformations described in the former paragraphs it is possible to generate a PO domain such that all the solutions satisfy the required constraints. This leads to the theorem described in the this section.

Definition. Two planning problems P and P', not necessarily of the same planning model, are equivalent modulo a plan transformation function ψ (in symbols $P \sim_\psi P'$) if s is a solution of P if and only if there exists a solution s' of P' such that $s = \psi(s')$.

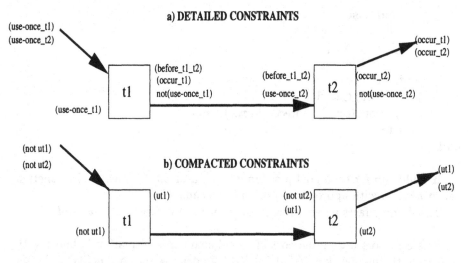

Figure1. Compacting dummy items

Definition. Given an ordinary action Op, we will denote respectively by vars(Op), precond(Op) e effect(Op), the variables, preconditions and effects of Op.

Theorem. TN planning is not more powerful than PO planning, in that for each TN planning problem $P = (I, S, G, O, A)$, there exists a PO planning problem $P' = \phi(P) = (\mathcal{I}', \mathcal{A}', \mathcal{G}')$ which is equivalent to P modulo ψ. ψ is the plan transformation function which substitutes respectively from a solution s' of P' the dummy actions op_{p_i} associated to each intermediate goal p_i by an achieve(p_i) node, the dummy actions op_{a_i} associated to execution goal and any non-dummy steps with a do(a_i) node, and the dummy actions op_{q_i} associated to each intermediate state q_i with a happen(q_i). Each node inherits the precedence constraints from its corresponding PO step.

Proof. We provide a constructive proof based on the following algorithm, which uses the methods defined in the previous sections for encoding TN constraints in a PO planning problems.

begin
$\quad\mathcal{I}' := \emptyset; \ \mathcal{A}' := \mathcal{A}; \ \mathcal{G}' := \emptyset;$
$\quad$**for** $n \in \mathcal{N}$ **do**
$\quad\quad u_n :=$new_cond();
$\quad\quad$**case** n **of**
$\quad\quad$happen(q) :
$\quad\quad\quad op_n :=$new_op(vars(q), $\neg u_n, u_n \wedge q$);
$\quad\quad$achieve(p) :
$\quad\quad\quad op_n :=$new_op(vars(p),$\neg u_n \wedge p, u_n$);
$\quad\quad$do(α) :
$\quad\quad\quad op_n :=$new_op(vars(α),$\neg u_n \wedge$precond(α), $u_n \wedge$effects(α));

> **end case**
> $A' := A' \cup \{op_n\}$
> $G' := G' \wedge u_n$
> $I' := I' \wedge \neg u_n$
> **end for**
> **for** $(n1, n2) \in O$ **do**
> $\mathrm{precond}(op_{n2}) := \mathrm{precond}(op_{n2}) \wedge u_{n1};$
> **end for**

end

It builds up for each goal g a dummy operator op_g by means of a function called *new_op*, with appropriate preconditions and effects.

The dummy facts u_g are created by means of the function *new_cond*.

It is easy to see that the cost of this domain transformation is linear with respect to the number $k = |I| + |S| + |G|$ ($|X|$ denotes the cardinality of the set X) of the nodes present in the task network, that is

- the number of actions A' is increased by k, with respect to the number of the original actions A, that is $|A'| = |A| + k$
- $|I'| = |I| + k$
- the number of goals G' is exactly k.

4.1 Example

Consider the following example: the user wants to send a file, which is located in a floppy disk, via ftp using a personal computer. The drive before this operation is empty and after the operation it must be empty again. The user also knows that at some moment the connection to Internet will be unavailable due to some network maintenance operations.

Although anyone can imagine an obvious solution of this problem, there is no way to model it in PO planning since there is no way of stating a "perform" goal and it is useless to have a goal equal to the initial state.

It is also impossible to state this problem in the ordinary HTN planning, because external events are not available.

The figure 2 shows the solution plan generated for our TN planning model.

Note that the solution plan also requires that the action send_file has to be executed before the event network maintenance.

On the other hand eject_disk is partially ordered with respect to network maintenance.

The dummy fact u_1 is added by the algorithm previously described to guarantee the existence of the dummy step representing the external event network maintenance.

Similarly, the dummy fact u_2 is added in order to send the file via ftp avoiding to send the file using another way, e.g. as an attachment of an e-mail message.

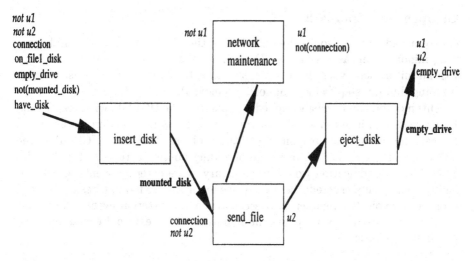

Figure2. The solution

5   Conclusions and Implementation Issues

Two main implementation strategies can be proposed for TN planning which attempt to use existing planners. The first strategy is based on a pure software reuse and it has a wider application; the second one requires some modifications to the planning algorithm and it can be applied only to certain PO planners.

A Black Box Approach: A TN Preprocessor

The result obtained for TN planning and the method of domain transformation used for proving the equivalence theorem suggest an interesting technique for obtaining a TN planner from an existing PO planner: the idea is to transform the initial domain (I, S, G, O, A) into the equivalent (I', A', G') and use the PO planner to solve the modified problem. Any solution for PO can then easily transformed in a solution plan for TN problem by replacing dummy actions and facts according to ψ.

The advantage of the approach is that the PO planner is reused as a black-box software module without any regard of its internal details. We applied this approach in implementing TNP, a task planner based on the TN model, which is implemented in Common LISP and which has been successfully demonstrated.

TNP acts as a preprocessor from TN problems to PO problems and then uses UCPOP [14] as a blackbox planner.

A trial version which trasforms domains written in the GRAPHPLAN [3] syntax has also been implemented and tested.

Although there is an obvious overload on the PO planner, due to the presence of dummy objects, the features of software reusing, fast implementation and linear time-space cost of problem compilation are apparent advantages of the domain transformation approach.

An Open Box Approach

This overload can be avoided by abandoning the black box approach and operating minor modifications in the PO planner, namely the planner should work with an initial plan where for every task and external event there exist a corresponding dummy step (which cannot be removed).

This method can be easily applied to a planner like UCPOP, which represents the current plan in its internal structures, as a network of action instances. In this case the network corresponding to the problem is given to UCPOP as the initial network, avoiding the overhead of adding dummy actions to the domain.

A further modification would be necessary if the external events to be handled are not totally ordered: the precedence maintenance module has to changed in order to avoid the planner to overconstraint the external events. Note that in the previous strategy we made the hypothesis that external events must be always totally ordered.

The method we have described in our paper is a reasonable method for dealing with tasks and external events when using planners which have no initial plan or which have internal structures not well suited for dealing with tasks and external events, like GRAPHPLAN.

Moreover this method can easily extended to handle with uncertain external events, as "tomorrow it will rain", by using a conditional planner as a target of the preprocessor (which needs minor changes), instead of a PO planning.

The encoding of problem constraints in the domain will be the subject of further investigations in order to analyze and to extend the number of constraints that can be encoded.

It could be also interesting to investigate these topics from the opposite point of view: trying to exploit, during plan generation, the constraints which are naturally embedded in a given domain.

It should be pointed out that the theoretical result of equivalence proved for TN and PO problems shows that only using an appropriate domain coding and solution decoding it is possible to reach the equivalence. The equivalence result does not deny that TN formalism is still more direct and expressive for task problem, but it points out that the machinery needed to solve a TN problem is basically, with the appropriate syntactic differences, a PO planner.

References

1. A. Barrett and D. Weld. *Schema Parsing: Hierarchical Planning for Expressive Language.* In Proceedings of AAAI-94
2. J. Blythe. *Planning with External Events.* In Proceedings of AIPS-94
3. A. Blum and M. Furst. *Fast planning through planning grpah analysis.* In Proceedings of IJCAI-95. To appear in Artificial Intelligence 1997
4. D. Chapman. *Planning for Conjunctive Goals.* Artificial Intelligence 32, 1987
5. K. Erol, J. Hendler, D.S. Nau. *Semantics for Hierarchical Task-Network Planning.* Tech. Rep. CS-TR-3239, Univ. of Maryland, March 1994

6. K. Erol, J. Hendler, D.S. Nau. *UMCP: A Sound and Complete Procedure for Hierarchical Task-Network Planning.* In Proceedings of AIPS-94

7. K. Erol, J. Hendler, D.S. Nau. *Complexity Results for HTN Planning.* Tech. Rep. CS-TR-3240, Univ. of Maryland, March 1994

8. K. Erol, J. Hendler, D.S. Nau. *HTN Planning: Complexity and Expressivity.* In Proceedings of AAAI-94

9. E.D.P. Pednault. *Synthesizing Plans That Contains Actions With Context-Dependent Effects.* Computational Intelligence, Vol. 4, 1988

10. S. Kambhampati. *A Comparative Analysis of Partial Order Planning and Task Reduction Planning* SIGART Bull. 1995

11. S. Kambhampati, J. Hendler. *A Validation Structure Based Theory of Plan Modification and Reuse.* Artificial Intelligence, May 1992

12. T.L. McCluskey, J.M. Porteous. *Planning Speed-up via Domain Model Compilation.* in New Direction in AI Planning. IOS Press 1996

13. E.D. Sacerdoti, *The nonlinear nature of plans.* In Proceedings of IJCAI 1975

14. J.S. Penberthy and D. Weld. *UCPOP: A Sound, Complete Partial Order Planner for ADL.* In Proceedings of KR-92, 1992.

15. Q. Yang. *Formalizing Planning Knowledge for Hierarchical Planning*, Computational Intelligence, Vol 6, pag. 12-24, 1990

Expressing Transformations
of Structured Reactive Plans

Michael Beetz[1] and Drew McDermott[2]

[1] University of Bonn, Dept. of Computer Science III, Roemerstr. 164,
D-53117 Bonn, Germany, beetz@cs.uni-bonn.de
[2] Yale University, Dept. of Computer Science, P.O. Box 208285, Yale Station,
New Haven, CT 06520-8285, USA, mcdermott@cs.yale.edu

Abstract. We describe XFRML, the transformation language of the planning system XFRM. XFRM is embedded in a simulated robot that performs jobs in a changing and partly unknown environment. XFRML allows XFRM to anticipate and forestall many common flaws in autonomous robot behavior that cannot be dealt with by other planning representations.

In order to diagnose execution failures in projected execution scenarios, XFRM has to infer whether or not particular parts of the plan were projected to be executed and why. The use of XFRML makes such inferences possible because XFRML not only represents the physical effects of plan execution, but also the process of plan interpretation, as well as temporal, causal, and teleological relationships among plan interpretation, the world, and the physical behavior of the robot.

1 Introduction

Autonomous robots acting in changing and partly unknown environments cannot commit in advance to a fixed course of action. Rather, they have to be flexible and make critical decisions when they acquire previously missing information while carrying out their plans. Thus, their plans must contain conditional, concurrent, and reactive subplans and cannot be constrained to be inflexible sequences of plan steps. To improve such flexible plans successfully, planning systems do not only have to project how the world will change as the robot executes its plan but also have to determine which parts of the plan were (projected to be) executed and why. In addition, the planning systems have to install their revisions in plans with complex internal structure.

To make the implementation of such planning systems possible, we will focus in this paper on a particular dimension of reasoning about plans and their projections: managing the complexity that is characteristic for the transformation of flexible structured plans. Over and above the difficult substantive issues about *what* plan transformations should be carried out, we must deal with formal issues about *how* to specify the transformations. For example, the "protection-violation avoidance" transformation [Sus77] is, in the classical framework, a matter of inserting a link. In a complex, structured plan, it is a complex editing operation that must respect the semantics of the plan language. In the past such transformations were represented as Lisp procedures, but the resulting codes were unintelligible and error-prone [McD92].

This paper describes XFRML (XFRM Plan Revision Language), a declarative notation for implementing general, common-sense plan revision methods. Using XFRML, XFRM reasons about and manipulates complex reactive plans by loading a projected execution scenario, diagnosing the causes of projected behavior flaws, and finally, applying plan transformation rules to produce better plans. XFRML is a PROLOG-like Horn clause language with fifty to sixty built-in predicates, which formalize relations on plans and the behavior they cause. These built-in predicates constitute a layer of abstraction that presents plans and their projections as if they were Horn clause databases. Using this abstraction, XFRM retrieves information from, and tests properties of, plans by means of concise, transparent queries that have a PROLOG-like semantics.

Utilizing the expressive power of XFRML, XFRM carries out a wide range of novel plan transformation methods, which forestall execution failures caused by sensing routines that overlook or misperceive objects, by unfaithful tracking of objects through their descriptions, by unreliable physical actions with undesired effects, or by interference between multiple threads of the robot's own plan. To anticipate and forestall such a wide spectrum of flaws XFRML reasons through the physical effects of plan execution as well as the plan interpretation, and the temporal, causal, and teleological relationships between plan interpretation, the world, and the behavior of the robot.

This paper is organized as follows: Section 2 sketches how the planning system XFRM that uses XFRML works and characterizes the plans XFRML reasons about. Section 3 provides examples of plan revision methods that can be expressed in XFRML and analyzes them to illustrate the different aspects of plan execution XFRML has to represent and reason about. The subsequent section describes the data structures representing projected execution scenarios that XFRML's built-in predicates operate on. Section 5 classifies and describes the most important XFRML predicates, gives examples of queries about projected execution scenarios and shows how they are formalized in XFRML. Section 6 demonstrates how plan revision methods can be formalized as XFRML plan revision rules.

2 The Planning System XFRM

XFRML is used by the planning system XFRM. This paper refers to a version of XFRM that is embedded in a simulated robot with limited sensing and effecting capabilities performing a varying set of complex tasks in a changing and partially unknown environment, a small world with various objects to be transported from place to place. The plans controlling our simulated robot are made robust by incorporating sensing and monitoring actions, and reactions triggered by observed events. XFRM is provided with a library of modular default plans that are efficient and cope with most eventualities. Using this library, XFRM computes a default plan for a set of tasks by retrieving and instantiating plans for individual tasks and pasting them together to form a parallel robot plan. While pasting default plans together is fast, it is prone to producing plans that may fail for contingencies. Hence, whenever the robot detects a contingency, XFRM will project the effects of this contingency on its current plan and revise the plan to make it more robust. Whenever XFRM thinks it has a plan that is better than the currently executed one, it will replace the current plan with the better one and restart the new plan.

Planning is implemented as a search in plan space. A node in the space is a proposed plan; the initial node is the default plan created using the plan library. A step in the space requires three phases. First, XFRM *projects* a plan to generate (randomly) sample execution scenarios for it. Then, in the *criticism* phase, XFRM examines these execution scenarios to estimate how good the plan is and to predict possible plan failures. It diagnoses the projected plan failures by classifying them in a taxonomy of failure models. The failure models serve as indices into a set of transformation rules that are applied in the third phase, *revision*, to produce new versions of the plan that are, we hope, improvements.

XFRML reasons about *structured reactive plans* (**SRPs**) written in RPL *(Reactive Plan Language)* [McD91], a LISP-like robot control language with conditionals, loops, local variables, processes, and subroutines. Plans can explicitly fail if they detect situations they cannot handle. RPL provides several high-level concepts (interrupts, monitors) to synchronize parallel actions, to make plans reactive, etc. Other reactive plan languages such as RAP [Fir89] or ESL [Gat96] are easily provided as macro languages on top of RPL. [McD91] (pg. 20), for instance, shows an implementation of RAP using RPL control structures.

One might argue in favor of simpler, more uniform plan representations, which are better suited for plan synthesis and learning. For the diagnosis and revision of complex, composite behaviors, however, it is more important that the plan language explicitly represents how behaviors interact. To demonstrate the advantages of such expressiveness let us look at two RPL constructs that specify the interaction of concurrent behaviors. The construct (WITH-POLICY p b), for instance, specifies that the behavior p is to be executed as a constraint on the behavior b. Thus, the RPL plan (WITH-POLICY (AVOID-OBSTACLES) (GO (X,Y))) tells the robot to go to (X,Y) subject to the constraint that the robot is to avoid any obstacle that is in it's way. A second control structure, TRY-ALL, specifies alternative methods for accomplishing a plan step that can be carried out concurrently. Consequently, (TRY-ALL (DETECT-DOOR-WITH-LASER) (DETECT-DOOR-WITH-CAMERA)) simultaneously tries to detect a door with its laser and visual sensors. It succeeds as soon as one of the methods does and fails only if both methods do.

Another important concept of SRPs are *variables* used for storing information about the world, doing simple program control (e.g., counters), and communication between different processes. Some variables are set by sensor readings. For instance, the fluents X-POS* and Y-POS* are continually updated by the robot's position estimation methods. Variables can be global, i.e., accessed from any part of the plan, or local, i.e., visible only within a limited scope in the plan.

Revising structured reactive plans requires XFRM to reason about full-fledged robot plans and diagnose various kinds of behavior flaws. To this end, XFRM must reason about the structure, function, and behavior of plans, and diagnose projected behavior flaws. To support this kind of reasoning, RPL provides declarative commands for goals, perceptions, and beliefs that can be used to make the structure of SRPs and the functions of subplans explicit and thereby provide XFRM with a (partial) model of its plan [BM92].

3 Plan Revision Rules

While revising SRPs is more difficult than revising partial-order plans it also enables planners to forestall additional types of plan failures. Let's illustrate this by looking at some of XFRM's plan revision rules that are implemented in XFRML and performed on SRPs:

1. *IF* a goal might be clobbered by an exogenous event *THEN* stabilize the goal state after achieving it, that is, spend efforts to prevent that the goal gets clobbered.
2. *IF* a goal might be clobbered by a robot action *THEN* make sure that the clobbering subplan is executed necessarily before the clobbered goal is achieved
3. *IF* a goal might be clobbered by a robot action and the robot notice it *THEN* reachieve the clobbered goals as the last step in your plan
4. *IF* a goal might be left unachieved because the robot overlooked an object *THEN* use another routine for sensing these objects
5. *IF* a goal might be unachieved because the robot had an ambiguous object description *THEN* achieve the goal for all objects satisfying the object description
6. *IF* the robot might achieve a goal *g* for an object *ob'* instead of the intended object *ob* because the robot made the description for *ob* ambiguous by changing the world *THEN* perform the subplan that caused the ambiguity after goal *g* is achieved.

Although, the plan revisions listed above look similar to those applied in other plan revision systems, most of them are novel. The second rule, for instance, works for arbitrary structured reactive plans instead of being limited to (hierarchical) partial-order plans. The third rule requires the planner to infer the beliefs of the robot at different stages in a projected execution scenario. The fourth rule requires the planner to predict (possibly using a probabilistic sensor model) how the computational state of the robot changes as it looks for an object and how the state would change if the sensor were perfect. The last two require decisions about whether the object descriptions used by the plan to find and manipulate objects are ambiguous. We know of no other plan revision system that can carry out these kinds of inferences.

Testing the applicability of the failure-type-specific plan revisions listed above requires XFRM to diagnose projected behavior flaws. In the diagnosis process the planning system must be able to carry out at least the following inferences: infer what the outcomes of subplans were and what they should have been; infer which parts of the plan terminated abnormally; and reconstruct the computational state of plan execution that influenced a control decision. The repair processes required by these six example revisions must carry out operations such as adding steps to the plan; reordering parts of the plan; introducing repetition of steps until some condition is satisfied; and changing operations on a single object into iterated operations on every element of a set of objects. Other revision methods remove steps from a plan, change variable bindings and arguments to routines, and introduce a more robust control structure. In general, plan revisions in XFRML are arbitrary transformations of RPL plan pieces.

To get a better sense of what entities and relations to include in our planning representation, we analyze a typical plan revision (number 1 above) more carefully and restate it as a plan transformation rule. The application condition of such a rule tests whether the revision is promising and the action part installs the revision in the plan:

<u>IF</u> 1. *GOAL(OB)* is clobbered by an exogenous event;
2. *DESIG* is a data structure returned by the sensing routine when the routine saw *OB*;
3. the robot tried to achieve *GOAL(DESIG)* with a plan named $P_{ACHIEVE(GOAL)}$; and
4. there exists a RPL variable *VAR* with value *DESIG*;

THEN REPLACE $P_{ACHIEVE(GOAL)}$
WITH SEQ $P_{ACHIEVE(GOAL)}$
STABILIZE(*GOAL(VAR)*).

The conditions of this plan revision rule refer to different aspects of plan execution: the first condition specifies what happened in the world, namely that a goal was destroyed by an event not under the control of the robot. The second condition relates a data structure used in the plan to the object it designates. The data structure *DESIG* is the computational result of sensing object *OB*. The third condition checks whether the robot controller has executed a subplan with the purpose to achieve *GOAL(DESIG)*. The last condition tests the existence of a variable in the SRP that has a description of the object *OB* as its value.

Most planning systems use representations that are simpler than XFRML. They either reason about how the world changes while the plan gets executed [AHT90] or about the process of plan interpretation [Dav92, McD85]. In the first case, the planning systems have to assume that the critical decisions about the course of actions are made during planning because they cannot represent and rationalize decisions made during plan execution. In the second case, they have to assume that the physical effects of the interpretation of a plan piece are exactly known in advance because they cannot predict how the world changes.

To diagnose conditions that typically prevent autonomous robots from accomplishing their jobs it is necessary to reason about the computational state of plan interpretation, the physical state of the world, as well as the relations between both of them. The way XFRM reasons about objects provides a good case in point. Because XFRM does not assume that arguments of plan steps denote objects in the world, it cannot represent just the "object." Instead, XFRM must reason about three closely related concepts: the *object* itself, the *object description*, which is generated by sensor routines and used for plan interpretation, and the RPL *variable*, which is the syntactic object in an RPL plan that, during plan interpretation, contains the object description as its value. Thus, to revise the plan such that the robot will make sure that a particular ball, say B-37 will not disappear after its delivery, the planner has to infer which designator *DES* in the process of plan interpretation describes B-37 and which variable *VAR* has *DES* as its value to make the appropriate plan transformation. Such detailed representations enable XFRM to differentiate failures caused by ambiguous, incorrect, and outdated object descriptions, and apply failure specific plan revision methods.

4 Execution Scenarios

The diagnosis of the behavior flaws above and the application of the corresponding plan revision methods requires the planning system not only to reason about the physical effects of plan execution but also the process of plan interpretation and the relations between both. To infer that a possible cause for an execution failure is an incorrect object description, the planner has to reconstruct the value of the RPL variable that should contain the object description and check whether this description describes the intended object correctly. Or, to diagnose a behavior flaw caused by a sensor error, the planner has to compare the value returned by a sensing routine with the value that a perfect sensor would return.

Therefore, when projecting a plan, XFRM generates an execution scenario, a data structure that records how the world and the state of plan interpretation change as the plan gets executed. An execution scenario consists of three components: the *task network*, the *timeline*, and the *code tree*, described in the subsequent paragraphs.

The task network stores information necessary to decide whether a given task has been tried, signalled a failure, what value it returned and to reconstruct the computational state at any state of plan interpretation. When the plan is executed, the plan interpreter generates stack frames, called *tasks* that correspond to the execution of a node in the code tree and record how the code subtree associated with the task was interpreted. When a plan is projected, the stack frames are preserved for later inspection by plan transformations.

Transformation rules also need to access the timeline that the projector uses to represent what happens in the world as the plan is executed. This is not a tree but a linear sequence of events and their results, synchronized with the task network. The events represent the start or end of an effector or sensing action, or an occurrence of an exogenous event. With each event there is associated a time instant and a set of *occasions*. Occasions are ground atomic statements that describe the state of the effectors and sensors, sensor data, and the environment. The event represents what happened at this time instant.

The final component of an execution scenario is the code tree of the projected plan. For carrying out plan revisions, SRPs are best thought of as code trees and their revision as replacing subtrees in code trees. Therefore, in an execution scenario, the projected plan is represented as a structure, called a *code tree*, which essentially duplicates the structure of the plan text, augmented with some further syntactic information. (For details, see [McD92].)

XFRM handles uncertainty implicitly: it randomly projects execution scenario from the given evidences and probabilistic action and exogenous event models and prior information. XFRM estimates the utility of a plan by taking the average utility over the projected scenarios and estimates the probability of a particular behavior flaw based on how often it occurred in the projected scenarios. As a consequence, XFRML does not have to consider uncertainty because it is only used for reasoning about individual scenarios.

5 Reasoning about Execution Scenarios

The syntax of XFRML is the usual PROLOG-in-LISP combination: parenthesized prefix notation, with variables indicated with "?". There are some general predicates providing basic utilities (arithmetic, unification) and the ability to call LISP code. New predicates are defined by sets of Horn clause rules of the form: $(\leftarrow P \text{ (and } Q_1 \ldots Q_n))$ where P is an atomic formula and $Q_1, \ldots, Q_n$ literals. The negation operator "THNOT" is implemented as negation by failure.

Below are some examples of tests that have occurred in XFRM's rules and can be performed on projected execution scenarios:

- The robot tried to get a ball from location $\langle 0,8 \rangle$ into its hand:

```
(AND (TASK-GOAL ?TSK (ACHIEVE (LOC ?DES HAND)))
     (HOLDS (VISUAL-TRACK ?DES ?OB) (DURING ?TSK))
     (HOLDS (AND (CAT ?OB BALL) (LOC ?OB (0,8))) (BEGIN ?TSK))).
```

In more detail, the robot has carried out a task ?TSK of the form (ACHIEVE (LOC ?DES HAND)) for a designator DES. While carrying out ?TSK the robot was for some time visually tracking the object described by DES by pointing the camera at the object ?OB where ?OB is a ball at location $\langle 0,8 \rangle$.

- The robot overlooked a ball at $\langle 0,8 \rangle$; that is, the routine for finding a ball at location $\langle 0,8 \rangle$ did not return an object description (RETURNED-VALUE ?P-TSK {}) although there was a ball at $\langle 0,8 \rangle$ (HOLDS (AND (CAT ?X BALL) (LOC ?X (0,8))) (TT ?P-TSK)).

```
(AND (TASK-GOAL ?P-TSK (PERCEIVE-1 (λ (?X) (AND (CAT ?X BALL) (LOC ?X (0,8))))))
     (RETURNED-VALUE ?P-TSK {})
     (HOLDS (AND (CAT ?X BALL) (LOC ?X (0,8))) (TT ?P-TSK)))
```

- After the execution of plan P the robot "knows" it has a ball from location $\langle 0,8 \rangle$ in its hand.

```
(AND (TASK-GOAL ?A-TSK (ACHIEVE (LOC ?DES HAND)))
     (HOLDS (TRACK ?DES ?OB) (DURING ?A-TSK))
     (HOLDS (AND (CAT ?OB BALL) (LOC ?OB (0,8))) (BEGIN-TASK TOP))
     (BELIEF-AT (LOC ?DES HAND) (END-TASK TOP)))
```

5.1 Accessing Code Trees

An essential prerequisite for revising SRPs is that the planning system can identify the parts of the plan it has to modify. The most important indexing technique for plan pieces in XFRML is the use of tasks. Every task corresponds to a piece of the code tree. The predicate (TASK-CODE-PATH *tsk cp*) holds if *cp* is the "codepath" of the subplan executed in order to perform *tsk*. A *codepath* specifies a subtree of a code tree by giving the labels of the branches that lead to it. Of course,

to use TASK-CODE-PATH, we have to have a task. One way is to use the relation
(TASK-GOAL *tsk goal*), which holds if *tsk* is a task annotated with the purpose *goal*.
The relation TASK-GOAL can be used to test whether the robot ever tried to get
something to location $\langle 0,10 \rangle$: (TASK-GOAL ?TSK (ACHIEVE (LOC ?DES $\langle 0,10 \rangle$))).

Another common plan revision is to add ordering relations between subplans
such that a particular task t_1 is executed necessarily before another given task t_2.
Since we cannot always directly reorder two tasks of interest (e.g., if one occurs
in an iteration of a loop), the planning system needs to determine an appropriate
ordering context. Thus, XFRML provides a predicate (ORDERING-CONTEXT t_1 t_2 t_{s1} t_{s2}
t_c) that is true if ordering t_{s1} before t_{s2} in the context of t_c is the weakest ordering
constraint that guarantees that t_1 is executed before t_2; t_c is a supertask of t_1
and t_2 in which the ordering constraint can be stored.

5.2 Predicates on Plan Interpretations

If a planner analyzes a plan failure in a plan in which the execution depends on
the plan's internal state, the planner will have to reconstruct the value of variables the plan is using at any time during projection. XFRML provides predicates
for referring to tasks, and, at a finer level, to the computational objects that
were built and used when tasks were executed.

(TASK-STATUS *tsk ti status*) holds if *status* is the status of *tsk* in the computational state *ti*. The status of tasks are either created, active, succeeded, failed,
or evaporated. Tasks may also return values when they succeed. For instance,
sensing tasks return data structures describing objects they have found in an
image. The relation (RETURNED-VALUE *tsk val*) holds if *val* is the value returned by
tsk. The relation (VALUE *var ti val*) where *ti* is either (BEGIN-TASK *tsk*) or (END-TASK *tsk*)
is true if *tsk* is in the scope of the plan variable *var* and *var* has the value *val* at
the start or end of *tsk*.

5.3 Predicates on Timelines

The purpose of plans is to change the world. XFRM represents how the world
changes during the execution of a plan in terms of *time instants, occasions,* and
events [McD92]. *Time instants* are points in time at which the world changes
due to an action or an exogenous event. An *occasion* is a stretch of time over
which a world state p holds and is specified by a proposition, which describes p,
and the time interval for which the proposition is true. New time instants are
generated by events that change the world.

Relations on timelines characterize the truth of a world state at a given time.
The relation (HOLDS *state t*) is true if *state* holds for t where *state* is a conjunction
of literals and t is the start or end of a task, the interval over which a task
was active (t = (TT *tsk*)), or a subinterval thereof (t = (DURING *tsk*)). Besides the
truth of states for time instants or intervals, XFRML provides relations describing
change and its cause. The relation (CLOBBERS *ev state ti*) holds if *ev* is the last event
occurring prior to *ti* that causes *state* to be false. Similarly, (CAUSES *ev state ti*)
holds if *ev* is the last event occurring prior to *ti* that causes *state* to hold.

5.4 Timelines and Plan Interpretation

The components described so far are also provided by other representations. What is missing in those representations, however, are the links between the representations for plan interpretation and change in the world. Thus, the fourth component of our conceptualization describes how plan interpretation and change in the world are related. An important class of relations between plan interpretation and the physical world are causal: SRPs start control routines and thereby change the world. Plans also ask the robot to sense its surrounding and thereby change their own computational state. The relation (ACTION *ev tsk*) holds if *ev* is an event caused by a robot action part of task *tsk*. A second class of relations is teleological: some subplans/tasks have the purpose to achieve, maintain, perceive, and stabilize a particular state. A third relationship is representational: data structures in SRPs are often used to describe objects and states in the world. **Teleological Relations.** The purpose of many subplans can be described in terms of the world states they are intended to achieve, maintain, or perceive. In RPL, the tasks of these subplans are annotated with declarative commands such as (ACHIEVE (LOC *des* (0,10))) (see [BM92]) which are viewed by the planner as annotations that indicate the purpose of a task/subplan and can be queried in XFRML using the (TASK-GOAL *t g*) predicate.

We still have to show how to test whether a task's purpose was to get a particular object, say *BALL-5*, to location ⟨0,10⟩. Here's how:

(AND (TASK-GOAL ?TSK (ACHIEVE (LOC ?DES (0,10))))
    (HOLDS (TRACK ?DES *BALL-5*) (DURING ?TSK)))

The first conjunct is satisfied if there exists a task of the form (ACHIEVE (LOC ?DES (0,10))). Since the first argument of the goal ?DES is a data structure describing an object and not the object itself, we check in the second condition that ?DES corresponds to the object *BALL-5*. One way to establish this correspondence is to check the condition (TRACK ?DES *BALL-5*), which is true if the robot tracked ?DES by pointing the camera at *BALL-5*. Teleological relations are important because the planner can use them to identify a task or subplan with a specified purpose. **Representational Relations.** Variables and data structures in SRPs often serve as internal models of aspects of the world. For instance, the variables X-POS* and Y-POS*, continually updated by the robot's odometer as the robot moves, provide the robot with an estimation of it's own position in the world. In this case we say that the robot believes it is at location ⟨X,Y⟩ if in this state, the value of X-POS* is *X* and the value of Y-POS* is *Y*. (see [RK86]) We take the relation (BELIEF-AT *state ti*) to mean that the robot believes that *state* holds in the world. The programmer has to provide axioms that define under which conditions the robot believes in *state* — usually in terms of constraints that the values of global variables must satisfy. Based on the axiomatization of (BELIEF-AT (LOC ROBOT (?X,?Y))) (below left), XFRM can check whether a possible cause for a execution failure is an incorrect odometer reading by asking the following XFRML query (below right).

(BELIEF-AT (LOC ROBOT (?X,?Y)) ?AT)	(?- (AND (BELIEF-AT (LOC ROBOT (?X,?Y))
← (VALUE X-POS* ?AT ?X)	(END-TASK *tsk*))
(VALUE Y-POS* ?AT ?Y)	(THNOT (HOLDS (LOC ROBOT (?X,?Y))
	(END-TASK *tsk*))

6 Plan Revision Rules

So far we've focused on how inferences are made about planner data structures. Now we turn our attention to how the results of these inferences are used to revise code trees. We will diagram plan-transformation rules

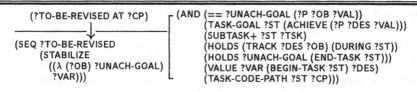

where *cond* is the applicability condition, (pl AT cp == pat) the input plan schema and *pl'* the output plan schema of the rule. The applicability condition is a conjunction of XFRML clauses. The input plan schema consists of a pattern variable to which the subplan with code path *cp* is bound and an optional pattern *pat* that is matched against the subplan *pl*. *pl'* is an RPL plan fragment containing pattern variables that get instantiated using the bindings produced by proving the applicability condition and matching the input plan schema. The rule is applicable if the application condition holds and the plan *pl* with code path *cp* matches the pattern *pat*. The resulting plan fragment replaces the input fragment in the revised plan.

```
(?TO-BE-REVISED AT ?CP)       ┌ (AND (== ?UNACH-GOAL (?P ?OB ?VAL))
─────────────────────────     │       (TASK-GOAL ?ST (ACHIEVE (?P ?DES ?VAL)))
            ↓                  │       (SUBTASK+ ?ST ?TSK)
(SEQ ?TO-BE-REVISED            │       (HOLDS (TRACK ?DES ?OB) (DURING ?ST))
     (STABILIZE                │       (HOLDS ?UNACH-GOAL (END-TASK ?ST)))
       ((λ (?OB) ?UNACH-GOAL)  │       (VALUE ?VAR (BEGIN-TASK ?ST) ?DES)
        ?VAR)))               └       (TASK-CODE-PATH ?ST ?CP)))
```

Figure 1. Example plan revision rule

Figure 1 shows the formalization of the first plan revision method discussed in section 4. Let ?UNACH-GOAL be the goal that is not achieved at the end of the task ?TSK, the task to execute the top-level plan. The revision replaces a plan step ?TO-BE-REVISED with a sequence (SEQ) consisting of ?TO-BE-REVISED followed by step stabilizing the previously achieved goal. The argument containing the λ-expression makes sure that the goal predicate is stabilized for the designator that is the value of varibale bound to ?VAR instead of the symbol bound to ?OB, which is meaningless at execution time. The revision rule is applicable under a set of conditions specifying that (a) The unachieved subgoal is of the form (?P ?OB ?VAL); (b) The robot has tried to achieve a goal (ACHIEVE (?P ?DES ?VAL)) as a subtask of ?TSK (c); (d) during this subtask the robot tracked ?DES by pointing the camera at object ?OB; (e) the unachieved goal holds at the end of subtask ?ST; (f) ?VAR is a variable in the environment of the subplan that has the value ?DES at the begin of task ?ST; and (g) the code path of ?ST.

7 Discussion

A notation for plan revision, such as XFRML, is difficult to assess. In this section we assess the significance of XFRML along several dimensions: the necessity of notations of this sort for robot control applications, the expressiveness and conciseness of the language, and the computational overhead.

Autonomous robots acting in realistic environments need a notation for plan revision methods because such robots exhibit many kinds of behavior flaws that cannot be prevented by existing plan revision methods. We have implemented models for about twenty five types of behavior flaws and about forty transformation rules [Bee96, BM94]. Most of which cannot be expressed in other planning representations. XFRML can express all the common-sense plan revisions listed in section 3. We can also express planning operations performed by classical planning systems such as means-end analysis [NS61] or the operations of the SNLP planning algorithm can [MR91].

XFRML can also express the rules used by other transformational planners, such as those described in [Sus77, Ham89]. To implement GORDIUS-like plan transformations, XFRM's projector would have to construct a dependency structure that justifies the executability of plan steps and their effects. We don't know how much of RPL could be handled by such dependency structures because the identification of causes and their effects is much more difficult in structured reactive plans. In SRPs, a specific behavior of the robot might be caused by subtle interactions of concurrent continuous control processes, or flawed behavior should be corrected by other processes. Such interactions and corrective behaviors are very difficult to represent as causal dependencies.

XFRML can be also applied to other reactive plan languages such as RAP [Fir89] and ESL [Gat96]. The easiest way to do this is to define the constructs provided by these languages as RPL macros and then use XFRM's tools for projecting reactive plans and representing code trees.

This paper complements previous research that has focussed on the basic algorithms for anticipating and forestalling execution failures in structured reactive plans [BM94] and on the design of structured reactive plans [BM92]. [BM94] makes already use of some XFRML predicates. XFRML, however, has been completely redefined since then.

You might have the impression that XFRML makes simple plan revisions complicated. The reason is that the XFRML plan revision methods are more precise than their counterparts used by other planners. As we have pointed out earlier, other planners make strong assumptions such as the assumption the robot is capable of referring to objects by their names or an one-to-one mapping between state transitions in the world and the the execution of plan steps. XFRML does not make these assumptions and therefore, has to infer the relationship between object descriptions generated by sensing routines and the objects they designate and between plan pieces and the events they cause. The pay-off is that XFRML can infer that the robot has a faulty or ambiguous object description, that the object changed its appearance without the robot noticing, and so on.

Another criterion for assessing XFRML is the conciseness of the notation. XFRML provides between fifty and sixty predicates; about half of them have been described in this paper. Considering that the notation is able to represent structured reactive plans, how the plans get interpreted, how the world changes, and the causal, teleological, and temporal relationships between these components, the number of built-in predicates is rather small. Many of the built-in predicates, especially the ones described in this chapter, are heavily used, that is, in most transformation rules we have written. XFRML is complete in the sense that any transformation that can be specified as a LISP program can also be specified as an XFRML transformation rule by using the EVAL predicate. However, these "escape" calls to LISP are exceptions and mainly used to perform small computations such as generating names for tags.

Besides expressiveness and conciseness, another criterion for the value of a notation is whether the overhead of using it is acceptable. In our application, the time for running an inference rule is negligible compared to the time for generating projections. For example, consider a routine plan for getting all objects from one place to another. The part of the default plan XFRM has to reason about is roughly 300 lines of RPL code long. The plan takes the system about four to five seconds to project. The projection contains more than eighty events that change the world state and more than five hundred tasks. Testing whether a projection satisfies the user's commands takes less than 0.03 seconds. Testing the applicability of transformation rules and installing the proposed revision takes much less than a second. There are two other speed-up techniques that the planning system does: caching temporal inferences and organizing the applicability conditions of a set of transformation rules in a discrimination net.

Finally, we have conducted experiments in a simulated changing world using a simulated robot with limited and noisy sensing and imperfect control [Bee96]. These experiments have shown that controllers that forestall flaws in robot behavior using XFRML are in situations that do not require foresight as efficient as fixed robot controllers and in situations that require foresight more reliable. Other experiments have demonstrated that controllers using XFRML can act competently in situations that can neither be handled by fixed nor by deliberative robot controllers.

Conclusion. Planning representations gain important expressive power by modeling the robot's physical behavior as well as the process of plan interpretation, and temporal, causal, and telelogical relationships between plan interpretation, the world, and the robots' behavior. This additional expressive power together with an expressive plan language enables planning systems to carry out a wide range of plan revision methods that cannot be implemented in other representations. Such plan revision methods can forestall execution failures caused by sensing routines that overlook or misperceive objects, by unfaithful tracking of objects, by unreliable physical actions, or by interference between concurrent actions of the robot.

We are currently implementing the control software of an autonomous mobile robot as structured reactive plans and apply the robot to office delivery tasks. In this setting, XFRM will be used to adapt the robot's default plans to contingent situations. Thus, the real test will be whether we can model the most important behavior flaws of an office delivery robot and the appropriate plan revision methods in XFRML without making significant extensions.

References

[AHT90] J. Allen, J. Hendler, and A. Tate, editors. *Readings in Planning*. Kaufmann, San Mateo, CA, 1990.

[Bee96] M. Beetz. *Anticipating and Forestalling Execution Failures in Structured Reactive Plans*. Ph.D. Thesis, Research Report YALEU/DCS/RR-1097, Yale University, 1996.

[BM92] M. Beetz and D. McDermott. Declarative goals in reactive plans. In J. Hendler, editor, *AIPS-92*, pages 3–12, Morgan Kaufmann, 1992.

[BM94] M. Beetz and D. McDermott. Improving robot plans during their execution. In Kris Hammond, editor, *AIPS-94*, pages 3–12, Morgan Kaufmann, 1994.

[Dav92] E. Davis. Semantics for tasks that can be interrupted or abandoned. In J. Hendler, editor, *AIPS-92*, pages 37–44, Morgan Kaufmann, 1992.

[Fir89] J. Firby. *Adaptive Execution in Complex Dynamic Worlds*. Technical report 672, Yale University, Department of Computer Science, 1989.

[Gat96] E. Gat. Esl: A language for supporting robust plan execution in embedded autonomous agents. In *AAAI Fall Symposium: Issues in Plan Execution*, Cambridge, MA, 1996.

[Ham89] K. Hammond. *Case-Based Planning*. Academic Press, Inc., 1989.

[McD85] D. McDermott. Reasoning about plans. In J. R. Hobbs and R. C. Moore, editors, *Formal Theories of the Commonsense World*, pages 269–317. Ablex, Norwood, NJ, 1985.

[McD91] D. McDermott. A reactive plan language. Research Report YALEU/DCS/RR-864, Yale University, 1991.

[McD92] D. McDermott. Transformational planning of reactive behavior. Research Report YALEU/DCS/RR-941, Yale University, 1992.

[MR91] D. McAllester and D. Rosenblitt. Systematic nonlinear planning. In *Proc. of AAAI-91*, pages 634–639, 1991.

[NS61] A. Newell and H. Simon. GPS, a program that simulates human thought. In Heinz Billing, editor, *Lernende Automaten*, pages 109–124. R. Oldenbourg, Munich, Germany, 1961.

[RK86] S. Rosenschein and L. Kaelbling. The synthesis of digital machines with provable epistemic properties. In *Proc. of the 1986 Conference on Theoretical Aspects of Reasoning about Knowledge*, pages 83–98, Monterey, CA, 1986.

[Sus77] G. Sussman. *A Computer Model of Skill Acquisition*, volume 1 of *Aritficial Intelligence Series*. American Elsevier, New York, NY, 1977.

Fast Probabilistic Plan Debugging

Michael Beetz[1] and Drew McDermott[2]

[1] University of Bonn, Dept. of Computer Science III, Roemerstr. 164,
D-53117 Bonn, Germany, beetz@cs.uni-bonn.de
[2] Yale University, Dept. of Computer Science, P.O. Box 208285, Yale Station,
New Haven, CT 06520-8285, USA, mcdermott@cs.yale.edu

Abstract. To improve the perfomance of robot action planners we must equip them with better and more realistic models of the robots' behavior and the physics of the world. These more realistic models together with the robots' lack of, and uncertainty in, information, however, yield so many ways the world might change as plan gets executed that the prediction of the *probability* of something happening gets infeasible.

In this paper, we discuss FPPD (Fast Probabilistic Plan Debugging), a plan revision technique that can, with high probability, forestall probable situation-specific execution failures: if the original plan is reliable for standard situations, then FPPD can debug the plan's flaws in nonstandard situations based on randomly projecting a small number of execution scenarios — even when considering various types of uncertainty and temporally complex behavior.

1 Introduction

Robot action planning, the generation and revision of control programs based on predictions of what might happen, aims at enabling robots to exhibit more competent behavior. Consider a delivery robot that learns during a delivery that the description of the object to be delivered is ambiguous. The robot then has to decide whether to deliver one object satisfying the description, all of them, or ask the orderer. Making a competent decision requires the robot to predict and assess the consequences of each course of action, and revise subplans accordingly while the plan is executed.

Planning the actions of autonomous mobile robots is difficult because robots often act in changing and partly unknown environments. In these settings, the robots' actions are temporally situated, that is it matters exactly when actions are executed, how long they take, and how they overlap with concurrent activities. Robots also lack essential information about their environments and are equipped with unreliable and inaccurate sensors and effectors.

To generate adequate behavior under such circumstances robot action planners must reason through *many kinds of uncertainty* and predict the effects of *temporally complex, possibly interfering activities.* Planning algorithms, such as SNLP [MR91], have been extended in various ways to handle more expressive action models and different kinds of uncertainty (about the initial state and the occurrence and outcome of events). Typically, these probabilistic planning systems compute bounds for the likelihood of, or probability distributions on, the states resulting from plan execution. Unfortunately, most extensions of the language for expressing probabilistic action models increase the number of things that might happen when a plan gets executed drastically. Planning algorithms that guarantee bounds for the probabilities of plan outcomes become prohibitively expensive even when abstracting away from important aspects of behavior such as reactions and interfering continuous events [Yam94].

Therefore, we research planning problems that do not require the computation of plans with guaranteed properties such as optimality or bounds on the probabilities of plan outcomes but still enable the robots to perform their jobs (on average) better than they possibly could without planning.

This paper studies **FPPD** (Fast Probabilisitic Plan Debugging), a planning technique that improves the behavior of agents by predicting probable execution failures and estimating the quality of a plan based on very few (3 - 4) randomly sampled execution scenarios. FPPD is cheap enough to enable agents to reason about very complex plans (200 - 400 lines of Lisp code) and various kinds of uncertainty and yet can achieve a very high rate (more than 95%) of carrying out necessary plan revisions and thereby improving plans. We will discuss why and under what conditions FPPD achieves such a high rate of improving plans.

2 The Agent Architecture

We have applied FPPD to a simulated robot equipped with limited sensing and effecting capabilities. The robot performs a varying set of tasks in a changing and partially unknown environment, a small world with various objects to be transported from place to place. The plans controlling our robot are made robust by incorporating sensing and monitoring actions, and reactions triggered by observed events.

The robot is provided with a library of modular routine plans that are efficient and cope with most eventualities. Using this library, the robot control system computes a routine plan for a set of jobs by retrieving and instantiating plans for individual jobs and pasting them together to form a parallel robot plan. While pasting routine plans together is fast, it is prone to producing plans that may fail for contingencies. Hence, whenever the robot detects a contingency, it will have to project the effects of this contingency on its current plan and revise the plan if necessary. Whenever the robot thinks it has a plan that is better than the currently executed one, it will replace the current plan with the better one and restart the new plan.

Thus, our robot starts with a routine plan that has a high expected utility with respect to the robot's prior (probabilistic) belief state about its actions, exogenous events and state of the environment. As the robot acts in its environments and takes observations it changes its belief state based on these observations. In particular, the belief state may depart from the prior belief state enough that the routine plan is likely to cause the robot to exhibit certain kinds of behavior flaws with high probability.

The goal of FPPD is to avoid these kinds of predictable behavior flaws. Thus, we design the routine plan such that it is appropriate under certain assumptions. Consider for instance, an office delivery robot. To make its plan efficient the controller of the delivery robot schedules its jobs. However, to determine a schedule for its delivery jobs, the robot has to assume that it knows when office doors are open and when they are closed. The best it can do is to guess the states of the doors based on its most recent observations and (probabilistic) prior information. Other assumptions include that the robot has all the information necessary to carry out its jobs successfully or that it has to accomplish only those jobs that are incorporated in its plan. As the robot acts in the environment, it monitors these assumptions. It scans the doors with its laser range finders whenever it passes them and processes emails containing new commands and information whenever they arrive.

Whenever the robot learns that a door assumed to be open is closed or vice versa or gets new information and commands, it checks whether its current plan is still appropriate and revises it when necessary. Often, it is not necessary to revise the current plan and therefore the robot keeps executing its current plan until the planner signals that a revision is necessary (see [BM96] for details).

The setting in which FPPD is to be used implies several requirements. The role of FPPD is enabling the robot to perform better than it possibly could without planning. To do so, FPPD doesn't have to make guarantees on the properties of the plans it computes. It is sufficient that it forestalls probable behavior flaws with a high probability and doesn't cost much if revisions are not necessary. On the other hand, FPPD has to be very fast with respect to the pace the execution of plans proceeds, reason through *many kinds of uncertainty* and predict the effects of *temporally complex, possibly interfering activities*.

In FPPD, planning is implemented as a search in plan space. A node in the space is a proposed plan; the initial node is the routine plan created using the plan library. A step in the space requires three phases. First, FPPD *projects* a plan to generate sample execution scenarios for it. Then, in the *criticism* phase, FPPD examines these execution scenarios to estimate how good the plan is and to predict possible plan failures. It diagnoses the projected plan failures by classifying them in a taxonomy of failure models. The failure models serve as indices into a set of transformation rules that are applied in the third phase, *revision*, to produce new versions of the plan that are, we hope, improvements.

3 Uncertainty and Temporally Complex Events

Autonomous robots have to deal with various sorts of uncertainty: missing and incorrect information about the state of the world; the duration and effects of robot actions and events; the occurrence of asynchronous, exogenous events; and the interference between simultaneous and overlapping events. In addition, plan execution is often driven by feedback loops and asynchronously arriving sensor readings. The various types of uncertainty yield a huge number of ways the execution of a plan might go.

The rich temporal structure of the behaviors generated by controllers of autonomous robots, increases the number of possible execution scenarios even more (see [AF94] for a discussion of important issues in the representation of temporally complex of actions and events). These behaviors cause changes in the world when they start, terminate, and change states while they are active. For example, going to a particular location causes the robot to steadily change its location. In addition, overlapping behaviors often interfere and cause effects that are very different from the ones they cause when run in isolation.

The prediction of many typical flaws of robot behavior such as overlooking or confusing objects and causing undesired side-effects requires detailed models of uncertainty and the temporal structure of robot behavior. We therefore use the temporal projector of the planning system XFRM [McD94] that provides a very expressive language for representing uncertain and temporally complex behavior. To project the effects of actions and events XFRM's projector determines (1) the situations in which events take place and (2) the events they overlap with.

XFRM's projector guesses the situations in which events take place based on the robot's prior perceptions and prior probabilistic models. Thus, to infer a certain aspect of the world the projector first determines whether stored data structures contain information concerning the query. If so, it guesses the answer based on this information and the probabilistic model of the sensor operation that provided the information. In addition, it considers the probability that the information might have become outdated and that projected actions and events might have changed the state. Without prior perceptions the projector guesses the answer based on prior probabilistic models of the number, kinds, locations, and features of objects typically spread out in the world.

The second task of the plan projector is the prediction of which events occur, when, and how long they take. Modelling an action such as grasping requires the projector to predict the events the grasping behavior causes. Grasping can be modelled as a single instantaneous event, as a sequence of instantaneous events, or as a continuous event, depending on the details required for planning. If the grasping behavior is approximated by a single instantaneous event the planner must assume that nothing can happen between the start and the end of a grasp. Approximating a grasp as a sequence of events say the begin of a grasp, getting contact with the object, and the end of the grasp, enables the planner to predict whether the robot carries the object when a grasp is interrupted. But it still cannot predict whether the arm will bump into an obstacle because it does not model how the arm extends to grasp the object, which requires modelling a grasp as a continuous event.

Often, even coarse-grained models of robot behavior must represent the robots' navigation behaviors as continuous events. Robots spend most of their time moving around and many actions are taken and events occur *while* the robot is moving. Consider, for example, a plan that asks the robot to go to some location and look for an empty box whenever the camera is not used. The effects of looking for empty boxes might be very different depending on when the routine gets activated (because the robot moves).

Another complication is that robot actions might non-deterministically cause different event sequences depending on the specific circumstances. For instance, the course of a grasp might depend on the rigidity or degree of wetness of the object. Besides asserting the events that take place during the execution of a plan we have to specify how these events change the world. This is done using context-dependent probabilistic effect rules that specify the propositions that the event causes to be true or not to hold any longer.

The projector also projects context-dependent (Poisson-distributed) events. Exogenous event models specify the average time in which an event occurs (depending on the context). Thus each time before the projector asserts a new event δ later from the last event it asks whether context condition holds and if so randomly decides whether an event has occurred within δ. If so it randomly generates a time δ' between 0 and δ at which the event is projected to occur.

4 Fast Probabilistic Plan Debugging

Before we analyze the impact of planning based on a small number of randomly generated execution scenarios, let us first explain how FPPD reasons about projected execution scenarios. To do this we first introduce four notions: *routine plans, behavior flaws, severity of behavior flaws*, and *cost/benefit computations* and then detail how FPPD works.

4.1 Routine Plans

Routine plans specify how robots are to respond to sensory input to accomplish its jobs. They are designed to reliably accomplish their purpose in standard situations by monitoring sensor readings and the feedback of the control processes, and locally recovering from many execution failures.

Consider, for instance, how routine plans might handle random events like objects slipping out of the robot's hand. Such events might occur at any time during deliveries and, as a consequence, the object might fall down at many different locations. If, however, the routine plan has a hardwired reaction that specifies that whenever the measured handforce drops to zero, then interrupt whatever you are doing, pick up the object again, and then continue with the delivery, then it often does not matter very much whether and where the object falls down because the robot will immediately pick it up again. Thus, the routine plan works fairly reliably when objects slip out of the robot's hand.

The use of routine plans relieves FPPD from having to guess situations, durations, and effects of actions exactly because it can expect its routine plans to work in any standard situation. It, therefore, only has to know the aspects in which the current state is non-standard. This requirement is easier to satisfy because now robots only have to monitor their surroundings for unusual features and guess the state based on the perceived features instead of steadily perceiving as much as possible.

4.2 Detecting and Eliminating Behavior Flaws

To eliminate behavior flaws FPPD does three things: it (1) infers probable behavior flaws, (2) determines the relative severity of the detected behavior flaws, and (3) judges the dominance of plans with respect to other ones.

Behavior Flaws are failures of a plan to achieve all commands completely. For example, a command *"get all the balls from location $\langle 0,8 \rangle$ to the location $\langle 0,10 \rangle$"* can be viewed as a sentence stating that all blocks that are at location $\langle 0,8 \rangle$ now, will be at $\langle 0,10 \rangle$; plus the tag: to be made true. Thus, a behavior flaw is any ball that is now at $\langle 0,8 \rangle$ and not at $\langle 0,10 \rangle$ when the plan is completed.

To eliminate the most severe behavior flaws first, FPPD has to deal with another complication: sometimes two occurrences of behavior flaws should be considered to be instances of the same behavior flaw. Thus, if two subgoals g_1 and g_2 of a command have not been achieved because a sensor program *sp* has overlooked the objects for which the goals should be achieved, the two occurrences of the flaws count as multiple occurrences of the same flaw. If, however, one object was overlooked and the other one disappeared before it was sensed or the two flaws are caused by different subplans, they are not considered to be the same. Merging instances of the same flaws cuts down the search space and enables the planner to recognize multiply occurring flaws as more severe.

We distinguish between two kinds of behavior flaws: *phantom flaws* and *predictable flaws*. A *phantom flaw* is a flaw caused by the execution of a routine plan in a standard situation. We call this flaw a phantom flaw because the planner will most likely not improve the plan by revising the routine plan to avoid this flaw (even though the flaw has been projected it is very unlikely to occur). We call a flaw *predictable*, if in situations that satisfy the condition c the examined plan will probably cause the flaw and c has been detected by the robot. FPPD uses the following criterion to discriminate between *predictable* and *phantom* flaws: a behavior flaw is predictable if and only if the flaw occurs at least j times in n projected execution scenarios. The accuracy of this discrimination procedure is determined by the choice of j and n.

The **Severity of Behavior Flaws** is a guess of how much the plan could be improved by eliminating the flaw. We take the value of the unachieved subgoal as an estimate of the severity. This typically overestimates the severity because plans resulting from plan revisions are often slower. However, by making behavior flaws look more severe than they are we can make sure that the planner tries to eliminate them [DP85]. Estimating the severity of a flaw is further complicated by the fact that the elimination of a behavior flaw might introduce new flaws. Approaches to deal with these complications are described in [Sim92, McD92].

Cost/benefit Computations. Agents should often try to accomplish as many of their jobs in as little time as possible. This kind of behavior is achieved by incorporating a utility model into FPPD that assigns benefits for accomplishing jobs from which costs for the time spent are subtracted. The utility model defines the score of a plan in a given execution scenario *es* with respect to the given commands. The benefit the robot gets for accomplishing individual commands depends on the commands and the degree to which they are accomplished.

4.3 Finding Predictable Behavior Flaws

The task of the plan projector is to take the current world model, a plan, probabilistic rules for generating exogenous events and guessing missing pieces of the
world model, probabilistic causal models of robot actions and generate *execution
scenarios* of the plan in order to find the predictable behavior flaws.[1]

Because of the uncertainty and lack of information the number of execution
scenarios that solve a given projection problem is too big to compute bounds for
different plan outcomes in reasonable amounts of time [Han90, KHW95, Kan92].

An alternative might seem to enumerate execution scenarios by projecting
the most likely outcomes of actions first. But this technique breaks down even in
very simple scenarios. Consider a biased dice: the probability that we roll a one
is fifty percent, while the probability of rolling all other numbers is ten percent.
Now, the robot has to project the plan "roll the dice until it shows a six" to
approximate the likelihood that the plan will roll a six. If projector is biased to
look at the most likely outcomes first, the plan will be predicted never to succeed
while in reality the plan will certainly succeed.

So far only Monte Carlo projection algorithms project such complex, probabilistic behavior [McD94, Yam94]. Thus, FPPD randomly samples a small number of execution scenarios. The Monte Carlo projection algorithm of FPPD uses
a conditional probability distribution for estimating the current state of the environment and the occurrence of exogenous events based on the robot's prior
observations and the current time (to account for the dynamics in the environment). The algorithm gets the robot's observations (mostly partial object and
state descriptions produced by sensing routines) and generates a set of n random
execution scenarios. In the second step a *behavior classifier* that is equipped with
a taxonomy of classes of behavior flaws detects, classifies, and collects the behavior flaws and merges the instances of behavior flaws that are occurrences of the
same flaw. The last step discriminates the collected flaws into predictable and
phantom flaws and returns the list of the predictable flaws ordered according to
their estimated severity.

5 Analysis of FPPD

The goal of FPPD is to eliminate severe predictable flaws while at the same time
avoid the elimination of phantom flaws. Since FPPD must revise plans while they
are executed it is crucial that debugging behavior flaws is much faster than executing plans. Therefore, FPPD can only afford to produce a small number of
candidate plans for avoiding one particular flaw and project for each candidate

---

[1] XFRM's probabilistic temporal projection algorithm is described in [McD92, McD94].
[McD94] gives a formal semantics of the representation language for probabilistic
and temporally complex behehavior, shows that a consistent set of causal models
has a unique model, and proves the algorithms for projecting execution scenarios to
be correct. That is, the algorithm computes as the number of projections approaches
infinity the accurate distribution of execution scenarios.

plan a small number of random execution scenarios. FPPD assumes that if a particular kind of behavior flaw is likely to occur due to a particular constellation of jobs or non-standard situation, the flaw will most likely show up in the projected execution scenarios.

Therefore, forestalling behavior flaws based on a few random execution scenarios might have the following unwanted effects:

1. the planner overlooks a predictable flaw;
2. the planner forestalls a phantom flaw instead of a predictable flaw;
3. the planner estimates a plan with predictable behavior flaws to be better than one without such flaws; and
4. the planner revises the plan to avoid a phantom flaw.

The rest of this section estimates the likelihood and analyzes the consequences of these negative effects.

To be more precise we consider a behavior flaw f that occurs in the perceived context c with the probability p. Further, let $X_i(f)$ represent the event that an instance of the behavior flaw f occurs in the ith execution scenario:

$$X_i(f) = \begin{cases} 1, & f \text{ occurs in the } i\text{th execution scenario,} \\ 0, & \text{otherwise} \end{cases} \tag{1}$$

The random variable $Y(f) = \sum_{i=1}^{n} X_i(f)$ represents the number of occurrences of the flaw f in n execution scenarios. Since the occurrence of behavior flaws in the randomly sampled execution scenarios are independent from each other, the value of $Y(f)$ can be described by the binomial distribution $b(n,p)$.

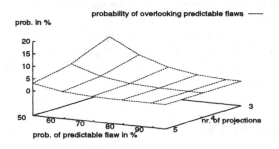

Figure 1. Probability of overlooking predictable flaws.

Using $b(n,p)$ we can consider the likelihood of the first negative effect of FPPD. Recall that FPPD considers a behavior flaw to be predictable iff it occurs at least j times in n projections. Thus the probability of overlooking a predictable flaw f with probability p in n execution scenarios is:

$$P(Y(f) < j) = \sum_{k=0}^{j-1} \binom{n}{k} * p^k * (1-p)^{n-k} \tag{2}$$

Figure 1 shows the probability of overlooking predictable flaws as a function of the probability of the predictable flaw and the number of projected execution scenarios for $j = 2$ (predictable flaws must occur at least twice). Setting j to 1 reduces the probability of overlooking predictable flaws at the cost of increasing the likelihood of chasing phantom flaws. Increasing j has the opposite effect.

The second problem of FPPD is that it might chase a phantom goal instead of predictable ones and therefore cause the planner to start too late with the elimination of a predictable flaw and missing the opportunity to install a necessary revision in time.

FPPD chases phantom flaws instead of predictable ones only if the severity of the phantom flaw is estimated to be at least as high as the one of the predictable flaws. Since routine plans are designed such that the probability of phantom flaws is very low, predictable flaws are likely to occur more often flaws and therefore, their severity is, with high probability, higher.

The following table shows the probability that the planner forestalls a phantom flaw instead of the predictable flaw for the case that $j = 1$ and the assumptions that the probability of phantom flaws is so small that the probability of multiple occurrences of the same phantom flaws are neglectable and all that flaws have the same severity; for the case that $j = 2$ this probability is neglectable:

prob. of the flaw	prob. of picking the phantom flaw based on x projections	
	$x = 3$	$x = 4$
50%	31.25%	18.75%
75%	3.95%	2.4%
90%	1.45%	0.4%

The third problem is that FPPD might estimate a plan that causes predictable flaws to be better than one that causes only phantom flaws. In the worst case, this might cause the robot to execute a plan containing predictable flaws until the planner has noticed its mistake (in our test domain typically under a minute). Since predictable behavior flaws are likely to occur more than once it is unlikely that the utility of a plan causing predictable flaws is estimated to be higher than the utility of one that causes no or only phantom flaws.

To avoid frequent chases of phantom flaws we use optimistic probabilistic models for the execution of sensing and action routines in standard situations.

To summarize, even for a small number of randomly generated execution scenarios is it very likely that FPPD will eliminate predictable behavior flaws. The likelihood of performing plan revisions to avoid phantom flaws can be minimized by using optimistic probabilistic models for the execution of sensing and action routines in standard situations. The results can be improved by increasing the number of execution scenarios that are generated and analyzed.

6 Experiments

An important metric for evaluating FPPD is the amount by which it improves the performance of the agent it controls [Zil95, CGHH89, PR90], which is measured in terms of how well the robot accomplishes its jobs and how long it takes. The agent's performance summarizes several measures such as the quality of the plan revisions, the time resources needed to compute these revisions, how robust plan revision is, and so on. To evaluate the impact of FPPD on agent behavior we have embedded FPPD into a simulated robot equipped with limited sensing and effecting capabilities. The robot performs a varying set of tasks in a changing and partially unknown environment, a small world with various objects to be transported from place to place.

To verify that FPPD can improve the robot's behavior in the simulated world we perform three kinds of experiments. (For a detailed description see [Bee96].) The first one demonstrates that for problems in which routine plans are adequate, the robot controller described in section 2 performs as well as the routine plan. The second one will show that if the probability distribution given to FPPD describes the world accurately, then FPPD will forestall probable behavior flaws with a high probability and will not make plans worse and thereby perform almost as well as a control system that uses a perfect oracle to pick the plan to be executed. The third experiment will show that FPPD can avoid behavior flaws that cannot be avoided by plans that are not modified during execution. Taken together these three experiments imply that FPPD enables an agent to perform better than it possibly could without planning. In all three experiments we have set $j = 2$ and $n = 4$; that is, a behavior flaw is predictable if it occurs at least twice in four projected execution scenarios.

The first experiment compares the performance of routine plans and control programs that apply FPPD in situations that do not require planning. Given a probability distribution on problems and situations we have drawn ten random problem instances and run each controller fifty times on each problem to get performance profiles for the controllers. Over the ten problem instances the difference between the mean of the time resources consumed by the routine plan and the controller applying FPPD did not differ more than 0.6%, the standard deviation not more than 1.2%. The difference in the least amount of time required to solve a problem instance did not differ more than 4.3% (average $< 1.4\%$). The difference in the maximal amount of time needed was smaller than 9.5% (average $< 2.3\%$). These results imply that the performance difference between routine plans and controllers that apply FPPD for problems in which routine plans are adequate are statistically insignificant.

The second experiment compares a controller applying FPPD with several other ones: a *routine plan*; a *cautious plan* that always acts as if interference caused by contingency c is probable; and a *clairvoyant controller* that uses a perfect oracle to choose the best course of action. We have performed the following experiment: the robot is to get all balls from one location to another one. While carrying out the task, the following contingencies may or may not occur: balls may disappear or change their shape, sensor programs may overlook objects or examine them incorrectly. FPPD is equipped with accurate probabilistic models of the contingencies. We run each controller in two scenarios: in one the contingency c occurs and in the other it does not. As expected, the cautious plans are significantly slower than the routine plan but achieve their subgoals reliably. The routine plan works well only if c does not occur; if c does occur, some are not delivered successfully. The controller with planning is as robust as the cautious plan. It is also on average less than 5% slower than the executing the best plan that achieves all the goals on a given trial. Planning costs are this low because FPPD plans during the idle time in which the interpreter was waiting for feedback from control routines. In terms of average benefit, the controller assisted by FPPD was better (337.0) than the cautious (321.0) and the routine plan (261.7). The experiment shows that FPPD can outperform robot controllers that do not plan. It also shows that under ideal conditions (exact probabilistic models; planning is fast compared to execution; the probability of predictable flaws in standard situations is very low and under certain conditions very high) as efficient as a system that knows the best plan to use on each occasion.

In our third experiment, we have made up ten problem instances that are characteristic for important classes of contingencies and cannot be handled adequately without predicting behavior flaws based on accurate models of uncertain and temporally complex behavior and revising plans to avoid the flaws. The problem instances comprised ones in which the robot was required to handle ambiguous object descriptions, had to deal with other robots, to handle deadlines, avoid subtle subplan interferences, and avoid overlooking objects. We have run the controller applying FPPD on each problem instance ten times. For each of these problem instances the success rate of the routine plan was less than fifty percent and the success rate of the controller applying FPPD more than ninety percent. This experiment shows that FPPD made it possible for the agent to act competently in a variety of situations that cannot be handled without projection and plan revision.

7   Related Work

Plan revision techniques can be classified into ones that reason about the structure of plans and the dependencies between plan steps [Kam90, HW92] and others that revise plans based on simulations/projections of plans (HACKER [Sus90], GORDIUS [Sim92], CHEF [Ham89]). There are several differences between FPPD and other plan revision techniques: (1) FPPD differs from other transformational planners in that it tries to adapt a simultaneously executed plan to specific situations to avoid particular flaws and thereby improve the agent's behavior instead of constructing a correct plan. (2) FPPD reasons about concurrent robot control programs and various kinds of uncertainty while CHEF, GORDIUS, and HACKER reason about plans with simple control structures and assume perfect knowledge.

Other planning systems that make plans more robust during their execution mainly address plan failures caused by nondeterministic outcomes of plan actions [DB90, DKKN93], or they plan for single, highly repetitive tasks [LH92]. FPPD, on the other hand, is able to diagnose a larger variety of failures (see [BM94]) and non-repetitive tasks. Another body of related work includes systems [Wil88] that revise plans to recover from failures that have already occurred.

Several variations of the classical planning problem have been proposed to reason about exogenous events; sensing actions, and uncertain and incomplete information. For example, the problems of generating plans that maximize the probability that a given goal G is true [KHW95, DHW94, Bly95, Han90] or that maximizes the expected utility [HR90, Wel90]. FPPD, on the other hand, does not reason about the exact probabilities of outcomes of plan execution. Probability is handled implicitly by the projector that generates random execution scenarios based on the given probability distributions. The planning approaches that maximize the probability of goal achievement only work if the plans are sequences of discrete plan steps and probability distributions describing the current state of the world are available. FPPD, on the other hand, reasons about plans that specify the concurrent execution of continuous control processes and has only sparse information about the current state of the world. FPPD's weaker methods suffice because the plans it reasons about are more robust and cause similar behavior in a range of standard situations. In addition, Monte Carlo projection methods often converge faster to the exact probability than other methods for probabilistic temporal projection (see [Yam94] for experiments and a detailed discussion).

8   Conclusions

This paper has described and discussed FPPD, a plan revision technique that enables agents acting in complex and partly unknown environments to achieve probably approximately competent behavior in contingent situations. Adequate behavior can only be produced with a high probability because the information available for planning is incomplete, uncertain, and possibly even false. The behavior can only be approximately competent because the agent starts executing its routine plan while looking for better plans. Thus, when the agent finds a better plan the resources spent for executing the routine plan might be wasted, or even worse, the effects of the routine plan must be reversed.

FPPD works because it uses detailed models of uncertain and temporally complex behavior. It can Forestall behavior flaws that are probable for a given contingent situation fast because FPPD can restrict itself to look for flaws that occur more than once in a small set of randomly sampled scenarios instead of trying to predict what will probably happen. For this method to work the plans FPPD reasons about have to be reliable for standard situations that is automatically correct local behavior flaws. In addition, FPPD has to distinguish between phantom flaws and predictable flaws, which can be done with a high success rate if the routine plans are reliable in standard situations and in the given scenarios the predictable flaws very likely.

We are currently implementing the control system of an autonomous mobile robot using routine plans and apply the robot to office delivery tasks. In this setting, FPPD will be used to adapt the robot's routine plans to contingent situations. The real test will be how much FPPD can improve the behavior of the office delivery robot.

References

[AF94]   J. Allen and G. Ferguson. Actions and events in interval temporal logic. Technical Report 521, University of Rochester, Computer Science Department, 1994.

[Bee96]   M. Beetz. *Anticipating and Forestalling Execution Failures in Structured Reactive Plans.* Ph.D. Thesis, Research Report YALEU/DCS/RR-1097, Yale University, 1996.

[Bly95]   J. Blythe. Ai planning in dynamic, uncertain domains. In *AAAI Spring Symposium on Extending Theories of Action*, 1995.

[BM94]   M. Beetz and D. McDermott. Improving robot plans during their execution. In Kris Hammond, editor, *AIPS-94*, pages 3–12, Morgan Kaufmann, 1994.

[BM96]   M. Beetz and D. McDermott. Local planning of ongoing behavior. In Brian Drabble, editor, *AIPS-96*, pages 3–12, Morgan Kaufmann, 1996.

[CGHH89]   P. Cohen, M. Greenberg, D. Hart, and A. Howe. Trial by fire: Understanding the design requirements for agents in complex environments. *AI Magazine*, pages 32–48, 1989.

[DB90]   M. Drummond and J. Bresina. Anytime synthetic projection: Maximizing the probability of goal satisfaction. In *Proc. of AAAI-90*, pages 138–144, 1990.

[DHW94]   D. Draper, S. Hanks, and D. Weld. Probabilistic planning with information gathering and contingent execution. In K. Hammond, editor, *Proc. 2nd. Int. Conf. on AI Planning Systems.* Morgan Kaufmann, 1994.

[DKKN93]   T. Dean, L. Kaelbling, J. Kirman, and A. Nicholson. Planning with deadlines in stochastic domains. In *Proc. of AAAI-93*, pages 574–579, 1993.

[DP85]   R. Dechter and J. Pearl. Generalized best-first search strategies and the optimality of A*. *Journal of the Association for Computing Machinery*, 32(3):505–536, July 1985.

[Ham89]   K. Hammond. *Case-Based Planning.* Academic Press, Inc., 1989.

[Han90]   S. Hanks. Practical temporal projection. In *Proc. of AAAI-90*, pages 158–163, Boston, MA, 1990.

[HR90]   P. Haddawy and L. Rendell. Planning and decision theory. *The Knowledge Engineering Review*, 5:15–33, 1990.

[HW92]   S. Hanks and D. Weld. Systematic adaptation for case-based planning. In J. Hendler, editor, *AIPS-92*, pages 96–105, Morgan Kaufmann, 1992.

[Kam90]   S. Kambhampati. A theory of plan modification. In *Proc. of AAAI-90*, Boston, MA, 1990.

[Kan92]   K. Kanazawa. *Reasoning about Time and Probability.* PhD thesis, Brown University, 1992.

[KHW95]   N. Kushmerick, S. Hanks, and D. Weld. An algorithm for probabilistic planning. *Artificial Intelligence*, 76:239–286, 1995.

[LH92]   D. Lyons and A. Hendriks. A practical approach to integrating reaction and deliberation. In J. Hendler, editor, *AIPS-92*, pages 153–162, 1992.

[McD92]   D. McDermott. Transformational planning of reactive behavior. Research Report YALEU/DCS/RR-941, Yale University, 1992.

[McD94]   D. McDermott. An algorithm for probabilistic, totally-ordered temporal projection. Research Report YALEU/DCS/RR-1014, Yale University, 1994.

[MR91]   D. McAllester and D. Rosenblitt. Systematic nonlinear planning. In *Proc. of AAAI-91*, pages 634–639, 1991.

[PR90]   M. Pollack and M. Ringuette. Introducing the tileworld: Experimentally evaluating agent architectures. In *Proc. of AAAI-90*, pages 183–189, Boston, MA, 1990.

[Sim92]   R. Simmons. The roles of associational and causal reasoning in problem solving. *Artificial Intelligence*, 53:159–207, 1992.

[Sus90]   G. Sussman. The virtuous nature of bugs. In J. Allen, J. Hendler, and A. Tate, editors, *Readings in Planning*, pages 111–117. Kaufmann, San Mateo, CA, 1990.

[Wel90]   M. Wellmann. *Formulation of Tradeoffs in Planning under Uncertainty.* Pitman and Morgan Kaufmann, 1990.

[Wil88]   D. Wilkins. *Practical Planning: Extending the AI Planning Paradigm.* Morgan Kaufmann, San Mateo, CA, 1988.

[Yam94]   E. Yampratoom. Using simulation-based projection to plan in an uncertain and temporally complex world. Technical Report 531, University of Rochester, CS Deptartment, 1994.

[Zil95]   S. Zilberstein. On the utility of planning. In M. Pollack, editor, *SIGART Bulletin Special Issue on Evaluating Plans, Planners, and Planning Systems*, volume 6. ACM, 1995.

Quantification in Generative Refinement Planning

Andrew Burgess and Sam Steel

University of Essex, Colchester C04 3SQ, UK
email: burga@essex.ac.uk, sam@essex.ac.uk

Abstract. This paper brings together a collection of new ideas from generative refinement planning with some more well established results from theorem proving. We add full quantification to a generative refinement planning framework, not by expanding to a *universal base* [9], but by Skolemizing. We apply our results to causal link planning which leads to a new conflict resolution strategy, a notion called *weakening the label*.

1 Introduction

The state of the art in handling explicit quantification within preconditions and effects of action schemata is unsatisfactory. Before UCPOP [9, 10], planners with expressive action languages represented plans as totally ordered sequences of actions (for example, PEDESTAL [4]) and the partial order planners were based on the restrictive STRIPS [2] representation (for example, TWEAK [1] and SNLP [3]). UCPOP introduces quantification into partial order planning with an action language based on Pednault's ADL [5, 7]. But universally quantified goals are expanded to a conjunction with the notion of a *universal base* and existential effects are not supported.

In this paper we present a truth criterion that handles quantification in preconditions and effects of action schemata. Although in its most general setting it appears intractable, by utilizing accumulators that take the form of causal links, it is shown that a planner can be implemented. In addition, the application of our findings to causal link planning leads to a new conflict resolution strategy, a notion called *weakening the label*.

We do not consider context-dependent effects in this paper although it is straightforward to extend the presented truth criterion to handle them. Our implementation does, however, cater for context-dependent effects. The reader is referred to [6, 8–10] for the details.

2 Generative Refinement Planning

Generative refinement planning systems model the effects that actions have on the world by considering the world, at any instant in time, to be in a particular *state*. The effect of an action is to cause the world to leave the current state and enter a different state. An action is therefore defined by a set of current-state/next-state pairs. This set specifies precisely what the effects of an action would be in each state of the world in which it can be performed.

A state is described by a set of *literals* of first order logic. A literal consists of a *predicate* and a *content* and may be negated. The content consists of an *n*-tuple of *terms* where n is said to be the *arity* of the predicate. A term is either a *constant* or a *parameter*. Unique constants may not denote the same object in the world, that is, they may not *codenote*. For example, the literal $on(a, ?P)$ consists of the predicate *on* and the pair of terms $(a, ?P)$ where a is a constant and $?P$ is a parameter.

An action is described by a *step*. A step has a finite number of *preconditions* or *goals* and a finite number of *effects*. The preconditions are a description of the *input states* in which the corresponding action can be executed. Similarly, the effects are a description of what changes in the world as a result of execution. In a generative refinement planning framework, actions are assumed to be deterministic, that is, for any given description of a valid input state, it is possible to construct a description of the *output state* from the effects. Preconditions and effects are also limited to sets of literals. We impose ordering constraints on steps to represent time. The complete set of steps that a planner can utilize is called the set of *action schemata*.

A plan is generated by repeatedly posting constraints and adding new steps to an initial *null plan*. A null plan consists of a start step whose effects encode the initial state of the world and a goal step whose preconditions encode the goal state. The only ordering constraint is that the initial step occurs before the goal step. During planning, the null plan is refined successively until it "justifiably" transforms the initial state of the world into the goal state. We put quotes around justifiably because unsound inference is characteristic of generative refinement planning. For example, not all ramifications of an effect, that is, logical consequences of an effect, are considered.

We now turn our attention to the representation of a plan. A plan only imposes the absolutely essential ordering constraints on its steps. Any linearization, that is, path through the steps that is consistent with the partial ordering, yields a valid plan. Planners that utilize this representation are said to practice *partial order planning* and must maintain the *consistency* of the ordering constraints. A set of ordering constraints is consistent if there exists at least one linearization that satisfies them.

Action schemata may be parameterized. Parameters should be thought of as place holders for future constants. When a new instance of an action schema, that is, a new step is introduced into a plan, not all of its parameters need be bound. Just as the bound parameters are constrained to codenote with the constants they are instantiated with, the unbound parameters may be constrained in another way. Such constraints on parameters are called *binding constraints*.

Binding constraints form an equivalence relation over parameters and constants. They come in two types. The first type is called a *codesignation constraint*. A codesignation constraint confines two pieces of syntax, at least one of which is a parameter, to denote the same object in the world. We write ?P $\approx$ **block4** to constrain a parameter[1] ?P to codenote with the constant **block4**. The second type of binding constraint is called a *non-codesignation constraint* which has the opposite effect of confining two items of syntax, at least one of which is a parameter, from denoting the same object. Similarly, we write ?P $\not\approx$ **block4** to constrain parameter ?P and constant **block4** from denoting the same object.

Recall that a consequence of representing plans as partially ordered sequences of actions is that one's planner is forced to maintain a consistent set of ordering constraints. Likewise, a consequence of parameterizing action schemata is that one's planner has to maintain a consistent set of binding constraints.

It is therefore apparent that during the planning process, a plan can be incomplete in two ways. Steps may only be partially ordered and only partially specified. A *completion* of a partially ordered partially specified plan is a *grounding* of parameters that is consistent with the binding constraints and a total ordering of the steps that is consistent with the partial ordering.

Planning terminates when a *goal plan* is found. A goal plan is a plan in which each of its completions is executable and leads to a goal state. Although many generative refinement planners output an arbitrary completion of a goal plan, leaving it in its most general form enables the agent to exploit its inherent concurrent nature. Any unbound parameter may be instantiated with an arbitrary constant during execution, providing it does not violate the binding constraints.

2.1 Causal Link Planning

In causal link planning, the establishment of a goal achieved through acting on the world is documented explicitly. This is represented by a data structure called a *causal link* [3]. A causal link traditionally comprises a triple of which two elements are steps. One step is called the link's producer (S_p) and the other the link's consumer (S_c). The remaining element of the link is the label, denoted by L. Precisely what L consists of depends on the action description language characterizing the planning algorithm. In the simplest case where action schemata may not be parameterized, L is just an effect of the producer and a precondition of the consumer. Such a causal link is written $S_c \xrightarrow{L} S_p$.

Clobberings in Causal Link Planning. When a new step is introduced into a plan, its effects must be checked against the labels of the causal links. If an effect of a new step is *possibly the negation* (in some binding of parameters) of a sentence that forms a label of a causal link and the new step *possibly occurs* (in some linearizations) between the associated producer and consumer, the new step is said to *clobber* that link. The standard way of dealing with such clobberings is to either *demote* or *promote* the clobberer. Demotion enforces a new ordering constraint on the steps where the clobberer is confined to execute before the

---

[1] We adopt the convention that a parameter must begin with a question mark (?). This helps to prevent confusion when other kinds of variable arise.

producer of the clobbered link. Similarly, promotion confines the clobberer to execute after the consumer of the clobbered link.

If an effect of a new step is a clobberer of a causal link only in a particular binding of parameters then a third way of resolving the conflict is to make that binding of parameters impossible. This is achieved with the addition of a non-codesignation constraint and is described further in Section 5.2.

Plans and their associated Justification Structures. A null plan can be viewed as the specification of a planning problem. In causal link planning, one takes a null plan, adds new steps and records explicit causal links between effects and preconditions until all goals are satisfied and no link is clobbered. The point here is that causal links form part of the justification that a plan meets its specification, but are not a part of the final plan. The output of a planning algorithm is simply a partially ordered (partially specified) set of steps. The agent that is going to use the plan need not see the associated *justification structure*, that is, the means by which the plan was generated. It is therefore important to distinguish a final plan from its associated justification structure.

2.2 Truth Criteria

An alternative approach to recording the interactions between steps explicitly is to recompute them repeatedly. This is achieved with a test called a *truth criterion*. A truth criterion specifies precisely the conditions in which a formula is true at a particular instant in a plan. This test provides a verification procedure that can be applied to a plan to determine that it meets its specification.

Chapman [1] specifies a modal truth criterion (MTC) for partially ordered, partially specified plans. He illustrates that to be able to determine the *necessary truth* of a literal, the action description language of preconditions and effects must be themselves confined to literals. A literal is necessarily true at some point in a partially ordered, partially specified plan if it is true in all completions at the same point. Fortunately, Chapman's result is misleading because in order to plan, it is not necessary to be able to determine the necessary truth of a literal. One can plan to *ensure* the necessary truth.

A truth criterion is not only used to verify that a plan meets its specification. It is also used the other way around to suggest ways of amending bad plans. A truth criterion approach to plan generation is not an opposite approach to causal link planning. Any causal link planner has an associated truth criterion. The difference between a truth criterion that utilizes causal links and one that does not is that in the former, the addition of causal links makes it explicitly clear which effect is supporting which goal in all completions[2]. In general, this is not the case, that is, different steps may support the same goal in different completions [1].

---

[2] Pednault illustrates with his "bomb and bucket" example [6] that in general, the establishing effect of a causal link is not necessarily the *final establisher*. We do not cater for this kind of reasoning.

3 Truth Criteria for Generative Refinement Planning

3.1 A Basic Truth Criterion

A truth criterion can have different equivalent forms, not all equally computationally useful. Chapman, having introduced the idea of a truth criterion, defined an obvious one and then showed it was equivalent to a different, more efficient, form, the modal truth criterion. Since we are not concerned with proposing an optimal planning system but with showing how generative refinement planning can be extended to cater for quantification, we shall stick with the more obvious criterion:

$p(T^*)$ **holds-before step** O if
> for all linearizations $<$ and for all bindings θ
>> there is a step E such that $E < O$
>>> and E has effect $p(U^*)$ such that $T^*\theta = U^*\theta$
>>> and for each precondition π of step E
>>>> π **holds-before step** E
>> and there is NO step C such that $E < C < O$
>>> and C has effect $\neg p(V^*)$ such that $T^*\theta = V^*\theta$

The first conjunct of the above criterion is concerned with establishment. For a literal P to be established before a step O, there must be a step E that occurs before O in *each* linearization of the plan. E need not be the same step in each linearization but it must have an effect Q such that in all binding of parameters (consistent with the binding constraints) P and Q *codesignate*. The final condition that must be satisfied is that all preconditions of the establishing effect hold before step E.

Two literals A and B *codesignate*, written $A \approx B$, if they are both negated or both are not, if their predicates are of the same arity and if their contents codesignate. During plan synthesis, one often needs to determine whether two literals can be made to codesignate. This process amounts to the unification of the two literals.

The second conjunct of the criterion tells us about clobbering. In each linearization and in each binding of parameters, a literal P established by a step E is clobbered by an intervening step C if C is in between E and O and has effect V such that the negation of V codesignates with P.

A step that clobbers a literal is part of a plan because one of its effects is being used elsewhere to support a different goal. There is no need, therefore, to ensure that a clobbering step has all its preconditions satisfied in order for it to be a clobberer.

3.2 A Truth Criterion for Quantification

We now relax the restriction that preconditions and effects must only consist of literals. Any well-formed formula of first order logic may form a precondition whereas any well-formed formula of first order logic that does not contain disjunction may form an effect. A consequence is that negation cannot operate over the effect language in general although existential quantification is permitted. The corresponding truth criterion is as follows.

> Formula F **holds-before step** O if
> > for all linearizations $<$ and for all bindings θ
> > > there is a step E such that $E < O$
> > > > and E has effect G such that $G\theta$ *establishes* $F\theta$
> > > > and for each precondition π of step E
> > > > > π **holds-before step** E
> > > and there is NO set of steps C such that
> > > > each $c_i \in C$ satisfies $E < c_i < O$
> > > > > and each $c_i \in C$ has effect H_i such that
> > > > > > $\& H_i \theta$ *clobbers* $F\theta$

In any linearization $<$ and in any binding of parameters θ, a formula F is established before a step O if there is a previous step E according to $<$ that has effect formula G and G under θ *establishes* F under θ. Although this is vague, an important feature is that the parameters are seen to be outside of the language of preconditions and effects, that is, the binding of parameters to constants is *not* a part of the procedure *establishes*. Clobbering is defined similarly with the different procedure *clobbers*.

A further generalization has been made in the above criterion to enable quantification to be dealt with in a satisfactory manner. What has been added is the possibility of *collective clobberings*. A collective clobbering is the collaboration of two or more steps such that each acting on its own has no impact but acting together clobber a formula.

In a linearization $<$ and a binding of parameters θ, a formula F that is established by a step E is clobbered by a set of steps C if each step $c_i \in C$ is in between E and the point under scrutiny according to $<$ and in addition each $c_i \in C$ has effect H_i such that the conjunction of all the H_i, written $\& H_i$, under θ *clobbers* F under θ.

4 Planning for Quantification

Determining whether an arbitrary formula of first order logic J establishes another arbitrary formula K amounts to illustrating that in all interpretations of constants, functions and relations and in all valuations of free variables in which J is true, K is also true. This is just the definition of logical consequence which is defined more formally as follows.

Definition 1. $J \models K$ if and only if for all interpretations I and for all valuations v if $I \models J[v]$ then $I \models K[v]$.

But because we consider parameters to be outside both our effect and goal languages and because we disallow variables to occur free, we have the following equivalence for formulas of our effect language F (where disjunction may not occur) and formulas of our goal language G.

Definition 2. F **establishes** G if and only if for all interpretations I if $I \models F$ then $I \models G$.

We define the notion of clobbering similarly.

Definition 3. F **clobbers** G if and only if there exists an interpretation I such that $I \models F$ and $I \not\models G$.

Recall that in Section 3.2, we introduced a truth criterion for quantification by utilizing the two black box procedures *establishes* and *clobbers*. Ideally, we would like the relation F *establishes* G to be true if F **establishes** G and vice versa. But because this is hard to achieve, we only insist on the former, that is, we only insist that *establishes* is sound but not complete. This applies similarly to the procedure *clobbers*. Underlying both the procedures *establishes* and *clobbers* is a theorem prover.

4.1 Refutation Theorem Proving

A theorem prover tries to determine whether F entails G, where F and G are arbitrary formulas of first order logic by searching for a *refutation*. A refutation is a proof by contradiction. We start with the formula F and a set of axioms and we assume $\neg G$. If we can then derive falsehood ($\#$), the only mistaken assumption is $\neg G$. Refutation theorem proving is sound and so it follows that G is a logical consequence of F.

In generative refinement planning systems, the process of determining a refutation between an effect literal P and a goal literal Q amounts to finding a binding of parameters θ such that $P\theta = Q\theta$. Refutation theorem proving, however, has more to offer us in terms of representation. For arbitrary formulas F and G, we have the following equivalence

$$F \models G \longleftrightarrow skolem(F), skolem(\neg G) \vdash \# \qquad (1)$$

where *skolem* is a function that converts a formula into its *Skolemized* form. The process of Skolemization translates a formula of first order logic into a different language that has no quantifiers. This is achieved by introducing new *Skolem terms*. The formula $(\forall X)(\exists Y)(p(X, Y))$, for example, Skolemizes to $p(X, \$(X))$ where $\$$ is a new Skolem function. The intuition here is that for every element in the domain of X, $\$$ provides an element from the domain of Y given by $\$(X)$ such that $p(X, \$(X))$.

Although we do not have the equivalence $F \leftrightarrow skolem(F)$, for an arbitrary formula F, what is apparent from (1) is that there is an interpretation of constants, functions and relations I_q such that $I_q \models F$ if and only if there is an interpretation of constants, functions, relations and Skolem terms I_s such that $I_s \models_s skolem(F)$. The relation $\models_s$ is defined inductively in the usual way except that the rules for universal and existential quantification are not included.

4.2 Establishment

We require the procedure *establishes* to have the following property for all effect formulas F and goal formulas G.

If F establishes G then F establishes G

We test whether F *establishes* G is true by Skolemizing both F and $\neg G$ and seeking a refutation. If we can show that there is a substitution of parameters θ and a substitution of universal variables ϕ such that $skolem(F)\theta\phi$ and $skolem(\neg G)\theta\phi$ are contradictory then the standard results of refutation theorem proving tell us that F *establishes* G.

We do not speak of Skolem constants as being introduced into a plan. They only crop up when we test F *establishes* G for effect F and goal G, that is, they form part of the justification that a plan meets its specification, but are not a part of the final plan.

The substitution of parameters is separated from the substitution of universal variables because the former affects the plan itself, that is, parameters are above our effect and goal languages whereas the latter exists temporarily to justify that the effect does indeed support the goal. During planning, one may have unbound parameters but inside the procedure *establishes* such parameters behave like ordinary constants. It is therefore impossible for a parameter to become bound with a Skolem term.

4.3 Clobbering

We implement *clobbers* similarly to *establishes* by utilizing theorem proving techniques but with some added machinery. Consider the following plan fragment.

In order to determine whether $(\exists X)(\neg p(X))$ *clobbers* $p(a)$ is true, we Skolemize $(\exists X)(\neg p(X))$ yielding $p(\$)$ and look for a substitution of parameters and universal variables such that $\neg p(\$)$ and $p(a)$ lead to contradiction. But clearly no such substitutions exist. Our procedure therefore returns false.

One can construct an interpretation, however, where $\$$ denotes the same object as a. The clobbering is then undeniable. What needs to be added is some machinery that allows Skolem constants to become "bound" to any other term. Skolem constants behave like ordinary constants in making establishment hard but they behave like variables in making clobbering easy. In this case $\$$ would become bound to a, illustrating that there is an interpretation of Skolem constants in which $\$$ denotes the same as a.

4.4   Skolemizing Action Schemata

In this section, we illustrate how an action schema can be Skolemized. This forms part of the internal workings of both the procedures *establishes* and *clobbers*. We stress that when reasoning about a plan, all preconditions and effects are seen to be in quantifier form. Skolemizing should be seen as only taking place inside the procedures *establishes* and *clobbers*.

An implementation may want to Skolemize action schemata before planning commences. The result is that the Skolemization procedure is removed from the implementation of *establishes* (and *clobbers*) and so improves efficiency. If this is done then one has to ensure that each time a precondition and effect is used by the implementation of *establishes* (and *clobbers*) then they are treated as if they are *freshly* Skolemized.

An important aspect of any implementation is that the universe should be organized in a structured way. In our implementation, a planning problem must specify a hierarchy of types. This fits in very naturally with quantification and Skolemization. Space forbids to discuss details. In this paper we assume that the universe is not typed only for clarity.

A STRIPS style action schema of the form

> action: $A(\overline{X})$
> preconditions: $P(\overline{X})$
> effects: $E(\overline{X})$

can be formulated as the situation calculus sentence

$$(\forall S)(\forall \overline{X})(holds(P(\overline{X}), S)) \rightarrow holds(E(\overline{X}), result(A(\overline{X}), S)))$$

In order to Skolemize an action schema, we first convert it to sentences of the situation calculus. We then Skolemize the resulting situation calculus sentences and convert them back into an action schema. For example, the schema

> action: $do\_nothing(?P)$
> preconditions: $(\forall X)(e(?P, X))$
> effects: $(\forall Y)(e(?P, Y))$

converts to the following sentence of the situation calculus

$$(\forall S)(\forall ?P) \qquad (holds((\forall X)(e(?P, X)), S) \rightarrow$$
$$holds((\forall Y)(e(?P, Y)), result(do\_nothing(?P), S)))$$

On Skolemizing that becomes

$$holds(e(?P, \$(S)), S) \rightarrow holds(e(?P, Y), result(do\_nothing(?P), S))$$

Recall that universal quantifiers in the antecedent of an implication behave like existential quantifiers in the consequent and vice versa. We do not let $ take ?P as an argument because parameters are seen to be outside our language of preconditions and effects and hence have no effect on Skolem terms. When converting back into a schema, the state variable is removed, yielding

action:	$do\_nothing(?\mathbf{P})$
preconditions:	$e(?\mathbf{P}, \$)$
effects:	$e(?\mathbf{P}, Y)$

There is an apparent asymmetry here in that an identical goal and effect Skolemize to different formulas. A universal precondition of the form $(\forall X)(p(X))$ that Skolemizes to $p(\$)$ should be interpreted as follows. If one can find support for $p(\$)$ independent of what $\$$ actually denotes, that is, in all interpretations of Skolem constants, then one has found support for $p(X)$ for all X.

The same intuition lies behind action schemata with existential effects. A Skolemized *run_lottery* schema might look like:

action:	$run\_lottery$
preconditions:	$every\_one\_has\_bought\_a\_ticket$
effects:	$millionaire(\$_1)$

In this context, $\$_1$ is a witness for an existential effect $(\exists M)(millionaire(M))$ but we know not what object $\$_1$ denotes.

5 Generalizing Causal Link Planning

In this section, we illustrate how one can utilize causal links that act like accumulators to enable the simple detection of collective clobberings.

A plan may only have a partial order on its steps and a step may only be partially specified. Explicit causal links are used to document the establishment of a goal and therefore the truth criterion of Section 3.2 is for a more general planner than the one described in this section.

5.1 Establishment and Clobbering

Recall that the establishment of a goal O by an effect E is documented in causal link planning by the construction of a new causal link that has label L. In a generative refinement planning framework, the relationship between literals E, L and O is $E\theta = O\theta = L$ for some binding of parameters θ. In this section, we relax the restriction that E, L and O need be identical literals. We define the relationship as follows.

$$E \text{ establishes } L \text{ and } L \text{ establishes } O$$

This generalizes causal link planning by enabling E to be a formula of our effect language and O a formula of our goal language. L is identical to E when a new causal link is constructed but as illustrated in the following sections, L may change during planning.

In causal link planning, the introduction of a new step forces one to look at each effect of the new step in turn and test whether it possibly clobbers each causal link. In this Section, we utilize the procedure *clobbers* to determine whether an effect of a new step clobbers a causal link. That is, for a possible clobbering effect C and causal link label L, we test whether

$$C \ clobbers \ L \qquad (2)$$

is true.

5.2 Weakening the Label

The usual approach to defuse a situation in which an effect C clobbers a causal link L is to *weaken the clobberer*. Weakening the clobberer means that C in (2) above is refined, yielding a weaker effect C' such that C' *clobbers* L is false.

Weakening the clobberer is more commonly known as *separation*. To be able to separate, there must be a non-empty substitution of parameters θ such that $C\theta$ *clobbers* $L\theta$. The weakening is achieved by the enforcement of a new non-codesignation constraint as the following plan fragment illustrates.

In this case, the weakened clobberer is $?P \neq a \rightarrow \neg p(a, ?P)$. The non-codesignation constraint is said to *separate the binding*. This strategy has no effect on the relationship between the establishing effect E, the label of the clobbered link L and the goal sentence O.

But what happens if ?P has already become bound to a? What we propose one can do is to *weaken the label of the causal link*, just as one weakens the clobberer by separation. One is now refining L in (2) above and in order to weaken this time, we must look inside the procedure *clobbers*. In order to weaken, it must be the case that for some (possibly empty) substitution of parameters θ and some non-empty substitution of universal variables ϕ, $skolem(C)\theta\phi$ together with $skolem(L)\theta\phi$ lead to absurdity. If ϕ is non-empty then one can weaken as follows.

The refinement of L to a new label L' such that C *clobbers* L' is false reduces the domain of a universal variable (X in the above plan fragment) as opposed to reducing the domain of a parameter under separation. The weakened label in this case is the formula $(\forall X)(X \neq a \rightarrow p(X, a))$.

For some establishing effect E, label L and goal sentence O where the relationship

$$E \ establishes \ L \text{ and } L \ establishes \ O$$

holds, it is always trivially the case that E *establishes* L' for any weakening L' of L. But it is not always the case, however, that the relationship L' *establishes* O remains intact. This has to be checked.

5.3 Collective Clobberings

Consider the following plan fragment. There is a clobbering here because when the domain of X contains only the singleton a, $\neg p(a)$ *clobbers* $(\forall X)(p(X))$ is true.

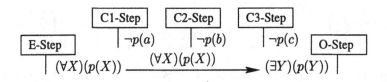

It is, however, reasonable to assume that the domain of X is non-trivial. Then $\neg p(a)$ ceases to be a clobberer. Now consider the scenario of Fig. 1. The problem

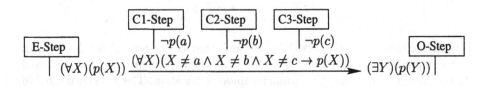

Fig. 1. A possible collective clobbering?

here is that there are three distinct clobberers. If one considers each clobberer acting individually then on the grounds of the preceding argument, one might conclude that there is no clobbering. If, however, one considers all three clobberers acting collectively, then things are not so straightforward. If the domain of X consists only of the three objects labelled a, b and c then there is no other distinct object that can act as witness for Y, that is, all three clobberers acting collectively exhaust the domain of Y. In this case, the collective clobbering is undeniable. Our process of weakening the label implicitly handles such situations as we now illustrate. If the process of weakening the label is iterated three times on Fig. 1, then one obtains the situation of Fig. 2. If the domain of Y is exhausted

Fig. 2. Weakening the label applied to Fig. 1

because a, b and c are the only members then one wants L' *establishes* O to be false. Thus, to ensure that there is a distinct object that can act as witness for the existential goal, one needs to place a *cardinality constraint* on the domain of Y. Providing the domain of Y contains at least one more distinct object other than a, b or c, then L' *establishes* O. The process of weakening the label therefore introduces a new kind of constraint on how small a domain may be.

6 Conclusion

In this paper, we illustrated how full quantification can be added to a generative refinement planning framework by utilizing techniques of refutation theorem proving. This involved the definition of the two procedures *establishes* and *clobbers* in which the process of Skolemization is buried. We used these procedures to generalize causal link planning, leading to a new conflict resolution strategy, a notion called weakening the label. We illustrated how the process of weakening the label enables collective clobberings to be detected and we further illustrated that as a by-product of weakening, a cardinality constraint may need to be placed on the domain of a type. A planner has been implemented in PROLOG that utilizes the techniques of this paper. We will present the implementation details in a forthcoming paper.

References

1. D. Chapman. Planning for conjunctive goals. In *Artificial Intelligence*, number 32, pages 333–377. 1987.
2. R.E. Fikes and N.J. Nilsson. Strips: a new approach to the application of theorem proving to problem solving. In *Artificial Intelligence*, volume 2, pages 189–208. 1971.
3. D. McAllester and D. Rosenblitt. Systematic nonlinear planning. In *9th Nat. Conf. on A.I.*, pages 634–639, July 1991.
4. D. McDermott. Regression planning. *International Journal of Intelligent Systems*, 6:357–416, 1991.
5. E.P.D. Pednault. Formulating multiagent, dynamic-world problems in the classical planning framework. In M.P. Georgeff and A.L. Lansky, editors, *Reasoning about actions and plans: proceedings of the 1986 workshop*, pages 47–82, Los Altos, California, 1986. Morgan Kaufmann.
6. E.P.D. Pednault. Synthesizing plans that contain actions with context-dependent effects. *Computational Intelligence*, 4(4):356–372, 1988.
7. E.P.D. Pednault. Adl: Exploring the middle ground between strips and the situation calculus. In *1st Int. Conf. on Principles of Knowledge Representation and Reasoning*, pages 324–332, 1989.
8. E.P.D. Pednault. Generalizing nonlinear planning to handle complex goals and actions with context-dependent effects. In J. Mylopoulos and R. Reiter, editors, *12th Int. Conf. Artificial Intelligence*, volume 1, 1991.
9. J.S. Penberthy and D.S. Weld. Ucpop: A sound, complete, partial order planner for adl. In *3rd Int. Conf. on Principles of Knowledge Representation and Reasoning*, pages 103–114, 1992. Available via FTP from /pub/ai at cs.washington.edu.
10. D. Weld. An introduction to least-commitment planning. *AI Magazine*, 1994. Available via FTP from pub/ai/ at cs.washington.edu.

Modal Tableaux for Reasoning About Actions and Plans

Marcos A. Castilho*, Olivier Gasquet, and Andreas Herzig

Université Paul Sabatier — IRIT — Applied Logic Group
118, route de Narbonne
TOULOUSE CEDEX 4
F31062 – FRANCE

URL: *http://www.irit.fr/ACTIVITES/EQ_ALG*
e-mail: {*castilho, gasquet, herzig*}*@irit.fr*
fax: +33 5.61.55.83.25

Abstract. In this paper we investigate tableau proof procedures for reasoning about actions and plans. Our framework is a multimodal language close to that of propositional dynamic logic, wherein we solve the frame problem by introducing the notion of dependence as a weak causal connection between actions and atoms. The tableau procedure is sound and complete for an important fragment of our language, within which all standard problems of reasoning about actions can be expressed, in particular planning tasks. Moreover, our tableaux are analytic and provide thus a decision procedure.

1 Introduction

In this paper we investigate tableau proof procedures for reasoning about actions and plans in a propositional modal language. There is a family of modal operators $[\alpha]$, where α is the name of an action, and a single modal operator $\Box$ to represent integrity constraints. Its dual modal operator $\Diamond$ can be used to formulate goals in planning tasks. We start with the logic of actions and plans $\mathcal{LAP}$, which is a simple multimodal logic where the logic of each $[\alpha]$ is the basic modal logic K, while that of $\Box$ is $S4$. $\Box$ interacts with every α in the sense that $\Box A \to [\alpha]A$.

$\mathcal{LAP}$ can be thought of as a simplified propositional dynamic logic (PDL) [Har84]: We claim that $\Box$ is sufficient to simulate the PDL iteration operator ($*$) in the standard reasoning about actions tasks. The difference between $*$ and $\Box$ is that the former semantically corresponds to reflexive and transitive closure, while the latter only *contains* reflexive and transitive closure. This makes that $\mathcal{LAP}$ is both compact and strongly complete, while PDL is not.

A tableau method for $\mathcal{LAP}$ can be defined straightforwardly by combining the tableau rules for the logics K and $S4$. Nevertheless, to effectively reason about actions and plans in $\mathcal{LAP}$ is difficult due to inertia: For every action only

---

* On leave from Universidade Federal do Paraná, Brazil

'very few' formulas change their truth value. For this reason, $\mathcal{LAP}$ tableau have to cope with a huge number of so-called frame axioms of the form $\Box(L \to [\alpha]L)$, L being a literal.

We could have recasted the solution of [Rei91] in our modal language, in a way similar to [DGL95]. There, the language of PDL is extended with converse (and also complement). We solve the problem in a conceptually simpler framework, by adapting the representation formalism (via the introduction of dependence relations), and in consequence the tableau reasoning mechanism. The story goes as follows:

1. For every action α and atomic formula P, whenever there are frame axioms $\Box(P \to [\alpha]P)$ and $\Box(\neg P \to [\alpha]\neg P)$ we say that P *is independent of* α (or α does not influence P). We drop such frame axioms and replace them by an *independence relation* between actions and atomic formulas. P is independent of α if and only if in any situation, the execution of α leaves the truth value of P unchanged.

2. In order to achieve representational economy, we do not write down the independence relation, but its complement, the dependence relation, which is supposed to be much smaller than the dependence relation, due to the hypothesis of inertia. In other words, we expect that for a given action α, almost all of the atoms P are independent of α. To check whether α and P are independent, we look up in the dependence relation whether $\alpha \rightsquigarrow P$ appears, and apply thus (a very simple version of) negation by failure. (This is the only nonmonotonic feature of our approach.)

3. To each dependence relation $\rightsquigarrow$ corresponds a logical system $\mathcal{LAP}_{\rightsquigarrow}$. We then adapt the tableau method for $\mathcal{LAP}$ to take into account the dependence relation: In the projection rule for α, every literal which is independent of α is preserved. This method is incomplete in the general case. We can show that it is complete for an important fragment of our language, and that after a normal forming step all standard problems of reasoning about actions and plans fall into that fragment. Completeness is proved w.r.t. a particular class of $\mathcal{LAP}$-models, viz. those models respecting the dependence relation: If P is independent of α, then the interpretation of P in worlds related by the accessibility relation associated to α is the same.

The rest of the paper is as follows: Section 2 contains language and terminology, and section 3 presents the logic of action and plans $\mathcal{LAP}$. In section 4 we show how to solve the frame problem by adding dependence relations to $\mathcal{LAP}$. Section 5 presents the tableau method, while in section 6 we show how it can be applied in planning tasks. Finally, in section 7 we discuss the characteristics of our approach.

2 Language and Terminology

In this section we present the logic of action and plans $\mathcal{LAP}$, and we state the terminology in terms of our modal language.

Let $ACT = \{\alpha, \beta, \ldots\}$ be the set of *atomic actions* (e.g. *"load"*, *"wait"* and *"shoot"*), and let $ATM = \{P, Q, \ldots\}$ be the set of *atoms* (e.g. *"Loaded"*). The set $LIT = \{L, L_1, \ldots\}$ of literals is made up by all atoms and their negations. $|.|$ is a function mapping literals to atoms, such that for every $P \in ATM$, $|P| = P$ and $|\neg P| = P$. The set FOR of *formulas* is defined in the usual way, in particular $[\alpha]A \in FOR$, if $A \in FOR$ and $\alpha \in ACT$. We read $[\alpha]A$ as "A after α", and $\Box A$ as "A is always true". (Hence $[\alpha]\bot$ expresses that α is inexecutable.) A formula without modal operators is *classical*.

We also use the standard *PDL* abbreviations $\langle\alpha\rangle A$ for $\neg[\alpha]\neg A$, $\Diamond A$ for $\neg\Box\neg A$, $[\alpha; \beta]A$ for $[\alpha][\beta]A$, $[\alpha \cup \beta]A$ for $([\alpha]A \wedge [\beta]A)$, $[A?]B$ for $A \to B$, $[\lambda]A$ for A and $[if\ A\ then\ \alpha\ else\ \beta]B$ for $((A \to [\alpha]B) \wedge (\neg A \to [\beta]B))$. We read λ as "do nothing", $A?$ as "continue if A holds", $\alpha \cup \beta$ as "do either α or β nondeterministically", $\alpha; \beta$ as "do α followed by β".

Reasoning about actions and plans involves three main concepts:

1. *Knowledge bases* (KB) are finite sets of formulas without the $\Box$-operator, e.g. $\{Walking, [shoot]Alive\}$. They represent factual knowledge (observations).
2. *Integrity constraints* (IC) are finite sets of formulas of the form $\Box A$ representing general laws. If A is a classical formula then $\Box A$ is a *static constraint* (IC_{stat}), e.g. $\Box(Walking \to Alive)$. (The ramification problem is generally viewed as the problem of taking into account such constraints.) Else $\Box A$ is a *dynamic constraint* (IC_{dyn}) which is used in particular to describe action laws. Among the latter there are *effect constraints* of the form $\Box(B \to [\alpha]C)$, where B and C are classical, e.g. $\Box(Loaded \to [shoot]Dead)$. If $C = \bot$ they are *inexecutability constraints*, (e.g. $\Box(\neg HasGun \to [shoot]\bot)$), and if $B = C$ they are *frame axioms*, e.g. $\Box(Alive \to [load]Alive)$. The frame problem is to avoid the explicit representation of frame axioms. Another form of action laws are *executability constraints* of the form $\Box(A \to \langle\alpha\rangle\top)$, where A is classical, e.g. $\Box(HasGun \to \langle shoot\rangle\top)$. We shall consider that IC is made up of static, effect, and executability constraints.
3. *Queries* are formulas whose derivability from the knowledge base under the integrity constraints is checked. Particular queries are *goals*, which are of the form $\Diamond A$ with A classical, e.g. $\Diamond\neg Alive$. These are intended to express that there is a plan leading to a state of affairs where A is true.

The different reasoning about actions tasks described in [San95] can be described as theorem proving problems in our modal framework. They typically involve a formula KB_1 describing (part of) the initial state of affairs, a sequence of actions $\pi = \alpha_1; \ldots; \alpha_n$ and a formula KB_2 describing (part of) the resulting state of affairs. *Prediction* means to prove $KB_1 \to [\pi]KB_2$, e.g. $Walking \to [wait; shoot]Dead$. *Postdiction* means to prove $\langle\pi\rangle KB_2 \to KB_1$, e.g. $\langle shoot\rangle Alive \to \neg Loaded$. *Planning* amounts to prove $KB_1 \to \Diamond KB_2$, e.g. $Loaded \to \Diamond Dead$. Then a plan π can be constructed from that proof.[1]

---

[1] Note that in the most general case, in prediction problems we do not know KB_2, and hence should not *find out whether* KB_2, but just *find* KB_2. The same is the case for KB_1 in postdiction. This requires abductive reasoning mecanisms.

3 Semantics of $\mathcal{LAP}$

Definition 1. *Models* for $\mathcal{LAP}$ ($\mathcal{LAP}$-models) are quadruples of the form $\mu = (W, (R_\alpha)_{\alpha \in ACT}, R_\square, \tau)$, where W is a set of worlds, $R_\square$ and each R_α are binary relations on W (accessibility relations), and $\tau : ATM \longrightarrow 2^W$ is an interpretation of atoms. We require $R_\square$ to be reflexive and transitive, and $R_\alpha \subseteq R_\square$ for every R_α.

The truth conditions are as usual, in particular:

- $\models^\mu_w [\alpha]A$ if for all $w' \in W : wR_\alpha w'$ implies $\models^\mu_{w'} A$;
- $\models^\mu_w \square A$ if for all $w' \in W : wR_\square w'$ implies $\models^\mu_{w'} A$.

Validity and satisfiability are defined as usual.

It is a standard result in multimodal logics that an axiomatics can be obtained by taking that of $S4$ for $\square$ and that of K for every $[\alpha]$, together with an interaction axiom $\square A \rightarrow [\alpha]A$ for every $[\alpha]$. As well, $\mathcal{LAP}$ is decidable, compact, and strongly complete [Cat89]. Semantic tableau for $\mathcal{LAP}$ can be obtained by combining the tableau rules for the logics K and $S4$, taking care of the inclusion relation between $\square$ and $[\alpha]$.[2]

Within $\mathcal{LAP}$, the frame problem is unsolved, i.e. we must explicitly write down all frame axioms.

4 Dependence and the Semantics of $\mathcal{LAP}_{\rightsquigarrow}$

Now we show how frame axioms can be represented economically by means of dependence relations, and how the semantics of $\mathcal{LAP}$ can be adapted appropriately.

Definition 2. A *dependence relation* is a binary relation $\rightsquigarrow \subseteq ACT \times ATM$. The complement of $\rightsquigarrow$ is noted $\not\rightsquigarrow$ and is called the *independence relation*.

$\alpha \rightsquigarrow P$ is read "P depends on α", or "α influences P". This expresses that after the execution of action α the truth value of P *may* change: There exists a state of affairs such that either P is true and becomes false after execution of α, or P is false and becomes true after execution of α. E.g. in the Yale shooting scenario, we have $load \not\rightsquigarrow Alive$, and $load \rightsquigarrow Loaded$, $shoot \rightsquigarrow Loaded$, $shoot \rightsquigarrow Alive$ (see example 5).

P is independent of α whenever the set of frame axioms contains both $\square(P \rightarrow [\alpha]P)$ and $\square(\neg P \rightarrow [\alpha]\neg P)$. The construction of $\rightsquigarrow$ allows us to drop all these frame axioms from the set of effect constraints. (Note that the $\rightsquigarrow$ is in the metalanguage.)

Suppose given some dependence relation $\rightsquigarrow$. Our reading of $\rightsquigarrow$ requires to constrain $\mathcal{LAP}$-models:

---

[2] Although such a combination is straightforward, Fabio Massacci [Mas97] has pointed out to us that we can no longer prove in the usual way that such tableau are in PSPACE. To our knowledge, there are currently no results in the literature concerning the complexity of $\mathcal{LAP}$.

Definition 3. An $\mathcal{LAP}_{\rightsquigarrow}$-*model* is an $\mathcal{LAP}$-model (satisfying the conditions of definition 1) such that for $\alpha \in ACT$, $P \in ATM$, and for every $w, w' \in W$ such that $wR_\alpha w'$

- if $\alpha \not\rightsquigarrow P$ then $w \in \tau(P)$ iff $w' \in \tau(P)$.

This condition says that if α does not influence P then the execution of α leaves unchanged the truth value of P.

A formula A is $\mathcal{LAP}_{\rightsquigarrow}$-valid ($\models_{\mathcal{LAP}_{\rightsquigarrow}} A$) iff $\models_w^\mu A$ for every world w of every $\mathcal{LAP}_{\rightsquigarrow}$-model μ.

Example 4 (The blocksworld).

$$KB = \{On_{1,2} \wedge On_{2,3} \wedge On_{3,Table}\}$$
$$\rightsquigarrow = \{puton_{i,j} \rightsquigarrow On_{i,j}, puton_{i,j} \rightsquigarrow Clear_j, puton_{i,j} \rightsquigarrow Holding_i,$$
$$take_{i,j} \rightsquigarrow On_{i,j}, take_{i,j} \rightsquigarrow Clear_j, take_{i,j} \rightsquigarrow Holding_i\}$$
$$IC = \{\Box[take_{i,j}]\neg On_{i,j}, \Box((Empty \wedge Clear_i \wedge On_{i,j}) \rightarrow \langle take_{i,j}\rangle\top),$$
$$\Box[puton_{i,j}]On_{i,j}, \Box((Holding_i \wedge Clear_j) \rightarrow \langle puton\rangle_{i,j}\top),$$
$$\Box(Empty \leftrightarrow \bigwedge_i \neg Holding_i), \Box(Holding_i \leftrightarrow \bigwedge_j \neg On_{i,j}),$$
$$\Box Clear_{Table}, \Box(Clear_j \leftrightarrow \bigwedge_i \neg On_{i,j}) \text{ for } j \neq Table,$$
$$\Box\neg(On_{i,k} \wedge On_{j,k}) \text{ for } i \neq j, \Box\neg(On_{i,j} \wedge On_{i,k}) \text{ for } j \neq k\}$$

Then $(KB \wedge IC) \rightarrow [take_{1,2}][puton_{1,Table}][take_{2,3}]Clear_3$ is $\mathcal{LAP}_{\rightsquigarrow}$-valid. As well, $(KB \wedge IC) \rightarrow \Diamond Clear_3$ is valid, i.e. there is a plan to clear block 3.

$\mathcal{LAP}_{\rightsquigarrow}$ has the same theoretical complexity as $\mathcal{LAP}$. This can be seen by the following transformation to $\mathcal{LAP}$: Given a dependence relation $\rightsquigarrow$ and a formula A, we reconstruct the set IC_{frame} of frame axioms that are relevant for A:

$$IC_{frame} = \{\Box(L \rightarrow [\alpha]L) : |L| \text{ occurs in } A, \text{ and } \alpha \not\rightsquigarrow |L|\}$$

Clearly, A is $\mathcal{LAP}_{\rightsquigarrow}$-satisfiable iff $A \wedge IC_{frame}$ is $\mathcal{LAP}$-satisfiable, and the size of $A \wedge IC_{frame}$ is linear in that of A.

Example 5 (The Yale Shooting Scenario (YSS)). We consider the classical scenario of [HM86] adapted by [Bak91]. Let *wait*, *load* and *shoot* be the actions of waiting, loading and shooting, respectively. Let the atoms *Loaded*, *Alive* and *Walking* represent "the gun is loaded", "the man is alive", and "the man is walking" respectively. The effect of the load action is that the gun is loaded and the effects of the shoot action is that unload the gun and also of killing the person if the gun is loaded. This action has no effect if the gun is unloaded. The wait action has no effect. We have domain knowledge that dead persons do not walk. Initially, the gun is unloaded and the man is walking and alive. This is represented in $\mathcal{LAP}_{\rightsquigarrow}$ by the sets below. It is easy to check that we have $\models_{\mathcal{LAP}_{\rightsquigarrow}} (KB \wedge IC) \rightarrow [load][wait][shoot](\neg Loaded \wedge \neg Alive \wedge \neg Walking).$:

$$\rightsquigarrow = \left\{ \begin{array}{l} load \rightsquigarrow Loaded, \\ shoot \rightsquigarrow Loaded, \\ shoot \rightsquigarrow Alive, \\ shoot \rightsquigarrow Walking \end{array} \right\}$$

$$IC = \left\{ \begin{array}{l} \Box(\textit{Walking} \to \textit{Alive}), \\ \Box\langle wait\rangle\top, \\ \Box\langle load\rangle\top, \\ \Box[load]Loaded, \\ \Box\langle shoot\rangle\top, \\ \Box[shoot]\neg Loaded, \\ \Box(Loaded \to [shoot]\neg Alive), \\ \Box(\neg Loaded \to ((Alive \to [shoot]Alive) \wedge (\neg Alive \to [shoot]\neg Alive))) \\ \Box(\neg Loaded \to ((\textit{Walking} \to [shoot]\textit{Walking}) \wedge (\neg Walking \to [shoot]\neg Walking))) \end{array} \right\}$$

$$KB = \{\neg Loaded,\ Alive,\ Walking\}$$

Note that after *wait* the independence *wait↛Loaded* is the warrant that the gun remains loaded after wait. Note also that the choice of a weak causal connection between actions and literals may force us to write down some additional (conditional) frame axioms.

Example 6 (Nondeterministic actions). We can illustrate by a modification of the blocksworld example that we can deal with nondeterministic actions: Suppose e.g. that we change the above definition of the action $puton_{i,j}$ (because the robot now is careless and may drop the block) to be $\Box[puton_{i,j}](On_{i,j} \vee On_{i,Table})$. We can still prove $\models_{\mathcal{LAP}_{\rightsquigarrow}}(KB \wedge IC) \to \Diamond Clear_3$, but no longer $\models_{\mathcal{LAP}_{\rightsquigarrow}}(KB \wedge IC) \to \Diamond On_{3,2}$.

Other nondeterministic actions can be formalized as well, such as tossing a coin, or throwing a coin on a chessboard [GKL95].

5 Automated Theorem Proving for $\mathcal{LAP}_{\rightsquigarrow}$

Suppose given some dependence relation $\rightsquigarrow$. In this section we show how to adapt $\mathcal{LAP}$ tableau to take into account $\rightsquigarrow$. We suppose the reader is familiar with tableau terminology. The presentation is in the style of [Gor92].

The tableaux calculus for $\mathcal{LAP}_{\rightsquigarrow}$ is defined by the set of tableau rules showed in figure 1, where:

- $\Box X = \{\Box A : A \in X\}$,
- $[\alpha]X = \{[\alpha]A : A \in X\}$,
- $\not\rightsquigarrow_\alpha X = \{L : L \in X \cap LIT \text{ and } \alpha \not\rightsquigarrow |L|\}$.

In fact, the rule $(K_{\not\rightsquigarrow}[\alpha])$ is the only non-standard tableau rule. It extends the standard one of modal logic K by the preservation of the set of independent

$$\frac{X;A;\neg A}{\bot}(\bot) \qquad \frac{X;\neg\neg A}{X;A}(\neg) \qquad \frac{X;A\wedge B}{X;A;B}(\wedge) \qquad \frac{X;\neg(A\wedge B)}{X;\neg A|X;\neg B}(\vee)$$

$$\frac{X;\Box A}{X;\Box A;A}(T\Box) \qquad \frac{Y;\Box X;\neg\Box A}{\Box X;\neg A}(4\Box) \qquad \frac{V;\Box X;[\alpha]Y;\not\leadsto_\alpha Z;\neg[\alpha]A}{\Box X;Y;\not\leadsto_\alpha Z;\neg A}(K_{\not\leadsto}[\alpha])$$

Fig. 1. Tableau rules for $\mathcal{LAP}_{\leadsto}$

literals. If this set was not preserved, then e.g. under $\alpha\leadsto P$ and $\alpha\not\leadsto Q$ no tableau for the $\mathcal{LAP}_{\leadsto}$-unsatisfiable formula $\Box(P\vee Q)\wedge\neg[\alpha]P\wedge\neg Q$ would close.[3]

Theorem 7 (Soundness). *If there is a closed $\mathcal{LAP}_{\leadsto}$-tableau for $\neg A$ then* $\models_{\mathcal{LAP}_{\leadsto}} A$.

The proof is in [CGH96].

Unfortunately this tableau calculus is incomplete: Suppose $\alpha\not\leadsto P$ and $\beta\not\leadsto P$. Then the formula

$$[\alpha]P\vee[\beta]\neg P \tag{1}$$

is $\mathcal{LAP}_{\leadsto}$-valid, but there is no closed $\mathcal{LAP}_{\leadsto}$-tableau for it. But completeness holds for a particular fragment:

Definition 8. A formula A is in *normal form* iff no compound dynamic operator appears in A, and for every subformula $[\alpha]B$ of A, B is of the form $B_1\vee B_2\vee \ldots\vee B_n$, and for $1\leq i\leq n$ one of the following holds:

- B_i is of the form $[\beta]C_i$
- B_i is of the form $\neg[\beta]C_i$
- B_i is a literal and $\alpha\leadsto|B_i|$

E.g. suppose $\alpha_1\leadsto P_1$, $\alpha_1\not\leadsto P_2$, $\alpha_2\not\leadsto P_1$ and $\alpha_2\leadsto P_2$. Then $\Box[\alpha_1](P_1\vee[\alpha_2]P_2)$ is in normal form, whereas $[\alpha_1]P_2$, $[\alpha_1]\Box P_1$, and $[\alpha_2][\alpha_1]P_2$ are not.

Formulas having $\Box$-operators in the scope of $[\alpha]$-operators, e.g. $[\alpha]\Box P$, cannot be put into normal form. Such kind of formulas would be used to express "from now on" laws, i.e. laws which are valid after the execution of an action. e.g. *Loaded* $\rightarrow$ *[shoot]$\Box$Dead* ("shoot causes the person to be definitively dead") or executability order of actions, e.g. $\Box[\alpha]\Box[\beta]\bot$ ("action α can not be executed before action β).

Luckily enough, the fragment of the language for which this can be done is sufficiently big to do our three reasoning tasks of section 2, named, prediction,

---

[3] The naive implementation of this rule may lead to an inefficient prover, because a (theoretical) huge number of atoms must be preserved each time the rule is applied. This is due to our hypothesis of inertia. This may be solved in practical cases by the implementation of a labelled tableau together with some strategy that allow us to just look up for independent literals when they are needed.

postdiction and planning. We were unable to find in the literature of reasoning about actions a domain that is not expressible in this sub-language.

We call a $\mathcal{LAP}_{\leadsto}$-formula *ordered* if no □-operator appears in the scope of any [α]-operator.

Theorem 9. *For every ordered formula there is an equivalent ordered formula in normal form.*

The proof is in [CGH96].

E.g. let $\alpha \leadsto P$, $\alpha \leadsto Q$ and $\alpha \not\leadsto R$. Then the formula $[\alpha](P \wedge [\alpha](R \vee \neg[\alpha]Q))$ takes the normal form $[\alpha]P \wedge (R \vee [\alpha][\alpha]\neg[\alpha]Q)$. As another example, if $\alpha \not\leadsto P$ and $\beta \not\leadsto P$, the formula 1 takes the normal form $P \vee \neg P$. It is easy to see that there is a tableau proof of the latter.

Theorem 10 (Completeness). *Let A be an ordered formula in normal form. If $\models_{\mathcal{LAP}_{\leadsto}} A$ then there is a closed $\mathcal{LAP}_{\leadsto}$-tableau for $\neg A$.*

The proof is in [CGH96]. It uses that our tableaux are analytic, and hence the tableau can be constructed in a way such that termination is ensured. Therefore our tableau method can be used as a decision procedure to check validity of ordered formulas A.[4]

Example 11 (YSS, cont.). A proof of $\models_{\mathcal{LAP}_{\leadsto}} KB \wedge IC \rightarrow [l][s](\neg L \wedge \neg A)$ (consider l to be *load*, s to be *shoot*, L to be *Loaded* and A to be *Alive*) is:

$$\frac{\neg(KB \wedge IC \rightarrow [l][s](\neg L \wedge \neg A))}{\underbrace{\frac{KB; IC; \neg[l][s](\neg L \wedge \neg A)}{\underbrace{\frac{KB; IC; \neg[l][s](\neg L \wedge \neg A); [l]L}{\underbrace{\frac{A; IC; \neg[s](\neg L \wedge \neg A); L}{A; IC; \neg[s](\neg L \wedge \neg A); L; L \rightarrow [s]\neg A}}_{(T\square)}}}_{(K_{\not\leadsto}[l])}}}_{(\wedge),several times}$$

$$\underbrace{\frac{A; IC; \neg[s](\neg L \wedge \neg A); L; \neg L}{\bot}}_{(\bot)} \qquad \underbrace{\frac{A; IC; \neg[s](\neg L \wedge \neg A); L; [s]\neg A}{\underbrace{\frac{A; IC; \neg[s](\neg L \wedge \neg A); L; [s]\neg A; [s]\neg L}{IC; \neg(\neg L \wedge \neg A); \neg A; \neg L}}_{(K_{\not\leadsto}[s])}}}_{(T\square)}$$

$$\underbrace{\frac{IC; \neg\neg L; \neg A; \neg L}{\bot}}_{(\bot)} \quad \underbrace{\frac{IC; \neg\neg A; \neg A; \neg L}{\bot}}_{(\bot)} \quad {}^{(\vee)}$$

Note how A (*Alive* ∈ KB) was preserved when rule $(K_{\not\leadsto}[l])$ was applied between lines 3 and 4 due to *load* $\not\leadsto$ *Alive*.

---

[4] The naive way of putting the formula in conjunctive normal form may cause exponential growth. In classical logic, this can be avoided by a more sophisticated algorithm where new atoms are introduced [Tse83,Sie87]. The resulting formula is satisfiability-equivalent to the original formula. Recently, this method has been extended to modal logic in [Mat93].

6 Plan Generation

Given a closed tableau for $KB \land IC \land \Box \neg G$, can we obtain a plan from that proof, i.e. a sequence of actions π such that $\models_{\mathcal{LAP}_{\leadsto}} (KB \land IC) \to \langle \pi \rangle G$? This will be the case if no negative occurrences of the $\Box$-operator occur in KB, IC and G.[5] Such a fragment is still large enough for our reasoning tasks of section 2: There, both KB and IC are conjunctions of formulas of the form $\Box A$, A containing no $\Box$-operator, and G is classical in the goal $\Diamond G$.

Here is the *plan generation algorithm* extracting a complex action π from the closed tableau for $IC \land KB \land \Box \neg G$:

1. Mark all occurrences of subformulas of G produced by the tableau rules (including G).
2. Mark all nodes where ($\bot$) has been applied to a marked formula (i.e. where a subformula of $\Box \neg G$ is 'responsible' for closure).
3. Mark all ancestor nodes of marked nodes.
4. Associate a plan to the root by bottom-up iteration.[6] Let n be some marked node in the tableau.
   - If the rule ($\bot$) has been applied to n, then the plan of n is λ.
   - If the rule ($\land$) has been applied to n, then the plan of n is that of the successor node.
   - If the rule ($\lor$) has been applied to n, and only one successor node is marked, then the plan of n is the plan of that successor node.
   - If the rule ($\lor$) has been applied to n, decomposing the formula $\neg(A_1 \land A_2)$, and both successor nodes are marked and have plans π_1 and π_2, then the plan of n is: "*if A_1 then π_1 else π_2*".
   - If the rule ($T\Box$) has been applied to n, then the plan of n is that of the successor node.
   - If the rule ($K_{\not\leadsto}[\alpha]$) has been applied to n, and the plan of the successor node is π_1, then the plan of n is: "$\alpha ; \pi_1$".

Theorem 12. *Let $KB \land IC \land \Box \neg G$ be $\mathcal{LAP}_{\leadsto}$-unsatisfiable, and let π be a complex action that has been associated to the root of some closed $\mathcal{LAP}_{\leadsto}$-tableau for it by the plan generation algorithm. If neither KB nor IC nor $\neg G$ contain negative occurrences of $\Box$ then $(KB \land IC) \to \langle \pi \rangle G$ is $\mathcal{LAP}_{\leadsto}$-valid.*

The proof is done by replacing $\Box \neg G$ by $[\pi] \neg G$ in the tableau. Then the same sequence of tableau rules as in the original tableau can be applied, and we can prove by induction that the latter leads again to a closed tableau. E.g. take the case

---

[5] This can be explained by the fact that in the tableau, if there is some negative occurrence of the $\Box$-operator, then one can "jump" to another world without identifying any specific action. If the transitions are only triggered by $\neg[\alpha]$, then a plan can be found by the composition of all actions that have been applied from the initial world to the last one.

[6] We suppose here that the root is marked. Else $IC \land KB$ would be unsatisfiable alone, and any plan would do.

of the rule ($\vee$) decomposing the node $X; \neg(A_1 \vee A_2)$ into $X; \neg A_1$ and $X; \neg A_2$. Suppose both $X; \neg A_1$ and $X; \neg A_2$ are marked and have plans π_1 and π_2. First, note that we must have $X = X' \cup \{\Box \neg G\}$ (because each of our tableau rules preserves boxed formulas). Then by induction hypothesis both $X'; [\pi_1]\neg G; \neg A_1$ and $X'; [\pi_2]\neg G; \neg A_2$ are closed. Now [*if* A_1 *then* π_1 *else* $\pi_2]\neg G \wedge \neg(A_1 \wedge A_2)$ abbreviates $(A_1 \rightarrow [\pi_1]\neg G) \wedge (\neg A_1 \rightarrow [\pi_2]\neg G) \wedge \neg(A_1 \wedge A_2)$, and the latter classically implies $([\pi_1]\neg G \wedge \neg A_1) \vee ([\pi_2]\neg G \wedge \neg A_2)$. Hence the node $X'; \Box \neg G; \neg(A_1 \vee A_2)$ must be closed. Finally, note that in unmarked nodes, $\Box \neg G$ is not 'responsible' for the contradiction, and hence $\Box$ can be instantiated without harm.

Example 13 (The blocksworld, cont.). Consider again example 4. As $\mathcal{LAP}_{\leadsto}$-tableaux are complete, a closed tableau for $KB \wedge IC \wedge \Box \neg(Clear_3 \wedge On_{3,Table})$ exists and the above algorithm will extracts a plan from it. The smallest one (coming from a smallest tableau) is $\pi = take_{1,2}; puton_{1,Table}; take_{2,3}; puton_{3,Table}$.

Generally there might be more than one closed tableau for a given formula $\neg A$, and in consequence an extracted plans might be unnecessarily complex. Clearly, the shorter the tableau proof, the simpler the extracted plan.

Note that the ($\vee$)-rule introduces conditional plans, and it might be impossible to check such conditions. Consider e.g. $IC = \{\langle \alpha_1 \rangle \top, \langle \alpha_2 \rangle \top\}$, and $KB = \{[\alpha_1]P \vee [\alpha_2]P\}$. There is a tableau proof that $(IC \wedge KB) \rightarrow \Diamond P$, which gives us the plan *if* $[\alpha_1]P$ *then* α_1 *else* α_2. But such a plan might not allow us to effectively act in order to obtain P. Take e.g. a game where there are two doors behind one of which there is a treasure, and read α_1 as "open the first door", α_2 as "open the second door", and P as "you get the treasure".

Note also that when a conditional plan is associated to a ($\vee$)-tableau rule, we can choose between A_1 and A_2 as a condition. This is of interest because it might be the case that A_2 can be tested, while A_1 cannot (or only in a more expensive way). In particular, the above example illustrates that it should be generally preferable to test classical formulas (instead of modal ones).

7 Discussion

We have presented a modal framework for reasoning about actions and plans, for which we have given a decision procedure. Although this framework is less expressive than propositional dynamic logic, it is expressive enough to deal with the standard reasoning about actions tasks of prediction, postdiction, and planning. The differences concerning the theoretical complexity remain to be established.

The main features of our approach can be summarized as follows: It is in terms of a family of *modal logics*, and allows to express *nondeterminism* and *indirect effects* of actions. It is based on the use of *dependence relations* and provides a *monotonic* solution to the frame problem. The decision procedure is based on a simple *tableau theorem prover*. Neither of these characteristics is novel alone, but, to the best of our knowledge, it is the first time that one approach unites *all* of such features:

(1) Modal logics and monotonic solutions to the frame problem: Modal logics (viz. *PDL* and extensions of it) have been used before to model reasoning about actions domains, e.g. in [Ros81,SB93,DGL95]. In [SB93] frame axioms are computed in a way similar to our construction of dependence relations, and in [DGL95] there is another monotonic solution to the frame problem in the style of [Rei91] and others, using converse and complement of actions.[7]

(2) The concept of dependence: The idea of adding information about dependence between actions and atoms is similar to the use of causality-like notions found in the literature on reasoning about actions. In this sense, dependence is a sort of weak causality. We just mention Sandewall's notion *occluded* [San95] and Kartha and Lifschitz' *releases* [KL94]. Nevertheless, contrarily to the approaches of Lifschitz *et col.*, it makes no sense in $\mathcal{LAP}_{\leadsto}$ to state a dynamic constraint $[\alpha]P$ without stating that P depends on α, while this might be the case e.g. in $\mathcal{AR}_0$. Dependence is also closely related with the next topic.

(3) Nondeterminism and indirect effects of actions: While nondeterministic actions can be handled in $\mathcal{LAP}_{\leadsto}$ in a straightforward way, actions with indirect effects (which are not covered by Reiter's solution) must be analysed in more depth. Although static integrity constraints such as $\square(Walking \rightarrow Alive)$ can be easily formulated, we must take care of the 'indirect dependences' of actions: The dependences of α must mention *all* the atoms that may be changed by the execution of α. E.g. if $\square(P \leftrightarrow Q)$ and $\alpha{\leadsto}P$ then we must also have $\alpha{\leadsto}Q$. For the time being this must be done by hand. The automatic generation of such derived dependences is subject of ongoing research. This motivates the formal study of the notion of dependence, and its relation to that of an integrity constraint. First results can be found in [FdCH96,Her97]. Anyway, there is a general feeling that that it is necessary to dispose of some causlity-like relation to solve the ramification problem [Lin95,MT95,Thi95,Thi97] and weak causality notion such as our goes into the same direction.

(4) Proof methods: $\mathcal{LAP}_{\leadsto}$ -tableaux need a preliminary step of normal form, as we have seen in section 5. But even if the naive algorithm is employed, in practical cases the size of the resulting formula should be close to that of the original one. One of the reasons is that action laws are already in normal form. (It would be strange to write down action laws $A \rightarrow [\alpha]C$ with C containing atoms that do not depend on α.) Furthermore, knowledge bases describing only the actual situation are in normal form. Hence it is only the goal which must be put in conjunctive normal form. Note that in planning problems, even this step is superfluous because the goal is already in normal form. Hence the complexity of

---

[7] This is opposed to minimization-based approaches, which are used in many formal systems dealing with the frame problem. Generally speaking, minimization is a particular reasoning mechanism which is added on top of a logic. Often things are formulated in the situation calculus, which means that we are in the framework of second-order logic. In our case there is no such minimization – or at least, it is a very simple one, which corresponds to the fact that we represent the dependence relation, while what is used in the procedure is the independence relation. Nevertheless, we have shown by a sound and complete translation [CGH96] that our formalism has at least the same expressive power as the minimization-based action logic $\mathcal{A}$ [GL93].

reasoning in our system is that of our tableau method. Unfortunately, as we have already pointed out, it seems that the theorectical complexity of our system is over PSPACE, which is the complexity of propositional STRIPS [Byl94].[8] Future work must be done in order to implement and evaluate the tableau method in practice. We have particular interest in the work of [GS96], which takes profit of existing SAT-algorithms for classical logic, and in that of [HSZ96], which presents a very efficient loop test for modal logic $S4$.

Acknowledgements We are grateful to Fabio Massacci, who has pointed out to us that our proof of PSPACE completeness in a previous version of this paper was erroneous. Thanks to Luis Fariñas del Cerro and two anonymous referees, whose comments helped to improve the presentation of the paper. This work was partially supported by CAPES (Brazil) under grants to the first author.

References

[Bak91]　A.B. Baker. Nonmonotonic reasoning in the framework of situation calculus. *Artificial Intelligence (AI)*, 49(1–3):5–23, may 1991.

[Byl94]　T. Bylander. The computational complexity of propositional STRIPS planning. *Artificial Intelligence (AI)*, 69(1–2):165–204, 1994.

[Cat89]　L. Catach. *Les logiques multi-modales*. PhD thesis, Université Paris VI, France, 1989.

[CGH96]　M.A. Castilho, O. Gasquet, and A. Herzig. Modal tableaux for reasoning about actions and plans. IRIT internal report, nov 1996.

[DGL95]　G. De Giacomo and M. Lenzerini. *PDL*-based framework for reasoning about actions. In *Proc. 4th Congresss of the Italian Association for Artificial Intelligence (IA*AI'95)*, number 992 in LNAI, pages 103–114. Springer-Verlag, 1995.

[FdCH96]　L. Fariñas del Cerro and A. Herzig. Belief change and dependence. In Yoav Shoham, editor, *Proc. 6th Conf. on Theoretical Aspects of Rationality and Knowledge (TARK'96)*, pages 147–162. Morgan Kaufmann Publishers, 1996.

[GKL95]　E. Giunchiglia, G. N. Kartha, and V. Lifschitz. Actions with indirect effects (extended abstract). In *Working notes of the AAAI-Spring Sysposium on Extending Theories of Actions*, 1995.

[GL93]　M. Gelfond and V. Lifschitz. Representing action and change by logic programs. *Journal of Logic Programming*, pages 301–321, 1993.

[Gor92]　R.P. Goré. *Cut-free sequent and tableau systems for propositional normal modal logics*. PhD thesis, University of Cambridge, England, 1992.

[GS96]　F. Giunchiglia and R Sebastiani. A SAT-based decision procedure for $\mathcal{ALC}$. In *Proc. Int. Conf. on Knowledge Representation and Reasoning (KR'96)*, pages 302–314, Cambridge, Massachussetts, 1996.

[Har84]　D. Harel. Dynamic logic. In D. Gabbay and F. Günthner, editors, *Handbook of Philosophical Logic*, volume II, pages 497–604. D. Reidel, Dordrecht, 1984.

[Her97]　A. Herzig. How to change factual beliefs using laws and independence information. In Dov M. Gabbay and Rudolf Kruse, editors, *Proc. Int. Joint Conf. on Qualitative and Quantitative Practical Reasoning (ECSQARU/FAPR-97)*, LNCS. Springer-Verlag, jun 1997.

---

[8] Unlike STRIPS, in our approach we can deal with nondeterminism and ramifications.

[HM86]   S. Hanks and D. McDermott. Default reasoning, nonmonotonic logics, and the frame problem. In *Proc. Nat. (US) Conf. on Artificial Intelligence (AAAI'86)*, pages 328–333, Philadelphia, PA, 1986.

[HSZ96]   A. Heuerding, M. Seyfried, and H. Zimmermann. Efficient loop-check for backward proof search in some non-classical propositional logics. In P. Miglioli, U. Moscato, D. Mundici, and M. Ornaghi, editors, *Proceedings of the 5th International Workshop TABLEAUX'96: Theorem Proving with Analytic Tableaux and Related Methods*, number 1071 in LNAI, pages 210–225. Springer-Verlag, 1996.

[KL94]   G. N. Kartha and V. Lifschitz. Actions with indirect effects (preliminary report). In *Proc. Int. Conf. on Knowledge Representation and Reasoning (KR'94)*, pages 341–350, 1994.

[Lin95]   F. Lin. Embracing causality in specifying the indirect effects of actions. In *Proc. of the 14th International Joint Conference on Artificial Intelligence (IJCAI'95)*, pages 1985–1991, Montreal, Canada, 1995.

[Mas97]   F. Massacci. Personal communication, may 1997.

[Mat93]   C. Mathieu. A resolution method for a non-monotonic multimodal logic. In S. Moral, editor, *Proc. ECSQUARU'93*, LNCS, pages 257–264. Springer-Verlag, 1993.

[MT95]   N. McCain and H. Turner. A causal theory of ramifications and qualifications. In *Proc. of the 14th International Joint Conference on Artificial Intelligence (IJCAI'95)*, pages 1978–1984, 1995.

[Rei91]   R. Reiter. The frame problem in the situation calculus: A simple solution (sometimes) and a completeness result for goal regression. *Artificial Intelligence and Mathematical Theory of Computation*, Papers in Honor of John McCarthy:359–380, 1991.

[Ros81]   S. Rosenschein. Plan synthesis: a logical approach. In *Proc. of the 8th International Joint Conference on Artificial Intelligence (IJCAI'81)*, pages 359–380, Academic Press, 1981.

[San95]   E. Sandewall. *Features and Fluents*. Oxford University Press, 1995.

[SB93]   W. Stephan and S. Biundo. A new logical framework for deductive planning. In *Proc. of the 13th International Joint Conference on Artificial Intelligence (IJCAI'93)*, pages 32–38, 1993.

[Sie87]   P. Siegel. *Représentation et utilisation de la connaissance en calcul propositionnel*. PhD thesis, Université d'Aix-Marseille II, Aix-Marseille, France, jul 1987.

[Thi95]   M. Thielscher. The logic of dynamic systems. In *Proc. of the 14th International Joint Conference on Artificial Intelligence (IJCAI'95)*, pages 1956–1962, Montreal, Canada, 1995.

[Thi97]   M. Thielscher. Ramification and causality. *Artificial Intelligence (AI)*, 89:317–364, 1997.

[Tse83]   G.S. Tseitin. On the complexity of derivations in propositional calculus. In Siekmann Wrightson, editor, *Automated Reasoning 2: Classical papers on computational logic*, pages 466–483, 1983.

A Time and Resource Problem for Planning Architectures

Amedeo Cesta and Cristiano Stella

IP-CNR
National Research Council of Italy
Viale Marx 15, I-00137 Rome, Italy
amedeo@pscs2.irmkant.rm.cnr.it

Abstract. This paper concerns the problem of resource reasoning in planning. It defines formally a constraint satisfaction problem, the Time and Resource Problem ($\mathcal{TRP}$), in which resource reasoning is seen as integrated with temporal reasoning. Two propagation techniques are introduced that reason about resource constraints in the $\mathcal{TRP}$ framework. The Profile Propagation technique, similar to time-tabling techniques, considers resource utilization in single instants of time (the time values) to synthesize necessary quantitative temporal constraints. The Order Propagation technique is more original. It observes single time points (the time variables) and their orderings to synthesize necessary qualitative temporal constraints.

1 Introduction

The problem of temporal reasoning in planning has been addressed in a number of works and various techniques for temporal constraint management are now commonly used. On the contrary, the problem of resource reasoning only recently has received attention [8, 6, 9]. Such a problem is increasingly relevant in planning architectures that address realistic problems. In such problems the distinction between planning and scheduling activities becomes vague and taking into account resource constraints during the problem solving phase starts to be important also from the point of view of search control.

This paper considers the possibility of representing resource constraints in a specialized module that can be called into play by a planner to check consistency of the current resource utilization. In this work we define a constraint system for time and resources and give properties useful to propagate effects of resource constraints. In the same spirit of works on temporal constraints like [5] we consider such a module independent from a particular planner and endowed with a set of interface primitives. Similarly to [5] we define a constraint satisfaction problem that we call Time and Resource Problem ($\mathcal{TRP}$) that characterizes the whole module.

After defining the $\mathcal{TRP}$ and its computational complexity (Section 2), the problem of propagating resource constraints is addressed in (Section 3) where two different propagation techniques are defined. Section 4 compares the paper results with other approaches. Section 5 presents an experimental evaluation that shows the interest of the propagation techniques.

2 The Time and Resource Problem

This section defines a mixed constraint system with time and resource constraint representation. It also introduces a set of primitives that allows to interface the constraint systems to the external world.

2.1 Time Representation

The chosen time representation is the Simple Temporal Problem (STP) as defined in [5]. For the purpose of this paper we assume to be endowed with the ability to define incrementally: (a) a set T of temporal variables t_i named time-points by using the primitive $DefineTimeVariable(t_i)$; (b) a set of binary constraints C between time-point by using the function $AddTimeConstraint(t_i, t_j, d)$. The function $AddTimeConstraint$ takes $t_i, t_j \in T$ and $d \in \mathbf{N}$ and define the following constraint:

$$t_j - t_i \leq d \tag{1}$$

The temporal variables t_i assume values on the set $\mathbf{N}$ and such values[1] should satisfy any constraint that considers t_i. Due to the restrictions of the STP, given a set of constraints, the possible values for the time variable t_i are included in an interval $[lb_i, ub_i]$. To compute the sets $[lb_i, ub_i]$ for any t_i a directed constraint graph $G_d(V_d, E_d)$ named *distance graph* is associated to the STP, where the set of nodes V_d represents the set of variables $\{t_1, \ldots, t_n\}$ and the set of edges E_d represents the set of constraints. The presentation of the temporal propagation algorithms is out of the scope of this paper.

2.2 Resource Representation

Given a set of resources R we define for each resource $r_j \in R$ a level of availability (or resource profile) $Q_j(t)$ that represents the available resource r_j over time.

A resource constraints is defined stating that the function $Q_j(t)$ is bounded to fall in an interval $[min_j, max_j]$ [2]. The two primitives $Produce(r, q, t_i)$ and $Allocate(r, q, t_i, t_j)$ are defined to modify resource availability. The primitive $Produce(r, q, t_i)$ associates a resource production of the quantity q to a temporal variable t_i [3]. The primitive $Allocate(r, q, t_i, t_j)$ represents the use of a quantity[4] q of the resource r between the time points t_i and t_j where $t_i \leq t_j$.

---

[1] In the following we will use the greek letter τ to indicate time instants: possible values for temporal variables.

[2] It is to be noted that $min_j = -\infty$ means no bound to consumptions, while $max_j = \infty$ means no bound to productions.

[3] A production of $-q$ indicates a resource consumption.

[4] Also in this case q can be either positive or negative.

The primitive $Allocate(r, q, t_i, t_j)$ may be represented in terms of the *Produce* by using the two productions $Produce(r, -q, t_i)$ and $Produce(r, q, t_j)$ and posting the constraint $t_i \leq t_j$. Such a primitive is explicitly defined because is very often used and the dependence between the two time points implied in the allocation is exploited to make propagation techniques more effective as shown later. By using such primitives it is possible to define for each resource r_j its usage $ru_{i,j}$ in the time-point t_i. A positive $ru_{i,j}$ represents a resource production, a negative $ru_{i,j}$ a resource consumption. If $ru_{i,j} = 0$ it means that the level of r_j is not modified in t_i.

When each time point t_i is assigned a value τ_i an availability level for each resource over time (named *resource profile*) may be defined as follows:

Definition 1. –Resource Profile– Let T be the set of time-points, for each resource r_j we call *resource profile* the temporal function:

$$Q_j(t) = \sum_{t_i \in T, \tau_i \leq t} ru_{i,j}$$

The function represents the available amount of the resource r_j over time. □

Definition 1 allows us to express a capacity constraint on a resource as a n-ary constraint on the time points that affect that resource. Considering that any $Q_j(t)$ is a piecewise constant function and its changes of value happen in the time instants where $ru_{i,j} \neq 0$ the constraint $min_j \leq Q_j(t) \leq max_j$ can be stated as follows:

Definition 2. –Resource Consistency– Let T_j be the set of time-points where $ru_{i,j} \neq 0$. A solution $\{t_1 = \tau_1, t_2 = \tau_2, \ldots t_n = \tau_n\}$ of an STP is consistent with respect to resource constraints if and only if for each resource r_j the following property holds:

$$\forall t_i \in T_j : min_j \leq \sum_{t_h \in T_j, \tau_h \leq \tau_i} ru_{h,j} \leq max_j \tag{2}$$

□

The primitives allow to represent a class of resources that involves large part of the taxonomy defined in the KRSL language proposal [11]. In particular, we can represent resources that are consumable/producible, reusable/non-sharable, and reusable/independently sharable. This can be done with different combinations of *Produce, Allocate, min,* and *max*.

2.3 Integrating Time and Resource Constraints

The whole constraint system may be expressed defining a new constraint problem the $\mathcal{TRP}$ (Time and Resource Problem).

Definition 3. $-\mathcal{TRP}-$ A *Time and Resource Problem* is a 7-ple

$$\mathcal{TRP} = <T, C, D, R, RU, MAX, MIN>$$

where: T is a set of time-points that may assume integer values; C is a set of temporal constraints $c_{i,j}$ of the kind $t_j - t_i \leq d_{i,j}$ with $d_{i,j} \in D$; R is a set of resources r_j which have an associated availability interval $[min_j, max_j]$ with $min_j \in MIN$ and $max_j \in MAX$; the function $RU : T \times R \to \mathbf{Z}$ represents the quantity of each resource used in any time-point. For each resource $r_j \in R$ a resource constraint is defined. A solution to a $\mathcal{TRP}$ is an assignment $\{t_1 = \tau_1, t_2 = \tau_2, \ldots t_n = \tau_n\}$ which is consistent with both time and resource constraints of the kind defined in equations 1 and 2. $\square$

A $\mathcal{TRP}$ can be represented with an hypergraph that we call *Time/Resource Net*. Unfortunately adding resource constraints to an STP causes some inconvenience due to the presence of n-ary resource constraints. The following theorem holds:

Theorem 4. $\mathcal{TRP}$ *is NP-complete.*

Proof sketch. a) for each assignment $\{t_1 = \tau_1, t_2 = \tau_2, \ldots t_n = \tau_n\}$ it is possible to check the constraint satisfiability in polynomial time ($\mathcal{TRP} \in NP$); b) the Job-Shop Scheduling problem, which is known to be NP-complete, is polynomially reducible to $\mathcal{TRP}$. $\square$

Known algorithms for NP-Complete problems are exponential. This involves that complete propagation algorithms in the Time/Resource Net may be impractical even on low size problems. In the rest of the paper we introduce incomplete techniques to propagate resource constraints that filter inconsistent solutions out from the search space.

3 Propagation Techniques

To propagate the resource constraints we have followed the idea of synthesizing new temporal constraints by reasoning on resource representation. This is what is usually done in scheduling to level the resource profiles (e.g., [4]). Here the attempt is to identify *necessary constraints*, that we call *implicit*, due to the verification of certain properties instead of synthesizing them heuristically as done in other approaches. This Section proposes two filtering techniques that partially propagate resource constraints: the first one reasons on single instant of time (the time values) defining a resource profile to synthesize necessary quantitative temporal constraints, the second one observes single time points (the time variables) and their orderings and synthesize necessary qualitative temporal constraints.

3.1 Profile-Propagation

The first technique requires the introduction of some preliminary concepts. The evaluation of a resource profile $Q_j(t)$ would require an assignment of a time value

τ_i to any time variable t_i that uses r_j. During the search for a solution such an assignment is not always available, as a consequence an approximate method to make deductions is needed. Our starting point is an observation also done in [6]: during problem solving at least lower and upper bounds may be given for each $Q_j(t)$. Such bounds can be called *optimistic resource profile* $orp_j(t)$ and *pessimistic resource profile* $prp_j(t)$ respectively. In particular $orp_j(t)$ $(prp_j(t))$ is a resource profile greater (lower) then any $Q_j(t)$ that can be obtained by completion of the current partial solution (that is $prp_j(t) \leq Q_j(t) \leq orp_j(t)$).

Before considering how to compute $orp_j(t)$ and $prp_j(t)$ let us give the basic properties they satisfy.

Proposition 5. *If for a resource r_j in an instant τ happens that $orp_j(\tau) < min_j$ or $prp_j(\tau) > max_j$ then the constraint system is inconsistent.*

Proposition 5 is used in [6] to check resource constraint inconsistency.

Proposition 6. *If for a given resource r_j in any instant τ happens that both $orp_j(\tau) \leq max_j$ and $prp_j(\tau) \geq min_j$ then any solution consistent with the current constraints is characterized by an admissible value for $Q_j(t)$.*

From Proposition 6 the following corollary follows:

Corollary 7. *If for any resource r_j in any instant τ happens that $orp_j(\tau) \leq max_j$ and $prp_j(\tau) \geq min_j$ then the constraint system is consistent.*

To compute the bound profiles we consider a resource r_j and the set $T_j(T_j \subseteq T)$ of the time-points in which the resource is modified. We remind that for any time point t_i the interval $[lb_i, ub_i]$ is computed and dynamically updated after any modification of the temporal network. Given any instant τ we can define two sets of time points: the set of time points $P_j(\tau)$ that are ordered before τ and the set of time point $I_j(\tau)$ about which the ordering with respect to τ is not deducible:

$$P_j(\tau) = \{t_i \in T_j \mid ub_i \leq \tau\}$$
$$I_j(\tau) = \{t_i \in T_j \mid lb_i \leq \tau \wedge ub_i > \tau\}$$

Given an assignment $\{t_1 = \tau_1, t_2 = \tau_2, \ldots t_n = \tau_n\}$ it should be clear that the sets $I_j(\tau)$ are empty because decisions have been taken. It is also clear that during the search process at any decision a subset of $I_j(\tau)$ is cut and inserted in $P_j(\tau)$. If we call $s_j(\tau)$ $(s_j(\tau) \subseteq I_j(\tau))$ the subset of $I_j(\tau)$ that falls in $P_j(\tau)$ in the final solution (by adding incremental choices to the current solution), we have:

$$Q_j(t) = \sum_{t_i \in P_j(t)} ru_{i,j} + \sum_{t_i \in s_j(t)} ru_{i,j}$$

that shows how the value of the resource profile is given by two terms (the first one of them known). As a consequence, to estimate the optimistic and pessimistic resource profiles we have to focus on two approximations for $s_j(t)$: $lb_j(t) \subseteq I_j(\tau)$ and $ub_j(t) \subseteq I_j(\tau)$ such that:

$$\sum_{t_i \in lb_j(t)} ru_{i,j} \leq \sum_{t_i \in s_j(t)} ru_{i,j} \leq \sum_{t_i \in ub_j(t)} ru_{i,j} \qquad (3)$$

The following subsets verify the equation 3:

$$lb'_j(t) = \{t_i \in I_j(t) \mid ru_{i,j} < 0\}$$
$$ub'_j(t) = \{t_i \in I_j(t) \mid ru_{i,j} > 0\}$$

With the two estimates we can compute the two bound profiles:

$$orp'_j(t) = \sum_{t_i \in P_j(t)} ru_{i,j} + \sum_{t_i \in ub'_j(t)} ru_{i,j}$$
$$prp'_j(t) = \sum_{t_i \in P_j(t)} ru_{i,j} + \sum_{t_i \in lb'_j(t)} ru_{i,j}$$

The computation of $orp'_j(t)$ and $prp'_j(t)$ and the verification of Proposition 5 and Corollary 7 allow to check for consistency of the current $\mathcal{TRP}$ network. This computation is equivalent to what is proposed in [6]. In fact it is possible to observe that the optimistic estimate consists in considering the consumption of resources as late as possible and the productions as early as possible. The pessimistic estimate can be obtained by reasoning the opposite way.

A more accurate estimate with respect to [6] may be obtained considering the duration constraints between the time points involved in an *Allocate* primitive. Without loss of generality, we assume that a single time-point can not be involved in more than one *Allocate*. With this assumption, we define a function $Link(t_i)$ such that $Link(t_i) = t_j$ if and only if either $Allocate(r, q, t_i, t_j)$ or $Allocate(r, q, t_j, t_i)$ have been performed ($Link(t_i) = \perp$ if t_i is not involved in any allocation). From the definition of *Allocate* it follows that $Link(t_i) \leq t_i$ for allocation of the kind $Allocate(r, q, t_j, t_i)$ and $Link(t_i) \geq t_i$ for $Allocate(r, q, t_i, t_j)$. It may be shown that when an optimistic and pessimistic estimate involve a time-point affected by an allocation a more accurate version of the estimate is the following (the subsets verify the equation 3):

$$lb_j(t) = \{t_i \in lb'_j(t) \mid \neg(Link(t_i) \in I_j(t) \wedge Link(t_i) \leq t_i)\}$$
$$ub_j(t) = \{t_i \in ub'_j(t) \mid \neg(Link(t_i) \in I_j(t) \wedge Link(t_i) \leq t_i)\}$$

With this new estimates of $s_j(t)$ it is possible to compute new bounds $orp_j(t)$ and $prp_j(t)$ more accurate of the previous ones.

Instead of stopping ourselves to this control for resource consistency, we use the bounds to synthesize new temporal constraints to be added in the STP problem. Those constraints are implied by the current situation (indicated with the operator $\Rightarrow$ in what follows). We can justify this technique with the following Theorem:

Theorem 8. *Let us consider a* Time/Resource Net *in which for any resource r_j the optimistic $orp_j(t)$ and pessimistic $prp_j(t)$ profiles have been defined. For any resource r_j, any instant τ, and any time point $t_i \in I_j(\tau)$ the following properties hold:*

$$(t_i \in ub_j(\tau)) \wedge (orp_j(\tau) - ru_{i,j} < min_j) \Rightarrow t_i \leq \tau$$
$$(t_i \in negset_j(\tau)) \wedge (orp_j(\tau) + ru_{i,j} < min_j) \Rightarrow t_i > \tau$$
$$(t_i \in posset_j(\tau)) \wedge (prp_j(\tau) + ru_{i,j} > max_j) \Rightarrow t_i > \tau \qquad (4)$$
$$(t_i \in lb_j(\tau)) \wedge (prp_j(\tau) - ru_{i,j} > max_j) \Rightarrow t_i \leq \tau$$

where:

$$negset_j(t) = \{t_i \in lb'_j(t) \mid \neg(Link(t_i) \in I_j(t) \wedge Link(t_i) \geq t_i)\}$$
$$posset_j(t) = \{t_i \in ub'_j(t) \mid \neg(Link(t_i) \in I_j(t) \wedge Link(t_i) \geq t_i)\}$$

We call the technique derived from Theorem 8 *Profile Propagation* (PP). It consists of detecting situations in which some of the conditions 4 of the Theorem hold in order to deduce the new quantitative temporal constraints to cut out inconsistent search space. An incremental algorithm to apply these filtering techniques has been implemented and has a complexity $O(n^2m)$ where n is the number of time-points and m is the number of resources. It is worth noting that Profile Propagation needs only the temporal information given by the admissible intervals $[lb_i, ub_i]$ for any time point t_i. As a consequence it can be used with a temporal algorithm that incrementally computes arc-B-consistency on the temporal network.

3.2 Order-Propagation

The Profile Propagation is the adaptation to the $\mathcal{TRP}$ of a class of techniques also known as "time-tabling" [10]. The presented formalization allowed us to define a second propagation technique that turns out to be more effective of the previous one but also more demanding in term of computational resources. The rationale for the new technique, named *Order Propagation* (OP) stands in observing the core of the Profile Propagation. In PP we observe the generic instant τ and the relative position with respect to τ of the time points that affect a certain resource. If we compute the path-consistency of the temporal network we know the relative position of any time-point with respect to the others because we compute the minimal distances on the graph G_d between any couple of time point. As a consequence, we can adapt the same observations done for the time instants to the time variables t_i and may repeat the same reasoning with respect to the t_i instead of the τ. We call d_{ij} the minimal distance on G_d (the shortest path as shown in [5]) from the time point t_i to the time point t_j (d_{ij} is the minimal integer l such that $t_j - t_i \leq l$).

For each resource r_j we identify the set $T_j (T_j \subseteq T)$ of the time-points in which the resource is used. Similarly to the previous discussion we define the set of time points $P_j(t_i)$ that are ordered before t_i and the set of time point $I_j(t_i)$ whose ordering with respect to t_i is not deducible. Observing that if $d_{ij} \leq 0$ it means that $t_j \leq t_i$ and that if $d_{ji} < 0$ it means that $t_j > t_i$, we may define the two sets as follows:

$$P_j(t_i) = \{t_h \in T_j \mid d_{ih} \leq 0\}$$
$$I_j(t_i) = \{t_h \in T_j \mid d_{ih} > 0 \wedge d_{hi} \geq 0\}$$

Indicating with $s_j(t_i)$ the subset of $I_j(t_i)$ that falls in $P_j(t_i)$ in the final solution, in which all the time points in T_j are ordered among them, we can again identify

$$Q_j(t_i) = \sum_{t_h \in P_j(t_i)} ru_{h,j} + \sum_{t_h \in s_j(t_i)} ru_{h,j}$$

In a way analogous to what done in the previous paragraph we can estimate an optimistic and pessimistic resource profile using the formulas:

$$LB'_j(t_i) = \{t_h \in I_j(t_i) \mid ru_{h,j} < 0\}$$
$$UB'_j(t_i) = \{t_h \in I_j(t_i) \mid ru_{h,j} > 0\}$$
$$LB_j(t_i) = \{t_h \in LB'_j(t_i) \mid \neg(Link(t_h) \in I_j(t_i) \wedge Link(t_h) \leq t_h)\}$$
$$UB_j(t_i) = \{t_h \in UB'_j(t_i) \mid \neg(Link(t_h) \in I_j(t_i) \wedge Link(t_h) \leq t_h)\}$$
$$ORP_j(t_i) = \sum_{t_h \in P_j(t_i)} ru_{h,j} + \sum_{t_h \in UB_j(t_i)} ru_{h,j}$$
$$PRP_j(t_i) = \sum_{t_h \in P_j(t_i)} ru_{h,j} + \sum_{t_h \in LB_j(t_i)} ru_{h,j}$$

The $ORP_j(t_i)$ and $PRP_j(t_i)$ satisfy also a Proposition and Corollary completely analogous to the one given above in which the generic instant τ is substituted by the generic t_i.

Also in this case we have used the properties for a propagation technique that is justified by the following theorem:

Theorem 9. *Let us consider a* Time/Resource Net *in which for any resource r_j the optimistic $ORP_j(t_i)$ and pessimistic $PRP_j(t_i)$ profiles have been defined. For any resource r_j, any $t_i \in T_j$, and any time point $t_h \in I_j(t_i)$ the following properties hold:*

$$(t_h \in UB_j(t_i)) \wedge (ORP_j(t_i) - ru_{h,j} < min_j) \Rightarrow t_h \leq t_i$$
$$(t_h \in NEGSET_j(t_i)) \wedge (ORP_j(t_i) + ru_{h,j} < min_j) \Rightarrow t_h > t_i$$
$$(t_h \in POSSET_j(t_i)) \wedge (PRP_j(t_i) + ru_{h,j} > max_j) \Rightarrow t_h > t_i \qquad (5)$$
$$(t_h \in lb_j(t_i)) \wedge (PRP_j(t_i) - ru_{h,j} > max_j) \Rightarrow t_h \leq t_i$$

where:

$$NEGSET_j(t_i) = \{t_h \in LB'_j(t_i) \mid \neg(Link(t_h) \in I_j(t_i) \wedge Link(t_h) \geq t_h)\}$$
$$POSSET_j(t_i) = \{t_h \in UB'_j(t_i) \mid \neg(Link(t_h) \in I_j(t_i) \wedge Link(t_h) \geq t_h)\}$$

We call the technique derived from Theorem 9 *Order-Propagation* (OP). It consists of detecting situations in which some of the four conditions of the Theorem hold in order to deduce the new qualitative temporal constraints to cut out inconsistent search space. An incremental algorithm to apply this filtering techniques has been implemented and has a complexity $O(n^2m)$ where n is the number of time-points and m is the number of resources. It is worth noting that Order-Propagation is inevitably more demanding from the computational side with respect to Profile-Propagation because it requires a more detailed temporal network. It needs the computation of the minimal distances between any couple of time points. As well known, arc-B-consistency on the temporal network is not sufficient to compute such minimal distances but path-consistency is needed. To this purpose we have adapted dynamic shortest path algorithms described in [2] to the temporal case.

4   Related Works

Resource reasoning has also been addressed in previous research on planning. The SIPE planner [15] is able to deal with consumable and producible resources but it does not allow an explicit representation of constraints to avoid conflicts or control the search space.

The HSTS architecture [8] addresses the problem of managing sharable resources, however it forces an over-constraining of the partial plan, since the sharable resources are managed specifying a total ordering of the activity within the plan.

O-Plan [6] addresses the managing of sharable resources using a criteria based on the optimistic and pessimistic resource profile in order to identify bounds violations. We started from the same basic observation concerning the bounds but investigated the synthesis of necessary new constraints that avoid bounds violations.

A different approach has been recently used in the IxTeT planner and described in [9]. In such system the resource management is entirely performed at search level. In particular, this technique consists of recognizing a potential conflict on the resource utilization and selecting in a heuristic way a further constraint able to avoid the conflict. It is worth noting that our techniques are somehow complementary to the one described in [9] and it would be interesting to use both the approaches in the same planner.

In [12] the problem MCJSSP is defined (Multiple-Capacitated Job-Shop Scheduling Problem), that is a generalization of the JSSP (Job-Shop Scheduling Problem) for resources with capacity greater than one. The paper presents techniques which currently represent the most efficient approach to address complex resource allocation problems through constraint-based methods. In such work constraint propagation is performed by two distinct techniques: the former is very similar to the Profile-Propagation, while the latter, which is called Sequencing-Checking, and can be considered an extension of the edge-finding technique [1] defined for the JSSP problem, is based on the analysis of the conflicts that arise between sets of operations. A theoretical comparison of sequencing-checking with our approach has not been done yet but an experimental comparison has been performed and it is described in Section 5.

4.1   *parc*Plan

The work reported in this paper is being developed from quite a while and previously described only in our native Italian language [14, 3]. In the meantime, an independent research has been published [7] which also uses orderings between time-points. Because of the similarities between the latter approach and ours we draw here a comparison.

In [7] a propagation technique for resource constraints is presented and applied to the *parc*Plan planner. The authors do not use time-tabling techniques like our Profile-Propagation. They start from a formalization, different from

$\mathcal{TRP}$, that considers only the *Allocate* primitive and propose a technique that can be compared with our Order-Propagation.

It is possible to prove that the deductions the *parc*Plan method allows to obtain are a proper subset of the deductions obtained by the Order-Propagation. Adapting the *parc*Plan propagation mechanism to the $\mathcal{TRP}$ it should assume the following form:

$$
\begin{aligned}
(t_h \in UB_j(t_i)) \wedge (ORP_j(t_i) = min_j) &\Rightarrow t_h \leq t_i \\
(t_h \in NEGSET_j(t_i)) \wedge (ORP_j(t_i) = min_j) &\Rightarrow t_h > t_i
\end{aligned}
\tag{6}
$$

It is possible to verify how both the relations use a stronger condition with respect to the corresponding relations (first two relations) in equation 5 of theorem 9. In fact, from the first relation in equation 5 we can notice that because $t_h \in UB_j$, from the definition of UB_j it follows that $ru_{h,j} > 0$. As a consequence, it is easy to deduce that the first relation in equation 6 is more restrictive than its correspondent in equation 5. A similar proof holds for the corresponding second relations. Furthermore, *parc*Plan does not use the deductions performed by the third and fourth relation of equation 5.

5 Experimental Evaluation

The performance of the approach implemented in the Time/Resource Net needs a deep evaluation on realistic problems. Here we describe some test performed in an experimental setting that although artificial gives some first reinforce in the results.

5.1 Setting

We have built an experimental apparatus creating a set of MCJSSP problems manipulating the benchmarks for JSSP proposed in [13]. The chosen problem setting is over-constrained with respect to the expressive power of $\mathcal{TRP}$. In fact MCJSSP represents only resource allocations, contains operations of fixed duration, and does not specify metric separation constraints between operations.

To simulate different styles of problem solving we have used two different search algorithms:

- *Instant-Search*: This is an algorithm with backtracking which selects, at each step, one of the un-scheduled operations and assigns to it the earlier possible start time. Such an algorithm is similar to the one used in [12] and is specialized for scheduling problems. Instant-Search is not a least-commitment algorithm, therefore it is not suitable to simulate the behavior of the most recent planning architectures. For this reason we have designed the second algorithm.
- *Order-Search*: This is a least-commitment search algorithm that instead of assigning time values to the temporal variables, posts ordering relationship between the time points which use the same resource. More specifically, at

each step an ordering is selected, among those not yet posted, that implies the least commitment for the solution.

Each experimental test consists in resolving a set of 250 MCJSSP problems using the two search algorithms defined with four different kinds of constraint propagation techniques:

- *Profile-Check*: it is essentially the technique used by the O-Plan planner [6]. It is not an actual propagation technique but a check for optimistic and pessimistic bound violation.
- *Profile-Propagation*: it is the technique defined in Subsection 3.1.
- *Sequencing-Checking plus Profile-Propagation*: it coincides with the constraint propagation performed by [12].
- *Profile-Propagation plus Order-Propagation*: it consists of the mixed execution of the two propagations techniques proposed here.

The first three propagation techniques coupled with the Instant-Search algorithm do not need the array of the minimal distances between each pair of time points, so they are associated with a temporal propagation that just achieves arc-consistency on the temporal network. Instead, in all other cases an algorithm that achieve path-consistency on the temporal network is used. In fact the Order-Search solver needs the minimal distance between each pair of time points.

The problems to solve are split into 5 classes of growing size. Each class is identified by 5 resources with capacity 2 (as in [12]) and a number of jobs respectively equal to 12,16,20,24 and 30. In this way we have obtained a total number of operations (of capacity 1) per problem respectively equal to 60,80,100,120 and 150. For each class 50 problems have been randomly generated using a technique similar to the one used in [12]. The module code has been implemented in Allegro Common Lisp on a Sun SPARC10 workstation.

5.2 Results

Table 5.2 shows, for each class (number of operations indicated with O60, O80, O100, O120 and O150) and for each kind of propagation, and for each search algorithm the number of solved problems (out of the 50 generated for each class) stopping the search after a fixed amount of time growing according to the class size and equal to, respectively, 100,200,250,300 and 400 seconds of CPU time.

Analyzing the table some observation can be done.

The Profile-Checking approach seems to have a limited effectiveness with problems of increasing size. It has a very low cost so in general it allows to visit more deeply the search space in the same time interval at its disposal.

The Sequencing-Checking is confirmed to perform quite well when couple with the Instant-Search algorithm as done in [12]. But its effectiveness is surprisingly limited when coupled with a least-commitment strategy like Order-Search.

The Profile-Propagation and Order-Propagation techniques, instead seem to be the most effective with this second kind of solver, therefore its reasonable to

Table 1. Experimental results: number of solved problems for each propagation technique

	Instant Search					Order Search				
	O60	O80	O100	O120	O150	OA60	O80	O100	O120	O150
Profile-Checking	48	25	0	0	0	20	23	15	13	4
Profile-Propagation	39	15	15	12	4	24	26	18	13	5
Sequencing-Checking + Profile-Propagation	50	45	42	40	35	20	26	9	4	0
Order-Propagation + Profile-Propagation	49	37	25	15	10	43	46	42	48	41

suppose that they should constitute an effective support for a planning architecture that adopts a least-commitment strategy.

Furthermore, the cross analysis between the two halves of the table shows that, on the problem set, the approach consisting of the Time/Resource module plus the least-commitment solver is as much efficient as the approach proposed in [12].

Of course more experimentation is needed to confirm the trends shown here. In particular experiments with a real planning architecture would be very helpful to confirm the behavior shown with least-commitment strategies.

6 Conclusions

This paper has defined a mixed time and resource problem $\mathcal{TRP}$ that formalizes in CSP terms the representation of resource constraints for planning systems. Furthermore a Time/Resource Net has been introduced that can be a powerful module to be inserted in a planning architecture to support search control in expressive domains. Two propagation techniques have been defined, Profile-Propagation and Order-Propagation, that allow to synthesize new implicit but necessary temporal constraints after reasoning on resource profiles. The effectiveness of the propagation techniques has been compared with other state-of-the-art techniques and shown to be quite competitive.

Acknowledgments

Authors' work was supported by Italian Space Agency, CNR Committee 12 on Information Technology (Project SCI*SIA), and CNR Committee 04 on Biology and Medicine.

References

1. D. Applegate and W. Cook. A Computational Study of the Job-Shop Scheduling Problem. *ORSA Journal on Computing*, 3:149–156, 1991.
2. G. Ausiello, G.F. Italiano, A. Marchetti Spaccamela, and U. Nanni. Incremental Algorithms for Minimal Length Paths. *Journal of Algorithms*, 12:615–638, 1991.
3. A. Cesta and C. Stella. Rappresentazione e gestione di vincoli su risorse in una architettura per la pianificazione (in Italian). In *Proceedings of the Fifth AI*IA Symposium. Naples, Italy*, 1996.
4. C. Cheng and S.F. Smith. Generating Feasible Schedules under Complex Metric Constraints. In *Proceedings 12th National Conference on AI (AAAI-94)*, 1994.
5. R. Dechter, I. Meiri, and J. Pearl. Temporal Constraint Networks. *Artificial Intelligence*, 49:61–95, 1991.
6. B. Drabble and A. Tate. The Use of Optimistic and Pessimistic Resource Profiles to Inform Search in an Activity Based Planner. In *Proceedings of the 2nd Int. Conf. on Artificial Intelligence Planning Systems (AIPS-94)*, 1994.
7. A. El-Kholy and B. Richards. Temporal and Resource Reasoning in Planning: the parcPLAN Approach. In *Proceedings of the 12th European Conference on Artificial Intelligence (ECAI-96)*, 1996.
8. R.E. Frederking and N. Muscettola. Temporal Planning for Transportation Planning and Scheduling. In *Proceedings of the IEEE International Conference on Robotics and Automation*, 1992.
9. P. Laborie and M. Ghallab. Planning with Sharable Resource Constraints. In *Proceedings of the International Joint Conference on Artificial Intelligence (IJCAI-95)*, 1995.
10. C. Le Pape. Three Mechanisms for Managing Resources Constraints in a Library for Constraint-Based Scheduling. In *Proceedings of the INRIA/IEEE Conference on Emerging Technologies and Factory Automation*, 1995. http://www.ilog.fr.
11. N. Lehrer. KRSL Reference Manual 2.0.2. ARPA/Rome Laboratory Planning and Scheduling Initiative. Technical report, ISX Corporation, 1993.
12. W.P.M. Nuijten and E.H.L. Aarts. Constraint Satisfaction for Multiple Capacitated Job-Shop Scheduling. In *Proceedings of the 11th European Conference on Artificial Intelligence(ECAI-94)*, 1994.
13. N. Sadeh. *Look-ahead Techniques for Micro-opportunistic Job-shop Scheduling*. PhD thesis, School of Computer Science, Carnegie Mellon University, Pittsburgh, PA, 1991.
14. C. Stella. Trattazione di vincoli su tempo e risorse in una architettura per la pianificazione automatica (in Italian). Master's thesis, Department of Computer and System Science, University of Rome "La Sapienza", February 1996.
15. D.E. Wilkins. *Practical Planning: Extending the Classical AI Planning Paradigm*. Morgan Kaufmann Pub.Inc., 1988.

Planning via Model Checking:
A Decision Procedure for $\mathcal{AR}$

Alessandro Cimatti[1], Enrico Giunchiglia[2],
Fausto Giunchiglia[1,3], Paolo Traverso[1]

[1] IRST, Povo, 38100 Trento, Italy
[2] DIST - University of Genoa, Viale Causa 13, 16145 Genova, Italy
[3] DISA - University of Trento, Via Inama 5, 38100 Trento, Italy

Abstract. In this paper we propose a new approach to planning based on a "high level action language", called $\mathcal{AR}$, and "model checking". $\mathcal{AR}$ is an expressive formalism which is able to handle, among other things, ramifications and non-deterministic effects. We define a decision procedure for planning in $\mathcal{AR}$ which is based on "symbolic model checking", a technique which has been successfully applied in hardware and software verification. The decision procedure always terminates with an optimal solution or with failure if no solution exists. We have constructed a planner, called MBP, which implements the decision procedure.

1 Introduction

A lot of research has focused on the problem of the expressiveness of formalisms for reasoning about action and change. This has lead to the development of various formalisms, e.g. action languages able to deal with the "frame problem" and the "ramification problem" (see for instance [7] and [11]). So far, however, little success has been obtained in the development of decision procedures which can be used as a basis for planning with these expressive formalisms.

The goal of this paper is to propose a new decision procedure for planning within an expressive formalism, able to handle, among other things, ramifications and non-deterministic effects. Our recipe is based on the following three ingredients:

1. Use a high level action language. This language must separate the language used to specify actions' effects, called the action description language, from the language used to ask questions about actions' effects, called the query language;
2. Give semantics to the action description language in terms of finite state automata. We need therefore to restrict to problems with a finite number of states. This hypothesis, though quite strong, allows us to treat several planning examples proposed in the literature so far;
3. Perform planning as "model based reasoning", that is, by verifying whether the automaton, as defined by a set of sentences of the action description language, satisfies the properties expressed by a query expressed in the query language.

Our proposal relies heavily on previous work. Proposal 1 is due to Lifschitz [11]. Furthermore, we use $\mathcal{AR}$ [7] as action description language. $\mathcal{AR}$ allows for ramification constraints, conditional effects, non deterministic actions, actions' preconditions, and non boolean fluents. Moreover, it allows for the definition of fluents as abbreviations of complex formulas. These features make $\mathcal{AR}$ one of the most powerful formalisms solving the "frame problem" and the "ramification problem". Proposal 2 is now standard practice in the development of action languages. Proposal 3 has been made within the Computer Science community and has led to the development of a very successful set of techniques and tools, nowadays grouped under the label of "model checking" (see, e.g., [5]). Our work relies on a specific technique known as "symbolic model checking" (see, e.g., [4]), used for industrial hardware and software verification. The possibility to apply model checking techniques to $\mathcal{AR}$ is due to the fact that in both cases semantics is given in terms of finite state automata. Other (minor) commonalities are the use of non boolean variables and non-determinism.

We have constructed a planner, called MBP (Model Based Planner), which implements the decision procedure described in this paper. As a consequence, MBP has some significant novel features. As far as we know, MBP is the first planner for $\mathcal{AR}$ and it is the first planner with a decision procedure able to handle ramifications, conditional effects, actions preconditions, nonboolean fluents and definitions at the same time. Moreover, given a planning problem, MBP always terminates with an optimal solution or with failure if no solution exists: this feature is not provided by several state of the art planners, e.g. UCPOP [14], and SATPLAN [10].

Finally, MBP opens up the possibility to investigate some challenging problems for future research. We have tested MBP with a few examples and the results are positive. The (still very limited number of) experiments we have performed show that MBP can be compared with state of the art planners like UCPOP and GRAPHPLAN. Future research should investigate how to implement different planning strategies and heuristics in MBP and then an extensive comparative analysis should be performed. Moreover, since MBP is able to plan with non-deterministic effects, this feature should be investigated in order to understand whether "planning via model checking" can be used to address the problem of the integration of plan generation within reactive planners which have to deal with non-deterministic domains.

This paper is structured as follows. In Section 2 we review $\mathcal{AR}$ and its semantics, which is given in terms of finite state automata. In Section 3, we introduce the query language and give semantics to the queries for temporal projection and planning in terms of properties on finite state automata. In Section 4, we show how to specify the finite state automaton of an action description in terms of a boolean formula. This step allows us to inherit the symbolic model checking techniques, as described for instance in [5]. Some of the results reported in this section adapt and extend analogous results presented in [6]. In Section 5 we describe the decision procedures for temporal projection and planning. In Section 6 we describe an implementation of the procedures and discuss some tests on some examples.

2 Action description language

An $\mathcal{AR}$ language is characterized by a finite nonempty set of *actions*, and a finite nonempty set of *fluents*, a subset of which is declared *inertial*. Each fluent F is associated to a finite nonempty set Rng_F of values (the *range* of F).

An *atomic formula* has the form $(F = V)$,[4] where F is a fluent, and $V \in Rng_F$. In case Rng_F is $\{T, F\}$, the fluent is said to be propositional and the atomic formula $F = T$ is abbreviated with F.

A *formula* is a propositional combination of atomic formulas.

Let A be an action, let F be an inertial fluent, and let C and P be formulas. In $\mathcal{AR}$ we can express that:

- C is true after we execute A in a state in which P is true. We do this with the *determinate effect proposition*

$$A \textbf{ causes } C \textbf{ if } P, \tag{1}$$

- F may non-deterministically change its value if we execute A in a state in which P is true. We do this with the *indeterminate effect proposition*

$$A \textbf{ possibly changes } F \textbf{ if } P, \tag{2}$$

- C is true in any state. We do this with the *constraint*

$$\textbf{always } C. \tag{3}$$

A scenario is formalized as a set of the above expressions, i.e. as an *action description*. In the following action description, *Load* and *DriveFast* are actions; *InTruck* and *InPlane* are propositional, inertial fluents:

$$
\begin{aligned}
&\textit{Load } \textbf{causes } \textit{InTruck } \textbf{if } (\neg \textit{InTruck} \land \neg \textit{InPlane}), \\
&\textit{Load } \textbf{causes } \textit{InPlane } \textbf{if } \textit{InTruck}, \\
&\textit{DriveFast } \textbf{possibly changes } \textit{InTruck } \textbf{if } \textit{InTruck}, \\
&\textbf{always } \neg(\textit{InTruck} \land \textit{InPlane}).
\end{aligned}
\tag{4}
$$

Let us consider now the semantics for $\mathcal{AR}$. A *valuation* is a function that associates to each fluent F an element of Rng_F. A valuation s is extended to atomic formulas as follows

$$s(F = V) = \begin{cases} T, & \text{if } s(F) = V, \\ F, & \text{otherwise.} \end{cases}$$

and to arbitrary formulas in the straightforward way. Consider an action description $\mathcal{A}$. A valuation s is said to be a *state* if, for every constraint (3) in $\mathcal{A}$, $s(C) = T$. For example, in the action description (4), there are three

---

[4] In [7], the authors use F is V instead of $F = V$.

states, corresponding to the three possible valuations satisfying the formula $\neg(InTruck \wedge InPlane)$.

The semantics of an action description is an automaton, i.e. a pair consisting of a set of states, and of a transition function Res mapping an action A and a state s into a set of states (which intuitively are the possible states resulting from the execution of A in s). The definition of Res incorporates the solution to the frame problem. Let $Res^0(A, s)$ be the set of states s' such that, for each determinate effect proposition (1) in $\mathcal{A}$, $s'(C) = \mathsf{T}$ whenever $s(P) = \mathsf{T}$. Then, $Res(A, s)$ is the set of states s' such that for any state s'' in $Res^0(A, s)$, $New_A(s, s'')$ is not a proper subset of $New_A(s, s')$. For any two states s and s', $New_A(s, s')$ is the set of formulas

$$F = s'(F)$$

such that

- F is inertial and $s'(F) \neq s(F)$, or
- for some indeterminate effect proposition (2) in $\mathcal{A}$, $s(P) = \mathsf{T}$.

The semantics of the action description (4) is the automaton shown in Figure 1.

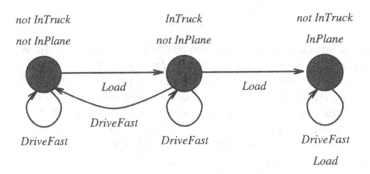

Fig. 1. The transition system for (4)

3 Query language

Both temporal projection and planning problems require the ability to compute the set of states resulting from the execution of a sequence of actions starting from a (partially specified) initial state. For example, in (4), we are interested in knowing the result of performing the action *Load* starting from an initial state in which the pack is neither in the truck nor in the plane.

As in [7], the initial state is specified with *initial conditions*, expressions of the form

$$\textbf{initially } C \tag{5}$$

where C is a formula. In the following, we speak about *domain descriptions* meaning the union of an action description and a set of initial conditions.

Consider a domain description $\mathcal{D}$. Our next step is to define $Res(A_1; \ldots; A_N)$ ($N \geq 0$) as the set of states possibly resulting from the execution of the sequence of actions $A_1; \ldots; A_N$ starting from an initial state. We define $Res(A_1; \ldots; A_N)$ in two steps. First, we define *Init* as the set of states s such that for each initial condition (5) in $\mathcal{D}$, $s(C) = \mathsf{T}$. Then we define $Res(A_1; \ldots; A_N)$ as follows:

- if $N = 0$, then we have the empty sequence of actions ϵ and $Res(\epsilon) = Init$;
- if $N > 0$, then $Res(A_1; \ldots; A_N)$ is

$$\{s' : s' \in Res(A_N, s''), s'' \in Res(A_1; \ldots; A_{N-1})\}.$$

A *temporal projection problem* is specified by an expression of the form

$$G \textbf{ after } A_1; \ldots; A_N \tag{6}$$

where G is a formula and $A_1, \ldots, A_N$ ($N \geq 0$) are actions. We say that (6) is *entailed* by $\mathcal{D}$ if $s(G) = \mathsf{T}$ *for each* state s in $Res(A_1; \ldots; A_N)$.

A *planning problem* is specified by an expression of the form

$$\textbf{goal } G \tag{7}$$

where G is a formula. We say that a sequence of actions $A_1; \ldots; A_N$ is a *solution* in $\mathcal{D}$ to a planning problem (7) if $s(G) = \mathsf{T}$, *for some* state s in $Res(A_1; \ldots; A_N)$. Notice that for a solution $A_1; \ldots; A_N$ of a planning problem, it might be the case that for some state s in $Res(A_1; \ldots; A_N)$, we have $s(G) = \mathsf{F}$. Of course, this is not possible in case of deterministic domains with fully specified initial state. The above definition is a generalization of the standard notion of solution to a planning problem usually given for such domains. On the other hand, executing a solution does not always guarantee the achievement of the goal.

4   Automaton specification

The idea underlying symbolic model checking is to manipulate sets of states represented as propositional formulas. We therefore perform a translation from an action description $\mathcal{A}$ into a propositional formula which directly codifies the transition relation of the finite state automaton described by $\mathcal{A}$. The crucial point is that this translation must codify in the automaton also the law of inertia in presence of ramification constraints. We perform the translation as follows. We introduce two variables F and F' for each fluent F in $\mathcal{A}$. The range of the variables F and F' is declared to be Rng_F. Intuitively, they represent the value of the fluent F in the current and next state. We have also a variable Act whose range is the set of actions of $\mathcal{A}$. Act is the action to be executed. In the following we assume that $F_1, \ldots, F_m$ $[F_{m+1}, \ldots, F_n,$ resp.$]$ are the inertial [not inertial, resp.] fluents of $\mathcal{A}$, listed according to a fixed enumeration. We will consider the assignments of values to variables satisfying

- the formula $State_F$, defined by

$$\bigwedge_{(\textbf{always } C) \in \mathcal{A}} C;$$

- and the formula Res_F, defined by

$$
\begin{aligned}
&Res_F^0 \wedge \\
&\neg \exists v_1 \ldots v_n (\ Res_F^0[F_1'/v_1, \ldots, F_n'/v_n] && \wedge \\
&\qquad \bigwedge_{1 \leq i \leq m} (v_i = F_i \vee v_i = F_i') && \wedge \\
&\qquad \bigvee_{1 \leq i \leq m} (v_i \neq F_i') && \wedge \\
&\qquad \bigwedge_{(\mathcal{A} \textbf{ possibly changes } F_i \textbf{ if } P) \in \mathcal{A}} ((Act = A \wedge P) \supset v_i = F_i'))
\end{aligned}
$$

$$(8)$$

where Res_F^0 is an abbreviation for

$$
State_F[F_1/F_1', \ldots, F_n/F_n'] \wedge \\
\bigwedge_{(\mathcal{A} \textbf{ causes } c \textbf{ if } P) \in \mathcal{A}} ((Act = A \wedge P) \supset C[F_1/F_1', \ldots, F_n/F_n']),
$$

and $\alpha[a/b]$ is the expression obtained substituting a with b in α.

An *assignment* is a set of pairs ⟨variable, value⟩ (notice that a valuation in the sense of $\mathcal{AR}$ is also an assignment). An assignment s *satisfies* a formula α if the formula resulting from the substitution of each variable w with $s(w)$ in α, is entailed by the unique name axioms for values. We can now formally state the fact that the conjunction of $State_F$ and Res_F captures the transition relation of the finite state automaton corresponding to $\mathcal{A}$.

Theorem 1. *Let A be an action, and let s, s' be two valuations of $\mathcal{A}$. Let σ be the the assignment $s \cup \{\langle F', V \rangle \mid s'(F) = V\} \cup \{\langle Act, A \rangle\}$. $s' \in Res(A, s)$ iff σ satisfies Res_F and $State_F$.*

In the hypotheses of the above theorem, it is easy to check that σ satisfies $State_F$ iff s is a state of $\mathcal{A}$. Now assume that s be a state (if it is not, the theorem trivially holds). The fact that σ satisfies Res_F iff $s' \in Res(A, s)$ needs some explanation. First, it is easy to check that $s' \in Res^0(A, s)$ iff the assignment σ satisfies Res_F^0. Then, we can reformulate the definition of $Res(A, s)$ given in Section 2 as the set of valuations s' such that

- $s' \in Res^0(A, s)$ (first line of (8)), and
- there does not exist a state $s'' \in Res^0(A, s)$ (second line of (8)) such that
  - for each inertial fluent F, either $s''(F) = s'(F)$ or $s''(F) = s(F)$ (third line of (8)); and
  - for some inertial fluent F, $s''(F) \neq s'(F)$ (fourth line of (8)); and
  - $s''(F) = s'(F)$ for each fluent F such that for some indeterminate effect proposition (2) in $\mathcal{A}$, $s(P) = \mathsf{T}$ (last line of (8)).

We can map $State_F$ and Res_F into quantifier free formulas. In the case of Example (4), $State_F \wedge Res_F$ is equivalent to the conjunction of (we abbreviate $F = \mathsf{T}$ and $F' = \mathsf{T}$ with F and F' respectively)

$$Act = Load \wedge \neg InTruck \wedge \neg InPlane \supset InTruck',$$
$$Act = Load \wedge InTruck \supset InPlane',$$
$$\neg(InTruck \wedge InPlane),$$
$$\neg(InTruck' \wedge InPlane'),$$

and

$$\neg(InTruck \equiv InTruck' \wedge InPlane \equiv InPlane') \supset$$
$$(Act = Load \wedge \neg InPlane \vee$$
$$Act = DriveFast \wedge InTruck \wedge \neg InTruck' \wedge \neg InPlane').$$

The passage to a propositional formula is then performed using the standard techniques of (i) mapping each variable with 2^n values into n independent variables with range $\{\mathsf{T}, \mathsf{F}\}$, and (after suitable substitutions in the formulas) (ii) for each variable w atomize $w = \mathsf{T}$ with w and $w = \mathsf{F}$ with $\neg w$.

5 Decision procedures

Our decision procedures work on the sets of states of the automaton. In the following, the procedures are defined for a given domain description, identified by the set of initial states $Init$ and the automaton specification, i.e. the transition relation Res_F. Figures 2 and 3 describe the procedures for temporal projection and planning problems, respectively. In both figures, we use standard set operators (e.g. $\subseteq, \backslash$), A[1,...,N] is an array of actions, and G denotes the set of states satisfying the formula G of $\mathcal{AR}$. Given two valuations s, s' and an action A, the expression Res(s, A, s') is satisfied when $s \cup \{\langle F', V\rangle \mid s'(F) = V\} \cup \{\langle Act, A\rangle\}$ satisfies Res_F.

Consider Figure 2. Intuitively, the loop computes the sequence of sets of all possible states resulting from the execution of the sequence A[1],...,A[N] and stores them into the array Exec[0,...,N]. Initially, the set of initial states $Init$ is assigned to Exec[0]. At each step i in the loop, Exec[i] stores the set of all possible states resulting from the execution of the i-th action A[i] from a state in Exec[i-1]. The final test, after the loop execution, checks whether all the states resulting from the execution of the action sequence, stored in Exec[N], satisfy G.

Theorem 2. temporal-projection(A[1,...,N],G) *returns* True *if the temporal projection problem* G *after* A[1];...;A[N] *is entailed by the domain description*, False *otherwise*.

The planning algorithm is presented in Figure 3. At each step of the loop, the set of states accessible after the execution of a number i of actions is generated and stored in Acc[i]. This is done by starting from previously unexplored (i.e.

```
function temporal-projection(A[1,...,N],G)

Exec[0] := Init;
for (i := 1,...,N)
 Exec[i] :=
  { s' : Res(s, A[i], s'), s ∈ Exec[i-1] }

if (Exec[N] ⊆ G)
 then return True
 else return False
```

Fig. 2. Temporal Projection Algorithm

new) states generated at previous step, contained in **New[i-1]**. This is similar to the computation performed in temporal projection, with the difference that all possible actions are considered. Indeed, the set **Acc[i]** is computed through **Res(s, A, s')** where **A** ranges over the set of all possible actions **Actions**. **New[i]** is computed as the set-difference of the accessible states **Acc[i]** with the accessible states at the previous step, i.e. **Acc[i-1]**. If **New[i]** is empty, then the entire space of accessible states has been covered without finding a goal, and **planner** returns **failure**. Otherwise, **planner** checks whether a state in **New[i]** is also a goal state (**New[i]** ∩ G) and stores the result in **Reached_goals**. If this is the case, **planner** calls **choose-plan** with argument i, i.e. the length of the plan. Intuitively, **choose-plan** builds a plan by traversing backwards the list of sets of states built by **planner**, and choosing one (of possibly many) action sequence leading to a goal state. The first step is to (arbitrarily) select one accessible goal state, namely **V[N]**. Then, at each j-th step, the set of pairs state-action **(s,A)** which can take to **V[j+1]** is generated and stored in **Back[j]**. One pair is arbitrarily chosen, and the action is stored in **A[j+1]**. The action reconstruction is necessary as the "forward" analysis performed by **planner** does not keep track of the actions which have been executed.

The planning procedure terminates, it is correct and complete, and finds optimal plans.

Theorem 3. **planner** *terminates.*

The proof is based on the fact that the sequence of sets **Acc[i]** is monotonic and has a least fixpoint (see [5] for a similar proof). There exists therefore an i such that **Acc[i]** = **Acc[i-1]**.

Theorem 4. *If* **planner**(G) *returns* **A[1,...,N]** *then* **A[1];...;A[N]** *is a solution to* **goal** G. *If* **planner**(G) *returns* **failure** *then there exists no solution to* **goal** G.

Theorem 5. *If there exists a solution to* **goal** G, *then* **planner**(G) *returns a solution of minimal length.*

function planner(G)
_____

```
Acc[0] := New[0] := Init;
i := 0;
while (New[i] != ∅)
 Reached_goals := (New[i] ∩ G);
 if (Reached_Goals != ∅)
  then return choose-plan(i);
 i := i + 1;
 Acc[i] := Acc[i-1] ∪
           { s' : Res(s, A, s'),
                 s ∈ New[i-1], A ∈ Actions };
 New[i] := Acc[i] \ Acc[i-1];
return failure;
```

_____

function choose-plan(N)
_____

```
V[N] := choose-element(Reached_Goals);
for (j := N - 1,...,0) do
 Back[j]  := { (s,A) : Res(s, A, V[j+1]),
                     s ∈ New[j+1] };
 (V[j],A[j+1]) := choose-element(Back[j]);

return A[1,...,N];
```

_____

Fig. 3. Planning Algorithm

The procedures for temporal projection and planning include the classical case of deterministic domains with fully specified initial state. In the deterministic case, temporal projection works on single states, since each Exec[i] is a singleton, while the planning procedure generates at most one state in Acc[i] and in New[i] for each action. In the case of non deterministic domains, the execution of an action can generate different states, and therefore Exec[i] can have more than one element, and Acc[i] and New[i] can have multiple states for each action.

6 Implementation and testing

We have implemented temporal-projection and planner in C language on top of SMV [5], a state-of-the-art symbolic model checker which has been successfully applied in hardware and software verification. We call the resulting system MBP (Model Based Planner). The data structures and algorithms of SMV constitute the basic building blocks of the temporal-projection and planner routines. SMV represents sets of states as OBDDs (Ordered Binary Decision Diagrams) [3; 5]. The main advantages of OBDDs are twofold. First, OBDDs give a very concise representation of sets of states. The dimension, i.e. the number of nodes, of an OBDD does not necessarily depends on the actual number of states. This fact provides the ability to represent extremely large sets of states and complex transition relations. Second, set theoretical operations, such as union and intersection, are implemented as very efficient operations on OBDD. This allows for an efficient implementation of our decision procedures.

An extensive comparative analysis of MBP is not one of the goals of this paper. Nevertheless, in order to have a preliminary test, we have looked for available implemented systems. Unfortunately, as far as we know, there are no such systems with an action language as expressive as $\mathcal{AR}$. Neither are there "standard" examples of significative complexity in the literature of theories of actions. All the examples we have found are toy examples, involving a very low number of states. As a first step, we have run MBP on some of these toy examples. On these examples, our procedures are extremely fast.

We have run a few examples and compared the results with two state-of-the-art planners, UCPOP [14] and GRAPHPLAN [2]. To do this, we had to shift to deterministic domains described by a subset of $\mathcal{AR}$. The results of the comparison are reported in Figure 4. (The time is in CPU seconds. A dash -- indicates that the system did not found a solution within the time limit of 3000 seconds).

	UCPOP	GRAPHPLAN	MBP
tsp.a	52	0.67	0.76
tsp.b	--	2023	62
tsp.c	--	--	49
fixit	--	0.26	3.6
logistic.a	--	2.5	80
logistic.b	--	12.4	1200

Fig. 4. Preliminary experimental evaluation

MBP is a total order planner, while both UCPOP and GRAPHPLAN are partial order planners. As a first test we have chosen a completely sequential problem: the "traveling salesman problem" (**tsp**). For this problem, we have considered various classes of tests, each characterized by the number of cities, and the probability of connection between two cities. Then we have run 30 random tests for each class. For low probability of connection and/or low number of cities, GRAPHPLAN is able to easily discover the existence/nonexistence of a plan and immediately halt. This is not true for UCPOP, where there is no mechanism for detecting the nonexistence of a plan. As such, we had to test the existence of a solution before submitting the problem to UCPOP. Interestingly, both GRAPHPLAN and UCPOP have shown a somehow counter-intuitive behavior: their performances decrease as the probability of connection increases, reaching -at a certain fixed number of cities- their worst at 100% connection probability. This is not the case for MBP, where we have what looks like an "easy-hard-easy" pattern and where the worst performance is obtained at 50% connection probability. With GRAPHPLAN we have been able to find solutions for up to 14 cities, while for UCPOP we had to stop at 10 cities (with a time limit of 3000 seconds). For tsp.c, GRAPHPLAN has not found a solution within 14800 seconds. In tsp.a, we considered 7 cities, with a 50% of connectivity between two cities. In tsp.b and tsp.c the number of cities is 14, the difference between the two examples is in the connectivity: 50% for tsp.b, and 80% for tsp.c. For MBP, an interesting parameter is the number of states, which, in the case of tsp.b and tsp.c is of the order of 10^7. Indeed, as the complexity increases, both UCPOP and GRAPHPLAN perform very badly compared to MBP.

GRAPHPLAN has been designed to solve efficiently problems with parallel actions, while tsp is a completely "sequential planning" problem. A higher level of parallelism can be exploited in the Fix Tire Problem [15] (fixit in Figure 4), where, indeed, GRAPHPLAN is faster than MBP. However, the fact that MBP is able to solve a notoriously difficult planning problem like fixit (MBP has generated and handled efficiently around 10^6 states) in less than 10 seconds is a very encouraging result.

Even if comparable with GRAPHPLAN on the fixit problem, MBP seems in general to decrease performance in domains which can be solved by plans with parallel actions. We have performed a test on logistic [18], a domain where most of the actions can be performed in parallel. logistic.a and logistic.b are two examples with different numbers of cities and packages (5 and 4, and 3 and 6, respectively). These examples are rather hard. UCPOP was unable to find a solution even for problems with 3 cities and 4 packages. Notice that GRAPHPLAN outperforms MBP. The number of reachable states (computed by MBP) is around 10^{13}. In this domain, MBP seems to suffer from the explosion of the number of states.

7   Conclusion and related work

In this paper we have described a model based decision procedure for $\mathcal{AR}$. This decision procedure enhances and integrates work and results developed in two different communities. We think that three are the main contributions of our work. First, as far as we know, MBP is the first planner for $\mathcal{AR}$ and, as such, it is the first planner to handle ramifications, conditional effects, actions preconditions, nonboolean fluents and definitions at the same time.

Second, given a planning problem, MBP always terminates with an optimal solution or with failure if no solution exists: this is not true for several planners (e.g. UCPOP and SATPLAN [10]) which are not guaranteed to terminate if given a planning problem with no solutions (unless we somehow limit the dimension of the search space in advance).

Third, we believe that our experimental results, though preliminary, are already very positive. MBP always performs better than UCPOP. Even though GRAPHPLAN performs better than MBP on the examples suited for non linear planners, MBP performs better on the one with a low degree of non-linearity.

Moreover we still have a lot of room for improvement. For instance, an extension of model based procedures to deal with parallel actions should improve performance on these domains significantly. Furthermore, the use of OBDDs in MBP is still naive. We expect that many techniques developed in the context of model checking and devoted to the reduction of the search space (e.g. conjunctive partitioning [5]) can be successfully applicable in this context.

More in general, our decision procedures are independent of the implementation with OBDDs. The procedures could in principle be reduced to a sequence of satisfiability problems. At each stage of the planning procedure, the satisfiability of the formula expressing the existence of a plan of length i should be tested. This is basically what is done, e.g., in SATPLAN, but with the bound on the plan length chosen a priori. The termination of the algorithm would be guaranteed by testing the unsatisfiability of the formula expressing that unexplored states exist. However, a problem with this approach is that at each step the formulas would become more and more complex. This would have to be handled appropriately. All of this is a topic of current research.

As far as the related work is concerned, to the best of our knowledge, the idea of planning via model checking is new and has never been proposed before. The translation from an action description language into a propositional formula is based on Winslett's possible models approach [19] (see also [13] for a similar usage of this approach). For other works stressing the importance of building planners with a powerful and neat formalism see [9; 14] and the work in deductive planning, where planning is seen as theorem proving (see for instance [17; 12; 8]). Deductive planning can be seen as an alternative approach to planning via model checking: in the latter approach, rather than defining a proof theory and generating plans by logical deduction, the decision procedures work on the models of an action description, i.e. on the space of the sets of states defining an automaton.

References

1. Andrew Baker. Nonmonotonic reasoning in the framework of situation calculus. *Artificial Intelligence*, 49:5–23, 1991.
2. Avrim Blum and Merrick Furst. Fast planning through planning graph analysis. In *Proc. of IJCAI-95*, pages 1636–1642, 1995.
3. R. E. Bryant. Symbolic Boolean manipolation with ordered binary-decision diagrams. *ACM Computing Surveys*, 24(3):293–318, September 1992.
4. J.R. Burch, E.M. Clarke, K.L. McMillan, D.L. Dill, and Hwang L.J. Symbolic model checking: 10^{20} states and beyond. *Information and Computation*, 98(2):142–170, 1992.
5. E. Clarke, O. Grunberg, and D. Long. Model checking. In *Proc. of the International Summer School on Deductive Program Design, Marktoberdorf*, 1994.
6. Enrico Giunchiglia. Determining ramifications in the situation calculus. In *Proc. of KR-96.*, 1996.
7. Enrico Giunchiglia, G. Neelakantan Kartha, and Vladimir Lifschitz. Representing action: Indeterminacy and ramifications. *Artificial Intelligence*, 1997. To appear.

8. Cordell Green. Application of theorem proving to problem solving. In *Proc. of IJCAI*, pages 219–240, 1969.

9. J. Hertzberg and S. Thiebaux. Turning an Action Formalism into a Planner – A Case Study. *Journal of Logic and Computation*, 4(5):617–654, 1994.

10. Henry Kautz and Bart Selman. Pushing the Envelope: Planning, Propositional Logic, and Stochastic Search. In *Proc. AAAI-96*, 1996.

11. Vladimir Lifschitz. Two components of an action language. In *Working Papers of the Third Symposium on Logical Formalizations of Commonsense Reasoning*, 1996.

12. Fangzhen Lin and Raymond Reiter. State constraints revisited. In *Working Papers of the Second Symposium on Logical Formalizations of Commonsense Reasoning*, 1993.

13. C. Pain-Barre and C. Schwind. Constructing Action Graphs for Planning. In *European Workshop on Planning (EWPS95)*, pages 373–388. Malik Ghallab, 1995.

14. J. Penberthy and D. Weld. UCPOP: A sound, complete, partial order planner for adl. In *Proc. of KR-92*, 1992.

15. Stuart Russel. Efficient memory bounded search algorithms. In *Proc. of ECAI-92*, pages 1–5, 1992.

16. Erik Sandewall. Features and fluents: A systematic approach to the representation of knowledge about dynamical systems. Technical Report LiTH-IDA-R-92-30, Linköping University, 1992.

17. W. Stephan and S. Biundo. A New Logical Framework for Deductive Planning. In *Proceedings of the 13th International Joint Conference on Artificial Intelligence (IJCAI-93)*, pages 32–38. Morgan Kaufmann, 1993.

18. Manuela Veloso. *Learning by analogical reasoning in general problem solving*. PhD thesis, 1992. CMU, CS Techn. Report CMU-CS-92-174.

19. M. Winslett. Reasoning about actions with a possible models approach. In *Proceedings of the 8th National Conference on Artificial Intelligence (IJCAI-93)*, pages 89–93, 1988.

Possibilistic Planning: Representation and Complexity

Célia Da Costa Pereira[1], Frédérick Garcia[1]
Jérôme Lang[2], and Roger Martin-Clouaire[1]

[1] INRA/BIA, Auzeville
BP 27, 31326 Castanet Tolosan cedex France
[2] IRIT, Université Paul Sabatier
118 Route de Narbonne, 31062 Toulouse cedex France

Abstract. A possibilistic approach of planning under uncertainty has been developed recently. It applies to problems in which the initial state is partially known and the actions have graded nondeterministic effects, some being more possible (normal) than the others. The uncertainty on states and effects of actions is represented by possibility distributions. The paper first recalls the essence of possibilitic planning concerning the representational aspects and the plan generation algorithms used to search either plans that lead to a goal state with a certainty greater than a given threshold or optimally safe plans that have maximal certainty to succeed. The computational complexity of possibilistic planning is then studied, showing quite favorable results compared to probabilistic planning.

1 Introduction

In a "classical" planning problem, it is assumed that actions are deterministic, the initial state is known and the goal is defined by a set of final states; a solution plan is then an unconditional sequence of actions that leads from the initial state to a goal state. However, most practical problems do not satisfy these conditions of complete and deterministic information. These strict assumptions can be relaxed in several directions including the following:

- Enabling the representation of *uncertainty about the initial state and/or the possible effects of actions*. This issue has lead to several approaches to *probabilistic planning* including ([19], [11], [31], [9], [13], [21]), and in particular, the Kushmerick et al.'s BURIDAN planner [25] for which the effects of actions as well as the initial state description are represented by means of probabilistic state operators that are a probabilistic extension of STRIPS' operators. A solution plan is there an unconditional sequence of actions leading to a goal state with a probability not less than a given threshold.
- Enabling the *flexible representation of goals*, replacing the set of goal states of classical planning by a preference ordering on goal states ([2] [17]) or a utility function ([22] ...) thus embedding the representation of the planning problem into decision theory.

- Taking account of different assumptions concerning *observability*. In a *fully observable* decision process, the current state is always known before the agent has to act so that an adequate solution consists in a conditional plan mapping each possible state at each time point to an actual decision. Such an assumption leads naturally to conditional planning, and in a decision-theoretic perspective to fully observable Markov decision processes (FOMDP) [3]. The other extreme case is *non-observability*, where the agent never gets any feedback from the process, which entails that one looks for an unconditional plan. Between these two extreme cases, *partially observable* decision processes enable the agent to gather some further information about the current state by performing tests (see for instance [7] [5]).
- Enabling the agent to interrupt the planner at any time after it has been launched ("anytime planning"), assuming thus that at any step of the planning process, the planner maintains a solution whose quality increases with execution time, eventually leading to an optimal solution.

This article considers the class of planning problems in which, firstly, the environment is *static* (which means that all changes that take place result from actions specified in the plan given by the agent), secondly, the goals are not flexible (i.e. defined by a set of goal states) and, thirdly, the environment is assumed to be *unobservable* during plan execution, thus requiring the search of non-conditional plans that must be robust to uncertainty. It outlines (see [10] for a detailed presentation) a possibilistic counterpart[1] of the Kushmerick et al.[25]'s approach in which possibility distributions [14] are used to represent the uncertainty both on the initial and subsequent states and on the outcomes of the execution of the context-dependent actions. Two notions of solution plans are used: γ-*acceptable plans* that lead to a goal state with a certainty greater than a given threshold γ, and *optimally safe plans* that lead to a goal state with maximal certainty.

An essential contribution expected from the possibility theory framework concerns the ability to represent more qualitatively and, thus more faithfully, what is known about the initial state and the possible effects of actions; the possibilistic approach is likely to be less sensitive to a lack of precision in the assessment of uncertainty. Using a model in which actions have possibilistic effects is particularly well-suited for cases in which the probabilities of the resulting effects of actions are not available, not very reliable, or hard to obtain, that is, in situation of partial or total ignorance about the immediate consequence of applying an action. Moreover, the notion of action with possibilistic effects properly generalizes the notion of nondeterministic actions by enabling the representation

---

[1] An alternative approach has been proposed by Chrisman [9] and further developed by Doan [13] which relies on a belief function represention that in essence amounts to express uncertainty by a set of probability distributions. The possibilistic representation used in this paper could be seen as a particular case of working with a set of probability distributions instead of a single one since a possibility (resp. necessity) measure is an upper (resp. lower) probability envelope [15].

of ordinal grading in the uncertainty that characterize the uncontrollable choice process through which the real effect of an action will be determined. What is represented is simply that one or several effects are normal in essence (nothing prevents them from occurring) and that some are more normal (less exceptional) than others, that is, some may be considered more plausible than others in the absence of any further information.

Besides its representational adequacy the possibilistic planning framework, as shown in this paper, has interesting properties of computational complexity compared to probabilistic planning. Indeed possibility theory is an *ordinal* model of uncertainty and the only operations needed in our framework are min, max and order reversal $(1 - .)$. This ordinal aspect of a possibilistic representation (contrarily to probabilistic representations which uses sum and product operators instead of max and min) can significantly reduce the complexity of plan generation: a core property is that the search of a γ-acceptable plan amounts to solve a planning problem strait-forwardly derived from the original possibilistic one and constituted only of pure (non graded) nondeterministic actions. This principle has led to the definition of three partial order planning algorithms, called NDP, POSPLAN and POSPLAN*.

Sections 2 and 3 provide a general description of the possibilitic planning approach. Section 4 presents complexity results for possibilitic planning and for pure nondeterministic planning that is encompassed as a special case.

2 Domain Representation in Possibilistic Planning

In this section we define the basic components of a possibilistic planning problem, and two different notions for a solution plan.

2.1 States and Actions

The facts or properties that need to be talked about in the application domain are represented in a finite propositional language by expressions that are conjunctions of atomic sentences (symbols) in either positive or negative form, i.e. conjunctions of literals. For convenience, we shall also occasionally represent an expression as the set of literals involved in the conjunction, an empty set representing no specification at all. A state is a complete description of the world at a time point, that is, a particular expression in which all atomic sentences of the language appear exactly once in a positive or negative form. A state is said to be satisfied by an expression ϵ (denoted $s \models \epsilon$) if and only if each literal of ϵ is in s. We define the set of states satisfied by an expression ϵ as $\mathcal{S}(\epsilon) = \{s \in S/s \models \epsilon\}$.

Definition 1 (uncertain states).
Let S denotes the set of all conceivable states. The uncertainty about the current state of the world is represented by a possibility distribution π over the set S of states such that $\max_{s \in S} \pi(s) = 1$. The initial state is described by the possibility distribution π_{init}.

π conveys what is known about the actual state of the world. $\pi(s)$ expresses to what extent it is possible that the real world state is s ; in particular, $\pi(s) = 0$ means that s is surely not the real world state, and $\pi(s) = 1$ means that nothing prevents s from being the real state. Note that there may be several states s such that $\pi(s) = 1$.

2.2 Possibilistic Actions

The actions considered here can be executed in any world state and their effect depends both on the execution-time state (context-dependent effect) and on chance (nondeterministic effect). The feasible nondeterministic results of the application of an action can be specified by a possibility distribution that enables a ranking of the possible outcomes on the scale of *normality* (i.e. non-exceptionality). More formally a possibilistic action is defined as follows.

Definition 2 (possibilistic actions).
A possibilistic action, denoted a, is a set of possibilistic effects $a = \{ep_i, i = 1, \ldots, m\}$, in which ep_i is the i-th possible effect defined by:

$$ep_i = <t_i, (\pi_{i1}, e_{i1}), \ldots, (\pi_{in_i}, e_{in_i}) >$$

where $\forall i, j$, t_i and e_{ij} are expressions, $\pi_{ij} \in]0, 1]$, such that

- *for all state s, there is a single i such that $s \models t_i$;*
- *for all i, $\max_{1 \leq j \leq n_i} \pi_{ij} = 1$.*

The ep_i's, the t_i's and the e_{ij}'s are called *possibilistic effects*, *discriminants* and *elementary consequences* respectively. The e_{ij}'s play the role of Add/Delete lists of the STRIPS action model: the state resulting from the change on a state s caused by e_{ij} is defined by:

$$Res(e_{ij}, s) = e_{ij} \cup \{l \in s \mid \bar{l} \notin e_{ij}\} .$$

If the context defined by t_i is verified before the execution of a, then it is possible at degree π_{ij} that effect e_{ij} is verified after the execution. If π_{ij} is equal to 1, then e_{ij} is a normal effect (i.e. nothing prevents it from occuring), else the smaller π_{ij} the more exceptional e_{ij}. For a given discriminant, the elementary consequences together with their associated degrees of possibility constitute a possibility distribution over the changes to the world.

Definition 3 (effect of a possibilistic action).
The result of executing action a on s is given by a possibility distribution on S defined by:

$$\pi[s'|s, a] = \begin{cases} \max_k \pi_{ik} & \text{if } s \in S(t_i) \text{ and } s' = Res(e_{ik}, s) \\ 0 & \text{otherwise} \end{cases} .$$

If the initial state is described by a possibility distribution π_{init} over S, then the effect of executing a is defined by the following possibility distribution:

$$\pi[s'|\pi_{init}, a] = \max_{s_0} \min(\pi[s'|s_0, a], \pi_{init}(s_0)) .$$

We will say that action a is *nondeterministic* if and only if $\forall s, s' \in S,\ \pi[s'|s, a] \in \{0, 1\}$.

2.3   Plans and Possibilistic Planning

We classically define a sequential plan as a totally ordered set of actions $\langle a_i \rangle_{i=0}^{N-1}$. A partially ordered plan is a pair $\mathcal{P} = (A, O)$ where A is a set of actions and O is a set of ordering constraints between these actions. A completion of $\mathcal{P}$ is a sequential plan $\mathcal{CP} = \langle a_i \rangle_{i=0}^{N-1}$ such that $A = \{a_0, \ldots, a_{N-1}\}$ and the total ordering $a_0 < \cdots < a_{N-1}$ is consistent with O.

The possibility to reach a given state s_N by executing a sequential plan of possibilistic actions $\langle a_i \rangle_{i=0}^{N-1}$ starting in a state s_0 is defined by:

$$\pi[s_N|s_0, \langle a_i \rangle_{i=0}^{N-1}] = \max_{(s_1 \ldots s_{N-1})} \min_{i=0 \ldots N-1} \pi[s_{i+1}|s_i, a_i] \ .$$

Let $Goals \subseteq S$ the set of the goal states, and π_{init} a possibility distribution over S that describes the initial state. The possibility and necessity measures to reach a goal state after the execution from π_{init} of the sequential plan $\langle a_i \rangle_{i=0}^{N-1}$ are then given by:

$$\Pi[Goals|\pi_{init}, \langle a_i \rangle_{i=0}^{N-1}] = \max_{s_0 \in S, s_N \in Goals} \min(\pi[s_N|s_0, \langle a_i \rangle_{i=0}^{N-1}], \pi_{init}(s_0))$$

$$N[Goals|\pi_{init}, \langle a_i \rangle_{i=0}^{N-1}] = \min_{s_0 \in S, s_N \in \overline{Goals}} \max(1 - \pi_{init}(s_0), 1 - \pi[s_N|s_0, \langle a_i \rangle_{i=0}^{N-1}]) \ .$$

Definition 4 (possibilistic planning problem).
A possibilistic planning problem Δ is a triplet $\langle \pi_{init}, \epsilon_{Goals}, A \rangle$ where π_{init} is the possibility distribution associated to the initial state, ϵ_{Goals} is an expression defining the set of goal states $Goals$ and A is the set of available possibilistic actions.

Given a possibilistic planning problem Δ, two criteria may be considered to define a *solution plan*: we say that a partially ordered plan is a γ-**acceptable plan** for Δ if $N[Goals|s_0, \mathcal{CP}] \geq \gamma$ for all totally ordered completion $\mathcal{CP}$ of $\mathcal{P}$; $\mathcal{P}$ is an **optimally safe plan**, or **optimal plan**, if $N[Goals|s_0, \mathcal{CP}]$ is maximal among all possible sequential plans for all totally ordered completion $\mathcal{CP}$ of $\mathcal{P}$.

3   Generation of Solution Plans

The algorithms we have developped [10] for solving a possibilistic planning problem are based on the equivalence between the search of γ-acceptable plans and the resolution of a derived planning problem that has only pure nondeterministic actions.

Definition 5 (from possibilistic to nondeterministic planning).
Let $\Delta = \langle \pi_{init}, \epsilon_{Goals}, \mathcal{A} \rangle$ a possibilistic planning problem and $\gamma \in]0, 1]$. The non-deterministic planning problem $\Delta_{1-\gamma}$ constructed from Δ is defined by $\Delta_{1-\gamma} = \langle \pi_{init1-\gamma}, \epsilon_{Goals}, \mathcal{A}_{1-\gamma} \rangle$ where $\pi_{init1-\gamma}(s) = 1$ if $\pi_{init}(s) > 1 - \gamma$ and 0 else, $\mathcal{A}_{1-\gamma} = \{a_{1-\gamma} \mid a \in \mathcal{A}\}$ such that if $a = \{\langle t_i, \ldots (\pi_{ij}, e_{ij}) \ldots \rangle\}$ then $a_{1-\gamma} = \{\langle t_i, \ldots (1, e_{ij}) \ldots \rangle \mid \pi_{ij} > 1 - \gamma\}$.

The distribution $\pi_{init1-\gamma}$ represents the set of initial states that have a possibility greater than $1 - \gamma$. The nondeterministic action $a_{1-\gamma} \in \mathcal{A}_{1-\gamma}$ is the result of transforming the action a in $\mathcal{A}$ by retaining only the effects having a possibility greater than $1 - \gamma$.

The following key result is the core of the possibilistic planning algorithms we outline next (the proofs of the following propositions are presented in [10]) :

Proposition 1 (equivalence).
A partial plan $\mathcal{P}$ is $\gamma-$acceptable for Δ if and only if it is 1-acceptable for $\Delta_{1-\gamma}$.

3.1 NDP: a Planning Algorithm for Nondeterministic Actions

NDP is a planning algorithm we have developed to solve nondeterministic planning problems. Like most of the classical planning algorithms, NDP explores a search tree of partial plans whose root is the null plan and the branches represent refinements of the current plan in order to establish subgoals or to confront threats on some already established causal links. The search stops when the current plan is recognized as a solution plan.

The main function of a planning algorithm like NDP is the refinement which transforms a partial plan $\mathcal{P}$ into a new partial plan $\mathcal{P}'$, by eliminating *flaws*. A flaw in $\mathcal{P}$ can be a subgoal not yet established, or a threat on a subgoal already established, that prevents $\mathcal{P}$ from being a solution plan.

Like in SNLP [27], UCPOP [29] or BURIDAN [25] NDP establishes a subgoal proposition p by adding a *causal link* between the effect of an operator that adds p and the action of which p is a precondition. More formally, if $a_j : t_k : p$ is a subgoal of $\mathcal{P}$ where $p \in t_k$ and t_k a discriminant of a_j in $\mathcal{P}$, and if $p \in e_{lm}$ where e_{lm} is an elementary consequence of a nondeterministic effect of the action a_i, then NDP can add the causal link $a_i : e_{lm} \xrightarrow{p} a_j : t_k$. Consequently, each proposition $q \in t_l$ becomes a new subgoal to establish. To each partial plan in the search graph is associated a set of subgoals $\mathcal{SG}$ and a set of causal links $\mathcal{CL}$. They are initialized with $\mathcal{SG} = \{end : \epsilon_{Goals} : q, \quad \forall q \in \epsilon_{Goals}\}$ and $\mathcal{CL} = \emptyset$.

A threat in a partial plan $\mathcal{P} = (A, O)$ is a pair $\langle a; l \rangle$ where l is a causal link $a' : e \xrightarrow{p} a'' : t$ in $\mathcal{CL}$ establishing a proposition p, and a is an action in A that potentially can delete p, i.e. one of its elementary consequences contains $\neg p$. In a classical propositional planner like SNLP, there are two ways to confront such a threat: you can add the constraint $a'' < a$ (*promotion*) or add the constraint $a < a'$ (*demotion*). NDP naturally keeps these two techniques. Due to the specificity of the problem of planning actions with context-dependent effects, the refinement function of NDP must in addition use another trick to protect a causal link as it is done in the two planners UCPOP and BURIDAN. In the NDP planner, we retain the *confrontation* form of BURIDAN. If $a : e$ is a threatening effect for a causal link l of $\mathcal{CL}$, NDP will try to make another non threatening effect $a : e'$ occur. This is done by adding to the discriminant of the causal link consumer a *safety proposition* sp unique to this threat, which becomes a new subgoal to achieve, and by adding to each non threatening elementary consequence $a : e'$ the proposition sp.

In classical planning with STRIPS-like operators, a polynomial truth criterion can be used to check whether or not a partial plan is a solution plan[8, 23]. In such a case the causal link structure is a way to simplify the management of this truth criterion. The problem of planning actions with context-dependent effects like in UCPOP is not as simple. It has been shown that the assessment problem for actions with context-dependent effect was NP-hard [8, 12]. We exhibit in Sect. 4 a similar result for non-deterministic action representation. Consequently, like in BURIDAN, we propose to check if a partial plan $\mathcal{P}$ is a safe plan by directly executing each of its totally ordered completions from each possible initial state.

3.2 Generating γ-Acceptable Plans and Optimal Plans

POSPLAN and POSPLAN* are the two planning algorithms we have developed to solve possibilistic planning problems.

Given a possibilistic planning problem Δ the possibilistic planning algorithm POSPLAN transforms it into a nondeterministic planning problem $\Delta_{1-\gamma}$. Then the nondeterministic planning algorithm NDP takes $\Delta_{1-\gamma}$ as input, and generates a partially ordered safe plan, which is γ-acceptable for Δ.

The link between γ-acceptable plans and optimal plans is clear: $\langle a_i \rangle_{i=1}^{N-1}$ is optimal if and only if it is γ-acceptable and $\forall \gamma' > \gamma$, there is no γ'-acceptable plan. Therefore a meta-algorithm for computing an optimal plan might consist in searching γ-acceptable plans with well-chosen successive values of γ. Several strategies can be thought of; they all require that the state transition degrees (i.e. the possibility degrees involved in the actions and the initial state) be ordered beforehand. Assume that $\{\alpha_i, i = 0, n\}$ is the set of possibility degrees named such that $0 = \alpha_0 < \alpha_1 < \alpha_2 < \ldots < \alpha_n < 1$ or, equivalently, $1 = \gamma_0 > \gamma_1 > \ldots > \gamma_{n-1} > \gamma_n > 0$ with $\gamma_i = 1 - \alpha_i$.

The POSPLAN* algorithm for generating optimal plans implements an increasing acceptability method. The principle is to consider successively the γ-acceptability levels $\gamma_n, \gamma_{n-1}, \ldots$ and to solve the corresponding non-deterministic planning problems $\Delta_{1-\gamma_i}$, until no solution can be found. The main characteristic of POSPLAN* is to avoid replanning from scratch at each iteration $\gamma_{i+1} \rightarrow \gamma_i$. Instead, POSPLAN* reuses the search tree developed so far and only realizes the updating of the current plan that is required to cope with the newly added elementary effects that have a possibility $\pi > 1 - \gamma_i$.

Let $\mathcal{P}$ be the current partial plan in the search tree, and γ_i the current acceptability level associated with $\mathcal{P}$. If $\mathcal{P}$ is not a solution plan for $\Delta_{1-\gamma_i}$, then $\mathcal{P}$ is classically refined into the new partial plan $\mathcal{P}'$, by considering the refinement method of NDP for the $\Delta_{1-\gamma_i}$ problem. In that case, the only action effects considered are the ones with a possibility greater than $1 - \gamma_i$. Conversely, if $\mathcal{P}$ appears to be a solution plan for $\Delta_{1-\gamma_i}$, then the current acceptability level of $\mathcal{P}$ becomes γ_{i-1} and γ_{max} is set to the value γ_i if necessary (see [10] for further details).

In other words, the first iteration amounts to search a plan made of actions restricted to their normal effects only. The successive iterations consist in incorporating the more and more exceptional effects.

The search by increasing acceptability has two worth-mentioning computational properties: POSPLAN* is "anytime" in the sense that it can supply a solution at any time (provided at least one exists and enough time has been allocated to its generation) and the supplied solution is all the better as the algorithm runs longer; the planning problems generated at each iteration are more and more difficult; consequently, the first iteration should be faster.

POSPLAN* can be considered as a hierarchical version of POSPLAN, and relies on an abstraction principle, similar to the ones that have been recently developed. In [32, 24, 18], hierarchal planning exploits a partitioning of the precondition propositions into abstraction level, such that within a given abstraction level only a subset of the subgoals are considered. The abstraction level definition is based on threatening constraints between operators, in order to minimize interaction between subgoals in different levels. In [4], abstractions for Markov decision processes are generated by eliminating not very relevant propositions, in regard to the utility function.

The soundness and completeness properties of NDP, POSPLAN and POSPLAN* have been established in [10]. In particular, the following proposition holds (an essential solution plan is a totally ordered solution plan such that no subplan can be a solution plan).

Proposition 2 (completeness of POSPLAN and POSPLAN*).
Let $\Delta = \langle \pi_{init}, \epsilon_{Goals}, \mathcal{A} \rangle$ be a possibilistic planning problem. If for $\gamma \in]0, 1]$ there exists an essential solution plan $\langle a_i \rangle_{i=0}^{N-1}$ such that $N[Goals|\pi_{init}, \langle a_i \rangle_{i=0}^{N-1}] \geq \gamma$ then $POSPLAN(\Delta, \gamma)$ will generate a partial solution plan $\mathcal{P}$ such that $\langle a_i \rangle_{i=0}^{N-1}$ is one of its completions. If γ_{max} is the greater γ_i such that there exists an essential solution plan $\langle a_i \rangle_{i=0}^{N-1}$ with $N[Goals|\pi_{init}, \langle a_i \rangle_{i=0}^{N-1}] = \gamma_i$ then $POSPLAN^*$ will generate a partial solution plan $\mathcal{P}$ with $N[Goals|\pi_{init}, \mathcal{P}] = \gamma_{max}$.

4 Computational Complexity

In this section we determine the complexity classes in which the various problems associated with possibilistic planning fall into. The methodology we use is inspired from recent results on probabilistic planning [20] [26] and on well-known results on planning with structured action representations [1] [6] [16].

Proposition 3.
Nondeterministic plan verification (NPV) is co-NP-complete.

Proof.
(a) Membership of the complementary problem $\overline{\text{NPV}}$ to NP is showed by the following nondeterministic algorithm which has as input $\langle \mathcal{A}, s_0, \epsilon_{Goals}, \langle a_0 \ldots a_n \rangle \rangle$:

1. guess a sequence $\langle s_1 \ldots s_n s_{n+1} \rangle$;
2. $\forall i$, verify that (s_i, a_i, s_{i+1}) is allowed by $\mathcal{A}$;
3. verify that $s_{n+1} \notin Goals$.

Steps 2 and 3 can be done in polynomial time, hence membership to NP.

(b) As to completeness, we give a polynomial reduction from the validity problem for DNF formulas (which is co-NP-complete) to NPV. Let $\varphi = D_1 \vee \ldots \vee D_m$ be a DNF formula on the alphabet $\{a_1, \ldots a_n\}$. We associate to φ the planning problem defined by the alphabet $\{d_1 \ldots d_m, g\}$, $s_0 = \{d_1, \ldots, d_m, g\}$, $\mathcal{A} = \{\texttt{fix}-a_1, \ldots \texttt{fix}-a_n, \texttt{look}\}$, $\epsilon_{Goals} = \{g\}$; action effects are defined by:

$$\texttt{fix}-a_i : \{\langle \emptyset, \{\overline{d_j}|a_i \in D_j\}, \{\overline{d_j}|\neg a_i \in D_j\} \rangle\};$$
$$\texttt{look} : \{\langle \{\overline{d_1}, \ldots, \overline{d_m}\}, \{\bar{g}\} \rangle\}.$$

Then, φ is valid iff $\langle \texttt{fix}-a_1, \ldots, \texttt{fix}-a_n, \texttt{look} \rangle$ is a good plan. Intuitively, the meaning of d_j is "disjunct D_j has not been violated yet by the current partial interpretation". g is set to **false** iff the interpretation violates *all* disjuncts (action **look** thus examines all disjuncts) and remains **true** otherwise; action $\texttt{fix}-a_i$ nondeterministically chooses a truth value for a_i; if this value is **true** (resp. **false**) then all disjuncts containing $\neg a_i$ (resp. a_i) are (i.e., become or remain) violated. Initially all disjuncts are not violated. It is rather easy to check that all executions of $\langle \texttt{fix}-a_1, \ldots, \texttt{fix}-a_n, \texttt{look} \rangle$ produce all models for the alphabet $a_1 \ldots a_n$ and that g remains true in all possible executions iff all models satisfy at least one of the disjuncts, i.e., if φ is valid. $\square$

As to plan existence, things are trickier. Classical STRIPS plan existence [6] is PSPACE-complete, so we cannot expect nondeterministic-STRIPS planning to be at a lower complexity level. It seems that it is actually *not* in PSPACE – all we can say is that it is in EXPTIME[2].

This point is left for further study. However, by adding the restriction that the plan length should be polynomially bounded (polynomial in the size of the input), we obtain nontrivial results:

Proposition 4.
Nondeterministic polynomial-length plan existence (NPPE) is Σ_2^P-complete[3].

---

[2] Note that unrestricted probabilistic plan existence [26] is EXPTIME-complete.

[3] $\Sigma_2^P = \text{NP}^{\text{NP}}$ is the class of decision problems that can be decided in polynomial time on a nondeterministic Turing machine using NP-oracles (see [30] [28]). The canonical

Proof.

(a) membership follows from the following algorithm:

    1. guess a plan $\langle a_0 \ldots a_l \rangle$;

    2. verify that it is a good plan for $\langle s_0, \mathcal{A}, \epsilon_{Goals} \rangle$.

Step 2 is done by a NP-oracle, and the rest of the algorithm is polynomial, because the length l of the plan is bounded by a polynomial function of the size of the input[4] hence NPPE $\in$ NP$^{\text{NP}} = \Sigma_2^P$.

(b) completeness is proved by the following polynomial reduction from 2-QBF to NPPE. Let $\exists a_1 \ldots \exists a_m \forall b_1 \ldots \forall b_p F$ be an instance of 2-QBF where F is under DNF, i.e., $F = D_1 \vee \ldots \vee D_m$. The associated instance of NPPE is defined by

$s_0 = \{\neg a_1 - \textbf{set}, \ldots \neg a_m - \textbf{set}, \neg b_1 - \textbf{set}, \ldots \neg b - \textbf{set}, d_1, \ldots d_n, g\}$;

$\epsilon_{Goals} = \{a_1 - \textbf{set}, \ldots a_m - \textbf{set}, b_1 - \textbf{set}, \ldots, b_p - \textbf{set}, g\}$;

$\mathcal{A} = \{a_1, \overline{a_1}, \ldots, a_m, \overline{a_m}, \textbf{fix} - b_1, \ldots, \textbf{fix} - b_p, \textbf{look}\}$, with

    $a_i : \{\langle \overline{a_i - \textbf{set}}, a_i - \textbf{set} \cup \{\overline{d_j} | \neg a_i \in D_j \} \rangle \}$;

    $\overline{a_i} : \{\langle \overline{a_i - \textbf{set}}, a_i - set \cup \{\overline{d_j} | a_i \in D_j \} \rangle \}$;

    $\textbf{fix} - b_i : \{\langle \overline{b_i - \textbf{set}}, b_i - \textbf{set} \cup \{\overline{d_j} | b_i \in D_j \} \cup \{\overline{d_j} | \neg b_i \in D_j \} \rangle \}$;

    $\textbf{look} : \{\langle \{\overline{d_1}, \ldots, \overline{d_m}\}, \{\overline{g}\} \rangle \}$

Actions a_i and $\overline{a_i}$ $(i = 1 \ldots m)$ are deterministic and fix the truth value of a_i to **true** and **false** respectively. $\textbf{fix} - b_i$ and $\textbf{look}$ are as in the proof of Proposition 4 (plus the extra variables $b_i - \textbf{set}$, needed here to ensure that all b_i's will be assigned a truth value in the plan). If G is attained by a plan, then necessarily this plan contains all $\textbf{fix} - b_j$'s (in any order) and for all i, either a_i or $\overline{a_i}$; then, it is a good plan iff the corresponding truth assignment of the a_i's satisfies the 2-QBF instance. $\qquad \square$

These results on nondeterministic planning can be immediately extended to possibilistic planning:

Proposition 5.
Deciding that $N(G|s_o, \langle a_o \ldots a_n \rangle) \geq \alpha$, $\alpha \in]0, 1]$ (ΠPV$\geq$) is co-NP-complete.

Proposition 6.
Deciding that there exists a plan P with polynomial length such that $N(G|s_o, P) \geq \alpha$, $\alpha \in]0, 1]$ (ΠPE$\geq$) is Σ_2^P-complete.

Proof. These are immediate corollaries from Propositions 4 (resp. 5) and 1. $\qquad \square$

Σ_2^P-complete problem is 2-QBF (for "quantified Boolean formula") [30]: show that $\exists a_1 \ldots \exists a_m \forall b_1 \ldots \forall b_p F(a, b)$, where the a_i's and b_j's are Boolean variables and F a formula built on them. The problem remains complete if F is under DNF.

[4] Here is why this result does not work without the restriction that plan length should be polynomially bounded: in the general case, the shortest good plan may have up to 2^n actions where n is the number of propositional variables ([6] for the deterministic case).

Proposition 7.
Deciding that $N(G|s_o, \langle a_o \ldots a_n \rangle) = \alpha$, $0 < \alpha < 1$ (ΠPV=) is DP-complete[5] [6].

Proof. It is based on the following lemma:
for $\beta < 1$, deciding that $N(G|s_o, \langle a_o \ldots a_n \rangle) > \beta$ is co-NP-complete.
The proof of the lemma is very similar to that of Proposition 4: indeed, we know that only a finite number of possibility values is used and we can thus define β^+ as the value immediately above β in the set $\{1-x \mid \exists s, a, s' \text{ s.t. } \pi(s'|a,s) = x\}$. It is clear that $N(G|s_o, \langle a_o \ldots a_n \rangle) > \beta$ iff $N(G|s_o, \langle a_o \ldots a_n \rangle) \geq \beta^+$, which (with Proposition 4) proves the lemma.
(a) membership: obvious since $N(G|s_o, \langle a_o \ldots a_n \rangle) = \alpha$ iff $N(G|s_o, \langle a_o \ldots a_n \rangle) \geq \alpha$ (NP) and not $(N(G|s_o, \langle a_o \ldots a_n \rangle) > \alpha$ (co-NP).
(b) completeness: immediate from Propositions 6 and 7. $\qquad\square$

Conclusions are twofold. First, it appears that possibilistic planning has (up to a linear factor) the same orders of complexity as nondeterministic planning. Second, these orders of complexity are far below those for the corresponding problems in probabilistic planning (also with compact representations): contrarily to possibilistic planning, probabilistic planning basically needs examining all paths (in the worst case), or at least to count them, to compute if the probability to reach the plan is higher than a given threshold. Goldsmith et al. [20] show that probabilistic plan evaluation with succinct representations is PP-complete (while the similar problem for possibilistic planning is co-NP-complete), and polynomial size probabilistic plan existence with succinct representations is NP^{PP}-complete (while the similar problem for possibilistic planning is Σ_2^P-complete). Since co-NP $\subseteq$ PP (the inclusion being likely to be strict), possibilistic planning appears to be easier than probabilistic planning.

5 Conclusions

The main goal of this paper was to present and analyse a possibilistic approach of planning under uncertainty. It was inspired by the work done on the BURI-DAN[25] planner that relies on a probabilistic representation of uncertainty. In practice, it seems more natural and easier to see actions in terms of normal and more or less exceptional effects rather than probable ones.

Besides its representational adequacy, the possibilistic approach has interesting computational properties since the search for γ-acceptable or optimally safe plans amounts to solve induced planning problems that have only crisp nondeterministic actions (i.e. each action having then only normal effects). Moreover,

---

[5] DP is the set of all languages which are the intersection of a language in NP and a language in co-NP. The canonical DP-complete problem is SAT-UNSAT: given two propositional formulas φ, ψ, decide that φ is satisfiable and ψ is not [28].

[6] Obviously, the similar problems for $\alpha = 1$ and $\alpha = 0$ are respectively co-NP-complete (Proposition 4) and co-NP-complete (complementary of the problem studied in the lemma).

in the case of optimal plan generation, the proposed sound and complete POS-PLAN* algorithm is an anytime least-commitment planner; it possesses the additional feature of iteratively solving derived planning problems that are progressively more complex and exploits at each iteration the partial plans developed in the previous ones. The POSPLAN* planner and, consequently, the NDP and POSPLAN algorithms have been implemented in Common Lisp reusing part of BURIDAN's code (in particular its SNLP basis).

The complexity results of the paper show that possibilistic planning is easier than probabilistic planning. They should however be relativized by the fact that the kind of problems suitable for the probabilistic and the possibilistic settings are very different in nature, hence the difficulty to compare these results on a single reference problem. Moreover, there may be efficient and much less complex approximations of probabilistic planning problems.

Acknowledgements The authors are grateful to an anonymous reviewer for pointing out the relevant works of Chrisman, Doan and Haddawy et al. (1995).

References

1. C. Bäckström. *Computational complexity of reasoning about plans*. PhD thesis, University of Linköping, 1992.
2. B. Bonet and H. Geffner. Arguing for decisions: a qualitative model for decision making. In *Proc. of UAI'96*, 1996.
3. C. Boutilier, T. Dean, and S. Hanks. *New Directions in AI Planning*, chapter Planning under uncertainty: structural assumptions and computational leverage, pages 157–172. IOS Press, Amsterdam, 1996.
4. C. Boutilier and R. Dearden. Using abstractions for decision-theoretic planning with time constraints. In *Proceedings AAAI*, pages 1016–1022, 1994.
5. C. Boutilier and D. Poole. Computing optimal policies for partially observable decision processes using compact representations. In *Proceedings AAAI'96*, pages 1168–1175, 1996.
6. T. Bylander. The computational complexity of propositional strips planning. *Artificial Intelligence*, 69:161–204, 1994.
7. A.R. Cassandra, L.P. Kaelbling, and M.L. Littman. Acting optimally in partially observable stochastic domains. In *Proceedings AAAI*, pages 1023–1028, 1994.
8. D. Chapman. Planning for Conjunctive Goals. *Artificial Intelligence*, 32, 1987.
9. L. Chrisman. Abstract probabilistic modeling of action. In *Proceedings AAAI*, pages 28–36, 1992.
10. C. Da Costa Pereira, F. Garcia, J. Lang, and R. Martin-Clouaire. Planning with graded nondeterministic actions: a possibilistic approach. *Int. J. of Intelligent Systems*, 12(12), 1997.
11. M. De Glas and E. Jacopin. An algebric framework for uncertain strips planning. In *Proceedings AIPS*, 1994.
12. T. Dean and M. Boddy. Reasoning about Partially Ordered Events. *Artificial Intelligence*, 36:375–399, 1988.
13. A. Doan. Modeling probabilistic actions for practical decision-theoretic planning. In *Proc. of AIPS'96*, 1996.

14. D. Dubois and H. Prade. *Possibility theory - an approach to computerized processing of uncertainty*. Plenum Press, 1988.

15. D. Dubois and H. Prade. Fuzzy sets and probability: misunderstanding, bridges and gaps. In *Proceeding of 2nd IEEE Int. Conf. on Fuzzy Systems*, pages 1059–1068, 1993.

16. H. Erol, D. Nau, and V.S. Subrahmanian. Complexity, decidability and undecidability results for domain-independent planning. *Artificial Intelligence*, 76:75–88, 1995.

17. H. Fargier, J. Lang, and R. Sabbadin. Towards qualitative approaches to multistage decision making. In *Proc. of IPMU'96*, 1996.

18. F. Garcia and P. Laborie. *New Directions in AI Planning*, chapter Hierarchisation of the Search Space in Temporal Planning, pages 217–232. IOS Press, Amsterdam, 1996.

19. R. Goldman and M. Boddy. Epsilon-safe planning. In *Proc. of UAI'94*, pages 253–261, 1994.

20. J. Goldsmith, M. Littman, and M. Mundhenk. The complexity of plan existence and evaluation in probabilistic domains. In *Proc. of UAI'97*, pages 182–189, 1997.

21. P. Haddawy, A. Doan, and R. Goodwin. Efficient decision-theoretic planning: Techniques and empirical analysis. In *Proc. of UAI'95*, pages 229–236, 1995.

22. P. Haddawy and P. Hanks. Issues in decision-theoretic planning: utility functions for deadline goals. In *Proc. of the 3rd Int. Conf. on Principles of Knowledge Representation and Reasoning (KR'92)*, pages 71–82, 1992.

23. S. Kambhampati and D.S. Nau. On the nature and role of modal truth criteria in planning. *Artificial Intelligence*, 1996.

24. C. Knoblock. Automatically generating abstractions for planning. *Artificial Intelligence*, 68:243–302, 1994.

25. N. Kushmerick, S. Hanks, and D.W Weld. An algorithm for probabilistic planning. *Artificial Intelligence*, 76:239–286, 1995.

26. M.L. Littman. Probabilistic propositional planning: representations and complexity. In *Proceedings AAAI*, pages 748–754, 1997.

27. D. McAllester and D. Rosenblitt. Systematic nonlinear planning. In *Proceedings AAAI*, pages 634–639, 1991.

28. C.H. Papadimitriou. *Computational complexity*. Addison-Wesley, 1994.

29. J.S. Penberthy and D. Weld. UCPOP: A sound, complete, partial-order planner for ADL. In *Proc. of the 3rd Int. Conf. on Principles of Knowledge Representation and Reasoning (KR'92)*, pages 103–114, 1992.

30. L. Stockmeyer. The polynomial-time hierarchy. *Theoretical Computer Science*, 3:1–22, 1977.

31. S. Thiébaux, J. Hertzberg, W. Shoaff, and M. Schneider. A stochastic model of actions and plans for anytime planning under uncertainty. *Int. J. of Intelligent Systems*, 10(2):155–183, 1995.

32. Q. Yang and J. D. Tenenberg. Abstracting a nonlinear least commitment planner. In *Proceedings AAAI*, pages 204–209, 1990.

Planning with Sensing for a Mobile Robot

Giuseppe De Giacomo, Luca Iocchi, Daniele Nardi, Riccardo Rosati

Dipartimento di Informatica e Sistemistica
Università di Roma "La Sapienza"
Via Salaria 113, 00198 Roma, Italy
<degiacomo,iocchi,nardi,rosati>@dis.uniroma1.it

Abstract. We present an attempt to reconcile the theoretical work on reasoning about action with the realization of agents, in particular mobile robots. Specifically, we present a logical framework for representing dynamic systems based on description logics, which allows for the formalization of sensing actions. We address the generation of conditional plans by defining a suitable reasoning method in which a plan is extracted from a constructive proof of a query expressing a given goal. We also present an implementation of such a logical framework, which has been tested on the mobile robot "Tino".

1 Introduction

In recent years there has been an attempt to reconcile the theoretical work on reasoning about action with the realization of agents, in particular mobile robots. Such a field of research has been referred to as *Cognitive Robotics* [10].

A mobile robot can indeed be regarded as an intelligent agent, that is designed both to achieve high-level goals and to be able to promptly react and adjust its behavior based on the information acquired through the sensors. Reactive capabilities are necessary to cope with the uncertainties of the real-world; action planning is important as well, if the robot is faced with situations where the knowledge of the environment is incomplete, subject to varying constraints. The integration of the two kinds of functionalities mentioned above is a critical issue in the design of intelligent agents.

The work reported in the present paper builds on a previous proposal [3], which provides a formal framework for reasoning about action derived from *dynamic logics* [16] and exploits the correspondence between such logics and *description logics*. A number of features that had been analyzed for description logics have proved useful for reasoning about action. Specifically, we have extended the language with an epistemic operator interpreted in terms of minimal knowledge, that allows us to express the knowledge about actions in such a way that we can effectively address the planning problem. We have implemented our proposal for reasoning about action on the mobile robot "Tino", which belongs to the *Erratic* family [8]. The implementation relies on the reasoning facilities offered by the knowledge representation system CLASSIC.

In this paper we extend the previous proposal with the ability of expressing sensing actions [18,11,6], i.e. knowledge producing actions that affect the agent's

Constructs	PDLs	DLs	DL Semantics
Atomic concept/proposition	A	A	$A^{\mathcal{I}} \subseteq \Delta$
Atomic role/action	R	R	$R^{\mathcal{I}} \subseteq \Delta \times \Delta$
Named individual	—	s	$s^{\mathcal{I}} \in \Delta$
True	tt	$\top$	Δ
False	ff	$\bot$	$\emptyset$
Conjunction	$C \wedge D$	$C \sqcap D$	$C^{\mathcal{I}} \cap D^{\mathcal{I}}$
Disjunction	$C \vee D$	$C \sqcup D$	$C^{\mathcal{I}} \cup D^{\mathcal{I}}$
Negation	$\neg C$	$\neg C$	$\Delta \setminus C^{\mathcal{I}}$
Universal quantification	$[R]C$	$\forall R.C$	$\{d \in \Delta \mid \forall d'. (d, d') \in R^{\mathcal{I}} \Rightarrow d' \in C^{\mathcal{I}}\}$
Existential quantification	$\langle R \rangle C$	$\exists R.C$	$\{d \in \Delta \mid \exists d'. (d, d') \in R^{\mathcal{I}} \wedge d' \in C^{\mathcal{I}}\}$
Inclusion assertion	$C \Rightarrow D$	$C \sqsubseteq D$	$C^{\mathcal{I}} \subseteq D^{\mathcal{I}}$ for every $\mathcal{I}$
Instance assertion	—	$C(s)$ $R(s_1, s_2)$	$s^{\mathcal{I}} \in C^{\mathcal{I}}$ $(s_1^{\mathcal{I}}, s_2^{\mathcal{I}}) \in R^{\mathcal{I}}$ for every $\mathcal{I}$

Table 1. Description logic $\mathcal{ALC}$

knowledge, but not the environment. We also extend the implementation with the ability of devising and executing conditional plans. From the point of view of the formalism, a new kind of axioms for sensing actions and the ability of propagating knowledge to successor states (in a controlled way) is introduced. From the point of view of the implementation, we design a more powerful method for devising the plan, and extend the capabilities of the plan execution component and of the underlying control system by providing new behaviors realizing the sensing actions.

The paper is organized as follows. We first recall the basic elements of our approach. We then focus on sensing actions and on the method for devising plans in the presence of this kind of actions. We finally describe the implementation of the new features in our robot "Tino".

2 Epistemic DL-based framework for representing actions

Our general framework for representing dynamic systems was originally proposed in [3]. It follows the lines of Rosenschein's work [16], based on propositional dynamic logics (PDLs) [9], and it makes use of the tight correspondence between PDLs and description logics (DLs) [19,4] that allows for considering PDLs and DLs as notational variants of each other. We use the notation of DLs, focusing on the well-known DL $\mathcal{ALC}$, corresponding to the standard PDL with atomic programs only. Table 1 summarizes the syntax and the semantics of $\mathcal{ALC}$ and the corresponding PDL. In addition, we use the two nonmonotonic modal operators: a *minimal knowledge operator* **K** and a *default assumption operator* **A**. These are interpreted according to the nonmonotonic modal logic *MKNF* [12], and give rise to the so-called autoepistemic description logic $\mathcal{ALCK}_{\mathcal{NF}}$ [5]. We do not have the space here to formally introduce such a logical framework, we refer the reader to [3] and [5]. Rather, we give an intuition of the underlying semantics.

The interpretation structures of DLs (PDLs) are essentially *graphs* labeled both on nodes and arcs. *Nodes*, called *individuals* in DLs, (states in PDLs) are labeled by *concepts* (formulae in PDLs) that denote properties of individuals. Arcs, called *links* in DL (state transitions in PDLs) are labeled by *roles* (actions in PDLs). Such interpretation structures can be concretely bound to the robot's behavior (possible courses of actions): individuals represent states of the robot and are labeled by concepts representing what is true in that state; links between individuals represent transitions between states of the robot, and are labeled by roles representing the actions that cause the state transition.

However, in general there is not enough information about the robot's environment to model its behavior by means of a single interpretation structure, since the robot's behavior will depend on external circumstances that will be known only at execution time. Rather, we model the robot's behavior with suitable axioms which reflect our (partial) knowledge and which are satisfied by *multiple* interpretation structures. As a consequence, in order to decide which action to perform next the robot can use only those facts that are "valid" in its current state, i.e. that are true in the representative of its current state in all possible interpretation structures. To do so the logical formalism must provide:

- A mechanism to isolate an individual representative of a given robot's state, in each possible interpretation, establishing a one-to-one mapping between the individuals in the different interpretation structures that represent the same robot's state.
- A mechanism to represent that a certain property (concept) is "valid" in a robot's state, i.e. true in the representatives of that state in all possible interpretations.

The minimal knowledge operator $\mathbf{K}$ gives us both the above mechanisms. On the one hand, it allows for isolating the representatives of robot's states in the different structures establishing a one-to-one mapping among them through the so-called *known individuals*. In general, known individuals will be only those that are explicitly *named* in some axiom (in our case, we will have a single such named individual, *init*, denoting the initial state of the robot) and those generated by a special use of $\mathbf{K}$ on roles denoting actions. On the other hand, it allows for denoting the "validity" of a property in a robot's state. In particular, an epistemic implication of the form $\mathbf{K}C \sqsubseteq D$ differs from the non-modal implication $C \sqsubseteq D$ since D is concluded for a given known individual only if C is necessarily true ("valid") for that known individual. This prevents forms of reasoning by cases such as the following: let $\Sigma = \{[C_1 \sqcup C_2](init), \mathbf{K}C_1 \sqsubseteq D, \mathbf{K}C_2 \sqsubseteq D\}$, then $\Sigma \not\models D(init)$, while let $\Sigma' = \{[C_1 \sqcup C_2](init), C_1 \sqsubseteq D, C_2 \sqsubseteq D\}$, then $\Sigma' \models D(init)$. Moreover, for $\mathbf{K}C \sqsubseteq D$ the contrapositive does not hold, i.e. $\neg D$ does not imply $\neg C$. Epistemic sentences $\mathbf{K}C \sqsubseteq D$ can be naturally interpreted in terms of *rules*, i.e. a forward reasoning mechanism.

The default assumption operator $\mathbf{A}$ allows for expressing justifications of default rules [15], and the combined usage of $\mathbf{K}$ and $\mathbf{A}$ allows for formalizing defaults in terms of modal formulas. We use it here in relation with sensing actions in a very specific way (see below).

3 Robot's behavior representation

We distinguish two kinds of robot's actions: *moving actions* and *sensing actions*. Both kinds of actions are considered *deterministic*, in the sense that a unique successor state will be generated by each action. We first focus on moving actions only as in [3], then in the next section we consider sensing actions as well. Here, we call moving actions all the actions that result in a change in the enviroment, like, for example, a change in the position of the robot. Like most approaches to reasoning about action [14,20] we express our knowledge in terms of a finite set of axioms forming a knowledge base Σ. Such axioms are partitioned in the classes below, each formalized in a specific way.

Static axioms (Γ_S)[1] They are used for representing background knowledge, which is invariant with respect to the execution of actions. Static axioms hold in every state, and they do not depend on actions. We formalize static axioms as $\mathcal{ALC}$ inclusion assertions, not involving action-roles, although in general they can involve other roles used for structuring concept (i.e. property) descriptions and form complex taxonomies of properties that are typical of DLs.

Action precondition axioms (Γ_P) They describe under which circumstances it is possible to execute an action. We formalize action precondition axioms through epistemic sentences of the form:

$$\mathbf{K}C \sqsubseteq \exists \mathbf{K}R_M.\top \tag{1}$$

where C is an $\mathcal{ALC}$ concept and R_M a moving action. This axiom can be read as: if C holds in the (known individual denoting the) current state s, then there exists a (known individual denoting a) state s' which is the R_M-successor of s.

Effect axioms (Γ_E) They specify the effects of executing an action R_M in a state satisfying certain *premises* C. We formalize effect axioms through epistemic sentences of the form:

$$\mathbf{K}C \sqsubseteq \forall \mathbf{K}R_M.\mathbf{K}D \tag{2}$$

where C and D are $\mathcal{ALC}$ concepts. This axiom can be read as: if C holds in the (known individual denoting the) current state s, then for each (known individual denoting an) R-successor s' of s, D holds in s' in all interpretations.[2]

Initial state description axioms (Γ_I) They specify the properties that hold in the initial state of the robot. We formalize them by introducing explicitly a named (and hence known) individual *init* denoting the initial state, and instance assertions of the form:

$$C(init) \tag{3}$$

where C is an $\mathcal{ALC}$ concept. This axiom can be read as: C holds in the state *init* in every possible interpretation.

The use of the **K** operator in the antecedent of the action precondition axioms restricts the applicability of an action to those states in which the precondition for the action are known by the agent. In the initial state, the only known

---

[1] Sometimes called *domain contraints* or *state constraints*.

[2] Note that, since actions are deterministic, there is at most one R-successor of s.

properties are those implied by the initial state description axioms and the static axioms; in any other state, the known properties are those implied by the effects of the last executed action (together with the static axioms).

We do not try to address the frame problem for moving actions by enforcing some general form of *common sense inertia law*: if a property C persists after a certain action R_M, the effect axiom $\mathbf{K}C \sqsubseteq \forall \mathbf{K}R_M.\mathbf{K}C$ must be included. Obviously some general default persistence mechanism would be highly desirable and in this paper we devise such a mechanism for the special case of sensing actions (see next section).

Planning problem In deductive planning one is typically interested in answering the following question: "Is there a sequence of actions that, starting from an initial state, leads to a state where a given property (the goal) holds?". This is captured in our framework by the following logical implication:

$$\Sigma \models PLAN\_FOR\_G(init) \tag{4}$$

where: (i) Σ is the knowledge base including the static axioms Γ_S, the action preconditions axioms Γ_P, the effect axioms Γ_E, and the initial state description axioms Γ_I; (ii) $PLAN\_FOR\_G(init)$ denotes that $PLAN\_FOR\_G$ holds in the initial state *init*, where $PLAN\_FOR\_G$ is *any* concept belonging to the set $\mathcal{P}_S$ defined inductively as: $\mathbf{K}G \in \mathcal{P}_S$; if $C \in \mathcal{P}_S$, then $\exists \mathbf{K}R_{M_i}.C \in \mathcal{P}_S$, for every moving action R_{M_i}.[3]

In other words, $PLAN\_FOR\_G$ stands for any concept expression of the form $\exists \mathbf{K}R_{M_1}.\exists \mathbf{K}R_{M_2}.\ldots.\exists \mathbf{K}R_{M_n}.\mathbf{K}G$ in which $n \geq 0$ and each R_{M_i} is a moving action, and it expresses the fact that from the initial state *init* there exists a sequence of successors (the same in every interpretation) that terminates in a state (the same in every interpretation) where G holds (in every interpretation).

4 Sensing

We now extend our framework in order to deal with sensing actions. Sensing actions are special actions that change the knowledge of the robot without changing the state of the external world in which the robot is embedded. Such an assumption may seem restrictive for sensing actions that can produce changes in the environment (i.e. sensing through the sonars may require motion). This is in fact not the case as we shall see later on, while it is useful to characterize sensing actions simply as knowledge producing actions.

We assume that the robot can sense certain facts represented by special atomic propositions, called *sensed propositions*; each sensed proposition is associated with a specific sensing action.

Action precondition axioms in Γ_P for the action R_S which senses the proposition S have the form:

$$\mathbf{K}C \sqcap \neg \mathbf{A}S \sqcap \neg \mathbf{A}\neg S \sqsubseteq \exists \mathbf{K}R_S.\top \tag{5}$$

---

[3] We use $\exists \mathbf{K}R_{M_i}.C$ as an abbreviation for $\exists \mathbf{K}R_{M_i}.\top \sqcap \forall \mathbf{K}R_{M_i}.C$. Indeed, since actions are assumed to be deterministic, the two concept expressions are equivalent.

where C is an $\mathcal{ALC}$ concept. It can be read as: if C holds in the current state s and the truth value of S is not known (i.e. it is consistent to assume both that S holds in s in every interpretation and that $\neg S$ holds in s in every interpretation), then it is possible to perform R_S, in the sense that there exists a unique R_S-successor s' of s which is the same in every interpretation.

Each sensing action R_S for the sensing proposition S has a *unique* **effect axiom** in Γ_E:

$$\mathbf{K}\top \sqsubseteq \forall \mathbf{K}R_S.\mathbf{K}S \sqcup \mathbf{K}\neg S \tag{6}$$

This axiom expresses that after having performed the action R_S the robot knows the truth value of the sensed proposition S, i.e. it knows *whether* S holds or not.

We enforce the following **frame axiom schemas** (Γ_{FR}):

$$\mathbf{K}\varphi \sqsubseteq \forall \mathbf{K}R_S.\mathbf{K}\varphi \tag{7}$$

one for each sensing action R_S, where φ stands for any $\mathcal{ALC}$ concept.[4] This propagates all concepts that hold in the current state s to the next state s'. The expression $\neg \mathbf{A}S \sqcap \neg \mathbf{A}\neg S$ in the premises of the precondition axioms for R_S prevents the execution of R_S in case either $\mathbf{K}S$ or $\mathbf{K}\neg S$ holds in the previous state. Hence, no contradiction may be generated from instances of the frame axiom schemas and the effect axiom for R_S.

Planning problem with sensing The robot's ability of sensing can be used to extend the notion of plan considered before to the notion of *conditional plan*. Indeed the robot may use its sensing capability to choose different courses of actions leading to a given goal, depending on the value of the sensed propositions. The planning problem then becomes:

$$\Sigma \models COND\_PLAN\_FOR\_G(init) \tag{8}$$

where: (i) Σ is the knowledge base including the static axioms Γ_S, the action precondition axioms Γ_P and the effect axioms Γ_E for both moving and sensing actions plus the frame axiom schema Γ_{FR} for the sensing actions, and the initial state description axioms Γ_I; (ii) $COND\_PLAN\_FOR\_G(init)$ denotes that $COND\_PLAN\_FOR\_G$ holds in the initial state, where $COND\_PLAN\_FOR\_G$ is *any* concept belonging to the set $\mathcal{P}_C$ defined inductively as follows:

1. $\mathbf{K}G \in \mathcal{P}_C$;
2. if $C \in \mathcal{P}_C$, then $\exists \mathbf{K}R_{M_i}.C \in \mathcal{P}_C$, for every moving action R_{M_i};
3. if $C_1, C_2 \in \mathcal{P}_C$, then $\exists \mathbf{K}R_{S_i}.(\mathbf{K}S_i \sqcap C_1) \sqcup (\mathbf{K}\neg S_i \sqcap C_2) \in \mathcal{P}_C$, for every sensing action R_{S_i}.

5 Plan generation

To the aim of generating plans in the framework proposed, we introduce the notion of *first-order extension* of a (epistemic) knowledge base $\Sigma = \Gamma_S \cup \Gamma_P \cup$

---

[4] In fact, a number of instances which is linear in the size of the knowledge base suffices (see the following section).

$\Gamma_E \cup \Gamma_{FR} \cup \Gamma_I$ containing the specification of the robot's behavior in the terms described above. Informally, the first-order extension of Σ (denoted as $FOE(\Sigma)$) is an $\mathcal{ALC}$ knowledge base which consists of: (1) the static axioms in Γ_S; (2) the specification of the initial state (the assertions on $init$ in Γ_I) augmented by the assertions which are consequences (up to renaming of individuals) of the epistemic sentences in Σ. The FOE of Σ provides a unique characterization of the knowledge that is shared by all the models of Σ, which is relevant wrt the planning problem.

In order to compute the first-order extension, we replace each sensing action R_S by two special actions R_S^+ and R_S^-. We denote by $\Gamma_E^{\pm}$ the set of effect axioms Γ_E in which those for the sensing actions R_S are replaced by:

$$\mathbf{K}\top \sqsubseteq \forall \mathbf{K} R_S^+ . \mathbf{K}S \qquad\qquad \mathbf{K}\top \sqsubseteq \forall \mathbf{K} R_S^- . \mathbf{K}\neg S.$$

We also use only a finite number of instances of the frame axiom schemas. We denote by $\Gamma_{IFR}^{\pm}$ the set of axioms:

$$\mathbf{K}C \sqsubseteq \forall \mathbf{K} R_S^+ . \mathbf{K}C \qquad\qquad \mathbf{K}C \sqsubseteq \forall \mathbf{K} R_S^- . \mathbf{K}C$$

obtained by: (1) instantiating the frame axiom schemas in Γ_{FR} for each concept C such that either $C(init) \in \Gamma_I$, or $\mathbf{K}C$ is in the postcondition of some effect axiom in Γ_E (i.e., C such that $\mathbf{K}D \sqsubseteq \forall \mathbf{K} R_M . \mathbf{K}C$, or $C, \neg C$ such that $\mathbf{K}\top \sqsubseteq \forall \mathbf{K} R_S . \mathbf{K}C \sqcup \mathbf{K}\neg C$ in Γ_E); (2) replacing each sensing action R_S by the two special actions R_S^+ and R_S^-.

The FOE of Σ is computed by the following algorithm:

ALGORITHM FOE
INPUT: $\Sigma = \Gamma_S \cup \Gamma_P \cup \Gamma_E \cup \Gamma_{FR} \cup \Gamma_I$
OUTPUT: $FOE(\Sigma)$

    PROCEDURE CREATE_NEW_STATE(s, R)
    begin
      $s' = $ NEW state name;
      $\mathcal{A}' = \mathcal{A} \cup \{R(s, s')\} \cup \{D(s') \mid D \in POST(s, R, \Gamma_S \cup \mathcal{A}, \Gamma_E^{\pm} \cup \Gamma_{IFR}^{\pm})\}$
      if there exists a state $s'' \in$ ALL_STATES **such that**
        $CONCEPTS(\Gamma_S \cup \mathcal{A}, s'') = CONCEPTS(\Gamma_S \cup \mathcal{A}', s')$
      then $\mathcal{A} = \mathcal{A} \cup R(s, s'')$
      else begin
        $\mathcal{A} = \mathcal{A}'$;
        ACTIVE_STATES = ACTIVE_STATES $\cup \{s'\}$;
        ALL_STATES = ALL_STATES $\cup \{s'\}$
      end
    end;
begin
  ACTIVE_STATES = $\{init\}$;
  ALL_STATES = $\{init\}$;
  $\mathcal{A} = \Gamma_I$;
  repeat
    $s =$ choose(ACTIVE_STATES);
    for each moving action R_M **do**
      if there exists $\mathbf{K}C \sqsubseteq \exists \mathbf{K} R_M . \top \in \Gamma_P$

        such that $\Gamma_S \cup \mathcal{A} \models C(s)$
    then
        CREATE_NEW_STATE(s, R_M);
    for each sensing action R_S **do**
    if there exists $\mathbf{K}C \sqcap \mathbf{A}S \sqcap \mathbf{A}\neg S \sqsubseteq \exists \mathbf{K}R_S.\top \in \Gamma_P$
        such that $\Gamma_S \cup \mathcal{A} \models C(s)$ **and** $\Gamma_S \cup \mathcal{A} \not\models S(s)$ **and** $\Gamma_S \cup \mathcal{A} \not\models \neg S(s)$
    then begin
        CREATE_NEW_STATE(s, R_S^+);
        CREATE_NEW_STATE(s, R_S^-)
    end;
    ACTIVE_STATES = ACTIVE_STATES $-\{s\}$
until ACTIVE_STATES = $\emptyset$;
return $\Gamma_S \cup \mathcal{A}$
end.

In the above algorithm, $CONCEPTS(\Gamma_S \cup \mathcal{A}, s) = \{C \mid \Gamma_S \cup \mathcal{A} \models C(s)\}$ denotes the set of concepts that are *valid* for the explicitly named individual s, occurring in the set of instance assertions $\mathcal{A}$, wrt the $\mathcal{ALC}$ knowledge base $\Gamma_S \cup \mathcal{A}$. $POST(s, R, \Gamma_S \cup \mathcal{A}, \Gamma_E^\pm \cup \Gamma_{IFR}^\pm) = \{D \mid \mathbf{K}C \sqsubseteq \forall \mathbf{K}R.\mathbf{K}D \in \Gamma_E^\pm \cup \Gamma_{IFR}^\pm \text{ and } \Gamma_S \cup \mathcal{A} \models C(s)\}$ denotes the effect of the application of the all triggered rules belonging to the set $\Gamma_E^\pm \cup \Gamma_{IFR}^\pm$ involving the action R in the state s, namely the set of postconditions (concepts) of the rules which are triggered by s.

Informally, the algorithm, starting from the initial state *init*, applies to each state the rules in the set $\Gamma_E^\pm \cup \Gamma_{IFR}^\pm$ which are triggered by such a state. A new state is thus generated, unless a state with the same properties has already been created. In this way the effect of the rules is computed, obtaining a sort of "completion" of the knowledge base.

The FOE is unique, that is, every order of extraction of the states from the set $ACTIVE\_STATES$ produces the same set of assertions, up to re-naming of states. Moreover, the algorithm terminates, that is, the condition $ACTIVE\_STATES = \emptyset$ is eventually reached, since the number of states generated is bound by the number of rules in $\Gamma_E^\pm \cup \Gamma_{IFR}^\pm$. More precisely, the number of generated states n_s is $n_s \leq 2^{n_r+1}$ with n_r equal to the number of rules in $\Gamma_E^\pm \cup \Gamma_{IFR}^\pm$, i.e., $n_r = n_{em} + 2n_{es} + 2n_{fr}(n_e + n_i)$, where: n_{em} and n_{es} are the number of effect axioms in Γ_E for moving and sensing actions respectively (n_{es} is equal to the number of sensing actions); $n_{fr} = |\Gamma_{FR}|$ is the number of frame axiom schemas (which is again equal to the number of sensing actions); $n_e = |\Gamma_E|$ is the total number of effect axioms; $n_i = |\Gamma_I|$ is the number of initial state description axioms in Γ_I. Observe that n_s depends essentially on the size of Γ_E and Γ_I.

Finally, the condition $CONCEPTS(\Gamma_S \cup \mathcal{A}, s) = CONCEPTS(\Gamma_S \cup \mathcal{A}', s')$ can be checked by verifying whether, for each concept C such that either $C(init) \in \Gamma_I$ or $\mathbf{K}C$ is in the postcondition of some axiom in Γ_E, $\Gamma_S \cup \mathcal{A} \models C(s)$ iff $\Gamma_S \cup \mathcal{A}' \models C(s')$.

Next we show that the notion of first-order extension constitutes the basis of a sound and complete planning method. More specifically, we show that the planning problem in Σ expressed by (8) can be reduced to an entailment problem in $FOE(\Sigma)$, by making use of the following translation function $\tau(\cdot)$.

Definition 1. Let C be a concept expression representing a plan (i.e. belonging to the set $\mathcal{P}_C$). Then, $\tau(C)$ is the concept expression obtained as follows:

1. if $C = \mathbf{K}G$ then $\tau(C) = \mathbf{K}G$;
2. if $C = \exists\mathbf{K}R_{M_i}.C_1$ then $\tau(C) = \exists\mathbf{K}R_{M_i}.\tau(C_1)$;
3. if $C = \exists\mathbf{K}R_{S_i}.(\mathbf{K}S_i \sqcap C_1) \sqcup (\mathbf{K}\neg S_i \sqcap C_2)$ then $\tau(C) = \exists\mathbf{K}R_{S_i}^+.\tau(C_1) \sqcap \exists\mathbf{K}R_{S_i}^-.\tau(C_2)$.

Theorem 2. Let $C \in \mathcal{P}_C$. Then, $\Sigma \models C(init)$ iff $FOE(\Sigma) \models \tau(C)(init)$.

6 Implementation

The framework previously presented has been actually used to describe the knowledge of the mobile robot Tino of the Erratic family [8]. In such implementation we use a restricted DL language to represent the robot's knowledge, which allows us to rely on the reasoning services provided by the well-known DL system CLASSIC [2]. In particular, we make use of the built-in instance checking mechanism to check the validity of a concept in a state, and of triggering of rules to propagate effects. However, CLASSIC does not provide an implementation for **K** and **A**, which are therefore handled by ad hoc attached procedures.

The planning procedure, given an initial state and a goal, generates a conditional plan that, when executed starting from the initial state, leads to a state in which the goal is satisfied. Furthermore, dynamic execution of plans is supervised by the monitor, which is responsible for integrating planning and control.

Generating conditional plans Conditional plans can in principle be generated in two steps. First, the FOE of the knowledge base is generated (using the algorithm above); such a knowledge base can be seen as an action graph representing all possible plans starting from the initial state. Then, such a graph is visited, building a term (the conditional plan) representing a tree in which: (i) sensing actions generate branches; (ii) each branch leads to a state satisfying the goal. Obviously, several strategies can be applied to implement this method, and they are not addressed in this paper.

A difficulty for conditional planners is the large number of states, due to the presence of different branches related to sensing actions. However, in most cases, the knowledge obtained by sensing actions does not need to be propagated through all moving actions. For example, when the robot senses whether a door is open, it could use this information just to decide whether or not to enter this door, and then forget it when the selected moving action is executed.

With respect to the propagation of sensed knowledge, we can distinguish the following two limit cases:

1. Sensed knowledge is propagated only through sensing actions, according to the frame axioms schemas Γ_{FR}. The sub-graph generated by a sequence of sensing actions is such that all its states that have an R_M-successor for some moving action R_M have in fact the same R_M-successor. In other words there is a confluence of edges labeled with R_M from the states in the sub-graph to a single successor state. In this case we get the "minimum" number of possible

resulting states. Observe that this confluence is the result of forgetting sensed knowledge acquired in the sub-graph.

2. Sensed knowledge is propagated through every action. This requires the use of explicit frame axioms for propagating sensed propositions through moving actions; such frame axioms are effect axioms of the form $KS \sqsubseteq \forall KR_M.KS$, one for each moving action R_M and for each sensed proposition S. In this case we get the "maximum" number of possible resulting states.

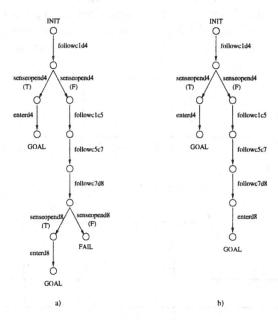

Fig. 1. Conditional plans

It is straightforward in our setting to model which (if any) knowledge acquired by sensing is propagated: it is sufficient to write explicit frame axioms about the persistence of the chosen sensed properties through moving actions. On the other hand, we assume that all knowledge is propagated thorough sensing actions by enforcing the related frame axioms schemas in Γ_{FR}.

Notice that, when sensed knowledge is not propagated through moving actions, we cannot actually make use of static axioms modeling relationships among sensed propositions, for example we cannot make use of the fact that at least one of the two doors leading to a room is open to show that a plan for reaching the room exists.

Our notion of plan is quite strong: we require a plan to exist whatever the truth values of sensed propositions are. We can introduce a weaker notion of conditional plan. In a *weak conditional plan* we only require that at least one branch will lead to the goal. It is straightforward to modify our formal notion of plan accordingly. Our planner is able to generate a weak conditional plan, if a strong one does not exist.

Let us consider now the following example: in the map of Fig. 2 a room is accessible from two different doors (named *Door4* and *Door8*), the robot is in the upper corridor and its goal is to reach this room. Suppose that the robot does not have any static knowledge about these doors. Then a strong conditional plan does not exist and the planner is able to generate the weak conditional plan graphically represented in Fig. 1a), which is a weak plan because there is a branch in which the plan fails, corresponding to the situation in which both the doors are closed. Suppose now that in the same situation we say the robot that at least one of the two doors is open, by adding the following static axiom:[5] $\top \sqsubseteq Door4Open \sqcup Door8Open$. In this case the strong plan of Fig. 1b) will be generated, in which, if the first door is known to be closed, then no sensing action is done on the other door, which is known to be open.

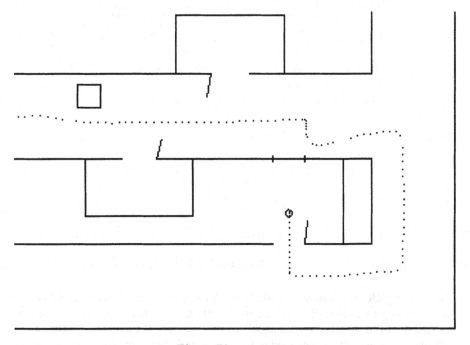

Fig. 2. Plan execution

In Fig. 2 a real execution of the strong plan is shown: the first door of the room is closed, while the second one is open; the robot, after reaching the first door, stops in front of it, executes the sensing action[6] and decides which action to perform next, that is it selects at run-time the right branch of the plan without an off-line replanning.[7]

---

[5] The disjunction, which is not present in CLASSIC, is simulated by the rules $\mathbf{K}Door4Closed \sqsubseteq Door8Open$ and $\mathbf{K}Door8Closed \sqsubseteq Door4Open$.

[6] Note that during a sensing action the robot can actually move, however such movements do not change its high-level state, such as, for example, being close to a door.

[7] Although it is not visible in the picture, the robot does not stop for sensing in front of the second door.

In the previous implementation (without sensing actions) such a goal would be achieved by attempting to enter the first door (roaming in front of the door during the plan failure time-out), and by generating a new plan after the failure of the action.

Dynamic execution of plans The reactive capabilities of the mobile robot Tino are based on a fuzzy controller [17,7], which provides integrated routines for sonar sensor interpretation, map building, and navigation. The control problem is decomposed into small units of control, called (low-level) *behaviors*, that are distinguished in reactive ones like avoiding obstacles, and (low-level) goal-oriented ones, like following a corridor. A blending mechanism is used to integrate reactive and goal-oriented behaviors, so that the robot can follow a corridor while avoiding obstacles.

The integration of planning and control in our robot is characterized by the mapping between high-level actions and goal-oriented behaviors. Indeed, high-level actions can be seen as goals to be achieved by the controller through the activation of appropriate behaviors. The dynamic execution of plans is achieved by a monitor responsible of integrating planning and control by both translating high-level actions into goal-oriented behaviors and scheduling the activation of such behaviors, taking care of choosing the correct branch of the plan according to the result of sensing actions. The monitor also checks the correct execution of the behaviors handling the possible plan failures and requests for replanning.

The introduction of sensing actions requires the design and implementation of *sensing behaviors*. We have extended the set of behaviors of the robot by adding the *SenseOpenDoor* one, that is able to determine whether a specified door is open. This behavior is based on sonar sensor interpretation and returns to the monitor a truth value, indicating the success of a sensing action, which will be used to decide which action to perform next. Notably, the robot moves while performing this behavior. However, the state is not specified by the absolute position of the robot, but rather by a property, such as being close to the door. The action *SenseOpenDoor* does not change the state of the robot since it is expected to leave the robot in the state close to the door, even if the actual position may have changed. Such a change does not matter as long as the subsequent action (for example entering the door) can be successfully accomplished.

7 Conclusions

In this paper we have proposed a logical framework for reasoning about action which provides for the formalization of sensing actions. In particular, we have shown that the use of the epistemic state of the agent (represented through the modal operators of **K** and **A**) allows for the formalization of sensing actions. Our approach has strong connections with previous research on logical formalization of knowledge-producing actions [18,13], which has pointed out the fact that a formalization of sensing actions must satisfy the properties of *non-forgetting* and *minimal learning*.

Our work on sensing is also related to [6], which presents a formalization of sensing actions based on an extension of STRIPS constructs. Sensing actions are distinguished by means of an annotation mechanism on the postconditions. A particular use of annotated propositions allows for expressing constraints on the plan, for example sensing the color of a door in order to enter into a room with a blue door is allowed, while painting a door blue in order to enter into such a room is forbidden. We are currently studying the possibility of adding plan constraints to our planner. In particular, we want to exploit the ideas reported in [1], which have been shown effective for speeding up the planning process.

Acknowledgments This research has been partially supported by MURST 60%. We gratefully thank Alessandro Saffiotti for his useful comments on an earlier version of the paper.

References

1. F. Bacchus and F. Kabanza. Using temporal logic to control search in a forward chaining planner. In *Proc. of the 3rd European Workshop on Planning*, 1995.
2. A. Borgida, R. J. Brachman, D. L. McGuinness, and L. Alperin Resnick. CLASSIC: A structural data model for objects. In *Proc. of ACM SIGMOD*, pages 59–67, 1989.
3. G. De Giacomo, L. Iocchi, D. Nardi, and R. Rosati. Moving a robot: the KR&R approach at work. In *Proc. of KR-96*, 1996.
4. G. De Giacomo and M. Lenzerini. Boosting the correspondence between description logics and propositional dynamic logics. In *Proc. of AAAI-94*, pages 205–212, 1994.
5. F. M. Donini, D. Nardi, and R. Rosati. Autoepistemic description logics. In *Proc. of IJCAI-97*, pages 136–141, 1997.
6. O. Etzioni, S. Hanks, D. Weld, D. Draper, N. Lesh, and M. Williamson. An approach to planning with incomplete information. *Proc. of KR-92*, 1992.
7. K. Konolige, K. Myers, E. Ruspini, and A. Saffiotti. The Saphira architecture: A design for autonomy. *Journal of Experimental and Theoretical Artificial Intelligence*, 9(1):215–235, 1997.
8. K. Konolige. Erratic competes with the big boys. *AAAI Magazine*, 2: 61–67, 1995.
9. D. Kozen and J. Tiuryn. Logics of programs. In *Handbook of Theoretical Computer Science*, pages 790–840. Elsevier, 1990.
10. Y. Lesperance, H. J. Levesque, F. Lin, D. Marcu, R. Reiter, and R. B. Scherl. A logical approach to high-level robot programming. In *AAAI Fall Symposium on Control of the Physical World by Intelligent Systems*, 1994.
11. H. J. Levesque. What is planning in presence of sensing? In *Proc. of AAAI-96*, pages 1139–1149, 1996.
12. V. Lifschitz. Minimal belief and negation as failure. *AIJ*, 70:53–72, 1994.
13. F. Lin and Y. Shoham. On non-forgetting and minimal learning. In *Proc. of the 1993 Int. Coll. on Cognitive Science*, 1993.
14. R. Reiter. *Representation and Reasoning for Dynamic Systems*, 1997. Forthcoming.
15. R. Reiter. A logic for default reasoning. *AIJ*, 13:81–132, 1980.
16. S. Rosenschein. Plan synthesis: a logical approach. In *Proc. of IJCAI-81*, 1981.
17. A. Saffiotti, K. Konolige, and E. H. Ruspini. A multivalued-logic approach to integrating planning and control. *AIJ*, 76(1-2):481–526, 1995.
18. R. Scherl and H. J. Levesque. The frame problem and knowledge producing action. In *Proc. of AAAI-93*, pages 689–695, 1993.
19. K. Schild. A correspondence theory for terminological logics: Preliminary report. In *Proc. of IJCAI-91*, pages 466–471, 1991.
20. M. Shanahan. *Solving the Frame Problem: A Mathematical Investigation of the Common Sense Law of Inertia*. The MIT Press, 1997.

Encoding Planning Problems
in Nonmonotonic Logic Programs

Yannis Dimopoulos, Bernhard Nebel, and Jana Koehler

Institut für Informatik, Universität Freiburg
Am Flughafen 17, D-79110 Freiburg, Germany
E-mail: <last name>@informatik.uni-freiburg.de

Abstract. We present a framework for encoding planning problems in logic programs with negation as failure, having computational efficiency as our major consideration. In order to accomplish our goal, we bring together ideas from logic programming and the planning systems GRAPHPLAN and SATPLAN. We discuss different representations of planning problems in logic programs, point out issues related to their performance, and show ways to exploit the structure of the domains in these representations. For our experimentation we use an existing implementation of the *stable models* semantics called SMODELS. It turns out that for careful and compact encodings, the performance of the method across a number of different domains, is comparable to that of planners like GRAPHPLAN and SATPLAN.

1   Introduction

Nonmonotonic reasoning was originally motivated by the need to capture in a formal logical system aspects of human commonsense reasoning that enable us to withdraw previous conclusions when new information becomes available. Logic programming systems accommodate nonmonotonic reasoning by means of a form of negation, called *negation as failure* (NAF). In their simplest form, nonmonotonic logic programs (also called normal logic programs) are sets of rules of the form $L \leftarrow A_1, A_2, \ldots, A_n, not\, B_1, not\, B_2, \ldots, not\, B_m$, where $n, m \geq 0$ and L, A_i, B_j are atoms. Atoms prefixed with the *not* operator are called *NAF literals* and can be intuitively understood as follows: *not B* is true iff all possible ways to prove B fail.

However, it is not always clear what "fail to prove" means. Logic programs can exhibit quite complicated structure, especially when some NAF literals depend on other NAF literals. Consider the following program P:

$$a \leftarrow not\, b$$
$$b \leftarrow not\, a$$

Different semantics give different "meaning" to the above program. Two of the most influential semantics for normal logic programs are the *stable models* semantics [6] and the *well-founded* semantics [13]. Under the 2-valued semantics of stable models, P has two models, one that assigns a the value true and b the value false, and another one that assigns the opposite values. Under the 3-valued well-founded semantics, both a and b are assigned the value *unknown*.

Here we are mainly interested in systems that implement the stable model semantics, but we will also use the well-founded model information for preprocessing and simplifying planning theories. Recent implementations of the stable model semantics include SLG [3], SMODELS [12], and the branch and bound method described in [14].

The relation between nonmonotonic logic programming and reasoning about action has been studied quite extensively in the literature, e.g. by Gelfond and Lifschitz [7]. In fact, there is some work on relating planning and logic programming, for example by using the *Event Calculus* in combination with abduction [4], or, similarly to what we describe here, logic programs and the stable model semantics or its variants [7,5,15]. Most of the research though is concerned more with the representational adequacy of logic programming as a formalism for representing theories of action and less with issues related to computational efficiency.

In this paper we present some preliminary results on representing planning problems in logic programming systems and discuss efficiency issues. For our encodings we borrow from the planning systems GRAPHPLAN [2] and SATPLAN [10]. The basic idea is simple: we encode the planning problems in such a way that the *stable models of the encodings correspond to valid sequences of actions*. Consequently, planning is the problem of finding a stable model that, for a certain time instant t, assigns true to all the fluents that belong to the final state. Action predicates that are true in the stable model and refer to time instants earlier than t, constitute a plan that achieves the goals.

In more detail, we present a number of different encodings of planning problems in logic programming and discuss nonmonotonic reasoning techniques that can be applied to them. Moreover we show how these representations can exploit the structure of the planning domains. Namely, in order to make the representation of the problems more compact we exploit the *post-serializability* property. Roughly speaking, a set of actions is post-serializable if, when applied in parallel and some of their preconditions contradict some of their effects, there is always an order such that if the actions are applied in this order, earlier actions never delete the preconditions of later ones.

We have conducted a number of experiments on problems taken from the planning literature. For these experiments we used SMODELS [12], a recent efficient implementation of the stable model semantics that seems to outperform other existing systems. It turns out that the combination of the above techniques gives an effective planning method. Its performance on a number of hard *blocks-world* and *logistics* problems, compares well with other existing systematic planning methods.

2 Stable Model Semantics and SMODELS

In this section we briefly review the stable model semantics and the SMODELS algorithm. Throughout the paper we assume basic knowledge of logic programming and familiarity with the planning systems GRAPHPLAN [2] and SATPLAN [10]. Due to space limitations we will not discuss the well-founded semantics [13].

A (normal) logic program is a set of rules of the form

$$L \leftarrow A_1, A_2, \ldots, A_n, not\ B_1, not\ B_2, \ldots, not\ B_m$$

where $n, m \geq 0$ and L, A_i, B_j are atoms. We assume that programs are ground, i.e., all atoms are ground. Let M be a set of atoms and P a normal logic program. We define as P^M the Horn program obtained from P by deleting (a) all rules that contain $not\ B_i$ for $B_i \in M$ (b) all NAF literals from the bodies of the remaining rules. The resulting program P^M is a Horn program as no NAF literal occurs in it. The semantics of a Horn program P_h is exactly its minimal model, denoted by $\mathcal{M}(P_h)$.

Definition 1. [6] A set of atoms M is a **stable model** of a normal logic program P iff $M = \mathcal{M}(P^M)$.

Example 2. Consider the following logic program P:

$m \leftarrow a$
$k \leftarrow b$
$a \leftarrow p, not\ b$
$b \leftarrow p, not\ a$
$p \leftarrow$

It is not difficult to see that both $M_1 = \{m, a, p\}$ and $M_2 = \{k, b, p\}$ are stable models of P. The well-founded model assigns true to p and unknown to all other atoms.

The above definition of stable model semantics is not constructive and can only be used to verify whether a set of atoms is a stable model of a program or not. In fact, determining whether a propositional logic program has a stable model is an NP-complete task.

SMODELS is an effective algorithm for computing the stable models of *function-free* normal logic programs. Non-ground programs are first grounded by a parser that is part of the system. The stable models of the resulting propositional program are computed by the SMODELS algorithm[1] that works roughly as follows. At each step, it first chooses a NAF literal to which it assigns a truth value (starting with the value false, meaning that the corresponding atom is excluded from the stable model currently under construction) and then it employs functions that propagate the assumed value in the program and check for conflicts

---

[1] For all experiments reported here we used SMODELS version 1.5 and the parser version 0.13.

with other values. If an inconsistency is detected, it backtracks and assigns a different value to the literal. Finally, it employs a heuristic for selecting the NAF literal on which it branches. We used this heuristic as it is.

It is important to note that since SMODELS branches only on NAF literals, *the search space consists only of atoms that occur negated in the program.* Atoms that occur only positively in the program are not choice points for the algorithm.

3   Representing Planning Problems

In this section we present the basic domain independent method for encoding plans in nonmonotonic logic programs. To facilitate discussion we assume that we are given a STRIPS-style specification of a planning problem L over a set of fluents F and a set of operators O. Moreover, we assume that the preconditions of the operators contain only positive literals.[2] With L we associate a logic program P_L as follows. For every fluent $fluent_i \in F$, P_L contains a set of rules

$$fluent_i(t) \leftarrow oper_j(t-1) \tag{1}$$

for every $oper_j \in O$ that contains $fluent_i$ in its add effects and every time instant t. For every operator $oper_i$, P_L contains the rule schemata

$$oper_i(t) \leftarrow precon_{i1}(t), \ldots, precon_{im}(t), switchon_i(t), not\ contradict_i(t)$$
$$contradict_i(t) \leftarrow controp_{i1}(t)$$
$$\ldots \tag{2}$$
$$contradict_i(t) \leftarrow controp_{in}(t)$$

where $precon_{ij}$ for $1 \leq j \leq m$ are the preconditions of operator $oper_i$, and $controp_{il}$, for $1 \leq l \leq n$, are operators that contradict with $oper_i$. An operator $oper_j$ contradicts with the operator $oper_i$ if the effects of $oper_j$ either contradict the effect of $oper_i$ (i.e., if applied in parallel lead to invalid world states) or are inconsistent with the preconditions of $oper_i$.[3] It is important to note that contradictory operators need not have different predicate names. In the *blocksworld* for example, the operator $move(X, K, Z, T)$ (where the arguments denote, from left to right, the object, the destination, the origin and the time instant) contradicts with $move(X, Y, Z, T)$ for $K \neq Y$, since a block can not move to two different places at the same time. Similarly, $move(L, Y, M, T)$ contradicts with $move(X, Y, Z, T)$ for $L \neq X$ and $Y \neq table$.

The *switchon_i* predicate implements the choice the system has at each time step t, between applying operator $oper_i$ or keeping it blocked. To realize this effect, we add for each *switchon_i* predicate the following two rules:

$$switchon_i(t) \leftarrow not\ blocked_i(t)$$
$$blocked_i(t) \leftarrow not\ switchon_i(t)$$

---

[2] Negative preconditions can be represented as in GRAPHPLAN [2], which adds only polynomial overhead [1].

[3] In GRAPHPLAN terminology this is called operator *interference*. We partly drop this restriction later in the paper by introducing the notion of post-serializable actions.

This pair of rules encodes a local (i.e., not influenced by choices on other literals in the program P_L) decision on the values of $switchon_i$ and $blocked_i$. By the stable model semantics, exactly one of these atoms will be true while the other will be false. If $switchon_i(t)$ gets the value true, operator $oper_i(t)$ can be applied, provided that the rest of the literals in the body of the rule with $oper_i(t)$ in the head are also true.

Finally, we need a set of rules to represent inertia. For each fluent $fluent_i$, P_L contains the rule:

$$fluent_i(t) \leftarrow fluent_i(t-1), not\ changefluent_i(t-1)$$

The rule simply states that a fluent that is true at time $t-1$ remains true at t unless an action changes its value to false. This change is encoded by the NAF literal $not\ changefluent_i(t-1)$ and a set of rules

$$changefluent_i(t) \leftarrow oper_j(t)$$

for every operator $oper_j(t)$ that has $fluent_i$ in its delete effects.

To the above we also add the fluents that are true in the initial state (time t_0), fix a number of time instants $t_0, t_1, \ldots, t_k$ and add type information. In this way we obtain the program P_L. Assume that the final state must contain a set of fluents $F_1, \ldots, F_n$. The planning problem then amounts to finding a stable model M of P_L that assigns true to the atoms $F_1(t_k), \ldots, F_n(t_k)$.

The translation we presented above is not the only possible. In fact, in many cases we can have more compact representations by omitting literals, rules or variables. Consider for instance, part of the encoding we used for the *fixit* domain [2], as depicted in Figure 1. It contains the definition of the rem-wheel ("remove wheel") predicate and some related fluents. In this logic program there is no *switchon* predicate for the rem-wheel operator, but the *blocked* predicate that may block the application of rem-wheel is directly attached to the operator definition. The *prevtime* predicate represents explicitly the relation between time instants. Since SMODELS cannot handle function symbols, all programs contain a set of assertions $prevtime(t_0, t_1)$, $prevtime(t_1, t_2)$, etc.

```
free(Y,T):-hub(Y),wheel(X),prevtime(T,T1),rem-wheel(X,Y,T1).

have(X,T):-hub(Y),wheel(X),prevtime(T,T1),rem-wheel(X,Y,T1).

rem-wheel(X,Y,T):-hub(Y),wheel(X),time(T),high(Y,T),on(X,Y,T),
unfastened(Y,T),not blocked11(X,Y,T).

blocked11(X,Y,T):-hub(Y),wheel(X),time(T),not rem-wheel(X,Y,T).

free(Y,T):-hub(Y),wheel(X),prevtime(T,T1),free(Y,T1),not occ(Y,T1).

occ(Y,T):-hub(Y),wheel(X),time(T),put-wheel(X,Y,T).
```

Fig. 1. The *fixit* domain

Moreover, by modifying slightly the above encoding it is possible to reduce the number of NAF literal. For instance, instead of representing operator interference through the rule schema (2) we can write:

$$oper_i(t) \leftarrow precon_{i1}(t), \ldots, precon_{im}(t), switchon_i(t)$$
$$inco \leftarrow oper_i(t), controp_{i1}(t)$$
$$\ldots$$
$$inco \leftarrow oper_i(t), controp_{in}(t)$$

$$(2')$$

and compute a stable model where the facts of the final state are true, but $inco$ is false. In this way we prohibit the parallel execution of contradicting actions, and avoid including in the program the NAF literal $not\ contradict_i(t)$ of rule schema (2). We call these encodings *constraint-based*. There are also other ways to "optimize" the logic programming representation of planning problems, which we will not discuss here due to space limitations.

The method we put forward differs from the encoding of planning problems in satisfiability proposed by Kautz and Selman [9], [10]. It is different from the propositional theories of [9] in that the logic program representation explicitly encodes contradictions between operators through the rule schemata (2). Moreover, it does not include axioms stating that actions imply their preconditions. The set of rules (2) and the *minimality* of the stable models suffice to ensure that an operator is applicable only if its preconditions hold. The logic programming representation is also different from the GRAPHPLAN-based encoding [10] in that it uses frame axioms instead of no-ops to solve the frame problem.

More importantly, the search spaces of SMODELS and propositional logic encodings are different. On one hand, the logic programming encoding introduces new predicate symbols in the problem representation (e.g., the *block* or *switchon* predicates) that do not appear in a STRIPS-style problem description. But on the other hand, recall that the search space for the SMODELS algorithm consists of NAF literals only.

4 Computing with Logic Programs

In this section we describe a number of different encodings of planning problems, discuss some efficient pre- and post-processing methods, and report on a number of experiments we conducted with the SMODELS system.

4.1 Linear Encodings

Recall that SMODELS computes the stable models of ground logic programs, therefore its performance (similar to GRAPHPLAN and SATPLAN) depends crucially on the number and the arity of the predicates of the input theory. For domains that contain predicates with high arity and variables with large domains, grounding can result in prohibitively large theories (here ground logic programs). Kautz and Selman [9] describe a method, called linear encoding, that splits operators with many arguments into a number of predicates with less

---

on(X,Y,T1):-prevtime(T1,T2),diff(X,Y),mvable(X),on(X,Y,T2),not move-obj(X,T2).

on(X,Y,T1):-prevtime(T1,T2),mvable(X),diff(X,Y),diff(X,Z),diff(Z,Y),
        on(X,Z,T2),move-obj(X,T2),move-dest(Y,T2).

clear(X,T):-mvable(X),time(T),not occ(X,T).

occ(X,T):-mvable(X),mvable(Y),time(T),on(Y,X,T).

move-obj(X,T):-mvable(X),clear(X,T),not otherobj(X,T),not blocked(X,T).

otherobj(X,T):- mvable(X),mvable(Y),diff(X,Y),move-obj(Y,T).

blocked(X,T):-mvable(X),not move-obj(X,T).

move-dest(X,T):-clear(X,T),mvable(Y),move-obj(Y,T),diff(X,Y),not otherdest(X,T).

otherdest(X,T):-diff(X,Y),move-dest(Y,T).

Fig. 2. *Blocks-world* with linear encodings

(in fact two) arguments. With this encoding, only one action can be applied at each time. Obviously, it is possible to obtain similar encodings for logic programming representations. Such a program for the *blocks-world* domain is depicted in Figure 2. Note that the representation explicitly requires that only one move action can be applied at each time.[4]

If the number of time steps is set to the length of the optimal plan, SMODELS is able to solve within reasonable time some hard *blocks-world* instances which are variants of those introduced in [10] (see Table 1). However, the algorithm seems to be quite sensitive to the "details" of the encoding. For instance, by replacing the rules for *move-obj, otherobj* and *blocked* of Figure 2 with the rules:

$move\text{-}obj(X,T): -mvable(X), time(T), clear(X,T), not\ blocked(X,T).$
$blocked(X,T): -mvable(X), mvable(Y), diff(X,Y), time(T), move\text{-}obj(Y,T).$
$blocked(X,T): -time(T), mvable(X), not\ move\text{-}obj(X,T).$

the runtime for the problem `bw-large.c` [10] increases by 40%. Nevertheless, the largest difference observed in the runtimes was never more than 70%. The phenomenon seems to be related to the heuristic used by the algorithm to select the branch literals.

4.2 Using the Well-Founded Semantics to Prune the Representation

The well-founded semantics [13] is essentially a 3-valued model that always exists, is unique for every logic program, and is traditionally considered to be a polynomial time "approximation" of the stable model semantics. Whenever the well-founded semantics assigns the value true to an atom, this atom will be true in all stable models and symmetrically, all atoms that are false in the well-founded model will be false in all stable models. The atoms that are not assigned

---

[4] A move action at time t is represented by *move-obj* and *move-dest* at time t.

a value in the well-founded model (unknown atoms) can have different values in different stable models. Although the well-founded semantics is too weak for planning problems (it is eager to assign the value unknown whenever confronted with a choice) it can be a useful and cheap preprocessing step that can reduce the size of planning problems.

To see how it works, consider a *blocks-world* problem with initial state $on(A, table)$, $on(B, A)$, $on(C, B)$. Clearly blocks B and A are occupied at time t_0 and the well-founded semantics will assign true to $occ(A, t0)$ and $occ(B, t0)$. Then, by the frame axiom (regardless of where C moves) $on(B, A), on(A, table)$ hold for time $t1$. Consequently $occ(A, t1)$ and $on(A, table, t2)$ hold. Therefore, we can omit ground rules and atoms that are not consistent with the above information, for instance we can omit the ground literal $on(A, C, t1)$ and all ground rules in which it occurs.

Using the information provided by the well-founded model, we can produce smaller ground instances. For the bw-large.c problem [10] for instance, the number of atoms reduces from 5,101 to 4,558 and the number of rules from 58,201 to 47,729 (see also Table 1). Computing the well-founded model never takes more than a few seconds.

4.3 Parallel Steps, Post-Serializability, and Weak Post-Serializability

Although linear encodings give compact representations, they have the disadvantage that they do not allow for parallel actions. Therefore, the number of time steps of a plan equals the number of actions in this plan. If we abandon linear encodings and adopt parallel actions, the arity of the operator predicates increases but at the same time we may obtain plans that achieve the goals in considerably fewer time steps. Therefore, it may happen that the size of the ground logic program also decreases and, more importantly, finding a solution becomes easier.

Clearly, the encoding we presented in Section 3 allows for parallel steps. For some domains however, it is possible to gain, by exploiting their structure, more parallelism during plan generation. First, we define some necessary notions. For a set of actions A, we define the *preconditions-effects graph* of A, denoted by A_G, to be the graph that contains a node for each action in A, and an edge from an action a_i to an action a_j if the preconditions of a_i are inconsistent with the effects of a_j.

Definition 3. A set of actions A that refer to the same time instant is *post-serializable* if (a) the union of their preconditions is consistent (b) the union of their effects is consistent and (c) the graph A_G is acyclic.

If a domain contains a set of post-serializable actions A, then we can apply these actions in parallel at a time instant t during plan generation, and then serialize them during a post-processing phase that works as follows: index with time t all actions that have in-degree 0 in A_G, remove these actions form A_G and index all actions that have in-degree 0 in the new graph with time $t + 1$. Repeat this procedure until all actions are removed and assume that the last time index used is $t + k$. Then assign time $t + k + 1$ to all actions that have been applied at time $t + 1$ in the original plan. In the next section, we will see some domains where the post-serializability property holds.

Consider now the *blocks-world* domain and suppose that we want to find plans that achieve goals expressed in terms of the *on* predicate. Assume that we encode the domain in a logic program that disables the operators $move(X, M, Z)$ and $move(K, Y, L)$ whenever the operator $move(X, Y, Z)$ is applicable, but it does not disable the operator $move(N, X, P)$. Clearly, this domain representation enables parallel execution of actions that are not post-serializable. Consider for example two blocks A and B that are on the table and clear. Then, the actions $move(A, B, table)$ and $move(B, A, table)$ can be applied in parallel, but they create a cycle since each of them deletes the *clear* precondition of the other. However, for planning problems that involve such sets of parallel actions, the *weak post-serializability* property may hold.

A set of actions A is *weakly post-serializable* if for the actions of A that refer to the same time instant the following conditions hold: (a) the union of their preconditions is consistent (b) there exists a function that maps the nodes of every possible cycle of A_G into a consistent set of acyclic actions such that all other actions of A remain valid with respect to the new set of actions and (c) if A achieves a consistent goal G, the new set of actions also achieves G.

Intuitively, a set of actions A is weakly post-serializable if whenever a cycle occurs in A_G, there is a way to break the cycle by replacing some of the actions in the cycle by other actions. Therefore, if the actions of a plan are weakly post-serializable, we can transform these actions into a valid plan, if one exists. Note that the action replacement must be local, i.e., no other actions of the plan must be affected. The way that cycles can be removed in the *blocks-world* domain is simple: move to the table one or more of the blocks involved in the cycle. This is a local replacement. Blocks that form a cycle cannot be cleared by any future actions and therefore they do not affect the rest of the plan. Figure 3 displays a weakly post-serializable move operator for the *blocks-world* domain. Observe that there is no rule that prohibits a block to move and at the same time another block to move on top of it[5]. Therefore in a state where blocks A, B and C are clear, the operators $move(A, B, t_i)$ and $move(B, C, t_i)$ can be applied in parallel. In the post-processing phase, the second action will be ordered before the first.

In terms of the logic programming approach we use here, all the above mean that it may be possible to remove from the representation some of the contradictions between the operators, and push the conflict resolution into the post-processing phase. This enables the planner to shorten plan length, and find an initial solution in fewer steps. This solution is then transformed, by post-processing, into the final plan.

---

[5] Observe also that the source of a block that moves is not specified in the move operator. This information can be easily derived in the post-processing phase from the *move* and *on* predicates.

```
move(X,Y,T):-moveable(X),time(T),block(Y),diff(X,Y),diff(X,Z),diff(Z,Y),
on(X,Z,T),clear(X,T),clear(Y,T),switchon(X,T),not other(X,Y,T).

other(X,Y,T):-moveable(X),time(T),block(Y),diff(X,Y),diff(Y,Z),move(X,Z,T).

other(X,Y,T):-moveable(X),moveable(Y),time(T),block(Y),diff(X,Y),diff(X,Z),
diff(Y,Z),move(Z,Y,T).

switchon(X,T):-moveable(X),time(T),not blocked(X,T).

blocked(X,T):-moveable(X),time(T),not switchon(X,T).
```

Fig. 3. *Blocks-world* with weakly post-serializable move operator

It turns out that action parallelism can have serious mitigating effects on the computation. For the 15 blocks problem bw-large.c, for instance, the method achieves the goals in 6 time steps (contrast this with the 14 steps of the linear encoding). Although in the parallel encoding the number of atoms and rules increases slightly, the overall runtime is smaller. The combination of parallel representation with well-founded model preprocessing reduces further the computation time (see Table 1). For the same problem, GRAPHPLAN with operators that allow parallel move actions, needs 31 minutes and 8 time steps. If we increase the number of blocks by two (problem bw-large.d), GRAPHPLAN finds a solution after 61 hours. The even larger problem bw-large.e with 19 blocks is practically unsolvable for GRAPHPLAN. The runtimes for SMODELS are given in Table 1. The rows showing GP-parallel in this table refer to an encoding that allows as much parallelism as GRAPHPLAN does. Note that it can be the case that grounding is more expensive than finding a solution.

Problem	Time/Actions	Atoms	Rules	Time
bw-large.c (linear)	14/14	5,101	58,201	1,482 (125)
bw-large.c (linear/well-found.)	14/14	4,558	47,729	1,110
bw-large.c (parallel)	6/20	5,572	65,851	483 (200)
bw-large.c (parallel/well-found.)	6/21	4,404	46,126	190
bw-large.d (parallel/constraint)	6/32	8,138	85,101	157 (639)
bw-large.d (GP-parallel/constraint)	9/36	11,874	169,102	450 (1,976)
bw-large.e (parallel/constraint)	7/37	11,623	139,499	365 (1,568)
bw-large.e (GP-parallel/constraint)	10/44	16,211	260,700	1,216 (4,270)
logistics.c (parallel)	8/68	2,529	10,531	18 (23)
trains.a (parallel/constraint)	8/39	1,957	7,786	647 (14)
trains.b (parallel/constraint)	7/34	2,234	13,746	1,261 (17)
trains.c (parallel/constraint)	8/42	2,514	15,942	5,989 (22)

Table 1. Runtimes for solving planning instances on a SUN ULTRA with 256M RAM. Times for grounding/parsing are given in brackets. All times are in CPU seconds. SMODELS was run with the *lookahead* option on.

4.4 Other Domains

We have tested the method on a number of other domains in order to obtain a more complete idea of its performance. The *fixit* domain, as it appears in GRAPHPLAN's distribution, is interesting because it contains a fairly large number (in fact 13) of operators and part of the actions are post-serializable (e.g., putting something in the boot and closing the boot at the same time). The performance of SMODELS (without well-founded preprocessing solved in 0.23 sec) is comparable to GRAPHPLAN (0.11 sec).

A more interesting domain is the *logistics* domain [10]. A number of packages are in different places in the initial state and the task is to deliver these packages to destinations specified in the final state, using the available resources (trucks and planes). This domain also contains post-serializable actions. The actions of loading a package to a truck/plane, unloading the package from a truck/plane and driving the truck/flying the plane can occur at the same time. During postprocessing all drive/fly actions will be delayed for one time step after the load and unload action with which they conflict.

This domain is hard even for GRAPHPLAN. GRAPHPLAN was not able to solve the problem logistics.c after running for 6 CPU hours[6]. If the number of time steps is set to the length of the optimal plan, SMODELS with parallel encoding and without well-founded model preprocessing solves this problem in 18 seconds. Part of the efficiency of the method can be attributed to the use of simple constraints that, although implied by the rules, help the algorithm to detect dead-ends earlier. These constraints are:

$inco : -veh(Y), obj(X), veh(Z), diff(Y, Z), in(X, Y, T), in(X, Z, T).$
$inco : -obj(X), loc(Y), loc(Z), diff(Y, Z), at(X, Y, T), at(X, Z, T).$
$inco : -veh(X), corloc(X, Y), corloc(X, Z), diff(Y, Z), at(X, Y, T), at(X, Z, T).$
$inco : -obj(X), loc(Y), at(X, Y, T), veh(Z), in(X, Z, T).$

where the predicate *corloc* contains the possible location of the vehicles. Like in a constraint-based encoding, SMODELS is asked to compute a stable model where the facts of the final state are true and *inco* is false. If during search, the assumed values derive *inco*, the algorithm backtracks immediately. Finally note that due to the high branching factor of the domain the well-founded model information is not of much help.

Similar to the *logistics* is the *trains* domain [8]. We are given a number of cars that can carry commodities and a number of engines that can be coupled with cars and move between cities that are connected by tracks. The task is to carry the commodities to their destinations. We can also require that the cars/engines are in specified locations in the final state. The main feature of the domain, in its UCPOP description, is a conditional *move* operator: if a car is coupled to an engine, it moves with the engine. Again, our encoding contains constraints similar to those of the *logistics* domain. We give some representative runtimes

---

[6] Kautz and Selman [10] report that for Walksat and *state-based encodings* the problem is solved in 1.9 seconds on a SGI Challenge/150 MHz. For other encodings and algorithms the problem is unsolvable (needs more than 10 hrs of CPU time).

for this domain in Table 1. The interesting point here is that although these theories are relatively small, they can be very hard for SMODELS.

The last set of experiments concerns the towers of Hanoi domain. SMODELS can solve the 4 blocks problem in a few seconds but the 5 blocks problem seems to be beyond its capabilities, at least for our encoding. Even though we have not applied the well-founded model preprocessing that can presumably reduce the complexity, the domain seems to have features that make it hard for the method; action parallelism is low and the constraints to be satisfied are very tight.

4.5 Other Issues

Finding a correct plan is not the only issue. Minimizing the number of actions is also important. This becomes especially important for systems like SMODELS that view planning as a constraint satisfaction problem. In fact, the plans synthesized by SMODELS often contain obviously redundant actions. This raises the question of what are good methods that remove redundant actions from plans. It seems that for domains like the *blocks-world* the problem is harder than for domains similar to *logistics*.

One possible way around this problem could be to give SMODELS' output, i.e., the set of actions that achieves the goal, as input to an efficient planner like GRAPHPLAN. If the number of (ground) operators (i.e., the actions in the initial plan) is small, it is possible that the planner will find a solution quickly and at the same time remove some of the redundant actions. The idea is related to the methods for ignoring irrelevant facts and operators during plan generation developed by Nebel *et al.* [11].

When using logic programming representations, we are confronted with another important issue. The run times we report above are for logic program representations with the number of time steps set to the length of the optimal plan. For practical problem solving, we can use binary search over the length of the plan [10] (or a similar method, depending on the size of the problem). This raises the question of how fast the algorithm fails in cases where the allowed plan length is less than necessary. For the *blocks-world* domain and the parallel encoding, the well-founded model information helps the system to determine unsolvability in a few seconds. Similarly for the *trains* problems of Table 1. For the *logistics* domain, proving unsolvability is harder, but still the difference between the performance of the method and GRAPHPLAN or SATPLAN is dramatic. For the logistics.c problem, if the allowed length is set to one less than the minimum, SMODELS reports that no stable model exists in 1,447 secs.

5 Conclusions

We presented techniques for encoding planning problems in nonmonotonic logic programs. We have provided some initial evidence that the combination of ideas from nonmonotonic reasoning and planning may deliver effective planning systems. We have also shown that planning problems constitute an interesting and challenging set of benchmarks for nonmonotonic reasoning system implementations.

In the future, we intend to work on a tighter integration of planning and nonmonotonic reasoning methods. One issue is how techniques used in GRAPHPLAN, like the automatic derivation of exclusive pairs, can be captured in the logic programming framework. Moreover, it is still open whether the branching heuristic can be modified in a way that it becomes more effective for logic programs that correspond to planning problems.

Acknowledgments

We would like to thank Alfonso Gerevini, Bertram Ludäscher and Ilkka Niemelä for their feedback.

References

1. C. Bäckström. Equivalence and tractability results for SAS$^+$ planning. *KR-92*.
2. A. Blum and M. Furst. Fast Planning Through Planning Graph Analysis. *Artificial Intelligence*, Vol. 90(1-2), 1997.
3. W. Chen and D.S. Warren. Computation of Stable Models and its Integration with Logical Query Processing. *IEEE Transactions on Knowledge and Data Engineering*, to appear.
4. M. Denecker, L. Missiaen and M. Bruynooghe. Temporal Reasoning with Abductive Event Calculus. *ECAI-92*.
5. P. M. Dung. Representing Actions in Logic Programming and its Applications in Database Updates. *ICLP-93*.
6. M. Gelfond and V. Lifschitz. The Stable Models Semantics for Logic Programs. *ICLP-88*.
7. M. Gelfond and V. Lifschitz. Representing Actions and Change by Logic Programs. *Journal of Logic Programming*, Vol. 17, 1993.
8. A. Gerevini and L. Schubert. Accelerating Partial-Order Planners: Some Techniques for Effective Search Control and Pruning. *Journal of Artificial Intelligence Research*, Vol. 5, 1996.
9. H. Kautz and B. Selman. Planning as Satisfiability. *ECAI-92*.
10. H. Kautz and B. Selman. Pushing the Envelope: Planning, Propositional Logic, and Stochastic Search. *AAAI-96*.
11. B. Nebel, Y. Dimopoulos and J. Koehler. Ignoring Irrelevant Facts and Operators in Plan Generation. *ECP-97*, this volume.
12. I. Niemela and P. Simons. Efficient Implementation of the Well-founded and Stable Model Semantics. *International Joint Conference and Symposium on Logic Programming*, 1996.
13. A. Van Gelder, K. Ross and J. Schlipf. The Well-founded Semantics for General Logic Programs. *Journal of the ACM*, Vol. 38, 1991.
14. V.S. Subrahmanian, D. Nau and C. Vago. WFS + Branch and Bound = Stable Models. *IEEE Transactions on Knowledge and Data Engineering*, Vol. 7, 1995.
15. V. S. Subrahmanian and C. Zaniolo. Relating Stable Models and AI Planning Domains. *ICLP-95*.

An Argument for a Hybrid
HTN/Operator-Based Approach to Planning

Tara A. Estlin* and Steve A. Chien and Xuemei Wang **

Jet Propulsion Laboratory, California Institute of Technology ***
4800 Oak Grove Drive, Pasadena, CA 91109-8099

Abstract. Work on generative planning systems has focused on two diverse approaches to plan construction. Hierarchical task network (HTN) planners build plans by successively refining high-level goals into lower-level activities. Operator-based planners employ means-end analysis to formulate plans consisting of low-level activities. While many have argued the universal dominance of a single approach, we present an alternative view: that in different situations either may be most appropriate. To support this view, we describe a number of advantages and disadvantages of these approaches in light of our experiences in developing two real-world, fielded planning systems.

1   Introduction

AI planning researchers have developed numerous approaches to the task of correct and efficient planning. Two main approaches to this task are *operator-based* planners and *hierarchical task network* (HTN) planners. While considerable work has been done in analyzing and formalizing each of these approaches [Chapman 1987, Erol et al. 1994], and some work has been done in comparing them from a theoretical standpoint [Kambhampati 1995, Minton et al. 1991], comparatively little effort has been devoted to comparing the two approaches in a more practical setting.

While both HTN and operator-based planners typically construct plans by searching in a plan-space, they differ considerably in how they express plan refinement operators. HTN planners generally specify plan modifications in terms of flexible task reduction rules. Operator-based planners perform all reasoning at the lowest level of abstraction and provide a strict semantics for defining operator definitions. By virtue of their representation, HTN planners more naturally represent hierarchy and modularity. In contrast, operator-based plan refinements are more general since they can cover many more planning situations.

---

 * Current address: Department of Computer Science, University of Texas at Austin, Austin, TX

 ** Current Address: Rockwell Science Center, Palo Alto, CA

*** This paper describes work performed by the Jet Propulsion Laboratory, California Institute of Technology, under contract with the National Aeronautics and Space Administration.

In this paper, we explain how a hybrid approach, which combines these two planning techniques, is an effective method for planning in real-world applications. In particular, we investigate the critical issue of planning representation. If domain knowledge can be naturally represented in a planning system then: (1) It will be easier to encode an initial knowledge base; (2) fewer encoding errors will occur, leading to a higher performance system; and (3) maintenance of the knowledge base will be considerably easier. Thus, an important measure for evaluating HTN and operator-based planning is how naturally each paradigm can represent key aspects of planning knowledge.

To evaluate representation abilities, we focus on four criteria: generality, hierarchy, flexibility, and efficiency. Generality describes the range of problem-solving situations that can be covered by a small amount of knowledge. Hierarchies allow common constraints, procedures, and patterns to be defined once yet used many times. Flexibility describes how easily a wide range of constraints can be accurately represented. Efficiency relates to how the representation influences the size of the planner's search space.

This paper describes a number of important representational issues that we have encountered in building two NASA planning systems [Chien et al. 1995]: Image Processing for Science Data Analysis (the MVP system) [Chien and Mortensen 1996] and Deep Space Network (DSN) Antenna Operations (the DPLAN system) [Chien et al. 1997]. The Multimission VICAR Planner (MVP) uses planning techniques to automatically generate image processing programs from user specified processing goals. MVP allows a user to specify a list of image processing requirements and then derives the required processing steps to achieve the input goals. Our second application concerns operating Radio Antennas. In this domain, the DPLAN planner is given a set of antenna tracking goals and equipment information. DPLAN then generates a list of antenna operation steps that will create a communications link with orbiting spacecraft.

Both of the planners described above employ a similar combination of HTN and operator-based planning techniques. Constructing and experimenting with these systems has helped us to closely examine many of the representation and efficiency trade-offs generated when using an integrated planning framework.

2   An Overview of HTN and Operator-based Planning

While we presume that the reader has a working knowledge of basic operator-based planning and HTN planning techniques, we briefly review the most salient differences of the two approaches.

An HTN planner [Erol et al. 1994] uses task reduction rules to decompose abstract goals into low level tasks. By defining certain reduction refinements, the user can direct the planner towards particular search paths. The user can also directly influence the planner by adding constraint information to a rule that would not strictly be derived from goal interaction analyses. HTN planners are thus considered very flexible in representing domain information. Unfortunately, this flexibility can often lead to numerous overly-specific reduction rules that can be difficult to understand.

In contrast, an operator-based planner [Penberthy and Weld 1992, Carbonell et al. 1992] reasons at a single level of abstraction – the lowest level. Actions are strictly defined in terms of preconditions and effects. Plans are produced through subgoaling and goal interaction analysis. All plan constraints are a direct consequence of goal achievements and precondition and effect analysis. This rigid representation is both a strength and a weakness. It is advantageous since it more explicitly directs the knowledge engineer in encoding a domain. Yet, it can also make certain aspects of a problem difficult to represent. For example, known ordering constraints can be difficult to encode if they cannot easily be represented in terms of preconditions and effects.

In an integrated HTN/operator framework, a planner can use multiple planning methods and reason about different types of planning goals. Both the MVP and DPLAN planners use a similar integration of HTN and operator-based planning methods. In these planners, domain information can be represented in either an HTN or operator format and both approaches can be used during planning to determine a problem solution. Domain information pertaining to these two planning techniques is kept separate; decompositional information is specified in decomposition rules, while items such as activity precondition and effects are kept in a separate schema list. This distinction is intended to allow a planner to apply a wider variety of planning techniques and to formulate domain information in a flexible and usable representation. These planners can also easily use additional domain information for more efficient and flexible planning.

Two very related systems to MVP and DPLAN are SIPE [Wilkins 1988] and O-Plan [Tate et al. 1994], which both allow for the integration of HTN and operator-based planning[4]. However, O-Plan and SIPE do not retain as much of an explicit distinction between HTN and operator-based planning techniques. Instead, plan formulation is primarily done using decomposition operators (or networks). Operator-based features such as preconditions and effects are added to these structures when necessary. In contrast, we support an approach in which HTN planning and operator-based techniques can be used in conjunction *or* as separate planning methods.

3 Representing Hierarchical and Modularity Information

Many of the obstacles in applying planning techniques to real-world problems can be characterized as representation difficulties. One advantage to employing an HTN planner is the ability to use abstract representation levels of domain objects and goals. Allowing abstract representations of these items enables us to represent domains in an object-oriented form, which is easier to write and reason about. This format also contributes to a more general domain knowledge base

---

[4] It is worth noting that these systems comprise 4 of the 5 applications recently described in [IEEE Expert 1996].

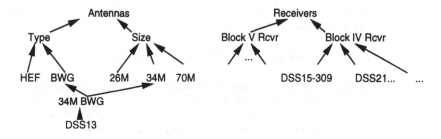

Fig. 1. Antenna and Receiver Hierarchies

that can be efficiently updated and maintained. Unlike operator-based planners, HTN planners provide direct support for this type of representation.[5]

3.1 Object and Goal Hierarchies

When using an HTN planner, different abstract levels of domain objects and goals can be represented by constructing an object or goal hierarchy. More detailed information such as object instances is at one end of a hierarchy, while very general information such as broad object types is at the other end. In the DSN domain, different types of equipment are often required for separate antenna activities. For example, many different types of antennas are currently represented in our domain. Our domain also includes several different types of receivers, which are used to receive data transmissions from orbiting spacecraft. In Figure 1 we show partial equipment hierarchies for antennas and receivers.

The main advantage to this type of representation is that decomposition rules can refer to either low- or high-level forms of a particular object or goal. In the DSN domain, a common antenna operation is performing a telemetry (or downlink) pass where information is transmitted from a spacecraft to an antenna. A telemetry pass usually requires one of several types of receivers depending on the type of antenna being used. The main steps of the pass may be very similar for different antennas even though different receiver types are required. By using object and goal hierarchies we can write just one telemetry decomposition rule to represent the general steps taken during this operation. For instance, in the telemetry rule shown in Figure 2, a general *perform-receiver-configuration* goal is asserted as a new goal.

Information pertaining to specific equipment is contained in smaller, more specialized rules. For instance, specific receiver configuration steps can be added separately by decomposing the *perform-receiver-configuration* goal. The rules listed in Figure 3 show two possible ways to break down this goal for either a Block-IV type receiver or a Block-V receiver. This format allows us to avoid writing multiple versions of the main telemetry rule.

---

[5] For a discussion of these issues in the context of representing reactive planning knowledge see [Firby 1996].

```
(decomprule default-telemetry-track
   lhs
      (initialgoals ((track-goal spacecraft-track telemetry ?track-id)))
   rhs
      (newgoals   ((g1 (perform-antenna-controller-configuration ?track-id))
                   (g2 (perform-exciter-n-transmitter-configuration ?track-id))
                   (g3 (perform-microwave-controller-configuration ?track-id))
                   (g4 (perform-receiver-configuration ?track-id))
                   (g5 (perform-telemetry-configuration ?track-id))
                   (g6 (move-antenna-to-point ?track-id))
                   (g7 (perform-receiver-calibration ?track-id)))
      constraints ((before g1 g6)
                   (before g7 g3)
                   (before g4 g7))))
```

Fig. 2. Telemetry Decomposition Rule

```
(decomprule default-telemetry-track
   lhs
      (initialgoals ((perform-receiver-configuration ?track-id)))
      conditions   ((CCN-equipment-assignment ?track-id ?equip)
                    ((isa ?equip BLOCK-IV-RECEIVER)))
   rhs
      (newgoals   ((configure-block-iv-receiver ?track-id ?equip))))

(decomprule configure-receiver2
   lhs
      (initialgoals ((perform-receiver-configuration ?track-id)))
      conditions   ((CCN-equipment-assignment ?track-id ?equip)
                    ((isa ?equip BLOCK-V-RECEIVER)))
   rhs
      (newgoals   ((configure-block-v-receiver ?track-id ?equip))))
```

Fig. 3. Two Decomposition Rules for Receiver Configuration

By allowing object and goal hierarchies, we can construct domains in an object-oriented approach. Domain information is easily understood and updated since domain details are kept separate from more general knowledge. For example, to understand the general steps of a telemetry operation, a user only has to view the main telemetry decomposition rule. If more low-level knowledge is desired, such as how to operate a particular piece of equipment, the user could search for rules that directly pertain to that equipment type. Knowledge maintenance is also more efficient. Most domain updates involve changes to only low-level steps. For instance, adding a new type of receiver to the domain, would not cause any rules that refer to more general receiver goals to be modified.

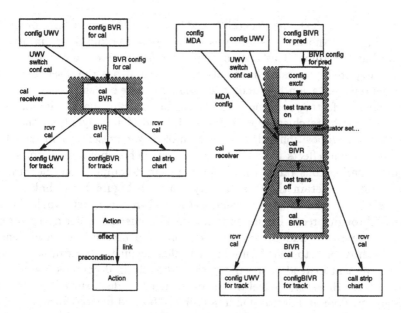

Fig. 4. VLBI Receiver Subplans

3.2 Modularity vs. Specialized Constraints

Unfortunately, a modular representation often makes it difficult to represent more specialized inter-modular constraints. These types of constraints refer to information inside of several different decomposition rules and are usually only applicable in certain situations. Defining these constraints forces the addition of more specialized rules and often causes a hierarchical representation of rules to be infeasible.

For example, when performing receiver calibration in the DSN domain, it is sometimes necessary for high-level rules to refer to specific receiver calibration steps. When using a Block-IV receiver, VLBI (Very Long Baseline Interferometry) telemetry tracks directly impose high-level ordering constraints on specific receiver calibration steps, instead of on a more general *calibrate-receiver* goal. Two different VLBI tracks are shown in Figure 4; the left uses a Block-V receiver and the right a Block-IV receiver. Low-level receiver calibration steps are shown in the shaded areas. In the Block-V case, receiver calibration is mapped onto a single general operator. However, in the Block-IV case it corresponds to five low-level steps which have constraints imposed on them by the telemetry rule. These constraints could be modified to refer to a more general goal (consisting of the shaded area), but then specialized constraint information would be lost. For instance, currently the *config-MDA* step and *config-exctr* step can be performed in parallel; however, if all ordering constraints are forced to refer to the entire shaded areas, such parallel execution would violate an ordering constraint.

One solution, which stays within the HTN framework, is to encode separate rules for tracks that require these inter-modular constraints. Unfortunately, this solution results in less rule generality and increases the complexity of the domain definition. Another possibility is to represent the knowledge in a purely operator-based format. This option often provides a more compact representation of required constraint information, however, it has the disadvantages of losing the representation hierarchy and requiring more search.

A more satisfactory solution is to incorporate operator-based planning techniques with the hierarchical representation. Instead of directly adding these constraints to decomposition rules, we can implicitly represent them by adding preconditions and effects to low-level track steps. This approach permits intermodular ordering constraints to be separate from decomposition rules, thereby allowing rules to retain their modularity. Thus, in Figure 4, the link between *config-MDA* and the low-level *calibrate-Block-IV-receiver* step would be represented through preconditions and effects. The relevant ordering constraints would eventually be added through operator-based precondition achievement. The only drawback to this formulation is that acquiring constraints through goal achievement instead of specifying them directly in decomposition rules increases search. However, we feel this is an adequate tradeoff since it allows us to represent our domain information in a more useful and flexible format.

Point 1: Hierarchy and Modularity *HTN approaches have the advantage of easily supporting a hierarchical representation. Operator-based approaches have the advantage of generality, since they can cover many planning situations unconsidered by the knowledge engineer. Yet, they are usually less efficient. A hybrid HTN/operator-based approach allows an encoding that supports hierarchy and generality, without requiring an overly large search space.*

4 Encoding Implicit Constraints

Another advantage to using a hybrid planning system is the ability to encode implicit constraint information. These are constraints that may not be obvious when defining decomposition rules or operators, but are still necessary for correct planning. Consider the following example. When performing a telemetry pass in the DSN domain, a required step is to position the antenna to point at a specified set of coordinates (represented by the goal *move-antenna-to-point*). However, for many pre-calibration steps, which prepare the antenna for a transmission, it is necessary to have the antenna in a stow position where stray transmissions are directed at a harmless location. The antenna is not moved to point at the final coordinates until most pre-calibration steps have been executed. Unfortunately, when defining the DSN domain, this constraint is often (accidentally) left out of many pre-calibration decomposition rules since it does not directly affect the success of pre-calibration activities.

One way to enforce this constraint is to explicitly add ordering constraints to all telemetry decomposition rules that specify *move-antenna-to-point* be ordered *after* any activity that could cause the antenna to transmit. Unfortunately, such a constraint may have to be specified numerous times if there are multiple rules to which it applies. Another option is to use operator-based precondition/effect analysis. We could add a precondition of *not(antenna-at-point)* to any pre-calibration activities that could cause antenna transmission. This prevents the *move-antenna-to-point* step from being ordered before any pre-calibration activities that use the transmitter. Unfortunately, this option requires a number of extra preconditions to be added and could possibly induce more search.

A better solution is to utilize both HTN and operator-based techniques. First we can add a protection to the main telemetry decomposition rule that forbids stray transmissions during the entire pre-cal process. Then, using operator-based methods, we can require any pre-calibration transmission action to have a conditional effect which violates this requirement when the condition *antenna-at-point* is satisfied. This strategy requires pre-calibration actions that cause transmissions to be ordered before the action *move-antenna-to-point* is executed, and it causes the least amount of knowledge maintenance.

Point 2: Implicit Constraints *An HTN approach offers great flexibility in specifying arbitrary constraints, but may require restating constraints multiple times (when no appropriate hierarchy exists). Operator-based methods can also be used to represent these constraints, however they often lead to a proliferation of operator preconditions. Hybrid methods offer the greatest flexibility in representing implicit constraints.*

5 Scripting vs. Declaring

Another notable difference between HTN and operator based approaches is that the HTN approach allows the encoding of specific action sequences while an operator-based approach often incurs significant search to construct this same sequence. Conversely, when operators can be combined in many different ways but still have interactions, an operator-based representation can be a more concise, natural method of encoding these constraints. In varying domains, or portions of one domain, different aspects of these representation tradeoffs are relevant. In order to demonstrate this tradeoff we performed an experiment where a knowledge engineer (KE) encoded a simplified portion of the MVP image processing domain [Chien and Mortensen 1996].[6] This portion represented a subproblem called image navigation.[7] The KE developed three planning models, one in which only operator-based techniques were used, one where only HTN techniques were used, and one where both techniques were used.

All possible steps of the image navigation problem are shown in Figure 5. In the most basic case the process would involve setup steps A.1 and A.2, and automatic navigation steps B.4 and B.5. However, in some circumstances all asterisked steps would also be added. For example, if there is an initial tiepoint file, step A.3 might be added.

---

[6] The knowledge engineer had some knowledge of the image processing application and had no knowledge of this paper or research topic.

[7] This is perhaps the most complex subproblem in this image processing domain. It involves 8 top-level goals and 40 operators; a typical plan might range from 20-50 operators.

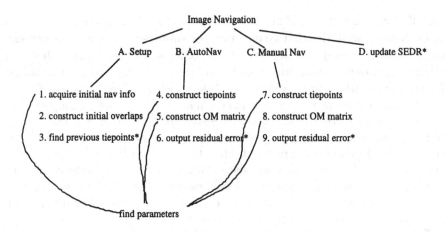

Fig. 5. MVP Navigation Process

Unfortunately, this is a very simplified navigation case. In most cases, the user would request a phase navigation process which would include more steps from both B and C. In these situations, manual navigation (C) would be performed to fine-tune the results of automatic navigation (B). To even more complicate matters, the exact specification of many steps depends on if other steps are being performed. For example, if residual error output is a requested goal, steps B.6 and C.9 must be executed. This requires that step B.5 and step C.8 have appropriate parameter settings to compute the residual output.

Furthermore, we have only listed the major component steps of navigating the image. There are also secondary steps that extract information from the image label. These secondary steps help appropriately select program parameters for each of the main steps listed in Figure 5. These extra details account for additional operators and steps in the plan not shown in Figure 5.

We compared the three knowledge bases constructed by the KE for this problem using the following measures: compactness of encoding, modularity (lack of repetition), and search efficiency. In Figure 6 we summarize the number of HTN rules, number of operators, and search required for the most complex problems in each of the encodings.

Fig. 6. Knowledge Encoding Statistics

Encoding	# HTN Rules	Operators	Search
Operators	0	8	26
Rules	15	NA	5
Hybrid	5	8	18

Based on our results, the pure operator-based representation is inefficient from a search perspective. While only a small subset of the operator combinations will actually be used in solving problems, this type of framework requires that the all operators be sufficiently accurate to rule out all other combinations. It is also difficult to debug the operators to ensure generation of only valid sequences. On writing a pure operator-based representation the KE said *"The operator KB was the most difficult to encode. One small change typically affected many operators and would require great re-testing. Because I had worked myself into a corner, I had to start from scratch a few times. For the final time, I realized that I needed to fully map the entire structure (including parameters) on paper."*

Representing this problem in a pure HTN framework is also difficult. Many complex combinations of dependencies and interrelations require numerous decomposition rules. Generally, there is one reduction rule for each basic sequence, and one rule for each combination of add-ons to the basic sequence. Unfortunately, this creates a proliferation of rules which are difficult to understand and maintain. The HTN encoding of this problem resulted in 4 rules to cover the automatic navigation process, 2 to cover the manual navigation process, and also a number of additional rules to address with previous tiepoint files (Step A.3). These rules account for the 15 rules required for the pure HTN representation.

In the combined HTN and operator-based framework it is possible to represent different parts of the plan generation process using operator-based and/or HTN methods. Basic sequences can be easily represented using HTN rules. More complex additions to each basic sequence can be represented through operator-based constructs such as preconditions and conditional effects. Once the basic sequence has been determined through decomposition, goal-achievement is used to add additional constraints or dependencies. The complex navigation problem discussed above can now be represented as a separate script. For example, the two basic navigation phases, automatic navigation and manual navigation, can be represented in an HTN framework. However, slight modifications from the default framework (such as whether or not to use an initial tiepoint file) can be linked in using operator-based planning techniques. This results in a reduced number of rules (compactness) and avoidance of redundancy in the KB. Avoiding redundancy is especially important since redundant portions of the KB must all be updated whenever one part is changed. This can lead to errors and increased maintenance costs.

Point 3: Scripting vs. Declaring *An HTN framework is more search efficient than an operator-based one in cases where only a few sequences of operators are valid. An operator-based framework is representationally much cleaner, however, it requires a more general set of operators that can correctly manage many possible execution paths. In a hybrid framework, we can interleave the two planning processes (and representations) to produce an efficient planner that supports a compact, maintainable representation.*

6 Other Representational Issues

6.1 Static Domain Information

One important issue in both operator-based and HTN-based planning is the ability to efficiently use static state information to assist in pruning the search space. Often, decomposition conditions or operator preconditions can be considered static if they will remain unchanged throughout the planning process. These conditions can usually be evaluated immediately, which will help to initially prune the search space. Different planners are able to take advantage of this static information in varying degrees. In our integrated planning framework, static preconditions occurring in decomposition rules are labeled as such and only variable bindings which satisfy them are generated when considering applicable decomposition rules. Thus, codesignation commitment to satisfy static conditions occurs, but unnecessary commitment for other subgoals and variables is avoided. These static conditions are related to filter conditions [Pryor and Collins 1992] in that they are a specific type of filter condition restricting the applicability of the operator. However, precisely because static conditions cannot be changed by operators, they can be easily evaluated by a partial order planner and used in determining the applicability of a decomposition rule or operator.

6.2 Nominal Plan Generation

It is often desirable to predict (and control) the plans that are generated for nominal or near-nominal conditions. For example, when the problem goals or initial state change slightly, it is often desirable for the output plan to also change only slightly. This is a strong user requirement in both the image processing and DSN antenna operations applications. In operator-based planners, it is often difficult to encode such preferences. The planner would typically only be required to generate a correct plan. In contrast, since HTN planning techniques are closer to scripting, HTN planners offer good control over nominal or near-nominal plan generation. Hybrid HTN/operator planning frameworks can thus also offer control over nominal plan generation.

6.3 Replanning

A key requirement of many real-world planning systems is the ability to replan when plan goals or other conditions change. Replanning generally requires basic knowledge of why certain goals and actions are present in the plan. This requires a basic level of operator-based information and is mostly supported through techniques such as precondition and effect analysis. HTN approaches often encourage the omission of this information from the domain knowledge since it is not required for normal planning. In order to replan, hybrid techniques must still maintain any relevant precondition and effect information. Therefore, if replanning is necessary, much of the ease of an HTN encoding approach is lost because a significant amount of operator-based information is still required.

6.4 Goal Modifiers

A relevant difference between operator-based and HTN planning is the number of goal modifiers that must be maintained. In operator-based planning, relevant goal modifiers are listed as arguments to the goal predicate. These modifiers then get propagated from goal to subgoal through operators. Thus, any parameters that are *possibly* relevant to a goal (and any of its subgoals) must be present as goal arguments. This procedure can result in long argument lists (often 10s of parameters), thereby increasing the difficulty of knowledge maintenance. In HTN planning, relevant modifiers are typically propagated top-down from abstract goals which expand into more specific activities. While this process still requires all possibly relevant parameters to be present, the expansions tend to result in short wide structures (e.g. an HTN rule expands a single goal into many goals). Thus, argument lengths quickly get shorter at lower levels of abstraction. Unfortunately, a hybrid approach requires goal arguments to support both HTN and operator-based planning and hence offers no advantage over either.

7 Conclusion

This paper has described a number of issues relevant in representing planning knowledge in operator-based and HTN-based paradigms. We have described the main tradeoffs of using either HTN or operator-based specifications to represent domain knowledge. In particular, we discuss how these different methodologies impact the naturalness of the representation. HTN approaches are strong at modular and hierarchical representation, however operator-based approaches usually provide a more compact representation of constraints. Hybrid representations are best at managing the tradeoff between generality and efficiency. Hybrid approaches are also most flexible at encoding implicit constraints. HTN/hybrid approaches offer most control over nominal plan generation, but operator-based techniques offer the most support for replanning. HTN approaches most cleanly represent goal argument regressions. Based on these criteria we conclude that neither the operator-based approach nor the HTN approach dominates the other. Rather, in some cases the operator-based representation is more appropriate and in other cases the HTN representation is more appropriate. Thus, it seems most prudent to advocate usage of hybrid HTN/operator techniques.

References

[Carbonell et al. 1992] Carbonell, J.G.; Blythe, J.; Etzioni, O.; Gil, Y.; Joseph, R.; Kahn, D.; Knoblock, C.; Minton, S.; Pérez, M. A.; Reilly, S.; Veloso, M.; and Wang, X. 1992. PRODIGY *4.0: The Manual and Tutorial*. Technical report, School of Computer Science, Carnegie Mellon University.

[Chapman 1987] D. Chapman, "Planning for Conjunctive Goals", 1987, *Artificial Intelligence 32*, 3.

[Chien and Mortensen 1996] S. A. Chien and H. B. Mortensen, "Automating Image Processing for Scientific Data Analysis of a Large Image Database," IEEE Transactions on Pattern Analysis and Machine Intelligence 18 (8): pp. 854-859, August 1996.

[Chien et al. 1997] S. Chien, A. Govindjee, T. Estlin, X. Wang, A. Griesel, R. Hill Jr., Automated Generation of Tracking Plans for a Network of Communications Antennas, Proc. 1997 IEEE Aerospace Conference, Aspen, CO, February, 1997.

[Chien et al. 1995] S. A. Chien, R. W. Hill Jr., X. Wang, T. Estlin, K. V. Fayyad, and H. B. Mortensen, "Why Real-world Planning is Difficult: A Tale of Two Applications," Proceedings of the Third European Workshop on Planning (EWSP95), Assisi, Italy, September 1995.

[Erol et al. 1994] K. Erol, J. Hendler, and D. Nau, "UMCP: A Sound and Complete Procedure for Hierarchical Task Network Planning," Proc. AIPS94, Chicago, IL, June 1994, pp. 249-254.

[Firby 1996] J. Firby, "Modularity Issues in Reactive Planning," Proc. AIPS96, Edinburgh, UK, May 1996, pp. 78-85.

[IEEE Expert 1996] AI Planning Systems in the Real World, IEEE Expert, December 1996, pp. 4-12.

[Kambhampati 1995] Kambhampati, S., A Comparative Analysis of partial order planning and task reduction planning, SIGART Bulletin, Special Issue on Evaluating Plans, Planners, and Planning, Vol 6, No. 1, January 1995.

[Minton et al. 1991] Minton S., J. Bresina, and M. Drummond, "Commitment Strategies in Planning: A Comparative Analysis," Proceedings AAAI-91.

[Penberthy and Weld 1992] J. S. Penberthy and D. S. Weld, "UCPOP: A Sound Complete, Partial Order Planner for ADL," Proceedings of the Third International Conference on Knowledge Representation and Reasoning, October 1992.

[Pryor and Collins 1992] G. Collins and L. Pryor, "Achieving the functionality of filter conditions in a partial order planner," Proceedings AAAI92, pp. 375-380.

[Tate et al. 1994] Tate, A., B. Drabble, and R. Kirby, "O-Plan2: An Open Architecture for Command Planning and Control," in *Intelligent Scheduling* (Eds. M. Fox and M. Zweben), Morgan Kaufmann, 1994.

[Wilkins 1988] D. Wilkins. *Practical Planning: Extending the Classical AI Planning Paradigm.* Morgan Kaufmann, 1988.

Natural Hierarchical Planning
Using Operator Decomposition

Maria Fox
Email:M.Fox@durham.ac.uk

Department of Computer Science,
University of Durham, South Road, Durham, UK

Abstract. Three approaches to hierarchical planning have been widely discussed in the recent planning literature: Hierarchical Task Network (HTN) decomposition, model-reduction and operator decomposition. Abstraction is used in different ways in these three approaches and this has significance for both efficiency and expressive power. This paper identifies four issues that arise in the use of abstraction in planning which have been treated in different ways in the three approaches identified above. These issues are discussed with reference to an approach to abstraction which combines elements of the HTN and operator-decomposition approaches. Particular comparison is made with the HTN approach in order to highlight some important distinctions between the task decomposition and operator decomposition planning strategies. The CNF (Common Normal Form) case study, used by Erol to demonstrate certain features of the HTN approach, is used as the basis for this comparison.

1 Introduction

Three approaches to hierarchical planning have been widely discussed in the recent planning literature: Hierarchical Task Network (HTN) decomposition, model-reduction and operator decomposition. Planners in the HTN tradition include NOAH, NONLIN, O-Plan and UMCP [13, 12, 3, 14, 4]. The model-reduction approach is based on an earlier approach known as model-relaxation [15], characterised by ABSTRIPS [11], and includes ALPINE/PRODIGY and HIGHPOINT [7, 1]. Operator decomposition planners have similarities with HTN planners but produce plans by goal achievement rather than task decomposition. Some examples, such as DPOCL [19, 18], have their roots in causal-link (POCL) planning in the style of UCPOP [9] and SNLP [8] whilst others, such as SIPE [16], are closer to the NOAH tradition.

There are important differences in how abstraction is achieved in these three approaches. For example, HTN planners do not allow effects to be associated with compound tasks, whilst operator decomposition planners typically do associate pre- and post-conditions with abstract operators. Model reduction planners have neither abstract operators nor compound tasks, but form abstract plans by ignoring certain literals in the domain language. These differences have significance for both efficiency and expressive power [1, 4].

This paper identifies four issues that arise in the use of abstraction in planning which have been treated in different ways in the three approaches identified above. These issues have been specifically addressed in the theory of abstraction implemented in AbNLP, a hierarchical planner in the POCL tradition, that exploits abstraction through operator decomposition. AbNLP combines operator decomposition with the notions of abstract plans and plan refinement, and can therefore be characterised as a cross between the HTN and operator decomposition styles. It is claimed that, as a result of its treatment of these issues, AbNLP provides a natural and expressive form of abstraction. Particular comparison is made with the HTN approach in order to highlight some important distinctions between the task decomposition and operator decomposition approaches. In order to provide a detailed example of the domain description language used in AbNLP, the way AbNLP works and how it differs from exemplars of the HTN approach, the CNF (Common Normal Form) case study used by Erol [4] is considered.

The paper is organised as follows: section 2 discusses four issues that arise in the use of abstraction in planning and the ways in which these four issues are addressed in the HTN and operator decomposition styles are then considered in detail and contrasted with their resolution in AbNLP. Model reduction is not considered in detail as the identification of abstraction levels with subsets of domain literals represents a different form of abstraction from that exploited in task refinement and operator decomposition. The planning algorithm AbNLP is described in section 3. In section 4 the CNF case study is used as an example of its operation and in order to provide a concrete comparison with HTN planning.

2 Contrasting different planning styles

One of the strongest motivations for using some form of abstraction in planning is the observation that people use it to great effect in their problem-solving. Much of the work on hierarchical planning was originally, at least in part, motivated by this observation [11, 12, 6, 15, 16, 13]. The following four features can be observed in the way people use abstraction.

1. The use of abstraction involves the deliberate loss of information;

2. Abstract plans have *intentional* meaning;

3. Abstraction levels can be mixed within a plan;

4. Abstract plans can contain operators which disappear from their refinements.

In the following discussion, the first of the four points is discussed as it arises in the discussion of the other three and is not given separate status.

2.1 Abstract plans have intentional meaning

A common proposal for the semantics of abstract plans is to interpret them in terms of their primitive completions. This is how Erol *et al.* interpret abstract plans in the HTN mechanism [5]. A problem is that abstract plans which have no primitive completions are meaningless under this interpretation. On first reading this seems reasonable because plans which cannot be realised seem, indeed, to be indistinguishable from meaningless plans. However, sensible abstract plans can be formed which convey the intentions of a planner in a way that is meaningful even if the plan turns out to have no completions. In Tenenberg's example [15] the abstract plan PrepareMeal has obvious intentional force even if it turns out to be unrealisable. The inability to interpret abstract plans in the HTN framework other than through their concrete completions arises from the lack of external structure associated with the methods that achieve non-primitive tasks. As Erol indicates, only primitive tasks are allowed to modify the state - the effects of non-primitive tasks are not known until they have been decomposed into primitives. Neither non-primitive tasks nor methods have pre- and post-conditions associated with them, so the intentional structure of an abstract plan cannot be revealed until the task network is refined.

The interpretation of primitive plans formed in the DPOCL system can be built upon the semantics of UCPOP, in which plans are interpreted as state-to-state functions. Since composite operators in the DPOCL framework have pre- and post-conditions it seems that an interpretation of abstract plans as transformations between sets of states might be possible, but the problems of managing the loss of information implied by the use of abstraction do not appear to have been considered in the current literature. The failure to consider interactions between different levels of abstractions within plans suggests that, although DPOCL is provably correct at the primitive level, the interpretation of its abstract plans is suspect - indeed, it seems that DPOCL would have to resort to backtracking heavily through refinement when inconsistencies present, but undetected, in abstract plans finally become apparent at primitive levels.

AbNLP is similar in style to DPOCL in having abstract, or composite, operators with pre- and post-conditions. Abstract plans are interpreted as transformations between sets of states and the problem of handling loss of information is managed using a mechanism which takes account of the destructive effect of abstract operators. The PrepareMeal operator can be said to destroy, in the sense of making unavailable, knowledge about whether there is meat (or indeed any other meal ingredient) in the fridge. This information can only be recovered after refinement, when a decision is made about which recipe to use.

AbNLP distinguishes between two kinds of deletion in the operator description language. The first kind is standard deletion, as performed by delete lists in the STRIPS language. The second kind is referred to as *information destruction*. Each abstract operator has an information destruction effect as part of its post-condition. This is called the *i-delete* list. If a proposition P appears on the i-delete list of an abstract operator then P can no longer be relied upon to hold following its application. For example, after the abstract movement of the large disc in the Towers of Hanoi, all atoms of the form $on(x, y)$, for discs x and pegs y, are i-deleted (see the example operators in section 2.2). This simply captures the fact that movement of the large disc might affect the positions of the other discs, but any such effects are not yet of concern to the planner. I-deletion is treated as normal deletion when considering interactions with established goals, because a proposition that has been i-deleted cannot be relied upon to be necessarily true. It is important to note that i-deleted propositions may in fact be either necessarily true or necessarily false (or neither of these) so to i-delete a proposition is not the same as asserting its possible truth (there may be no completions in which the proposition is asserted).

The use of i-deletes ensures that abstract plans are sound with respect to the domain axioms. The details of how they are used are discussed with reference to the CNF example in section 4.

2.2 Abstraction levels can be mixed within a plan

Abstraction levels can be mixed within task networks in the HTN framework because primitive tasks can occur alongside non-primitive tasks so that primitive operators can be introduced into plans at any level of refinement. Constraints which cannot be resolved at the current level are placed on a "promissory list" and a plan becomes inconsistent as soon as any constraint on the promissory list is violated. However, interactions between primitive and non-primitive components may not be fully revealed until the non-primitive components have been significantly expanded, at which point it may emerge that unsustainable promises were made much earlier in the plan development process. This could entail considerable unnecessary plan development effort. The problem arises from an inability to prevent unsustainable promises from being committed to when insufficient information was available to determine whether they could be kept.

In planners which exploit rigid abstraction hierarchies, formed by partitioning either domain literals or actions [7, 17], abstraction levels cannot be mixed within plans. This simplifies consistency maintenance but at the expense of flexibility and expressive power. DPOCL allows intermingling of composite and non-composite operators but, as noted above, the problems associated with dealing with interactions between them are not fully addressed. It is possible that serious problems in this regard have not been encountered in applications of DPOCL because it has been applied mainly in discourse planning contexts in which, typically, operators do not have delete lists [10]. None of the example operators presented in the DPOCL literature have negative effects.

AbNLP has been designed specifically to allow the correct management of interactions between operators at different levels of abstraction. The use of i-deletes to handle the loss of information associated with the application of abstract operators allows less abstract operators to follow more abstract ones in a plan only if their *filters* are unaffected by both the delete and i-delete lists of the abstract operator. Filters in AbNLP are preconditions which can be made necessarily true by constraint addition, but not by the addition of new steps. This is the only type of precondition that operators (both abstract and primitive) can have in AbNLP.

In AbNLP an abstract operator can be said to characterise a transformation from *all* states in its input set to *some* state in its output set. The sizes of these sets correspond to the extent of the planner's knowledge of the actual state at the corresponding stage of the planning process. The most abstract operators have no filters so that they can be applied regardless of the state of knowledge of the planner. Less abstract operators, which usually have more filters, can be applied when more knowledge is available. If the filters of an operator cannot be satisfied then a more abstract version of that operator must be used in its stead. As a consequence of information loss, at certain points in the development of an abstract plan there may not be sufficient information available for the planner to ascertain whether a certain condition is asserted or not. Abstract operators can be used to continue the process of plan development under these conditions.

The following operators are taken from the representation used by AbNLP of the Towers of Hanoi domain. MoveDisc is a primitive operator and corresponds to the single STRIPS operator required for this domain. MoveLarge is an abstract operator which can be applied regardless of the positions of the discs and has the effect that the large disc is on peg Y. The positions of the other discs are unknown - the movement of the large disc ensures that the medium disc cannot be clear for a move to any peg (the *clear* predicate is only satisfied if no disc is on top of the disc to be moved and no smaller disc is on its destination peg). Any knowledge about the contents of the pegs (other than what is asserted by this operator) is lost (through i-deletion). Literals containing "dollared" variables in the delete and i-delete lists are universally quantified - that is, they are deleted/i-deleted for *all* values of those variables.

The second goal in the body is tied to the codas of both goals. Codas are discussed in the following section.

MoveLarge(Y)	MoveDisc(D,X,Y)
Pre:	Pre: on(D,X), top(D,X), under(D,Q)
Add: id1:on(large,Y)	top(Z,Y), smaller(D,Z)
id2:top(large,Y)	Add:on(D,Y)
Del: clear(medium,$X)	top(Q,X)
IDel: on($X,$Y)	under(D,Z)
top($X,$Y)	top(D,Y)
{Body: id3:clear(large,Y).	Del: on(D,X)
id4:on(large,Y) → id1,id2.	top(D,X)
tcons: (id3,id4)}	under(D,Q)
	top(Z,Y)

An abstract plan to transform the state in which all of the discs are on peg a into a state in which the large disc is on peg c and the medium disc is on peg b would be as follows:

$$MoveLarge(c) \rightarrow MoveMedium(b)$$

The abstract MoveMedium operator is required because the position of the medium disc is i-deleted by the MoveLarge operator. After refinement it will become apparent that the medium disc is moved to peg b in the process of moving the large disc to peg c, so that expansion of the MoveMedium step is unnecessary. The unexpanded operator is then removed from the plan without consideration of the goals in its body. This is different from the HTN technique of satisfying goals which are already asserted with dummy tasks.

2.3 Steps in abstract plans can disappear on refinement

The standard way of expanding abstract operators (or tasks) in decomposition planners is to substitute them for partially ordered steps. The expansion of abstract plan components into steps allows the specification of what to *do*, rather than what to *achieve*, which Erol claims allows the expression of certain types of goals which cannot be easily captured as propositions. An example arises when scheduled behaviour is required (do A then do B). However, the CNF example in section 4 shows that goals of this kind can be captured naturally in a propositional way using abstraction, without the need to take a task-decomposition approach to solving them.

The heuristic advantage offered by the task decomposition approach taken in HTN planning is that much of the conflict resolution work that might be involved in the expansion of a compound task has already been resolved in the constraint formula associated with the expansion. Given that, when two compound tasks are ordered, the whole expansion of the first task must be constrained to be before the whole expansion of the second, its interaction with the rest of the plan is kept to a minimum. Of course, this reduces the flexibility with which an abstract plan can be refined.

Allowing abstract operators to have effects creates the problem of relating these effects correctly to the expansions of abstract operators on refinement of an abstract plan. Yang [17] requires each decomposition of an operator that achieves l to contain a sub-task with effect l that is not undone by any other subtask in the expansion (the *unique main subtask*). This ensures that each expansion achieves the effects of the abstract operator. DPOCL requires that all steps in the decomposition of a composite operator come within the start and end points of the interval occupied by the composite operator in the abstract plan. For each of the composite operator's effects there must be a sequence of steps in the decomposition which culminates in its achievement. This is a less restrictive constraint than that imposed by Yang.

An abstract operator in AbNLP has two parts: its *shell* and its *body*. The shell consists of the filters of the operator, its add list, delete list and i-delete list. Every proposition on the add list is associated with a time identifier, called a *coda*. The goals in the body are partially ordered and there is at least one goal in the body associated with every coda in the shell. Thus, there may not be unique achievers for high level effects, and main effects are not distinguished from the other effects of the abstract operator. The association between a goal g and a coda c is that g must persist until c in the refined plan. In other words, g achieves, or contributes to the achievement of, the add effect with coda c in the refined plan. The coda c has significance in the abstract plan as the end of the interval over which the add effect is required to remain asserted.

When an operator is expanded the goals in its body can interleave with other goals and operators in the refined plan provided that the refined plan remains consistent with all of the constraints imposed at the abstract level. A new constraint is added requiring g to be asserted over an interval including c. This ensures that the add effect in the shell of the operator is perpetuated in the refined plan. If two abstract operators are ordered in the abstract plan then every goal in the body of the first operator must persist over an interval that includes the moment of application of the second operator. This does not prevent the intervals associated with the goals in the body of the second operator from starting before the first operator. DPOCL cannot achieve this flexibility because of the requirement that constraints between abstract operators entail the same constraint between their entire expansions.

An advantage of specifying expansions in terms of goals rather than steps is that abstract operators can disappear in refined plans if all of the goals in their bodies are already asserted over the necessary intervals. The restriction to goals does not restrict the kinds of goals that can be expressed, as the CNF example demonstrates. Further, the way in which information loss is handled means that abstract operators can be added to a plan which, after refinement, are found to be redundant. AbNLP allows the expansion of abstract operators to be postponed until it is certain that the work they entail is required. If it transpires that the operator is redundant it is removed from the plan. UMCP does not permit the removal of composite tasks - they have to be decomposed into goal tasks before they can be replaced with dummy steps.

3 The planning process of AbNLP

AbNLP begins with a complete picture of the world, the initial state, and a conjunction of goals characterised by a set of acceptable configurations of the world. Goals are expressed as intervals over which certain propositions must hold. The goals are placed on a *commitment stack*. AbNLP works by interleaving planning episodes with refinement. Each planning episode involves achieving all outstanding goals, using as many primitive operators as possible (since this converges faster towards finished plans) but using abstract operators when primitives cannot be applied. This differs from approaches in which planning adheres to a strict action hierarchy [17]. A non-linear planning process in the style of UCPOP is used, except that no sub-goaling is done on the filters of operators. Refinement occurs when there are no goals remaining to be achieved.

On refinement, the decision is made as to whether to expand, postpone or drop abstract operators. If an operator is expanded the goals in its body are added to the commitment stack and the constraints in the body are added to the global constraints sets. Postponed operators are placed on the commitment stack during plan refinement so that they can be reconsidered for expansion at the appropriate point in the refined plan. This means that the objects retrieved from the stack are either goals or postponed expansions.

Each postponed expansion has one or more *keys* associated with it, which are the goals it was used in the plan to achieve. The expansion is only done if there is sufficient information available to confirm that at least one of the keys has not been *i-achieved* over the required interval. A key is i-achieved over an interval if it is either asserted over that interval or i-deleted during that interval in the current plan. The i-deletion of a key means that the key may, in fact, be asserted as required. If there is still doubt, then the effort of expansion is postponed again. The following algorithm indicates the process by which AbNLP proceeds towards a primitive solution using the hierarchical planning techniques discussed above.

```
To plan:
1 WHILE there are postponed operators or commitments in the plan DO
2       WHILE the commitment stack is non-empty DO
3           pop commitment c from commitment stack
4           IF c is a goal
5           THEN achieve c
6           ELSE    IF any key for c is not possibly i-achieved
7                   THEN expand c
8                   ELSE IF all keys for c are possibly achieved
9                        THENFOReach key, k, of c DO
10                            SE-achieve k
11                       drop c
12                  ELSE postpone c
13      place all abstract operators and postponed commitments into commitment
        stack, topologically sorted, earliest at the top
14      inherit all ordering and variable-binding constraints and causal links
        attached to the initial state or to primitive operators
```

```
To achieve c
1 identify a possibly achieving step, existing or new, o
2 add ordering and variable-binding constraints to make o a necessary achiever
        for c
3 add promotion, demotion or separation constraints to ensure that nothing deletes
        or i-deletes c
4 IF o is a new step
5 THEN  FOR each precondition, p, of o DO
6           SE-achieve p
7           add promotion, demotion or separation constraints to ensure o does not
            conflict with existing causal links
```

SE-achieve is identical to Achieve, except that no new step may be introduced into the plan.

4   The CNF example

The CNF domain is an artificial domain used by Erol to demonstrate that HTN planning in UMCP has an expressive advantage over functor-free STRIPS. This domain provides a useful example with which to contrast the HTN approach exemplified by UMCP with the natural approach to abstraction exemplified by AbNLP. Most significantly, solving problems in the CNF domain involves setting goals which, it has been claimed, require the use of tasks to capture. Second, the domain is small and yet non-trivial, and has the advantage of having been presented in full in the UMCP literature making it available for full comparison. Third, it is small enough to allow the main features of AbNLP to be demonstrated in action using reasonably uncomplicated examples.

CNF is a formal language domain specified in terms of two context free grammars. The goal is to find a string common to the languages generated by the two grammars. Thus, the initial state consists of the rules for any two context free grammars (with terminals a and b and rules for non-terminals having at most two symbol expansions) and plans correspond to the common strings with symbols from the two grammars strictly alernating to ensure equivalent outputs. The operator set consists of operators for expanding the non-terminals of the two grammars in a way that ensures strict turn-taking between them. The initial state contains the assertion that it is G1's turn and the goal is expressed so that each grammar takes precisely the same number of turns.

A peculiar feature of this domain for state-based planning is that simple-establishment [2] is not necessarily advantageous. For example, if the construction of a common string requires that a particular non-terminal be expanded twice it is not helpful for the planner to spend a long time exploring the path in which the first expansion is re-used. The HTN encoding of this domain avoids this problem by simply requiring two decompositions of the same expansion task. As will be seen, the representation of the domain in AbNLP requires that symbols be "unexpanded" directly after their expansion so that the planner is unable to reuse achieved expansion goals.

Erol's encoding of the domain includes the following set of primitive operators and methods. Only the operators and methods for the first symbol of each grammar are given - analogous operators and methods exist for the other symbols of the grammars.

(operator Fa1()	(operator Fa2()	(declare-method G(v)	(declare-method G(v)
:pre: ((¬ turn))	:pre: ((turn))	:expansion ((n Fa1))	:expansion ((n Fa2))
:post: ((Pa)(turn)))	:post: ((¬ Pa)(¬ turn)))	:formula (veq v a1))	:formula (veq v a2))

(declare-method G(v)	(declare-method G(v)
:expansion ((n do_nothing))	:expansion ((n1 G v1) (n2 G v2))
:formula (veq v dummy))	:formula (and (ord n1 n2) (initially (R v v1 v2))))

Two context free languages are defined for which UMCP is to find a common string. These are: $\{a^n b^n | n \geq 0\}$ and $\{(ab)^n | n \geq 1\}$. The corresponding grammars are:

$$\begin{aligned} G1 : S &\to \epsilon \\ S &\to aQ \\ Q &\to Sb \end{aligned} \qquad\qquad \begin{aligned} G2 : S &\to ab \\ S &\to aQ \\ Q &\to bS \end{aligned}$$

The initial state contains the rules for these grammars and the fact that it is G1's turn initially. The goal is expressed as the requirement that the compound tasks (G S1) and (G S2) are expanded and that, following this, it is G1's turn again (both strings are of the same length).

UMCP produces the following correct plan:

$$Fa1 \to Fa2 \to do\_nothing \to do\_nothing \to Fb1 \to Fb2$$

in which the *do_nothing* steps are unordered with respect to Fa2.

An effective encoding of the CNF domain in AbNLP contains the following primitive operators, the first of which corresponds to Erol's Fa1 and Fb1. There is an analogous operator for the other grammar which is not shown here. There is no *do_nothing* operator but the *unexpand* is required for the reasons explained above.

```
expandG1(N)                    unexpand(N)
Var: N                         Var: N,G
Pre: turn(G1)                  Pre: expanded(N,G)
     terminal(N)               Add:unexpanded(N)
Add:expanded(N,G1)             Del: expanded(N,G)
     turn(G2)                  econs: N ≠ dummy
Del: turn(G1)
     unexpanded(N)
```

The most abstract operator in the set is *TopExpand*, which is used to expand non-terminals. *N* must be a non-terminal and an application of *TopExpand* loses information about whose turn it is, since the work involved in its expansion might involve turn-taking but the details are not available at this level. Thus, this operator i-deletes *turn($G)*. The other post-condition effects in the shell of *TopExpand* are self-explanatory. The identifier *id*1 is the coda associated with the add effect.

The body contains three ordered goals. The first identifies an appropriate rule yielding the labels *X* and *Y*, which are terminals or non-terminals of the appropriate grammar. The goals are ordered so that *X* is *MidExpanded* before *Y*. Expanding a symbol involves waiting for the turn of the appropriate grammar, performing the expansion and then unexpanding so that the expansion cannot be reused. This is expressed through the *MidExpand* operator.

The final body-goal is associated with the coda of the add effect and is therefore the goal which can be said to complete achievement of this effect at the refined level.

The *MidExpand* operator for the first grammar is shown here - there is an analogous one for the second grammar. It is responsible for expanding and unexpanding a label and it loses information about whose turn it is, as does *TopExpand*.

```
TopExpand(N)                        EstablishTurn(G)
Var: N,X,Y,G                        Var: G
Pre: non_terminal(N,G)              Pre:
Add:   id1:expanded(N,G)            Add:  id1:turn(G)
Del:   unexpanded(N)                Del:
IDel:  turn($G)                     IDel:
{Body: id3:rule(N,X,Y,G).           {Body:  id2:turn(G1) → id1.}
       id4:mid_expanded(X,G).
       id5:mid_expanded(Y,G) → id1.
 tcons: (id4,id5)}

                    MidExpandG1(N)
                    Var: N
                    Pre: symbol_of(N,G1)
                    Add:   id1:mid_expanded(N,G1)
                    Del:   unexpanded(N)
                    IDel:  turn($G)
                    {Body:  id2:turn(G1).
                            id3:expanded(N,G1).
                            id4:unexpanded(N) → id1.
                     tcons:  (id2,id3)
                             (id3,id4)}
```

The initial state contains all of the grammar rules and asserts that it is the turn of G1 initially. The goal is expressed as the conjunction

$$expanded(s1, G1) \land expanded(s2, G2) \land turn(G1)$$

At the most abstract level the plan is as follows:

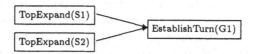

Because *TopExpand* loses information about whose turn it is it is necessary to achieve the final goal at this level using an *EstablishTurn(G1)*. Expansion of this operator is postponed when the plan is refined because the fact that the two *TopExpand* applications are unordered means that it is not possible to determine whether the work involved in actually establishing G1's turn will be needed. On refinement of the plan the goals in the bodies of the *TopExpand* operators are achieved yielding the following plan in which the body of *EstablishTurn* has been postponed.

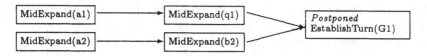

On refinement of this plan there is still insufficient information available to determine whose turn it is, because *MidExpand* i-deletes this information. The expansion of *EstablishTurn* is postponed again.

The finished plan at the next level is:

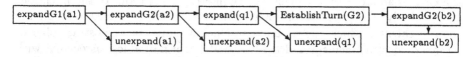

At this level it is apparent that turn(G1) is established at the end of the sequence of turn-taking and the unexpanded operator *EstablishTurn* has, accordingly, been dropped from the plan.

The final plan is produced after a further 3 plan refinements and a total of 38 goal achievements.

5 Conclusions

The CNF example demonstrates that the ability to order goals in the bodies of abstract operators makes it possible to express goals identified as tasks in the HTN literature. For example, the compound task of making a round trip to New York [4] would be expressed in AbNLP as the goal *madeRoundTrip(X, Y)* which would be achieved by an abstract operator with the strictly ordered goals *at(X)*, *at(Y)* and *at(X)* in its body.

The CNF example shows how information loss is modelled through the use of i-deletes in AbNLP. It also shows that Abstract operators which seem to play a role in an abstract plan (such as *EstablishTurn*) can be dropped if it transpires that the work involved in expanding them will not, after all, be necessary. The abstract plans shown in section 4 have meaning by virtue of the effects of the abstract operators within them, which clearly convey the intentions behind them. In later refinements of the plan (not shown here) primitive expand operators are interleaved with *MidExpands* and *TopExpands*, clearly demonstrating that AbNLP allows levels of abstraction to be mixed within planning levels. Thus, the four features described as fundamental to the natural exploitation of abstraction have been shown in operation in this example.

The artificiality and simplicity of the domain prevents several features of AbNLP from being clearly conveyed. The most important of these is that AbNLP allows goals from the bodies of abstract operators to be interleaved even when the abstract operators were ordered prior to refinement. This point was made in section 2.3 - the freedom to do this is made possible by way in which the association between body goals and the add effects they achieve is realised in constraints in the refined plan. In this domain the operators are not rich enough to show off the coda mechanism to the best advantage. In more richly structured operators, in which abstract operators may have more than one effect, several of the body goals may be tied to codas rather than just the last goal in the body being tied to the one and only coda in the shell. Further, it is possible for more than one body goal to be tied to the same coda. In this example however, it is the sequencing of the goals in the body that achieves the add effect of the abstract operator, so it is only the last goal in the body that needs to be associated with the add effect.

The main features of AbNLP have been discussed and demonstrated through the CNF example: abstract plans can be interpreted in terms of the intentions they embody; the purposes of goals in the bodies are expressed through the coda mechanism which allows the intentional structure of an abstract plan to be inherited on refinement and the deliberate information loss associated with the use of abstraction is properly managed through information deletion and its subsequent recovery following the refinement of abstract plans.

References

1. F. Bacchus and Q. Yang. Downward refinement and the efficiency of hierarchical problem solving. *Artificial Intelligence*, 71(1), 1994.
2. D. Chapman. Planning for conjunctive goals. *Artificial Intelligence*, 29, 1987.
3. M. Drummond. Refining and extending the procedural net. In *Proceedings of IJCAI-85*, 1985.
4. K. Erol. *Hierarchical Task Network Planning: Formalization, Analysis and Implementation*. PhD thesis, University of Maryland, 1995.
5. K. Erol, J. Hendler, and D.S. Nau. Semantics for hierarchical task network planning. Technical Report CS-TR-3239 UMICS-TR-94-31, Department of Computer Science, University of Maryland, USA, 1994.

6. H. Kautz. A formal theory of plan recognition and its implementation. In J.F. Allen, H.A. Kautz, R.N. Pelavin, and J.D. Tenenberg, editors, *Reasoning about plans*. Morgan-Kaufmann, 1991.

7. C. Knoblock. Automatically generating abstraction for planning. *Artificial Intelligence*, 68:2, 1994.

8. D. McAllester and D. Rosenblitt. Systematic non-linear planning. In *Proceedings of IJCAI-91*, 1991.

9. J.S. Penberthy and D.S. Weld. UCPOP: A sound and complete partial order planner for ADL. In *Proceedings of KR-92, the 3rd International Conference on Principles of Knowledge Representation and Reasoning*, 1992.

10. C. Reed, D.P. Long, and M. Fox. Context and focussing in argumentative discourse planning. In *Proceedings of the International Conference on Context*, 1997.

11. E.D. Sacerdoti. Planning in a hierarchy of abstraction spaces. *Artificial Intelligence*, 5, 1974.

12. E.D. Sacerdoti. *A structure for plans and behaviour*. American Elsevier, 1977.

13. A. Tate. Project planning using a hierarchical non-linear planner. Technical report, Department of Artificial Intelligence, University of Edinburgh, 1976.

14. A. Tate, B. Drabble, and J. Dalton. O-PLAN: A knowledge-based planner and its application to logistics (url: ftp://ftp.aiai.ed.ac.uk/pub/documents/1996/96-arpi-oplan-and-logistics.ps). In *Advanced Planning Technologies*. Morgan Kaufman, 1996.

15. J. Tenenberg. Abstraction in planning. In J.F. Allen, H.A. Kautz, R.N. Pelavin, and J.D. Tenenberg, editors, *Reasoning about plans*. Morgan-Kaufmann, 1991.

16. D. Wilkins. *Practical planning: extending the classical AI paradigm*. Addison-Wesley, 1988.

17. Q. Yang. Formalizing planning knowledge for hierarchical planning. *Computational Intelligence*, 6, 1990.

18. R. M. Young and J. D. Moore. DPOCL: A principled approach to discourse planning. In *Proceedings of the 7th International Workshop on NLG*, 1994.

19. R. M. Young, M. E Pollack, and J. D. Moore. Decomposition and causality in partial order planning. In *Proceedings of the Second International Conference on AI and Planning Systems*, 1994.

Planning, Learning, and Executing in Autonomous Systems

Ramón García-Martínez
Departmento de Computación
Facultad de Ingeniería
Universidad de Buenos Aires
Bynon 1605. Adrogue (1846)
Buenos Aires. Argentina
email: rgm@mara.fi.uba.ar

Daniel Borrajo
Departamento de Informática
Escuela Politécnica Superior
Universidad Carlos III de Madrid
28911 Leganés (Madrid), España

dborrajo@ia.uc3m.es

Abstract. Systems that act autonomously in the environment have to be able to integrate three basic behaviors: planning, execution, and learning. Planning involves describing a set of actions that will allow the autonomous system to achieve high utility (a similar concept to goals in high-level classical planning) in an unknown world. Execution deals with the interaction with the environment by application of planned actions and observation of resulting perceptions. Learning is needed to predict the responses of the environment to the system actions, thus guiding the system to achieve its goals. In this context, most of the learning systems applied to problem solving have been used to learn control knowledge for guiding the search for a plan, but very few systems have focused on the acquisition of planning operator descriptions. In this paper, we present an integrated system that learns operator definitions, plans using those operators, and executes the plans for modifying the acquired operators. The results clearly show that the integrated planning, learning, and executing system outperforms the basic planner in a robot domain.

Keywords: Planning, unsupervised machine learning, autonomous intelligent systems, theory formation and revision.

1 Introduction

Autonomous intelligent behavior is an area with an emerging interest within Artificial Intelligence researchers [6, 10, 13, 14]. It integrates many areas, such as robotics, planning, and machine learning. This integration opens many questions that arise when designing such systems, such as how operator descriptions can be *incrementally* and *automatically* acquired from the planning/execution cycle, or how a planner can use incomplete and/or incorrect knowledge, as mentioned in [17]. With respect to learning, autonomous systems must generate theories of how their environment reacts to their actions, and how the actions affect the environment. Usually, these theories are partial, incomplete and incorrect, but they can be used to plan, to further modify those theories, or to create new ones.

Among the different types of machine learning techniques, those based on observation and discovery are the best modelers for human behavior [5]. Thus, it is interesting to study how an autonomous system can automatically build planning operators that model its environment [6, 7]. In this context, machine learning applied to planning has mainly focused on learning control knowledge in many different ways such as: macro-operators, control knowledge, or cases. There is also currently a big trend on learning state transition probabilities in the context of reinforcement learning [15, 18]. However, very few have approached the generalized operators acquisition problem [3, 17], which is crucial when dealing with systems that must *autonomously* adapt to a changing environment.

We present in this paper a system, LOPE,[1] that integrates planning, learning, and execution in a closed loop, showing an autonomous intelligent behavior. Learning planning operators is achieved by observing the consequences of executing planned actions in the environment [7].[2] In order to speed up the convergence, heuristic mutations of the observations have been used. Also, probability distribution estimators have been introduced to handle the contradictions among the generated planning operators. The learning technique integrates ideas from genetic algorithms (mutation as a learning operator), reinforcement learning (dealing with operator success probabilities and rewards), and inductive learning (generalization and specialization learning operators). The learning mechanism allows not only to acquire operator descriptions, but also to adapt those descriptions to changes in the environment. The results show how the learning mechanism outperforms the behavior of the base planner with respect to successful plans (plans that achieve self-proposed goals).

Section 2 describes the general architecture of the LOPE system, defining its architecture and top-level algorithm. Section 3 defines the representation that will be used in the paper for situations, observations and planning operators. Section 4 presents the learning model and its components. Section 5 defines the planner. Section 6 explain the performed experiments. And, finally, Section 8 draws the conclusions of the work.

2 General System Description

The integrated system learns, plans and executes in a simulated world according to the robot model described and used by many authors, such as [10, 12]. In this context, a model of the environment refers to a mapping between perceived situations, performed actions, and expected new situations, which is different from high-level models of the environment used by classical planners. The autonomous agent type of world are two-dimensional grids, where each position of the grids can have different elements, such as obstacles, energy points, or be empty. The objective of the LOPE system is to learn operators that predict the effect of actions in the environment, by observing the consequences of actions.

---

[1] LOPE stands for Learning by Observation in Planning Environments.

[2] When we talk about environment, we do not refer to a unique setup, but to the generic concept of environment.

The system can be described as an exploring robot that perceives the environment, applies actions, and learns from its interaction with the world. At the beginning, the system perceives the initial situation, and selects a random action to execute in the environment. Then, it loops over a code that executes an action, perceives the resulting situation and utility of the situation (explained in section 4), learns from observing the effect of applying the action in the environment, and plans for further interactions with the environment. The top-level goal of the planning algorithm is implicit in the system: achieving a situation with the highest utility; the goal is not an input to the system. This fact does not remove generality to the overall architecture, since the function that computes the utility can be changed to the one that reflects other types of goals. Figure 1 shows an schematic view of the architecture, where the allowed actions is the set of actions that the robot can perform in the environment.

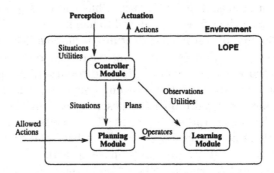

Fig. 1. Architecture of the Integrated System.

3 Representation

For LOPE, as for many other systems, there is a difference between the world states, common to classical planning, and the observations it perceives. While classical planners are mainly interested in the high-level descriptions of the states (e.g. on(A,B) in the blocksworld), LOPE builds its operators based on the perceptions it gets from its sensors. Its "states" are the inputs it receives from its sensoring system. Currently, there is no post-processing of its inputs for translating them into high-level descriptions. The model of the sensoring system is a modified version of the one proposed by [10], who suggested a system with 24 sectors, distributed in three levels. We use a model with eight sectors in two levels (close and distant sensing), and three regions (Left, Frontal, and Right) as shown in Figure 2. The values of each sector conform a binary vector of eight positions that describe each situation. A value of 1 in a position of the vector means that the corresponding sensor has detected something in its sector.

Previous work of the authors developed early versions of the learning mechanism [7, 8]. The representation was based on the model proposed in [6], in which an observation (also called experience unit) had the following structure:

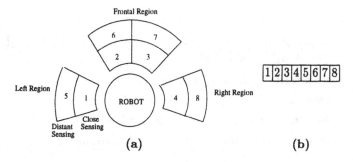

Fig. 2. Divisions of the sensoring system (a) and its internal representation (b)

[Initial Situation, Action, Final Situation]

Observations were directly used as planning operators. In this paper, while the concept of observation does not change, the representation of operators is extended, by the addition of features that allow to determine their planning/execution acceptability. The proposed planning operator model has the following structure and meaning:

PLANNING OPERATOR: O_i		
Feature	**Description**	**Values**
C	Initial Situation (conditions)	s-vector
A	Action	action
F	Final Situation	s-vector
P	Times that the operator O_i was successfully applied (the expected final situation, F, was obtained)	integer
K	Times that the action A was applied to C	integer
U	Utility level reached applying the action to the initial situation, C, of the operator	real 0..1

where *s-vector* is a vector of eight positions and each position can have a 0, 1, or ?. The value ? means "it does not matter the value of that position". We have used the following actions for the value *action*: go, turn-left, turn-right, and stop. U is a function of the distance of the robot to the closest energy point. It is computed by the environment as

$$U(S,P) = \frac{1}{|\, 1 - d(S,P)\,|}$$

where S is the robot position, P is the closest energy point, and $d(S,P)$ is the distance between S and P. Then, this measure is given to the system as an input.

4 Learning Planning Operators

We will first define the concepts of similar and equal operators needed for the learning method, to further detail the learning method, present an example, and discuss the mutation heuristics.

4.1 Definitions

Given two operators $O_1 = [C_1, A_1, F_1, P_1, K_1, U_1]$ and $O_2 = [C_2, A_2, F_2, P_2, K_2, U_2]$, and an observation $o = [S_1, A, S_2]$, we say that:

- The two operators are **similar** if $C_1 = C_2$ and $A_1 = A_2$.
- The two operators are equal if $C_1 = C_2$, $A_1 = A_2$, and $F_1 = F_2$.
- The observation is **similar** to the operator O_1 if $S_1 \subseteq C_1$ and $A = A_1$.
- The observation **confirms** the operator O_1 if $S_1 \subseteq C_1$, $A = A_1$, and $S_2 \subseteq F_1$.

4.2 Learning Algorithm

Suppose a situation S_1 is perceived by the system, and there exists a set of operators, $\mathcal{O}$, such that each operator is of the form $O_i = [C, A, F, P, K, U]$. If the system applies the action A, arriving at a situation S_2, the learning method processes this checking whether it is *similar* to any operator.

- If it is *similar*, it checks to see if the observation *confirms* the operator. Then, it rewards all such operators and punishes *similar* ones. If a *similar* operator exists, but there is none that is *confirmed* by the observation, it creates a new operator, punishes *similar* operators to the new one, and mutates those *similar* operators. The operators generated by the mutation procedure reward *equal* operators and punish *similar* ones.
- If it does not find a *similar* operator for the input observation, it creates a new one.

Punishing operators means incrementing the number of times that the pair (condition,action) of *similar* operators to O has been observed. The effect of incrementing their K is equivalent to punishing them. Also, *rewarding* operators means incrementing the P and K of a successful operator, with the equivalent effect of rewarding it. With respect to the utility, the system will record, for each operator, the utility of the highest-utility situation achieved by applying the operator action to the operator condition situation.[3]

4.3 Example of Learning Episodes

Suppose that the robot does not have any knowledge on how the environment will react to actions that are applied by the robot. We will see now how the system builds a set of operators from the observations o_1, o_2 and o_3, that do not have to necessarily be observed in consecutive instants of time, since other actions could have been applied in the middle.

$$o_1 = (00001001, GO, 00000000) \text{ with } U = U_1$$
$$o_2 = (00001001, GO, 00001111) \text{ with } U = U_2$$
$$o_3 = (00001001, GO, 00000000) \text{ with } U = U_3$$

---

[3] Since the final situation can be generalized, there might be more than one utility. Only the highest is stored.

After observing o_1, according to the algorithm described before, it generates a new operator $O_1=[00001001,\text{GO},00000000,1,1,U_1]$. When it later observes o_2, it finds out that there is a similar operator, O_1. Thus, it first includes the new operator $O_2 = [00001001, GO, 00001111, 1, 2, U_2]$ into the set of operators $\mathcal{O}$. Then, it punishes the similar operators (only O_1 in this case), changing it to be $O_1 = [00001001, GO, 00000000, 1, 2, U_1]$. Then, it calls the mutation heuristics to create mutated observations. Among other mutation heuristics, the retraction heuristic, would generate the mutated observation $m = [00001001, GO, 0000????, U]$, where U would be U_1 in this case. Since it now finds that there are similar operators, O_1 and O_2, it adds a new (mutated) operator, $O_3 = [00001001, GO, 0000????, 1, 3, U_1]$, and punishes all similar operators by incrementing their K, leaving $\mathcal{O}$ as:

$$O_1 = [00001001, GO, 00000000, 1, 3, U_1]$$
$$O_2 = [00001001, GO, 00001111, 1, 3, U_2]$$
$$O_3 = [00001001, GO, 0000????, 1, 3, U_1]$$

For LOPE, the new mutated operator O_3 predicts what will be the final situation after applying the action GO to the initial situation 00001001 as well as O_1 and O_2 do. This is why $P_{O_3} = 1$. A value of three would mean a stronger relation between O_3 and O_1/O_2. When it observes o_3, which is a *confirmation* of operators O_1 and O_3, it rewards all operators equal to the observation (O_1 and O_3), and punishes all operators that are similar (O_2). Since it rewards both operators O_1 and O_2, the K of all operators gets increased to 5. The final set of operators is:

$$O_1 = [00001001, GO, 00000000, 2, 5, U_1]$$
$$O_2 = [00001001, GO, 00001111, 1, 5, U_2]$$
$$O_3 = [00001001, GO, 0000????, 2, 5, U_1]$$

4.4 Heuristic Mutation of Operators

The heuristic mutation of operators is based on the heuristics defined in [9] and [11]. Hayes-Roth proposed a set of heuristics for revising a faulty (buggy) theory, in the framework of theory revision. We selected which heuristics were applicable for the chosen vector representation, and transformed those for correcting violated expectations of plans.

- **Retraction:** generalizes an operator predicted situation so that it is consistent with the new observation.

- **Exclusion:** restricts the conditions of the operator, so that it does not apply to the observed situation again.

- **Avoidance:** also restricts the applicability conditions of the operator by conjoining negated preconditions that are sufficient for not predicting the observed situation again. Since the implementation of this heuristic in the chosen vector representation arrived to a similar procedure as the previous one, we did not use this heuristic.

- **Inclusion:** generalizes the operator conditions, so that it will later apply in the observed situation.

- **Assurance:** generalizes the conditions of the operator, so that it can be applied in the future to assure the predicted effects. Again, the implementation of this heuristic was similar to the previous one, so it was not used.

Salzberg heuristics are used to correct prediction violations. He proposed the following heuristics for revising predicting rules in a racing domain. We also transformed those heuristics to the vector representation. As in the previous case, we did not implement all heuristics, given that some of them do not have an equivalent when one does not have a knowledge-rich domain theory as Salzberg had.

- **Inusuality:** restricts the condition of an operator, so that it will not longer apply to the observed initial situation.

- **Ignorance:** assigns the fault of using an operator to unknown relations. Salzberg used a propositional representation with variable length, and since we are using a vector-based representation (fixed length representation), we could not use this heuristic.

- **Guilty:** has a set of predefined possible causes of fault in an operator, such that when a fault appears, the heuristic checks whether one of those causes is present in the observed situation. We did not implement this heuristic, since we could not find such a set of predefined causes, such as "when the first two bits are 1 in the situation", given that this domain does not have a rich domain theory.

- **Conservationism:** is a meta-heuristic that selects the mutation heuristic (from the Salzberg ones), that proposes less modifications in the conditions of an operator.

- **Simplicity:** is a generalization of the Hayes-Roth retraction heuristic in that it generalizes several operators into one.

- **Adjustment:** when the P/K ratio of an operator falls below a given threshold, it is very unlike that the operator will correctly predict any situation. If it is a generalization of a set of operators (for instance, by application of the simplicity heuristic), this heuristic generates other combinations of those operators that will increase the ratio.

5 Planning

The planner builds a sequence of planning operators[4] that allows to efficiently reach the top-level goal of having the highest utility (being on top of an energy point) by being on a situation which yields such utility. In case another domain requires a more classical high-level set of goals (as in the case of the blocksworld

---

[4] In this case, the term operator and action are equivalent with respect to planning and execution, given that operators do not have variables.

or logistics transportation), a richer representation would be needed. The planning and learning components would have to be changed accordingly, but the overall architecture and techniques would still be valid.

Since each operator has its own utility, the planner will try to build plans that transform each current situation into the situation described by the condition of the operator with the highest utility; that is, the operator that achieves the highest utility situation (its final situation). Therefore, these conditions are subgoals of the top-level goal. The resulting plan will allow the execution module to perform a set of actions that interact with the environment in such a way that it arrives to a situation in which the action of the highest utility operator can be executed (the conditions are met), thus achieving that level of utility.

5.1 Building a Plan

The planning algorithm proceeds as follows. At the beginning, there are no operators, so the system generates a default plan by randomly selecting whether to act randomly, or to act by curiosity/exploration (by approaching a close obstacle).[5] If the system already has some operators, it builds a list of goals, each of them is a pair (situation,operator), where situation is the final situation of the operator. This list is ordered by decreasing values of the utility of their respective operators. For each subgoal, the planner tries to find a plan that can transform the current situation S into one of the subgoals. Since it first tries the goals with higher utilities, and it stops when it finds a plan, the planner will find a plan for achieving the highest utility reachable goal. If the planner cannot find a plan for any goal, it generates a default plan according to the default planning procedure described above.

In order to create a plan to achieve a goal, the planner creates a graph by backward chaining on the goal. Since the goals are pairs (situation,operator), the root of the search tree will be the situation, that will only have one successor labeled with the operator of the goal. For each situation in the search tree, it creates a node, and a successor for each operator whose final situation matches that situation, and continues backwards until it cannot expand more nodes. Goal loops (repetition of the same situation in the path from a node to the root) are detected and search stops under those nodes. When it finishes the expansion of the tree, if the current situation appears in the graph, there exists at least one plan that can achieve the goal from the current situation.

As an example of how this algorithm proceeds, suppose that the system already built the set of operators shown in Figure 3(a), where there are two actions A_1 and A_2, and five situations S_1 to S_5. The search space corresponding to those operators is shown in Figure 3(b), where each node represents a situation, and each arc is labeled with a tuple (A, P, K, U), where A is the action of the operator, that transforms a situation into another, P and K are the features that capture the information on success probability (explained in subsection 5.2), and U is the operator utility.

---

[5] The system is close to an obstacle when there is a 1 on any element of the input vector.

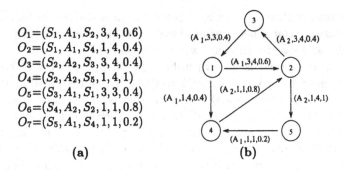

$O_1 = (S_1, A_1, S_2, 3, 4, 0.6)$
$O_2 = (S_1, A_1, S_4, 1, 4, 0.4)$
$O_3 = (S_2, A_2, S_3, 3, 4, 0.4)$
$O_4 = (S_2, A_2, S_5, 1, 4, 1)$
$O_5 = (S_3, A_1, S_1, 3, 3, 0.4)$
$O_6 = (S_4, A_2, S_2, 1, 1, 0.8)$
$O_7 = (S_5, A_1, S_4, 1, 1, 0.2)$

(a)

(b)

Fig. 3. Example of planning operators (a) and their graph representation (b).

Given that search space, if the planner tries to find a plan to achieve the higher utility reachable goal from the current situation S_1, it would first generate the list of pairs (goal-situation,operator) in descendent order of utility. In this case, the list would be:

$$[(S_5, O_4)(S_2, O_6)(S_2, O_1)(S_4, O_2)(S_3, O_3)(S_1, O_5)(S_4, O_7)]$$

As (S_5, O_4) has the highest utility level, the system builds the search tree shown in Figure 4, where the root is the situation S_5, its only successor is the condition part of the operator O_4: situation S_2, and the arcs are labeled with the actions and operators that transform a situation in another. Search stops under nodes of situations S_3 (twice) and S_5 since the only way to obtain those situations is from situation S_2 which would cause a goal loop.

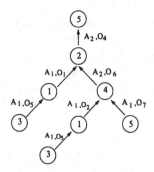

Fig. 4. Search tree generated when planning to achieve situation S_5 from S_1.

There are two plans that reach S_5 from S_1: $O_1 \circ O_4$[6] (actions A_1 and A_2) and $O_2 \circ O_6 \circ O_4$ (actions A_1, A_2, and A_2). The planner selects the shortest plan, which is $O_1 \circ O_4$ ($A_1 \circ A_2$).

---

[6] o represents the composition of operations.

5.2 Stochastic Planning

In order to estimate the probability of success of plans, the planner is based on an extension of the theory of stochastic automata. The knowledge that the system has at a given time, the set of planning operators, can be viewed as a model of how its environment will react to the system's actions. The quotient P_{O_i}/K_{O_i} of a given operator O_i, is the probability estimator of the fact that given the action A_{O_i} applied to a situation S_j that matches the operator conditions $(S_j \subseteq C_{O_i})$ results in a situation S_k that verifies the predicted effects of the operator $(S_k \subseteq F_{O_i})$. We have shown in our previous work that this estimator is an unbiased estimator that follows a multinomial probability distribution. Therefore, the knowledge that the system has of the effects of an action A_i at a given instant can be represented by the transition matrix M_{A_i}, that has on the (j, k) position the quotient P_{O_i}/K_{O_i} of the operator whose action is A_i, its conditions are S_j, and the predicted effects S_k [2].

The Ps and Ks of the plan operators can be used in the evaluation of the plans that are generated. This "a priori" estimation of the plan success probability, allows to discard plans with a low probability of success $(P/K < \tau)$, where τ is a user-defined threshold. This property is critical when the system must act without supervision.

As an example, in the previous plan, the transition matrix M_{A_1} associated to the action A_1, the transition matrix M_{A_2} associated to the action A_2, and the transition matrix M_P of the plan $P = A_1 \circ A_2$ are:

$$
\begin{array}{c}
\begin{array}{cccccc}
 & S_1 & S_2 & S_3 & S_4 & S_5
\end{array} \\
\begin{array}{c} S_1 \\ S_2 \\ S_3 \\ S_4 \\ S_5 \end{array}
\left[\begin{array}{ccccc}
0 & \frac{3}{4} & 0 & \frac{1}{4} & 0 \\
0 & 0 & 0 & 0 & 0 \\
1 & 0 & 0 & 0 & 0 \\
0 & 0 & 0 & 0 & 0 \\
0 & 0 & 0 & 1 & 0
\end{array}\right] \\
M_{A_1}
\end{array}
\times
\begin{array}{c}
\begin{array}{cccccc}
 & S_1 & S_2 & S_3 & S_4 & S_5
\end{array} \\
\begin{array}{c} S_1 \\ S_2 \\ S_3 \\ S_4 \\ S_5 \end{array}
\left[\begin{array}{ccccc}
0 & 0 & 0 & 0 & 0 \\
0 & 0 & \frac{3}{4} & 0 & \frac{1}{4} \\
0 & 0 & 0 & 0 & 0 \\
0 & 1 & 0 & 0 & 0 \\
0 & 0 & 0 & 0 & 0
\end{array}\right] \\
M_{A_2}
\end{array}
=
\begin{array}{c}
\begin{array}{cccccc}
 & S_1 & S_2 & S_3 & S_4 & S_5
\end{array} \\
\begin{array}{c} S_1 \\ S_2 \\ S_3 \\ S_4 \\ S_5 \end{array}
\left[\begin{array}{ccccc}
0 & \frac{1}{4} & \frac{9}{16} & 0 & \frac{3}{16} \\
0 & 0 & 0 & 0 & 0 \\
0 & 0 & 0 & 0 & 0 \\
0 & 0 & 0 & 0 & 0 \\
0 & 1 & 0 & 0 & 0
\end{array}\right] \\
M_{A_P}
\end{array}
$$

From the analysis of M_{A_P}, the probability that the plan P applied to the situation S_1 achieves the situation S_2 is $\frac{1}{4}$, the probability that the plan P applied to the situation S_1 achieves the situation S_3 is $\frac{9}{16}$, and the probability that the plan P applied to the situation S_1 achieves the situation S_5 is $\frac{3}{16}$.

6 Experiments and Results

We performed two experiments to test the behavior of LOPE. In the first one, we averaged the results of running 50 experiments. In each experiment the initial setup (environment and position of the robot) was randomly selected, and LOPE performed 8000 cycles of learning, planning and execution. We compared four versions of the system: the base planner, in which operators are created directly from the observations, following Fritz et al. work [6]; the base problem solver using operators learned using heuristic mutation [7]; the base problem solver estimating for each operator its probability of success [8]; and the base problem solver, in which operators are mutated, and a probability estimator is assigned to each operator.

We used the percentage of successful plans when comparing these four versions of the system, and the results of the experiment are shown in Figure 5 (a). These results clearly show that the combination of mutation and probability estimation outperform the base planner behavior, and, also, the separate use of any of them. The combined use of mutation and probabilities make the system converge towards a 80% of success plans, while the base planner converges towards half of it (around 40%).

The second experiment was performed to show the generality of the learned knowledge, as the knowledge transfer from one setup (environment and initial position of the robot) to another. We randomly generated a set of setups, W, and averaged the results of running 50 times the following experiment: a setup w was randomly selected from W; 8000 cycles were run on w; another setup $w' \neq w$ was chosen from the set W; 8000 cycles were run on w', using the learned operators in w; and results were collected. The results are shown in Figure 5(b) where it is shown that the use of previously learned knowledge, even in another setup, improves the initial behavior as well as the convergence of the overall system, with respect to the results in Figure 5(a). For instance, while, in the first experiment, the 70% of success plans was achieved at around 3200 cycles, in the second experiment, the same success ratio was achieved at 1500 cycles.

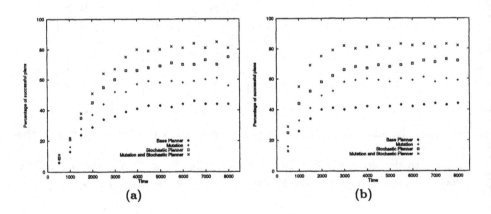

(a) (b)

Fig. 5. Results of comparing four versions of the system with respect to successful planning (a) and knowledge transfer.

7 Related Work

The GINKO system [1] and the LIVE system [12] integrate perception, action and learning. They both differ from the proposed architecture in the fact that they do not take into account reinforcement nor heuristic-based refinement of operators. Christiansen [4] also addresses the problem of learning operators (task theories) in a robotic domain. However, in his work there is no revision process as our heuristic-based refinement process. DYNA [15] integrates reinforcement learning, planning and reacting based on approximated dynamic programming. It differs from our work in the fact that the reinforcement procedure is local to an operator, while, in our case, the reinforcement of an operator explicitly implies the punishment of similar ones (global reinforcement).

OBSERVER [17] integrates planning and learning. Wang proposes an incremental approach for operators revision, where operators evolve during the execution of the system. However, there is no memory of past versions of the operators as in LOPE. Another difference relies in the representation language for operators. Her work used the representation language of PRODIGY4.0 operators [16] that is based on predicate logic, since its goal is to perform classical high-level planning. Our approach uses a representation that is closer to the inputs and outputs of a more reactive system, with low-level planning.

8 Conclusions

There are many real world problems where there is no domain theory available, the knowledge is incomplete, or it is incorrect. In those domains, autonomous intelligent systems, defined as systems that learn, self-propose goals, and build plans to achieve them, sometimes are the only alternative to acquire the needed domain description. In this paper, we have presented an architecture that learns a model of its environment by observing the effects of performing actions on it. The LOPE system autonomously interacts with its environment, self-proposes goals of high utility for the system, and creates operators that predict, with a given probability estimator, the resulting situation of applying an action to another situation. Learning is performed by three integrated techniques: rote learning of an experience (observation) by creating an operator directly from it; heuristic mutation of incorrect learned operators; and a global reinforcement strategy of operators by rewarding and punishing them based on their success in predicting the behavior of the environment. The results show that the integration of those learning techniques can greatly help an autonomous system to acquire a theory description that models the environment, thus achieving a high percentage of successful plans.

References

1. M. Barbehenn and S. Hutchinson. An integrated architecture for learning and planning in robotic domains. *Sigart Bulletin*, 2(4):29–33, 1991.
2. Calistri-Yeh. *Classifying and Detecting Plan Based Misconceptions for Robust Plan Recognition*. PhD thesis, Department of Computer Science. Brown University, 1990.

3. Jaime G. Carbonell and Yolanda Gil. Learning by experimentation: The operator refinement method. In R. S. Michalski and Y. Kodratoff, editors, *Machine Learning: An Artificial Intelligence Approach, Volume III*, pages 191–213. Morgan Kaufmann, Palo Alto, CA, 1990.

4. Allan Christiansen. *Automatic Acquisition of Task Theories for Robotic Manipulation*. PhD thesis, School of Computer Science, Carnegie Mellon University, Pittsburgh, PA, March 1992.

5. B. Falkenhainer. A unified approach to explanation and theory formation. In J. Shrager and Langley P., editors, *Computational Models of Scientific Discovery and Theory Formation*. Morgan Kaufmann, 1990.

6. W. Fritz, R. García-Martínez, J. Blanqué, A. Rama, R. Adobbati, and M. Samo. The autonomous intelligent system. *Robotics and Autonomous Systems*, 5(2):109–125, 1989.

7. Ramón García-Martínez. Heuristic theory formation as a machine learning method. In *Proceedings of the VI International Symposium on Artificial Intelligence*, pages 294–298, México, 1993. LIMUSA.

8. Ramón García-Martínez and Daniel Borrajo. Unsupervised machine learning embedded in autonomous intelligent systems. In *Proceedings of the 14th IASTED International Conference on Applied Informatics*, pages 71–73, Innsbruck, Austria, 1996.

9. Frederick Hayes-Roth. Using proofs and refutations to learn from experience. In R. S. Michalski, J. G. Carbonell, and T. M. Mitchell, editors, *Machine Learning, An Artificial Intelligence Approach*, pages 221–240. Tioga Press, Palo Alto, CA, 1983.

10. S. Mahavedan and J. Connell. Automatic programming of behavior-based robots using reinforcement learning. *Artificial Intelligence*, 55:311–365, 1992.

11. Stephen Salzberg. Heuristics for inductive learning. In *Proceedings of the Ninth International Joint Conference on Artificial Intelligence*, pages 603–609, Los Angeles, CA, 1985.

12. W. Shen. Discovery as autonomous learning from enviroment. *Machine Learning*, 12:143–165, 1993.

13. Reid Simmons and Tom M. Mitchell. A task control architecture for mobile robots. In *Working Notes of the AAAI Spring Symposium on Robot Navigation*, 1989.

14. Peter Stone and Manuela M. Veloso. Towards collaborative and adversarial learning: A case study in robotic soccer. *To appear in International Journal of Human-Computer Systems (IJHCS)*, 1996.

15. Richard Sutton. Integrated architectures for learning, planning, and reacting based on approximating dynamic programming. In *Proceedings of the Seventh International Conference on Machine Learning*, pages 216–224, Austin, TX, 1990. Morgan Kaufmann.

16. Manuela Veloso, Jaime Carbonell, Alicia Pérez, Daniel Borrajo, Eugene Fink, and Jim Blythe. Integrating planning and learning: The PRODIGY architecture. *Journal of Experimental and Theoretical AI*, 7:81–120, 1995.

17. Xuemei Wang. Planning while learning operators. In B. Drabble, editor, *Proceedings of the Third International Conference on Artificial Intelligence Planning Systems (AIPS96)*, pages 229–236, Edinburgh, Scotland, May 1996.

18. C. J. C. H. Watkins and P. Dayan. Technical note: Q-learning. *Machine Learning*, 8(3/4):279–292, May 1992.

Combining the Expressivity of UCPOP with the Efficiency of Graphplan

B. Cenk Gazen and Craig A. Knoblock

Information Sciences Institute and
Department of Computer Science
University of Southern California
Marina del Rey, CA 90292

Abstract. There has been a great deal of recent work on new approaches to efficiently generating plans in systems such as Graphplan and SATplan. However, these systems only provide an impoverished representation language compared to other planners, such as UCPOP, ADL, or Prodigy. This makes it difficult to represent planning problems using these new planners. This paper addresses this problem by providing a completely automated set of transformations for converting a UCPOP domain representation into a Graphplan representation. The set of transformations extends the Graphplan representation language to include disjunctions, negations, universal quantification, conditional effects, and axioms. We tested the resulting planner on the 18 test domains and 41 problems that come with the UCPOP 4.0 distribution. Graphplan with the new preprocessor is able to solve every problem in the test set and on the hard problems (i.e., those that require more than one second of CPU time) it can solve them significantly faster than UCPOP. While UCPOP was unable to solve 7 of the test problems within a search limit of 100,000 nodes (which requires 414 to 980 CPU seconds), Graphplan with the preprocessor solved them all in under 15 CPU seconds (including the preprocessing time).

1 Introduction

One of the important issues in planning is how to define domains and problems. There is a trade-off between the expressiveness and manageability of a formal domain definition language. On one hand, a practical language should be as high-level as possible so that the domain engineer can represent planning problems easily, accurately and naturally. On the other, the more complex the language, the harder it is for the planner to solve the problems.

Some of the planners that support a high-level language are ADL [1], Prodigy [2] and UCPOP [3]. UCPOP is a partial order planner that supports a very expressive domain definition language. The characteristic features of such a language are negations, conditional effects, disjunctive preconditions, universal and existential quantification, axioms, and facts. Given these constructs, it is usually possible to find a natural representation for a given domain.

Graphplan [4] is a graph algorithmic planner that runs much faster than traditional planners but supports a minimal language for defining domains and problems. In Graphplan, a domain is represented by a set of operators, each of which is defined by a list of parameters, a list of propositions as preconditions, and a list of add and delete effects. A problem is represented by a typed set of objects, a list of propositions as initial conditions, and a list of propositions as the goal. For most domains, this language is awkward to use, although once the domain is defined in this language, problems can be solved much faster than it is possible with UCPOP.

One approach to support a more expressive language is to extend the 'Planning Graph' of Graphplan [5]. Another is to develop a preprocessor that translates domains from an expressive representation language into a simpler one. Advantages of the second approach are that it is conceptually simple and that it is not necessarily specific to one planner. On the other hand, it cannot handle some language constructs as efficiently as a high-level planner can.

In this paper, we present a set of algorithms that transform a UCPOP domain and problem into an equivalent Graphplan domain and problem, although the same methods can be used with other fast planners, notably SATplan [6], that are based on simple representations. The goal is to make the best of both planners. UCPOP supports a rich set of domain definition language features, but is much slower compared to Graphplan, which only supports a minimal language.

The preprocessor takes as input a UCPOP domain and problem, and generates an equivalent pair in Graphplan's language by applying rewriting rules step by step. The result of each step is an equivalent representation of the domain where some of the language constructs have been replaced with simpler ones.

2 Rewriting UCPOP domains as Graphplan domains

In UCPOP, domains are defined by operators, axioms, facts, and safety constraints [7]. Problems are defined by a list of initial conditions and a goal expression. UCPOP operators are represented by a list of parameters, a precondition expression, and an effect expression. The last two are arbitrarily nested first-order logic expressions, although some semantically meaningless (in a planning problem) expressions are not allowed. The restriction follows from the fact that operators should have deterministic effects. The expressions can be formed using negations, conjunctions, disjunctions, implications, and quantification. When used in effect expressions, implications have different semantics and are called conditional effects. The semantics are different because the antecedent of a conditional effect is evaluated with respect to the set of propositions that hold before the operator is applied, whereas the consequent refers to the resulting set. Quantifications can be either universal or existential.

An axiom is a rule that allows the planner to deduce a proposition from the current set of valid propositions. UCPOP supports a restricted form of axioms, where an axiom can only deduce a single proposition. A fact is an arbitrary piece of code that is executed during planning. In UCPOP, they can only appear in the preconditions of operators. Safety constraints are conditions that the planner must maintain throughout the plan.

Although both are based on the STRIPS representation [8], Graphplan has a very restrictive language as compared to UCPOP. A Graphplan domain definition consists of a list of operators. Each operator has a list of parameters, a list of preconditions, a list of 'add' effects and a list of 'delete' effects. The last three lists are assumed to be conjunctions. The precondition list contains propositions that need to hold before the operator can be applied. The application of an operator results in the propositions in the 'add' list to be added to the current set of valid propositions, whereas those propositions in the 'delete' list are removed from the same set. The restrictiveness of Graphplan's language comes from the fact that both preconditions and effects are lists and not arbitrary expressions.

Interestingly, this lack of expressive power in the domain definition language does not place an inherent limitation on the types of problems that Graphplan can solve. The preprocessor we have developed can automatically transform UCPOP domains into Graphplan domains. The current implementation handles all the UCPOP features except facts and safety constraints. We are working on extending the preprocessor to support facts, but safety constraints are better supported explicitly by a planner than with preprocessing.

In our preprocessing approach, we make two assumptions about the domains. First, we assume that objects are not created dynamically. This means that a list of all objects in the domain is available to the preprocessor. Second, we assume that all objects have types. However, this is not a limiting assumption as it is always possible to assign the same type (e.g., object) to every object in the domain. It is also possible to have multi-typed objects. For example, a plane can be typed both as a vehicle and a flying-object. If type information is available, our preprocessor can generate a smaller domain, which in turn makes Graphplan run more efficiently.

The preprocessor is structured as six layers (Figure 1). Each layer processes some specific language construct and generates output that is input to the next layer. The top layer accepts the domain definition from the user while the bottom layer creates the domain in Graphplan's language.

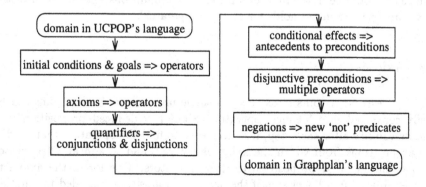

Fig. 1. Preprocessing Layers

2.1 Initial Conditions and Goals

Since initial conditions and goals can contain high-level language constructs, the first step is to convert them into operators. In general, this makes it unnecessary to make special case versions of the algorithms to process the initial conditions and goals.

Given: initial condition expression i; goal expression g; list of operators l_o

let o_{init} be a new operator with precondition (init-problem) and
   effect (and i (not (init-problem)))
let o_{goal} be a new operator with precondition g and effect (goal-achieved)
add o_{init} and o_{goal} to l_o
set the new initial condition to be (init-problem)
set the new goal to be (goal-achieved)

For example, the following problem definition:

(problem blocks :inits (forall (block ?x) (clear ?x))
                   :goal (or (on a table) (exists (block ?x) (clear ?x))))

would be transformed into:

(problem blocks :inits (init-problem)
              :goal (goal-achieved))
(operator init-operator :precondition (init-problem)
                  :effect (and (forall (block ?x) (clear ?x)) (not (init-problem))))
(operator goal-operator :precondition (or (on a table) (exists (block ?x) (clear ?x)))
                  :effect (goal-achieved))

Creating these kinds of operators is a standard planning technique. However, it introduces two extraneous steps when introduced in preprocessing, and these steps need to be removed from the final plan or simply ignored. On the other hand, Graphplan's efficiency is not affected in any significant way as the only operator that is applicable at the first step is the 'init-operator'. After its application, the second level of propositions of the planning graph is exactly the same as it would be in the first level if the initial conditions were stated directly. A 'symmetric' argument holds for the 'goal-operator'.

2.2 Axioms

UCPOP restricts axioms to asserting a single proposition. Such axioms can be easily converted into 'deduce' operators. Since any deduced proposition may lose its validity after each step, it is necessary to find the operators that modify the propositions from which the axiom is derived, and to add an effect which negates the deduced proposition to these operators. This forces the axiom to be re-evaluated in a latter step if the deduced proposition is needed for another operator.

Given: axiom a; list of operators l_o

let o be a new operator
set the precondition of o to context(a) where
   context(a) is an expression that must be true before the axiom can be applied
set the effect of o to implies(a) where
   implies(a) is the single deduced proposition, with predicate p of n arguments
for each op in l_o
   if effect(op) contains any predicate in context(a)
     add (forall $(v_1\ v_2\ \ldots\ v_n)$ (not $(p\ v_1\ v_2\ \ldots\ v_n)$))) to effect($op$)
add o to l_o

For example,

```
(axiom is-clear :context (or (eq ?x Table) (not (exists (obj ?b) (on ?b ?x))))
              :implies (clear ?x))
(operator put-on :parameters (obj ?x) (obj ?y) (obj ?d)
              :precondition (and (on ?x ?d) (clear ?x) (clear ?y))
              :effect (and (on ?x ?y) (not (on ?x ?d))))
```

would be transformed into:

```
(operator deduce-is-clear :parameters (obj ?x)
                  :precondition (or (eq ?x Table)
                                    (not (exists (obj ?b) (on ?b ?x))))
                  :effect (clear ?x))
(operator put-on :parameters (obj ?x) (obj ?y) (obj ?d)
              :precondition (and (on ?x ?d) (clear ?x) (clear ?y))
              :effect (and (forall (?v1) (not (clear ?v1)))
                           (and (on ?x ?y) (not (on ?x ?d)))))
```

Having axioms in a language makes the operator definitions cleaner and less error-prone by allowing the deducible effects that are repeated in many operators to be stated in a single axiom. In a way, preprocessing undoes that, and although the resulting domain is not as compact, its correctness is preserved. Since a conservative approach is followed in invalidating the deduced propositions, in the worst case an axiom may need to be asserted after each step. For example, the 'put-on' operator above does not have to assert (not (clear ?x)) because ?x is still clear after this action, but because it does, the axiom needs to be applied to re-assert (clear ?x) if another action requires (clear ?x) later.

2.3 Quantifiers

In this layer, universal quantifiers are expanded into conjunctions and existential quantifiers into disjunctions. Because dynamic creation of objects is not allowed and all the objects are explicitly declared, the expansion is straightforward. The preprocessor rewrites the quantified expression as a conjunction or disjunction of expressions. Each of these expressions is generated by instantiating the quantified variable with each of the objects that the variable can denote.

Given: a list of objects l_{ob} and a quantified expression $(q \ (t \ v) \ e)$ where
$q \in \{forall, exists\}$; t is a type; v is the quantified variable; e is an expression
for each $ob \in l_{ob}$ s.t. type$(ob) = t$
   $e_i =$ instantiate v with ob in e
if existential(q)
   replace $(q \ (t \ v) \ e)$ with (or $e_1 \ e_2 \ldots e_n$)
else // universal(q)
   replace $(q \ (t \ v) \ e)$ with (and $e_1 \ e_2 \ldots e_n$)

   Given the object definition '(block a) (block b) (block c)', the preprocessor
will expand the expressions on the left into those on the right:

(forall (block ?x) (clear ?x))	(and (clear a) (clear b) (clear c))
(exists (block ?x) (clear ?x))	(or (clear a) (clear b) (clear c))

   The expansion of quantifiers over all the objects is where the static domain
assumption is necessary. Since it is assumed that a list of all the objects in the
domain is available to the preprocessor, the expansion can be done easily. Our
second assumption that all objects are typed is also useful at this layer, because
the expansion is done only over the objects that have the corresponding type. In
the worst case, where a quantified variable can range over all the objects in the
domain (i.e., all objects have the same type), the expansion contains as many
terms as there are objects. After the expansion, a domain in which only a few
objects belong to each type will be more compact than an equivalent domain
where all the objects have the same type. In practice, expansion of quantified
expressions proved to be an acceptable preprocessing technique because most
quantified variables can be restricted to range over a small number of objects.

2.4 Conditional Effects

Conditional effects are translated into simpler expressions by moving the antecedents into the preconditions. By definition, the consequent of a conditional
effect is asserted only when the antecedent holds before the operator is applied.
An equivalent way to represent such an operator is to use two operators: one
with the antecedent in the preconditions and the consequent in the effects, and
another with the negation of the antecedent in the preconditions and the consequent removed from the effects (Figure 2).

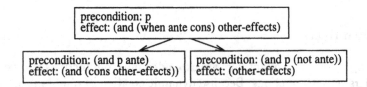

Fig. 2. Transforming Conditional Effects

   More generally, an operator can have multiple conditional effects, which may
appear either as separate conjuncts or as nested conditional effects. An example

of the former is (and (when p q) (when r s)), and an example of the latter is (when p (when q r)). Both cases are handled by applying the expansion of Figure 2 recursively to the resulting operators until all the conditional effects are eliminated.

This expansion generates an exponential number (in terms of the number of conditional effects) of operators, but in some cases it can avoid the problem by partially evaluating the antecedent and replacing the operator with a simplified one which does not have the conditional effect. Depending on the outcome of the evaluation, the consequent can be added to or removed from the effects.

Given: an operator o with precondition p and effect (and $e_1 \, e_2 \ldots e_n$)

if for some i, e_i is a conditional effect (when $a_i \, c_i$)
    if can-partially-evaluate(a_i)
        if a_i evaluates to true
            replace e_i with c_i in the effect
        else // a_i evaluates to false
            remove e_i from the effect
        recursively apply algorithm to o
    else // partial evaluation is not applicable
        recursively apply algorithm to the operator with precondition
            (and $p \, a_i$) and effect (and $e_1 \, e_2 \ldots e_{i-1} \, c_i \, e_{i+1} \ldots e_n$)
        recursively apply algorithm to the operator with precondition
            (and p (not a_i)) and effect (and $e_1 \, e_2 \ldots e_{i-1} \, e_{i+1} \ldots e_n$)
else // no conditional effects in the effect
    add o to the set of operators

Here are example operators:
```
(operator move-briefcase
     :parameters (location ?x) (location ?y)
     :precondition (at ?x)
     :effect (and (not (at ?x)) (at ?y)
              (when (money-in) (and (not (money-at ?x)) (money-at ?y))))))
(operator deduce-table-clear
     :effect (and (when (eq a table) (clear a)) // after expansion of (forall (obj ?x) ...)
              (when (eq b table) (clear b)) // over obj = {a, b, table}
              (when (eq table table) (clear table)))))
```
And how they would be rewritten:
```
(operator move-briefcase-1 :parameters (location ?x) (location ?y)
                           :precondition (and (at ?x) (money-in))
                           :effect (and (not (at ?x)) (at ?y)
                                    (not (money-at ?x)) (money-at ?y)))
(operator move-briefcase-2 :parameters (location ?x) (location ?y)
                           :precondition (and (at ?x) (not (money-in)))
                           :effect (and (not (at ?x)) (at ?y)))
(operator deduce-table-clear :effect (clear Table)))
```
An expansion of the 'deduce-table-clear' operator would result in 2^3 operators, but with partial evaluation only one operator is created. The partial evaluation technique requires the preprocessor to determine the static predicates of the

domain. As a first approximation, this can be done by finding those predicates that do not appear in the effects of any operator.

In some cases, although an antecedent contains only static predicates, the arguments of the predicates are parameters of the operator. Since the parameters are not bound during preprocessing, the truth value of the antecedent cannot be determined. Our solution is to expand the operators by instantiating over those parameters that appear in the antecedent. The antecedents in the following operator cannot be evaluated because ?boxy is not bound.

```
(operator push-box
    :parameters (?boxx ?boxy ?roomx)
    :precondition ...
    :effect ... (when (neq box1 ?boxy) ...) (when (neq box2 ?boxy) ...) ...)
```

The preprocessor instantiates ?boxy and creates multiple operators, so that partial evaluation is possible. One of the new operators is:

```
(operator push-box-box1
    :parameters (?boxx ?roomx)
    :precondition ...
    :effect ... (when (neq box1 box1) ...) (when (neq box2 box1) ...) ...)
```

At worst, this technique generates $(\text{\# of objects})^{(\text{\# of parameters})}$ operators, but this number is certainly much smaller than $2^{\text{\# of objects}}$. In fact, Graphplan needs to do the expansion internally (for uninstantiated parameters) to build the planning graph, so it can still work efficiently.

However, partial evaluation is not always possible, in which case the number of operators created from a single operator is 2^n, where n is the number of conditional effects of that operator. Although n is generally a small number, it can get large when conditional effects are combined with universal quantifiers:

```
(forall (block ?x) (when (not (painted ?x)) (color ?x blue)))
```

The previous preprocessing layer would generate as many conditional effects as there are blocks, and removing them would create $2^{\text{\# of blocks}}$ operators. Although this is a significant theoretical limitation of the preprocessing approach, the problem does not occur often. In fact, in all the test domains, all occurrences of universally quantified conditional expressions could be expanded by using partial evaluation.

2.5 Disjunctions

A disjunction in the precondition of an operator is eliminated by creating multiple operators such that each new operator has one of the disjuncts in its precondition and the exact same effect as the original operator (Figure 3).

Given: an operator o with precondition (or p_1 p_2 ... p_n) and effect e

for each p in $\{p_1$ p_2 ... $p_n\}$
    let o_i be a new operator with precondition p and effect e
    add o_i to the set of operators
remove o from the set of operators

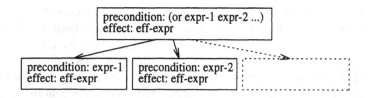

Fig. 3. Transforming Disjunctions

In the example below, the first operator, 'move', will be transformed into the next two operators, 'move-1' and 'move-2'.

```
(operator move :parameters (location ?x) (location ?y)
              :precondition (or (and (at ?x) (adj ?x ?y)) (and (at ?x) (adj ?y ?x)))
              :effect (and (at ?y) (not (at ?x))))
(operator move-1 :parameters (location ?x) (location ?y)
               :precondition (and (at ?x) (adj ?x ?y))
               :effect (and (at ?y) (not (at ?x))))
(operator move-2 :parameters (location ?x) (location ?y)
               :precondition (and (at ?x) (adj ?y ?x))
               :effect (and (at ?y) (not (at ?x))))
```

Unlike universally quantified conditional effects, we are not faced with an exponential blow-up problem for existentially quantified preconditions. This is because the number of operators generated for such an operator is proportional only to the number of disjuncts in the precondition of the operator.

2.6 Negations

Graphplan supports negated propositions in the effects through the use of 'delete' lists. However, negations are not allowed in the preconditions. As suggested in the Graphplan package, it is possible to work around this restriction by introducing a new predicate not-p when it is necessary to use the negation of p in the preconditions. Of course, the effects of all the operators need to be modified to keep p and not-p consistent. The 'normal' operators and the 'init-operator' require different processing. When 'normal' operators assert p, the preprocessor modifies the effects to also delete not-p. Similarly, when they assert the negation of p, that effect is changed to assert 'not-p' and delete p. The algorithm below processes the 'normal' operators.

Given: a list of operators l_o

for each p that appears as (not p) in some precondition(o) s.t. $o \in l_o$
   create a new predicate not-p
   for each $o \in l_o$ s.t. o is not the 'init-operator'
      if $(p \ldots) \in$ effect(o), add (del (not-p $\ldots$)) to effect(o)
      if (not $(p \ldots)) \in$ effect(o)
         replace it with (not-p $\ldots$)
         add (del $(p \ldots)$) to effect(o)
      if (not $(p \ldots)) \in$ precondition(o), replace it with (not-p $\ldots$)
replace all other negated effects (not $(p \ldots)$) with (del $(p \ldots)$)

The next algorithm modifies the 'init-operator' to initialize the world such that it is consistent and 'closed' for all the predicates. By default, the initial conditions are always consistent and closed for predicates that do not have negated predicates introduced by the algorithm above. However, this is not true for those that do have negated predicates. When the truth of some proposition is asserted by two predicates p and not-p, the initial conditions must contain either one or the other. Since the initial conditions do not contain propositions with the latter predicate initially, the algorithm must add such propositions to the effect expression of the 'init-operator'.

Given: the init-operator o_{init}; a list of predicates that have negated predicates l_p

for each p in l_p

   for each $inst$ $(p$ arg_1 arg_2 ... $arg_n)$ of p

     if $inst \notin$ effect(o_{init}) // effect(o_{init}) are the initial conditions

       add (not-p arg_1 arg_2 ... arg_n) to effect(o_{init})

For example, assuming 'at' appears as (not (at ...)) in some precondition, the first domain below would be transformed into the second:

```
(problem p :objects (location bank) (location home) (location office)
          :inits (at office)
(operator go :parameters (location ?x) (location ?y)
             :precondition (at ?x)
             :effect (and (not (at ?x)) (at ?y)))
```

```
(problem p :objects (location bank) (location home) (location office)
          :inits (not-at home) (not-at bank) (at office)
(operator go :parameters (location ?x) (location ?y)
             :precondition (at ?x)
             :effect (not-at ?x) (del (at ?x)) (del (not-at ?y)) (at ?y))
```

This transformation can result in a huge set of initial conditions because the number of possible instantiations of a single predicate is proportional to (# of objects)$^{(\text{\# of parameters})}$. In practice, this is not a problem because the number of parameters of any predicate is usually a small number.

3 Results

We ran the preprocessor+Graphplan pair on all the problems that come with the UCPOP 4.0 package. The preprocessor was implemented in about 600 lines of Lisp code. Both the preprocessor and UCPOP were run in Lucid Common Lisp on a Sun Ultra I workstation. Graphplan was originally written in C and its executable was run on the same machine.

Table 1 shows a comparison of the running times. UCPOP was able to find a solution faster than the preprocessor+Graphplan pair in only 13 problems among 41, but even that figure is misleading because all of those 13 problems are 'trivial' in the sense that the solutions are found in under one second. In fact, for 9 of them, both planners find solutions in less than 0.1 seconds. Moreover, UCPOP is much slower on harder problems even in domains where it did better than Graphplan on trivial problems of the same domain.

Two domains that caused trouble were the 'office-world' and the 'strips-world'. For the 'office-world' domain, there was not much we could do because in that domain objects are created dynamically and our static-world assumption does not hold. The 'strips-world' domain presented a number problems. First the domain contained a fact, which the preprocessor was not ready to handle. Fortunately, the fact was not a necessary part of the domain and the planning problems could be stated without using facts. The resulting simpler domain was still not solvable by UCPOP, but it was also not easy to preprocess because of the universally quantified conditional effects. Here is a typical operator from the 'strips-world' domain:

```
(operator push-box
        :parameters (?boxx ?boxy ?roomx)
        :precondition ...
        :effect (and (forall (?1) (and (when (neq ?1 ?boxx) (not (next-to robot ?1)))
                                       (when (neq ?1 ?boxy) (not (next-to ?boxx ?1)))
                                       (when (and (neq ?1 robot) (neq ?1 ?boxy))
                                             (not (next-to ?1 ?boxx)))))
                (next-to ?boxy ?boxx) (next-to ?boxx ?boxy)  (next-to robot ?boxx)))
```

The effects assert that all 'next-to' propositions (with the exception of three) that refer to the robot or to either of the parameters ?boxx or ?boxy do not hold after this operator is applied. The three exceptions are those that appear in the last line. Expanding this operator without partial evaluation would generate 2^{36} operators because there are 12 objects that ?1 can denote and there are 3 conditional effects for each instantiation. Fortunately, all the antecedents involve static predicates, so partial evaluation is possible. Both problems of this domain are solved in about 10 seconds, whereas UCPOP fails after almost 1000 seconds with a search limit of 100,000 nodes. In this particular domain, preprocessing time dominates the planning time because a lot of partial evaluation needs to be done by the preprocessor, but the resulting domain is relatively simple for Graphplan.

Finally, it is also important to compare the quality of solutions generated by the planners. Since Graphplan always finds the plan with the least number of steps, its solutions are guaranteed to have equal or fewer steps than UCPOP's. In the set of problems we have experimented with, Graphplan's solutions are exactly the same as UCPOP's except in 'uget-paid' where UCPOP adds an extra step. The quality of Graphplan's solutions does not really show up because most of the test problems are simple and UCPOP fails to return a solution for the more difficult ones.

4 Discussion

Automated translation from a high-level domain definition language into a simpler one makes it possible to use simple but fast planners in complicated domains. Graphplan is one example of such a planner, but the same approach will also work with SATplan, which in some domains can perform an order of magnitude better than Graphplan. In fact, a similar rewriting approach [6] is followed to

Table 1. Comparison of UCPOP and Preprocessor+Graphplan

DOMAIN	PROBLEM	UCPOP (s)	Preprocessor (s)	Pre.+GP (s)
blocks-world-domain	suss.-anomaly	0.04	-	0.04
	tower-invert3	0.06	-	0.05
	tower-invert4	0.43	-	0.18
road-operators	road-test	0.02	-	0.01
hanoi-domain	hanoi-3	80.13	-	0.13
	hanoi-4	423 (NS)	-	1.54
ferry-domain	test-ferry	0.49	-	0.03
molgen-domain	rat-insulin	0.83	0.01	0.28
robot-domain	r-test1	0.02	0.02	0.04
	r-test2	9.76	0.01	0.07
monkey-domain	monkey-test1	0.14	-	0.07
	monkey-test2	0.82	-	0.17
	monkey-test3	253.87	-	0.51
briefcase-world	get-paid	0.01	-	0.02
	get-paid2	0.05	0.01	0.05
	get-paid3	0.25	0.01	0.13
	get-paid4	0.13	-	0.12
init-flat-tire	fixit	524 (NS)	0.01	0.24
	fix1	0.01	0.01	0.04
	fix2	0.02	-	0.02
	fix3	0.66	0.01	0.07
	fix4	0.03	0.01	0.02
	fix5	0.01	0.01	0.02
ho-world	ho-demo	0.02	0.03	0.05
fridge-domain	fixa	0.42	0.02	0.54
	fixb	408 (NS)	0.02	1.45
mcd-blocksworld	mcd-suss.-ano.	0.07	0.01	0.08
	mcd-tower-invert	414 (NS)	0.02	1.02
mcd-bw-axiom	mcd-sussman	0.03	-	0.03
	mcd-tower	0.07	-	0.05
uni-bw	uget-paid	0.01	0.03	0.06
	uget-paid2	0.06	0.02	0.08
	uget-paid3	1.46	0.03	0.32
	uget-paid4	0.13	0.03	0.33
sched-world-domain2	sched-test1a	0.01	0.13	0.15
	sched-test2a	0.01	0.25	0.28
prodigy-bw	prodigy-sussman	0.36	-	0.04
	prodigy-p22	695 (NS)	0.01	1.51
strips-world	move-boxes	980 (NS)	9.29	10.21
	move-boxes-1	961 (NS)	9.30	13.31
init-flat-tire2	fixit2	18.15	0.01	0.19
AVERAGE*		10.84	0.47	0.82

NS : No solution within the set search limit, which was 100,000 nodes.
-   : '0', i.e., less than the minimum value the timer could show.
*   : Average only for the solved problems.

encode planning problems into SAT. The input language for the SAT encoding algorithms is similar to the output from our preprocessor. By combining the two, SATplan can be used to solve problems defined in the language of UCPOP.

From a theoretical point of view, the expansion of conditional effects is a serious limitation of the preprocessing approach because the number of operators generated by the transformation is exponential in terms of the number of conditional effects. However, preprocessing is still a practical technique in that, for most problems, the exponential blow-up can be avoided by partial evaluation or object typing or both. Also, it is possible to avoid the problem altogether by using a planner, such as IPP [5], that can handle conditional effects efficiently.

One interesting improvement to the preprocessor is to eliminate some of the operators from a domain by looking at the problem at hand. This can be done similar to the way Graphplan builds planning graphs except by starting from the goals instead of from the initial conditions. When some operators are eliminated, it might also be possible to determine that more predicates are in fact static, thus making room for more partial evaluation than is possible initially. Although in trivial domains this optimization will not help much, in larger domains such an approach can reduce the set of operators for many problems.

Another extension is preprocessing facts. The same backward chaining algorithm that is used to find the relevant operators can also be used to determine the facts that are relevant to the problem being solved. The relevant facts can then be added to the initial conditions as normal propositions.

References

1. Edwin P.D. Pednault. ADL: Exploring the middle ground between STRIPS and the situation calculus. In *Proc. 1st. Int. Conf. On Principles of Knowledge Representation and Reasoning*, 1989.
2. Steven Minton, Craig A. Knoblock, D. Koukka, Yolanda Gil, Robert L. Joseph, and Jaime G. Carbonell. Prodigy 2.0: The manual and the tutorial. Technical report, Department of Computer Science, Carnegie Mellon University, 1989.
3. Daniel S. Weld. An introduction to least commitment planning. *AI Magazine*, 15(4), 1994.
4. Avrim L. Blum and Merrick L. Furst. Fast planning through planning graph analysis. *Artifical Intelligence*, 90(1-2):281–300, 1997.
5. Jana Koehler, Bernhard Nebel, Jörg Hoffman, and Yannis Dimopoulos. Extending planning graphs to an ADL subset. In *Proc. ECP-97*, Toulouse, France, 1997.
6. Henry Kautz and Bart Selman. Pushing the envelope: Planning, propositional logic, and stochastic search. In *Proc. AAAI-96*, Portland, OR, 1996.
7. A. Barrett, Dave Christianson, Marc Friedman, Chung Kwok, Keith Golden, Scott Penberthy, Ying Sun, and Daniel Weld. UCPOP user's manual, version 4.0. Technical report, Department of Computer Science and Engineering, University of Washington, 1995.
8. Richard E. Fikes and Nils J. Nilsson. STRIPS: A new approach to the application of theorem proving to problem solving. *Artificial Intelligence*, 2(3/4):189–208, 1971.

Bounded Parameter Markov Decision Processes

Robert Givan and Sonia Leach and Thomas Dean

Department of Computer Science, Brown University
115 Waterman Street, Providence, RI 02912, USA
http://www.cs.brown.edu/people/{rlg,sml,tld}
Phone: (401) 863-7600   Fax: (401) 863-7657
Email: {rlg,sml,tld}@cs.brown.edu

Abstract. In this paper, we introduce the notion of a *bounded parameter Markov decision process* (BMDP) as a generalization of the familiar *exact* MDP. A bounded parameter MDP is a set of exact MDPs specified by giving upper and lower bounds on transition probabilities and rewards (all the MDPs in the set share the same state and action space). BMDPs form an efficiently solvable special case of the already known class of MDPs with *imprecise parameters* (MDPIPs). Bounded parameter MDPs can be used to represent variation or uncertainty concerning the parameters of sequential decision problems in cases where no prior probabilities on the parameter values are available. Bounded parameter MDPs can also be used in aggregation schemes to represent the variation in the transition probabilities for different base states aggregated together in the same aggregate state.

We introduce *interval value functions* as a natural extension of traditional value functions. An interval value function assigns a closed real interval to each state, representing the assertion that the value of that state falls within that interval. An interval value function can be used to bound the performance of a policy over the set of exact MDPs associated with a given bounded parameter MDP. We describe an iterative dynamic programming algorithm called *interval policy evaluation* which computes an interval value function for a given BMDP and specified policy. Interval policy evaluation on a policy π computes the most restrictive interval value function that is sound, *i.e.*, that bounds the value function for π in every exact MDP in the set defined by the bounded parameter MDP. We define *optimistic* and *pessimistic* notions of optimal policy, and provide a variant of value iteration [Bellman, 1957] that we call *interval value iteration* which computes a policies for a BMDP that are optimal in these senses.

1   Introduction

The theory of Markov decision processes (MDPs) provides the semantic foundations for a wide range of problems involving planning under uncertainty [Boutilier *et al.*, 1995a, Littman, 1997]. In this paper, we introduce a generalization of Markov decision processes called *bounded parameter Markov decision processes* (BMDPs) that allows us to model uncertainty in the parameters that comprise an MDP. Instead of encoding a parameter such as the probability of making a transition from one state to another as a single number, we specify a range of possible values for the parameter as a closed interval of the real numbers.

A BMDP can be thought of as a family of traditional (exact) MDPs, *i.e.,* the set of all MDPs whose parameters fall within the specified ranges. From this perspective, we may have no justification for committing to a particular MDP in this family, and wish to analyze the consequences of this lack of commitment. Another interpretation for a BMDP is that the states of the BMDP actually represent sets (aggregates) of more primitive states that we choose to group together. The intervals here represent the ranges of the parameters over the primitive states belonging to the aggregates. While any policy on the original (primitive) states induces a stationary distribution over those states which can be used to give prior probabilities to the different transition probabilities in the intervals, we may be unable to compute these prior probabilities—the original reason for aggregating the states is typically to avoid such expensive computation over the original large state space.

BMDPs are an efficiently solvable specialization of the already known *Markov Decision Processes with Imprecisely Known Transition Probabilities* (MDPIPs). In the related work section we discuss in more detail how BMDPs relate to MDPIPs.

In a related paper, we have shown how BMDPs can be used as part of a strategy for efficiently approximating the solution of MDPs with very large state spaces and dynamics compactly encoded in a factored (or implicit) representation [Dean *et al.*, 1997]. In this paper, we focus exclusively on BMDPs, on the BMDP analog of value functions, called *interval value functions*, and on policy selection for a BMDP. We provide BMDP analogs of the standard (exact) MDP algorithms for computing the value function for a fixed policy (plan) and (more generally) for computing optimal value functions over all policies, called *interval policy evaluation* and *interval value iteration* (IVI) respectively. We define the desired output values for these algorithms and prove that the algorithms converge to these desired values in polynomial-time, for a fixed discount factor. Finally, we consider two different notions of optimal policy for an BMDP, and show how IVI can be applied to extract the optimal policy for each notion. The first notion of optimality states that the desired policy must perform better than any other under the assumption that an adversary selects the model parameters. The second notion requires the best possible performance when a friendly choice of model parameters is assumed.

2 Exact Markov Decision Processes

An (exact) Markov decision process M is a four tuple $M = (Q, A, F, R)$ where Q is a set of states, A is a set of actions, R is a reward function that maps each state to a real value $R(q)$,[1] and F is a state-transition distribution so that for

---

[1] The techniques and results in this paper easily generalize to more general reward functions. We adopt a less general formulation to simplify the presentation.

$\alpha \in \mathcal{A}$ and $p, q \in \mathcal{Q}$,

$$F_{pq}(\alpha) = \Pr(X_{t+1} = q | X_t = p, U_t = \alpha)$$

where X_t and U_t are random variables denoting, respectively, the state and action at time t. When needed we will write F^M to denote the transition function of the MDP M.

A *policy* is a mapping from states to actions, $\pi : \mathcal{Q} \to \mathcal{A}$. The set of all policies is denoted Π. An MDP M together with a fixed policy $\pi \in \Pi$ determines a Markov chain such that the probability of making a transition from p to q is defined by $F_{pq}(\pi(p))$. The *expected value function* (or simply the *value function*) associated with such a Markov chain is denoted $V_{M,\pi}$. The value function maps each state to its *expected discounted cumulative reward* defined by

$$V_{M,\pi}(p) = R(p) + \gamma \sum_{q \in \mathcal{Q}} F_{pq}(\pi(p)) V_{M,\pi}(q)$$

where $0 \leq \gamma < 1$ is called the *discount rate*.[2] In most contexts, the relevant MDP is clear and we abbreviate $V_{M,\pi}$ as V_π.

The optimal value function V_M^* (or simply V^* where the relevant MDP is clear) is defined as follows.

$$V^*(p) = \max_{\alpha \in \mathcal{A}} \left(R(p) + \gamma \sum_{q \in \mathcal{Q}} F_{pq}(\alpha) V^*(q) \right)$$

The value function V^* is greater than or equal to any value function V_π in the partial order $\geq_{\text{dom}}$ defined as follows: $V_1 \geq_{\text{dom}} V_2$ if and only if for all states q, $V_1(q) \geq V_2(q)$.

An optimal policy is any policy π^* for which $V^* = V_{\pi^*}$. Every MDP has at least one optimal policy, and the set of optimal policies can be found by replacing the max in the definition of V^* with arg max.

3 Bounded Parameter Markov Decision Processes

A *bounded parameter MDP* is a four tuple $\mathcal{M} = (\mathcal{Q}, \mathcal{A}, \hat{F}, \hat{R})$ where $\mathcal{Q}$ and $\mathcal{A}$ are defined as for MDPs, and $\hat{F}$ and $\hat{R}$ are analogous to the MDP F and R but yield closed real intervals instead of real values. That is, for any action α and states p, q, $\hat{R}(p)$ and $\hat{F}_{p,q}(\alpha)$ are both closed real intervals of the form $[l, u]$ for l and u real numbers with $l \leq u$, where in the case of $\hat{F}$ we require $0 \leq l \leq u \leq 1$.[3] To ensure that $\hat{F}$ admits well-formed transition functions, we require that for

---

[2] In this paper, we focus on expected discounted cumulative reward as a performance criterion, but other criteria, *e.g.*, total or average reward [Puterman, 1994], are also applicable to bounded parameter MDPs.

[3] To simplify the remainder of the paper, we assume that the reward bounds are always tight, *i.e.*, that for all $q \in \mathcal{Q}$, for some real l, $\hat{R}(q) = [l, l]$, and we refer to l as $R(q)$. The generalization to nontrivial bounds on rewards is straightforward.

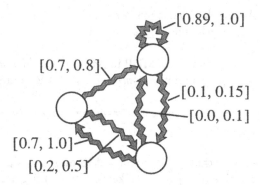

Fig. 1. The state-transition diagram for a simple bounded parameter Markov decision process with three states and a single action. The arcs indicate possible transitions and are labeled by their lower and upper bounds.

any action α and state p, the sum of the lower bounds of $\hat{F}_{pq}(\alpha)$ over all states q must be less than or equal to 1 while the upper bounds must sum to a value greater than or equal to 1. Figure 1 depicts the state-transition diagram for a simple BMDP with three states and one action.

A BMDP $\mathcal{M} = (\mathcal{Q}, \mathcal{A}, \hat{F}, \hat{R})$ defines a set of exact MDPs which, by abuse of notation, we also call $\mathcal{M}$. For exact MDP $M = (\mathcal{Q}', \mathcal{A}', F', R')$, we have $M \in \mathcal{M}$ if $\mathcal{Q} = \mathcal{Q}'$, $\mathcal{A} = \mathcal{A}'$, and for any action α and states p, q, $R'(p)$ is in the interval $\hat{R}(p)$ and $F'_{p,q}(\alpha)$ is in the interval $\hat{F}_{p,q}(\alpha)$. We rely on context to distinguish between the tuple view of $\mathcal{M}$ and the exact MDP set view of $\mathcal{M}$. In the definitions in this section, the BMDP $\mathcal{M}$ is implicit.

An *interval value function* $\hat{V}$ is a mapping from states to closed real intervals. We generally use such functions to indicate that the given state's value falls within the selected interval. Interval value functions can be specified for both exact and BMDPs. As in the case of (exact) value functions, interval value functions are specified with respect to a fixed policy. Note that in the case of BMDPs a state can have a range of values depending on how the transition and reward parameters are instantiated, hence the need for an interval value function.

For each of the interval valued functions $\hat{F}$, $\hat{R}$, $\hat{V}$ we define two real valued functions which take the same arguments and give the upper and lower interval bounds, denoted $\overline{F}$, $\overline{R}$, $\overline{V}$, and $\underline{F}$, $\underline{R}$, $\underline{V}$, respectively. So, for example, at any state q we have $\hat{V}(q) = [\underline{V}(q), \overline{V}(q)]$.

Definition 1. For any policy π and state q, we define the interval value $\hat{V}_\pi(q)$ of π at q to be the interval

$$\left[\min_{M \in \mathcal{M}} V_{M,\pi}(q), \max_{M \in \mathcal{M}} V_{M,\pi}(q) \right]$$

In Section 5 we will give an iterative algorithm which we have proven to converge to $\hat{V}_\pi$. In preparation for that discussion we now state that there is at least one specific MDP in $\mathcal{M}$ which simultaneously achieves $\overline{V}_\pi(q)$ for all states q (and likewise a specific MDP achieving $\underline{V}_\pi(q)$ for all q).

Definition 2. For any policy π, an MDP in $\mathcal{M}$ is π-*maximizing* if it is a possible value of $\arg\max_{M \in \mathcal{M}} V_{M,\pi}$ and it is π-*minimizing* if it is in $\arg\min_{M \in \mathcal{M}} V_{M,\pi}$.

Theorem 3. *For any policy π, there exist π-maximizing and π-minimizing MDPs in $\mathcal{M}$.*

This theorem implies that $\underline{V}_\pi$ is equivalent to $\min_{M \in \mathcal{M}} V_{M,\pi}$ where the minimization is done relative to $\geq_{\text{dom}}$, and likewise for $\overline{V}$ using max. We give an algorithm in Section 5 which converges to $\underline{V}_\pi$ by also converging to a π-minimizing MDP in $\mathcal{M}$ (likewise for $\overline{V}_\pi$).

We now consider how to define an optimal value function for a BMDP. Consider the expression $\max_{\pi \in \Pi} \hat{V}_\pi$. This expression is ill-formed because we have not defined how to rank the interval value functions $\hat{V}_\pi$ in order to select a maximum. We focus here on two different ways to order these value functions, yielding two notions of optimal value function and optimal policy. Other orderings may also yield interesting results.

First, we define two different orderings on closed real intervals:

$$[l_1, u_1] \leq_{\text{pes}} [l_2, u_2] \iff \begin{cases} l_1 < l_2, \text{ or} \\ l_1 = l_2 \text{ and } u_1 \leq u_2 \end{cases}$$

$$[l_1, u_1] \leq_{\text{opt}} [l_2, u_2] \iff \begin{cases} u_1 < u_2, \text{ or} \\ u_1 = u_2 \text{ and } l_1 \leq l_2 \end{cases}$$

We extend these orderings to partially order interval value functions by relating two value functions $\hat{V}_1 \leq \hat{V}_2$ only when $\hat{V}_1(q) \leq \hat{V}_2(q)$ for every state q. We can now use either of these orderings to compute $\max_{\pi \in \Pi} \hat{V}_\pi$, yielding two definitions of optimal value function and optimal policy. However, since the orderings are partial (on value functions), we must still prove that the set of policies contains a policy which achieves the desired maximum under each ordering (*i.e.*, a policy whose interval value function is ordered above that of every other policy).

Definition 4. The *optimistic optimal value function* $\hat{V}_{\text{opt}}$ and the *pessimistic optimal value function* $\hat{V}_{\text{pes}}$ are given by:

$$\hat{V}_{\text{opt}} = \max_{\pi \in \Pi} \hat{V}_\pi \text{ using } \leq_{\text{opt}} \text{ to order interval value functions}$$
$$\hat{V}_{\text{pes}} = \max_{\pi \in \Pi} \hat{V}_\pi \text{ using } \leq_{\text{pes}} \text{ to order interval value functions}$$

We say that any policy π whose interval value function $\hat{V}_\pi$ is $\geq_{\text{opt}}$ ($\geq_{\text{pes}}$) the value functions $\hat{V}_{\pi'}$ of all other policies π' is *optimistically (pessimistically) optimal*.

Theorem 5. *There exists at least one optimistically (pessimistically) optimal policy, and therefore the definition of $\hat{V}_{\text{opt}}$ ($\hat{V}_{\text{pes}}$) is well-formed.*

The above two notions of optimal value can be understood in terms of a game in which we choose a policy π and then a second player chooses in which MDP M in $\mathcal{M}$ to evaluate the policy. The goal is to get the highest[4] resulting value function $V_{M,\pi}$. The optimistic optimal value function's upper bounds $\overline{V}_{\text{opt}}$ represent the best value function we can obtain in this game if we assume the second player is cooperating with us. The pessimistic optimal value function's lower bounds $\underline{V}_{\text{pes}}$ represent the best we can do if we assume the second player is our adversary, trying to minimize the resulting value function.

In the next section, we describe well-known iterative algorithms for computing the exact MDP optimal value function V^*, and then in Section 5 we will describe similar iterative algorithms which compute the BMDP variants $\hat{V}_{\text{opt}}$ ($\hat{V}_{\text{pes}}$).

4 Estimating Traditional Value Functions

In this section, we review the basics concerning dynamic programming methods for computing value functions for fixed and optimal policies in traditional MDPs. In the next section, we describe novel algorithms for computing the interval analogs of these value functions for bounded parameter MDPs.

We present results from the theory of exact MDPs which rely on the concept of normed linear spaces. We define operators, VI_π and VI, on the space of value functions. We then use the Banach fixed-point theorem (Theorem 6) to show that iterating these operators converges to unique fixed-points, V_π and V^* respectively (Theorems 8 and 9).

Let $\mathcal{V}$ denote the set of value functions on $\mathcal{Q}$. For each $v \in \mathcal{V}$, define the (sup) *norm* of v by

$$\|v\| = \max_{q \in \mathcal{Q}} |v(q)|.$$

We use the term *convergence* to mean convergence in the norm sense. The space $\mathcal{V}$ together with $\|\cdot\|$ constitute a complete normed linear space, or *Banach Space*. If U is a Banach space, then an operator $T : U \to U$ is a *contraction mapping* if there exists a λ, $0 \le \lambda < 1$ such that $\|Tv - Tu\| \le \lambda \|v - u\|$ for all u and v in U.

Define $VI : \mathcal{V} \to \mathcal{V}$ and for each $\pi \in \Pi$, $VI_\pi : \mathcal{V} \to \mathcal{V}$ on each $p \in \mathcal{Q}$ by

$$VI(v)(p) = \max_{\alpha \in \mathcal{A}} \left(R(p) + \gamma \sum_{q \in \mathcal{Q}} F_{pq}(\alpha) v(q) \right)$$

$$VI_\pi(v)(p) = R(p) + \gamma \sum_{q \in \mathcal{Q}} F_{pq}(\pi(p)) v(q).$$

In cases where we need to make explicit the MDP from which the transition function F originates, we write $VI_{M,\pi}$ and VI_M to denote the operators VI_π and VI as just defined, except that the transition function F is F^M.

Using these operators, we can rewrite the expression for V^* and V_π as

$$V^*(p) = VI(V^*)(p) \quad \text{and} \quad V_\pi(p) = VI_\pi(V_\pi)(p)$$

---

[4] Value functions are ranked by $\ge_{\text{dom}}$.

for all states $p \in Q$. This implies that V^* and V_π are fixed points of VI and VI_π, respectively. The following four theorems show that for each operator, iterating the operator on an initial value estimate converges to these fixed points.

Theorem 6. *For any Banach space U and contraction mapping $T : U \to U$, there exists a unique v^* in U such that $Tv^* = v^*$; and for arbitrary v^0 in U, the sequence $\{v^n\}$ defined by $v^n = Tv^{n-1} = T^n v^0$ converges to v^*.*

Theorem 7. *VI and VI_π are contraction mappings.*

Theorem 6 and Theorem 7 together prove the following fundamental results in the theory of MDPs.

Theorem 8. *There exists a unique $v^* \in V$ satisfying $v^* = VI(v^*)$; furthermore, $v^* = V^*$. Similarly, V_π is the unique fixed-point of VI_π.*

Theorem 9. *For arbitrary $v^0 \in V$, the sequence $\{v^n\}$ defined by $v^n = VI(v^{n-1})$ $= VI^n(v^0)$ converges to V^*. Similarly, iterating VI_π converges to V_π.*

An important consequence of Theorem 9 is that it provides an algorithm for finding V^* and V_π. In particular, to find V^*, we can start from an arbitrary initial value function v^0 in V, and repeatedly apply the operator VI to obtain the sequence $\{v^n\}$. This algorithm is referred to as *value iteration*. Theorem 9 guarantees the convergence of value iteration to the optimal value function. Similarly, we can specify an algorithm called *policy evaluation* which finds V_π by repeatedly apply VI_π starting with an initial $v^0 \in V$.

The following theorem from [Littman *et al.*, 1995] states a convergence rate of value iteration and policy evaluation which can be derived using bounds on the precision needed to represent solutions to a linear program of limited precision (each algorithm can be viewed as solving a linear program).

Theorem 10. *For fixed γ, value iteration and policy evaluation converge to the optimal value function in a number of steps polynomial in the number of states, the number of actions, and the number of bits used to represent the MDP parameters.*

5 Estimating Interval Value Functions

In this section, we describe dynamic programming algorithms which operate on bounded parameter MDPs. We first define the interval equivalent of policy evaluation $I\hat{V}I_\pi$ which computes $\hat{V}_\pi$, and then define the variants $I\hat{V}I_{opt}$ and $I\hat{V}I_{pes}$ which compute the optimistic and pessimistic optimal value functions.

5.1 Interval Policy Evaluation

In direct analogy to the definition of VI_π in Section 4, we define a function $I\hat{V}I_\pi$ (for *interval value iteration*) which maps interval value functions to other interval value functions. We have proven that iterating $I\hat{V}I_\pi$ on any initial interval value function produces a sequence of interval value functions which converges to $\hat{V}_\pi$ in a polynomial number of steps, given a fixed discount factor γ.

$I\hat{V}I_\pi(\hat{V})$ is an interval value function, defined for each state p as follows:

$$I\hat{V}I_\pi(\hat{V})(p) = \left[\min_{M \in \mathcal{M}} VI_{M,\pi(p)}(\underline{V})(p), \ \max_{M \in \mathcal{M}} VI_{M,\pi(p)}(\overline{V})(p) \right].$$

We define $\underline{IVI}_\pi$ and $\overline{IVI}_\pi$ to be the corresponding mappings from value functions to value functions (note that for input $\hat{V}$, $\underline{IVI}_\pi$ does not depend on $\overline{V}$ and so can be viewed as a function from $\mathcal{V}$ to $\mathcal{V}$—likewise for $\overline{IVI}_\pi$ and $\underline{V}$).

The algorithm to compute $I\hat{V}I_\pi$ is very similar to the standard MDP computation of VI, except that we must now be able to select an MDP M from the family $\mathcal{M}$ which minimizes (maximizes) the value attained. We select such an MDP by selecting a function F within the bounds specified by $\hat{F}$ to minimize (maximize) the value—each possible way of selecting F corresponds to one MDP in $\mathcal{M}$. We can select the values of $F_{pq}(\alpha)$ independently for each α and p, but the values selected for different states q (for fixed α and p) interact: they must sum up to one. We now show how to determine, for fixed α and p, the value of $F_{pq}(\alpha)$ for each state q so as to minimize (maximize) the expression $\sum_{q \in Q} (F_{pq}(\alpha)V(q))$. This step constitutes the heart of the IVI algorithm and the only significant way the algorithm differs from standard value iteration.

The idea is to sort the possible destination states q into increasing (decreasing) order according to their $\underline{V}$ ($\overline{V}$) value, and then choose the transition probabilities within the intervals specified by $\hat{F}$ so as to send as much probability mass to the states early in the ordering. Let $q_1, q_2, \ldots, q_k$ be such an ordering of Q—so that, in the minimizing case, for all i and j if $1 \le i \le j \le k$ then $\underline{V}(q_i) \le \underline{V}(q_j)$ (increasing order).

Let r be the index $1 \le r \le k$ which maximizes the following expression without letting it exceed 1:

$$\sum_{i=1}^{r-1} \overline{F}_{p,q_i}(\alpha) + \sum_{i=r}^{k} \underline{F}_{p,q_i}(\alpha)$$

r is the index into the sequence q_i such that below index r we can assign the upper bound, and above index r we can assign the lower bound, with the rest of the probability mass from p under α being assigned to q_r. Formally, we choose $F_{pq}(\alpha)$ for all $q \in Q$ as follows:

$$F_{pq_j}(\alpha) = \begin{cases} \overline{F}_{p,q_i}(\alpha) & \text{if } j < r \\ \underline{F}_{p,q_i}(\alpha) & \text{if } j > r \end{cases}$$

$$F_{pq_r}(\alpha) = 1 - \sum_{i=1, i \ne r}^{i=k} F_{pq_i}(\alpha)$$

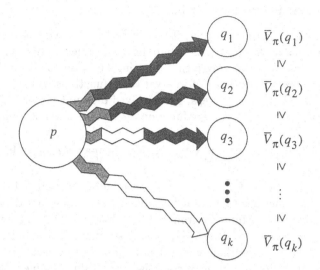

Fig. 2. An illustration of the basic dynamic programming step in computing an approximate value function for a fixed policy and bounded parameter MDP. The lighter shaded portions of each arc represent the required lower bound transition probability and the darker shaded portions represent the fraction of the remaining transition probability to the upper bound assigned to the arc by F.

Figure 2 illustrates the basic iterative step in the above algorithm, for the maximizing case. The states q_i are ordered according to the value estimates in $\overline{V}$. The transitions from a state p to states q_i are defined by the function F such that each transition is equal to its lower bound plus some fraction of the leftover probability mass.

Techniques similar to those in Section 4 can be used to prove that iterating $\underline{IVI}_\pi$ ($\overline{IVI}_\pi$) converges to $\underline{V}_\pi$ ($\overline{V}_\pi$). The key theorems, stated below, assert first that $\underline{IVI}_\pi$ is a contraction mapping, and second that $\underline{V}_\pi$ is a fixed-point of $\underline{IVI}_\pi$, and are easily proven[5].

Theorem 11. *For any policy π, $\underline{IVI}_\pi$ and $\overline{IVI}_\pi$ are contraction mappings.*

Theorem 12. *For any policy π, $\underline{V}_\pi$ is a fixed-point of $\underline{IVI}_\pi$ and $\overline{V}_\pi$ of $\overline{IVI}_\pi$.*

These theorems, together with Theorem 6 (the Banach fixed-point theorem) imply that iterating $I\hat{V}I_\pi$ on any initial interval value function converges to $\hat{V}_\pi$, regardless of the starting point.

Theorem 13. *For fixed γ, interval policy evaluation converges to the desired interval value function in a number of steps polynomial in the number of states, the number of actions, and the number of bits used to represent the MDP parameters.*

---

[5] The min over members of $\mathcal{M}$ is dealt with using a technique similar to that used to handle the max over actions in the same proof for V^*

5.2   Interval Value Iteration

As in the case of VI_π and VI, it is straightforward to modify $I\hat{V}I_\pi$ so that it computes optimal policy value intervals by adding a maximization step over the different action choices in each state. However, unlike standard value iteration, the quantities being compared in the maximization step are closed real intervals, so the resulting algorithm varies according to how we choose to compare real intervals. We define two variations of interval value iteration—other variations are possible.

$$I\hat{V}I_{opt}(\hat{V})(p) = \max_{\alpha \in A,\ \leq_{opt}} \left[\min_{M \in \mathcal{M}} VI_{M,\alpha}(\underline{V})(p),\ \max_{M \in \mathcal{M}} VI_{M,\alpha}(\overline{V})(p) \right]$$

$$I\hat{V}I_{pes}(\hat{V})(p) = \max_{\alpha \in A,\ \leq_{pes}} \left[\min_{M \in \mathcal{M}} VI_{M,\alpha}(\underline{V})(p),\ \max_{M \in \mathcal{M}} VI_{M,\alpha}(\overline{V})(p) \right]$$

The added maximization step introduces no new difficulties in implementing the algorithm. We discuss convergence for $I\hat{V}I_{opt}$—the convergence results for $I\hat{V}I_{pes}$ are similar. We write $\overline{IVI}_{opt}$ for the upper bound returned by $I\hat{V}I_{opt}$, and we consider $\overline{IVI}_{opt}$ a function from $\mathcal{V}$ to $\mathcal{V}$ because $\overline{IVI}_{opt}(\hat{V})$ depends only on $\underline{V}$. $\overline{IVI}_{opt}$ can be easily shown to be a contraction mapping, and it can be shown that $\hat{V}_{opt}$ is a fixed point of $I\hat{V}I_{opt}$. It then follows that $\overline{IVI}_{opt}$ converges to $\overline{V}_{opt}$ in polynomially many steps. The analogous results for $\underline{IVI}_{opt}$ are somewhat more problematic. Because the action selection is done according to $\leq_{opt}$, which focuses primarily on the interval upper bounds, $\underline{IVI}_{opt}$ is not properly a mapping from $\mathcal{V}$ to $\mathcal{V}$, as $\underline{IVI}_{opt}(\hat{V})$ depends on both $\underline{V}$ and $\overline{V}$. However, for any particular value function V and interval value function $\hat{V}$ such that $\overline{V} = V$, we can write $\underline{IVI}_{opt,V}$ for the mapping from $\mathcal{V}$ to $\mathcal{V}$ which carries $\underline{V}$ to $\underline{IVI}_{opt}(\hat{V})$. We can then show that for each V, $\underline{IVI}_{opt,V}$ converges as desired. The algorithm must then iterate $\overline{IVI}_{opt}$ convergence to some upper bound $\overline{V}$, and then iterate $\underline{IVI}_{opt,\overline{V}}$ to converge to the lower bounds $\underline{V}$—each convergence within polynomial time.

Theorem 14. *A. $\overline{IVI}_{opt}$ and $\underline{IVI}_{pes}$ are contraction mappings.*
B. For any value functions V, $\underline{IVI}_{opt,V}$ and $\overline{IVI}_{pes,V}$ are contraction mappings.

Theorem 15. *$\hat{V}_{opt}$ is a fixed-point of $I\hat{V}I_{opt}$, and $\hat{V}_{pes}$ of $I\hat{V}I_{pes}$.*

Theorem 16. *For fixed γ, iteration of $I\hat{V}I_{opt}$ converges to $\hat{V}_{opt}$, and iteration of $I\hat{V}I_{pes}$ converges to $\hat{V}_{pes}$, in polynomially many iterations in the problem size (including the number of bits used in specifying the parameters).*

6   Policy Selection, Sensitivity Analysis, and Aggregation

In this section, we consider some basic issues concerning the use and interpretation of bounded parameter MDPs. We begin by reemphasizing some ideas introduced earlier regarding the selection of policies.

To begin with, it is important that we are clear on the status of the bounds in a bounded parameter MDP. A bounded parameter MDP specifies upper and lower bounds on individual parameters; the assumption is that we have no additional information regarding individual exact MDPs whose parameters fall with those bounds. In particular, we have no prior over the exact MDPs in the family of MDPs defined by a bounded parameter MDP.

Policy selection Despite the lack of information regarding any particular MDP, we may have to choose a policy. In such a situation, it is natural to consider that the actual MDP, *i.e.,* the one in which we will ultimately have to carry out some policy, is decided by some outside process. That process might choose so as to help or hinder us, or it might be entirely indifferent. To minimize the risk of performing poorly, it is reasonable to think in adversarial terms; we select the policy which will perform as well as possible assuming that the adversary chooses so that we perform as poorly as possible.

These choices correspond to optimistic and pessimistic optimal policies. We have discussed in the last section how to compute interval value functions for such policies—such value functions can then be used in a straightforward manner to extract policies which achieve those values.

There are other possible choices, corresponding in general to other means of totally ordering real closed intervals. We might for instance consider a policy whose average performance over all MDPs in the family is as good as or better than the average performance of any other policy. This notion of average is potentially problematic, however, as it essentially assumes a uniform prior over exact MDPs and, as stated earlier, the bounds do not imply any particular prior.

Sensitivity analysis There are other ways in which bounded parameter MDPs might be useful in planning under uncertainty. For example, we might assume that we begin with a particular exact MDP, say, the MDP with parameters whose values reflect the best guess according to a given domain expert. If we were to compute the optimal policy for this exact MDP, we might wonder about the degree to which this policy is sensitive to the numbers supplied by the expert.

To explore this possible sensitivity to the parameters, we might assess the policy by perturbing the parameters and evaluating the policy with respect to the perturbed MDP. Alternatively, we could use BMDPs to perform this sort of sensitivity analysis on a whole family of MDPs by converting the point estimates for the parameters to confidence intervals and then computing bounds on the value function for the fixed policy via interval policy evaluation.

Aggregation Another use of BMDPs involves a different interpretation altogether. Instead of viewing the states of the bounded parameter MDP as individual primitive states, we view each state of the BMDP as representing a set or *aggregate* of states of some other, larger MDP.

In this interpretation, states are aggregated together because they behave approximately the same with respect to possible state transitions. A little more precisely, suppose that the set of states of the BMDP $\mathcal{M}$ corresponds to the set of *blocks* $\{B_1, \ldots, B_n\}$ such that the $\{B_i\}$ constitutes the partition of another MDP with a much larger state space.

Now we interpret the bounds as follows; for any two blocks B_i and B_j, let $\hat{F}_{B_i B_j}(\alpha)$ represent the interval value for the transition from B_i to B_j on action α defined as follows: $\hat{F}_{B_i B_j}(\alpha) = \left[\min_{p \in B_i} \sum_{q \in B_j} F_{pq}(\alpha), \ \max_{p \in B_i} \sum_{q \in B_j} F_{pq}(\alpha)\right]$ Intuitively, this means that all states in a block behave approximately the same (assuming the lower and upper bounds are close to each other) in terms of transitions to other blocks even though they may differ widely with regard to transitions to individual states.

In Dean *et al.* [1997] we discuss methods for using an implicit representation of a exact MDP with a large number of states to construct an explicit BMDP with a possibly much smaller number of states based on an aggregation method. We then show that policies computed for this BMDP can be extended to the original large implicitly described MDP. Note that the original implicit MDP is not even a member of the family of MDPs for the reduced BMDP (it has a different state space, for instance). Nevertheless, it is a theorem that the policies and value bounds of the BMDP can be soundly applied in the original MDP (using the aggregation mapping to connect the state spaces).

7   Related Work and Conclusions

Our definition for bounded parameter MDPs is related to a number of other ideas appearing in the literature on Markov decision processes; in the following, we mention just a few such ideas. First, BMDPs specialize the MDPs with imprecisely known parameters (MDPIPs) described and analyzed in the operations research literature[White and Eldeib, 1994, White and Eldeib, 1986, Satia and Lave, 1973]. The more general MDPIPs described in these papers require more general and expensive algorithms for solution. For example, [White and Eldeib, 1994] allows an arbitrary linear program to define the bounds on the transition probabilities (and allows no imprecision in the reward parameters)— as a result, the solution technique presented appeals to linear programming at each iteration of the solution algorithm rather than exploit the specific structure available in a BMDP. [Satia and Lave, 1973] mention the restriction to BMDPs but give no special algorithms to exploit this restriction. Their general MDPIP algorithm is very different from our algorithm and involves two nested phases of policy iteration—the outer phase selecting a traditional policy and the inner phase selecting a "policy" for "nature", *i.e.*, a choice of the transition parameters to minimize or maximize value (depending on whether optimistic or pessimistic assumptions prevail). Our work, while originally developed independently of the MDPIP literature, follows similar lines to [Satia and Lave, 1973] in defining optimistic and pessimistic optimal policies.

Bertsekas and Castañon [1989] use the notion of aggregated Markov chains and consider grouping together states with approximately the same residuals. Methods for bounding value functions are frequently used in approximate algorithms for solving MDPs; Lovejoy [1991] describes their use in solving partially observable MDPs. Puterman [1994] provides an excellent introduction to Markov decision processes and techniques involving bounding value functions.

Boutilier and Dearden [1994] and Boutilier *et al.* [1995b] describe methods for solving implicitly described MDPs and Dean and Givan [1997] reinterpret this work in terms of computing explicitly described MDPs with aggregate states.

Bounded parameter MDPs allow us to represent uncertainty about or variation in the parameters of a Markov decision process. Interval value functions capture the resulting variation in policy values. In this paper, we have defined both bounded parameter MDP and interval value function, and given algorithms for computing interval value functions, and selecting and evaluating policies.

References

[Bellman, 1957] Bellman, Richard 1957. *Dynamic Programming.* Princeton University Press.

[Bertsekas and Castañon, 1989] Bertsekas, D. P. and Castañon, D. A. 1989. Adaptive aggregation for infinite horizon dynamic programming. *IEEE Transactions on Automatic Control* 34(6):589–598.

[Boutilier and Dearden, 1994] Boutilier, Craig and Dearden, Richard 1994. Using abstractions for decision theoretic planning with time constraints. In *Proceedings AAAI-94.* AAAI. 1016–1022.

[Boutilier *et al.*, 1995a] Boutilier, Craig; Dean, Thomas; and Hanks, Steve 1995a. Planning under uncertainty: Structural assumptions and computational leverage. In *Proceedings of the Third European Workshop on Planning.*

[Boutilier *et al.*, 1995b] Boutilier, Craig; Dearden, Richard; and Goldszmidt, Moises 1995b. Exploiting structure in policy construction. In *Proceedings IJCAI 14.* IJCAII. 1104–1111.

[Dean and Givan, 1997] Dean, Thomas and Givan, Robert 1997. Model minimization in Markov decision processes. In *Proceedings AAAI-97.* AAAI.

[Dean *et al.*, 1997] Dean, Thomas; Givan, Robert; and Leach, Sonia 1997. Model reduction techniques for computing approximately optimal solutions for Markov decision processes. In *Thirteenth Conference on Uncertainty in Artificial Intelligence.*

[Littman *et al.*, 1995] Littman, Michael; Dean, Thomas; and Kaelbling, Leslie 1995. On the complexity of solving Markov decision problems. In *Eleventh Conference on Uncertainty in Artificial Intelligence.* 394–402.

[Littman, 1997] Littman, Michael L. 1997. Probabilistic propositional planning: Representations and complexity. In *Proceedings AAAI-97.* AAAI.

[Lovejoy, 1991] Lovejoy, William S. 1991. A survey of algorithmic methods for partially observed Markov decision processes. *Annals of Operations Research* 28:47–66.

[Puterman, 1994] Puterman, Martin L. 1994. *Markov Decision Processes.* John Wiley & Sons, New York.

[Satia and Lave, 1973] Satia, J. K. and Lave, R. E. 1973. Markovian decision processes with uncertain transition probabilities. *Operations Research* 21:728–740.

[White and Eldeib, 1986] White, C. C. and Eldeib, H. K. 1986. Parameter imprecision in finite state, finite action dynamic programs. *Operations Research* 34:120–129.

[White and Eldeib, 1994] White, C. C. and Eldeib, H. K. 1994. Markov decision processes with imprecise transition probabilities. *Operations Research* 43:739–749.

Planning and Search Techniques for Intelligent Behaviour of Battlefield Entities

R. T. Hepplewhite & J. W. Baxter
Defence Evaluation and Research Agency
St. Andrews Road,
Malvern,
Worcestershire. WR14 3PS
United Kingdom

Abstract

Computer Generated Forces (CGFs) are becoming increasingly important in battlefield simulations, in particular for reducing the number of operators required to control entities when training only a few military commanders. These entities must operate in a spatially and temporally continuous dynamic domain, react to any situation in a realistic but non-deterministic manner, using potentially uncertain information about the world. This paper describes our "broad agent" approach for implementing intelligent entities in battlefield CGFs, which attempts to avoid using rules covering every possible contingency but instead uses more fundamental principles to derive plans for achieving objectives. These agents are linked in a Command and Control (C^2) hierarchy. An agent's behaviour is implemented as rule-sets executed by a tool-kit, developed to support generic agent architectures and interactions between agents. When the agent receives an objective it generates alternative plans by considering possible sequences of actions and using high level principles selects the most appropriate plan for the current situation. This plan is then acted upon, and may include giving objectives to subordinate agents. The results presented throughout this paper have shown that by considering sequences from only a few actions the agents are capable of generating complex plans.

1. Introduction

The costs of performing live military exercises to train future commanders are becoming increasingly prohibitive. Hence, CGFs are increasingly being used to simulate battlefield entities and their interactions to provide commanders with appropriate training and experience. The trainees control their forces as in a real exercise, except the behaviour of the units is computer generated. These simulators inter-operate (for example using the Distributed Interactive Simulation, DIS, protocols) to give the appearance that the commander is operating in a realistic scenario.

Although this training method is more cost effective, it still requires many operators (to control opposing and flanking forces). The intelligence level of entities in many systems is such that the operator frequently has to intervene to correct inappropriate actions of the entities which detracts from the high level strategic planning and so degrades training value. It is therefore desirable to increase the level of automation and intelligence of the CGF systems to reduce the supervision required. This has lead to a large number of CGF research activities [Ceranowicz 1994; McEnany et al., 1994]

2. Characteristics of the Problem

The process of planning within the battlefield is complex. The agent has to take account of many factors, including:

- Movement and intention of enemy forces.
- Uncertain, incomplete and out of date information ("Fog of War").
- Terrain features.
- The overall objective of the force.
- Co-ordination of its actions with other entities.

In order that an agent provides a realistic training experience it is necessary that it not merely reacts to current situations, but is proactive in the environment. This implies the agents are capable of planning actions into the future predicting the probable outcome. This requires a more general planning system, which we are investigating by using "broad agents" [Bates et al., 1991]. In addition, complex behavioural models are usually too computationally expensive to use in CGF systems. However, in mitigation more than one course of actions may be acceptable, and it is generally sufficient that the CGF chooses a plausible course of actions. Hence, a heuristic methodology of planning appears suited to modelling behaviour [Meliza et al., 1995].

Thus the approach is not to implement detailed rules for particular situations but raise the level of decision making by endowing agents with knowledge of the principles of manoeuvres and constraints about the world. This allows orders to be issued as objectives, rather than instructions, which the agent can plan for itself how to achieve. We have identified five principles which a CGF should exhibit if it is to seem realistic for training purposes.

- Exhibiting Appropriate Actions: the agent should be capable of acting in any situation it may encounter. Agents based on prescribed rules often exhibit pathological behaviour when faced with situations which do not match the specific situation the rules were intended for. Our approach overcomes these problems by considering the effects different courses of actions would produce and so generate the most appropriate plan for the situation as a whole.

- Acting at Tempo: tempo, an important tactic, is where a force executes sequences of events, or multiple activities more quickly than the opposition is able to keep pace with. Thus a commander needs to adapt quickly to changes in situation whilst maintaining the overall objective. The agent architecture has the facility to respond to a situation quickly by invoking reactive behaviour, but still developing in the background an overall plan of action.

- Acting Co-operatively: it is essential that the agents act co-operatively to provide greater effectiveness of a unit. Effective co-operation results from a hierarchical command and control structure which includes the re-allocation of roles following attrition. For this reason and because it corresponds to real C^2 systems, we use a hierarchy of command agents.

• Operator Interaction: ultimately the CGF system must interact with a human operator who provides the overall battle plan, and can modify the actions of units if required. Therefore, the communication between the operator and the entities must be in a form which is clearly understandable, and in a familiar format [Ceranowicz *et al.*, 1994b].

• Plausible but not Predictable Behaviour: in order for the trainee to be convinced they are battling against a real opponent, the behaviour of the entities must be plausible both in the short term and by the overall strategy displayed. This also includes unpredictability of the opponent. Our approach intends to overcome these problems, by considering different courses of actions and selecting either the best, or one from the 'n' best plans and thereby introducing uncertainty.

3. Agent Tool-Kit

The framework for the agents has been developed in collaboration with Aaron Sloman at Birmingham University as a "SimAgent" tool-kit, written in Poplog [Sloman *et al.*, 1995]. The "SimAgent" tool-kit executes multiple agents, controls the message passing between them and allows physical simulation of the agents.

Since, the precise agent architecture was not initially known the tool-kit needed the facility to support different architectures between the agents, and possibly a number of sub-architectures within the agent to support all its functionality. Thus, the tool-kit does not unnecessarily restrict the ontology space. Also, the agents need to interact with each other and possibly with other entities. Therefore, the agents must be physically simulated. This can be achieved either using modules internal to the tool-kit, or by enabling the agents to control the actions of a separate simulation system. The tool-kit has three main attributes.

3.1. Agent Scheduling

The tool-kit scheduler is responsible for the correct running of the agents. The scheduler runs in a two pass operation. Firstly, it allows the agents to perform their mental processes. Secondly, it passes messages between agents and runs any physical simulation, or external actions of the agents. This ensures the behaviour is generally independent of the order of the agents, because all agents get to perform sensor and thinking activities before the actual state of any entity changes. The ability to apply resource limits during the first step enables the agents to be constrained to run in real time by limiting the processing time they have. This requires the use of real-time AI techniques.

3.2. Agent Mechanisms

Each agent has an associated collection of rule-sets. A rule-set contains a collection of condition-action rules interacting via a number of databases. The condition action components of a rule are not limited to a particular style, since they can invoke any POP11 function, it is possible to call other languages such as C++, Prolog, etc. The rule-sets are a method of grouping similar behaviour components. The rules can switch between rule-sets and databases, push them on a stack, restore them, etc. (c.f. SOAR [Laird 1993]).

Although learning is not included in our implementation, it is supported in the tool kit. A rule can introduce new rules or rule-sets within an agent.

3.3. Agent Actions

Inevitably the agents will want to perform actions based on their motivations, thus the agents require physical simulation. To allow interaction with other entities, using DIS, we use an external simulation. The external simulation returns messages back to the agents reporting changes in state, or information from sensors.

Figure 1. shows the relationship between the agent objects, agent rule-sets, the tool-kit and remote simulation.

4. Broad Agents

An entity's intelligence is based on a "broad agent" architecture [Bates *et al.*, 1991]

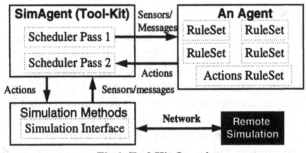

Fig 1. Tool-Kit Overview.

implemented within a C^2 hierarchy. A broad agent is designed to have a broad but shallow range of capabilities, instead of a few very detailed behaviours. The C^2 hierarchy enables commands to be devolved from high level commanders to subordinates and so each agent need only consider the appropriate level of detail.

The scenario being developed to demonstrate the agents' behaviour is based on a battle group formation. Currently the implementation extends to one tank squadron shown in Figure 2. We have not embodied learning behaviour into the agent in the present implementation because it was felt that a lot of behavioural principles could be extracted from Doctrine Manuals.

Each agent within the hierarchy is based on the same broad agent architecture, Figure 3 shows the basic design. The fundamental properties of this design are:

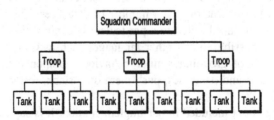

Fig. 2. Example Squadron Composition.

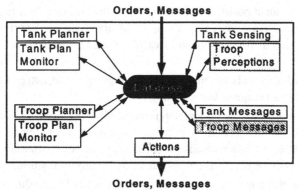

Orders, Messages

Fig. 3. Example Troop Commander Architecture.

• It contains a 'central database', through which all the rule-sets communicate. This database can be partitioned on a keyword, each sub-database holding related data, allowing searching to be performed much more efficiently.

• Individual rule-sets can be identified to perform fundamental tasks, although their operation may be inter-linked. Separating functionality enables parallelism of the rule-sets.

• The modules only simulate the agent's intelligence and do not perform any actual physical modelling. To perform actions the agent sends instructions to the physical simulator, and receives confirmation back about the action via its sensors. This allows separation of the intelligence modelling from the physical simulation.

• The design of the intelligence is generic to any position in the C2 hierarchy.

• Additional or modified behaviour can be easily implanted into the agent by simply loading different, or additional rule-sets into the agent. Thus, if the troop commander is destroyed, the second in command of the unit takes charge of the unit. This is achieved by the new troop commander inheriting the troop commander rule-sets and continuing the campaign. However, the new troop commander does not obtain the database from the previous commander, but, in accordance with military doctrine already knows the objective in hand.

As the agents can interact with other simulation entities, it is necessary for the agents to run in real time. This is achieved by constraining the amount of processing an agent can perform on a cycle.

The behaviour of the tank agents is observed by using them to control tanks in a simple simulation linked with the agent Tool-Kit during a small tank battle scenario.

5. Squadron Agent

The Squadron Commander agent is currently capable of performing the planning for a squadron delay order. A delaying order requires the squadron to hinder the passage of enemy forces through an area. The delay order is passed from a superior commanding agent describing the area in which the squadron is to deploy, and the general direction of enemy approach. The squadron commander decides where to place the troops within the deployment area for best effect. In doing this the squadron commander must consider a number of features of the problem, including:

• Finding hull down positions (positions where the hull of a tank is protected from direct fire) on the terrain, avoiding assumptions about terrain features. Also, points must be found across the deployment area to ensure the whole area infront can be covered.

• Deciding which combinations of hull down positions to assign to the troops so obtaining the best coverage of the terrain.

• Ensuring troops provide mutual support (i.e. covering fire). This may imply sub-optimal coverage of the terrain, it is better for unit to have support it if gets into difficulty. This does have the advantage of reducing the search space significantly, by removing combinations of points cheaply at an early stage of planning.

• Time scale of the operation, how long the agent has before the units must be in position ready.

• Manoeuvre and retreat lines, alternative cover points, and safe retreat routes for re-grouping.

• Protection of key features.

The current planner executes a fairly prescribed sequence of activities. An activity is associated with a "mental" process necessary in order for the agent to achieve the objective. The planner creates activities as required to perform the necessary functions. Activities can execute in parallel or multiple times with different parameters to allow any-time planning. Thus currently activities exist for the first three features listed above. Having decided on a possible solution, the agent then issues orders to the troop commanders to occupy the hull down locations.

In delaying the enemy it is very important to minimise the hidden areas (dead ground) in which the enemy forces could manoeuvre. Hence, the commander must consider the total area covered by the different combinations of the hull down positions. To do this the commander generates a binary map of points which are visible from the hull down position in consideration, taking into account the limited field of view of a tank, and the range of the weapon system available.

Coverage maps, such as that shown in Figure 4, are generated for each of the hull down positions, but only combined for combinations of points which satisfy the mutually supportive requirement. This dramatically reduces the memory requirement and improves performance considerably compared to examining all the hull down position combinations.

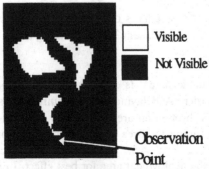

Fig. 4. Example of coverage map.

Once a coverage map has been generated for a combination of points, an estimate must be made of its "effectiveness". A set of positions which provide better cover should have a low cost associated with it, poor coverage, which could allow enemy to easily slip through the defences should have a high cost. Currently the cost is based on:

- Total area of coverage.
- Threshold depth of coverage across the area.
- Mean square of the coverage depth across the area.

Examples of good and bad coverage are shown in Figure 5. This highlights how the three costing measures used can enable combinations of troop deployment options to be compared and ones which give good depth and breadth of coverage to be selected.

These costs are combined using a vector of weights, and the plan with lowest cost is selected. The cost selector continuously detects new options associated with a particular plan and assesses these against the current best plan. Thus a plan is ready at an early stage and may improve with time as better options emerge as they are generated.

The use of these 'anytime' planning techniques is vital to get good performance in real time. An initial plan can be quickly made and selected while the planning routine goes on to consider other, perhaps more favourable options.

Figure 6 shows an example of the planned deployment of troops by the squadron commander to delay the advance of an enemy force. The supposed enemy approach is

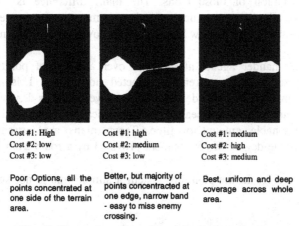

Cost #1: High	Cost #1: high	Cost #1: medium
Cost #2: low	Cost #2: medium	Cost #2: high
Cost #3: low	Cost #3: low	Cost #3: medium
Poor Options, all the points concentrated at one side of the terrain area.	Better, but majority of points concentracted at one edge, narrow band - easy to miss enemy crossing.	Best, uniform and deep coverage across whole area.

Fig. 5. Examples of good and bad coverage maps.

in the direction of the arrow, and the squadron has been ordered to deploy in the area marked. The troop positions, marked by arrows, are seen to be within mutual support range of each another, and positioned just behind folds in the terrain for concealment, but offering good visibility of the terrain in front of them.

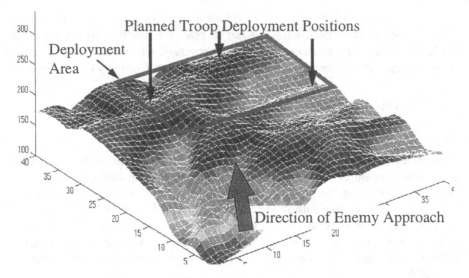

Fig. 6. Squadron deployment of troops

6. Troop Agent

The troop commander agents and tank commander agents are very similar in that they produce plans for movement orders together with re-planning criteria and monitor the execution of those plans. The main difference is that the troop commander plans take longer to calculate and cover movements of several kilometres over the terrain rather than the few hundred meters over which the tank commander agent plans.

The troop commander agents make plans over a series of points based upon 'significant' terrain features, currently abstracted ridge lines. This is designed to enable troop commanders to consider large scale moves, such as driving round a hill, as a single step, and reduces the search space significantly to enable the planning to occur in a reasonable amount of time. Troop plans are currently based on consideration of the degree of concealment provided by a route from known enemy positions

To represent a ridge in the planning system a simple line is not sufficient, some

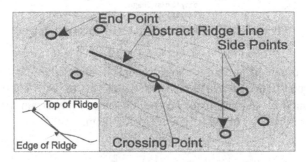

Fig. 7. Example of ridge line abstraction.

idea of the size of the ridge is also important and potential crossing points. The ridge lines are abstracted manually and a simple algorithm used to extract the edge points. An example is shown in Figure 7.

6.1. Costing of routes

The cost function uses a combination of traversal time and exposure to enemy units. To model the effect of terrain, traversal time is based on the slope of the terrain profile. The speed reduction depends on how close the slope is to the maximum vehicle gradient. Only upward slopes have an effect and 'impassable' slopes are given an arbitrarily slow speed. The exposure of a route is calculated by using line of sight to find what percentage of a route segment (sampled at 50m intervals) is visible to observer positions. The costs are combined by multiplying the cost of exposed sections by a constant indicating the relative importance of speed and concealment.

6.2. The search mechanism

The search is a variant of A* modified to work with complete routes over a fully connected graph. The search is required to find the lowest cost solutions in the available time.

The search starts by considering the cost of the route direct from the start to the goal and then considers all single stage routes (routes which travel via a single intermediate node). This gives an upper bound on the route cost and also identifies the direction in which search can be carried out with the lowest apparent branching factor. A* search then proceeds, expanding in the direction with the lowest apparent branching factor. The heuristic function used is the straight line distance divided by the maximum speed of the vehicle. In general the branching factor at each node would appear to be the number of nodes in the graph. In practice it is considerably lower than this since nodes can be rejected if the expected path cost through them exceeds the current lowest cost plan. When a lower cost route to a node is found the planner checks the (known) cost to directly complete the route to see if this provides a cheaper route than has been found so far and updates its plan accordingly. This means that at any time the best known route can be executed, allowing the troop commander to respond quickly when necessary. The search terminates when no node has any possible extensions which could yield a lower cost route.

Figure 8 shows how the initially high cost for a route was improved over time with an initial very fast reduction in cost as the search quickly identified how to avoid areas

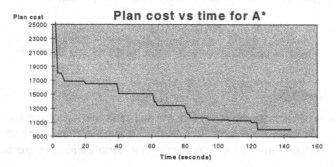

Figure 8. Plan cost against Planning Time

which were very exposed to the enemy and then showing a steady improvement as the route was refined.

6.3. Executing troop level plans

The route planner has been incorporated into the troop commander which uses it to plan routes for the troop to follow. Routes are planned based on known enemy positions. The troop commander may re-plan the route if an enemy which was not previously known about is detected. The behaviour this produces can be seen in Figure 9.

The blue troop initially planned to cross the ridge in front of it and proceed towards their goal along the northern edge of the ridge. As it reached the top of the hill one of the tanks spotted the red troop in the valley and informed the troop commander. This resulted in a re-plan which caused the blue troop commander to adjust its plan to

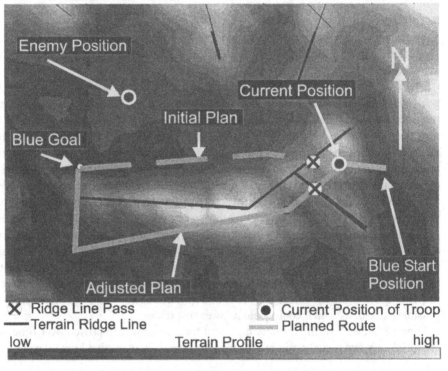

Fig. 9. Initial troop plan and a re-plan on spotting the enemy.

follow the southern slopes of the ridge instead, first crossing the smaller ridge to the SW.

7. Tank Agents

The tank agent is responsible for driving the tank and operating its weapons. At this level the situation can change very quickly so in general tanks are only concerned with the immediate future so only generate short term plans. The troop commander issues an objective to the tank agent giving a location to move to which may include additional constraints.

The tank agent then plans to move to the location to arrive at a specific time. Included in the plan is an indication how long it should remain valid until a re-plan may be required. To generate a plan the agent considers sequences of simple actions. Associated with performing each action is a cost in time, distance and exposure to risk. Actions which are not appropriate to the situation by violating a constraint or not conforming to a high level principle, are rejected thereby reducing the search space. To evaluate the cost associated with risk, the agent performs a simple simulation of the action into the future and the interactions with other agents. This includes assessing the likely changes in threat to the agent, e.g. moving into a more exposed area. An A* search algorithm is used to find a course of actions with lowest cost and hence generate a plan.

Currently the agent can generate plans by considering sequences of eight actions: advance to goal; veer left or right; follow ridge-line; retreat from threat (move away but remain facing the threat); advance to threat; face threat (stops movement and sets to face the threat); run away; and hold in place.

Tests have been conducted at the tank level by adjusting the weights the planner uses associated with time taken, distance and exposure to risk. This affects the way in which the agents behave in a given situation, and thus a "personality" can be attributed to the agents in terms of their risk taking behaviour. This has been demonstrated in a scenario involving two opposing troops of three tanks, whose starting positions and final goals are such that they have to cross each others path.

In the scenario where both troops are cautious, shown in Figure 10, the troops tend to hover at the limits of maximum firing range trying to work their way around each other and occasionally exchange shots. The red force has to take a large detour since the tanks cannot move directly to their goal without exposing their flanks to fire from the blue troop. The blue troop on the other hand simply delays its advance and moves towards the goal when the red troop has retreated out of range. In the risky vs. risky scenario the two groups come into sight of each other when they reach A. When they come within range at B both groups launch into an immediate assault and a fight ensues. Neither group is prepared to postpone its actions in order to avoid a fight but do alter their approach to the goal to face the enemy.

These scenarios demonstrate that appropriately different behaviours can be achieved by simply changing the risk parameter the agents find acceptable. This shows that different command styles can be easily emulated.

8. Results and Conclusions

This paper has summarised a number of planning techniques within the agents in a C^2 hierarchy, and presented results for each implementation. Using a hierarchy of agents is proving a useful method of dividing the problem of planning over terrain. Deriving a plan immediately at the lowest level of detail proves to be too computationally expensive, and usually has to be discarded whenever the situation changes. However, by using a C^2 hierarchy the high level commander considers detail at a larger scale suitable for the next level down. Using this information the subordinate commander further refines the plan suitable for their subordinates, but the

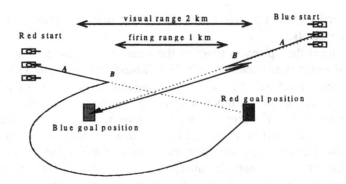

Fig. 10. Combat between two 'cautious' groups.

plan search space has already been considerably reduced. Thus the agents are able to generate plans much more quickly. Changes in the situation at the low levels does not necessarily affect the high level plans. Thus, only partial re-planning is necessary reducing the computational effort required to maintain plausible plans.

Compared to systems that use explicit rules for situations, our agents are able to consider the effect of their actions in context of the situation. Our agents are not constrained to a limited set of situations but exhibit appropriate behaviour in a wide range of situations with relatively few rules.

The performance of our agents is directly attributable to their effective use of terrain. However, developing planning systems that efficiently use the terrain to good effect in context of the situation is no trivial matter, and our current research is developing methods of terrain reasoning. Thus the focus of our current research is the further development of terrain reasoning algorithms.

References

[Bates *et al.*, 1991] J. Bates, A. B. Loyall and W. S. Reilly. *Broad Agents*. Sigart Bulletin, 1991.

[Ceranowicz, 1994] A. Ceranowicz. ModSAF Capabilities. In *Proceedings of the 4th Conference on Computer Generated Forces and Behavioural Representation*, pages 3-8, Orlando, Florida, May 4-6 1994. Institute for Simulation and Training.

[Ceranowicz *et al.*, 1994b] A. Ceranowicz, D. Coffin, J. Smith, R. Gonzalex and C. Ladd. Operator Control of Behaviour in ModSAF. In *Proceedings of the 4th Conference on Computer Generated Forces and Behavioural Representation*, pages 9-16. Orlando Florida May 4-6 1994. Institute for Simulation and Training.

[Laird *et al.*, 1993] J. E. Laird, B. L. Clave, A. Erik and D. Roberts. Soar User's Manual (V6), 1993. University of Michigan, Carnegie Mellon University.

[McEnany *et al.*, 1994] B. R. McEnany and H. Marshall. CCTT SAF Functional Analysis. In *Proceedings of the 4th Conference on Computer Generated Forces and Behavioural Representation*, pages 195-207. Orlando Florida May 4-6 1994. Institute for Simulation and Training.

[Meliza *el al.*, 1995] L. L. Meliza and E. A. Varden. Measuring Entity and Group Behaviours of Semi-Automated Forces. In *Proceedings of the 5th Conference on Computer Generated Forces and Behavioural Representation.* Pages 181-192. Orlando Florida May 9-11 1995. Institute for Simulation and Training.

[Sloman *et al.*, 1995] A. Sloman and R. Poli. SIM_AGENT: A tool-kit for exploring agent designs. ATAL-95 Workshop on Agent Theories, Architectures, and Languages, IJCAI-95 Montreal, August 1995.

Understanding and Extending Graphplan

Subbarao Kambhampati, Eric Parker and Eric Lambrecht[†]
Department of Computer Science and Engineering
Arizona State University, Tempe AZ 85287-5406
http://rakaposhi.eas.asu.edu/yochan.html; {rao,ericpark,eml}@asu.edu

Abstract

We provide a reconstruction of Blum and Furst's Graphplan algorithm, and use the reconstruction to extend and improve the original algorithm in several ways. In our reconstruction, the process of growing the planning-graph and inferring mutex relations corresponds to doing forward state-space refinement over disjunctively represented plans. The backward search phase of Graphplan corresponds to solving a binary dynamic constraint satisfaction problem. Our reconstruction sheds light on the sources of strength of Graphplan. We also use the reconstruction to explain how Graphplan can be made goal-directed, how it can be extended to handle actions with conditional effects, and how backward state-space refinement can be generalized to apply to disjunctive plans. Finally, we discuss how the backward search phase of Graphplan can be improved by applying techniques from CSP literature, and by teasing apart planning and scheduling (resource allocation) phases in Graphplan.

1. Introduction

Blum and Furst's Graphplan algorithm [1995] has recently emerged as the fastest planner for solving classical planning problems. Despite its impact, currently there exists very little critical analysis of the algorithm, its sources of strength and its relation to the traditional planning algorithms. In this paper, we will show that significant surface differences notwithstanding, the Graphplan algorithm can actually be best understood in terms of forward state-space refinement over disjunctive partial plans that correspond to a unioned representation of the forward state-space search tree. Normally, direct refinement of these disjunctive plans (called "planning-graphs" in Graphplan parlance) tends to result in reduced "pruning power." To counter this, Graphplan infers and propagates information about disjuncts that cannot together hold in any solution (called "mutex" relations in Graphplan parlance). The mutex inference process can be seen as a generalization of the standard refinement strategies in the presence of disjunctive plans, and helps Graphplan in producing a planning-graph that is a close "upper bound" approximation to the forward state-space search tree. Solution extraction involves searching for a sequence of actions that is part of the disjunctive plan, and solves the planning problem. This can be done by a backward search over the planning-graph structure. The search problem here corresponds closely to a binary dynamic constraint satisfaction problem [Mittal & Falkenhainer, 1990].

Our reinterpretation of Graphplan, summarized above, explains the role of such properties as "interference" relations, "mutex" relations and "action parallelism" in the algorithm, and also clarifies their relative impact on its performance. Our reconstruction also helps us place Graphplan in the pantheon of refinement planners. The connection between Graphplan and forward state-space refinement suggests improving Graphplan by making it goal-directed, and extending it to handle more expressive actions. The connec-

---

[†] This research is supported in part by the NSF NYI award IRI-9457634, the ARPI Initiative grant F30602-95-C-0247 and the ARPA AASERT grant DAAH04-96-1-0231. We would like to thank Avrim Blum and Dan Weld for helpful discussions on Graphplan, and Mark Peot and David Smith for making their Lisp implementation of Graphplan available to us.

tion between the backward search on the planning-graph and the dynamic constraint satisfaction problem suggests improvements to backward search by exploiting techniques from constraint satisfaction (c.f. [Tsang, 1993]).

The rest of the paper presents our reconstruction of the Graphplan algorithm, and elaborates on the insights it affords and the extensions it suggests. The paper is organized as follows: In Section 2, we will reconstruct the Graphplan algorithm starting from a generalized forward state-space search. In Section 3, we discuss the insights offered by our reconstruction. Section 4 presents a variety of ways of improving the efficiency and coverage of the Graphplan algorithm, including making Graphplan goal directed through means-ends analysis (4.1), supporting propagation of mutex information in the backward direction (4.2), empowering Graphplan to handle more expressive action representations (4.3), improving Graphplan's backward search phase with the help of CSP techniques (4.4), and teasing apart planning and scheduling in Graphplan (4.5). Section 5 summarizes the contributions of this paper.

2 Reconstructing Graphplan from Forward State-space Search

2.1 Generalized Forward State-space search

Let us start our reconstruction of Graphplan with a simple example domain containing 6 operators -- $O_1, O_2, ... O_6$, and a No-OP (do nothing action), all of whose preconditions and effects are shown on the top in Figure 1. Now consider the process of forward state-space search starting from the initial state (R,W). Recall that this involves applying every applicable action to the initial state to compute new states, and applying operators to the resultant states iteratively. A portion of the search tree resulting from this process is shown on the bottom left in Figure 1 (in solid lines). Each path in this tree corresponds to a partial plan. Planning ends when one of the states in the search tree contains all the goals. The path to that state is output as the plan.

Although this process normally leads to "sequential" or totally ordered plans, we can easily extend the idea to allow for a special form of parallelism in the solutions. This is done by projecting the sets of actions that are independent of each other (i.e., they don't delete each others preconditions or added effects) together [Drummond, 1989] [1]. For the search tree on the bottom left in Figure 1, the portion of the tree produced by allowing the projection of independent action sets is shown in dashed lines. For example, since O_1 and O_2 are independent and have their preconditions satisfied in the initial state, we can apply the action set (O_1, O_2) together to the state (R,W) to get the state (P,Q) at the second level, from where we can apply O_4 to get Z in the third level. If our goal is Z, we can terminate in the third level with the solution $[O_1, O_2]$--O_4. This plan is said to be two time steps long, with the first time step containing two actions. The semantics of the parallelism is that in the first time step, we can execute O_1 and O_2 concurrently, and in the second step we execute O_4. It should be easy to see that as long as we allow the projection of all independent action sets, any complete search strategy (such as breadth first) is guaranteed to find us the shortest plan (in terms of number of time steps). If we only project single actions, the first time Z appears in a state is at the fourth level. In other words, allowing the projection of independent action sets reduces the solution depth (while increasing the branching and redundancy in the search tree). The total number of actions in the solution however remain the same.[2]

---

[1] This is however very different from the kind of partial order found in plan space plans. In particular, within a given branch of the projection tree, the positioning of the operators with respect to time steps is strictly fixed; this positioning is what gives the state information at the next level.

[2] It is possible to reduce the redundancy in this search tree by first pre-processing the domain to partition actions into maximal sets of non-interfering actions, and then doing search by projecting each of the action sets, rather than individual actions. Since not all actions in an action set may be simultaneously applicable in a given state, projection will involve stripping the action set of inap-

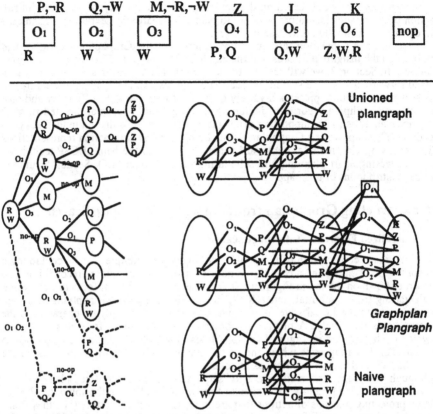

Figure 1. Interpreting Graphplan as a disjunctive forward state-space refinement planner. On the left is a portion of the search tree generated by a forward state-space search. The portion in dashed lines show the branches produced by allowing the parallel projection of independent actions. On the right are three different disjunctive representations of the tree.

2.2 Planning-graph as a compact representation for the search tree

A big problem with forward state-space search (that it shares with many other planning algorithms), is that the search (projection) tree can grow exponentially large even for very small problems. One way of getting a handle on the forward branching would be to somehow consider all the states in a given level *together*, rather than as separate nodes in the search tree. In particular, seeing the states as sets of propositions, we can try to union the sets together to get the collection of propositions from which all the states in that level are made up. These unions are roughly (see below) equivalent to what the Graphplan algorithm calls "proposition lists." We shall call the resulting structure a *"unioned planning-graph"*.

The unioned planning-graph for our example is shown at the top right in Figure 1. The proposition lists at various levels are shown in ovals. The proposition list at the first

---

plicable actions. Finally, since not all the actions in an action set may not be relevant to the final goal, the sequence of action sets that is returned upon termination will have to be post-processed to eliminate irrelevant actions. This can be done in polynomial time with the help of the causal structure of the solution plan.

level is the union of just the initial state, and is thus (R,W). At the second level, it is (P,Q,M,W,R), and at the third level, it is (Z, P, Q, M, W, R).

We can relate the proposition lists at successive levels in terms of actions that can be taken between these levels. Specifically, the unioned planning-graph in Figure 1 contains, between every two consecutive proposition lists, all the actions taken between those levels in the corresponding state-space projection tree shown in Figure 1. The actions in the planning-graph can be connected to the elements in the preceding proposition list that comprise their preconditions, and the elements in the following proposition list that comprise their effects. Since the actions are only connected to the propositions they change, the persistence of propositions during action execution is not explicit in the planning-graph. To make the persistences explicit, a set of "no-op" actions -- one for the persistence of each of the propositions -- are introduced. In the unioned planning-graph in Figure 1, these correspond to the direct connections between the propositions in consecutive levels.

Loosely speaking, the unioned proposition list at level i in the planning-graph can be seen as a compact "disjunctive" representation of the b^i states (assuming a branching factor b) at the ith level of the corresponding state-space search tree. Thus a unioned planning-graph does seem to provide a compact representation for curtailing the growth of forward state-space search. Before we can make this representation the basis for an efficient planning algorithm, we need to decide how the planning-graph structure is grown, and how solutions are extracted from it.

2.3 Growing and searching planning-graphs

Although the unioned planning-graph itself can be grown by generating and converting the state-space search tree, this is clearly very inefficient as it will have the overhead of classical state-space planning. We can reduce the cost significantly if we are willing to get by with a planning-graph structure that is an (upper bound) approximation to the unioned planning-graph.

Specifically, one simple way of growing a planning-graph would be to add all actions (including no-ops) whose preconditions are subsets of the current proposition list, and construct the proposition list at the next level as the union of the effects of all these actions.[3] We shall call the resultant structure the *"naive planning-graph."* The naive planning-graph for our example problem is shown in Figure 1. Note that O_5 (in the second level of the naive planning-graph) is not present in the state-space search tree in Figure 1 (and thus also absent from the unioned planning-graph in Figure 1), making the naive planning-graph an upper bound approximation to the unioned planning-graph. In contrast to the exponential cost of generating the state-space search tree, the naive planning-graph is a polynomial-sized structure that can be generated in polynomial time (the main savings in generation cost comes because the planning-graph contains at most one instance of each action at each level, as against the possibly exponential number in the corresponding level of the state-space search tree).

To do solution extraction, we need to prove to ourselves that there is a sequence of legal states culminating in a state where all the goals are satisfied. This can be done by essentially following the dependency links between actions and proposition list elements. For example, to see if we have a successful plan for goals (P, Z) in the planning-graph shown in Figure 1, we check if there are actions supporting P and Z in that level. Z is supported by O_4 while P is supported by O_1 and no-op. Since we need only one support for each goal, we consider each support of P in turn. Suppose we pick O_1 for P (leaving no-op as a backtrack choice) and O_4 for Z. We then have to ensure that the preconditions of these two actions are satisfied in the previous proposition list. This leads to the recursive goal set (R, P, Q) at the previous level. At this point, we have single supports to all three goals—no-op for R, O_1 for P and O_2 for Q. These actions cannot occur together

---

[3] An even simpler way would be to introduce all actions at all levels. This is the idea used by Kautz and Selman [1996] in their linear encodings.

since R is deleted by O_1. We can think of this as O_1 interfering with no-op. At this point we can backtrack, consider the remaining choice, no-op, as the support for P, and we will be able to succeed.

The termination process discussed above can be cast as a *dynamic constraint satisfaction problem (DCSP)* [Mittal & Falkenhainer, 1990]. The DCSP is a generalization of the Constraint Satisfaction Problem [Tsang, 1993], that is specified by a set of variables, activity flags for the variables, the domains of the variables, and the constraints on the legal variable-value combinations. In a DCSP, initially only a subset of the variables is active, and the objective is to find assignments for all active variables that is consistent with the constraints among those variables. In addition, the DCSP specification also contains a set of "activity constraints." An activity constraint is of the form: "if variable x takes on the value v_x, then the variables y,z,w... become active." The correspondence between the planning-graph and the DCSP should now be clear. Specifically, the propositions at various levels correspond to the DCSP variables, and the actions supporting them correspond to the DCSP domains. The action interference relations can be seen as DCSP constraints -- if a_1 and a_2 are interfering with each other, and p_{11} and p_{12} are supported by a_1 in the planning-graph while p_{21} and p_{22} are supported by a_2, then we have the constraints: $p_{11}=a_1$ => $p_{21} \neq a_2$, $p_{12}=a_1$ => $p_{21} \neq a_2$, etc. Activity constraints are implicitly specified by action preconditions: supporting an active proposition p with an action a makes all the propositions in the previous level corresponding to the preconditions of a active. Finally, only the propositions corresponding to the goals of the problem are "active" in the beginning.

2.4 Improving growth and search of planning-graphs

The naive planning-graph can be exponentially larger (in terms of actions per level) than the unioned planning-graph (to see this, consider a situation where the preconditions of all domain actions hold in a proposition list, but only a few subsets of the proposition list actually correspond to legal states). Thus, growing and searching it may actually be worse than doing state-space search.

Thankfully, we can improve our approximation to the unioned planning-graph by tracking information as to which subsets of the proposition list do not belong to legal states. For example, if we recognize that (Q,W) is not part of any legal state at the second level of the search tree in Figure 1, we could avoid projecting the action O_5 (which has preconditions Q,W) from this proposition list. This type of information can also control the backward search for a solution on the planning-graph. For example, if we know that (R, P, Q) is not a part of any legal state at the second level, we could backtrack as soon as we get this as our recursive goal set.

Unfortunately, keeping track of all illegal subsets of a proposition list can in general require both too much computation (since we don't have access to the state-space search tree) and memory (as there can be an exponential number of illegal subsets of a proposition list in the worst case). However, even knowing *some* of the illegal subsets of the proposition lists can help us. An interesting middle ground is to keep track of all 2-sized illegal subsets alone (since there are only at most n^2 such subsets). This is the idea behind Graphplan's "mutex" relations—two elements in a proposition list are said to be mutex if they belong to the set of 2-sized illegal subsets.

The nice thing about pair-wise mutex relations is that they can be inferred efficiently through incremental constraint propagation. We start by generalizing the mutex relations to hold between pairs of interfering actions. Although the Graphplan algorithm assumes a specific definition of interference -- viz., actions interfere if the effects of one violate the preconditions or effects of the other, the definition of interference between actions is really up to the designer of the domain, and only needs to capture the requirements for concurrent execution [Reisig, 1982].[4] Starting with the actions in the first level, we can

---

[4] It is instructive to note that optimal solution length depends on the interference definition used. For example, if the domain doesn't allow any concurrency, we can consider every pair of actions to be interfering. In this case, optimal solutions will be sequential. Similarly, we can weaken the

consider any pair of actions that interfere to be mutex. The mutex relation can then be propagated to any effects of the actions in the next proposition list (as long as those effects are not being supported by other non-interfering actions). In particular, in the example we have been following, O_1 and the no-op leading to R are interfering as the former deletes R. Thus, R and P are mutex at the second level proposition list. Similar reasoning shows that Q and W are mutex.

As expected, mutex information curtails the growth of the planning-graph and helps in termination check. Since (Q,W) are found to be mutex, there is no point in projecting O5 from the first level proposition list, as is shown in the Graphplan planning-graph in Figure 1 (mutex relations are not shown in the figure). Similarly, since R and P are mutex at the second level, the backward search for the goals P and Z can be terminated as soon as we reach the second level proposition list.

In the context of our observation in the previous section that the planning-graph can be seen as a DCSP, the mutex propagation can be seen as inferring additional variable-value constraints. The mutex propagation process however is different from the standard notion of "constraint propagation" in the CSP. To see this, note that the mutex propagation routines use the constraints among variables (propositions) at one level to derive implicit constraints among the variables at the next level. In contrast, normal constraint propagation procedures use the constraints among a given set of variables to derive new constraints among the same set of variables.

3 Discussion

The reconstruction of the Graphplan algorithm in terms of forward state-space projection reduces the mystery regarding the antecedents of the algorithm. We recognize that both the fact that plans produced by Graphplan can contain multiple actions within each step, and the fact that Graphplan terminates with smallest plan (in terms of time-steps), are consequences of the properties of the corresponding forward state-space search tree. Similarly, we recognize that the planning-graph is an *approximation* to the disjunctive (unioned) representation of the state-space search tree—with the approximation becoming finer and finer as we maintain bookkeeping information about illegal subsets of proposition lists. We have shown that mutex relations can be understood as inferring information about 2-sized illegal subsets.

Our reconstruction shows that the ability to refine disjunctive partial plans, rather than action parallelism, is the more important innovation of the Graphplan algorithm. In particular, it is easy to make Graphplan produce only serial plans by changing our definition of action interference, and considering every pair of non no-op actions to be interfering. This serial version of Graphplan will have the same tradeoffs with respect to Graphplan as normal forward state-space search will have with search with projection of independent action sets. Specifically, in situations where the domain does allow parallelism, the parallel planning-graph can terminate with fewer levels than the serial planning-graph. More importantly, the serial version of Graphplan will still outperform normal state-space planners. We verified this observation by comparing a state-space planner based on Graphplan data-structures to a serial version of Graphplan.

Our account also gives us some insights into the tradeoffs offered by the propagation of mutex relations. The first point we note is that mutex relations help in generating a planning-graph that is a finer approximation to the unioned planning-graph. The approximation to the unioned planning-graph provided by the mutex relations will in general differ from the exact unioned planning-graph since mutex identifies only 2-sized illegal subsets but not the 3- and higher-sized ones. Because of this difference, some illegal projections are still left in the planning-graph. In our example in Figure 1, the Graph-

---

interference to hold only between actions one of which deletes the preconditions or *useful* effects of the other (notice that Graphplan considers violation of any effect, not just useful effects). This weaker interference relation will lead to more parallel (and thus shorter) solutions than Graphplan.

plan planning-graph includes O_6, with preconditions Z, R, and W, in the third level actions, and the proposition K in the level four propositions, although it is easy to see from the search tree that O_6 cannot be applied from any of the states in level 3.

While the approximation can be further improved by 3- and higher sized mutex relations, whether or not the cost of computing the mutex relations is offset by the improvements in planning-graph size and the time to search it depends on what percentage of action interactions in the domain are pair-wise (as against three-, four-, or n-ary interactions).[5] The amazing practical success of 2-sized mutex relations can be explained by the relative rarity of higer-order interactions between actions in most classical planning domains. This rarity is to a certain extent due to a lack of global resource constraints in the classical planning domains. 2-sized mutexes may thus not be as effective when we consider more complex domains containing such global constraints. To illustrate, consider a variation of the blocksworld domain where the blocks have non-uniform sizes, with super-blocks that can, for example, hold two blocks on top of them. In such a scenario, suppose we are considering three actions all of which attempt to stack a distinct block on top of the same super-block. These three actions together are interacting, while no two of them are interacting.

The connection between the planning-graph and the dynamic constraint satisfaction problem provides insights into the operation of the backward search phase of the Graphplan algorithm. In essence, the Graphplan algorithm uses a systematic backtracking search strategy [Tsang, 1993] for solving the dynamic CSP—computing a satisfying assignment at one level, and recursing on the variables that are activated in the next level. Upon failure to compute a satisfying assignment at any level, the algorithm backtracks to the previous level. The memoization phase in Graphplan can be seen as a special form of no-good learning [Kambhampati, 1997b]. The connection also makes it clear that the specific details of the backward search algorithm used in Graphplan are by no means unique. There exist other possible ways of solving dynamic CSP algorithms that are worth considering. These include variable and value ordering heuristics as well as full no-good based learning schemes. We shall elaborate these in Section 4.4.

3.1 Graphplan as a refinement planner

Most existing AI planners fall under the rubric of refinement planners. Kambhampati et. al [1995,1996,1997c] provide a general model for refinement planning. Our reconstruction of Graphplan from forward state-space planning helps us interpret it as an instance of this generalized refinement planning. Specifically, the planning-graph structure of Graphplan can be seen as a "partial plan" representation. An action sequence belongs to the candidate set of the planning-graph if it has a prefix that contains some subset of actions from each of the levels of the planning-graph, contiguous to each other. For example, any action sequence with a prefix O_1-O_2-O_4-O_6 will be a candidate of the planning-graph shown in Figure 1 (since O_1, O_2 belong to the first level actions, O_4 belongs to the second level actions and O_6 belongs to the third level). O_1-O_2-O_4-O_6 itself is one of the minimal candidates of the planning-graph. Similarly, no action sequence that has a prefix O_6 can be a candidate of this planning-graph. The relation between the naive, unioned and Graphplan planning-graphs can be formally stated by saying that the candidate set of the naive planning graph is a superset of the candidate set of the Graphplan planning-graph, which in turn is a superset of the candidate set of unioned planning-graph.

The forward "planning-graph growing" phase corresponds to the refinement operation. The inference and propagation of mutex constraints can be seen as a legitimate part of the

---

[5] Even binary interactions between actions can eventually lead to higher-level interactions between propositions. Graphplan algorithm does remember higher level mutex relations between propositions by caching ("memoizing") failing goal sets. Graphplan algorithm works because these higher order relations are a small subset of the total number, and can be learned upon failure. In a domain with a significant number of non-binary action interactions, higher order interactions between propositions will be much more prevalent and cannot be postponed to the learning stage without a drastic hit on performance.

refinement process since the addition of mutex constraints reduces the candidate-set of the planning-graph. The backward search phase of Graphplan corresponds to "solution extraction"—to see if any of the minimal candidates of the planning-graph correspond to a solution. It is thus easy to see that solution extraction is helped by the reduction in the candidate-set of the planning-graph that is achieved through the inference of mutex constraints.

The interesting thing about this analogy is that unlike traditional refinement planners, such as the forward state-space planner or the partial-order planner, which search among various partial plans during the refinement phase, Graphplan considers only one partial plan and thus does not incur *any* premature commitment. As we saw, this single plan is approximately equal to a unioned or "disjunctive" representation of all the partial plans in the forward state-space search. While there is no search among partial plans in Graphplan, its solution extraction process is costlier than that used by a forward state-space refinement.

All this brings up a very important insight: If Graphplan can do so well by refining disjunctive plans using forward state-space refinements, might it not be possible to duplicate this success in the context of backward state-space, plan-space and task-reduction refinements? Kambhampati [1997a] considers this question and outlines the challenges involved in developing such planners.

4 Extending Graphplan

4.1 Making Graphplan goal-directed

The strong connection between forward state-space refinement and Graphplan suggests that Graphplan can suffer some of the same ills as the former. Specifically, in many realistic domains, there will be too many actions that are applicable in any proposition list, unduly increasing the width of the planning-graph structure. Indeed, we (as well as other researchers) found that despite its efficiency, Graphplan can easily fail in domains where many actions are available and only few are relevant to the top level goals of the problem. There are several ways of making Graphplan goal-directed.

One simple way of reducing the width of the planning-graph would involve constructing and using *operator graphs* for the problem. Operator graphs [Smith & Peot, 1996] symbolically back-chain on the goals of the problem to isolate actions of the domain that are potentially relevant for solving the problem. Although not every action in the graph is guaranteed to be relevant for the solution, we can guarantee that all solutions consist only of operators from the operator graph. Thus, restricting attention to these actions in the planning-graph expansion phase will reduce the width of the planning-graph. The cost of operator graph construction is itself quite low since the graph contains at most one instance of each precondition and action.

The operator graphs may still not be able to reduce the width of the graph sufficiently however. In particular, the fact that an action is relevant to the problem doesn't imply that it is to be considered in each action level of the planning-graph. In order to predict the relevance of an action to a given level, we have developed a novel way by adapting means-ends analysis [McDermott, 1996] to Graphplan. Our approach, called Mea-Graphplan [Parker & Kambhampati, 1997]., involves first growing the planning-graph in the backward direction by regressing goals over actions, and then using the resulting structure as a guidance for the standard Graphplan algorithm. Growing the backward planning-graph involves regressing proposition lists over "relevant" actions. In particular, for every proposition p in the kth level proposition list (counting from the goal state side), we introduce all actions (include the dummy *"preserve-p"* action) that have p in their effects list into the $(k+1)^{th}$ level action list. Actions are introduced only if they are not already present at that level. The proposition list at the $(k+1)^{th}$ level then consists of the preconditions of all the actions introduced at the $(k+1)^{th}$ level. Suppose we have grown the planning-graph in this way for j levels, and would like to search for the solution in the graph. The j-level backward planning-graph structure shows all actions that are relevant at each level of the forward planning-graph. We can now run the standard Graphplan algorithm, making it consider only those actions that are present at the corresponding level of the backward planning-graph. Alternately, we can also mark the propositions in the jth level that are present in the initial state as "*in*" and propagate the "*in*" flags to actions and propositions at the earlier levels (an action is in if all its preconditions are in, and a proposition is in if any of its supporting actions are in). If this process results in the goal propositions being marked in, we can commence a mutex propagation phase on the part of the graph that is marked "*in*", followed by a backward search phase.

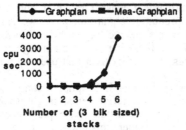

Figure 2. Performance improvement achieved by making Graphplan goal directed

Notice that the planning-graph considered by either of these approaches is significantly smaller than both the pure backward planning-graph (since some of the actions may not actually have their preconditions satisfied in the preceding action level) and the standard planning-graph (since we only consider actions that are relevant to the goals). This leads to a dramatic reduction of plan-graph building cost in problems containing many irrelevant actions. Figure 2 compares Mea-Graphplan with the standard Graphplan algorithm on a set of blocks world problems. Each problem consists of some k 3-block stacks in the initial state, which are to be individually inverted in the goal state. The graph plots the cpu time as k is increased (the planners were written in Lisp and run on a Sparc 10). Notice the dramatic increase in the cost of planning suffered by Graphplan as compared to Mea-Graphplan. The main reason for this turns out to be the graph build time. For values of k greater than 6, Mea-Graphplan still solves the problem while Graphplan runs out of memory.

4.2 Propagating mutexes in the backward direction

Although Mea-Graphplan generates the planning-graphs in the backward direction, it ultimately uses the forward state-space refinement ideas to infer and propagate mutex relations. A variation on this theme would involve doing the inference and propagation in the backward direction also, thus developing a Graphplan algorithm based completely on backward state-space refinement. Although it would look at first glance that no useful information can be propagated in the backward direction, we have found that the information about "goals that will never be required together" can be gainfully propagated.

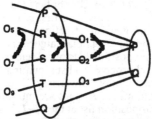

Figure 3. Propagating mutexes in the backward direction (mutexes shown as black links)

Specifically, two actions are said to be backward mutex if (a) they are statically interfering, i.e., the effects of one violate the preconditions or "useful" effects (the effects of the action that are used to support propositions in the planning graph) of the other, or (b) they have the exact same set of useful effects, or (c) the propositions supported by one action are pair-wise mutex with the propositions supported by the other. Two propositions are backward mutex if all the actions supported by one are pair-wise mutex with all the actions supported by the other. To illustrate this, consider the example shown in Figure 3. Here, O_1 and O_2 are mutex since they are solely supporting P. This leads to a mutex relation between R and S (since they are supporting actions that are mutex). Finally, O_5 and O_7 are mutex since they are supporting propositions that are mutex. Our preliminary studies[6] show that these propagation rules derive a reasonably large set of mutex relations on the planning-graph. We are investigating their utility in controlling search both by themselves and in concert with forward mutexes. We are also considering the effectiveness of the backward mutexes in controlling the search of the planning-graph in the forward direction (which corresponds to a variant of the network flow problem).

4.3 Handling more expressive action representations

Although the Graphplan algorithm is originally described only for propositional actions, there is nothing in the algorithm that inhibits it from being extended to more "expressive" action representations such as the ones used in UCPOP [Penberthy & Weld, 1992]. The UCPOP representation allows negated preconditions and goals, conditional and quantified effects in the actions, as well as disjunctive preconditions. We will briefly discuss how each of these can be handled.

Negated preconditions and goals are quite straightforward to handle, if we allow proposition lists to contain both positive and negative literals. Disjunctive preconditions can be handled by allowing actions at the kth level to be connected to multiple sets of preconditions at $(k-1)^{th}$ level. Finally, universally quantified effects can essentially be expanded into a conjunction of unquantified conditional effects. Notice that this expansion does not increase the number of actions.

The treatment of conditional effects is more interesting. One obvious approach would be to convert each action with conditional effects into a set of actions *without* conditional effects. However, this approach often leads to an exponential blow-up in the number of actions. A better approach is to handle conditional effects directly. Doing this requires several minor modifications to the Graphplan algorithm. We shall illustrate these with the help of the example in Figure 4. Here, there are five actions, O_0, ..., O_4. The actions O_3 and O_4 have conditional effects, as shown on the left-hand side of the figure. Suppose that we are starting from the initial state shown at the left-most proposition list of the planning graph and are interested in achieving goals K and M. The planning-graph will be grown as shown in the figure (to avoid clutter, we only show the persistence actions that will be useful in solving the problem, and avoid showing O_3 in the first level). The first iteration is straightforward with one small exception--we explicitly introduce negated propositions, and support persistence of negated propositions from the initial state by using the closed world assumption (e.g. $\neg J$, which is true in the initial state by closed world assumption, persists to the second proposition list). The actions O_1 and O_2 are interfering and thus the propositions (P, W) and ($\neg$R, W) are marked as mutex. The extension at the second level involves actions with conditional effects. Propositions corresponding to conditional effects are handled with conditional establishment links. For example, L is provided by O_3 if P is true in the previous state. Thus we support L with a link to O_3 and its antecedent proposition P in the previous level. Unconditional establishment can be seen as a special case where the antecedent link is omitted (to signify that no special antecedents are required); see the effect K of O_3.

Next, we need to generalize the mutex propagation to work in the presence of conditional establishments. We do this as follows: two (conditional) establishment paths are

---

[6] This is part of joint work with Dan Weld.

mutex if (a) the action supporting one is mutex with the action supporting the other, or (b) one of the antecedents of the first conditional establishment is mutex with one of the antecedents of the second one, or (c) one of the antecedents of the first conditional establishment is mutex with the consequent of the second conditional establishment (or vice versa). The clauses "b" and "c" of course are the generalizations needed to handle conditional effects. Two propositions are mutex if each of the establishments of the first proposition is mutex with each of the establishments of the second proposition.

Applying this rule, we find that L and M are mutex at the third level since P, which is an antecedent of L, is mutex with W, which is an antecedent of M. Notice that O_3 and O_4 are themselves not marked mutex. In fact, the action mutex rules remain unchanged: two actions are marked mutex if either (a) one of the preconditions of one of the actions is mutex with one of the preconditions of the other action, or (b) if the unconditional effects of one of the actions deletes a precondition or an unconditional effect of the other action.

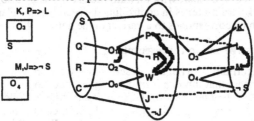

Figure 4. Example illustrating direct handling of conditional effects (mutexes shown as black links)

Coming back to our example, the goals K and M are present in the third level proposition list and backward search can commence. Since some of the goals may be supported by conditional establishments, in addition to the primary preconditions of the selected actions the backward search must also subgoal on the secondary causation preconditions, and further consider preservation preconditions for all the subgoals with respect to all the selected actions. In our example, K can be supported by O_3, and M can be supported by the conditional establishment $[O_4, W]$. Thus, we must subgoal on S, which is the precondition of O_3, as well as W, which is the causation precondition of M with respect to O_4. Furthermore, we must ensure that neither of the selected actions violate any of these subgoals. Since O_4 has a conditional effect ¬S, we must post the preservation precondition of S with respect to O_4, which is ¬J. Since none of the selected actions violates ¬J, we can stop with the three subgoals S, W and ¬J. Since all of these can be supported at the next level through unconditional establishments with the resulting subgoals being true in the initial state, the backward search succeeds.

4.4 Improving Graphplan backward search using CSP techniques

The connection between the planning-graph and the dynamic constraint satisfaction problem suggests several possible improvements for the backward search phase of Graphplan. Considering such improvements is further motivated by the fact that compiling the planning-graph into a SAT instance and solving it using SAT solving techniques has been shown to out-perform standard Graphplan [Kautz & Selman, 1996; Bayardo & Schrag, 1997]. The current understanding in the CSP literature (c.f. [Frost & Dechter, 1996; Bayardo & Schrag, 1997]) is that the best systematic search algorithms for the standard CSP involve forward checking (a form of constraint propagation), dynamic variable ordering, dependency directed backtracking and no-good learning. Of these, the Graphplan backward search uses only memoization -- a limited form of no-good learning. Thus, it is worth considering the utility of the other three ideas as well as the full-fledged no-good learning. Supporting forward checking involves filtering out the conflicting actions from the domains of the remaining goals, as soon as a particular goal is assigned. Dynamic variable ordering involves selecting for assignment the goal that has the least number of remaining establishers. Preliminary results[7] show that these techniques can bring about significant improvements in Graphplan's performance. For example, Graphplan is able to solve a blocks world benchmark problem 8 times faster with the "least number of remaining establishers" variable ordering heuristic as compared with that of the "most number of remaining establishers." These results also show that contrary to Blum & Furst's speculations [1995] "goal ordering" does have a practical impact on Graphplan.

As discussed in [Kambhampati, 1997b], in general a failure explanation (no-good) for the dynamic CSP specifies a set of assigned variables (with their assignments) and a set of unassigned variables. The semantics of such a failure explanation are that if it is part of any search node produced in solving that DCSP, then none of the branches under that search node can lead to a solution. In this context, Graphplan memos can be seen as a subset of possible failure explanations -- those that only name unassigned variables. Failure explanations consisting of both assigned and unassigned variables can help in situations where most ways of achieving a set of subgoals at a level k fail, but a small fraction succeed. In such cases, no memos can be learned, and without generalized failure explanations Graphplan will be forced to repeat failing assignments many times. It would be interesting to investigate the utility of a full-fledged learning strategy, involving the explanation of failures at leaf nodes, and regression and propagation of leaf node failure explanations to compute interior node failure explanations, along the lines described in [Kambhampati, 1997b]. Not only does such a strategy promise to increase learning opportunities, it could also make the existing memos more "general". Specifically, Graphplan stores all of the goals of a failing goal set at a level k, even if the failure is actually due to the presence of only a small subset of them.[8] Full-fledged learning will help alleviate this situation, making the stored goal sets more likely to be useful in other branches of the search..

4.5 Teasing planning and scheduling apart in Graphplan

By now it is well-known that despite its efficiency, Graphplan can perform poorly on some problems. This can happen for one of two reasons -- first, due to irrelevant actions in the domain the planning-graph grows too fast, using up all existing memory. This can be handled to a large extent by making Graphplan goal-directed (see Sections 5.1 and 5.2). Another class of problems, exemplified by the benchmarks used in Kautz and Selman's SATPLAN experiments [1996] are hard because they require too much effort in the backward search phase. An analysis of these problems reveals that the main reason for the difficulty here is that Graphplan combines the planning and scheduling (resource allocation) phases, making the combined problem much harder to solve. To understand this, note that in a blocks world problem like bw-large-a in the SATPLAN suite, Graphplan finds a plan that is correct save the ordering of the actions in one of the early iterations, but spends enormous time in the next several iterations effectively "linearizing" this plan to handle the resource restrictions imposed by the availability of a single hand. The inefficiency of this approach is apparent when we realize that during these later iterations, Graphplan is not only looking at the approximately correct plan, but also the rest of the search space. This approach results in a degradation of Graphplan's performance when given additional resources (e.g., the number of robot hands are increased beyond 2 in blocks world) -- a decidedly counter-intuitive behavior. A much better alternative would thus involve separating the planning and scheduling phases in Graphplan, terminating planning as soon as a plan that is correct modulo resource allocation is found, and then starting a separate scheduling phase with this single plan as the

---

[7] This is part of joint work with Dan Weld.
[8] Notice that this is different from the "subset memoization" that is employed in the Graphplan implementation. which involves checking if any subset of the current goal set is matching a stored memo. Here we are interested in storing a smaller memo to begin with (so both normal and subset memoizations have a better chance of succeeding).

input. Our preliminary investigations show that such a strategy often leads to dramatic improvements in the efficiency of plan generation. We are currently in the process of completing the formalization and evaluation of this idea [Srivastava & Kambhampati, 1997].

5 Conclusion

In this paper, we have provided a rational reconstruction of Blum and Furst's Graphplan algorithm starting from forward state-space search. This reconstruction has shown that Graphplan's planning-graph data structure is an upper-bound approximation to the unioned representation of the state-space search tree, with the mutex propagation making the approximation finer. The backward search phase corresponds to solving a dynamic constraint satisfaction problem. We used the reconstruction to clarify the role and relative tradeoffs offered by "action parallelism" and "mutex propagation" in the Graphplan algorithm, and to interpret Graphplan as a refinement planner. We have also used our understanding to sketch a variety of ways of extending the Graphplan algorithm, including making Graphplan goal-directed, empowering it to handle more expressive action representations, supporting backward propagation of mutex information, improving backward search by exploiting CSP techniques and teasing apart planning and scheduling in Graphplan. Further details and evaluation of these extensions will be described in a forthcoming extended version of this paper.

References

Barrett, A. and Weld, D. 1994. Partial Order Planing: Evaluating possible efficiency gains. *Artificial Intelligence*, 67(1):71-112.

Blum, A. and Furst, M. 1995. Fast planning through planning graph analysis. In *Proc. IJCAI-95* (Extended version appears in *Artificial Intelligence, 90(1-2)*)

Bayardo, R. and Schrag, R. 1997. Using CSP look-back techniques to improve real-word SAT instances. In *Proc. AAAI-97.*

Frost, D and Dechter, R. 1994. In search of best constraint satisfaction search. In *Proc. AAAI-94.*

Drummond, M. 1989. Situated control rules. In *Proceedings of the First International Conference on Knowledge Representation and Reasoning*, 103-113. Morgan Kaufmann.

Kambhampati, S., Knoblock, C., and Yang, Q. 1995. Planning as refinement search: A unified framework for evaluating design tradeoffs in partial order planning. *Artificial Intelligence*, 76(1-2):167-238.

Kambhampati, S. and Yang, X. 1996, On the role of disjunctive representations and constraint propagation in refinement planning. In *Proceedings of the fifth International Conference on Principles of Knowledge Representation and Reasoning*. 35-147.

Kambhampati, S. 1997a. Challenges in bridging plan synthesis paradigms. In Proc. IJCAI-97.

Kambhampati, S. 1997b. On the relations between intelligent backtracking and explanation-based learning in planning and constraint satisfaction. *rakaposhi.eas.asu.edu/pub/rao/jour-ddb.ps.*

Kambhampati. S. 1997c. Refinement planning as a unifying framework for plan synthesis. *AI Magazine.* 8(2).

Kautz, H. and Selman, B. 1996. Pushing the envelope: Planning Propositional Logic and Stochastic Search. In *Proceedings of National Conference on Artificial Intelligence.* 1194-11201

McDermott, D. 1996. A Heuristic estimator for means-ends analysis in planning. In: *Proceedings of 3rd International Conference on AI Planning Systems. AAAI Press.* 142-149.

Mittal, S. and Falkenhainer, B. 1990. Dynamic Constraint Satisfaction Problems. In *Proc. AAAI-90.*

Parker, E and Kambhampati, S. 1997. Making Graphplan goal-directed. Forthcoming.

Reisig, W. 1982. *Petrie Nets: An Introduction.* Springer-Verlag.

Smith, D and Peot, M. 1996. Suspending recursion in partial order planning. In *Proc. 3rd Intl. Conference on AI Planning Systems.*

Srivastava, B and Kambhampati, S. 1997. Teasing apart planning and scheduling in Graphplan. Forthcoming.

Tsang, E. *Constraint Satisfaction.* Academic Press. 1993.

Extending Planning Graphs to an ADL Subset

Jana Koehler, Bernhard Nebel, Jörg Hoffmann, and Yannis Dimopoulos

Institute for Computer Science
Albert Ludwigs University
Am Flughafen 17
79110 Freiburg, Germany
<last-name>@informatik.uni-freiburg.de

Abstract. We describe an extension of GRAPHPLAN to a subset of ADL that allows conditional and universally quantified effects in operators in such a way that almost all interesting properties of the original GRAPHPLAN algorithm are preserved.

1 Introduction

Planning with planning graphs [1] has received considerable attention recently. The impressive performance and in particular the theoretical properties such as soundness, completeness, generation of shortest plans, and termination on unsolvable problems motivated us to use the approach as the kernel algorithm for our own planner IP^2. But GRAPHPLAN also has its limitations. First, its performance can decrease dramatically if too much irrelevant information is contained in the specification of a planning task [7]. Second, its simple representation language is restricted to pure STRIPS operators – no conditional or universally quantified effects are allowed and it was unclear whether the underlying planning algorithm could be extended to more expressive formalisms [1, 3, 6].

---

name: **move-briefcase**
par: l_1:location, l_2:location
pre: at-b(l_1)
eff: ADD at-b(l_2), DEL at-b(l_1)
$\forall x$:object [in(x) $\Rightarrow$ ADD at(x,l_2), DEL at(x,l_1)].

Fig. 1. Operator with conditional and universally quantified effects

In principle, sets of STRIPS operators can be used to encode conditional effects. For example, the *move* operator from the well-known Briefcase domain that specifies that all objects which are inside a briefcase move whenever the briefcase moves (Fig. 1) can be equivalently translated into a set of operators – one operator for each possible subset of objects, i.e., moving the empty briefcase, moving the briefcase with one object inside, with two etc. But such an encoding leads to exponentially more operators which can make even small planning problems practically intractable, see [5]. These observations motivated us to directly embed operators with conditional and universally quantified effects into planning graphs, while other features of ADL [8] that are e.g., available in UCPOP [9] can be reasonably handled by preprocessing [3].

2 A Semantics for Parallel ADL Plans

One of the distinguished features of GRAPHPLAN is its ability to produce *shortest* plans in the sense that it exploits maximal parallelism of actions in the plan – a property one would like to carry over to more expressive operators.

Definition 1. An *operator* is a 4-tuple consisting of

1. a *name*, which is a string,
2. a *parameter list* of typed variables,
3. the *precondition* φ_0, which is a conjunction of atoms, and
4. the *effect* as a conjunction of possibly universally quantified formulas that are of the form $\varphi_i \Rightarrow \alpha_i, \delta_i$ where φ_i is the so-called effect condition (limited to a set of atoms) and α_i, δ_i are the actual effects (also limited to sets of atoms with α_i being the Add effects and δ_i being the Del effects).

Note that as in GRAPHPLAN no explicit atomic negation is available in our language. Instead we model atomic negation by introducing an additional predicate *not-p(x)* if $\neg p(x)$ is needed. The universal quantifier may be absent and in the case of an unconditional effect $\varphi_i = \emptyset$ holds. An example of a valid operator is shown in Fig. 1. An example of a non-valid effect representation is $\varphi_i \Rightarrow \forall x : \text{ADD } p(x)$, because the effect condition lies outside the scope of the universal quantifier.

Definition 2. The set of all ground atoms is denoted with P. As usual, a *state* $S \subseteq P$ is a set of ground atoms.

Definition 3. An *action* o is a ground instance of an operator and has the form:[1]

$$o : \varphi_0$$
$$\alpha_0, \delta_0;$$
$$\varphi_1 \Rightarrow \alpha_1, \delta_1;$$
$$\vdots$$
$$\varphi_n \Rightarrow \alpha_n, \delta_n.$$

---

[1] The ground instance of a universally quantified effect $\forall x \ [\varphi_i(x) \Rightarrow \alpha_i(x), \delta_i(x)]$ is the conjunction of ground instances $\bigwedge_{k=0}^{n} [\varphi_i([x/a_k]) \Rightarrow \alpha_i([x/a_k]), \delta_i([x/a_k])]$ if the domain $\text{DOM}(x)$ of the typed quantified variable x is $\{a_0, a_1, \ldots, a_n\}$.

The $\varphi_i, \alpha_i, \delta_i$ are sets of ground atoms with φ_0 denoting the preconditions of o, α_0 being the *Add* list and δ_0 being the so-called *Delete* list of o. A conditional effect contains the effect condition φ_i, Add list α_i and Delete list δ_i.

Figure 2 shows a ground instance of the *move* operator for DOM(*object*)= {*letter*, *toy*} and DOM(*location*) = {*office*, *home*}.

name: **move-briefcase**	
par: office, home: location	
pre: at-b(office)	
eff: ∅	⇒ ADD at-b(home), DEL at-b(office);
in(letter)	⇒ ADD at(letter,home), DEL at(letter,office);
in(toy)	⇒ ADD at(toy,home), DEL at(toy,office).

Fig. 2. A possible ground instance of the *move* operator

In the following, we define the result of applying a single action to a given state.

Definition 4. Let *Res* be a function from states and sequences of actions to states. The result of applying a single-action sequence $\langle o \rangle$ to a state S is defined as

$$Res(S, \langle o \rangle) = \begin{cases} (S \cup A(S,o)) \setminus D(S,o) & \text{if } \varphi_0 \subseteq S \\ \text{undefined} & \text{otherwise} \end{cases}$$

with

$$A(S,o) = \bigcup_{\varphi_i \subseteq S, i \geq 0} \alpha_i \qquad \text{and} \qquad D(S,o) = \bigcup_{\varphi_i \subseteq S, i \geq 0} \delta_i .$$

The result of applying a sequence of actions to a state is recursively defined as usual.

For a planning language of simple STRIPS actions, the definition of *Res* can be extended to a set of parallel actions in a straightforward way [1] such that the resulting state is uniquely defined. However, when conditional effects are allowed, it is very difficult and even too restrictive to guarantee the uniqueness property of *Res* [5]. Therefore we define a function R that yields a set of resulting states.

Definition 5. Let S be a set of states and R be a function from sets of states and sequences of sets of actions to sets of states. The result of applying a one-set sequence of parallel actions $\langle Q \rangle = \langle \{o_1, \ldots, o_n\} \rangle$ is defined as:

$$R(S, \langle Q \rangle) = \begin{cases} \{T \subseteq P \mid S \in \mathcal{S}, q \in Seq(Q), T = Res(S,q)\} & \text{if } Res(S,q) \text{ defined} \\ & \forall S \in \mathcal{S}, q \in Seq(Q) \\ \text{undefined} & \text{otherwise} \end{cases}$$

with $Seq(Q)$ denoting the set of all linearizations of the action set $Q = \{o_1, \ldots, o_n\}$. In the special case of the empty sequence we obtain $R(\mathcal{S}, \langle\rangle) = \mathcal{S}$. The result of applying a sequence of sets of parallel actions is defined as

$$R(\mathcal{S}, \langle Q_1, \ldots, Q_n \rangle) = \begin{cases} R(R(\mathcal{S}, \langle Q_1, \ldots, Q_{n-1} \rangle), \langle Q_n \rangle) & \text{if } R(\mathcal{S}, \langle Q_1, \ldots, Q_{n-1} \rangle) \\ & \text{is defined} \\ \text{undefined} & \text{otherwise .} \end{cases}$$

3 Planning Graphs for an ADL Subset

The algorithm to construct planning graphs for a given planning problem in the ADL subset of operators differs not very much from the original algorithm described in [1].

Definition 6. A *planning problem* $\mathcal{P}(\mathcal{O}, D, I, G)$ is a 4-tuple where $\mathcal{O}$ is the set of operators, D is the domain of discourse (a finite set of typed objects), and I (the initial state) and G (the goal state) are sets of ground atoms.

Given $\mathcal{O}$ and D, the set of all actions O is the set of possible ground instances of all operators in $\mathcal{O}$.

Definition 7. As in GRAPHPLAN, we define a *planning graph* $\Pi(N, E)$ as a directed leveled graph with the set of nodes $N = N_O \cup N_F$ where N_O and N_F contain the sets of action nodes and ground atom (also called fact) nodes with $N_O \cap N_F = \emptyset$, respectively. The set of edges $E = E_P \cup E_A \cup E_D$ is split into the three disjoint sets E_P, the precondition edges ($N_F \times N_O$) and E_A, E_D which contain the Add effect edges and Del effect edges ($N_O \times N_F \times 2^{N_F}$).[2]

In a leveled graph, action and fact nodes are arranged in alternating levels and each level is associated with a time step (a natural number). The smallest level $N_F(0)$ comprises fact nodes (one per atom from the initial state I) and is followed by a level of action nodes $N_O(0)$, followed by $N_F(1), N_O(1), N_F(2), \ldots, N_F(max)$, i.e., the graph starts and ends with a fact level. Edges are restricted to link only nodes from two adjacent levels. All this is identical to GRAPHPLAN.

Furthermore, we keep the original notion that two actions *interfere* if one unconditionally deletes a precondition or an unconditional ADD effect of the other, i.e., they cannot simultaneously be executed in *any* world state considering only their unconditional effects. This implies that conditional effects are ignored when defining *interference* between actions, because whether two actions

---

[2] We write effect edges as triples $N_O \times N_F \times 2^{N_F}$ where an edge is drawn between an action node $o \in N_O$ and its effect (a fact node) $f \in N_F$ that is labeled with a set of fact nodes, which represents the (conjunctive) effect condition under which o achieves f.

interfere based on their conditional effects cannot be decided in advance, but depends on the specific state in which the actions are to be executed. We also adopt GRAPHPLAN's original notion that if two actions are mutually exclusive of each other no possible state of the world exists where both could be executed.

Definition 8. Two actions are *mutually exclusive* of each other

- at time step 0: iff they interfere;
- at time step $n \geq 1$: iff they interfere or the actions have competing needs.

Definition 9. Two actions o_1 and o_2 at an action level $N_O(n \geq 1)$ have *competing needs* iff there exist facts $f_1 \in \varphi_0(o_1)$ and $f_2 \in \varphi_0(o_2)$ that are mutually exclusive.

Definition 10. Two facts $f_1, f_2 \in N_F(n \geq 1)$ are *mutually exclusive* iff there is no non-exclusive pair of actions $o_1, o_2 \in N_O(n-1)$ or no single action $o \in N_O(n-1)$ that conditionally or unconditionally adds f_1 and f_2.

Intuitively, facts are exclusive if no possible state of the world can make both true – considering only their unconditional effects.

Definition 11. An action o is *applicable in a fact level* $N_F(n)$ iff $\varphi_0(o) \subseteq N_F(n)$ and all $f \in \varphi_0(o)$ are non-exclusive of each other.

Based on the previous definitions, IP^2 is *optimistic* when building planning graphs, i.e., analysis and resolution of conflicts between actions caused by conditional effects are deferred to the planning phase. Although actions are non-exclusive if potential conflicts between their conditional effects occur, one can sometimes propagate exclusivity information from preconditions and effect conditions to conditional effects [5].

Technically, planning graphs are constructed in the following way: Given a planning problem, the set of actions is determined as all possible ground instances of all operators. The atoms from the initial state form the first fact level $N_F(0)$. Each action level $N_O(n)$ contains two kinds of action nodes: so-called no-ops (one per atom in $N_F(n)$) and "ordinary" action nodes (one per action that is applicable in $N_F(n)$). No-ops are GRAPHPLAN's solution to the frame problem. For each fact $f \in N_F(n)$, a no-op nop_f is added to $N_O(n)$ with precondition $\varphi_0(nop_f) = \{f\}$ and the only unconditional effect $\alpha_0(nop_f) = \{f\}$. For each "ordinary" action node o, precondition edges between each fact in $N_F(n)$ that is a precondition of o and the action node are established. IP^2 planning graphs differ from GRAPHPLAN only wrt. the effect edges and how the next fact level $N_F(n+1)$ is built. Given a conditional effect $\varphi_i(o) \Rightarrow \alpha_i(o), \delta_i(o)$, IP^2 first proceeds over the individual Add effects $f \in \alpha_i(o)$. They are added to $N_F(n+1)$ iff the following conditions are satisfied:

1. $\varphi_i(o) \subseteq N_F(n)$
2. all facts in $\varphi_i(o)$ are non-exclusive of each other in $N_F(n)$
3. all facts in $\varphi_i(o)$ are non-exclusive of the facts in $\varphi_0(o)$ in $N_F(n)$

The first two conditions imply that the effect condition is applicable, similar to Definition 11. Condition 3 tests if precondition and effect condition can ever hold in the same state – although one can assume that any "reasonable" operator definition will satisfy this condition.

Since one action can achieve the same atomic effect f under different effect conditions, more than one edge can exist between an action node and a fact node in the next level. For each atomic Del effect $f \in \delta_i(o)$, the same tests are performed on the effect condition $\varphi_i(o)$ and a Del edge is established if $f \in N_F(n + 1)$. After each level is completed, the mutual exclusive pairs of facts in $N_F(n + 1)$ and actions in $N_O(n)$ are determined. The planning graph construction terminates when all goal atoms occur in $N_F(max)$ or if the goal state is unreachable, see Theorem 13.

Given the following sets of actions $\{Op1, Op2, Op3\}$ together with the initial state $I = \{d1, d2, d3, x, y, z\}$ and goals $G = \{a, b, c\}$, Fig. 3 shows the generated planning graph (without no-ops).

Op1
pre: d1
eff: ADD a, DEL d1.

Op2
pre: d2
eff: ADD b, DEL d2;
      y ⇒ ADD x;
      x ⇒ DEL a.

Op3
pre: d3
eff: ADD c;
      y ⇒ ADD x;
      z ⇒ ADD y.

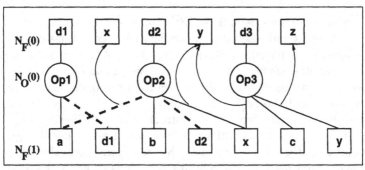

Fig. 3. An example planning graph. The delete edges are drawn with dashed lines and each conditional effect edge has a pointer to its effect condition. The three actions are non-exclusive because they interfere only over their conditional effects.

Planning graphs for the ADL subset inherit all properties of the original planning graphs as described in [1]: First, their size is polynomially restricted in their depth and in the number of actions and facts in the initial state. Second, fact levels grow monotonically, which allows us to incorporate the original "level-off" test into IP^2 that defines a simple and sufficient, but not necessary criterion that a planning problem has no solution.

Definition 12. Let Mutex(n) be the set of all exclusive pairs at fact level n. We say that the planning graph has *leveled off* at level n iff $|N_F(n)| = |N_F(n + 1)|$ and $|\text{Mutex}(n)| = |\text{Mutex}(n + 1)|$.

Theorem 13. *[Blum & Furst 95] A planning problem $\mathcal{P}(\mathcal{O}, D, I, G)$ has no solution if its planning graph has leveled off at time step n and either*

1. *one atomic goal is not contained in $N_F(n)$ or*
2. *at least two goal atoms are marked as mutually exclusive.*

4 Finding a Valid Plan in Planning Graphs

The first part of the planning algorithm is identical to GRAPHPLAN: The planning graph is built until the goals are reached for the first time or the graph has leveled off and it turns out that the goal state is not reachable. Note that the planning graph contains only the initial fact level $N_F(0)$ if $G \subseteq I$, i.e., if the goal state holds already in the initial state. If the goals are unreachable, $\perp$ ("no solution exists") is returned. If they are already satisfied in the initial state, $\langle\rangle$ ("empty plan") is returned.

A. initial creation of planning graph
   call the planning graph generation algorithm
   returns $\Pi(N, E)$ or $\perp$ /* shortest graph containing goals */
      max /* the number of proposition levels generated */
      Mutex(n)/* all exclusive pairs at level n */
   if *max* $= 0$ then return $\langle\rangle$ and stop planning.
   if $\Pi(N, E) = \perp$ then return $\perp$ and stop planning.

If none of the special cases applies, a recursive search algorithm search(n) over the planning graph is initialized that starts at the last fact level ($n = max$) and terminates when actions from level $N_O(n-1)$ have been successfully selected to achieve the goals at fact level $N_F(n)$ for all levels $1 \leq n \leq max$. The search algorithm differs in three points from its GRAPHPLAN predecessor:

1. the input, which is a pair of sets,
2. the selection procedure for actions at each level, which takes into consideration that an action can possibly achieve the same goal atom under different effect conditions, and
3. the resolution of conflicts caused by conditional effects.

The input consists of two sets of facts instead of only one: (1) the *goals* $\mathcal{G}_n$ that have to be achieved at level n by selecting actions at $N_O(n-1)$ and (2) so-called *negative goals* C_n that the selected actions have to avoid, i.e., no state in which $\mathcal{G}_n$ is established must entail C_n.[3] If one of the negative goal atoms were established by the selected actions, effect conditions of undesired conditional effects would be made true leading to harmful interaction among actions that were selected to achieve the goals at level $n + 1$.

---

[3] Note that the input is $\mathcal{G}_{max} = G$ and $C_{max} = \emptyset$ for the initial call search(*max*).

B. level-guided expansion and search

```
loop
/* initialization of search parameters /*
n                        := max /* current level */
G_max                    := G /* fixed goal set at max level */
∀ G_{1≤n≤max-1}          := ∅ /* variable goal set at other levels */
∀ C_{1≤n≤max}            := ∅ /* negative goals at level n */
∀ Δ_{0≤n≤max-1}          := ∅ /* set of selected edges at each level */
call search(max) /* find plan in given planning graph */
if FAILURE
   then if G_max is unsolvable (Theorem 14)
           then return ⊥ and stop planning
           else call expand(max + 1) /* expand graph by one level */
        endif
   else plan found: return set of used actions at each level
endif
endloop
```

Given a set of goal atoms $\mathcal{G}_n \subseteq N_F(n)$ and a set of negative goals $\mathcal{C}_n \subseteq N_F(n)$, action selection proceeds as follows: First, a set of Add edges $\Delta_{n-1} \subseteq E_A(n-1)$ is selected at action level $N_O(n-1)$ that enable the atoms in the goal set $\mathcal{G}_n$. In contrast to GRAPHPLAN that selects an action, IP^2 selects a particular Add edge that is linked to the goal, because the same action can achieve a goal atom under different types of effects (conditional or not) or under different effect conditions. By selecting an edge, an action is chosen indirectly (marked as "used").

1. choice point: select set of Add edges Δ_{n-1}

```
for each goal atom g ∈ G_n
    if a "used" action o ∈ N_O(n-1) has an unconditional Add edge to g
       then Δ_{n-1} := Δ_{n-1} ∪ {(o, g, ∅)} and G_n := G_n \ g
       /* skip goals that are already unconditionally achieved */
       else select edge (o, g, φ_i(o)) of an action o such that
       a) already "used" actions at level n − 1 and o are non-exclusive
       b) o does not unconditionally
            - delete a goal g ∈ G_n or effect condition of another selected edge
            - add a negative goal c ∈ C_n
       c) no already "used" action unconditionally deletes an atom in φ_i(o)
    endif
endfor
```

The conditions a) to c) guarantee that the "used" actions are independent of each other wrt. their preconditions, unconditional effects, effect conditions of used conditional effects, and that no negative goal is unconditionally added.

Given the example in Fig. 3 and the goals $\mathcal{G}_1 = \{a, b, c\}$ and $\mathcal{C}_1 = \emptyset$, the planner has as its only choice the edges $(Op1, a, \emptyset)$, $(Op2, b, \emptyset)$, and $(Op3, c, \emptyset)$. All conditions are satisfied, i.e., the actions are non-exclusive and no unconditional Del effects occur.

As a next step, IP^2 computes the goals at level $n-1$ based on the preconditions and effect conditions of the selected Add edges. If the resulting set $\mathcal{G}_{n-1}$ is mutually exclusive, the planner backtracks to a new choice of edges, because mutually exclusive goals can never be achieved in the same state.

2. compute goal set $\mathcal{G}_{n-1}$:
$\mathcal{G}_{n-1} := \bigcup_k \varphi_0(o_k) \cup \bigcup_k \varphi_i(o_k)$ with $(o_k, g, \varphi_i(o_k)) \in \Delta_{n-1}$
`/* note that` $\varphi_i(o_k) = \emptyset$ `for an unconditional effect */`

In the small example from Fig. 3, this step is trivial, because all selected edges are unconditional and the new goals $\mathcal{G}_0$ are obtained as the preconditions $\{d1, d2, d3\}$ of the actions.

Now, the action set can be tested for minimality. For each used action, all unconditional Add edges and all conditional Add edges are collected, whose effect conditions are completely contained in the new goals $\mathcal{G}_{n-1}$. The action set is minimal if each action (which can also be a no-op) achieves at least one goal fact that is not achieved by any other action considering the collected edges. If the action set is non-minimal, the planner backtracks and the next choice of edges and actions is computed.

Now, the planner can determine the new negative goals $\mathcal{C}_{n-1}$. This process is quite complex and comprises two main tasks:

1. The planner has to decide if negative goals from the set $\mathcal{C}_n$ are explicitly destroyed by actions at level $n - 1$ or progressed through the set $\mathcal{C}_{n-1}$.
2. The selected actions at level $n - 1$ are tested for interference caused by conditional effects. To prevent harmful conditional effects, atoms from the corresponding effect conditions are added to the new negative goals $\mathcal{C}_{n-1}$.

For the first task, the planner checks if there is a negative goal c in the set $\mathcal{C}_n$ that is non-exclusive of the new goals $\mathcal{G}_{n-1}$ and that is added by a no-op. This means that c holds in the state where $\mathcal{G}_{n-1}$ is achieved and that it could "survive" the execution of the selected actions at time step $n - 1$ if the no-op is non-exclusive of the selected actions, i.e., there is no action in the set Δ_{n-1} that deletes c. The planner can deal with this conflict in two ways: either by adding c to the set of new negative goals $\mathcal{C}_{n-1}$ or by selecting a Del edge from a new or already used action to destroy c. In the first case, we obtain the first entry for the new negative goals. In the second case, the new goals have to be augmented by the preconditions (and possibly effect conditions) of the selected action. Note that this action needs to be a valid choice wrt. interference with already used actions as tested in Part 1 of the search algorithm. To avoid the generation of non-optimal plans, progression is tried first and in the second case, Del edges of used actions are preferred.

3. deal with negative goals $\mathcal{C}_n$:
determine the set $\mathcal{C}_n^-$ of negative goals in $\mathcal{C}_n$ that are non-exclusive of $\mathcal{G}_{n-1}$
$\mathbb{C} = \emptyset$ `/* initialization */`
for all $c \in \mathcal{C}_n^-$

```
   if c is Add effect of a no-op
      then C := C ∪ {c}
      else nothing
   endif
endfor
for all c ∈ C choice point:
   progress c as a new negative goal: Cₙ₋₁ := Cₙ₋₁ ∪ {c}
   or
   select a Del edge from E_D(n − 1)
   Δₙ₋₁ := Δₙ₋₁ ∪ {(o, c, φᵢ(o))}
   Gₙ₋₁ := Gₙ₋₁ ∪ φ₀(o) ∪ φᵢ(o)
endfor
```

For the second task, the planner has to deal with conditional interference among actions that was totally ignored until now. The difference between the two types of effects is that unconditional effects always occur when an action is selected, while conditional effects additionally require the effect condition to hold. This gives the planner the possibility to prevent an undesired conditional effect by making sure that its effect conditions do not hold in the state in which the action is executed. But IP^2 does not know which specific linearization will be chosen for execution because it selects a set of "parallel" actions. Therefore, it has to address two tasks:

1. By forming a set of negative goals at level $n - 1$ it guarantees that the undesired effect condition does not hold in the state in which the "parallel" action set is executed.
2. By testing that no action in the parallel set adds the undesired effect condition it guarantees that any linearization leads to a valid execution sequence.

Four different possibilities for conditional interference have to be tested: A selected action is not allowed to conditionally delete a goal (an atom from the set G_n), a precondition of another selected action (an atom from the set G_{n-1}), an effect condition of a desired conditional effect (also an atom from G_{n-1}), or to conditionally add a negative goal from the set C_n.

If the planner discovers conditional interference, it checks if the effect conditions $\varphi_i(o)$ of a harmful conditional effect are contained in the set G_{n-1}. In this case, backtracking to choose a new Δ_{n-1} is necessary, because $\varphi_i(o)$ is causally linked to the new goals G_{n-1}, i.e., whenever they are achieved, the context for the harmful side effect is established as well. If actions at level $N_O(0)$ have harmful conditional effects, backtracking is also necessary because the effect conditions hold in the initial state, which cannot be altered by IP^2. On all levels $n \geq 1$, the set $\varphi_i(o) \setminus G_{n-1}$ of effect condition atoms that are not in the new goal set is added to a set of sets S and a (not necessarily minimal) hitting set for S forms the set of new negative goals C_{n-1}. This means, one element out of each set in S is selected to form C_{n-1}, because a conditional effect is only achieved if the effect condition as a whole (set) is established, i.e., preventing one single atom per effect condition already avoids the undesired effect. Considering the set difference $\varphi_i(o) \setminus \mathcal{G}_{n-1}$ avoids that goals and negative goals overlap.

In the example from Fig. 3, the planner finds out that $Op2$ deletes the goal a under condition x, which becomes the first new negative goal, i.e., $C_0 = \{x\}$. Now the planner has to resolve the "linearization problem" by making sure that no selected action adds any of the new negative goals in C_0. The planner checks if any used actions other than $Op2$ add x, which is the case for $Op3$ that adds x under condition y. This means, if $Op3$ is executed before $Op2$ in a state in which y holds, the condition x becomes true and $Op2$ will delete the goal a. Therefore, y must be added as a new negative goal to make sure that this effect is prevented as well. If the effect conditions were a set of atoms instead of a singleton, one of the atoms would be selected as a new negative goal, i.e., the planner has a choice point. Since C_0 has been extended, the whole test is repeated with $C_0 = \{x, y\}$. Fortunately, only $Op3$ can add the effect condition y of its own harmful conditional effect and this does not matter. Thus, a fixed point is reached and all effect conditions of effects that potentially add new negative goals are already prevented by C_0. But since $C_0 \neq \emptyset$, no plan can be extracted.

4. compute negative goals C_{n-1}
    for all actions o marked as "used" in $N_O(n-1)$
        if exists an edge $(o, g, \varphi_i(o)) \in E_D(n-1)$ with $g \in \mathcal{G}_n$ or $g \in \mathcal{G}_{n-1}$ or
        $(o, g, \varphi_i(o)) \in E_A(n-1)$ and $g \in C_n$
        then add $\varphi_i(o) \setminus \mathcal{G}_{n-1}$ to the set of sets $\mathbb{S}$
        else nothing
        endif
    endfor
    if $\emptyset \in \mathbb{S}$ (exists $\varphi_i(o) \subseteq \mathcal{G}_{n-1}$) or $[n = 1$ and $\mathbb{S} \neq \{\emptyset\}]$ (actions at level $N_O(0)$)
        then backtrack
        else <u>choice point</u>: choose C_{n-1} as a hitting set for $\mathbb{S}$
    endif
    complete C_{n-1} by effect conditions of used actions that add atoms in C_{n-1}
    if $\mathcal{G}_{n-1}$ and C_{n-1} are disjoint
        then invoke search$(n-1)$
        else backtrack
    endif

The completion process fails if an effect condition is completely contained in $\mathcal{G}_{n-1}$, because this would make $\mathcal{G}_{n-1}$ and C_{n-1} overlap (a relevant fact had to be made true and false at the same time), or if an action unconditionally adds a new negative goal. During backtracking, all choices of new negative goals (i.e., hitting sets) are tried before a different choice of Δ_{n-1} becomes necessary.

If all possible choices of actions to achieve the goals at level n have failed, the planner has to backtrack to action level n to change one of the sets $\mathcal{G}_n$, C_n because it has proven the pair to be unsolvable.

Backtracking at the maximum level of the graph is not possible and leads to a failure of search(max) on the planning graph, i.e., no valid plan could be extracted. The planning graph is extended by another action and fact level and the planner searches again on the extended graph. This process of interleaved graph expansion and search terminates if either a set Δ_n was successfully selected at each level of the graph – the plan is the set of all actions that are marked as "used" – or the problem turns out to be unsolvable, cf. Theorem 14.

Theorem 14. *Let the planning graph for a planning problem* $\mathcal{P}(\mathcal{O}, D, I, G)$ *be leveled off at some level* n. *Let* $m \geq n$ *be the current maximum fact level. The problem* $\mathcal{P}(\mathcal{O}, D, I, G)$ *is unsolvable if and only if extending the planning graph to level* $m + 1$ *and searching the extended graph leads to the same number of goal/negative goal pairs at level* n, *i.e.,* $|\{\langle \mathcal{G}_n^m, \mathcal{C}_n^m \rangle\}| = |\{\langle \mathcal{G}_n^{m+1}, \mathcal{C}_n^{m+1} \rangle\}|$.

See [5] for the proof where we also show that this unsolvability test remains valid under subset memoization.

Theorem 15. *Let* $\mathcal{P}(\mathcal{O}, D, I, G)$ *be a planning problem. If* IP^2 *returns a parallel plan* $\mathcal{P} = \langle O_1, O_2, \ldots O_n \rangle$ *then*

$$\bigcap R(I, \langle O_1, O_2, \ldots, O_n \rangle) \supseteq G$$

holds, i.e., $\mathcal{P}$ *is a solution.*

To prove soundness we rely on the semantics as developed in Definition 5 and proceed by induction over the length of the plan. Completeness follows from soundness and the fact that IP^2 terminates on unsolvable planning problems. The generation of shortest plans cannot always be guaranteed wrt. our liberal execution semantics. Certain special cases of conditional interference can result in an unnecessary separation of actions [5].

5 Selected Results from the Empirical Evaluation

In the empirical evaluation [5] we were mainly interested in the following questions:

1. Does the extension to a more expressive language lead to a computational overhead?
2. How does IP^2 compare to other planners supporting operators with conditional and universally quantified effects such as Prodigy [2] and UCPOP?

Due to space restrictions we can only sketch a few of the results here and have to refer the reader to [5]. To answer Question 1, we compared IP^2 to GRAPHPLAN on the original GRAPHPLAN test suite. On most of the examples, IP^2 can outperform GRAPHPLAN because we have not simply extended GRAPHPLAN's code, but made significant changes where we thought to have a more efficient solution. We also ran both systems on SATPLAN [4] examples to evaluate the influence of our improved algorithm for subset memoization yielding convincing results. To answer Question 2, we compared IP^2 to UCPOP and Prodigy in the Briefcase domain and a variant of the Scheduling domain. In both domains, IP^2 can usually outperform the other systems. We show the results for the Scheduling domain in Table 1.

Table 1. IP^2, Prodigy, and UCPOP in the scheduling domain

Problem	time steps	actions	UCPOP	Prodigy	IP^2
sched1	3	6	0.94	2.07	0.95
sched2	5	8	4.20	10.27	1.29
sched3	6	9	4.80	56.71	1.57
sched4	7	11	103.00	2.42	1.63
sched5	9	16	-	78.28	5.01
sched6	9	17	-	37.8	6.19

6 Conclusion

We have presented an extension of planning graphs to a subset of ADL that preserves allmost all interesting theoretical properties of the original GRAPHPLAN algorithm. A detailed empirical evaluation showed that this extension of the original GRAPHPLAN system comes with no computational overhead if carefully implemented and that it competes very well with other planners that support ADL subsets. The resulting system is the kernel algorithm of our own interference progression planner IP^2 that we intend to use as the planning algorithm for a mobile robot platform.

References

1. A. Blum and M. Furst. Fast planning through planning graph analysis. *Artificial Intelligence*, 90(1–2):279–298, 1997.
2. E. Fink and M. Veloso. Prodigy planning algorithm. Technical Report CMU-94-123, Carnegie Mellon University, 1994.
3. B. Gazen and C. Knoblock. Combining the expressivity of UCPOP with the efficiency of Graphplan. In Steel [10].
4. H. Kautz and B. Selman. Pushing the envelope: Planning, propositional logic, and stochastic search. In *AAAI-96*, pages 1194–1201.
5. J. Koehler, B. Nebel, J. Hoffmann, and Y. Dimopoulos. Extending planning graphs to an ADL subset. Technical report, 1997. http://www.informatik.uni-freiburg.de/~ koehler/ipp.html.
6. D. McDermott. A heuristic estimator for means-ends analysis in planning. In *AIPS-96*, pages 142–149.
7. B. Nebel, Y. Dimopoulos, and J. Koehler. Ignoring irrelevant facts and operators in plan generation. In Steel [10].
8. E. Pednault. ADL: Exploring the middle ground between STRIPS and the Situation Calculus. In *KR-89, Morgan Kaufman*, pages 324–332.
9. J. Penberthy and D. Weld. UCPOP: A sound, complete, partial order planner for ADL. In *KR-92, Morgan Kaufman*, pages 103–113.
10. S. Steel, editor. *Proceedings of the 4th European Conference on Planning*, LNAI. Springer, 1997.

Breaking Security Protocols as an AI Planning Problem

Fabio Massacci

Dipartimento di Informatica e Sistemistica
Università di Roma I "La Sapienza"
via Salaria 113, Roma
e-mail:massacci@dis.uniroma1.it

Abstract. Properties like confidentiality, authentication and integrity are of increasing importance to communication protocols. Hence the development of formal methods for the verification of security protocols. This paper proposes to represent the verification of security properties as a (deductive or model-based) logical AI planning problem. The key intuition is that security attacks can be seen as plans. Rather then achieving "positive" goals a planner must exploit the structure of a security protocol and coordinate the communications steps of the agents and the network (or a potential enemy) to reach a security violation. The planning problem is formalized with a variant of dynamic logic where actions are explicit computation (such as cryptanalyzing a message) and communications steps between agents. A theory of computational properties is then coupled with a description of the particular communication protocols and an example for a key-distribution protocol is shown.

1 Introduction

The development and formal verification of security protocols is one of the key requirement for modern distributed systems which face the need of secure communication over an insecure network.

The key idea is to rely on cryptographic primitives (shared and public key encryption, hashing etc.) to guarantee security properties viz. confidentiality, integrity or authentication (see [8,11,16,27] for an introduction).

Yet the presence of well designed cryptographic primitives is far from guaranteeing such security properties. On the contrary, most "secure" systems are not broken by cryptographic attacks, but rather by exploiting operational blunders [4] and logical errors in the protocol design [1,6,17]. The subtlety of logical faults may even be such that a protocol may become a standard (e.g. a version of the CCITT X.509) before being proved badly broken [6].

Logical errors can be prevented by formal verification and a number of techniques have been developed for the logical analysis of security protocols [19]. Formal systems abstract away the cryptographic details and develop a theory of actions (communication and computing) where some messages can be "opened" by an agent only if she has the corresponding (secret) key.

For a formal analysis one can use *logics of knowledge and belief* in the same spirit of the works of Halpern et al [9] for high-level reasoning about communication protocols. After the seminal paper on the BAN logic [6] those logics have become a large family, e.g. [2,12,29,30]. At the other end of the spectrum, researches have described *protocols as traces of atomic actions*, modeling explicitly the properties low-level of the network. The finite states approach (based on the process algebra CSP and model checking [17,26] or on states enumeration methods [19,20]) can be used to find attacks whereas the approach based on induction can be used to prove properties such as secrecy and authenticity [23].

1.1 Security Verification as a Planning Problem

At this stage one may start wondering: this is surely interesting but... what formal verification has to do with planning?

Undoubtedly the use of logic and theorem proving techniques for reasoning about action is a backbone of deductive planning [13,25,18,28,5] and the use of proof tactics borrowed from interactive theorem provers [22] is the basis for both tactical planning and the verification of security properties [23].

The similarity is tighter for verification systems based on traces: they have a sophisticated modeling of the actions available to the legitimate participants, of the computing power of a potential enemy and of his abilities to tamper (read, destroy or spoof) legitimate messages [17,19,20,23,26]. This is just (low-level) reasoning about action in disguise.

Yet one may argue that deductive planning and formal verification share the same tools (logic and theorem proving) but have different objectives. It is so because we are used to think that in a planning problem we *accomplish something "good"*: from stacking blocks on a table to moving a mechanical arm, from avoiding collisions between a moving robot and other objects, to complex scheduling of satellites. The second point is that we often assume that *multi-agent planning is cooperative*.

To represent the verification of security protocol as a classical AI planning problem we need to change slightly our perspective: we need a "disruptive" planner, who wants to exploit the available (legitimate or illegitimate) actions to achieve unwanted effects and somehow deceive some of the agents. The task of the planner is then to break the systems.

In a nutshell we simply need to *model security attacks as plans* in a suitable formalism for reasoning about actions, communications and computations. A planning task which is interesting for its characteristics:

- the planner must combine legitimate and "illegitimate" steps of the protocol to construct an attack, somehow coordinating the bad and good agents involved in the communication;
- "illegitimate" steps are strongly constrained: they must "look like" legitimate steps, for instance the attacker can redirect a message, or modify a message by replacing the name of the sender with her own name, but must always respect the format of the messages foreseen by the protocol;

– not all undesirable states correspond to attacks (i.e. valid plans) we are only interested in attacks where, according to some of the legitimate parties of the protocol, "everything seems to go smoothly";
– among possible action we have to make explicit the computational activity of the agents, and thus we have to cope with knowledge changing actions;
– we want to describe the initial condition sparingly (e.g. only the secrecy of some long term cryptographic keys) and let the planner figure out the rest;
– not all security violations are possible for a given protocol and thus we may fail to find a plan in that case.

If we chose a formalism based on dynamic logic [15] which has been successfully applied to planning (see e.g. [25,28,7]) we can use deduction to show that a plan (an attack) exists and, most important, use the proof to generate the attack. We can also try to prove that no plan exists and hence that the particular security property represented by the negation of the planning goal is attained.

Notice that we are not bound to deductive planning. Model-generation planning [14] may be equally well suited.

As an aside remark, computational complexity is not an issue here. At first because protocols are usually short and second and foremost because the plan construction is once-off. If we can find an attack to a protocol, the protocol will be revised or the threat model[1] will be changed. Indeed we are not using the planner for (repeated) actions but rather for verification and trading time (ex-ante) for avoiding problems (after implementations) is worth the trouble.

Reusing previous plan (attacks) to check a modified protocol can also be configured as a problem of re-usable planning: trying to adapt past plans to a modified description of the environment and available actions.

In the rest of the paper we give a high-level introduction to security protocols (§2) . On the technical side we introduce a dynamic logic for modeling communication and computation (§3). Then we explain how to transform it into a planning problem (§4), model the general communication and computing properties (§5) and discuss possible extensions (§6).

2 A High Level View of Security Protocols

We sketch some characteristics and goals of security protocols to make the paper self-contained[2]. Security protocols can be succinctly described as follows [8]:

> What distinguishes a cryptographic protocol from any other algorithm is the underlying model of computation. In a cryptographic protocol, two or more participants communicate with each other over a clearly defined communication network. Each participant may function asynchronously... and has access to a basic set of cryptographic utilities.

---

[1] The attacks we are worried about and that the protocol guarantee to fight off.
[2] An introduction to security protocols can be found in [8,21,16] and an high level analysis in [6,11]. A practical overview can also be found in [27].

Furthermore each participant has a basic computational power... may apply cryptographic transformation, make decision and generate messages. [...] a participant may combine a priori knowledge with the properties of the messages he generates and receives to determine a property of the communication system... In a worst case analysis of a protocol one must assume that a participant may try to subvert the protocol.

As stated above, one of the key aspects of cryptographic protocols is the use of cryptographic primitives (see [8,6]). Here, we can consider such cryptographic primitives at an high level of abstraction. The key intuition is to regard them as *computationally hard functions with trapdoors*.

For example, consider the case of encryption. At an high level it is simply a function from strings (messages) to strings which needs a subsidiary string (the key) to be computed. Inverting the function (getting the original messages from the encrypted one) without knowing the key is extremely hard (in some cases even impossible). The knowledge of the key provide us with a trapdoor through the computational barrier. Thus, if we give an encrypted message to a number of agents, we may assume than only those who have the key will be able to read it. We may exploit this assumption to achieve useful properties [21,27] in an anonymous and untrusted medium such an electronic network, where everybody can pretend to be anybody else.

For instance, to know whether *Alice* is alive, *Bob* can send a message encrypted with a key that only she knows. If he gets the original message in reply, then he can be "sure" that *Alice* has read it (indeed she has decrypted it). It seems simple, yet it is easy to get it wrong [6,1]: the key must be secret, it must not be distributed to the "wrong guys", *Bob* text must be difficult to guess etc.

In this framework there is a number of security properties and goals that we may want to establish. We (informally) describe some of them and refer to [1,6,11,31] for some of the subtleties involved:

Secrecy: a message is only disclosed to its intended recipients;

Freshness: a certain message is recent, and is not an old replay of a previously used (and possibly compromised) one;

Authenticity: a message, which should come from a certain participant of the protocol, did indeed come from its legitimate sender;

Proof of Identity: a certain type message may be uniquely attributed to a particular participants in the protocols;

Non-repudiation: a participant may not deny of having sent a message or having received a message.

Such properties are usually determined by the use of some cryptographic primitives. For instance proof of identity can be determined by using electronic signatures (e.g. public and private key cryptography).

2.1 A Practical Example: Challenge Response

To show some practical examples we use the standard notation [6] for representing security protocols. *Principals* (agents) involved in the communications are denoted by $A, B, C, E \ldots$. Typically E represents the environment (or a possible enemy) whereas A and B the legitimate parties of the protocol.

Messages, denoted by M, are constructed from unspecified atomic strings, principals' names, cryptographic keys etc. using functions $f(M_1, \ldots, M_n)$. Some functions, e.g. encryption, are denoted by special symbols and we follow such use in the sequel.

Nonces[3] are denoted by N (possibly with mnemonic indices) whereas keys for symmetric encryption are denoted by K and the corresponding encryption of message M is $\{M\}_K$. Private and public keys are sometimes denoted by SK and PK and the corresponding encryptions are $eSK\{M\}$ and $ePK\{M\}$, following [11] in the use of ISO notation. Messages concatenation is denoted by the standard $\{M, M'\}$.

A *protocol* is a sequence of steps $A \rightarrow B: M$, where M is a message:

$$1.\ A \rightarrow B: M_1$$
$$2.\ B \rightarrow A: M_2$$
$$3.\ A \rightarrow B: M_3$$

corresponds to a protocol where A starts by sending M_1 to B. After B has received M_1 he can send M_2 to A which finally replies with M_3.

Below are some challenge-response protocols from the ISO-10181 standard:

protocol 1 - Nonce-Crypto	protocol 2 - Crypto-Nonce
1. $A \rightarrow B: N_a$	1. $A \rightarrow B: ePK_B\{N_a\}$
2. $B \rightarrow A: eSK_B\{N_a\}$	2. $B \rightarrow A: N_a$

Loosely speaking, the "task" of both protocols is to "convince" A that B is "alive" or, more properly, that somebody which can use B's signature is alive.

Here the underlying cryptographic primitive is public key cryptography. The idea is that there are two keys: one secret (the private key SK_B), and one widely available (the public key PK_B). The high-level functioning of the cryptographic primitive can be easily described: if you encrypt a message with one key you need the other to decrypt it, and viceversa.

The left protocol is initiated by A which sends a nonce (i.e. a random challenge) to B which reply by encrypting the nonce with his private secret key (i.e. signing the challenge). The intuition is that only B knows his secret key and thus only B can "sign" N_a. Still A can easily verify it since the public key PK_B is known. So she takes the message that she receives back and tries to decrypt it with PK_B. If she gets back N_a than she can be "sure" that only B could have done it. So, if she gets it quickly, she could conclude that B is alive.

In the second protocol, A encrypts the nonce N_a with B's public key. Then B decrypts this message with his secret private key and sends back N_a. The same reasoning seems to apply here, but what happens if somebody else can guess N_a? For instance, if A just use a sequence of integers generated by a counter for subsequent N_as? The second protocol can therefore be broken by anybody who can guess A challenges (see [30]).

---

[3] A nonce="number used once" is (usually) just a random number, see [16,27].

3 A Dynamic Logic for Security Protocols

To represent formally the actions and the communication properties involved in a security protocols we use a variant of dynamic logic [15], since its use for planning is simple and well-known [25,28] and it suits well to such problem.

The basic components are four: *principals, messages, protocols and formulae*. In comparison with standard dynamic logic [15] protocols play the role of actions and messages could be compared to first order terms.

Principals and messages have been already introduced in §2.

Formulae, denoted by φ, ψ, are constructed from the atomic components A made M (A synthesized message M), A recv M (A received message M or M is a sub message in a message received by A), A sent M, A has M or A has M with the obvious meaning.

Composed formulae are obtained with the boolean connectives $\neg\varphi$, $\varphi \Rightarrow \psi$ and the modal one $[\pi]\varphi$, whose meaning is that after any possible run of protocol π, property φ holds. Other connectives are abbreviations such as $\wedge$, $\vee$ or $\langle\pi\rangle\varphi \equiv \neg[\pi]\neg\varphi$ which says that is it possible to run π and end in state where φ holds.

Protocols are formed as programs [15] from atomic actions: $A \rightarrow B : M$ which means that principal A attempted to sends a message M to B; A *makes* M when A tries to compose message M; and A *reads* M if A tries to cryptanalyze M.

The use of "attempt" in the intuitive explanations above is due to the particular nature of the problem (§2): A may try to send the message to B, but B may not actually receive it because the "enemy" intercepted it.

The (standard) operators are sequential composition $(\pi_1 ; \pi_2)$, non deterministic choice $(\pi_1 \cup \pi_2)$, iteration (π^*), converse (π^-) and test $(\varphi?)$, where φ is a formula. Nondeterministic choice can be used to model the possibility of an opponent to replace some of the legitimate steps of the protocol and the converse operator π^- can be interpreted as "before running π".

Notice that the whole system could be reformulated using the notation and semantics of [28] in particular is sufficient to use the relations $add - r$ and $delete - r$ of [28] where r is instantiated to the relations $\cdot$made$\cdot$, $\cdot$recv$\cdot$ etc.

The semantics can be given by using Kripke models as done in [28] or using runs and interpreted systems [2,9,29]. There is not substantial difficulties except for the enforcement of the constraints due to cryptographic primitives.

4 The Design of the Planning Problem

To map our problem into a planning problem we need to:

- define explicitly the computational properties of principals i.e. define the actions for composition and (crypt)analysis of messages (and also what information the agents gain from these operations);
- represent the communications between agents by actions which can either satisfy general properties or be tailored to the particular protocol;

– formalize the ability and the behavior of a potential enemy (sometimes the network itself), which may interfere with the regular running of the communications protocols;
– identify the typology of security violations which we may consider as relevant goals G for planning attacks;
– finally the initial conditions IC will be typically determined by the (informal) assumptions of the protocol (e.g. private keys are secret, honest principals generates fresh nonces etc.).

Remark 1. Defining the (disruptive) behavior of the network or the "enemy" is essential for the problem to make sense and indeed any attacking plan to exists.

Indeed legitimate agents will try to follow the protocol as closely as possible unless they are mislead by somebody. Thus, for any (attacking) plan to exists we must devise this somebody which can deviate from the rules. The key point is that meaningful deviations must not be so arbitrary to be unmanageable: the attacker may destroy, replay or change messages but only to the extent that her messages still look like those of the original protocol.

The global properties of the network GC, viz. the computational properties, the communications possibilities and the behavior of the network (or the potential enemy), will be the classical post - and pre-conditions for the planning problem [25,28]. We sometimes also use the terminology of [24] and refer to constraints of the form $\varphi \Rightarrow [\pi]\psi$ as successor state axioms and to those of the form $\langle \pi \rangle \psi \Leftrightarrow \varphi$ as preconditions.

Once we have set the logical framework, the plan is the $\pi?$ such that $GC \models IC \Rightarrow \langle \pi? \rangle G$ as in [28].

4.1 Security Violations as Goals

A number of possible *planning goals*, i.e. security violations, can be devised in term of confidentiality, authenticity and freshness.

For instance a violation of *confidentiality* is represented by the goal E has M_s where M_s is a message supposed to be secret, such as the session key of a key K_{ab} of the Needham-Schroeder protocol (§2).

We can also represent *impersonation* either from the point of view of the initiator (A received a message apparently from B who is not there) or the respondent. In this case somebody can impersonate B and yet mislead A into thinking that everything went smoothly: she have sent all its messages and received all "right" messages "coming" from B, yet none of such message ever come from be. So she may simple have achieved the result of giving her credit card number to some villain... This state of affairs can be easily described with the following formula:

$$\bigwedge_i A \text{ sent } M_{ai} \wedge \bigwedge_j A \text{ recv } M_{bj} \wedge \bigwedge_j \neg B \text{ sent } M_{bj}$$

Where M_{ai} are the messages A is supposed to send B during a correct run of the protocol and M_{bj} are the one she is supposed to receive from B. We can weaken the bad effects we are planning by changing the $\bigwedge_k$ into a disjunctions or by dropping some conjuncts etc.

In some cases we may require something stronger than simply sending a messages: for instance, for *cash protocols*, it is not only important that A sent a message but she has actually made it (in practice has signed the main message). In this case we can replace $A\,\mathsf{sent}\,M$ with $A\,\mathsf{sent}\,M \wedge A\,\mathsf{made}\,M$ and similarly replace $\neg B\,\mathsf{sent}\,M$ with $\neg B\,\mathsf{made}\,M$.

Another issue is *freshness*: we may reach a state where everything is fine for A, who receives a new key, while B received an old compromised key.

$$A\,\mathsf{recv}\,M_a \wedge \neg A\,\mathsf{had}\,M_a \wedge B\,\mathsf{recv}\,M_b \wedge B\,\mathsf{had}\,M_b$$

It is worth noting that also here we have to cope with the frame problem. Moreover we can also use a formalization based on planning as model generation rather than deduction as in [14]. We leave further details to the full paper.

5 Modeling the Communication Environment

We inherit directly all the axioms and properties of standard dynamic logic with converse [15]. If we wanted to redefine the basic primitives in terms of the *add* and *delete* operator of [28] then we would have to import also their axioms.

5.1 Computational Abilities of Agents: Synthesis

The next step is the definition of the computational properties of the principals involved in the communication wrt the synthesis of messages.

In traditional security analysis, either based on authentication logics such as [6] or traces and states enumeration [20,26], it is assumed that all principals, including the potential enemy E, have the same computational power w.r.t. cryptographic primitives. For simplicity we follow the same approach here but we could also devise differentiate principals with different computational power by changing the applicable axioms.

The first part regards the ability of *composing messages*: we have traditional successor state axioms of the form $\varphi \Rightarrow [\pi]\psi$ [24,25] and local constraints:

$$\neg A\,\mathsf{has}\,M \Rightarrow [A\ makes\ M]A\,\mathsf{made}\,M$$
$$A\,\mathsf{made}\,M \Rightarrow A\,\mathsf{has}\,M$$

Notice that we put the negation of $\cdot\,\mathsf{has}\,\cdot$ in the precondition of the successor state axioms because we want to be conservative: we want to derive that A "constructed" M only if this was really necessary.

The next set of axioms depends on the particular function we need to use in our protocols and are just preconditions:

$$\langle A\ makes\ f(M_1, \ldots, M_n)\rangle\top \Leftrightarrow \Phi^f_{make}(A\,\mathsf{has}\,M_1, \ldots, A\,\mathsf{has}\,M_n)$$

Typically Φ^f will be a boolean conjunction of its arguments, thus matching the intuition that for constructing a function we need to have all its arguments.

For instance in the case of encryption and concatenation:

$$\langle A \, makes \, \{M\}_K \rangle \top \; \Leftrightarrow \; A \, \text{has} \, M \wedge A \, \text{has} \, K$$
$$\langle A \, makes \, \{M_1, M_2\} \rangle \top \; \Leftrightarrow \; A \, \text{has} \, M_1 \wedge A \, \text{has} \, M_2$$

This is equivalent to say that to encrypt a message one, of course, need both the message and the key.

Atomic messages, such as nonces and keys, may have particular properties. For instance we may want private key of the challenge response protocols (§2) to be unguessable by the enemy:

$$\langle E \, makes \, PK_B \rangle \top \; \Leftrightarrow \; \perp$$

If we use deductive planning just to look for the existence of plans, we can drop the axiom altogether.

On the contrary the nonces of the Crypto-Nonce challenge response protocol may or may not be guessable according the axiom we choose:

$$A \, \text{made} \, N_a \; \Rightarrow \; \langle E \, makes \, N_a \rangle \top$$

implies that it is possible for E to guess the nonce generated by A. For instance this may happen if A uses simply a counter to generate her nonces.

On the contrary the formula below implies that nobody can guess A nonces[4].

$$A \, \text{made} \, N_a \; \Rightarrow \; \neg \, \langle E \, makes \, N_a \rangle \top$$

5.2 Computational Abilities of Agents: Cryptanalysis

The ability of *analyzing messages* is essential. We have some general successor state axioms and some local conditions such as

$$\top \Rightarrow [A \, reads \, f(M_1, \ldots, M_n)](A \, \text{has} \, M_1 \wedge \ldots \wedge A \, \text{has} \, M_n)$$
$$A \, \text{recv} \, M \Rightarrow A \, \text{has} \, M$$

Notice that the axiom just state *if* A can analyze a function f then she can recover its components and we can well have functions which she cannot analyze. The precondition axioms for the cryptanalysis of a functions depends of course on the function itself and has the general form:

$$\langle A \, reads \, f(M_1 \ldots M_n) \rangle \top \; \Leftrightarrow \; A \, \text{has} \, f(M_1 \ldots M_n) \wedge \Phi^f_{read}(A \, \text{has} \, M_1 \ldots A \, \text{has} \, M_n)$$

For the limited version of public key cryptography we used in our challenge response protocol (§2) we can defined the following properties:

$$\langle A \, reads \, eSK\{M\} \rangle \top \; \Leftrightarrow \; A \, \text{has} \, eSK\{M\} \wedge A \, \text{has} \, PK$$
$$\langle A \, reads \, ePK\{M\} \rangle \top \; \Leftrightarrow \; A \, \text{has} \, ePK\{M\} \wedge A \, \text{has} \, SK$$

---

[4] In theory the possibility of guessing the right answer is never zero but, for practical purposes, we may be satisfied that it is negligible.

We have the property of agents to *remember* the data they have got. We can represent it as follows (π_0 is any atomic action):

$$A \text{ has } M \Rightarrow [\pi_0]A \text{ has } M \qquad A \text{ made } M \Rightarrow [\pi_0]A \text{ made } M$$
$$A \text{ had } M \Rightarrow [\pi_0]A \text{ had } M \qquad A \text{ recv } M \Rightarrow [\pi_0]A \text{ recv } M$$

Remark 2. Properties of key and nonces must be carefully added since they may easily lead to inconsistency.

We can also assume that all principals have the names of other principals, i.e. that $A \text{ has } B$ is an axiom.

5.3 Modeling the Communication, the Network and the Enemy

Some postconditions and some preconditions are independent of the protocol. The first axioms provide us with a simple mechanism for handling freshness:

$$A \text{ has } M' \Rightarrow [A \rightarrow B : M]A \text{ had } M'$$
$$A \text{ has } M' \Rightarrow [B \rightarrow A : M](A \text{ recv } M \Rightarrow A \text{ had } M')$$
$$\neg C \text{ had } M' \Rightarrow [A \rightarrow B : M]\neg C \text{ had } M' \quad \text{for } C \neq A, B, E$$

In the second implication we impose that A must have received M. If M is going to be intercepted by E then A may not realize that "time is passing" (i.e. some external event is happening).

Next we have *non-interference* among principals (only the intended recipient of a message can receive it) and *sending*, where $C \neq B, E$:

$$\neg C \text{ recv } M \Rightarrow [A \rightarrow B : M]\neg C \text{ recv } M$$
$$\top \Rightarrow [A \rightarrow B : M]A \text{ sent } M$$

The other *communication properties* depends on the protocol and the choice of the explicit or implicit encoding of the enemy as the network.

We can choose to *explicitly model the enemy as she were in charge of the network*. This is usually done in traced based systems [17,19,26] and is common in the informal analysis of protocols. In this case, for each step $A \rightarrow B : M$ we must add the following preconditions

$$\langle E \rightarrow B : M \rangle \top \Leftrightarrow E \text{ recv } \{B, M\}$$
$$\langle A \rightarrow E : \{B, M\}\rangle \top \Leftrightarrow A \text{ has } M \wedge \Phi_{send}(A, M, protocol)$$

In a nutshell, the enemy (the network) can forward any message that she has received, while "good" principals should follow the protocol (or at least believe that they are following it).

The formula $\Phi_{send}(A, M, protocol)$ states that this is the correct time for A to send M. So, if M is supposed to be the n-th message in the "normal" protocol run then $\Phi_{send}(A, M, protocol)$ describes A's viewpoint up to the $n-1$th message: A has sent all message she was supposed to sent and she has received all messages she was supposed to receive (if the protocol was followed by all parties involved).

For instance in the Crypto-Nonce challenge (§2) we have:

$$\langle B \to A: N_a \rangle \top \;\Leftrightarrow\; B \text{ has } N_a \wedge B \text{ recv } e\,PK\{N_a\}$$

We must also add the following state successor axioms:

$$\top \Rightarrow [A \to E: M]E \text{ recv } M \qquad \top \Rightarrow [E \to B: M]B \text{ recv } M$$

In this case we can assume that, once that the enemy has decided to deliver the message, she will deliver it, and similarly that all messages sent to the network at least arrive there. Then the enemy may decide not to pass them forward.

If we choose the *implicit modeling* of the enemy then our formalization requires more care. At first we may assume that the enemy is *tapping the lines* the network and *sending spoof messages*:

$$\top \Rightarrow [A \to B: M]E \text{ recv } M \qquad E \text{ has } M \Rightarrow \langle E \to A: M \rangle \top$$

Remark 3. The axioms for spoof messages is too general. Indeed we are only interested in M which respects the format of the messages of the desired protocols. It can be replaced by a series of more definite axioms.

With this replacement, if we limit the number of nonces, keys and agents, we can map the system into PDL and make it decidable. We must transform the precondition axioms for the steps of the protocol into a set of axioms of the form:

$$\langle A \to B: M \rangle \Phi^i_{rec}(A, M, protocol) \;\Leftrightarrow\; A \text{ has } M \wedge \Phi_{send}(A, M, protocol)$$

The different $i = 1, \dots m$ will determine the possible outcomes of the actions: they could be $A \text{ recv } M$ or $\neg A \text{ recv } M$. If also the enemy may and may not receive messages then we may have more cases.

In alternative we can assume that messages are always delivered, replace Φ^i_{rec} with $\top$, add then axiom $[A \to B: M]B \text{ recv } M$ and then model the "blocking" of messages as agents that do not respond[5].

Finally, following an idea of [23], we can also add *oops messages* where a principal "accidentally" looses the session key at the end of the protocol.

6 Discussion

In this paper we have shown how the formal verification of security protocols can be naturally represented as an interesting AI planning problem.

Using a dynamic logic one can represent the communication and computing actions which can be used by legitimate and illegitimate participants in a protocol. Then finding an attack is equivalent to find a plan which leads to a state which violates some security requirement. In the present formalization all conditions are (implicitly) universally quantified and, by setting the number

---

[5] Notice that we have a possibility formula for the precondition axiom so we may validate Φ_{send} without actually choosing the subsequent step.

of different nonces, keys and principals we could transform it into a problem in dynamic propositional logic by grounding the properties on a subset of the Herbrand universe, in a fashion similar to the technique used in [14], and thus getting a decidable problem.

For a full modeling of protocols with potentially infinite participants or runs, such as [23] further developments are necessary. The simplest way is to introduce actions for generating new nonces. Such actions would also make the model closer to the semantics of [2,29]. The (necessary) trade off is that "term-creating" actions will affect the decidability of the planning problem.

A further step towards a full-fledge modeling is the introduction of time: a number of protocols use time-stamps rather than nonces and reasoning about actions and time becomes essentials. Also in this direction AI techniques are available [3] and the corresponding planning methods could be applied.

Acknowledgments

A large part of this work has been carried while the author was at the Computer Laboratory, University of Cambridge (UK). Discussions with A. Gordon, R. Needham and L. Paulson on security protocols and L. Carlucci Aiello, G. De Giacomo and D. Nardi on planning were invaluable. A special thank to the Computer Laboratory and Larry Paulson for their hospitality in Cambridge. This work have been partly supported by MURST-40% grant.

References

1. M. Abadi and R. Needham. Prudent engineering practice for cryptographic protocols. *IEEE Trans. on Software Engineering*, 22(1):6–15, 1996.
2. M. Abadi and M. Tuttle. A semantics for a logic of authentication. In *Proc. of the 10th ACM Symp. on Principles of Distributed Computing*, pp. 201–216, 1991.
3. J. Allen. Towards a general theory of action and time. *AIJ*, 23:123–154, 1984.
4. R. Anderson. Why cryptosystems fail. In *Proc. of the 1st ACM Conf. on Communications and Computer Security*, pp. 217–227. ACM Press, 1993.
5. S. Biundo. Present-day deductive planning. In C. Bäckstrom and E. Sandewall, editors, *Current Trends in AI Planning*, pp. 1–5. ISO Press, 1994.
6. M. Burrows, M. Abadi, and R. Needham. A logic for authentication. *ACM Trans. on Computer Systems*, 8(1):18–36, 1990. Also available as Res. Rep. SRC-39, DEC - System Research Center, 1989.
7. G. De Giacomo and M. Lenzerini. PDL-based Framework for Reasoning about Actions In *Proc. of the Italian Conf. on Artificial Intelligence (AI*IA-95)*, vol. 992 of *LNAI*, pp. 103–114. Springer-Verlag, 1995.
8. R. De Millo, L. Lynch, and M. Merrit. Cryptographic protocols. In *Proc. of the 14th ACM Symp. on Theory of Computing (STOC-82)*, pp. 383–400, 1982.
9. R. Fagin, J. Halpern, Y. Moses, and M. Vardi. *Reasoning about Knowledge*. The MIT Press, 1995.
10. M. Fitting. *Proof Methods for Modal and Intuitionistic Logics*. Reidel, 1983.
11. D. Gollmann. What do we mean by entity authentication. In *Proc. of the 15th IEEE Symp. on Security and Privacy*, pp. 46–54. IEEE Comp. Society Press, 1996.

12. L. Gong, R. Needham, and R. Yahalom. Reasonign about belief in cryptographic protocols. In *Proc. of the 9th IEEE Symp. on Security and Privacy*, pp. 234–248. IEEE Comp. Society Press, 1990.

13. C. Green. Application of theorem proving to problem solving. In *Proc. of the 1st Internat. Joint Conf. on Artificial Intelligence (IJCAI-69)*, pp. 219–239, 1969.

14. H. Kautz and B. Selman. Planning as satisfiability. In *Proc. of the 10th European Conf. on Artificial Intelligence (ECAI-92)*, pp. 359–363. John Wiley & Sons, 1992.

15. D. Kozen and J. Tiuryn. Logic of programs. In J. van Leeuwen, editor, *Handbook of Theoretical Computer Science*, vol. II, chap. 14, pp. 789–840. Elsevier Science, 1990.

16. A. Liebl. Authentication in distributed system: A bibliography. *Operating Systems Review*, 27(4):31–41, October 1993.

17. G. Lowe. Some new attacks upon security protocols. In *Proc. of the 10th IEEE Computer Security Foundations Workshop*, pp. 162–169. IEEE Comp. Society Press, 1996.

18. Z. Manna and R. Waldinger. How to clear a block: Plan formation in situational logic. *J. of Automated Reasoning*, 3:343–377, 1987.

19. C. Meadows. Formal verification of cryptographic protocols: A survey. In *Advances in Cryptology - Asiacrypt 94*, vol. 917 of *LNCS*, pp. 133–150. Springer-Verlag, 1995.

20. C. Meadows. Analyzing the Needham-Schroeder public key protocol: A comparison of two approaches. In E. Bertino, H. Kurth, G. Martella, and E. Montolivo, editors, *Proc. of the 4th European Symp. on Research in Computer Security*, vol. 1146 of *LNCS*, pp. 351–364. Springer-Verlag, 1996.

21. R. Needham and M. Schroeder. Using encryption for authentication in large networks of computers. *Communications of the ACM*, 21(12):993–999, 1978.

22. L. Paulson. *Isabelle: A Generic Theorem Prover*, vol. 828 of *LNCS*. Springer-Verlag, 1994.

23. L. Paulson. Proving properties of security protocols by induction. Technical Report TR409, Computer Laboratory, Univ. of Cambridge (UK), 1996.

24. R. Reiter. The frame problem in the situation calculus: A simple solution (sometimes) and a completeness result for goal regression. In V. Lifschitz, ed., *Artificial Intelligence and Mathematical Theory of Computation: Papers in Honor of John McCarthy*, pp. 359–380. Academic Press, 1991.

25. S. Rosenschein. Plan synthesis: A logical perspective. In *Proc. of the 7th Internat. Joint Conf. on Artificial Intelligence (IJCAI-81)*, pp. 331–337, 1981.

26. S. Schneider. Security properties and CSP. In *Proc. of the 15th IEEE Symp. on Security and Privacy*, pp. 174–187. IEEE Comp. Society Press, 1996.

27. B. Schneier. *Applied Cryptography: Protocols, Algorithms, and Source Code in C.* John Wiley & Sons, 1994.

28. W. Stephan and S. Biundo. A new logical framework for deductive planning. In *Proc. of the 13th Internat. Joint Conf. on Artificial Intelligence (IJCAI-93)*, pp. 32–38. Morgan Kaufmann, 1993.

29. P. Syverson and P. van Oorschot. On unifying some cryptographic protocols logics. In *Proc. of the 13th IEEE Symp. on Security and Privacy*. 1994.

30. G. Wedel and V. Kessler. Formal semantics for authentication logics. In Elisa Bertino, Helmut Kurth, Giancarlo Martella, and Emilio Montolivo, editors, *Proc. of the 4th European Symp. on Research in Computer Security*, vol. 1146 of *LNCS*, pp. 219–241. Springer-Verlag, 1996.

31. J. Zhou and D. Gollmann. Observations on non-repudiation. In Kim Kwangjo and Matsumoto Tsutomu, editors, *Advances in Cryptology - Asiacrypt 96*, vol. 1163 of *LNCS*, pp. 133–144. Springer-Verlag, 1996.

Time-Oriented Skeletal Plans: Support to Design and Execution

Silvia Miksch[1], Yuval Shahar[2], Werner Horn[3], Christian Popow[4], Franz Paky[5], Peter Johnson[6]

[1] Vienna University of Technology, Institute of Software Technology, Resselgasse 3/188, A-1040 Vienna, Austria, email: silvia@ifs.tuwien.ac.at

[2] Section on Medical Informatics, Stanford University, Stanford, CA 94 305 - 5479, USA email: shahar@smi.stanford.edu

[3] Austrian Research Institute for Artificial Intelligence (ÖFAI) & Department of Medical Cybernetics and Artificial Intelligence, University of Vienna, Freyung 6, A-1010 Vienna, Austria, email: werner@ai.univie.ac.at

[4] NICU, Department of Pediatrics, University of Vienna, Währinger Gürtel 18-20, A-1090 Vienna, Austria, email: popow@vm.akh-wien.ac.at

[5] Department of Pediatrics, Hospital of Mödling, Weyprechtgasse 12, A-2340 Mödling, Austria, email: franz.paky@magnet.at

[6] The Sowerby Unit for Primary Care Informatics, University of Newcastle, 21 Claremont Place, Newcastle Upon Tyne, NE2 4AA, UK, email: pete@mimir.demon.co.uk

Abstract. Skeletal plans are a powerful way to reuse existing domain-specific procedural knowledge. In the **Asgaard** project, a set of tasks that support the design and the execution of skeletal plans by a human executing agent other than the original plan designer are designed. The underlying requirement to develop task-specific problem-solving methods is a *modeling language*. Therefore, within the Asgaard project, a time-oriented, intention-based language, called **Asbru**, was developed. During the design phase of plans, Asbru allows to express durative actions and plans caused by durative states of an observed agent. The intentions underlying these plans are represented explicitly as temporal patterns to be maintained, achieved or avoided. We will present the underlying idea of the Asgaard project and explain the time-oriented Asbru language. Finally, we show the benefits and limitations of the time-oriented, skeletal plan representation to be applicable in real-world, high-frequency domains.

1 Motivation and Introduction

We are motivated by the need for knowledge-based support in the medical domain. Health care providers are faced with two problems: (1) the information overload resulting from modern equipment, and (2) improving the quality of health care through increased awareness of proper disease management techniques. *Clinical protocols* and *guidelines* should solve the difficulties. Clinical guideline refers to a general principle by which a course of actions is determined and clinical protocol refers to a general class of therapeutic interventions. In the following, we will use clinical guideline and protocol interchangeable.

Appropriate clinical protocols are only available for a very limited class of clinical problems. They are not adjusted to the patient data-management system, they are partly vague and incomplete concerning their intentions and their temporal and context-dependent representation, and most often they are outdated after being developed. Extracting and formulating the knowledge structure for clinical protocols is a non trivial task. The context implicit in the protocols must be made explicit.

1.1 Automated Support to Protocol-Based Care

During the last few years, there have been several efforts to create automated reactive planners to support the process of protocol-based care over periods of time. In the *prescriptive* approach, active interpretation of the guidelines is given; examples include ONCOCIN (Tu et al. 1989) in the oncology domain and the DILEMMA project (Herbert et al. 1995), the EON architecture (Musen et al. 1996), the PROMPT project (Fox et al. 1997) and the PRESTIGE project (Gordon et al. 1997), as general architectures. In the *critiquing* approach, the program critiques the physician's plan rather than recommending a complete one of its own. This approach concentrates on the user's needs and assumes that the user has considerable domain-specific knowledge (Miller 1986).

Several approaches to the support of guideline-based care encode guidelines as elementary state-transition tables or as situation-action rules dependent on the electronic medical record (Sherman et al. 1995), but do not include an intuitive representation of the guideline's clinical logic, and have no semantics for the different types of clinical knowledge represented. Other approaches permit hypertext browsing of guidelines via the World Wide Web (Barnes and Barnett 1995), but do not use the patient's electronic medical record.

The most favored attempts capturing and supporting clinical procedures, are *flow diagrams* and *flowcharting tools*. The medical experts are mostly used to working with these techniques. However, it is quite difficult to cope with all possible orders of plan execution and all the exception conditions that might arise. Clinical protocols are a way of pre-compiling decisions that must be made, in which experts knowledge is distilled into a form of procedural knowledge. The trouble is that this by necessity can only cover a small subset of the possible situations and possible paths through. Additionally, medical experts have a lot of difficulties to define their metrics for measuring the success or failure of an individual action. The best experts often have their own personal metrics by which they judge the success or failure of an action they have taken. But these metrics are usually very arbitrary, based on empirical factors, and difficult to extract from the expert. They may differ from one expert to another quite widely. The expert cannot usually be pushed into providing the evidence for these metrics.

1.2 Skeletal Plans

A common strategy for the representation and the reuse of domain-specific procedural knowledge is the representation of that knowledge as a library of skeletal plans. Skeletal plans are plan schemata at various levels of detail that capture the essence of the procedure, but leave room for execution-time flexibility in the achievement of particular (Friedland and Iwasaki 1985). Thus, they are usually reusable in different contexts. The idea was proposed to reduce complexity of planning, called skeletal-plan refinement. Instead of planning in an unconstrained search space, the skeletal-plan refinement method relies on available abstraction (or skeletal) plans which were refined in the context of a particular problem. Later similar ideas were exploited to create automated reactive planners, such as ONCOCIN (Tu et al. 1989), SPIN (Uckun 1994), and a KADS model for hierarchical skeletal plan refinement (Aitken and Shadbolt 1994).

1.3 Modeling Languages

On the one hand, workers in medicine and medical informatics have recognized the importance of protocol-based care to ensure a high quality of care since the 1970s. A group of investigators, working through the American Society for Testing and Materials (ASTM), has defined a standard procedural language, known as the Arden syntax (Hripcsak et al. 1994). The Arden syntax encodes situation-action rules. Developers of the Arden syntax have promoted this Pascal-like language because of the pressing needs to facilitate exchange of guidelines among health-care institutions using existing software technology. This standard has significant limitations: The language currently supports only atomic data types, lacks a defined semantic for making temporal comparisons or for performing data abstraction, and provides no principled way to represent clinical guidelines that are more complex than individual situation-action rules (Musen et al. 1995). Therefore the Arden syntax is not applicable for our purposes.

On the other hand, computer-oriented knowledge interchange languages (e.g., KIF (Genesereth and Fikes 1992)), ontologies or models for knowledge sharing (e.g., Gruber (1993); Guarina and Giaretta (1995)), and general purpose languages to support planning (e.g., PROPEL language (Levinson 1995), O-Plan2 (Tate et al. 1994) were introduced. These traditional (plan-execution) representations have significant limitations and are not applicable in dynamic changing environments, like medical domains: (1) they assume instantaneous actions and effects; (2) actions often are continuous (durative) and might have delayed effects and temporally-extended goals (Bacchus and Kabanza 1996); (3) there is uncertainty and variability in the utility of available actions; (4) unobservable underlying processes determine the observable state of the world; (5) a goal may not be achievable; (6) parallel and continuous execution of plans is necessary. The requirements of plan specifications in clinical domains (Tu et al. 1989; Uckun 1994) are often a superset of the requirements in typical toy-problem domains used in planning research.

A sharable skeletal-plan-execution language needs to be expressive with respect to temporal annotations and needs to have a rich set of parallel, sequential, and iterative operators. Thus, it should enable designers to express complex procedures in a manner similar to a real programming language (although typically on a higher level of abstraction). The language, however, also requires well-defined semantics for both the prescribed actions and the task-specific annotations, such as the plan's intentions and effects, and the preferences (e.g., implicit utility functions) underlying them. Thus, the executing agent's (e.g., the physician's) actions can be better supported, leading to a more flexible dialog and, in the case of the clinical domains, to a better acceptance of automated systems for guideline-based care support. Clear semantics for the task-specific knowledge roles also facilitate acquisition and maintenance of these roles.

With these requirements in mind, we have developed a time-oriented, intention-based, and sharable language, called **Asbru**. The Asbru language is part of the **Asgaard** project (Shahar et al. 1996a), in which we are developing task-specific problem-solving methods that perform design, execution, and critiquing tasks in medical domains. (In Norse mythology, Asgaard was the home and citadel of the gods. It was located in the heavens and was accessible only over the rainbow bridge, called Asbru.)

Section 2 gives an overview about the Asgaard project. Section 3 and 4 explains the various components of the time-oriented, intention-based language Asbru. Section 5 characterizes the medical problem of artificial ventilated newborn infants and illustrates how it is represented in Asbru. In the last section we evaluate Asbru's applicability identifying it's strengths and limitations.

2 The Asgaard Project

The **Asgaard** project outlined some useful task-specific problem-solving methods to support both designer and executor of skeletal plans. The project is oriented to support therapeutic issues. The problem-solving methods are divided in tasks, which are performed during *design time* and *execution time* of a skeletal plan (Table 1). Each task can be formulated as answering a specific set of questions. A more detailed description can be found in (Shahar et al. 1996a).

Table 1. Overview of the support tasks during design and execution time

Time	Task	Questions to be answered
Design time	Verification	Are the intended plans compatible with the prescribed actions?
	Validation	Are the intended states compatible with the prescribed actions and intended plans?
Execution time	Applicability of plans	What skeletal plans are applicable this time to this world?
	Execution of plans	What should be done now according to the execution-plan's prescribed actions?
	Recognition of intentions	Why is the executing agent executing a particular set of actions, especially if those actions deviate from the skeletal plan's prescribed actions?
	Critique of the executing agent's actions	Is the executing agent deviating from the prescribed actions or intended plan? Are the deviating actions compatible with the author's plan and state intentions?
	Evaluation of the plan	Is the plan working?
	Modification of an executing plan	What alternative actions or plans are relevant at this time for achieving a given state intention?

3 The Asbru Language: Basic Concepts

Asbru can be used to design specific plans as well as support the performance of different reasoning and executing tasks. During the design phase of plans, Asbru provides a powerful mechanism to express durative actions and plans caused by durative states of an observed agent (e.g., many actions and plans need to be executed in parallel or every particular time point). These plans are combined with intentions of the executing agent of plan. They are uniformly represented and organized in the *guideline-specification library*. During the execution phase an applicable plan is instantiated with distinctive arguments and state-transition criteria are added to execute and reason about different tasks.

3.1 Meaning of "Intention-based"

The meaning of *intentions* in general and for planning tasks in particular has been examined in philosophy (Bratman 1987) and in artificial intelligence (Pollack 1992). We view intentions as temporally extended goals at various abstraction levels (Bacchus and Kabanza 1996). Intentions are *temporal patterns* of actions or states, to be maintained, achieved, or avoided.

3.2 Meaning of "Temporal Pattern" and "Time annotations"

Intentions, world states, and prescribed actions are *temporal patterns*. A temporal pattern is (1) a *parameter proposition*: a parameter (or its abstraction), its value, a context, and a time annotation; (2) a *combination* of multiple parameter propositions (Shahar and Musen 1996b); or (3) a *plan-state* associated to an instantiated plan (plan pointer) and a time annotation.

The *time annotation* we use allows a representation of uncertainty in starting time, ending time, and duration (Dechter et al. 1991; Rit 1986). The time annotation supports multiple time lines (e.g., different zero-time points and time units) by providing *reference annotations*. We define temporal shifts from the reference annotation to represent the uncertainty in starting time, ending time, and duration, namely earliest starting shift (ESS), latest starting shift (LSS), earliest finishing shift (EFS), latest finishing shift (LFS), minimal duration (MinDu), and maximal duration (MaxDu). The temporal shifts are associated with time units (e.g., minutes, days) or domain-dependent units. Thus, our temporal annotation is written as ([ESS, LSS], [EFS, LFS], [MinDu, MaxDu], REFERENCE). Figure 2 illustrates our time annotation. ESS, LSS, EFS, LFS, MinDu, and MaxDu can be "unknown" or "undefined" to allow incomplete time annotation.

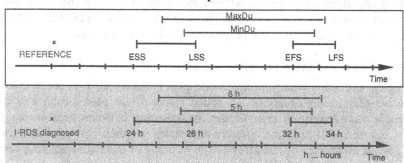

Fig. 2. A schematic illustration of the Asbru time annotations. The upper part of the figure presents the generic annotation. The lower part shows a particular example representing the time annotation [[24 HOURS, 26 HOURS], [32 HOURS, 34 HOURS], [5 HOURS, 8 HOURS], I-RDS-diagnosed]), which means "starts 24 to 26 hours after I-RDS was diagnosed, ends 32 to 34 hours after the I-RDS was diagnosed , and lasts 5 to 8 hours".

For example, the parameter proposition "the level of blood gas is normal or above the normal range in the context of controlled ventilation-therapy for at least three hours, using the activation of the plan as reference point", is written in Asbru as:

```
(STATE(BG) (OR NORMAL ABOVE-NORMAL) controlled-ventilation
    [[ _, _], [_, _], [180 MIN,_], *self*])
```

To allow temporal repetitions, we define sets of cyclic time points (e.g., MIDNIGHTS, which represents the set of midnights, where each midnight occurs exactly at 0:00 A.M., every 24 hours) and cyclic time annotations (e.g., MORNINGS, which represents a set of mornings, where each morning starts at the earliest at 8:00 A.M., ends at the latest at 11:00 A.M., and lasts at least 30 minutes). In addition, we allow certain short-cuts such as for the current time, whatever that time is (using the symbol *NOW*), or the duration of the plan (using the symbol *). Thus, the Asbru notation enables the expression of interval-based intentions, states, and prescribed actions with uncertainty regarding starting, finishing, duration, and the use of absolute, relative, and even cyclical (with a predetermined granularity) reference annotations. All domain-dependent time annotations, units, and time abstractions have to be defined in advance to be applicable in all plans in the guideline-specification library. The definitions ensure that site-specific practice can be clarified and specified (e.g., DAYS start at 0:00 am or DAYS start at 7:00 am). In addition, a sampling-frequency argument specifies the frequency of sampling the external-world's data, such as when verifying the applicability of a particular plan. Thus, we define a sampling frequency for examining the plan's state-transition criteria (see Sect. 3.4).

3.3 Decomposition and "Semantic" Stop-Condition

A *plan* in the guideline-specification (plan) library is composed hierarchically, using the Asbru syntax, of a set of plans with arguments and time annotations. A decomposition of a plan into its subplans is always attempted by the execution interpreter, unless the plan is not found in the guideline-specification library, thus representing a nondecomposable plan (informally, an *action* in the classical planning literature). This can be viewed as a "semantic" stop-condition. Such a plan is referred to the agent for execution, which may result in an interaction with a user or an external calling of a program. Plans have return values.

3.4 Plan States and State-Transition Criteria

During the execution phase, an applicable plan is instantiated. A set of mutually exclusive *plan states* describes the actual status of the plan during execution. Particular *state-transition criteria* specify transition between neighboring plan states. Figure 3 illustrates the different plan states and their corresponding transition criteria mentioned on the arrows. The meaning of the state-transition criteria is explained in Sect. 4.3. We distinguish between plan states during the plan-selection phase (left-hand side of Fig. 3) and between plan states during the execution phase (right-hand side of Fig. 3). For example, if a plan has been activated, it can only be completed, suspended, or aborted depending on the corresponding criteria. The gray triangle on the right-hand side of Fig. 3 includes the three basic states; these should always be defined. The suspended state is optional and is available for more complex plan types. A suspended plan can be either reactivated or restarted. The reactivation depends on the reactivate condition. The restart condition is defined implicitly: first, abort an activated plan and then restart it from the considered state.

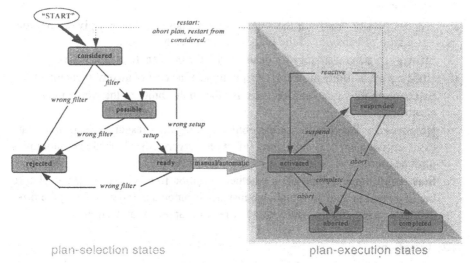

Fig. 3. The plan-instance states and their associated state-transition criteria used in Asbru.

4 Components of Asbru

A plan consists of a name, a set of arguments, including a time annotation (representing the temporal scope of the plan), and five components: **preferences**, **intentions**, **conditions**, **effects**, and a **plan body** which describes the actions to be executed. The general arguments, the time annotation, and all components are optional. A subplan has the same structure (Fig. 4a). An example is given in Fig. 4b, the example is described in Sect. 5.

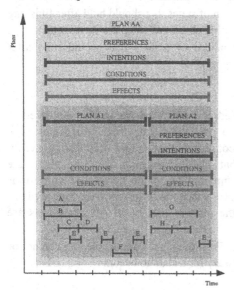

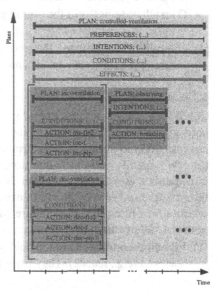

Fig. 4a. Graphical representation of a clinical-guideline specification in Asbru.

Fig. 4b: Subplans of the treatment protocol for immature respiratory distress syndrome.

4.1 Preferences

Preferences bias or constrain the selection of a plan to achieve a given goal and express a kind of behavior of the plan. We distinguish between:

(1) **Strategy**: a general strategy for dealing with the problem (e.g., aggressive);

(2) **Utility**: a set of utility measures (e.g., minimize the cost or inconvenience);

(3) **Select-method**: a matching heuristic for the applicability of the whole plan (e.g., exact-fit);

(4) **Resources**: a specification of prohibited or obligatory resources (e.g., in certain cases of treatment of a pulmonary infection, surgery is prohibited and antibiotics must be used);

(5) **Start-conditions:** an indication whether transition from a ready generic plan to the started state of an actual plan instance is automatic (after applying the *filter* and *setup* preconditions—see below) or requires approval of the user.

4.2 Intentions

Intentions are high-level goals at various levels of the plan, an annotation speci-fied by the designer, which supports tasks such as critiquing and modification. Intentions are temporal patterns of executing-agent actions and external-world states that should be maintained, achieved, or avoided. We define four categories of intentions:

(1) **Intermediate-state:** the state(s) that should be maintained, achieved, or avoided during the applicability of the plan (e.g., the blood-gas levels are slightly below to slightly above the target range);

(2) **Intermediate-action:** the action(s) that should take place during the execution of the plan (e.g., minimize level of mechanical ventilation);

(3) **Overall-state-pattern:** the overall pattern of states that should hold after finishing the plan (e.g., patient had less than one high blood-gas value per 30 minutes);

(4) **Overall-action-pattern:** the overall pattern of actions that should hold after finishing the plan (e.g., avoid hand-bagging).

4.3 Conditions

Conditions are temporal patterns, sampled at a specified frequency, that need to hold at particular plan steps to induce a particular state transition of the plan instance. We do not directly determine conditions that should hold during execu-tion. We specify different conditions that enable transition from one plan state into another (see Fig. 3). A plan is completed when the completed conditions become true, otherwise the plan's execution suspends or aborts. Aborting a plan's execution is often due to a failure of the plan or part of it. All conditions are optional. We distinguish between:

(1) **Filter-preconditions** need to hold initially if the plan is applicable, but can not be achieved (e.g., female). They are necessary for a state to become possible;

(2) **Setup-preconditions** need to be achieved to enable a plan to start (e.g., inspiratory oxygen concentration F_iO_2 is less than 80%) and allow a transition from a `possible` plan to a `ready` plan;

(3) **Suspend-Conditions** determine when an `activated` plan has to be suspended – certain conditions (*protection intervals*) need to hold (e.g., blood gas has been extremely above the target range for at least five minutes);

(4) **Abort-Conditions** determine when an `activated`, `suspended`, or `reactivated` plan has to be aborted (e.g., the increase of the blood-gas level is too-fast for at least 30 seconds);

(5) **Complete-conditions** determine when an `activated` or `reactivated` plan has to be completed successfully (e.g., returning to spontaneous breathing);

(6) **Reactivate-Conditions** determine when a `suspended` plan has to be reactivated (e.g., blood gas level is back to normal or slightly increased).

4.4 Effects

Effects describe the functional relationship between the plan arguments and measurable parameters (e.g., the *dose* of insulin is inversely related to the level of blood glucose) or the overall effect of a plan on parameters (e.g., administration of insulin decreases the blood glucose). Effects have a likelihood annotation—a probability of occurrence.

4.5 Plan-Body

The plan body is a set of plans to be executed in parallel, in sequence, in any order, or in some frequency. We distinguish among several types of plans: *sequential, concurrent,* and *cyclical*. Only one type of plan is allowed in a single plan body. A sequential plan specifies a set of plans that are executed in sequence; for continuation, all plans included have to be completed successfully. Concurrent plans can be executed in parallel or in any order. We distinguish two dimensions for classification of sequential or (potentially) concurrent plans: the number of plans that should be completed to enable continuation and the order of plan execution. The continuation condition specifies the names of the plans that must be completed to proceed with the next steps in the plan. A cyclical plan (an EVERY clause) includes a plan that can be repeated, and optional temporal and continuation arguments that can specify its behavior.

5 Treatment Protocols for Artificial Ventilated Newborn Infants

Artificial ventilation has greatly contributed towards the improvement of the mortality and morbidity of premature newborn infants. However, standardized clinical treatment protocols for immature respiratory distress syndrome (I-RDS) are partly vague and incomplete concerning their intentions and their temporal and context-dependent representation. Therefore, we acquired the implicit or not mentioned intentions and conditions from domain experts.

Figure 5 illustrate the top-level treatment protocol for I-RDS. After I-RDS is diagnosed, a plan dealing with limited monitoring possibilities is activated, called

initial-phase. Depending on the severity of the disease, three different kinds of plans can follow, **controlled-ventilation**, **permissive-hypercapnia**, or **crisis-management**. Only one plan at a time can be activated, however the order of execution and the activation frequency of the three different plans depend on the severity of the disease. The brackets in Fig. 5 illustrate this. Additionally, it is important to continue with the plan **weaning** only after a successful completion of the plan **controlled-ventilation**. After a successful execution of the plan **weaning**, the extubation should be initiated. The extubation can be either a single plan **extubation** or a sequential execution of the subplans **cpap** and **extubation**.

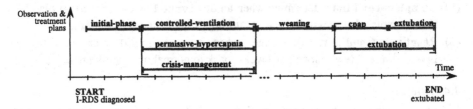

Fig. 5. Treatment protocol for immature respiratory distress syndrome (I-RDS).

The following specification shows the treatment protocol I-RDS in Asbru syntax:

```
(PLAN I-RDS-therapy                  (PLAN one-of-controlled-ventilation
   <... parts deleted ...>              <... parts deleted ...>
(DO-ALL-SEQUENTIALLY                  (DO-SOME-ANY-ORDER
   (initial-phase)                       (controlled-ventilation)
   (one-of-controlled-ventilation)       (permissive-hypercapnia)
   (weaning)                             (crisis-management)
   (one-of-cpap-extubation)))          CONTINUATION-CONDITION
                                           controlled-ventilation))
```

The continuation condition specifies which subplans must be completed successfully to continue with the next plan. In the subplan **one-of-controlled-ventilation** the CONTINUATION-CONDITION guarantees that it is only possible to start the plan **weaning**, when plan **controlled-ventilation** had been completed successfully. The alternative subplans **permissive-hypercapnia** or **crisis-management** are applied too, however the whole plan **one-of-controlled-ventilation** will never be completed successfully without a final successful completion of subplan **controlled-ventilation**.

Figure 4b is a zoom-in of Fig. 5 showing the subplan **controlled-ventilation** and its possible subplans using the Asbru language. In Fig. 4b two notations are used: uppercase letters followed by colons (":") indicate elements of Asbru and lowercase letters indicate particular plans, subplans, or actions. The plan **controlled-ventilation** is decomposed into two subplans, decreasing or increasing the ventilation setting (plan **inc-ventilation** and **dec-ventilation**) and the plan **observing**. The frequency of these two plans cannot be specified in advance. The number of activation periods depends on the health condition of the patient. The points (●●●) in Fig. 4b indicate these unknown repetitions. The subplan **inc-ventilation** is decomposed into three subplans, **inc-fio2**, **inc-f**, or **inc-pip**. These three subplans are nondecomposable plans (actions). Additionally, only one of these three actions can be activated at each time period, which is illustrated with the brackets. The same decomposition holds for the subplan **dec-ventilation**. The subplan `controlled-ventilation` is written in Asbru syntax:

```
(PLAN controlled-ventilation
(PREFERENCES (SELECT-METHOD BEST-FIT))
(INTENTION:INTERMEDIATE-STATE
    (MAINTAIN STATE(BG) NORMAL controlled-ventilation *))
(INTENTION:INTERMEDIATE-ACTION
    (MAINTAIN STATE(RESPIRATOR-SETTING) LOW controlled-ventilation *))
(SETUP-PRECONDITIONS
    (PIP (<= 30) I-RDS *now*)
    (BG available I-RDS
            [[_, _], [_, _],[1 MIN,_](ACTIVATED initial-phase-1#)]))
(ACTIVATED-CONDITIONS AUTOMATIC)
(ABORT-CONDITIONS ACTIVATED
    (OR (PIP (> 30) controlled-ventilation
            [[_, _], [_, _], [30 SEC, _], *self*])
        (RATE(BG) TOO-STEEP controlled-ventilation
            [[_, _], [_, _], [30 SEC,_], *self*])))
    (SAMPLING-FREQUENCY 10 SEC))
(COMPLETE-CONDITIONS
    (FiO2 (<= 50) controlled-ventilation
        [[_, _], [_, _], [180 MIN, _], *self*])
    (PIP (<= 23) controlled-ventilation
        [[_, _], [_, _], [180 MIN, _], *self*])
    (f (<= 60) controlled-ventilation
        [[_, _], [_, _], [180 MIN, _], *self*])
    (patient (NOT DYSPNEIC) controlled-ventilation
        [[_, _], [_, _], [180 MIN, ], *self*]))
    (STATE(BG) (OR NORMAL ABOVE-NORMAL)
        controlled-ventilation [[_, _], [_, _], [180 MIN,_], *self*])
    (SAMPLING-FREQUENCY 10 MIN))
(DO-ALL-SEQUENTIALLY
    (one-of-increase-decrease-ventilation)
    (observing)))
```

The intentions of subplan `controlled-ventilation` are to maintain a normal level of the blood-gas values and the lowest level of mechanical ventilation (as defined in the context of controlled ventilation therapy) during the span of time over which the subplan is executed. This subplan is activated immediately, if peak inspiratory pressure PIP $\leq$ 30 and the transcutaneously assessed blood-gas values are available for at least one minute after activating the last plan instance **initial-phase** (as reference point). The subplan must be aborted, if abort condition becomes true. The sampling frequency of the abort condition is 10 seconds. The subplan is completed successfully, if the complete condition becomes true. The body of the subplan `controlled-ventilation` consists of a sequential execution of the two subplans.

6 Benefits and Limitations

Applying the Asbru language to represent time-oriented skeletal plans is a very effective tool to acquire the domain knowledge needed in a structured way. The semantics for the task-specific knowledge facilitate acquisition and maintenance. Asbru places a particular emphasis on an expressive representation for time-oriented actions and world states in combination with the underlying intentions as temporal patterns to be maintained, achieved or avoided. It allows the use of different granularities and reference points to represent multiple time lines.

Asbru's representation includes the duration of actions, their success or failure, and allows time annotation of events, actions/plans, and world states with uncertainty in their appearances. Asbru has a rich set of sequential, concurrent, or cyclical operators, which enables the expression of complex procedures. Preferences, intentions, conditions, effects, and actions, are specified as various levels depending on their occurrence and evidence. The expressive representation results in an uniformly represented and organized guideline-specification library.

Nevertheless, the expressive representation of Asbru still has some limitation. In general, the medical experts were hard pressed to fill all the slots of the Asbru language and there was very little procedural, pre-compiled knowledge (protocols) found. The flexibility of the time annotation is one of the main benefits of Asbru. The ability to select different reference points is heavily used in the I-RDS protocols. Further, the ability to define different sampling intervals as shown in the above example is essential in high-frequency domains. On the one hand, it is the only way to be able to react fast in critical situations. On the other hand, it allows checking by long-term stability on a 10 minutes sampling frequency with appropriate filtering of data. In summary, the acquisition of the temporal patterns and time annotations needed is still quite difficult. In real-world high-frequency domains, the temporal dimensions are often vague or unknown.

7 Conclusion

Representing complex execution plans, such as clinical protocols, and the intentions underlying them in a sharable and acquirable form is imperative for useful, flexible automated assistance in the execution of these plans. In the manifold domains of clinical medicine and intensive care, such a task-specific representation is crucial for dissemination of modern clinical knowledge, since the use of clinical protocols will set up standards in the provision of high quality of care.

We outlined the basic concepts of an effective time-oriented representation of skeletal plans, called Asbru and proved the applicability of the Asbru syntax in the context of ventilator management in neonatal intensive care, which is based on the accurate analysis of high-frequency data.

Acknowledgements: We greatly appreciate the support given to the Austrian Research Institute of Artificial Intelligence (ÖFAI) by the Austrian Federal Ministry of Science and Transport, Vienna. Y. Shahar is supported by grants LM05708 and LM06245 from the National Library of Medicine, IRI-9528444 from the National Science Foundation. Computing resources were provided by the Stanford CAMIS project, funded under Grant No. LM05305 from the National Library of Medicine.

References

Aitken, J. S., Shadbolt, N.: Knowledge Level Planning. In Bäckström, C., Sandewall, E. (eds.), *Current Trends in AI Planning*, IOS Press, Amsterdam (1994) 33–45

Bacchus, F., Kabanza, F.: Planning for Temporally Extended Goals, *Proc. of the 13th Nat. Conference on Artificial Intelligence (AAAI-96)*, AAAI Press/The MIT Press, Menlo Park (1996) 1215–1222

Barnes, M., Barnett, G. O.: An Architecture for a Distributed Guideline Server, In Gardner, R. M. (ed.) *Proc. of the Annual Symposium on Computer Applications in Medical Care (SCAMC-95)*, Hanley & Belfus (1995) 233–237

Bratman, M. E.: *Intention, Plans and Practical Reason,* Harvard Univiversity Press, Cambridge, MA (1987)

Dechter, R., Meiri, L., Pearl, J.: Temporal Constraint Networks. *Artificial Intelligence, Special Volume on Knowledge Representation,* 49(1-3) (1991) 61–95

Fox, J., Johns, N., Rahmanzadeh, A.: Protocols for Medical Procedures and Therapies: A Provisional Description of the PROforma Language and Tools, In Keravnou, E. et al. (eds.), *Proc. of the 6th Conference on Artificial Intelligence in Medicine Europe (AIME-97),* Springer, Berlin (1997) 21–38

Friedland, P. E., Iwasaki, Y.: The Concept and Implementaion of Skeletal Plans. *Journal of Automated Reasoning,* 1(2) (1985) 161–208

Genesereth, M. R., Fikes, R. E.: *Knowledge Interchange Format, Version 3.0 Reference Manual.,* Computer Science Department, Stanford Univ., Tech.Report Logic-92-1 (1992)

Gordon, C., Johnson, P., Waite, C., Veloso, M.: Algorithm and Care Pathway: Clinical Guidelines and Healthcare Processes, In Keravnou, E. et al. (eds.), *Proc. of 6th Conference on Artificial Intelligence in Medicine Europe (AIME-97),* Springer, Berlin (1997) 66–69

Gruber, T. R.: *Toward Principles for the Design of Ontologies Used for Knowledge Sharing, Knowledge Systems Laboratory,* Stanford Univ., TR KSL 93-04 (1993)

Guarina, N., Giaretta, P.: Ontologies and Knowledge Bases. In Mars, N. J. I. (ed.) *Towards Very Large Knowledge Base,* IOS Press, Amsterdam (1995)

Herbert, S. I., Gordon, C. J., Jackson-Smale, A., Renaud Salis, J.-L.: Protocols for Clinical Care. *Computer Methods and Programs in Biomedicine,* 48 (1995) 21–26

Hripcsak, G., Ludemann, P., Pryor, T. A., Wigertz, O. B., Clayton, P. D.: Rationale for the Arden Syntax. *Computers and Biomedical Research,* 27 (1994) 291–324

Levinson, R.: A General Programming Language for Unified Planning and Control. *Artificial Intelligence, Special Volume on Planning and Scheduling,* 76(1-2) (1995)) 319–375

Miller, P. L.: *Expert Critiquing System: Practice-Based Medical Consultation by Computer* Springer, New York, NY (1986)

Musen, M. A., Gennari, J. H., Eriksson, H., Tu, S. W., Puerta, A. R.: PROTÉGÉ-II: A Computer Support for Development of Intelligent Systems from Libraries of Components, *Proc. of the 8th World Congress on Medical Informatics (MEDINFO-95)* (1995) 766-770

Musen, M. A., Tu, S. W., Das, A. K., Shahar, Y.: EON: A Component-Based Approach to Automation of Protocol-Directed Therapy. *Journal of the American Medical Information Association,* 3(6) (1996) 367–388

Pollack, M.: The Use of Plans. *Artificial Intelligence,* 57(1) (1992) 43–68

Rit, J.-F.: Propagating Temporal Constraints for Scheduling, *Proc. of the 5th Nat. Conference on Artificial Intelligence (AAAI-86),* Morgan Kaufmann, Los Altos (1986) 383–8

Shahar, Y., Miksch, S., Johnson, P.: A Task-Specific Ontology for Design and Execution of Time-Oriented Skeletal Plans, In Gaines, B. (ed.) *Proc. of the 10th Knowledge Acquisition for Knowledge-Based Systems Workshop,* Banff, Alberta, Canada, 1996a.

Shahar, Y., Musen, M. A.: Knowledge-Based Temporal Abstraction in Clinical Domains. *Artificial Intelligence in Medicine, Special Issue Temporal Reasoning in Medicine,* 8(3) (1996b) 267–298

Sherman, E. H., Hripcsak, G., Starren, J., Jender, R. A., Clayton, P.: Using Intermediate States to Improve the Ability of the Arden Syntax to Implement Care Plans and Reuse Knowledge, In Gardner, R. M. (ed.) *Proc. of the Annual Symposium on Computer Applications in Medical Care (SCAMC-95)* Hanley & Belfus (1995) 238–242

Tate, A., Drabble, B., Kibry, R.: O-Plan2: An Open Architecture for Command, Planning, and Controll. In Zweber, M. et al. (eds.), *Intelligent Scheduling,* Morgan Kaufmann, San Francisco, (1994) 213–239

Tu, S. W., Kahn, M. G., Musen, M. A., Ferguson, J. C., Shortliffe, E. H., Fagan, L. M.: Episodic Skeletal-Plan Refinement on Temporal Data. *Com. of ACM,* 32(1989) 1439–1455

Uckun, S.: *Instantiating and Monitoring Skeletal Treatment Plans,* Knowledge Systems Laboratory, Stanford Univ., KSL 94-49 (1994)

SINERGY: A Linear Planner Based on Genetic Programming

Ion Muslea

Information Sciences Institute / University of Southern California
4676 Admiralty Way
Marina del Rey, CA 90292 (USA)
muslea@isi.edu

Abstract. In this paper we describe SINERGY, which is a highly parallelizable, linear planning system that is based on the genetic programming paradigm. Rather than reasoning about the world it is planning for, SINERGY uses artificial selection, recombination and fitness measure to generate linear plans that solve conjunctive goals. We ran SINERGY on several domains (e.g., the briefcase problem and a few variants of the robot navigation problem), and the experimental results show that our planner is capable of handling problem instances that are one to two orders of magnitude larger than the ones solved by UCPOP. In order to facilitate the search reduction and to enhance the expressive power of SINERGY, we also propose two major extensions to our planning system: a formalism for using hierarchical planning operators, and a framework for planning in dynamic environments.

1 Motivation

Artificial intelligence planning is a notoriously hard problem. There are several papers [Chapman 1987, Joslin and Roach 1989, Bylander 1992] that provide in-depth discussions on the complexity of AI planning, and it is generally accepted that most non-trivial planning problems are at least NP-complete. In order to cope with the combinatorial explosion of the search problem, AI researchers proposed a wide variety of solutions, from search control rules [Weld 1994, Etzioni 1993, Minton 1996] to abstraction and hierarchical planning [Knoblock 1991 and 1994] to skeletal planning [Friedland 1985]. However, even though the above-mentioned techniques may dramatically narrow the search space, there is no guarantee that the corresponding planning algorithms will gracefully scale up for real-world problems.

As a reaction to the shortcomings of the traditional planners, during the last couple of years we witnessed the occurrence of new type of planning systems: the stochastic planners. This new approach to AI planning trades in the completeness of the planner for the speed up of the search process. Planners like SatPlan [Kautz and Selman 1996] or PBR [Ambite and Knoblock 1997] are at least one order of magnitude faster than the classic planning systems, and they are also capable of handling significantly larger problem instances.

In this paper we present SINERGY, which is a general-purpose, stochastic planner based on the genetic programming paradigm [Koza 1992]. Genetic Programming (GP) is an automatic programming technique that was introduced as an extension to the genetic algorithms (GA) [Holland 92], and it uses evolution-like operations (e.g., reproduction and cross-over) to generate and manipulate computer programs. In [Koza 1992 and 1994, Spector 1994, Handley 1994], the authors used GP to solve several problems that are similar to the ones encountered in AI planning (e.g., the Sussman anomaly, the robot navigation problem, and an unusual variant of the block world problem). Even though their domain-specific solutions cannot be considered general-purpose planning systems, the experimental results showed that GP has great potential for solving large instances of traditional AI planning problems.

Based on the encouraging results obtained by both stochastic planners and GP-based problem solving techniques, we decided to formalize and fully-implement a general-purpose AI planner that relies on the genetic programming paradigm. Rather than reasoning about the world it is planning in, SINERGY uses artificial selection, recombination and fitness measures to generate linear plans that solve conjunctive goals. We must emphasize that SINERGY has an expressive power equivalent to the one offered by UCPOP: it provides conditional effects, disjunctive preconditions, and both universal and existential quantifiers. We tested our planner on several domains, and the experimental results show that SINERGY is capable of handling problem instances that are one to two orders of magnitude larger than the ones solved by UCPOP.

2 Genetic Programming

Genetic Programming represents a special type of genetic algorithm in which the structures that undergo adaptation are not data structures, but hierarchical computer programs of different shapes and sizes. The GP process starts by creating an initial population of randomly-generated programs and continues by producing new generations of programs based on the Darwinian principle of "the survival of the fittest". The automatically-generated computer programs are expressed as function composition, and the main breeding operations are *reproduction* and *cross-over*. By reproduction we mean that a program from generation i is copied unchanged within generation $i+1$, while the cross-over takes two parent-programs from generation i, breaks each of them in two components, and adds to generation $i+1$ two children-programs that are created by combining components coming from different parents.

In order to create a GP-based application, the user has to specify a *set of building-blocks* based on which the population of programs is constructed, and an *evaluation function* that is used to measure the fitness of each individual program. There are two types of primitive elements that are used to build a program: *terminals* and *functions*. Both terminals and functions can be seen as LISP-functions, the only difference between them consisting of the number of arguments that they are taking: terminals are not allowed to take arguments, while functions take at least one argument. The *individuals* generated by the GP system represent computer *programs* that are built by *function composition* over the set of terminals and functions. Consequently, GP imposes the *closure property*: any value returned by a function or a terminal must represent a valid input for any argument of any function in the function set.

As we have already mentioned, the GP problem specification must include a domain-specific *fitness evaluation function* that is used by the GP system to estimate the "fitness" of each individual of a generation. More specifically, the fitness function takes as input a GP-generated program P, and its output represents a measure of how appropriate P is to solve the problem at hand (in this paper, lower fitness values mean better programs). In order to estimate the fitness of an GP-generated program, the evaluation function uses a set of *fitness cases*. Each fitness case is a tuple *<in-values, desired-out-values>* that has a straightforward meaning: for the given *in-values*, a "perfectly fit" program should generate the *desired-out-values*. In terms of AI planning, the *in-values* represent the initial world status, while the *desired-out-values* can be seen as the goals to be achieved.

Once the terminals, functions, fitness cases and fitness function are specified, the user has only to select a few running parameters (e.g., number of programs per generation, number of generations to be created, maximum size of a program) and to let the GP system evolve the population of programs. Both cross-over and reproduction are performed on randomly chosen individuals, but they are biased for highly fit programs. Such an approach has two major advantages: on one hand, the "highly fit" bias leads to the potentially fast discovery of a solution, while on the other hand, GP is capable of avoiding local minima by also using in the breeding process individuals that are less fit than the "best" offsprings of their respective generations. Although GP problem solvers are not complete (i.e., if there is a solution to the problem, GP-based systems are not guaranteed to find it), the experimental results show that they are usually able to find close-to-optimal solutions for a wide range of problems, from robotics to pattern recognition to molecular biology.

3 Planning as Genetic Programming

Even though there are several exceptions (e.g., NOAH [Sacerdoti 1975]), the vast majority of the AI planners define their planning actions in a declarative manner that is based on the one used by STRIPS [Fikes and Nilsson 1971]. In contrast, SINERGY takes a different approach and requires a procedural description of the planning operators. SINERGY relies on a procedural description of the planning actions because its underlaying, GP-based problem solver has to execute in simulation each plan in order to estimate its fitness. However, as Table 1 shows, the different nature of traditional AI planners and our GP-based planner (i.e., reasoning about plans *vs.* generating and executing genetically-created plans) does not prevent the two categories of planning systems to have similar interfaces.

Table 1. Interface Comparison: Traditional AI Planning Systems *vs.* SINERGY

	Traditional AI Planners	SINERGY
Input	- initial state - set of goals - set of operators - additional information (search control rules, memory of plans, etc.)	- initial state - set of goals - set of operators - additional information (fitness evaluation functions)
Output	Plan: a (partially ordered) sequence of fully instantiated operations	Plan: a *linear* sequence of fully instantiated operations

In order to find a solution for the problem at hand, SINERGY uses an approach resembling the one described in [Kautz and Selman 1996]: it converts an AI planning problem P_1 to a problem P_2 of a different nature, it solves P_2 based on a stochastic approach, and it converts the result to a solution for P_1. However, while Kautz and Selman turned the AI planning problem to an equivalent satisfiability problem, SINERGY converts the AI planning problem to a GP problem (Figure 1).

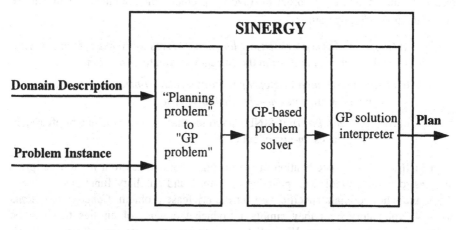

Fig. 1. The SINERGY approach to AI planning

The SINERGY approach to solving AI planning problems has three main advantages. First of all, GP problem solving is by its very nature a highly parallelizable process. The most expensive operation in terms of CPU-time is the fitness evaluation, and it is easy to see that a GP-based planner scales up gracefully to any number of parallel processors: the fitness evaluations of different plans represent completely independent processes that can by easily performed on different processors. Second, the SINERGY approach to AI planning facilitates problem solving in dynamic environments. As each plan simulation has to be executed step by step, we can create a framework that would allow the dynamic update of the planning environment after the execution of each operation in the plan (e.g., for the robot navigation problem, we can define mobile obstacles that move on predefined trajectories). Third, SINERGY provides a flexible way to express goal priorities by requiring the definition of a fitness evaluation function for each goal-predicate (see the next section). Domain implementers can use weight-factors to express the relative importance of each goal type, and, consequently, plans that solve a larger number of higher-importance goals will have a better fitness value and will be preferred during the selection and recombination process.

GP-based problem solvers rarely find optimal solutions for the problems at hand, but the above mentioned advantages together with SINERGY's ability to find close-to-optimal solutions for large, complex problem instances makes the GP-based approach to AI planning an alternative to be taken into account and a serious candidate for further research investigations.

4 Specifying a Planning Domain for SINERGY

In this section we analyze the domain representation features offered by SINERGY. In order to make this process as intuitive as possible, we will present an example of a domain description for the briefcase problem (BP). In a few words, we can define BP as follows: given a number of briefcases ($B=\{B_1, B_2, \dots, B_n\}$), objects ($O=\{O_1, O_2, \dots, O_m\}$), and locations ($L=\{L_1, L_2, \dots, L_k\}$), we want to deliver each object O_i to its respective destination L^i_j. In order to solve the problem, the planning system can use one of the following operators:

a) *(move-briefcase a-briefcase a-location)*: moves *a-briefcase*, together with all the objects in it, from the current location to *a-location*.

b) (put-in *an-object a-briefcase*): if *an-object* and *a-briefcase* are at the same location, puts *an-object* in *a-briefcase*.

c) (take-out *an-object*): if SINERGY finds that *an-object* is in a briefcase, say *B*, it takes *an-object* out of *B*.

In SINERGY, any specification of the planning domain has four main descriptive sections: concepts, predicates, planning operators, and auxiliary functions. Figure 2 shows the whole domain specification for the briefcase problem. *Concept definitions* are self-explanatory, and they simply introduce the *types* of entities that can be manipulated by the planner. We will focus first on *predicate specifications*, which require several important comments, and we will continue our discussion by analyzing the *planning operators* and the *auxiliary functions*.

Any SINERGY predicate can be used both to describe the state of the world (e.g., a given object is *at* a given location or *in* a briefcase) and to specify a goal (e.g., the object *obj* must be transported *at* a given location or put *in* a briefcase). As the planning problem is converted to a GP one, each predicate must have a corresponding fitness evaluation function. Even though in our example the fitness evaluation functions are extremely simple (i.e., they just count the number of unsatisfied goals), a fitness evaluation function might be arbitrarily complex: it can use heuristics like the Manhattan distance (e.g., for the robot navigation problem), or it might include weight-factors that would allow the user to define a hierarchy of the goals based on their relative importance (i.e., the more important a type of a goal, the larger its weight-factor will be).

As we have already seen, SINERGY does not reason about plans, but instead uses artificial selection and recombination to create plans that are likely to have a better fitness measure than the ones in the previous generation. In order to evaluate the fitness of a given plan P, which is a linear sequence of fully instantiated planning operators $p_1, p_2, \dots, p_l$, SINERGY sets the world status to the given initial state S_0, and it successively simulates the execution of each operator p_i in the plan. At the end of the plan execution, the planner computes the fitness of P based on the formula

$$\sum_{i=1}^{n} FitnessEvaluationFunction_{Predicate_i}(CurrentState, Goals)$$

```
;; Concept definitions.
(defvar *concepts* '(object briefcase location))

;;Predicate definitions: pairs <predicate fitness-eval-fct>.
(defvar *predicates* '((in in-fitness) (at at-fitness)))

(defun in-fitness( relevant-goals )
 (number-of-unsatisfied-goals relevant-goals))

(defun at-fitness( relevant-goals )
 (number-of-unsatisfied-goals relevant-goals))

;; Operator definitions (names and number of arguments).
(defvar *planning-operators*
        '( (move-briefcase 2) (take-out 1) (put-in 2) ))

(defun put-in( arg-1 arg-2 )
 (let ((an-object (convert-to arg-1 'object))
       (a-briefcase (convert-to arg-2 'briefcase)))
  (when ;; PRECONDITIONS
     (equal (get-location an-object) (get-location a-briefcase))
     ;; EFFECTS
     (add-fact `(in ,an-object ,a-briefcase))))
 arg-1)

(defun take-out( arg-1 )
 (let ((an-object (convert-to arg-1 'object)))
   (when ;; PRECONDITIONS
     (is-fact `(in ,an-object ,(get-briefcase an-object)))
     ;; EFFECTS
     (delete-fact `(in ,an-object ,(get-briefcase an-object)))))
 arg-1)

(defun move-briefcase ( arg-1 arg-2 )
 (let((a-briefcase (convert-to arg-1'briefcase))
      (a-location (convert-to arg-2 'location)))
   (when ;; PRECONDITIONS
     (not (is-fact `(at ,a-briefcase ,a-location)))
     ;; EFFECTS
     (for-all 'object #'do-move (list a-briefcase a-location))

     (delete-fact `(at ,a-briefcase ,(get-location a-briefcase)))
     (add-fact `(at ,a-briefcase ,a-location))))
 arg-1)
;; Auxiliary functions.
(defun do-move ( obj br to )
  (when (is-fact `(in ,obj ,br))
        (delete-fact `(at ,obj ,(get-location obj)))
        (add-fact `(at ,obj ,to))))

(defun get-location (object)
  (find-attribute-value '?location `(at ,object ?location)))

(defun get-briefcase (object)
  (find-attribute-value '?briefcase `(in ,object ?briefcase)))
```

Fig. 2. The Domain Description for the Briefcase Problem.

Planning operators are defined as a collection of Lisp functions that are used as terminals and functions by the GP problem solver. In order to keep track of the world status during a plan execution, SINERGY provides the predefined functions *add-fact* and *delete-fact* that must be used by the planning operators whenever they change the world status. As a direct consequence of the procedural definition of the planning operators, the use of disjunctive preconditions and conditional effects is a trivial task in SINERGY. Furthermore, our planning system offers additional features that make its domain description language extremely powerful and expressive. First, SINERGY allows users to define *auxiliary functions* that can be invoked within the operators. For instance, in our BP example, *get-location* and *get-briefcase* are used to determine the current location, respectively the briefcase that contains a given object. Second, SINERGY provides both universal and existential quantifiers that have the following syntax:

for-all *concept-name auxiliary-function-name additional-arguments*

exists *concept-name auxiliary-function-name additional-arguments*

In the definition of the *move-briefcase* operator we used the universal quantifier to apply an action to all instances of the *object* concept, but both types of quantifiers can also be used in the goal specification of any problem instance.

SINERGY also provides a domain-independent solution to a major problem related to the different nature of AI planning and GP: planning operators are "strongly typed" (i.e., each argument of an operator must be of a well-defined, pre-established type), while the GP functions introduced in [Koza 1992] are "typeless" because they always rely on the *closure property*, which ensures that any value returned by a function or terminal represents a valid actual parameter for any function in the function set. In order to solve this problem, we used the following approach: in addition to the user-defined terminals (i.e., planning operators that take no arguments), the GP problem solver uses a supplementary set of terminals $T_s = \{ t_1,$ $t_2, ...t_n \}$. For a given problem instance, SINERGY automatically generates T_s in such a way that the value returned by a terminal t_i can be converted to a unique object name of *any* type defined within the planning universe. Consequently, each planning operator must convert its parameters to objects of the desired type by invoking the SINERGY-provided *convert-to* function.

Finally, for a given planning domain, the user has to specify the instance of the problem to be solved (Figure 3). The variable **concept-instances** defines the domain objects of each type (e.g., briefcases, locations, or objects-to-be-moved), while **init-state** and **goal-state** are used by SINERGY to generate a fitness case for the GP problem solver. Based on the information in **concept-instances**, SINERGY also creates the internal data structures that allow the *convert-to* function to uniformly map GP entities to valid domain objects.

5 An Example of Plan Evolution Based on Genetic Recombination

In order to better understand how SINERGY creates new plans from the existing ones, we will analyze an example of plan construction that is based on the GP cross-over operation. Let us suppose that SINERGY tries to solve the BP instance that is presented in Figure 3. Based on the BP domain description, our planner generates an empty set of GP terminals and three GP functions: *take-out*, *put-in*, and *move-*

briefcase (*take-out* has one argument, while *put-in* and *move-briefcase* require two arguments).

```
(defvar *concept-instances*
 '( (object (o1 o2)) (briefcase (b1)) (location (l1 l2 l3))))
(defvar *init-state* '((at o1 l1)(at o2 l3) (at b1 l1)))
(defvar *goal-state* '((at o1 l2))))
```

Fig. 3. The Definition of a Simple BP Instance.

After analyzing the domain description, SINERGY examines the problem instance and generates the additional set of terminals T_s that was briefly discussed in the previous section. As it is beyond the scope of this paper to explain the algorithms based on which T_s and the corresponding data structures are generated (for details see [Muslea 1997]), let us accept without further proof that for the given BP instance SINERGY creates a set of six additional terminals $T_s = \{t_1, t_2, t_3, t_4, t_5, t_6\}$, and the function *convert-to* provides the mappings described in Table 2. The information from Table 2 must be interpreted as follows: the function call (*convert-to* (t_2) *'location*) returns the location name l_2, while the function call (*convert-to* (t_6) *'object*) returns the object name o_2. Note that for concepts that have a unique instance (e.g., *briefcase*) all terminals are mapped to the unique object name, while for concepts with several instances, each object name corresponds to the *same* number of distinct terminals from T_s.

Table 2. CONVERT-TO mapping of terminals to domain objects.

CONVERT-TO	location	object	briefcase
t_1	l_1	o_1	b_1
t_2	l_2	o_2	b_1
t_3	l_3	o_1	b_1
t_4	l_1	o_2	b_1
t_5	l_2	o_1	b_1
t_6	l_3	o_2	b_1

Now let us suppose that in Generation 1 the GP system creates the two random programs *P1* and *P2* presented in Table 3. Both *P1* and *P2* are expressed as function compositions over the sets of GP terminals and functions. During the plan-simulation phase, the GP problem solver executes the programs *P1* and *P2* by starting with the inner-most functions (i.e., the terminals t_1 and t_2) and ending with the outmost ones (e.g., *take-out*, respectively *move-briefcase*). If we use the *convert-to* function to map each occurrence of the terminals t_1 and t_2 to *object names* of the types specified in each planning operator, the programs *P1* and *P2* can be interpreted as the equivalent linear plans <(*put-in* o_1 b_1), (*take-out* o_1)>, respectively <(*take-out* o_2), (*move-briefcase* b_1 l_2)>. As none of these two plans satisfies the goal (*at* o_1 l_2), the GP problem solver will create a new generation of programs.

In Table 3, we assumed that in order to create the second generation, the GP system applies the cross-over operator to the plans $P1$ and $P2$. As the recombination process arbitrarily breaks each parent in two components, let us suppose that in the current example the GP system chooses to interchange the high-lighted portions of $P1$ and $P2$, which leads to the creation of the new plans $C1$ and $C2$. Even though the child-plan $C1$ is useless and contains redundant operators, the plan $C2$ represents a solution to our BP instance because after its simulated execution the goal $(at\ o_2\ l_2)$ is satisfied. As a final note, we must emphasize that most of the GP-generated plans are similar to $C1$ in the sense that they include redundant operators, and, in many cases, the preconditions of the fully-instantiated operators are not satisfied (e.g., during the simulation of $C1$, none of the operators can be actually executed because the object o_1 is not in the briefcase b_1). However, after multiple recombinations, plan fragments might fit together in such a way that a newly created plan solves the problem at hand.

Table 3. Programs $P1$ and $P2$ are recombined into $C1$ and $C2$.

	GP-generated Programs	GP Functions Executed During Plan Simulation	Equivalent Linear AI Plans
$P1$	(take-out *(put-in (t_1) (t_2)))*	1: (put-in (t_1) (t_2)) 2: (take-out (t_1))	1: (put-in o_1 b_1) 2: (take-out o_1)
$P2$	(move-briefcase *(take-out (t_2))* (t_2))	1: (take-out (t_2)) 2: (move-briefcase (t_2) (t_2))	1: (take-out o_2) 2: (move-briefcase b_1 l_2)
$C1$	(take-out *(take-out (t_2)))*	1: (take-out (t_2)) 2: (take-out (t_2))	1: (take-out o_2) 2: (take-out o_2)
$C2$	(move-briefcase *(put-in (t_1) (t_2))* (t_2))	1: (put-in (t_1) (t_2)) 2: (move-briefcase (t_1) (t_2))	1: (put-in o_1 b_1) 2: (move-briefcase b_1 l_2)

6 Experimental Results

In order to have an accurate image of SINERGY's capabilities, we ran our planner on three different domains: the single robot navigation problem (RNP), the 2-robot navigation problem (2RNP), and the briefcase problem (BP). In this paper, we define RNP as follows: given a rectangular m-by-n table T with k blocks located in its grid-cells, a robot R must navigate from its current position CP to the desired position DP. In order to reach DP, the robot can use any of the eight available operations: *move* (north/south/east/west) to an unoccupied neighboring cell, or *push* (north/south/east/west) a block located in a neighboring cell X to an empty cell Y that is right behind X. 2RNP is similar to RNP, but it requires that both robots reach their respective destination. RNP is an extremely hard problem because of the high level of interaction among the operators' effects (i.e., if the robot pushes a block to an inappropriate location, it may bring the universe into a status from where the problem is not solvable anymore), and 2RNP is even harder because the two robots might have conflicting goals.

For all our experiments, we ran SINERGY on a maximum of 1000 generations of 200 individuals each. The population size is extremely small in terms of GP problem solvers, but due to our hardware limitations (we ran the experiments on a single-processor, non-dedicated SUN-4 machine) we could not afford to consistently use a larger population. However, we made a few experiments on 50 generations of 2000 individuals, and the solution was found in significantly fewer generations because the larger initial population increases the chances of finding well-fit plans from the very first generation. For each of the three domains mentioned above, we ran SINERGY on more than 100 problem instances, and our results for the most difficult instances are presented in Tables 4, 5 and 6.

Table 4. Results for the Single Robot Navigation Problem

Instance	Description	Generation of First Solution
RNP-1	4x4 table, 6 obstacles	1
RNP-2	another 4x4 table, 6 obstacles	1
RNP-3	8x8 table, 18 obstacles (requires at least 6 PUSH-es)	10
RNP-4	50x50 table, no obstacles	150
RNP-5	100x100 table, no obstacles	317
RNP-6	100x100 table, same obstacles positions as in RNP-1	354
RNP-7	100x100 table, same obstacles positions as in RNP-2	333
RNP-8	100x100 table, same obstacles positions as in RNP-3	353

In Table 4, we show the results of running SINERGY on several difficult instances of RNP that UCPOP was not able to solve. Based on the experimental results, we can make several important observations. First, SINERGY is capable of solving hard problem instances that are two orders of magnitude larger than the ones solved by UCPOP (note: for both RNP and 2RNP we used a fitness evaluation function based of the Manhattan distance between the position reached by the robot and the desired position). For instance, in RNP-8 we have a 100-by-100 table with 18 blocks that completely obstruct the way from the initial position (0,0) to the destination (99,99), and the robot must perform two complicated sequences of PUSH operations (one to get away from its initial location, and another one to make its way toward the final destination). Second, SINERGY is capable of creating better plans (i.e., closer to the optimal solution) once it finds a first solution. For example, SINERGY found a first solution for RNP-6 at generation 354 (it had 293 operations, while the optimal plan required only 206 actions), but by the time it reached generation 867, our planner kept improving the plan and was able to deliver a solution with only 216 operations. Finally, SINERGY is especially well fit to solve hard problem instances. While on easy instances, like small tables with no blocks, UCPOP is faster than SINERGY, the GP-based approach is more appropriate for problem instances that have a higher level of difficulty.

Table 5. Results for the 2-Robot Navigation Problem

Instance	Description	Generation of First Solution
2RNP-1	8x8 table, no obstacles	9
2RNP-2	8x8 table, 2 obstacles	14
2RNP-3	8x8 table, 5 obstacles	24
2RNP-4	8x8 table, 10 obstacles	49
2RNP-5	100x100 table, 18 obstacles	-

The experiments presented in Table 5 are of a different nature: for 2RNP, we tested SINERGY's performance on domain specifications that are totally unfit for the GP approach. That is, rather than extending the domain representation for RNP such that both the *move* and *push* operators take an additional parameter that denotes the robot-to-perform-the-action, we decided to use the same set of operators, and to interpret a generated plan as follows: by default, all the even operators are performed by $robot_1$, while the odd ones are executed by $robot_2$. It is easy to see that such a representation is not fit for GP-based problem solvers: if the recombination of two parent-plans $P_1 = <a_1, a_2, ..., a_n>$ and $P_2 = <b_1, b_2, ..., b_m >$ generates the children-plans $C_1 = <a_1, a_2, ..., a_{2k+1}, b_{2l+1}, b_{2l+2}, ..., b_m>$ and $C_2 = <b_1, b_2, ..., b_{2l}, a_{2k+2}, a_{2k+3}, ..., a_n>$, the operators $b_{2l+1}, b_{2l+2}, ..., b_m$ from C_1 and $a_{2k+2}, a_{2k+3}, ..., a_n$ from C_2 will be executed by different robots than the ones that executed them within the original plans P_1 and P_2. However, despite the inappropriate encoding of the plans, SINERGY is capable of finding a solution for all medium-size test-instances.

Table 6. Results for the Briefcase Problem

Instance	Description	Generation of First Solution
BP-1	4 objects, 5 locations, 1 briefcase	59
BP-2	5 objects, 5 locations, 1 briefcase	42
BP-3	5 objects, 5 locations, 5 briefcases	42
BP-4	10 objects, 10 locations, 1 briefcase	66
BP-5	10 objects, 10 locations, 2 briefcases	68
BP-6	10 objects, 10 locations, 5 briefcases	136
BP-7	10 objects, 10 locations, 10 briefcases	-

Finally, our last set of tests was performed for the briefcase problem (Table 6). We used the domain specification presented in Figure 2, and the experimental results are similar to the ones obtained for the RNP domain: on easy instances (e.g., all objects must be transported to the same place and are initially stored at the same location) UCPOP solves the problem faster than SINERGY, but on complex problem instances (e.g., large number of objects, each of them being initially located at a different location) SINERGY is still capable of solving the problem, while UCPOP is unable to cope with the increased level of difficulty. By analyzing the results of SINERGY in the three domains that we considered, we can conclude that our planner significantly outperforms UCPOP for all difficult test-instances, but it is slower than UCPOP on most of the easy ones.

7 Future Work

We plan to extend SINERGY by adding two major features. First, we would like to facilitate the search reduction by introducing hierarchical planning operators. The new version of SINERGY would allow users to create several levels of abstraction, each of them being described by a distinct set of operators and predicates. For instance, if we consider a combination of the briefcase problem and the robot navigation problem (*BRNP*), at the higher level of abstraction each robot could perform the three BP operations (*put-in, take-out,* and *move-to*), and SINERGY would not be concerned with any navigation details. Once the planner finds a solution at the higher level of abstraction, it translates each fully-instantiated (*move-to robot$_i$ location$_j$*) operator into a goal (*at robot$_i$ x$_j$ y$_j$*) that must be solved at a lower level of abstraction. In order to satisfy the newly generated goals, SINERGY must solve the navigation problem based on a different set of operators (e.g. *move, rotate,* or *push*). The use of hierarchical planning operators might be extremely beneficial for domains like *BRNP*, in which achieving the goal (*at object 100 13*) involves a long sequence of *move* and *push* operators, followed by a single *take-out* action.

Second, we would like to allow users to define planning problems that involve dynamic environments. For instance, in the robot motion problem, we could define two distinct types of obstacles: fixed blocks and mobile blocks. Fixed blocks could change their positions only if they are pushed by a robot, while mobile blocks would be continuously changing their positions based on predefined trajectories. As candidate plans are executed in simulation, after performing each planning operation SINERGY could update the position of the mobile blocks based on the predefined trajectory functions. We believe that the ability of SINERGY to plan in dynamic environments would represents a major advantage of our approach because most real-world problems must be solved in dynamic environments, and traditional planners are generally unable to cope with such environments.

8 Conclusions

The major contribution of this paper consists of providing a domain-independent mapping of any AI planning problem into an equivalent GP problem. In final analysis, we can conclude that SINERGY is a general-purpose AI planning system that is capable of solving large, complex problem instances. By supporting disjunctive preconditions, conditional effects, and both existential and universal quantifiers, SINERGY provides users with a domain description language that has an expressive power equivalent to the one offered by UCPOP. Our initial results show that SINERGY outperforms UCPOP on all the difficult examples it was tested on. Furthermore, the highly parallelizable nature of GP makes us believe that running SINERGY on a relatively low-power, parallel machine would allow our planner to easily solve problem instances at least two orders of magnitude larger than the ones presented in this paper.

Even though SINERGY is an incomplete planner that does not generally find the optimal solution for a given problem, its practical ability to solve complex problems and to improve the quality of its initial solution makes it a valuable tool for dealing with hard problems. We plan to enhance SINERGY by adding hierarchical operators and a formalism for handling dynamic universes, and we expect the new version to provide both a faster planning process and significantly more expressive power.

9   References

Ambite, J.L., Knoblock, C.: Planning by Rewriting: Efficiently Generating High-Quality Plans. In *Proceedings of AAAI-97* 706-713, 1997.

Bylander, T.: Complexity Results for Extended Planning. In *Artificial Intelligence Planning Systems: Proceedings of First International Conference* 20-27, 1992.

Chapman, D.: Planning for Conjunctive Goals. *Artif Intelligence* 32 (1987) 333-377.

Etzioni, O.: Acquiring search-control knowledge via static analysis. *Artificial Intelligence* 62 (1993) 255-302.

Fikes, R., Nilsson, N.: STRIPS: A New Approach to the Application of Theorem Proving to Problem Solving. In *Artificial Intelligence* 2 (1971) 189-208.

Friedland P., Imasaki, Y.: The Concept and Implementation of Skeletal Plans. *Journal of Automated Reasoning* 1 (1985), 161-208.

Handley, S.: The Automatic Generation of Plans for a Mobile Robot via Genetic Programming with Automatically Defined Functions. In *Advances in Genetic Programming*, K.E. Kinnear Jr., Editor. MIT Press, 391-407, 1994.

Holland, J.H.: *Adaptation in Natural and Artificial Systems*. MIT Press, 1992.

Joslin, D., Roach, J.: A Theoretical Analysis of Conjunctive-Goal Problems. *Artificial Intelligence* 41(1989) 97-106.

Kautz, H., Selman, B.: Pushing the Envelope: Planning, Propositional Logic, and Stochastic Search. In *Proceedings of AAAI-96* 1194-1201, 1996.

Knoblock, C.: Automatically Generating Abstractions for Planning. *Artificial Intelligence*, 68(1994) 243-302.

Knoblock, C.: Search Reduction in Hierarchical Problem Solving. In *Proceedings of the National Conference on Artificial Intelligence* 686-691, 1991.

Koza, J.: *Genetic Programming II*. MIT Press, 1994.

Koza, J.: *Genetic Programming*. MIT Press, 1992.

Minton, S.: Is There Any Need for Domain-Dependent Control Information?: A Reply. In *Proceedings of AAAI-96* 855-862, 1996.

Muslea, I.: A General-Purpose AI Planning System Based on the Genetic Programming Paradigm. *Late Breaking Papers at GP-97* 157-164, 1997.

Sacerdoti, E.: The Nonlinear Nature of Plans. In *Advance Papers of the Fourth International Conference on Artificial Intelligence* (IJCAI-75) 204-214, 1975.

Spector, L.: Genetic Programming and AI Planning Systems. In *Proceedings of Twelfth National Conference of Artificial Intelligence* 1329-1334, 1994.

Weld, D.: An Introduction to Least-Committed Planning. *AI Mag.* 15(1994) 27-60.

A Case Study on Mergeability of Cases with a Partial-Order Planner

Héctor Muñoz-Avila & Frank Weberskirch

University of Kaiserslautern, Dept. of Computer Science
P.O. Box 3049, D-67653 Kaiserslautern, Germany
E-mail: {munioz|weberski}@informatik.uni-kl.de

Abstract. Retrieving multiple cases is supposed to be an adequate retrieval strategy for guiding partial-order planners because of the recognized flexibility of these planners to interleave steps in the plans. Cases are combined by merging them. In this paper, we will examine two different kinds of merging cases in the context of partial-order planning. We will see that merging cases can be very difficult if the cases are merged eagerly. On the other hand, if cases are merged by avoiding redundant steps, the guidance of the additional cases tends to decrease with the number of covered goals and retrieved cases in domains having a certain kind of interactions. Thus, to retrieve a single case covering many of the goals of the problem or to retrieve fewer cases covering many of the goals is at least equally effective as to retrieve several cases covering all goals in these domains.

1 Introduction

In case-based reasoning (CBR) systems, the performance of the adaptation phase depends on the adequacy of the retrieval criteria [Koehler, 1994] [Francis and Ram, 1995b]. For example, if CBR is used to guide the search process of a domain-independent planner, inadequate retrieval criteria may result in a lower performance of the problem solving process compared to first-principles planning in state-space [Veloso, 1994] and partial-order planning [Hanks and Weld, 1995] [Francis and Ram, 1995a] [Ihrig and Kambhampati, 1996].

Retrieving several cases covering different parts of the problem is a recurrent idea in case-based planning (CBP) [Veloso, 1994] [Francis and Ram, 1995a] [Ihrig and Kambhampati, 1996]. Cases are combined by *merging* them. A general definition of merging has been presented in [Kambhampati et al., 1996]. The basic idea is to replay decisions of the retrieved cases independent of the decisions replayed from the other cases. These independently replayed cases are completed into a solution by the first-principles planner. We will see that this form of merging, which we called *eager merging*, is not too useful for a partial-order planner like SNLP [McAllester and Rosenblitt, 1991]. We will analyze the reasons for this and provide experiments supporting our analysis.

A more elaborated merging method is to consider the replayed decisions to avoid adding steps that already have been introduced [Veloso, 1994,Ihrig and Kambhampati, 1996]. In this way redundancy in a plan is reduced. This method, which we called *non-redundant merging*, has been shown to be effective in guiding the planning process. However, we will see that in domains having a certain kind of interactions, the guidance tends to decrease with problem size. Thus, to retrieve a single case covering much of the goals of the problem or to retrieve fewer cases covering much of the goals is at least equally effective as to retrieve several cases covering all goals in these domains.

The paper is organized as follows: first, we briefly recall the SNLP paradigm and present a domain used throughout the paper. Section 3 discusses eager merging in the context of partial-order planning. The next section presents non-redundant merging and a first observation about this method. Section 5 defines a certain form of interactions and analyzes its effects on non-redundant merging. Then, empirical results are presented. Finally, related work is discussed and conclusions are made.

2 Partial-Order Planning and an Example Domain

In this work we will concentrate on a CBP scenario where we have a partial-order planner, SNLP, as the base level planner. Formally, a partially ordered plan [McAllester and Rosenblitt, 1991] is a 4-tuple (S, L, CL, B), where S is the set of plan steps, L is a set of *links* between steps in S, CL is the subset of L containing the causal links, and, B is a set of *constraints* on the variables bindings. L contain causal links and ordering links and induces a partial order, $<_L$, for executing steps in S. A causal link, $s_1 \rightarrow p@s_2$, captures causal dependencies between steps by indicating the step s_1 achieving a precondition p of another step s_2. Ordering links are added to solve threats. A *threat* to a causal link $s_1 \rightarrow p@s_2$ occurs if there is a third plan step s_3 that has as effect p or $\neg p$ and that is parallel to $s_1 \rightarrow p@s_2$, that is, neither $s_3 <_L s_1$ nor $s_2 <_L s_3$ holds. If the effect of s_3 is p the threat is said to be *positive* otherwise it is said to be *negative*. Positive threats must be solved to avoid redundancy in plans in that the same goal is achieved by two parallel steps. Negative threats must be solved to ensure the consistency of the plan.

Planning with SNLP [McAllester and Rosenblitt, 1991] proceeds by *establishing open conditions* and *resolving conflicts*. To establish an open precondition, a step in S is selected or a new step is added to S such that one of its effects matches the open precondition. For each establishment of a precondition a causal link is added. To solve a threat to a causal link $s_1 \rightarrow p@s_2$ caused by a step s_3, an ordering link is added such that $s_3 <_L s_1$ or $s_2 <_L s_3$.[1]

---

[1] Originally, SNLP proposed another variant to solve threats called *separation*. With separation, binding constraints on the variables are added that make it impossible to match the effect of s_3 with the precondition $p@s_2$. However, [Smith and Peot, 1993] show that ignoring separable threats does not affect correctness or completeness of

Example Domain. A domain frequently referred to in the planning literature is the domain of process planning (see [Hayes, 1987], [Kambhampati et al., 1991], [Gil, 1991], [Karinthi et al., 1992], [Britanik and Marefat, 1995], [Nau et al., 1995], [Muñoz-Avila and Weberskirch, 1996a]), particularly the manufacturing process of mechanical workpieces. To manufacture a workpiece, several so-called machining operations are performed to transform a given piece of raw material into design specifications. Typically, a piece of raw material is clamped on a machine and a cutting tool is used to remove layers of raw material. The process continues by changing the cutting tool or the clamping position to machine areas of the workpiece. A basic restriction is that at any time of the machining process the workpiece is *clamped* from at most one position and a limited number of cutting tools can be *held*. In the specification used in [Muñoz-Avila and Weberskirch, 1996b], an order, $\prec$, for achieving the machining goals can be predefined based on the geometry of the workpiece [Muñoz-Avila and Weberskirch, 1996a]. Thus, problem descriptions consist not only of the initial and final state, (I, F), but of the order $\prec$. The 3-tuple $(I, F, \prec)$ is called an *extended problem description*. The order $\prec$ can be seen as an additional restriction that any solution must meet.

3 Eager Merging of Cases

Eager replay has been shown to be an adequate reuse strategy for partial-order planners such as SNLP [Ihrig and Kambhampati, 1994]. Reuse with *eager replay* is done in two phases. First, the decisions taken in the retrieved case are replayed in the new situation as long as they don't produce inconsistencies. Once this phase is finished, a so-called *skeletal plan* is obtained that may contain open preconditions and threats. Then, the skeletal plan is completed by first-principles planning.

When several cases are retrieved, the question of how to merge them arises. A first approach is to replay each retrieved case and let the planner do the merging. We called this *eager merging* as it corresponds to the straightforward use of eager replay for multiple cases. To examine the limitations of eager merging we recall the definition of mergeability of plans [Kambhampati et al., 1996]:

Definition 1 (Mergeability of Plans). Given a plan P_1 for achieving a goal g_1. P_1 is **mergeable** with respect to a plan P_2 for achieving a goal g_2 if there is a plan P extending P_1 and P_2 achieving both g_1 and g_2.

In addition, the plans are said to be **simple mergeable** if every step in P is present in either P_1 or P_2 and the number of steps in P is equal to the number of steps in P_1 and P_2 (that is, only ordering links are added).

The definition of mergeability does not exclude that backtracking takes place in finding P. The point is that no backtracking should take place in the plan

---

SNLP. Additionally, the search space without separation is at most the same as with separation.

refinement steps that added plan steps, links, or constraints in P_1 or in P_2. In CBP, a maximal gain is expected if a case base is given that is constituted of mergeable plans. If the cases can be replayed totally in the the context of the new problem, the mergeability condition ensures that the planner will not need to revise decisions taken in the cases during the completion phase. It may not always be possible to replay the cases completely, however if the cases are small in terms of the number of goals solved (e.g., one-goal cases), this situation is likely to occur. The strategy of storing small cases has been explored before to decrease the size of the case base [Ihrig and Kambhampati, 1996].

Mergeability turns out to be a strong requirement. A first indication of how strong this requirement is can be derived from the following definition:

Definition 2 (Parellelizability of Goals). Given two goals g_1 and g_2. If any two plans P_1 and P_2 achieving g_1 and g_2 are mergeable, then g_1 and g_2 are said to be **parallelizable**.

[Kambhampati et al., 1996] show that if a set of goals is parallelizable, then the goals are trivially serializable[2] and that the opposite direction does not hold. That is parellelizability is a stronger requirement than trivial serializability. We found that in the context of partial-order planning mergeability is indeed a very restrictive condition:

Proposition 3. *Suppose that first-principles planning is done with SNLP. Then, a plan P_1 for achieving a goal g_1 is mergeable with respect to a plan P_2 for achieving a goal g_2 if and only if P_1 and P_2 are simple mergeable.*

Proof. Planning in SNLP proceeds by solving threats and establishing open (unachieved) preconditions. New steps are added to a plan, only to achieve open preconditions. Because P_1 and P_2 are complete plans (they achieve g_1 and g_2), only threats may occur (interactions between P_1 and P_2). Thus, P_1 and P_2 can be extended to a plan achieving g_1 and g_2 if and only if the threats can be solved. That is, if only ordering links need to be added to extend these plans.∎

This simple result shows that mergeability is a very strong requirement for partial-order planning with SNLP. For example, as explained before, in the domain of process planning there are always interactions between two machining plans because the use of the cutting tools needs to be rationalized. In the specification used [Munoz-Avila and Weberskirch, 1996b], not only ordering links must be added between the holding steps to solve the threats, but new steps must be introduced as well for performing the operation that unmounts the tool from the holding machine, *MakeToolHolderFree*. The same situation occurs if the specification of [Gil, 1991] is used (the unmount operation is called *Release-from-holding-device* there). As a result, proposition 1 shows that machining plans are

---

[2] Given two goals g_1 and g_2, if any plan achieving g_1 can be extended to a plan achieving g_1 and g_2, then g_1, g_2 is said to be a *serialization order*. If g_1, g_2 and g_2, g_1 are serialization orders then g_1 and g_2 are said to be *trivially serializable* [Korf, 1987,Barrett and Weld, 1994,Kambhampati et al., 1996].

not mergeable for SNLP. In the logistics transportation domain [Veloso, 1994], it is easy to find situations, where new steps must be added to extend the cases.

4   Non-Redundant Merging of Cases

A disadvantage of eager merging is that the solution obtained may be very large because several steps are repeated unnecessarily. Therefore, another form of merging, which we denote as *non-redundant merging*, has been proposed [Veloso, 1994,Ihrig and Kambhampati, 1996]. During the replay phase, opportunities to establish preconditions are considered in the following way: before replaying a step to establish an open precondition, the system checks if the precondition can be established with a step in the current subplan (i.e., the subplan already obtained from the cases replayed before). If this is possible, the step is not replayed and the precondition is left open. During the completion process, the first-principles planner prefers to establish the conditions left open by the replay process by using the available steps. New steps are added only if no completion of the plan by using the steps available is possible. If more than two cases are involved, the process is done stepwise: the first two are merged and extended to obtain a complete subplan (i.e., a subplan containing no open preconditions and no threats). The third case is then merged with the current subplan and so on. The rationale behind non-redundant merging is to take advantage of opportunities to establish the open preconditions using steps that were not available because the cases were solved separately.

Example. The way the interactions between the goals affect the non-redundant merging process is illustrated with the example in figure 1 (*cs*, *hs* and *ms* denote clamping, holding and machining steps respectively): it shows two subplans for *machined(ctr)* and *machined(ucut)* when the non-redundant form of merging was used and the subplan for *machined(ctr)* was generated before the subplan for *machined(ucut)* (threats are depicted with double arrows). A step *cs(left)* was not replayed (depicted with a dashed box) because another step *cs(left)* in the other subplan establishes the precondition *clamped(left)*. As a result, the part of the case achieving the preconditions of *cs(left)* is not replayed, too.

Based on the non-redundant form of merging plans, *non-redundant mergeability of plans*, the notion of *simple non-redundant mergeability of plans* and *non-redundant parellelizability of goals* can be defined. We define non-redundant mergeability of plans for illustration purposes:

Definition 4 (Non-Redundant Mergeability). Given two plans P_1 and P_2, then $P_2 \setminus P_1$ denotes the plan that remains after pruning plan steps from P_2 achieving goals that can be established by using steps in P_1. Plan steps that were added to achieve a precondition of a pruned step, are pruned as well.

Given plan P_1, P_2 for achieving the goal g_1, g_2. Plan P_1 is *non-redundant mergeable* with respect to P_2 if there is a plan P extending P_1 and $P_2 \setminus P_1$ achieving both g_1 and g_2.

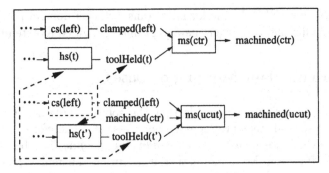

Fig. 1. Interactions between two subplans.

Clearly, the mergeability of plans implies their non-redundant mergeability and the parellelizability of goals implies their non-redundant parellelizability. Non-redundant merging is more flexible than eager merging. For example, in the specification of the domain of process planning used, if the machining goals are achieved in an order consistent with $\prec$, the plans are non-redundantly mergeable even though they are never mergeable. The two subplans depicted in Figure 1 are non-redundant mergeable: the precondition *clamped(left)* can be established with the existing step *cs(left)* and an unmount step can be added an ordered between *hs(t)* and *hs(t')*. Machining goals are also $\prec$-constrained trivially serializable [Muñoz-Avila and Weberskirch, 1996b].[3] However, examples can be found of goals that are trivially serializable and not non-redundantly parellelizable. We will now show that non-redundant parallelizability is also an stronger requirement than trivial serializability.

Proposition 5. *If a set of goals* $g_1, ..., g_n$ *is non-redundant parallelizable, then it is trivially serializable.*

Proof. We will prove this result for two goals. Let P_1 be a plan achieving g_1. We will show that P_1 can be extended to a plan achieving g_1 and g_2. Let P_2 be any plan achieving g_2 and SEQ_2 the sequence of refinement steps to obtain P_2. Let $SEQ_{P_2 \setminus P_1}$ be the subsequence of refinement steps in SEQ_2 achieving $P_2 \setminus P_1$. Because, g_1 and g_2 are non-redundantly parallelizable, there must be a plan P_3 extending P_1 and $P_2 \setminus P_1$ that achieves g_1 and g_2. Let SEQ_3 be the sequence of refinement steps to obtain P_3 by extending P_1 and $P_2 \setminus P_1$. Then, P_1 can be extended to a plan achieving g_1 and g_2 by following the sequences of refinement steps $SEQ_{P_2 \setminus P_1}$ and then SEQ_3. This shows that g_1, g_2 is a serialization order. In the same way it can be shown that g_2, g_1 is also a serializiation order. Thus, g_1, g_2 are trivially serializable. ■

---

[3] $\prec$-constrained trivially serializable is a restricted form of trivial serializability for extended problem descriptions, $(I, F, \prec)$, in which only orders consistent with $\prec$ are taken into account (and not all the permutations of the goals).

5 Positive Interactions and Non-redundant Merging

When following the non redundant merging method, it can be observed that once the replay phase is finished, no *positive* threats between the current subplan (i.e., the subplan obtained after merging the previous cases) and the replayed case occur. The reason for this is that positive threats indicate that the same effect has been obtained in the subplan and the replayed case, which is the kind of redundancy that non redundant merging avoids. In the example in Figure 1, which only involves two goals, one of the subgoals of the machining step achieving the first goal is left open and as a result a significant portion of the case is not replayed. The kind of interactions occuring can be formalized as follows:

Definition 6 (Conflict between goals). A set of goals G is said to be *in conflict*, if for every two subplans P_i and P_j achieving g_i and g_j in G, there is a step in P_i that threatens a causal link in P_j and vice versa.

We also say that P_i and P_j interact. If there are positive (negative) threats, the interactions are said to be positive (negative).

In the domain of process planning, machining goals are *always* in conflict. Negative interactions between subplans indicate violations to the restrictions on the clamping operation (i.e., the workpiece can only be clamped from one position at a time). In the specification used in [Muñoz-Avila and Weberskirch, 1996b], only one tool can be held at a time. Thus, there are always at least two interactions between machining subplans, one caused by the clamping steps and the other one caused by the holding steps. Given that in this specification any workpiece can be clamped by using at most 6 different clamping operations, there are always positive interactions when at least 7 cases are merged. We will see in the experiments that as the number of positive interactions increases, the guidance provided by the additional cases tends to be small as more cases are merged and more goals are covered.

Notice that in the logistics transportation domain goals might not be in conflict. For example, a subplan in which a truck picks an object in one location, moves to other location and drops the object does not interact with a subplan performing the same operations in a different city.

6 Evaluating the Merging Strategies

We performed experiments to evaluate the different merging strategies in partially ordered plans based on SNLP.

Domains: We performed experiments with the domain of process planning, an artificial domain[4] and the logistics transportation domain.

---

[4] The artificial domain is an extension of the ART-1D-RD [Kambhampati, 1993], in that two new operators were added that rationalize the use of the resources hf and he instead of adding and deleting them directly in the actions A_i. This domain is similar to the domain of process planning in that goals are in conflict.

Problems: We constructed a sequence of single-goal problems (15 for the domain of process planning, 12 for the transportation domain and 8 for the artificial domain). To observe the way the positive interactions affect the merging process, sequences of $n+1$-goal problems were constructed by adding a goal randomly selected from the sequence of single-goal problems to each problem of the sequence of n-goal problems. The constructed problems were revised to avoid repetitions. In this way, we ensured that when several cases were retrieved, all the goals in the problem are covered. The construction of the case base reflects an ideal situation because in practice it is unlikely that all the goals of the problem are covered. However, this situation is appropiate to compare the merging methods because a maximal gain is expected from CBP.

Retrieval and adaptation: The similarity assessment used was the footprinted similarity metric and the case base was constructed in the way of Prodigy/Analogy [Veloso, 1994]. For each problem, the retrieval strategy followed was to retrieve one-goal cases such that all goals of the problem are covered. The retrieved cases were merged in eager-merging and non-redundant-merging modes. For the domain of process planning the goals were merged in an order consistent with $\prec$.

The data obtained with pure SNLP is intended as a reference to compare the merging algorithms and not to show the advantages of CBP over first-principles planning. [Veloso, 1994,Ihrig and Kambhampati, 1996] already observed benefits of CBP over first-principles planning. As explained before, the construction of the case base was biased towards obtaining maximal gains with CBP.

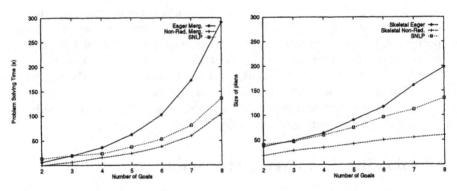

Fig. 2. (a) Problem solving time and (b) plan size for the domain of process planning

Results. Figures 2, 3 and 4 compare data obtained with the domain of process planning, the artificial domain and the logistics transportation domain. Part (a) of these figures shows the problem solving time by using eager and non-redundant merging and SNLP. Parts (b) shows the size (i.e., $S + L$) of the skeletal plans

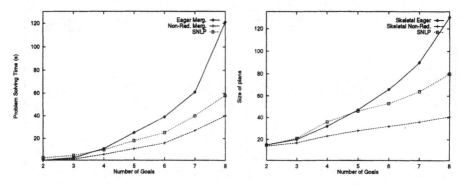

Fig. 3. (a) Problem solving time and (b) size for the artificial domain

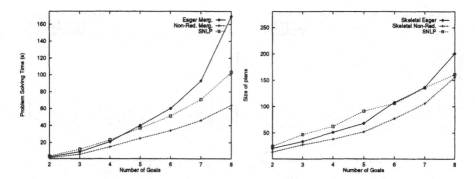

Fig. 4. (a) Problem solving time and (b) skeletal plan size for the logistics transportation domain

obtained with eager and non-redundant merging and the size of the solution plans obtained by SNLP.

Common to the three domains is that the worst performance is obtained with the eager merging mode (it is outperformed by SNLP). Eager merging seems to be an inadequate choice when the base level planner is SNLP corroborating in this way Proposition 1. In the domain of process planning and the artificial domain this result reflects the fact that subplans are always nonmergeable. In the transportation domain some of the skeletal subplans generated were mergeable. Thus, the performance with the eager merging mode is slightly better compared to the other domains. With the non-redundant mode, the difference between the size of the skeletal plan and the solution plan is a measure for the effort needed in the completion phase. For example, the effort for completition in the transportation domain (see Figure 4 (a)) is less than in the other two domains because the skeletal plans are comparatively larger (see Figure 4 (b)).

Figure 5 compares (a) the number of positive interactions and (b) the total number of interactions occuring in these domains. Because no positive interactions can occur after non redundant merging, the positive interactions are mea-

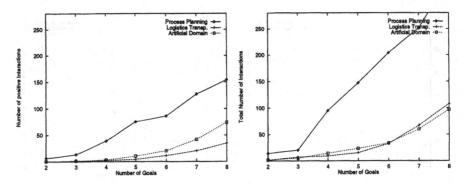

Fig. 5. (a) Number of positive interactions and (b) total number of interactions

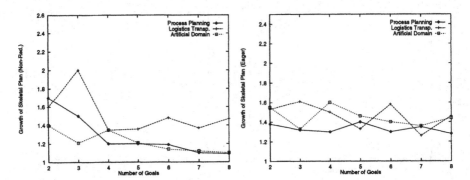

Fig. 6. Growth of skeletal plan size with the (a) non-redundant and (b) eager merging

sured by observing the eager-merging mode. The difference between the skeletal plan in eager-merging mode with the skeletal plan in non-redundant-merging mode reflect the percentage of the cases that was not replayed because of the positive interactions. Particularly, in the domain of process planning and the artificial domain, it can be observed that for solving the 8-goal problems, a significant part of the cases was not replayed (more than 70%). This is the result of the positive interactions, which in both situations correspond to approximately 50% of the interactions (see Figure 5).

Related to this issue, notice that as the number of goals increases, the guidance provided by the additional cases retrieved with the non-redundant merging mode decreases in the domain of process planning and the artificial domain. Figure 6 (a) compares the relative growth of the plans in the three domains for non-redundant merging whereas part (b) compares this growth for eager merging. The relative growth for n goals was measured by dividing the average size of the plans for n goals by the average size of the plans for n-1 goals. It can be observed that for the process planning domain and the artificial domain the relative growth of the skeletal plan generated in non-redundant mode decreases with the number of goals (see Figure 6). Notice that for both domains there is a significant increase in the number of positive interactions (see Figure 5). This supports our claim that in domains were goals are in conflict, the guidance provided by the additional cases retrieved tends to decrease with the number of goals. These results suggest that in these domains retrieving a single case covering as much of the goals as possible or fewer cases is an equivalent strategy because merging additional cases is worthless after several goals have been solved. Notice, that the growth of the skeletal plans obtained with eager merging does not decrease with the number of goals.

In contrast to the other two domains, in the logistics transportation domain the guidance provided by the additional cases with non redundant merging does not decrease as more goals have been solved and correspondly the number of positive interactions does not increase in a significant way. This shows that in domains were goals are not in conflict, retrieving several cases and using non-redundant merging is indeed an adequate choice.

7 Related Work

The idea of avoiding redundancy during replay of multiple cases was first proposed in Prodigy/Analogy [Veloso, 1994]. Prodigy/Analogy uses a mixed-initiative strategy to switch the search control between case-based and first-principles. The basis for this strategy is the fact that Prodigy searches in the space of states instead of the space of plans as in our work. Selecting the kind of base-level planner depends on the characteristics of the particular domain [Kambhampati et al., 1996,Barrett and Weld, 1994,Veloso and Blythe, 1994]. For the specification of the domain of process planning being used here, there is theoretical evidence that a partial-order planner such as SNLP is a better choice [Muñoz-Avila and Weberskirch, 1996b].

derSNLP+EBL [Ihrig and Kambhampati, 1996] is a cased-based planner searching in the space of plans. derSNLP+EBL applies the following strategy: in principle, several single-goal cases are retrieved, each covering a goal of the problem. Non redundant merging is used to combine them. If decisions in the subplans achieving the goals need to be revised to obtain a solution, this solution is stored as a new multi-goal case. If in future retrieval episodes the same situation is encountered, the multi-goal case is retrieved instead of the single-goal cases. Based on the results of this paper, we affirm that in domains where goals are in conflict this method results in an improvement of the performance of the planning process as the result of the multi-goal cases learned but not of the merging method itself. As the number of goals increases, the process of merging cases serves mainly to construct multi-goal cases.

Although not in the context of partial-order planning, previous work has shown that merging subplans into a solution is NP-complete [Karinthi et al., 1992,Yang et al., 1992]. The same work, however, shows that there are instances of the problem that can be solved in polinomial time. An algorithm for merging is presented containing several operations, one of which involves merging the same step occuring in different plans into a single step. This operation is comparable to prefering existing establishing oportunities of the non redundant merging method.

8 Conclusion

We explored eager and non redundant merging in the context of CBP with a partial-order planner. We have seen that eager merging has a very limited applicability because of the strong requirements that it makes on the cases so that they can be combined. In particular for SNLP we saw that mergeability is equivalent to simple mergeability. Non redundant merging is more flexible but we have seen that the guidance provided decreases by the additional cases retrieved as the number of goals being solved increases in domains where goals are in conflict and subplans have positive interactions. The empirical results show that the guidance provided by the additional cases tends to be small as more cases are merged and more goals are covered. Thus retrieving a single cases covering much of the goals or fewer cases is an effective retrieval strategy.

References

[Barrett and Weld, 1994] Barrett, A. and Weld, D. (1994). Partial-order planning: Evaluating possible efficiency gains. *Artificial Intelligence*, 67(1):71–112.

[Britanik and Marefat, 1995] Britanik, J. and Marefat, M. (1995). Hierarchical plan merging with application to process planning. In *Proceedings of IJCAI-95*, pages 1677–1683.

[Francis and Ram, 1995a] Francis, A. G. J. and Ram, A. (1995a). A domain-independent algorithm for multi-plan adaptation and merging in least-commitment planning. In Aha, D. and Rahm, A., editors, *AAAI Fall Symposium: Adaptation of Knowledge Reuse*, Menlo Park, CA. AAAI Press.

[Francis and Ram, 1995b] Francis, A. J. and Ram, A. (1995b). A comparative utility analysis of case-based reasoning and control-rule learning systems. In *Proceedings ECML-95*, number 912 in Lecture Notes in Artificial Intelligence.

[Gil, 1991] Gil, Y. (1991). A specification of manufacturing processes for planning. Technical Report CMU-CS-91-179, School of Computer Science, Carnegie Mellon University, Pittsburg.

[Hanks and Weld, 1995] Hanks, S. and Weld, D. (1995). A domain-independent algorithm for plan adaptation. *Journal of Artificial Intelligece Research*, 2.

[Hayes, 1987] Hayes, C. (1987). Using goal interactions to guide planning. In *Proceedings of AAAI-87*, pages 224–228.

[Ihrig and Kambhampati, 1994] Ihrig, L. and Kambhampati, S. (1994). Derivational replay for partial-order planning. In *Proceedings of AAAI-94*, pages 116–125.

[Ihrig and Kambhampati, 1996] Ihrig, L. and Kambhampati, S. (1996). Design and implementation of a replay framework based on a partial order planner. In Weld, D., editor, *Proceedings of AAAI-96*. IOS Press.

[Kambhampati, 1993] Kambhampati, S. (1993). On the utility of systematicity: Understanding tradeoffs between redundancy and commitment in partial-order planning. In *Proceedings of IJCAI-93*, pages 116–125.

[Kambhampati et al., 1991] Kambhampati, S., Cutkosky, M., Tenenbaum, M., and Lee, S. (1991). Combining specialized reasoners and general purpose planners: A case study. In *Proceedings of AAAI-91*, pages 199–205.

[Kambhampati et al., 1996] Kambhampati, S., Ihrig, L., and Srivastava, B. (1996). A candidate set based analysis of subgoal interactions in conjunctive goal planning. In *Proceedings of the 3rd International Conference on AI Planning Systems (AIPS-96)*, pages 125–133.

[Karinthi et al., 1992] Karinthi, R., Nau, D., and Yang, Q. (1992). Handling feature interactions in process-planning. *Applied Artificial Intelligence*, 6:389–415.

[Koehler, 1994] Koehler, J. (1994). Flexible plan reuse in a formal framework. In *Current Trends in AI Planning*, pages 171–184. IOS Press, Amsterdam, Washington, Tokio.

[Korf, 1987] Korf, R. (1987). Planning as search: A quantitative approach. *Artificial Intelligence*, 33:65–88.

[McAllester and Rosenblitt, 1991] McAllester, D. and Rosenblitt, D. (1991). Systematic nonlinear planning. In *Proceedings of AAAI-91*, pages 634–639.

[Muñoz-Avila and Weberskirch, 1996a] Muñoz-Avila, H. and Weberskirch, F. (1996a). Planning for manufacturing workpieces by storing, indexing and replaying planning decisions. In *Proceedings of the 3nd International Conference on AI Planning Systems (AIPS-96)*. AAAI-Press.

[Muñoz-Avila and Weberskirch, 1996b] Muñoz-Avila, H. and Weberskirch, F. (1996b). A specification of the domain of process planning: Properties, problems and solutions. Technical Report LSA-96-10E, Centre for Learning Systems and Applications, University of Kaiserslautern, Germany.

[Nau et al., 1995] Nau, D., Gupta, S., and Regli, W. (1995). AI planning versus manufacturing-operation planning: A case study. In *Proceedings of IJCAI-95*.

[Smith and Peot, 1993] Smith, D. and Peot, M. (1993). Postponing threats in partial-order planning. In *Proceedings of AAAI-93*, pages 500–506.

[Veloso, 1994] Veloso, M. (1994). *Planning and learning by analogical reasoning*. Number 886 in Lecture Notes in Artificial Intelligence. Springer Verlag.

[Veloso and Blythe, 1994] Veloso, M. and Blythe, J. (1994). Linkability: Examining causal link commitments in partial-order planning. In *Proceedings of the 2nd International Conference on AI Planning Systems (AIPS-94)*, pages 13–19.

[Yang et al., 1992] Yang, Q., Nau, D., and Hendler, J. (1992). Merging separately generated plans with restricted interactions. *Computational Intelligence*, 8(2):648–676.

Ignoring Irrelevant Facts and Operators in Plan Generation

Bernhard Nebel, Yannis Dimopoulos, and Jana Koehler

Institut für Informatik,
Albert-Ludwigs-Universität,
D-79100 Freiburg, Germany
E-mail: ⟨*last name*⟩@informatik.uni-freiburg.de

Abstract. It is traditional wisdom that one should start from the goals when generating a plan in order to focus the plan generation process on potentially relevant actions. The GRAPHPLAN system, however, which is the most efficient planning system nowadays, builds a "planning graph" in a forward-chaining manner. Although this strategy seems to work well, it may possibly lead to problems if the planning task description contains irrelevant information. Although some irrelevant information can be filtered out by GRAPHPLAN, most cases of irrelevance are not noticed.

In this paper, we analyze the effects arising from "irrelevant" information to planning task descriptions for different types of planners. Based on that, we propose a family of heuristics that select relevant information by minimizing the number of initial facts that are used when approximating a plan by backchaining from the goals ignoring any conflicts. These heuristics, although not solution-preserving, turn out to be very useful for guiding the planning process, as shown by applying the heuristics to a large number of examples from the literature.

1 Introduction

It is traditional wisdom that one should start from the goals when generating a plan in order to focus the plan generation process on potentially relevant actions. The GRAPHPLAN system [2], however, which is the most efficient planning system nowadays, builds a "planning graph" in a forward-chaining manner, applying all actions that are possible. While GRAPHPLAN works well on most of the examples known from the literature, one might suspect that larger examples containing information that is irrelevant for a particular task lead to performance problems. In fact, irrelevant information can lead to huge planning graphs even when GRAPHPLAN's feature for filtering out irrelevant facts is used.

Although, at first sight, it might seem to be pathological to have task specifications that contain irrelevant information, this situation occurs naturally when one wants to handle larger domains with varying and diverse goals. For instance, in a robotics domain one may want the robot to transport things, to guide people, to clean rooms, etc. In this case, one wants a domain description with all the necessary operators and the static domain specification. For a given goal and initial state, most of the domain might be irrelevant, however. Further, even the toy examples from the literature sometimes contain some form of "irrelevant information," which, if removed, leads to better performance of the planning process.

For traditional planning systems that perform a backward-chaining search from the goal to the initial state, irrelevance is supposedly not a problem because such planning systems consider only actions that are relevant for solving the planning problem. Planning systems that do forward-chaining from the initial state may, however, run into performance problems. They probably explore possibilities that can never contribute to achieve the goal. However, when comparing GRAPHPLAN with a traditional backward-chaining planner, such as UCPOP [11], GRAPHPLAN is so much faster than UCPOP that GRAPHPLAN's larger sensitivity to irrelevance does not matter much. Nevertheless, "irrelevant information" can be a serious problem for GRAPHPLAN, as is shown below.

In order to bring the best of the two worlds together, one might think of mixing the backward-chaining with the forward-chaining approach. The basic idea for creating top-down expectations in a planning system is quite simple: do backward-chaining from the goals to the initial facts using the operators and ignoring any conflicts between operator applications. This creates an AND-OR tree, where the AND-nodes are the goals or the preconditions of an (instantiated) operator and the OR-nodes are single ground atoms which can be generated by different (instantiated) operators. However, how long should we grow this tree and what paths are relevant in this tree? Further, if we select paths in the AND-OR tree, what should we do with the nodes on the selected paths? Finally, how can we make sure that growing this tree does not result in an exponential explosion?

In the GRAPHPLAN system, these questions are answered as follows. Grow the tree as long as new ground atoms are produced, consider all paths as relevant and take all ground atoms on these paths as relevant. Finally, since a fixpoint computation is used instead of creating the tree explicitly, the computational costs are bounded polynomially in the number of ground atoms. While this is an efficient and safe strategy, since it does not exclude any solution, it is also very weak. In almost all cases we considered, it does not lead to any reduction in computational costs.

A heuristic guiding the planning process should be *efficient* and *solution preserving*, i.e., it should not exclude possible solutions. Since determining relevant information in planning is usually as hard as planning itself, satisfying both requirements probably leads to quite weak heuristics as in the case of the GRAPHPLAN system. We propose a heuristic based on minimizing the use of initial facts when backchaining from the goals to the initial facts, which is similar to McDermott's *greedy regression graph* heuristic. Based on that, we determine the information which is most likely relevant for the planning process. This heuristic is not solution preserving, but it is computationally very efficient and turns out to be quite effective for a large number of domains. Further, for McDermott's [9,10] *grid world* examples and for a number of examples used by Kautz and Selman [7], our heuristics proved to be very effective, reducing GRAPHPLAN's planning time significantly.

The rest of the paper is structured as follows. The next section discusses the notion of "relevance" and "irrelevance" in plan generation. In Section 3, we then show the effects "irrelevant information" can have on different planning systems. A family of heuristics to determine potentially useful information from the description of a planning task is described in Section 4, and the empirical results of applying these heuristics to a large number of examples are given in Section 5. In Section 6 we discuss the results and conclude.

2 What is "Irrelevant" in Plan Generation?

Sometimes it is intuitively obvious that a planning task description contains irrelevant information. For example, if in a STRIPS [5] blocks-worlds planning task the blocks can have a color, then the colors are irrelevant – provided the goal description does not mention colors or if there are no operators to paint blocks.

There are more subtle cases, however. For example, if a block can be painted while the robot holds it and if the goal description contains information that the color of the block should be the same as in the initial state. Of course, the painting operation is irrelevant. However, it is not obvious how to detect this in a domain-independent way.

An even more subtle case is a blocks-world planning task with a number of additional blocks sitting on the table which are not mentioned in the goal description. These blocks are clearly irrelevant for finding a plan of stacking the relevant blocks, but they are considered by plan generation systems, leading to serious performance problems.

Trying to make the notions of *relevance* and *irrelevance* more concrete, one notes that there are at least two levels on which we can discuss these notions. First of all, there is the *external level*. A planning task description may contain type information, initial facts, and operators that are not needed for a solution.[1] Secondly, we can consider the *internal level* of the planning system. Here, we can consider ground operators or ground facts as relevant or irrelevant. In the following, we refer to operators, type information, initial facts, other ground facts, and instantiated operators as **pieces of information**.

Regardless of the level and the type of information, one can distinguish between different degrees of irrelevance. First of all, a piece of information may never be part of any solution for a given planning task, i.e., it is **completely irrelevant**. Secondly, a piece of information may appear in some plans, but it is not necessary for generating a plan. We call this **solution irrelevance**. If plan length is an issue, one can define the notion of **solution-length irrelevance** in a similar way. Unfortunately, however, these "semantic" notions of irrelevance are

---

[1] The goal description is, of course, never irrelevant!

computationally as hard as planning itself, at least for the case of propositional STRIPS, which is PSPACE-complete [3,1].

Theorem 1. *For propositional* STRIPS, *deciding* complete irrelevance *and* solution irrelevance *of a piece of information in a planning task description is* PSPACE-*complete under polynomial Turing-reductions.*[2]

Proof sketch. Membership in PSPACE follows from the following simple facts. A fact or operator is *solution-irrelevant*, if its removal does not change the plan existence property, which is in PSPACE, i.e., two calls to an oracle deciding plan existence suffice to decide solution irrelevance. Further, a fact or operator is *completely irrelevant* if adding something to the planning task that makes the fact or operator necessary for achieving the goals changes the plan existence property.

PSPACE-hardness of *solution irrelevance* follows, since by adding an operator or fact to a planning task description that must be used in any plan, we can decide plan existence of the original problem by deciding solution irrelevance of the new piece of information in the modified problem.

PSPACE-hardness of complete irrelevance follows because plan existence can be decided by deciding complete irrelevance of all facts or operators. ∎

Approaching the notion of irrelevance from a more syntactic point of view, we consider the process of *chaining* between ground facts. We say that a fact φ **generates** ψ iff there is an operator o that can be instantiated to a (type-consistent) ground operator g in a way such that φ is a precondition of g and ψ is an add-effect of g. Based on this definition we say that φ_0 is **reachable by backchaining** from φ_n iff there exists a sequence of facts $\varphi_0, \varphi_1, \ldots, \varphi_n$ such that φ_i generates φ_{i+1}. Similarly, φ_n is **reachable by forward-chaining** from φ_0 iff φ_0 is reachable by backchaining from φ_n.

Using these notions, one can distinguish between *goal irrelevance* and *initial-state irrelevance*. A piece of information is **goal irrelevant** if it cannot be reached by backchaining from the goals, and a piece of information is **initial-state irrelevant** if it cannot be reached by forward-chaining from the initial state. Both notions imply complete irrelevance and are easily computable. GRAPHPLAN can filter out both kinds of irrelevant information. Initial-state irrelevant information is filtered out in building the planning graph, goal irrelevant information can be filtered out by using an option that leads to computing the ground facts reachable by backchaining from the goals. However, as pointed out above, these notions are also very weak and do not cover the more subtle cases mentioned in the beginning of this section.

3   Empirical Effects of Irrelevance

As mentioned in the Introduction, one would expect that traditional backward-chaining planners will have less difficulties with solution-irrelevant pieces of in-

---

[2] Using an appropriate definition for solution-length, one could prove the same for solution-length irrelevance.

formation than the GRAPHPLAN system. In order to test this hypothesis, we set up two sets of modified blocks-world planning tasks.

In the first set, we added colors and a paint operation to the blocks world, where the paint operation has three parameters, namely the block, its previous color, and its new color. Further, painting can only be performed if the robot holds the block. Finally, we specify in the initial conditions that all blocks are white and require in the goal description that they are still white. In the second set of examples, we took ordinary blocks-world planning tasks and added superfluous blocks that sit on the table and are clear. In both sets we varied the number of relevant blocks and the number of irrelevant details, i.e., colors and superfluous blocks.

The results[3] shown in Fig. 1 seem to confirm the hypothesis that backward-chaining planners such as UCPOP[4] are not as much affected as GRAPHPLAN by solution-irrelevant information.[5] The number of colors in a planning task description does not seem to affect the search process of UCPOP at all, while the colors seem to present a problem for GRAPHPLAN. Further, the effect of superfluous blocks for UCPOP is much less dramatic than for the GRAPHPLAN-system.

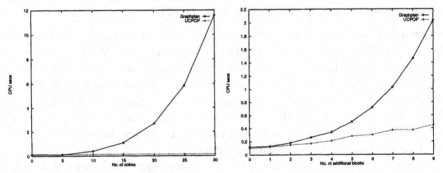

Fig. 1. CPU time for stacking 2 blocks when colors or other blocks are present

These results are quite interesting in themselves because they demonstrate that there are cases where UCPOP can outperform GRAPHPLAN. Having a closer look at GRAPHPLAN, one notes that the increase of runtime is mainly caused by the effort to generate the planning graph. In other words, the conjecture that creating a planning graph in a forward-chaining manner can lead to performance problems in the presence of irrelevant information seems to be justified. However, if we vary the number of relevant pieces of information as well, the picture changes. In Fig. 2, the x-axis measures the number of relevant blocks (note the log-scale for the CPU time).

---

[3] These and the following results were obtained by a single trial for each data point on a SPARCstation 4/110 with 64MB main memory.

[4] In all our experiments, we used the *zlifo* search strategy [6].

[5] Note that the colors are not goal-irrelevant because colors are mentioned in the goal description. For this reason, GRAPHPLAN cannot detect their irrelevance.

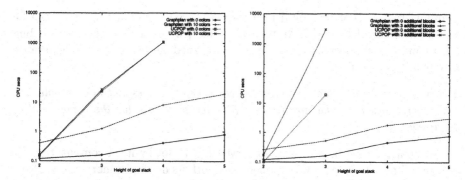

Fig. 2. CPU time for stacking n blocks when colors or other blocks are present

Although GRAPHPLAN seems to be affected by irrelevance in our examples much more than UCPOP, GRAPHPLAN is so much faster that this does not matter. Nevertheless, GRAPHPLAN's sensitivity to irrelevance can be quite serious. For example, a blocks-world planning task with eight blocks and ten colors cannot be solved by GRAPHPLAN without recompiling the planning system using a larger data structure for storing nodes in the planning graph. Further, in the examples with irrelevant blocks, the memory requirements grow with number of blocks regardless of whether the blocks are relevant or not. Since those memory requirements are so severe that they can fill up the memory of ordinary workstations with 64 MB even for planning tasks containing only 15 blocks, any attempt to reduce memory consumption is worthwhile. Finally, the runtime requirements grow with the total number of blocks. In fact, 15 blocks seemed to be the maximum number of blocks GRAPHPLAN could handle in one hour for our example set. So, removing any single irrelevant block can help in making a planning task practically solvable.

4 Selecting Relevant Information by Backchaining and Minimizing the Use of Initial Facts

As sketched above, one can straight-forwardly create top-down expectations in the planning process by backchaining from the goals creating an AND-OR-tree, where the AND-nodes are sets of ground facts (goals or the preconditions of an action) and the OR-nodes are single ground facts that can be generated by different operators. We call such a tree a **fact-generation tree**.

An OR-node of a fact-generation tree is considered to be **solved** if it is an initial fact or if one of its immediate children is solved. An AND-node is solved if all of its children are solved. The entire fact-generation tree is solved if the AND-node corresponding to the goals is solved. The fact-generation tree can be grown until it is solved or a preset depth is reached without a solution.

This is a very crude approximation to the planning process because the state of the world and delete-effects of operators are completely ignored. However, it provides us with a straight-forward and sound method for deciding that a planning task cannot be solved in d steps (where non-conflicting steps can be executed in parallel as in GRAPHPLAN). In fact, we used this method to debug our planning task specifications, which often turned out to be unsolvable because of trivial typing errors.

Proposition 2. *If a fact-generation tree of depth d does not have a solution, then there does not exist any $\lfloor (d-1)/2 \rfloor$-step plan to solve the corresponding planning task.*

Although the method is straight-forward, it is not by itself computationally efficient. Since the tree grows exponentially with its depth, memory and runtime costs can be quite high even for moderate branching and depth. *Memoizing* the results for each ground fact together with the level in the tree and reusing the result if the new search node is as close to the leave nodes as the memoized results makes the process more efficient.[6] With memoizing, every ground fact will be created at most once per OR-level in the search tree, restricting the number of explored nodes polynomially in the depth of the tree and the size of the instantiated planning task description.

Proposition 3. *Creating a fact-generation tree of depth d can be done in time polynomial in $d \times n \times m$, where n is the number of ground facts and m is the number of ground operators.*

While it suffices to propagate the values *true* and *false* in a fact-generation tree in order to detect unsolvability, we need more sophisticated ways to compute a solution if we want to compute the pieces of information that are probably relevant for the planning process. The idea is to determine a **minimum set of initial facts** (i.e., a set with a minimal number of elements) that are necessary to solve the fact-generation tree. Since there are in general different ways to generate a fact, we determine for every AND- and OR-node the set of sets of initial facts that could be used to generate this particular node. We call these sets of sets **possibility sets**.

In order to illustrate this idea, we present a small artificial example. STRIPS-operators will be written as

$$N : P \rightsquigarrow A/D,$$

where N is the name of the operator, P is the set of preconditions, A is the set of add-effects, and D is the set of delete-effects. We use the following set of operators:

$$O1: \{a, b\} \rightsquigarrow \{x, z\} \, / \, \{a\}$$
$$O2: \{b, c\} \rightsquigarrow \{x\} \quad / \, \emptyset$$
$$O3: \quad \{c\} \rightsquigarrow \{y\} \quad / \, \{c\}$$

Further, we assume that $\{a, b, c\}$ is the set of initial facts and $\{x, y\}$ is the set of goals. Then, as demonstrated in Fig. 3, the possibility set for the goals is $\{\{a, b, c\}, \{b, c\}\}$, and the minimum set of initial facts that solves the fact-generation tree is $\{b, c\}$.

---

[6] This means, we effectively create a directed graph instead of a tree.

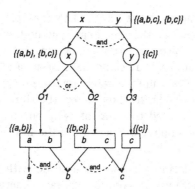

Fig. 3. Example for computing a minimum set of initial facts that can be used to solve the fact-generation tree

The computation of such possibility sets is computationally expensive, however. At each AND-node, the elements of the possibility set result from computing the union over all choices of picking elements from the possibility sets of the OR-nodes immediately below the AND-node. For example, the possibility set of the AND-node $\boxed{x\ y}$ in Fig. 3 is obtained by computing $\{a, b\} \cup \{c\}$ and $\{b, c\} \cup \{c\}$. In general, we may get a possibility set at an AND-node with a number of elements that is the product of the cardinalities of the sets at the OR-nodes immediately below the AND-node. This implies that the number of elements of these sets can grow exponentially with the breadth and depth of the fact-generation tree. Further, there does not seem to be an easy way out here. The problem of computing a minimum set of initial facts solving the fact-generation tree is a computationally hard problem.

Theorem 4. *Computing a minimum set of initial facts that solves a fact-generation tree is* NP-*hard for propositional* STRIPS.

Proof sketch. Follows by a straight-forward reduction of the *hitting set* problem to the problem at hand. ∎

Since the computation of minimum sets of initial facts that are necessary for solving the fact-generation tree is intended to be a heuristic for determining the relevance of pieces of information, we are not forced to compute all elements of a possibility set, however. Further, even non-optimal sets of initial facts can be useful. For this reason, we use a crude approximation. At every node we store only the 10 smallest sets computed so far.

Having computed the (approximation of a) possibility set for the goals, there is the question of what to do with the result. First of all, we must decide what to do in case the possibility set has more than one element. Different methods are conceivable:

1. use the union over all elements in the possibility set,
2. use the union over all set-inclusion minimal sets,
3. use the union over all minimum sets, or
4. pick a minimum set.

Running the heuristic on all the GRAPHPLAN examples and some other examples revealed that most of the time the fourth method, which we call **one-best-set** method, is a good choice. Sometimes, however, this led to longer plans than necessary, because resources that could have been used were removed. Worse yet, in the *rocket* examples it unfortunately removes one rocket so that the planning task becomes unsolvable. In those cases, the third method, which we call **all-best-sets** method, proved to be a safe way out. Finally, for some of McDermott's *grid world* examples, we had to use the first method, called **all-sets** method.

Secondly, we must decide what we want to do with this **set of probably relevant initial facts**. Since the creation of a fact-generation tree is only a very crude approximation of the planning process, initial facts that are necessary for solving the planning task might have been missed. We used three methods of selecting "probably relevant" pieces of information with an increasing degree of restriction:

1. Consider all *objects* mentioned in the set of probably relevant initial facts as relevant and filter out initial facts that contain irrelevant objects.
2. Consider only the *initial facts* in the set of probably relevant initial facts as relevant.
3. Consider only those *ground operators* as relevant that appear in the fact-generation tree and can be generated by the set of probably relevant initial facts.

These methods can be justified as follows. In domains containing a graph that has to be traversed (e.g., McDermott's [9] *Manhattan world*), where undirected edges are represented by pairs of initial facts, often only the first method is useful. The second method is useful if the fact-generation tree is similar to a final plan in that it makes use of all the relevant initial facts. The third method is useful if in building the fact-generation tree all ground operators are used that are necessary for the real plan.

It turned out that for different planning domains different strategies are effective. In the blocks-world domain, for example, a solved fact-generation tree often contains all the necessary ground operators to solve the planning task. In general, it seems to be a good *meta-heuristic* to try the third strategy first, since if it is unsuccessful, GRAPHPLAN fails fast. Then one should try the second and then the first strategy. Since determining the set of "probably relevant initial facts" is also only approximate, this sequence should be interleaved with the *one best set* and *all best sets* strategies described above. In case, we do not get a solution in this way, one may still run the planner on the original problem. In this way, we get (theoretical) completeness although the family of heuristics itself is not solution preserving (see also [4]).

5 Empirical Results

We implemented the family of heuristics described above as a C-program that can be used as a filter for GRAPHPLAN,[7] and tested them on a large set of examples. Applying our heuristics to the examples in Section 3 revealed that they effectively remove the irrelevant information in our blocks-world planning tasks. The CPU time of GRAPHPLAN on the problems and the CPU time of the heuristics combined with GRAPHPLAN are shown in Fig. 4.

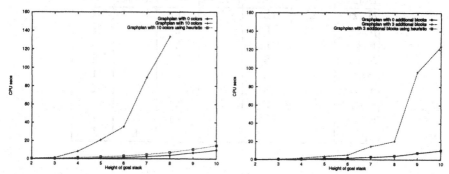

Fig. 4. Graphplan CPU time for stacking n blocks when colors or other blocks are present and when using the heuristic

In order to get an idea of how the heuristics behave on different domains, we ran them on the GRAPHPLAN examples. Runtime is not an issue here, because all problem are solved in a few seconds. More interesting is the question whether the heuristics are *solution-length preserving* or *solution preserving*. An answer to this question is given in Table 1.

In 55% of all examples, it was feasible to use the ground operators that appear in the fact-generation tree basing the selection on the one-best-set method. If the all-best-sets method is used, 86% of the examples could be solved. In case of the *logistics* and *mblocks* domains, however, basing the selection on *one best set* leads to longer plans, because useful resources are removed. In the *rockets* domain, the removal of one of the rockets leads to unsolvability.[8] Even worse is the *tsp* domain. Here, we have to base the selection of relevant information on the *objects* that appear in the set of probably relevant initial facts. The reason is that the undirected edges in the graph are represented by two ground facts, standing for two directed edges. In building the fact-generation tree, however, often only one of those facts is used, i.e., we only traverse the edge in one direction, while in the final plan we must also use the other direction.

More interesting planning tasks are, of course, those that are hard for GRAPH-PLAN. One such set of hard tasks is the test set that has been used to demonstrate

---

[7] The program can be obtained from the authors.

[8] If in the planning task description one could distinguish between usable resources and the initial state information, the heuristic would have a much better way to decide what is relevant.

Table 1. Solution- and solution-length preserving properties of the different heuristics for different domains. An "S" means that the particular heuristic did not change the solution-existence property for all the examples considered, an "L" means that the plans have the same length. If the letter is in parentheses, it means that some examples did not have the property.

	select ground operators		select initial facts		select objects	
	one best set	all best sets	one best set	all best sets	one best set	all best sets
Domain						
blocks	(L)	(L)	L	L	L	L
fixit	L	L	L	L	L	L
fridge	L	L	L	L	L	L
link	S	S	S	S	S	S
logistics	S	L	S	L	S	L
mblocks		S	S	L	S	L
monkey	L	L	L	L	L	L
rocket		(L)		(L)		L
tsp					L	L

the performance of SATPLAN [7]. The results for applying our heuristics are given in Table 2.

Table 2. Time steps and actions of generated plan and CPU time on a Sun Ultra 1/170 needed for plan generation on SATPLAN examples. "–" indicates that no solution was found.

	GRAPHPLAN		GRAPHPLAN with heuristic selecting ground operators				GRAPHPLAN with heuristic selecting initial facts			
			one best set		all best sets		one best set		all best sets	
Task	time /act.	CPU secs	time /act.	CPU secs	time /act.	CPU secs	time /act.	CPU secs	time /act.	CPU secs
rocket_ext.a	7/34	107	–	0.2	–	0.2	8/27	0.4	7/34	108
rocket_ext.b	7/30	498	–	0.2	–	0.3	10/29	17	7/30	499
logistics.a	11/54	1954	13/51	928	11/54	1654	13/51	3355	11/54	1955
logistics.b	13/45	767	15/42	218	13/45	655	15/42	707	13/45	768
bw_large.a	12/12	1.8	12/12	0.8	12/12	0.8	12/12	0.9	12/12	0.9
bw_large.b	18/18	319	18/18	26	18/18	26	18/18	44	18/18	44

Although the planning tasks descriptions were not intentionally designed to have irrelevant information in it, it turned out that the bw_large examples contain irrelevant facts. Further, also the logistics and rocket_ext examples contain more initial facts than necessary to generate a solution. However, in these cases the facts correspond to resources which, if removed, lead to longer plans. In any case, applying the heuristics seems to pay off on this set of examples. If too much information is removed, GRAPHPLAN is very fast in detecting this. Further, overall planning time is reduced in almost all cases.

Another interesting planning task is McDermott's [9] *Manhattan world* example.[9] GRAPHPLAN cannot handle it because the memory requirements are too high. Even on an SunUltra I workstation with 1 GB memory, GRAPHPLAN could not find a plan and failed with a memory overflow after 24 CPU hours. Applying our heuristic to the *Manhattan world* example (using *one-best-sets* with *relevant objects* for filtering) returned a reduced planning task after 14 CPU seconds on a Sun Ultra 1/170 . Running GRAPHPLAN on this reduced task resulted in a plan with length 40 after another 12 CPU seconds.[10] McDermott [10] reported that his UNPOP planner needs 16 CPU minutes on average to find a plan with an average length of 52.[11] We also ran our heuristics on the *Sokoban* examples suggested by J. Eckerle and adapted by McDermott [10] with similar results.

6 Discussion and Conclusion

Starting from the observation that the GRAPHPLAN system is highly sensitive to irrelevant information in the planning task description, we developed a family of heuristics aimed at identifying relevant information. These heuristics are very similar to McDermott's [9] *greedy regression graph* heuristic. Minor differences are that AND-nodes are completely instantiated in our case while they may contain variables in McDermott's system. Further, McDermott uses best-first search or discrepancy-search, while we used a simple iterative deepening search. One main difference is that we base our selection on minimum sets of initial facts necessary to solve the fact-generation tree, while McDermott bases his selection on the minimal number of actions. The most striking difference is, however, that we run our heuristic once before planning starts, while McDermott uses his heuristic each time before extending the plan by an action. Nevertheless, our approach results in quite reliable predictions most of the time.

Despite its simplicity, the heuristics turned out to be very useful. In many domains, the most constraining heuristic gives solution-preserving results and reduces planning time considerably. Further, the heuristic enables GRAPHPLAN to find plans for McDermott's *grid world* examples.

Although we used the heuristic only in combination with GRAPHPLAN, it can, of course, be combined with any other planner based on the STRIPS formalism such as SATPLAN [7]. We already extended the heuristics to deal with conditional

---

[9] We used a representation of the domain tailored to GRAPHPLAN, e.g., the conditional operators are transformed to a set of unconditional operators. Further the grid is encoded as a graph so that our heuristic can identify probably relevant objects.

[10] McDermott [9] claimed that 43 steps is the optimum for the example, but in fact only 40 steps are necessary.

[11] McDermott's results were obtained on a SPARCstation 2, which is approximately 15 times slower than a Sun Ultra 1/170.

operators and integrated it in our extension of the GRAPHPLAN-planner [8] with promising results.

Acknowledgements

We would like to thank Alfonso Gerevini and the anonymous reviewers for comments on an earlier version of this paper.

References

1. C. Bäckström. Equivalence and tractability results for SAS$^+$ planning. In B. Nebel, W. Swartout, and C. Rich, editors, *Principles of Knowledge Representation and Reasoning: Proceedings of the 3rd International Conference (KR-92)*, pages 126–137, Cambridge, MA, Oct. 1992. Morgan Kaufmann.
2. A. L. Blum and M. L. Furst. Fast planning through planning graph analysis. *Artificial Intelligence*, 90(1-2):279–298, 1997.
3. T. Bylander. The computational complexity of propositional STRIPS planning. *Artificial Intelligence*, 69(1-2):165–204, 1994.
4. T. A. Estlin and R. J. Mooney. Multi-strategy learning of search control for partial order planning. In *Proceedings of the 13th National Conference of the American Association for Artificial Intelligence (AAAI-96)*, Portland, OR, July 1996. MIT Press.
5. R. E. Fikes and N. Nilsson. STRIPS: A new approach to the application of theorem proving to problem solving. *Artificial Intelligence*, 2:189–208, 1971.
6. A. Gerevini and L. Schubert. Accelerating partial-order planners: Some techniques for effective search control and pruning. *Journal of Artificial Intelligence Research*, 5:95–137, 1996.
7. H. A. Kautz and B. Selman. Pushing the envelope: Planning, propositional logic, and stochastic search. In *Proceedings of the 13th National Conference of the American Association for Artificial Intelligence (AAAI-96)*, pages 1194–1201, Portland, OR, July 1996. MIT Press.
8. J. Koehler, B. Nebel, J. Hoffmann, and Y. Dimopoulos. Extending planning graphs to an ADL subset. In *Proc. European Conference on Planning 1997*, Toulouse, France, September 1997.
9. D. McDermott. A heuristic estimator for means-ends analysis in planning. In *Proceedings of the 3rd International Conference on Artificial Intelligence Planning Systems (AIPS-96)*, pages 142–149. AAAI Press, Menlo Park, 1996.
10. D. McDermott. Using regression-match graphs to control search in planning. Manuscript submitted for publication, 1997.
11. J. S. Penberthy and D. S. Weld. UCPOP: A sound, complete, partial order planner for ADL. In B. Nebel, W. Swartout, and C. Rich, editors, *Principles of Knowledge Representation and Reasoning: Proceedings of the 3rd International Conference (KR-92)*, pages 103–114, Cambridge, MA, Oct. 1992. Morgan Kaufmann.

A Tabu Search Strategy to Solve Scheduling Problems with Deadlines and Complex Metric Constraints

Angelo Oddi * and Amedeo Cesta

IP-CNR
National Research Council of Italy
Viale Marx 15, I-00137 Rome, Italy
{oddi,amedeo}@pscs2.irmkant.rm.cnr.it

Abstract. In this paper a *Relaxable Metric Scheduling Problem* (*RMSP*) is defined that extends the classical job shop scheduling problem with the use of complex temporal metric constraints and with the possibility of making the distinction between *relaxable* and *not-relaxable* constraints explicit. The paper proposes and experimentally evaluates a *tabu search* procedure to improve a previously created heuristic solution to the *RMSP*. The tabu procedure uses the idea of relaxing some temporal constraints to "navigate" the search space and to find a solution. In particular, it tries to produce either a solution where there are no relaxations or a solution where only the constraints classified as relaxable are violated. Experimental results on scheduling problems of increasing size demonstrate the usefulness of the proposed approach.

1 Introduction

Scheduling problems are an important class of constraint satisfaction problems which have many practical applications [14]. A classical formalization of the problem, generated in the manufacturing domain, is the *Job Shop Scheduling Problem* (JSSP) [6], which involves synchronizing the production of *n jobs* in a facility with *m resources*. The production of a given job requires the execution of a sequence of operations (or activities). Each operation has a specific processing time and its execution requires the exclusive use of a designated resource. Each job has associated a ready time and a deadline, and its production must be accomplished within this interval. It is possible to formulate two versions of this problem with respect to the fact that deadlines and ready times are relaxable or not. The relaxable version of the problem models many practical applications where, rather than finding an exact solution (where all the constraints are satisfied), a solution which represents an agreement between conflicting constraints is searched. There are several motivations to choose this approach to solve a

---

* Part of this work was developed during the author's Ph.D. program in Medical Computer Science at the Department of Computer and System Science of the University of Rome "La Sapienza".

scheduling problem. Firstly, greedy heuristic methods are not infallible, and the possibility of search failure increases when the problem grows in size. Chronological backtracking is one possibility to find a solution in those cases, but its systematicity generally implies high computational cost. Secondly, it may be the case that there is no solution which satisfies all the original constraints, but at the same time some constraints are relaxable and the only possible solution is to find an agreement on the operated violations.

In the scheduling literature, two type of constraints are distinguished: *hard* and *soft* or not-relaxable and relaxable. Examples of relaxable time constraints are the deadlines of set of jobs in a factory domain or staff turns in a medical-resource domain. This type of constraints are generally relaxable because the people or things involved in the scheduling process can accept the violations at an additional cost, that is, the schedule is physically possible even if relaxations are not desirable. Other type of constraints cannot be relaxed. For example, in the HSTS domain (a scheduling problem for the Hubble Space Telescope [9]) the constraints imposed by the visibility of a star, in order to take its picture, cannot be relaxed for the simple motivation that the star could not be visible anymore. Another important issue is that sometimes JSSP is not enough to represent physical constraints in a work environment. For example, let us suppose to work in a medical domain, where jobs represent care protocols and activities are care units. In the hypothesis to consider a simple care protocol which represents two basic actions in order for a patient to take an X-ray: 1) to swallow a preparation to make some organs evident; 2) take an X-ray on the machine. A simple precedence constraint is not enough to represent the real constraints between the two previous actions. In fact, the preparation will be effective after a minimum time and it will become ineffective after a maximum time. A way to enrich the JSSP model is to introduce constraints on the jobs' activities where it is possible to impose that the difference in time between the end-time of an activity and the start-time of the next must be greater than (or equal to) a minimum value and less than (or equal to) a maximum value. Generally this type of constraints represents scheduling constraints which cannot be relaxed as in the example of the medical protocol.

In this paper, we propose and evaluate the use of a *tabu search* strategy for solving job shop scheduling problems with deadlines and complex metric constraints. The problem is also used in [3] where the authors developed highly effective, greedy heuristics for this class of problems based on simple measures of temporal sequencing flexibility, and in [12] where a set of stochastic procedures were proposed which are a randomized counterpart of the deterministic ones tested in [3]. The aim of this paper is to propose a method which is able to manage scheduling problems where it is unlikely to find a solution where all the constraints are satisfied. The tabu search algorithm will be used to "navigate" in the space of the relaxed solutions from an initial one, in order to find a further solution where the total amount of violations operated on the constraints is sensibly reduced and in particular all the violations on the hard constraints are removed.

The paper is organized as follows: Section 2 introduces the scheduling problem and reminds the basic temporal representation for a solution. Section 3 briefly introduces the greedy algorithm that builds an initial solution. Section 4 illustrates the basic idea to explore the space of the relaxed solution and gives the tabu search algorithm used to improve a solution. Section 5 proposes some experiments which show the usefulness of the search strategy introduced. Section 6 draws some conclusions.

2 Problem Definition

As we said in the previous Section, the problem solved in this paper was considered in [3, 12] in a version where constraints can not be violated. Here we consider a new definition of the problem called *Relaxable Metric Scheduling Problem* (RMSP) which involves synchronizing the use of a set of resources $R = \{r_1 \ldots r_m\}$ to perform a set of jobs $J = \{j_1 \ldots j_n\}$ over time. The processing of a job j_i requires the execution of a sequence of n_i activities $\{a_{i1} \ldots a_{in_i}\}$, and the execution of each activity a_{ij} is subject to a set of constraints that can be violated only in the case it is specifically indicated. The type of constraints are the following:

- *resource availability* - each a_{ij} requires exclusive use of a single resource $r_{a_{ij}}$ for its entire duration.
- *processing time constraints* - each a_{ij} has a minimum and maximum processing time, $proc_{ij}^{min}$ and $proc_{ij}^{max}$, such that $proc_{ij}^{min} \leq e(a_{ij}) - s(a_{ij}) \leq proc_{ij}^{max}$, where the variables $s(a_{ij})$ and $e(a_{ij})$ represent the start and end times respectively of a_{ij}.
- *separation constraints* - for each pair of successive activities a_{ij} and $a_{i(j+1)}$, $j = 1 \ldots (n_i - 1)$, in job j_i, there is a minimum and maximum separation time, sep_{ik}^{min} and sep_{ik}^{max}, such that $\{sep_{ik}^{min} \leq s(a_{i(k+1)}) - e(a_{ik}) \leq sep_{ik}^{max} : k = 1 \ldots (n_i - 1)\}$.
- *job release and due dates* - Every job j_i has a release date rd_i, which specifies the earliest time that any a_{ij} can be started, and a due date dd_i, which designates the time by which all a_{ij} must be completed. We suppose that this type of constraint can be violated in the final solution.

There are different ways to formulate this problem as a *Constraint Satisfaction Problem* (CSP). In [3, 12], the problem is treated as one of establishing precedence constraints between pairs of activities that require the same resource, so as to eliminate all possible conflicts in resource use. In CSP terms, a decision variable O_{ijr} is defined for each pair of activities a_i and a_j requiring resource r, which can take one of two values: $a_j\{before\}a_i$ or $a_i\{before\}a_j$. As we said above, in order to get a solution we can violate some constraints. With *violation* we indicate a tuple $(c, \delta_{lb}, \delta_{ub})$ where c is a constraint of the form $a \leq tp_j - tp_i \leq b$ and δ_{lb}, δ_{ub} are two values greater or equal to zero, such that, $0 \leq a - \delta_{lb} \leq b + \delta_{ub}$, which represent the amount of violation operated on the constraint c. We define as a *violated solution* a couple $< A, V >$, where $A = \{o_{ijr}\}$ is a set of assignments to the decision variables O_{ijr} consistent with all the time constraints (below we will give an exact definition of this concept) and $V = \{(c, \delta_{lb}, \delta_{ub})\}$ is a set of violations operated on the time constraints which make time-feasible the solution obtained. In other words, without the violations it should not be possible to order every set of activities which request the same resource. The problem is to determine a *feasible solution*, that is, a relaxed solution such that it satisfies all constraints which cannot be violated and the total amount of violation (the sum of the values δ_{lb} and δ_{ub}) on the other constraints is as low as possible.

2.1 Managing Temporal Information

To support the search for a consistent assignment to the set of decision variables O_{ijr} introduced above, we can define for any $RMSP$ a directed graph $TM(TP, E)$ called *time map* [4], where the set of nodes TP represents time-points or temporal variables (i.e., the origin point, the horizon point and the start and end time points, $s(a_i)$ and $e(a_i)$, of each activity a_i) and the set of edges E represents temporal distance constraints between couple of time-points (that is, the time constraints listed in the itemization of Section 2). Every temporal constraint has the general form $a \leq tp_j - tp_i \leq b$ and is represented in the graph $TM(TP, E)$ as a direct edge (tp_i, tp_j) with label $[a, b]$. Each time point $tp_i \in TP$ has associated an interval $[lb_i, ub_i]$ of the possible time instants, or temporal values, where the event associated to the time-points may happen. The time-point tp_1, the origin point, has associated the constant interval $[0, 0]$.

The graph $TM(TP, E)$ corresponds to a *Simple Temporal Problem* (STP) [5], the computation of the intervals $[lb_i, ub_i]$ and the check for problem's consistency (a problem is inconsistent when there exists at least an empty interval $[lb_i, ub_i]$) can be polynomially determined via shortest path computations on a directed graph $G_d(V_d, E_d)$ called *distance graph* [5]. The graph G_d is obtained from the time map $TM(TP, E)$ as follows: (a) the set of nodes $V_d = TP$; (b) the set of edges E_d is built from the set E considering for each constraint $a \leq tp_j - tp_i \leq b \in E$ two weighted edges in the set E_d: the first one directed from tp_i to tp_j with weight b, the second one directed from tp_j to tp_i with weight $-a$. In G_d the usual definitions of path and path's length on a weighted graph are assumed: a path is sequence of consecutive edges $(tp_1, tp_2), (tp_2, tp_3) \ldots (tp_{n-1}, tp_n)$; the length of a path is the sum of the weights associated to the sequence of edges. $d(i, 1)$ is the length of the shortest path on G_d from the time point tp_i to the origin point tp_1 and $d(1, i)$ is the length of the shortest path from the origin point tp_1 to the time point tp_i. A negative cycle is a closed path with negative length. As shown in [5], the interval $[lb_i, ub_i]$ of time values associated to the generic time variable tp_i is computed on the graph G_d as the interval $[-d(i, 1), d(1, i)]$. In [5] is also shown that an STP is consistent iff there are no negative cycles in its graph G_d.

A search for a solution to $RMSP$ can proceed by repeatedly adding new precedence constraints into TM in order to resolve conflicts in the use of resources and efficiently recomputing [1, 2, 11] shortest path lengths to confirm that TM (and G_d) remains consistent.

3 Finding an Initial Solution by Relaxing Constraints

A local search method works starting from an initial solution built with another method. The algorithm currently used to create the initial solution is a greedy procedure largely inspired by [3]. The algorithm iteratively selects decision variables O_{ijr} (which represent conflicts) and assigns them values on the basis of a measure of temporal flexibility leaved in the domain after the value of a variable is assigned. After a decision is taken, the temporal constraints are propagated and a new conflict is considered until all the decision variables have a fixed value. During the search process, it might happen that the domain of a decision variable becomes empty. This means that the insertion of a precedence constraint to resolve the conflict has induced temporal inconsistencies (a set of negative cycles on the graph G_d). The original algorithm described in [3] stops, because a *dead-end* is reached. On the contrary, the present greedy algorithm looks for a *violated solution*. It detects negative cycles in the distance graph, chooses one cycle and fixes it by relaxing a constraint on the cycle. When inserting relaxations the heuristic tries to maintain the solution as safe as possible. There are two mechanisms whose aim is to get an acceptable violated solution: the first one tries to minimize the amount of violations of the time constraints; the second one, uses a simple priority heuristic, which, in order to reduce the probability to get a violated solution, selects first relaxable time constraints, and in the case there is no one of the previous type, selects not-relaxable time constraints. For lack of space we are not able to insert a complete description of the algorithm which is included in [11].

4 A Tabu Search Approach to Improve a Solution

Tabu search [7, 8] is a local search approach recently applied with success to a large set of combinatorial optimization problems. In this Section we introduce a tabu search approach to solve the *RMSP*.

The tabu meta-heuristic is based of the notion of *move*. A move is a function which transforms one solution into another. For any solution S, a subset of moves applied to S is computed. The subset of moves produces a subset of solutions called the *neighborhood of S*. A tabu search algorithm starts from an initial solution S_0, and at each step i searches the neighborhood of the current solution in order to find a new solution (a neighbor) S_i that has the best value of a given objective function. At this point the neighbor S_i becomes the current solution and the search process is iterated to find a new best neighbor S_{i+1}. In order to prevent cycling, it is not allowed to turn back to solutions visited in the previous $MaxSt$ steps. Where $MaxSt$ is the max length of the so-called *tabu list*, a list of forbidden moves. Whenever a move from a current solution to its neighbor is made, the inverted move is inserted in the tail of the *tabu list* whose length is kept less or equal to $MaxSt$ by removing its head. During the search process, in order to find a near-optimal solution for the problem, at each step a "global" best solution S^* is updated. A tabu move might happen to be interesting with respect to the current solution. In order to perform this move, an *aspiration function* is defined which, under certain conditions, accepts a forbidden move. Generally, the definition of aspiration function is such that a forbidden move is accepted when it generates a neighbor which improve the solution S^*. The search process is performed until at least one of the following conditions becomes true: 1) the objective function of the solution is close to a known lower bound; 2) the algorithm performs $MaxIter$ steps without improving S^*; 3) a time limit is reached. To apply *tabu search* to a particular problem, the definition of structural elements, such as move, neighborhood, tabu list, aspiration function, etc., is needed. With respect to the classical job shop scheduling problem, the $RMSP$ uses a more sophisticated time model (the STP [5]). A tabu approach to $RMSP$ needs an extension of the algorithms presented in [10, 13] to deal with temporal information. Our tabu procedure extensively uses algorithms to modify the time map. To perform a move it is needed to remove some temporal constraints and add other ones. This is achieved by using incremental algorithms [2, 11] which work on the STP model and quite efficiently can add and remove temporal constraints in incremental style. At each modification they update only the part of the time map really affected by the change.

4.1   A Running Example

To explain the way our tabu procedure works we introduce an example. Let us consider a simple problem with two resources and two jobs, where each job has two activities. Figure 1 contains a representation of a violated solution for the problem but it is also useful to understand the problem formulation. To maintain the figure simple we have represented the time map instead of the graph G_d.

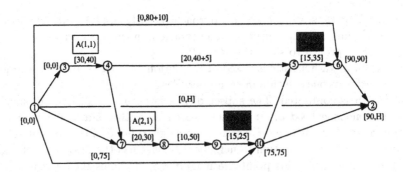

Fig. 1. A initial violated solution for the example

$A(i,j)$ means that activity A belongs to job job_i and is executed in position j. In Figure 1, white activities request the resource r_1, and grey activities request r_2. Time-points tp_1 and tp_2 represent the start and end of the time line (the origin point and horizon point). The edge (tp_1, tp_2) is the *horizon constraint* which constrains all the activities in a fixed time horizon of amplitude H (the exact value of H is not relevant here, we can suppose a value much greater than any deadline in the problem). The four activities $A(1,1)$, $A(1,2)$, $A(2,1)$ and $A(2,2)$ are depicted "anchored" to the *time map*. Each of them has a start and end time (for example, tp_3 and tp_4 are the start-time and end-time of $A(1,1)$). Edges (tp_3, tp_4), (tp_5, tp_6), (tp_7, tp_8) and (tp_9, tp_{10}) are the *time processing* constraints. Edges (tp_4, tp_5) and (tp_8, tp_9) are the *separation* constraints. Edges (tp_1, tp_3), (tp_1, tp_6), (tp_1, tp_7) and (tp_1, tp_{10}) are the *job release and due dates* constraints. All edges are labeled with intervals $[a, b]$, when these are not explicitly shown the default label $[0, H]$ should be assumed. Edges (tp_4, tp_7) and (tp_{10}, tp_5) included in Figure 1 are not part of the problem formulation but are inserted to resolve the conflicts in the use of resources. We can suppose to build a solution to the problem by inserting first the constraint (tp_4, tp_7) (without generating time inconsistencies) and second the constraint (tp_{10}, tp_5). In this latter case two negative cycles are induced on the graph G_d derived from the time map. The first one is $1 \to 6 \to 5 \to 10 \to 9 \to 8 \to 7 \to 4 \to 3 \to 1$ with length -10 can be canceled by changing the label 80 of (tp_1, tp_6) to the value $80 + 10$. The second one $4 \to 5 \to 10 \to 9 \to 8 \to 7 \to 4$ with length -5 can be removed by modifying the label 40 of the edge (tp_4, tp_5) to $40 + 5$. In this way we obtain the particular conflict-free *violated solution* in the figure.

4.2 Defining a Move in the *RMSP*

Similarly to [10, 13], a move in the *RMSP* is a transformation of a solution S by swapping a couple of activities (a_i, a_j) which require the same resource.

It is worth observing that the swap of two activities can generally create a state of temporal inconsistency in the time map. There are at least two ways to resolve this problem: either to only consider the subset of moves which do not produce time inconsistency, or to introduce some violations between the time constraints and try to repair such violations during the tabu search process to arrive again to a feasible solution. This second choice has the advantage of exploring more deeply the search space and will be used in the following, but at the same time, it is computationally more expensive, as can be seen observing the tabu algorithm below. The neighborhood of a solution S is a set of new solutions which may involve violations of time constraints. In the following we consider moves that swap activities (a_i, a_j) when the following conditions hold:

1. (a_i, a_j) are consecutive on the resource r;
2. (a_i, a_j) are on a shortest path in the graph G_d.

It is worth reminding that two activities are on a shortest path if considered the time points $e(a_i)$ and $s(a_j)$ or $e(a_j)$ and $s(a_i)$ on the graph G_d an edge exists which connects $e(a_i)$ and $s(a_j)$ or $e(a_j)$ and $s(a_i)$ and belongs to the shortest path either from or to the time origin tp_1.

A violation (Section 2) is a tuple $(c, \delta_{lb}, \delta_{ub})$, where c is a temporal constraint in the time map, δ_{lb} and δ_{ub} are the violations operated respectively on the lower and upper bound of the constraint's label $[a, b]$. Under the restrictions stated by Conditions 1 and 2 it is possible to prove [11] that the time inconsistencies can be removed by violating only the upper bounds of either a separation or a deadline constraints. In other words, we can consider only violations of the form $(c, 0, \delta_{ub})$ that can be written as (c, δ). In a similar way, a *restoration* is a couple (c, δ), where c is a temporal constraints and δ is the reduction value for the upper bound constraint to restore the original value.

With the previous assumptions the definition of *move* is the following:

Definition 1. Given a violated solution, a move mv on a resource r is defined as the tuple $(r, acts, rlx, res)$, where $acts$ is a couple of activities (a_i, a_j) which satisfies Condition 1 and 2, $rlx = \{(c_i, \delta_i)\}$ is a set of violations on the time constraints and $res = \{(c_j, \delta_j)\}$ is a set of possible restorations operated after the swap of the couple of activities.

The definition does not specify a method to violate and restore constraints, this is a matter of the specific heuristics adopted. The previous definition is general enough to be applied with the STP temporal model.

4.3 The Tabu Search Algorithm

In Figure 2 the tabu search algorithm for the $RMSP$ is shown that manages an initial solution S_0. As input the algorithm is given the initial solution S_0, the parameters $MaxIter$ and $MaxSt$, and the objective functions f_{obj}. The algorithm uses two variables S^* and S_{min}, which represent respectively the current optimal solution and the best solution found in the exploration of a neighborhood. In the case the algorithm explores a sequence of $MaxIter$ neighborhood without an improvement of the solution S^*, then the algorithm stops (Step 2). A neighborhood is searched between Steps 4 and 10, where is found the solution S_{min}. The idea of *aspiration function* is implemented at Step 8 where a tabu move is accepted in the case it improves S^* and the current S_{min}. Finally, when a solution S_{min} is found, the move $move_{min}$ is added to the *tabu-list* (Step 13) and the variable S^* is updated.

The core of the algorithm consists of the two sub-primitives *Get-Neigth-Moves* and *Make-Move*.

The *Get-Neigth-Moves* implements the definition of neighborhood. By using Definition 1 two different neighborhoods are introduced: (a) the set of moves is computed for each resource. This choice analyzes deeply the search space, but at the same time is quite expensive; (b) the set of moves is computed only for a randomly selected resource .

The procedure *Make-Move* makes the swap of the couple of activities (a_i, a_j) specified by the move mv. It is essentially composed by a sequence of application of three primitives that work on the time-map: *Remove, Insert-with-Relax* and *Restore-Heuristic*. To explain how the procedure works we use Figure 3 in which a swap is performed between activities $A(1, 2)$ and $A(2, 2)$ starting from the solution of Figure 1.

The *Make-Move(mv)* performs the following steps:

TABU-STP$(S_0, MaxIter, MaxSt, f_{obj})$
1. $S^* ::= S_0; S_{min} ::= S_0;$
2. **while not**(Last-Iteration($MaxIter$)) **do begin**
3.   Get-Neigth-Moves(S_{min});
4.   **while not**(Neighborhood-Empty) **do begin**
5. $move ::=$ Select-Move(S_{min});
6. $S_{curr} ::=$ Make-Move($move$);
7.   **if** Tabu-Move($move$)
8.   **then if** Aspiration-Func($S_{curr}, S^*, S_{min}, f_{obj}$) **then** $S_{min} ::= S_{curr}$
9.   **else if** Improves($S_{curr}, S_{min}, f_{obj}$) **then** $S_{min} ::= S_{curr}$
10.   **end**
11. **if** Improves(S_{min}, S^*, f_{obj})
12.   **then begin**
13.   Update-Tabu-List($move_{min}, MaxSt$)
14. $S^* ::= S_{min}$
15.   **end**
16. **end**

Fig. 2. TABU-STP algorithm

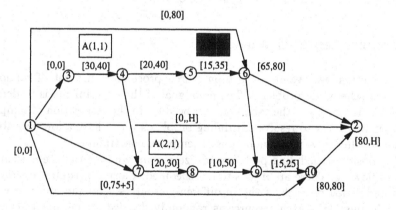

Fig. 3. Feasible solution obtained after the swap of the activities $A(1,2)$ and $A(2,2)$

1. *Remove*: it incrementally deletes time constraints from the time map. In the example the constraint (tp_{10}, tp_5) is removed.
2. *Insert-with-Relax*: it tries to insert a precedence constraint between a couple of time-points. If the insertion gives a consistent situation it stops, otherwise (when a time inconsistency is detected) the procedure iteratively: (1) gets one of the negative cycle created on the graph G_d; (2) selects a constraint on the negative cycle and relaxes it; (3) propagates the effect of the relaxation in the graph G_d. The previous sequence of steps continues until all the negative cycles induced by the insertion on the precedence constraints are deleted

and a time-feasible solution is reached. In the example, the new constraint (tp_6, tp_9) is inserted and the effects are propagated in the time map. The new insertion generates a time inconsistency. In fact, the negative cycle $1 \rightarrow 10 \rightarrow 9 \rightarrow 6 \rightarrow 5 \rightarrow 4 \rightarrow 3 \rightarrow 1$ is induced whose length is -5 . This inconsistency can be resolved by relaxing one or more constraints along the cycle. The same criterion explained in Section 3 is used, the algorithm selects the label 75 on the constraint (tp_1, tp_{10}) and relaxes it to the value $75 + 5$.

3. *Restore-Heuristic*: it tries to restore the original constraint by scanning the set of violations V operated on the solution. For each element (c, δ), where c has the form $a \leq tp_j - tp_i \leq b$, it tries to insert the new constraint $a \leq tp_j - tp_i \leq b - \delta$. If the insertion is consistent the element (c, δ) is deleted from the set V, otherwise the method tries to repair the next violation. In the example, the labels on constraints (tp_1, tp_6) and (tp_4, tp_5) are restored to the original values, in fact the modification of the network removes both the negative cycles mentioned in Section 4.1.

The solution obtained in the example is now feasible, because as a consequence of the move also the separation constraint (tp_4, tp_5) is restored to the original value. The only relaxed constraint in the new solution is a deadline constraint that is feasible according to the definition of $RMSP$.

5 Experimental Evaluation

In this Section, we evaluate the tabu search procedure on a set of randomly generated scheduling problems. The main goal of the experiments is to demonstrate the usefulness of the tabu search procedure in the restoration of temporal constraints. We try to resolve scheduling problems which have a low probability to have a solution without violations of temporal constraints.

We consider scheduling problems of size $n \times m$, whose structure is sketched in the following. There are n jobs to be scheduled. Each job requires operations to be performed on each of the m different resources, and the order in which each job must visit each resource is randomly decided. Experiments concern problem sets of 50 instances at each of three different sizes: 8×3, 12×3 and 12×4. The problem sets are generated following the generation scheme used in [3] adapted to generate particularly hard instances. We indicate with $U[x, y]$ a random number in the interval $[x, y]$ generated with a uniform distribution. The minimum processing time of activities is chosen as $U[10, 50]$, and the maximum processing time is generated by multiplying the minimum processing time by the value $(1+p)$, where $p = U[0, 0.4]$. Separation constraints $[a, b]$ between every two consecutive operations in a job are generated with $a = U[0, 10]$ and $b = U[40, 50]$. All the ready times rd_i of the jobs are fixed to 0 and the deadlines dd_i are fixed to a common value M. The value of M is calculated by the follow formula $M = (n - 1)p_{bk} + \sum_{i=1}^{m} p_i$, where p_{bk} is the average minimum processing time of operation on the bottleneck resource, and p_i is the average minimum processing time of operation on resource r_i. The bottleneck resource is the resource with maximum value of the sum of the minimum processing time of the activities which requests the resource. In order to generate hard scheduling problems with a low probability to have an "exact solution", we have introduced a parameter called *Slack* which controls the amplitude of the allocation windows of the jobs (see Section 2) $[rd_i, dd_i]$. In practice, the real windows for a job j_i is $[Slack * rd_i, Slack * dd_i]$. For *Slack* we have used the value 0.8. This is used to shrink the original time window to make the satisfaction of the constraints harder.

In the experiments we use the following objective function:

$$f_{obj}(S) = \alpha_{sep} v_{sep}(S) + \alpha_{dl} v_{dl}(S)$$

where $v_{sep}(S)$ represents the sum of the violation values on the separation constraints and $v_{dl}(S)$ represents the sum of the violation values on the deadline constraints. α_{sep} and α_{dl} are numeric coefficients whose aim is to focus the tabu search on a specific type of violation. In these experiments we fixed $\alpha_{sep} = 8$ e $\alpha_{dl} = 1$, in order to focus the procedure on the restoration of separation constraints. Finally, we complete the setting of tabu parameters as follows. For each class of problem $MaxSt$ is 9. For problems 8×3 $MaxIter$ is 9; for problems 12×3 $MaxIter$ is 36 and for problems 12×4: $MaxIter$ is 72.

As said in Section 4.3 two different definitions of neighborhood are used. For problems 8×3, the neighborhood of a solution is the set of moves that satisfy Definition 1. As we have said, this choice analyzes deeply the search space, but at the same time it is time expensive and we can use it only on small problems. For problems 12×3 and 12×4, the neighborhood is built by considering only the moves on a randomly chosen resource.

The procedure and the experimental setting were implemented in *Allegro Common Lisp* on a SUN Sparc 10 workstation. Table 1 shows the results obtained for the three different classes of problem. For each class results are shown relative to: (a) the application of the heuristic method described in Section 3 (lines labeled HEU); (b) the application of the tabu procedure to the previous solution (lines labeled TABU). Lines labeled with $\Delta\%$ simply show the percent variations of the results obtained before and after the application of the tabu procedure. Each line labeled with HEU or TABU reports the following data: N_r denotes the number of instances which have violations on the time constraints; N_{sep} denotes the number of instances which have violations on the separation constraints; N_{dl} denotes the number of instances which have violations on the deadline constraints; R_{sep} denotes the average amount of violations (in time units) operated on the separation constraints; R_{dl} denotes the average amount of violations (in time units) operated on the deadline constraints; *CPU-time* denotes, in seconds, the average cpu-time needed to produce the solution.

The lines labeled with $\Delta\%$ show the usefulness of the tabu procedure on highly constrained scheduling problems. In particular, column N_{sep} shows that the tabu procedure makes respectively feasible 90%, 82% and 64% of the unacceptable initial solutions. Moreover, even if all the problems presents violations on the deadlines constraints, in the case of problems 8×3 and 12×3, the value R_{dl} is reduced.

Table 1. *TABU-STP*'s performance on 8 × 3, 12 × 3 and 12 × 4 problem sets

Problem	Strategy	N_r	N_{sep}	N_{dl}	R_{sep}	R_{dl}	CPU-time(sec)
	HEU	50	39	50	54.3	77.9	5.8
8 × 3	TABU	50	4	50	21.7	55.8	44.4
	Δ%	0	90.0	0	60.0	28.0	-
	HEU	50	40	50	58.5	162.9	27.5
12 × 3	TABU	50	7	50	5.0	152.3	142.9
	Δ%	0	82.0	0	91.0	6.0	-
	HEU	50	44	50	101.5	210.1	62.9
12 × 4	TABU	50	16	50	16.6	221.4	498.6
	Δ%	0	64	0	84.0	-5.0	-

Observing the cpu-times shown in Table 1, it is quite evident that the algorithms are computationally expensive. This is mainly due to the explicit consideration of metric constraints. In the heuristic method HEU, the main source of time complexity is the update of the array of distances $d(i, j)$. This array is extensively used to build an effective method [3, 11] to solve scheduling problems with metric constraints. Every time a new conflict is resolved, $d(i, j)$ is updated, and in the case some constraints are violated, this is done by a sequence of operations of constraints detection, relaxation and updating of the array $d(i, j)$. The last sequence of operations is quite expensive with respect to the situation where no violation is allowed. For example, in the case of instances of problems 12 × 4 which does not need violations the average solution time should be about 10-15 seconds instead of 62 seconds.

As far as the tabu search algorithm is concerned we observe that these results are not definitive, they represent an intermediate step towards a more elaborate tabu search strategy to effectively scale on larger problems. Here we have introduced a methodology to cope with the problem and demonstrated the usefulness of the definition of *move* given in an STP framework.

6   Conclusions

The aim of this paper is to present the application of a tabu strategy to solve scheduling problems which need the STP temporal model. The defined tabu search procedure uses a definition of *move* based on the violation and restoration of temporal constraints. It can be implemented by using some efficient algorithms, described in [2, 11], that dynamically manage temporal constraints. The idea of relaxing and restoring temporal constraints allows to work with temporarily violated solutions and can be used "to navigate" the search space in order to find a feasible solution from a violated one.

In an experimental study on randomly generated scheduling problems of increasing scale, the local search procedure was found to significantly improve a start solution obtained with a heuristic strategy. The particular use of tabu search is an interesting step in solving scheduling problems with relaxable deadlines and complex metric constraints which have a low probability to have an "exact solution".

Acknowledgments

We would like to thank the ECP anonymous reviewers for their useful comments. Authors' work was supported by Italian Space Agency, CNR Committee 12 on Information Technology (Project SCI*SIA), CNR Committee 04 on Biology and Medicine, and Italian Ministry of Scientific Research. Angelo Oddi is currently supported by a scholarship from CNR Committee 12 on Information Technology.

References

1. G. Ausiello, G.F. Italiano, A. Marchetti Spaccamela, and U. Nanni. Incremental Algorithms for Minimal Length Paths. *Journal of Algorithms*, 12:615–638, 1991.
2. A. Cesta and A. Oddi. Gaining Efficiency and Flexibility in the Simple Temporal Problem. In *Proceedings of the Third International Conference on Temporal Representation and Reasoning (TIME-96)*. IEEE Computer Society Press, 1996.
3. C. Cheng and S.F. Smith. Generating Feasible Schedules under Complex Metric Constraints. In *Proceedings 12th National Conference on AI (AAAI-94)*, 1994.
4. T.L. Dean and D.V. McDermott. Temporal Data Base Management. *Artificial Intelligence*, 32:1–55, 1987.
5. R. Dechter, I. Meiri, and J. Pearl. Temporal Constraint Networks. *Artificial Intelligence*, 49:61–95, 1991.
6. S. French. *Sequencing and Scheduling: an Introduction to the Mathematics of the Job-Shop*. Hellis Horwood Lim., 1982.
7. F. Glover. Tabu Search – Part I. *ORSA Journal of Computing*, 1:190–206, 1989.
8. F. Glover. Tabu Search – Part II. *ORSA Journal of Computing*, 2:4–32, 1990.
9. N. Muscettola. HSTS: Integrating Planning and Scheduling. In M. Zweben and M.S. Fox, editors, *Intelligent Scheduling*. Morgan Kaufmann, 1994.
10. E. Nowicki and C. Smutnicki. A Fast Taboo Search Algorithm for the Job Shop Problem. *Management Science*, 42:797–813, 1996.
11. A. Oddi. *Sequencing Methods and Temporal Algorithms with Application in the Management of Medical Resources*. PhD thesis, Department of Computer and System Science, University of Rome "La Sapienza", 1997.
12. A. Oddi and S.F. Smith. Stochastic Procedures for Generating Feasible Schedules. In *Proceedings 14th National Conference on AI (AAAI-97)*, 1997.
13. P.J.M Van Laarhoven, E.H.L. Aarts, and J.K. Lenstra. Job Shop Scheduling by Simulated Annealing. *Operations Research*, 40:113–125, 1992.
14. M. Zweben and M.S. Fox, editors. *Intelligent Scheduling*. Morgan Kaufmann, 1994.

Contingency Selection in Plan Generation

Nilufer Onder[1] and Martha E. Pollack[1,2]

[1] Department of Computer Science
[2] Intelligent Systems Program
University of Pittsburgh, Pittsburgh PA 15260, USA

Abstract. A key question in conditional planning is: how many, and which of the possible execution failures should be planned for? One cannot, in general, plan for all the failures that can be anticipated: there are simply too many. But neither can one ignore all the possible failures, or one will fail to produce sufficiently flexible plans. We describe a planning system that attempts to identify the contingencies that contribute the most to a plan's overall value. Plan generation proceeds by extending the plan to include actions that will be taken in case the identified contingencies fail, iterating until either a given expected value threshold is reached or the planning time is exhausted. We provide details of the algorithm, discuss its implementation in the Mahinur system, and give initial results of experiments comparing it with the C-Buridan approach to conditional planning.

1 Introduction

Classical AI plan generation systems assume static environments and omniscient agents, and thus ignore the possibility that events may occur in unexpected ways—that contingencies might arise—during plan execution. A problem with classical planners is, of course, that things do not always go "according to plan." In contrast, universal planning systems and more recent MDP-based systems make no such assumption. They produce "plans" or "policies" that are functions from states to actions. However, the state space can be enormous, making it difficult or impossible to generate complete policies or truly universal plans.[3]

Conditional planners take the middle road. They allow for conditional actions with multiple possible outcomes and for sensing actions that allow agents to determine the current state[1, 3, 4, 5, 10, 11]. A key question in conditional planning is: how many, and which of the possible execution failures should be planned for?

In this paper, we describe Mahinur, a probabilistic partial-order planner that supports conditional planning with contingency selection. Mahinur implements an iterative refinement planning algorithm that identifies the contingencies that contribute the most to the plan's overall value, and gives priority to the contingencies whose failure would have the greatest negative impact. We concentrate on two aspects of the problem, namely, planning methods for an iterative conditional planner and a method for computing the negative impact of possible sources of failure. We present experimental data from our current implementation, and compare our system with other probabilistic conditional planners.

---

[3] Thus Dean et al.[2] describe an algorithm to construct an initial policy for a restricted set of states, and incrementally increase the set of states covered.

2 Planning with Contingency Selection

We start with a basic idea: a plan is composed of many steps that produce effects to support the goals and subgoals, but not all of the effects contribute equally to the overall success of the plan. Of course, if plan success is binary—plans either succeed or fail—then in some sense all the effects contribute equally, since the failure to achieve any one results in the failure of the whole plan. However, as has been noted in the literature on decision-theoretic planning, plan success is not binary. Some plans may do a better job than others of achieving the stated goals. Similarly, some contingencies that arise during plan execution may have more impact on plan outcome than other contingencies.

In this paper, we focus on the fact that the goals that a plan is intended to achieve may be decomposable into subgoals, each of which has some associated value. For example, consider a car in a service station and a plan involving two goals: installing the fallen front reflector and repairing the brakes. The value of achieving the former goal may be significantly less than the value of achieving the latter. Consequently, effects that support only the former goal (e.g., getting the reflector from the supplier) contribute less to the overall success of the plan than the effects that support only the latter (e.g., getting the calipers). Effects that support both goals (e.g., having placed a call to the supplier) will have the greatest importance. This suggests that it may be most important to have a back-up plan to handle the possibility of the supplier having already closed for the day; almost as important to have a back-up plan in case the supplier is out of calipers; and less important to have a back-up plan in case the supplier is out of reflectors. Of course, in reality the importance of having back-up plans will also depend on the likely difficulty of replanning "on-the-fly" for particular contingencies. But in this paper, we concentrate on simpler methods for calculating the impact of any contingency on plan success, assuming that all on-the-fly calculations are equally difficult. More sophisticated techniques that give up this assumption can later be folded into the process, and used within the conditional planning algorithm we present.

The high level specification of our iterative conditional planning algorithm is shown below:

1. **Skeletal plan**: Construct a skeletal plan.
2. **Plan refinement**: While the plan is below the given
   expected value threshold:
   2a. Select the contingency whose failure has the highest
       expected disutility.
   2b. Extend the plan to include actions to cover the failure.

The algorithm first finds a *skeletal plan*, i.e., a minimal plan with nonzero probability of success. During each iteration, a contingency whose failure will have a maximal *disutility* is selected. The plan is then extended to include actions to take in case the selected contingency fails. Iterations proceed until the expected value of the plan exceeds some specified threshold or the planning time is exhausted.

This algorithm depends crucially on the notions of contingencies and their expected values. However, before defining those, we will describe the prior approaches taken to conditional planning.

3 Prior Approaches

The literature on conditional planning mirrors the broader literature on plan generation in having both total-order and partial-order representations for plans. Total-order conditional planners include the Plinth[5] and the Weaver[1] systems. Although these systems do not directly focus on the problem of intelligently selecting contingencies to plan for, they do in practice make such selections using heuristics. The developers of the Plinth system have conjectured that, although partial-order representations are frequently more efficient in unconditional planning, they are likely to be unwieldy for conditional planning. One of our research aims has been to explore this conjecture, and we have therefore focused on partial-order approaches to conditional planning.

The most well-known probabilistic partial-order planner is C-Buridan[3]. C-Buridan constructs conditional plans in a somewhat indirect fashion. In some situations, there will be more than one operator that can achieve a goal G. To increase the support for G, C-Buridan may introduce multiple steps into the plan, only to realize that those steps conflict with one another. To resolve the conflict, it has a special mechanism for introducing an observation action. The observation action will have two possible outcomes, and C-Buridan will split the plan into two branches, associating each branch arbitrarily with one of the conflicting outcomes. Consider the example from the C-Buridan paper[3]. It involves a part which must be processed. Two alternative actions, SHIP and REJECT, both have an effect PROCESSED; thus, C-Buridan will insert both a SHIP and a REJECT step into the plan. Both will have a precondition of NOT-PROCESSED, and an effect of PROCESSED, and hence C-Buridan detects a traditional threat in the plan. The threat cannot be resolved by step ordering, so C-Buridan inserts an observation step into the plan, and splits the plan into two contexts. The final plan is the correct one: CHECK-PART; SHIP IF GOOD; REJECT IF BAD.

Unfortunately, there are three drawbacks to C-Buridan's approach of forming conditional plans. First, and most consequential to our research, in the process of constructing plans, C-Buridan does not reason about whether particular branches of conditional plans are worth constructing. It is only *after* the branch is constructed that C-Buridan recognizes it as a branch and places it into one context of an observation action. For instance, in the example above, C-Buridan first inserts the SHIP and REJECT actions into the plan, to provide added support to the PROCESSED goal, and only then recognizes those actions as alternative contingencies. But what is needed is to reason ahead of time about the value of addressing these particular alternatives.

Second, as is, this approach can find only a restricted range of conditional plans, and will not find those in which the observation step should follow an initial step, to determine whether a second step should be taken. For instance, suppose that the probability of a PAINT action succeeding is 50%. One natural way to ensure that a part has at least a 75% chance of being painted is to include two PAINT actions in the plan. Assume, though, that a part should be painted once (say because it will result in an overly thick coat of paint). A reasonable conditional plan would be PAINT; CHECK-IF-SUCCESSFUL; PAINT IF NOT SUCCESSFUL. However, for this problem, C-Buridan would insert two PAINT steps, and then try to resolve their incompatibility by inserting an observation step *before* them (see Sect. 7 for one fix that we used in our implementation of C-Buridan).

The third problem involves the way in which C-Buridan links the outcomes of observation steps to later actions in the plan. The alternative outcomes of observation steps are labeled with arbitrary strings, called *observation labels*, that do not relate to propositions. The planner simply has to try every possible pairing of observation labels and subsequent actions into distinct contexts, resulting in needless expansion of the search space.

4 The Mahinur System

Our approach to conditional planning combines the Buridan system[8] for managing probabilistic actions with a CNLP-style[10] approach to handling contingencies.[4] Given the problems outlined in the previous section, we needed to keep several features of the CNLP system that C-Buridan had chosen to modify. We also added mechanisms for intelligent contingency selection.

Unlike the systems discussed above, CNLP does not include mechanisms for reasoning about probabilistic outcomes. But it does construct conditional plans to account for foreseen sources of uncertainty. That is, CNLP actions may have multiple possible outcomes. When the planner uses one of the outcomes of such an action to establish a precondition, it realizes that the goal cannot be achieved in every possible completion of the plan. To resolve this, it duplicates the goal, and marks it so that it can only be supported by actions that do not depend on the outcome that was just used. The actions that are inserted to support the new goal then constitute the "other" branch of the conditional plan.[5]

4.1 Actions and Contingencies

We build on the representation for probabilistic actions that was developed for Buridan[8, p. 247]. *Causal actions* are those that alter the state of the world. For instance, the PAINT action depicted both graphically and textually in Fig. 1 has the effects of having the part painted (PA) and blemishes removed (‾BL) 95% of the time when the part has not been processed (‾PR).

Definition 1. A causal action N is defined by a set of *causal consequences*:

$$N : \{< t_1, \rho_{1,1}, e_{1,1} >, \ldots, < t_1, \rho_{1,l}, e_{1,l} >, \ldots,$$
$$< t_n, \rho_{n,1}, e_{n,1} >, \ldots, < t_n, \rho_{n,m}, e_{n,m} >\} .$$

For each i, j: t_i is an expression called the consequence's *trigger*, and $e_{i,j}$ is a set of literals called the *effects*. $\rho_{i,j}$ denotes the probability that the effects in $e_{i,j}$ will be produced given that the literals in t_i hold. The triggers are mutually exclusive and exhaustive. For each effect e of an action, $RESULT(e, st)$ is a new state that has the negated propositions in e deleted from, and the non-negated propositions added to st.

---

[4] C-Buridan also builds on Buridan; hence its name.

[5] With CNLP, the branches do not rejoin, whereas with C-Buridan they can. Methods for rejoining branches have not been explored in the context of CNLP style algorithms.

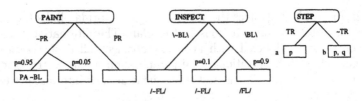

PAINT: { <{~PR},0.95,{PA,~BL}>, <{~PR},0.05,{}>,<{PR},1,{}> }

INSPECT: { <\~BL\{},1,{},/~FL/>, <\BL\{},0.1,{},/~FL/>, <\BL\{},0.9,{},/FL/> }

Fig. 1. Example actions.

Conditional plans also require *observation actions* so that the executing agent will know which contingencies have occurred, and hence, which actions to perform. Observational consequences are different from causal consequences in that they record two additional pieces of information: the *label* (marked with //) shows *which proposition's* value is being reported on, the *subject* (marked with \\) shows *what the sensor looks at*. The subject is needed when an aspect of the world is not directly observable and the sensor instead observes another (correlated) aspect of the world. For instance, a robot INSPECTing a part might look at whether it is blemished (\BL\), to report whether it is flawed (/FL/). Note that the label and the subject are not arbitrary strings—they are truth-functional propositions.

Definition 2. An **observation action** N is a set of *observational consequences*:

$$N : \{< sbj_1, t_1, \rho_{1,1}, e_{1,1}, l_{1,1} >, \ldots, < sbj_1, t_1, \rho_{1,l}, e_{1,l}, l_{1,l} >, \ldots,$$
$$< sbj_n, t_n, \rho_{n,1}, e_{n,1}, l_{n,1} >, \ldots, < sbj_n, t_n, \rho_{n,m}, e_{n,m}, l_{n,m} >\} .$$

For each i, j: sbj_i is the *subject* of the sensor reading, t_i is the *trigger*, $e_{i,j}$ is the set of any *effects* the action has, and $l_{i,j}$ is the label that shows the *sensor report*. $\rho_{i,j}$ is the probability of obtaining the effects and the sensor report. The subjects and triggers are mutually exclusive and exhaustive. In our framework we wanted to keep the ability to represent faulty sensors as introduced by C-Buridan, by representing the relationship between the subject and the report. But, unlike a trigger, a subject proposition is not meant to be achieved by the planner.

An important issue in the generation of probabilistic plans is the identification of equivalent consequences. We define *contingencies* to be subsets of outcomes of probabilistic actions. For instance, if we paint a part, we may or may not succeed in having the part painted properly. Having the part painted is one contingent outcome of the paint action; not having it is another. A deterministic action is simply one with a single (contingent) outcome. The contingencies of a step are relative to the step's intended use. For instance, if the rightmost step in Fig. 1 is used to support p, then {a,b} is its single contingency, but if it is used to support q, then {a} and {b} are alternative contingencies.

4.2 Plan Representation

We define a planning problem in the usual way, as a set of initial conditions encoded as a start step (START: $\{< \emptyset, \rho_1, e_1 >, \ldots, < \emptyset, \rho_n, e_n >\}$), a goal (GOAL:

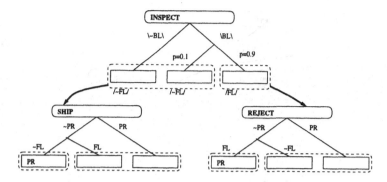

Fig. 2. Observation links.

$\{< \{g_1, \ldots, g_n\}, 1, \emptyset >\})$, and an action library. We assume that each top-level goal g_i has value $val(g_i)$. A plan in our framework has two sets of steps and links (causal and observational), along with binding and ordering constraints.

Definition 3. A **partially ordered plan** is a 6-tuple, $< T_c, T_o, O, L_c, L_o, S >$, where T_c and T_o are causal and observation steps, O is a set of temporal ordering constraints, L_c and L_o are sets of causal and observation links, and S is a set of open subgoals. It is important to note that both types of links emanate from contingencies rather than individual outcomes. For instance, in Fig. 2, SHIP will be executed if INSPECT reports /FL/, and REJECT will be executed otherwise.

Definition 4. A **causal link** is a 5-tuple $< S_i, c, p, c_k, S_j >$. Contingency c of step S_i is the link's *producer*, contingency c_k of step S_j is the link's *consumer*, and p is the *supported proposition* $(S_i, S_j \in T_c \cup T_o)$.

Definition 5. An **observation link** is a 4-tuple $< S_i, c, l, S_j >$. Contingency c is the collection of consequences of $S_i \in T_o$ that report l. An observation link means that $S_j \in T_c \cup T_o$ will be executed only when the sensor report provided by S_i is l.

Often the planner needs to reason about all the steps that are subsequent to a particular observation. We therefore define a *composite step* as a portion of the plan graph rooted at an observation action. Although composite steps are an important part of our overall framework we will omit the formal definitions for brevity in this paper (See [9] for the general definitions).

4.3 Expected Disutility

The importance of planning for the failure of any particular contingency can be seen to be a factor of two things: the probability that the contingency will fail, and the degree to which the failure will affect the overall success of the plan. To compute the former, one needs to know both the probability that the action generating the particular contingency will be executed, and the conditional probability of the contingency given the action's occurrence. Computing the latter is

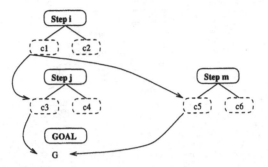

Fig. 3. Computing expected disutility.

more difficult. In this paper, however, we make two strong simplifying assumptions. First, we assume that the top-level goals for any planning problem can be decomposed into utility-independent[6] subgoals having fixed scalar values. Second, we assume that all failures are equally difficult to recover from at execution time. With these two assumptions, we can compute the *expected disutility* of a contingency's failure: it is the probability of its failure, multiplied by the sum of the values of all the top-level goals it supports. Planning for the failure of a contingency c means constructing a plan that does not depend on the effects produced by c, i.e., a plan that will succeed even if c fails.

The main idea in computing the expected value of a contingency c is to find out which top-level goal(s) will fail if the step fails to produce c. For example, suppose that contingency c_1 of step S_i establishes a proposition p for contingency c_3 of step S_j and for contingency c_5 of step S_m (Fig. 3). Suppose also that the trigger expressions for c_3 and c_5 contain other propositions which will become true with probability k_3 and k_5 just before their respective steps are executed. Then, the support provided along the path that has more probability of success is more valuable. We call k_i *the probability that c_i will support the goal*. If a contingency directly supports a goal, then k is 1. As an example, suppose that c supports top-level goal g_i in two ways: along one path with probability 0.7, and along another with probability 0.8. If c fails, the most that will be lost is the support for g_i with probability 0.8, and thus the expected value of c is $0.8 \times val(g_i)$. Therefore, while propagating the values to a contingency, we take the maximum support it provides for each top-level goal.

Definition 6. Expected value of a contingency: Suppose that contingency c has outgoing causal links to consumer contingencies $c_1, \ldots, c_n$ and possibly an outgoing observation link to step S. Assume that k_i is the probability that c_i supports goal g, and k_{n+1} is the probability that S supports g. Then, the expected value of c with respect to g is:

$$evg(c,g) = \begin{cases} val(g), & \text{if } c \text{ directly supports } g, \\ max(k_1, \ldots, k_{n+1}) \times val(g), & \text{otherwise.} \end{cases}$$

---

[6] The utility of one subgoal does not depend on the degree to which other goals are satisfied[6].

For z top-level goals, the expected value of c is, $EV(c) = \sum_{i=1}^{z} evg(c, g_i)$.

We next consider the computation of expected disutility of a contingency's failure. To begin, we need to compute the probability that a given state will occur after the execution of a sequence of actions.[7]

Definition 7. The probability of a state after a (possibly null) sequence of steps is executed:

$$P[st'|st, <>] = \{1, \text{if } st' = st; 0, \text{otherwise.}\}$$

$$P[st'|st, < S >] = \sum_{<t_i, \rho_{i,j}, e_{i,j}> \in S} \rho_{i,j} P[t_i|st] P[st'|RESULT(e_{i,j}, st)]$$

$$P[st'|st, < S_1, \ldots, S_n >] = \sum_{u} P[u|st, < S_1 >] P[st'|u, < S_2, \ldots, S_n >]$$

where S_1 is a causal step.[8] The action sequence is a total ordering consistent with the partially ordered plan.

The expected disutility of a contingency c is the product of the probability that the action generating c will be executed, the conditional probability of c's failure given the action's occurrence, and the expected value of c.

Definition 8. Expected disutility of the failure of a contingency: Let c be a contingency of step S_i. If the condition for c is $< \{t_1, \rho_1\}, \ldots, \{t_m, \rho_m\} >$, then the expected disutility of c is defined as

$$P[S_i \text{ is executed}] \times (1 - (\sum_{k=1}^{m} \rho_k P[t_k| < S_1, \ldots, S_{i-1} >])) \times EV(c) .$$

5 The Planning Algorithm

We can now see how the algorithm in Sect. 2 works. After forming a skeletal plan, it selects a contingency c whose failure has maximal expected disutility. Suppose that c has an outgoing causal link $< S_i, c, p, c_k, S_j >$ (Fig 4, left). Because the proposition supported by c is p, the planner selects an observation action, S_o, that reports the status of p and inserts it ordered to come after S_i. Two contingencies for S_o are formed: c_1 contains all of S_o's outcomes that produce the label $/p/$, and c_2 contains all the other outcomes. The causal link $< S_i, c, p, c_k, S_j >$ is removed and an observation link $< S_o, c_1, /p/, S_j >$ is inserted to denote that S_j will be executed when the sensor report is $/p/$. In addition, a causal link, $< S_i, c, sbj, c_1, S_o >$ is inserted (Fig. 4, right). This link prevents the insertion of an action that would perturb the correlation between the subject and label propositions. Conditional planning then proceeds in the CNLP style: the goal is duplicated and labeled so that it cannot receive support from the steps that depend on contingency c_1 of the observation step.

---

[7] The probability of an expression e with respect to a state st is defined as: $P[e|st] = \{1, \text{if } e \subseteq st; 0, \text{otherwise.}\}$.

[8] We will be omitting the formal definition with the observation steps for brevity. The main idea is to recursively calculate the result of a sequence of steps for each branch.

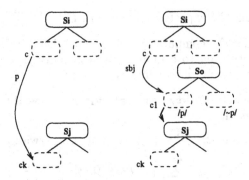

Fig. 4. Inserting a new observation action.

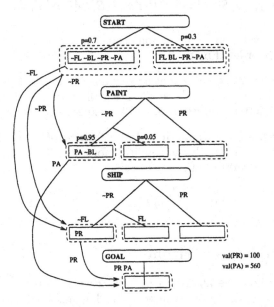

Fig. 5. The skeletal plan.

6 Example

The following example is based on the example presented in the C-Buridan paper. The goal is to process(PR) and paint(PA) parts. Initially, 30% of the parts are flawed(FL) and blemished(BL), the rest are in good condition. The "correct" way of processing a part is to reject it if it is flawed, and to ship it otherwise. We assign 100 as the value of processing a part, and 560 as the value of painting. The action library contains the SHIP, REJECT, INSPECT and PAINT actions.

The Mahinur planning system starts by constructing a skeletal plan, and nondeterministically chooses the SHIP action to process the part. Two contingencies of SHIP are constructed (shown in Fig. 5 in dashed boxes): the first one produces PR, and the second does not. A causal link that emanates from the first contingency is established for PR.

The triggers for the first contingency are adopted as subgoals (¬PR,¬FL), and both are supported by START. For START, two different sets of contingencies are constructed: one with respect to ¬PR, and one with respect to ¬FL. When PAINT is inserted to support the PA goal, and the ¬PR trigger of the first contingency is supported by START, the skeletal plan is complete. The skeletal plan contains three contingencies whose disutilities of failure must be calculated (the contingency for ¬PR of START has no alternatives). The expected disutilities for the first contingencies of START, PAINT, and SHIP are $0.3 \times 100 = 30$ (for ¬FL), $0.05 \times 560 = 28$ (for PA), and $0.3 \times 100 = 30$ (for PR), respectively.

Mahinur chooses to handle the first contingency with the higher expected disutility, namely the first contingency of START. Because ¬FL is the proposition supported by that contingency, an action that inspects the value of FL is inserted before SHIP (Fig. 6). The causal link supporting ¬FL is removed and an observation link from the ¬FL report is inserted. The INSPECT step looks at BL to report about FL. Therefore, the first contingency of START is linked to INSPECT to ensure that an action that alters the value of BL cannot be inserted between START and INSPECT (BL and FL are correlated). The new branch is then completed. For the duplicated goal, a new REJECT action is inserted to support PR, and the existing PAINT step is used to support PA yielding the plan shown in Fig. 6. If the success threshold has not been met, Mahinur will plan for additional contingencies. Note that existing conditional planners can solve this problem, but the plan generated will be the same regardless of the value assigned to the top-level goals. Within our framework, the planner is sensitive to the values assigned to each goal and is able to focus on different parts of the plan based on the disutility of contingencies.

7 Implementation and Experiments

Mahinur is implemented using C-LISP Common Lisp on a PC running Linux. We conducted preliminary experiments on two sets of problems. In the first set, we used synthetic problems that had an increasing number of goals, and thus an increasing number of potential failures (Problem 1 has one goal and one action that can fail, problem 2 has two goals and one action that can fail for each goal, and so on). For each problem, Table 1 shows the total run time for solving the problem and the amount of time used for disutility calculation as the expected utility threshold is increased and more iterations of conditional planning are performed.[9] As expected, runtime increases exponentially with the size of the problem; disutility calculation, however, is insignificant.

For the second set of experiments (Table 2), we implemented the C-Buridan algorithm on top of Buridan. We used the same support functions for conditional planning (context propagation, checking context compatibility) and the same ranking function as in Mahinur. To fix the problem we discussed in Sect. 3, namely, the problem of C-Buridan always inserting observation actions before both of the conflicting actions, we introduced a threat resolution mechanism that nondeterministically places only one of the conflicting actions into a context of an observation step. We implemented the Mahinur algorithm in two ways:

---

[9] The problem marked with a * terminated with a LISP out-of-memory error.

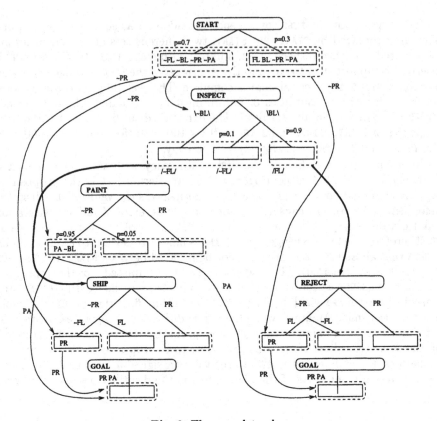

Fig. 6. The complete plan.

	Problem 1		Problem 2		Problem 3	
Iterations	Run	Disutility	Run	Disutility	Run	Disutility
0	0.01	0.01	0.03	0.01	0.08	0.01
1	0.14	0.01	0.56	0.01	3.92	0.02
2	0.42	0.01	11.28	0.02	335.21	0.03
3	1.67	0.02	229.22	0.03	4368.43	0.05
4	9.11	0.03	3558.87	0.04	*	-

Table 1. Run time and disutility calculation time in seconds (experiment 1).

Mahinur(a) forms contingencies but puts a plan in the search space for each outcome in a contingency; Mahinur(b) selects one of the outcomes randomly.[10]

To demonstrate the advantage of directly planning for contingencies, we used a domain which contains a single PAINT operator. Painting a part repeatedly increases the probability of success by 0.5^n, where n is the number of repetitions. It is an error to paint a part if it succeeded on the last try, thus the plan has to contain an observation action to check whether the part was painted, and repeat

---

[10] The experiments marked with a * terminated when the search limit of 20,000 nodes was reached.

Problem	C-Buridan	Mahinur (a)	Mahinur (b)
PAINT (t=0.75)	184	33	16
PAINT (t=0.875)	17,341	187	49
PAINT (t=0.9375)	*	1018	131
PAINT (t=0.9688)	*	5851	247
PAINT (t=0.9844)	*	*	512
SHIP-REJECT	*	250	40
TIREWORLD	*	278	47
TRANSPORT PACKAGE	1,190	52	40
TREATMENT	*	22	14

Table 2. Number of nodes visited (experiment 2).

the PAINT step only if it has not been successful. Comparing the second column of results (C-Buridan) to the first one (Mahinur(a)) in Table 2, we see that Mahinur expanded significantly fewer nodes as the probability threshold(t) is increased. This is because the planning process concentrates on directly planning for contingencies. In contrast, the problem quickly became hard for C-Buridan because of additional branching that results from overly frequent attempts to handle conflicts by conditional branching. We observed a similar explosion of the search space on the SHIP-REJECT problem, a standard textbook problem on conditional planning (TIREWORLD[12]), and examples from conditional planning literature (TRANSPORT PACKAGE[1] and TREATMENT[7]).

Comparing the last column to the second column displays a second advantage of forming contingencies. The search space is decreased by heuristically selecting one outcome in a contingency rather than generate a plan for each outcome.

It is important to note that the disutility calculation we use is heuristic: we consider only the intended use of each action (as shown by the causal links) rather than the exact contribution to the plan, and we consider one total ordering for the disutility calculation. In $EV(c)$, we summarize the contribution of c to the achievement of each goal. One alternative to our method of calculation is to evaluate the exact probability of a goal failing given that c is not achieved. We will empirically compare the heuristic and exact approaches in upcoming work.

8 Summary and Related Work

We presented an approach to partial-order conditional planning that directly reasons about the value of planning for alternative contingencies. Other relevant work includes the recent decision-theoretic planning literature, e.g., the Pyrrhus system[13] which prunes the search space by using domain-specific heuristic knowledge, and the DRIPS system[7] which uses an abstraction hierarchy.

Our approach combines the Buridan mechanism for managing probabilistic actions with a CNLP-style of conditional branch formation and adds techniques for identifying contingencies and computing their effect on overall plan success. In this paper, we concentrated on constructing conditional branches as a method of increasing the probability of success of a plan. Our next step is to incorporate methods for reducing the probability of failure by adding more supporting actions. Our conjecture is that by concentrating on the "right" contingency using the disutility calculation, the planner will be more flexible to produce better plans quickly. Experimental assessment with a much larger "real-world" domain and extensions to utilize richer utility functions will be forthcoming.

Acknowledgments. This work has been supported by a scholarship from the Scientific and Technical Research Council of Turkey, by the Air Force Office of Scientific Research (Contract F49620-96-1-0403), by an National Science Foundation Young Investigator's Award IRI-9258392, and by National Science Foundation Award IRI-9619579.

References

1. Jim Blythe and Manuela Veloso. Analogical replay for efficient conditional planning. In *Proc. 14th Nat. Conf. on Artificial Intelligence*, pages 668–773, 1997.
2. T. Dean, L. P. Kaelbling, J. Kirman, and A. Nicholson. Planning under time constraints in stochastic domains. *Artificial Intelligence*, 76:35–74, 1995.
3. Denise Draper, Steve Hanks, and Daniel Weld. Probabilistic planning with information gathering and contingent execution. In *Proc. 2nd Int. Conf. on AI Planning Systems*, pages 31–36, 1994.
4. Oren Etzioni, Steve Hanks, Daniel Weld, Denise Draper, Neal Lesh, and Mike Williamson. An approach to planning with incomplete information. In *Proc. 3rd Int. Conf. on Principles of Knowledge Repr. and Reasoning*, pages 115–125, 1992.
5. Robert P. Goldman and Mark S. Boddy. Epsilon-safe planning. In *Proc. 10th Conf. on Uncertainty in Artificial Intelligence*, pages 253–261, 1994.
6. Peter Haddawy and Steve Hanks. Utility models for goal-directed decision-theoretic planners. Technical Report 93-06-04, Department of Computer Science and Engineering, University of Washington, 1993.
7. Peter Haddawy and Meliani Suwandi. Decision-theoretic refinement planning using inheritance abstraction. In *Proc. 2nd Int. Conf. on AI Planning Systems*, pages 266–271, 1994.
8. Nicholas Kushmerick, Steve Hanks, and Daniel S. Weld. An algorithm for probabilistic planning. *Artificial Intelligence*, 76:239–286, 1995.
9. Nilufer Onder and Martha E. Pollack. Contingency selection in plan generation. In *AAAI Fall Symp. on Plan Execution: Problems and Issues*, pages 102–108, 1996.
10. Mark A. Peot and David E. Smith. Conditional nonlinear planning. In *Proc. 1st Int. Conf. on AI Planning Systems*, pages 189–197, 1992.
11. Louise Pryor and Gregg Collins. Planning for contingencies: A decision based approach. *Journal of Artificial Intelligence Research*, 4:287–339, 1996.
12. Stuart J. Russell and Norvig. *Artificial Intelligence: A Modern Approach*. Prentice Hall, Englewood Cliffs, NJ, 1994.
13. Mike Williamson and Steve Hanks. Optimal planning with a goal-directed utility model. In *Proc. 2nd Int. Conf. on AI Planning Systems*, pages 176–181, 1994.

Approaching the *Plans are Programs* Paradigm Using Transaction Logic

Marcus V. Santos[1] and Marcio Rillo[2]

[1] University of Toronto, D.L. Pratt Building, 6 King's College Road,
Canada, M5S 1A1
marcus@cs.toronto.edu
Tel: (416) 978-6610 Fax: (416) 978-4765

[2] Universidade de São Paulo, L.S.I., Av. Prof. Luciano Gualberto 158, trav. 3,
São Paulo - SP - Brazil - 05508-900
rillo@lsi.usp.br
Tel: (011) 818-5659 Fax: (011) 818-5665

Abstract. Transaction logic ($\mathcal{TR}$) is a formalism that accounts for the specification and execution of update phenomena in arbitrary logical theory, specially logic programs and databases. In fact, from a theoretical standpoint, the planning activity could be seen as such a kind of phenomenon, where the execution of plan actions update a world model. This paper presents how a planning process can be specified and formally executed in $\mathcal{TR}$. We define a formal planning problem description and show that goals for these problems may be represented not only as questions to a final database state, but also as the invocation of complex actions. The planning process in this framework can be considered as an executional deduction of a $\mathcal{TR}$ formula. As a highlight of this work we could mention that it provides a clean and declarative approach to bridging the gap between formal and real planning. The user not only "programs" his planning problem description, but also gains a better understanding of what is behind the semantics of the plan generation process.

1 Introduction

Due to the characteristics of real applications such as incomplete information, changes in dynamic worlds, and nondeterminism, approaches based on plan synthesis tend to be too demanding computationally. Aiming to overcome this difficulty, we directed our efforts to a subclass of deductive planning, namely, the *"plans are programs"* paradigm[3]. Though this planning paradigm is a big step towards bridging the gap between formal and applied research, the approaches developed so far suffer from a tremendous burden: the *frame problem*.

Essentially, this planning paradigm entails that instead of searching for a sequence of actions that would take an agent from an initial world state to a final goal state, the idea is to find a legal execution for a high-level nondeterministic program. This is the core idea of the research carried on by Levesque *et. al* [9],

---

[3] [1] presents a survey on the deductive planning field.

which uses situation calculus [11, 8] as the basis of a programming language for steering robots. Based on dynamic logic [7], Stephan/Biundo [14] use a similar approach, although they are more concerned with the data structures inherent to world situations.

As far as the modeling of changes in the world is concerned, the majority of works based on deductive planning address this issue via the axiomatization of action effects through action formalisms. As a result, in order to subdue the *frame problem*, most logics require a large number of complex formulae to completely describe even a simple action. It is reasonable to admit that the gap originates from this axiomatization process.

Using transaction logic ($\mathcal{TR}$) [3] as the planning specification tool, we adopt an orthogonal approach to the action effects axiomatization. Instead of focusing on the axiomatization process, we center on the specification and execution of complex actions. We argue that in many common applications the frame problem is not an issue. A reasonable support to this proposition are the practical/applied researches developed so far. In these practical situations, elementary actions are usually specified procedurally; the hard work is to combine them in a suitable way.

As clearly presented by Bonner/Kifer [3, 2], $\mathcal{TR}$ fulfills exactly this lack by providing a suitable logical tool to combine actions. Once the frame problem is solved for elementary actions (via oracles[4]), the solution is propagated to complex actions.

Therefore, to address the *plans are programs* paradigm using $\mathcal{TR}$, we firstly define a language through which the user can specify with relative expressiveness a classical planning problem description, i.e., the initial world state, the domain knowledge, a goal and a set of actions composed of primitive and complex actions. Some points concerning the use of $\mathcal{TR}$ in this description are worth-mentioning. First, since $\mathcal{TR}$ was originally designed to deal with database updates, the current world state is always materialized and accessible during the planning process. Hence, to infer if some condition (fluent) is valid in a world state (situation), there is no need to unwind actions back to the initial situation.[5] Another point is that $\mathcal{TR}$ enables the definition of different abstraction levels during action specification, i.e., the user is not restricted to define elementary actions. In a logic programming style, he can compose complex actions as well.

As far as the goal representation is concerned, since in $\mathcal{TR}$ there is no difference between queries and updates, goals for problem descriptions can be represented not only as a query that must be valid in a final world state, but also as formula invoking simple queries or any previously defined action (elementary or complex).

Another important characteristic of our formalization which enables a semantic analysis of the planning process, is that the generation of a plan to a certain

---

[4] [2] presents two interesting oracles, namely, the classical and situation oracles. Through these oracles it is possible to do "low-level" reasoning using an action formalism, and complex action specification and execution in $\mathcal{TR}$.

[5] Process usually known in the AI literature as *regression*.

goal could be realized through the internal $\mathcal{TR}$ inference system. In this way, each planning step, each world state update can be formally described through the sequents of the $\mathcal{TR}$ executional deduction process.

The rest of the paper is organized as follows: in Section 2 we present the essentials of $\mathcal{TR}$ programming. Those readers more acquainted with this logic could skip this section. In Section 3 we present how elementary and complex actions can be defined in the logic. We also present alternatives to optimize an action system for real implementation. In Section 4 we describe a planning problem description in this logical framework. In this analysis we focus on the representation of different forms of goal representations.

2 The Essence of $\mathcal{TR}$ Programming

$\mathcal{TR}$ is a formalism basically applicable to the study of problems related to the update phenomena. In planning this kind of problem is very common, since the execution of actions in real environments could be modeled by suitable updates applied to a set of logic formulae. Generally, considering $\mathcal{TR}$ a programming system, its interaction with the user should be similar to logic languages like PROLOG or relational database systems. The user would build rules which describe transactions, ask for the execution of certain transactions and the system would answer presenting solutions to the transaction or updating the database. An important difference between $\mathcal{TR}$ and PROLOG is that updates in PROLOG are not logical. If the user performs a database update and afterwards, for some reason, the execution fails, the database is not rolled back to its original state.

2.1 Syntax

The $\mathcal{TR}$ syntax is similar to that of classical first order logic, except for the fact that it has an additional binary operator, $\otimes$, called *serial conjunction*, which gives the user the facility to combine transactions and execute them sequentially. For instance, the expression $a \otimes b$ denotes a serial conjunction which informally means: "First execute transaction a, and then execute transaction b". Transaction formulae are defined as follows:

1. An atomic formula is an expression of the form $p(t_1, ..., t_n)$, where p is a predicate symbol, and $t_1, ..., t_n$ are function terms as in first-order-logic.
2. If ψ and ϕ are transaction formulae, then so are the following expressions:
   - $\psi \wedge \phi$, $\psi \vee \phi$, $\psi \otimes \phi$, $\psi \oplus \phi$, and $\neg\phi$[6].
   - $(\forall X)\phi$ and $(\exists X)\phi$, where X is a variable.

---

[6] The serial disjunction is dual to the serial conjunction, and is defined as $\neg a \otimes \neg b \leftrightarrow \neg(b \oplus a)$.

Bonner and Kifer [3] also introduced the shuffle operator, &, which is used to represent transactions where the order of satisfaction is not relevant, e.g., $(a \otimes b) \vee (b \otimes a)$, could be represented more synthetic-ally as $a\&b$.

We used a more restrictive $\mathcal{TR}$ serial-Horn version which allows the user to program transactions. A $\mathcal{TR}$ serial-Horn program consists of two parts: the *transaction base*, which is a finite set P of serial-Horn rules specifying the user defined transactions, and the *database* consisting of a set D of first order logic formulae, where the transaction base can insert and remove formulae. Serial-Horn rules are expressions of the form:

$$p(X_1, X_2, ..., X_n) \leftarrow \alpha \qquad (1)$$

where $p(X_1, X_2, ..., X_n)$, $(n \geq 0)$, is an atomic formula and α is a serial conjunction of the form $a_1 \otimes a_2 \otimes ... \otimes a_k$, $(k \geq 0)$.

The $\mathcal{TR}$ semantics of a database state is defined by a special mechanism called state data oracle, O^d, i.e., it is a parameter of the logic. To each state identifier, i, $O^d(i)$ is a set of first order formulae representing the truths about the database state. Depending on the application domain, different kinds of state data oracles can be used. In this paper we used the generalized Horn oracle where $O^d(i)$ is a set of generalized Horn rules.

Since $\mathcal{TR}$ is directed to the formal specification of update phenomena, it provides a way to specify elementary updates. As explained in [3], rather then committing to a fixed set of elementary transitions, this kind of transition is also treated as a *parameter* of the logic, i.e., they are specified through the transition oracle, O^t, which is a function that maps pairs of states to sets of variable free atomic formulae. In this work the atomic formulae $ins(b)$ and $del(b)$ represent, respectively, elementary state transitions which insert and delete a formula b from the database, i.e., $ins(b) \in O^t(D, D + \{b\})$ and $del(b) \in O^t(D, D - \{b\})$[7].

2.2 Model Theory

The $\mathcal{TR}$ semantics is built on the concept of sequence of database states named paths. Like the modal logic semantics, a structure consists of a set of states and each state represents a database. However, the truths in $\mathcal{TR}$ are not defined on arcs between database states, but on paths.

Definition: (Path structure) [3] Let L be a language having a state data oracle, O^d, and a state transition oracle, O^t. A path of length k on L is a finite and arbitrary sequence of state identifiers, $\langle D_1, ..., D_k \rangle$, where $k \geq 1$. The set of all paths in L is called $Paths(L)$. A *path structure* M on L is the triple $\langle U, I_f, I_{path} \rangle$, where:

- U is a set called domain of M;
- I_f is an interpretation of function symbols occurring in L;

---

[7] The operators $+$ and $-$ denote, respectively, set union and difference.

- I_{path} is a mapping from every path in $Paths(L)$ to a semantic structure in $Struct(U, I_f)$. The set $Struct(U, I_f)$ is the set of all classical first order structures on L of the form $\langle U, I_f, I_p \rangle$, where I_p is the mapping that interprets the predicate symbols P as a relation in U; U and I_f are interpreted in the same way as in M.

Definition: (Model) A *path structure* (M) is a model of a $\mathcal{TR}$ formula ϕ, written $M \models \phi$, iff $M, \pi \models \phi$ for every path π.

Definition: (Executional Entailment) Let P be a transaction base, D an initial database, ϕ a transaction formula and $D_0, ..., D_n$ a sequence of database states. Then $P, D_0, ..., D_n \models \phi$ is true iff $M, \langle D_0, ..D_n \rangle \models \phi$ for every model, M, of P.

For any transaction base P, any sequence of database states $D_0, ..., D_n$, and any transaction formulae α and β, the following statements are true:

- If $P, D_0, ..., D_n \models \alpha$ and $P, D_0, ..., D_n \models \beta$ then $P, D_0, ..., D_n \models \alpha \wedge \beta$.
- If $P, D_0, ..., D_i \models \alpha$ and $P, D_i, ..., D_n \models \beta$ then $P, D_0, ..., D_n \models \alpha \otimes \beta$.
- If $\alpha \leftarrow \beta$ is in P, and $P, D_0, ..., Dn \models \beta$ then $P, D_0, ..., Dn \models \alpha$.
- If $\alpha \in O^t(D_0, D_1)$ then $P, D_0, D_1 \models \alpha$.
- If $\psi \in O^d(D_0)$ then $P, D_0 \models \psi$ where ψ is a first order formula.

2.3 Proof Theory

In the $\mathcal{TR}$ serial-Horn version, an inference is successful if and only if it finds an execution path to the transaction ϕ, i.e., a sequence of database states $D_0, \cdots, D_n$ in such a way that $P, D_0, \cdots, D_n \models \phi$. The inference system is composed of one axiom and three inference rules:

Axiom: $P, D \cdots \vdash ()$.

Inference Rules: In rules 1-3 bellow, σ is a substitution, a is an atomic formula and *rest* is a serial conjunction.

1. **Defining transactions**: if $b \leftarrow \phi$ is a rule from P, b and a unify with the m.g.u σ, then

$$\frac{P, D \cdots \vdash (\exists)(\phi \otimes rest)\sigma}{P, D \cdots \vdash (\exists)(a \otimes rest)}$$

2. **Querying the database**: if $a\sigma$ and $rest\sigma$ share no variables and $O^d(D) \models_c a\sigma$, then

$$\frac{P, D \cdots \vdash (\exists)rest\sigma}{P, D \cdots \vdash (\exists)(a \otimes rest)}$$

3. **Performing elementary updates**: if $a\sigma$ and $rest\sigma$ share no variables and $a\sigma \in O^t(D_1, D_2)$, then

$$\frac{P, D_2 \cdots \vdash (\exists)rest\sigma}{P, D_1 \cdots \vdash (\exists)(a \otimes rest)}$$

Definition: (Executional Deduction) Let P be a transaction base. An *executional deduction* of a transaction, Φ, is any deduction, i.e., a sequence of sequents, that satisfies the following conditions:

1. the initial sequent has the form $P, D' \cdots \vdash ()$, for some database D';
2. the final sequent has the form $P, D \cdots \vdash (\exists)\phi$, for some database D;
3. each sequent is obtained from the previous sequent by one of the inference rules.

3 Actions in the $\mathcal{TR}$ Framework

Essential to the formalization of a planning process is the definition of an action system. In the $\mathcal{TR}$ framework, an action is a serial-Horn rule which can invoke other actions, simple queries or elementary updates applied to a world state described as a set of classical Horn rules. Therefore, considering $\mathcal{L}$ a language of the $\mathcal{TR}$ serial-Horn version, an instance of an action system Σ is the triple:

$$\Sigma = \langle \mathcal{D}, \mathcal{K}, \mathcal{A} \rangle$$

where,

- $\mathcal{D} \subseteq \mathcal{L}$ consists of a world state, is a set of classical Horn rules such that each atomic rule σ, $\sigma \in \mathcal{D}$, is considered *essential*, and the others are considered *non-essentials*; only *essential* rules can be updated in the database.[8]
- $\mathcal{K} \subseteq \mathcal{L}$ represents the domain knowledge, is a set of classical Horn rules;
- $\mathcal{A} \subseteq \mathcal{L}$ is the action definitions. An action definition α, $\alpha \in \mathcal{A}$, can be elementary or complex. Elementary action definitions are defined in terms of the elementary state transitions of the transition oracle, O^t, mentioned in Section 2.1. Complex actions, in the general case, are serial-Horn rules which can invoke any action from the set of action definitions, and any rule from $\mathcal{D}$ or $\mathcal{K}$.

We mentioned in Section 1 that our approach focuses on complex actions specification and execution rather then elementary actions axiomatization. Besides this, we also argued that many common situations could be formally addressed even if we do not consider the frame problem an issue. Therefore, to support these claims we implemented an example similar to the one presented in [12]. Though it is just a toy example, the provided $\mathcal{TR}$ modeling approach can be straightforwardly extended to more real and complex situations. Figure 1 depicts this environment where a robot executes household tasks moving objects from place to place. We illustrate the concepts presented in this Section defining the following action system:

World state - $\mathcal{D}$ (D_0): $\left\{ \begin{array}{lll} on(tv, tpshelf) & on(box, duct) & on(book, btmshelf) \\ on(ball, book) & clear(tv)) & clear(box) \\ clear(floor) & clear(ball) & rounded(ball) \end{array} \right.$

---

[8] We borrowed from Lifschitz the notion of essential\non-essential formulae [10] and used this concept in [4] to define the soundness of action operators specified in $\mathcal{TR}$.

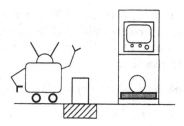

Fig. 1.

Domain knowledge - $\mathcal{K}$:

$$damage(tv) \leftarrow on(X, Y) \wedge on(Y, tv)$$

$$aired\_room \leftarrow \neg on(X, duct)$$

$$safe\_environ \leftarrow \neg damage(tv) \wedge aired\_room$$

These classical Horn-rules define the domain constraints. In this case it is not allowed to stack two objects on top of the television, and no object can be placed on the air duct. It is important to note that the serial-Horn conditions permit such rules (generalized Horn rules) in the database [3].

Action definitions - $\mathcal{A}$ (elementary actions):

$pickup(X) \leftarrow$
    $clear(X) \otimes on(X, Y) \otimes$ } Elementary action preconditions.
    $del(on(X, Y)) \otimes ins(clear(Y))$ } Elementary state transitions.
$putdown(X, Y) \leftarrow$
    $clear(Y) \otimes X \neq Y \otimes$
    $\neg\, rounded(Y) \otimes Y \neq duct \otimes$ } Elementary action preconditions.
    $ins(on(X, Y)) \otimes del(clear(Y))$ } Elementary state transitions.

Action definitions - $\mathcal{A}$ (complex actions):

$move(X, Y) \leftarrow pickup(X) \otimes putdown(X, Y)$
$achieve\_on(X, Y) \leftarrow achieve\_clear(X) \otimes achieve\_clear(Y) \otimes move(X, Y)$
$achieve\_clear(X) \leftarrow clear(X)$
$achieve\_clear(X) \leftarrow on(Y, X) \otimes achieve\_clear(Y) \otimes move(Y, Z) \otimes Z \neq X$
$achieve\_safety \leftarrow achieve\_clear(tv) \otimes achieve\_clear(duct)$

3.1 Action executional deduction

Now that we specified the whole set of action definitions, it would be worth to present how can an action be executed in the $\mathcal{TR}$ framework. While analyzing this process, we will emphasize the characteristics of the logical framework which motivate its use in planning.

Basically, the execution of an action in $\mathcal{TR}$ is a theorem proof procedure. Therefore, to invoke a transaction formula, $?\text{-} \phi$, is equivalent to obtain a proof to the executional entailment $P, D_0 \cdots, D_n \models \phi$. Suppose we wanted the robot to execute the following transaction:

$$achieve\_on(book, floor) \otimes safe\_environ$$

which means: "move the book to the floor and verify if the environment is safe afterwards." We present the executional deduction (proof) of this formula next:[9]

Sequents	Inference rule
$P, D_0 \cdots \vdash$	1
$achieve\_on(book, floor) \otimes safe\_environ$	
$if\ \ P, D_0 \cdots \vdash achieve\_clear(book) \otimes$	1

$$\underbrace{}_{\beta}$$

$achieve\_clear(floor) \otimes move(book, floor) \otimes safe\_environ$	
$if\ \ P, D_0 \cdots \vdash on(Y, book) \otimes achieve\_clear(Y) \otimes move(Y, Z) \otimes \beta$	2
$\cdots$	$\cdots$

Through inference rule 2 (Section 2.3), Y is unified to *ball*. Then,

$if\ \ P, D_0 \cdots \vdash achieve\_clear(ball) \otimes move(ball, Z) \otimes \beta$	1
$\cdots$	$\cdots$

Since $clear(ball) \in D_0$, the derivation of $achieve\_clear(ball)$ is straightforward. Therefore, continuing from transaction $move(ball, Z)$ and applying inference rule 1:

$if\ \ P, D_0 \cdots \vdash pickup(ball) \otimes putdown(ball, Y) \otimes \beta$	1

The actual world state, D_0, satisfies the preconditions of the elementary action $pickup(ball)$. Therefore, this action removes the atom $on(ball, book)$ from the database and inserts $clear(book)$ updating the database from D_0 to $D_1 = D_0 - on(ball, book)$ and from D_1 to $D_2 = D_1 + clear(book)$. Now proving $putdown(ball, Y)$ through inference 1:

$if\ \ P, D_2 \cdots \vdash clear(Y) \otimes X \neq Y \otimes \neg rounded(Y) \otimes Y \neq duct \otimes$	2
$\quad ins(on(X, Y)) \otimes del(clear(Y)) \otimes \beta$	

Using inference rule 2 we unified Y with constant *box*, such that $clear(Y) \in D_1$. Then, checked the other action preconditions and updated the database from D_2 to $D_3 = D_2 + on(ball, box)$, and from D_3 to $D_4 = D_3 - clear(box)$. To prove β, i.e., $achieve\_clear(floor) \otimes move(book, floor) \otimes safe\_environ$, we decided to omit the proof steps of transaction $achieve\_clear(floor)$, and continued the derivation from transaction $move(book, floor) \otimes safe\_environ$.

$\cdots$	$\cdots$
$if\ \ P, D_4 \cdots \vdash move(book, floor) \otimes safe\_environ$	1
$if\ \ P, D_4 \cdots \vdash pickup(book) \otimes putdown(book, floor) \otimes safe\_environ$	1

---

[9] Due to the limited space we omitted some trivial steps in the proof. Although, we give the necessary informal explanations concerning what happens during these steps.

Since D_4 satisfies the preconditions of $pickup(book)$, this action will cause two transitions in the database. The new database state, D_6, satisfies the preconditions of action $putdown(book, floor)$, which causes one transition in the database, i.e., from D_6 to $D_7 = D_6 + on(book, floor)$.[10] Now is time to prove the last transaction:

$$\cdots \qquad \qquad \cdots$$
$$if \ P, D_7 \cdots \vdash safety\_action \qquad \qquad 1$$
$$if \ P, D_7 \cdots \vdash \neg damage(tv) \wedge aired\_room \qquad 2$$

Since the air duct is still blocked, i.e., $on(box, duct) \in D_6$, it is straightforward to prove through classical SLD resolution applied to the generalized Horn rules in the database that the last transaction is not valid at D_6. Even if we backtrack undoing the database updates, there is no explicit action which moves the box from the air duct. Therefore it is impossible to prove that from the initial database state, D_0, we can execute $achieve\_on(book, floor) \otimes safe\_environ$. Although, if we specify the initial formula in such a way that the robot provides the necessary safety conditions before trying to move the book, i.e.,

$$achieve\_safety \otimes achieve\_on(book, floor) \otimes safe\_environ \qquad (2)$$

this formula can be now executed from the initial world state.

3.2 Optimization and backtracking

The action system mentioned in the previous example represents an intuitive formalization for the robot example. As a second step towards implementing this system in a computer, we used some programming techniques to optimize the amount of backtracking and eliminate the possibility of destructive interaction between subgoals.

First concerning backtracking, as we mentioned in the example, to certify that the elementary action will update the world state in a desired way, we placed suitable preconditions before the invocation of elementary state transitions. A good programming technique that we can use to reduce the amount of backtracking is to reinforce the pre- and postconditions in the complex actions as well, especially if the action presents different effects for the same precondition. Since accomplished database updates can be rolled back during backtracking in $\mathcal{TR}$, if the inference system chooses the wrong action effect, this effect can be undone if a postcondition is not satisfied. For example, suppose we define an action α which has one precondition and n different effects:

$$\alpha \leftarrow prec \otimes effect$$
$$effect \leftarrow effect_1$$
$$effect \leftarrow effect_2$$
$$\vdots$$
$$effect \leftarrow effect_n$$

---

[10] We defined the transition oracle, O^t, relative to this example in such a way that the elementary transition $del(clear(floor))$ does not cause any change to the database state, i.e., the floor is always is clear.

In this case, even though the inference system chooses one action effect nondeterministically, if we invoke α inside another action, we guarantee the achievement of the intended effect if we place a suitable postcondition after invoking α.

We can apply this strategy to the specification of action $achieve\_on(X, Y)$. If we want that it can be executed only in a safe environment, we place action $achieve\_safety$ as a precondition. In effect, $achieve\_clear(Y)$ is a nondeterministic action, since to clear Y the robot can place an eventual object that happens to be on Y at any place. Therefore, if we want that $achieve\_on$ does not cause any hazard, we place the environment constraint as postcondition. By this way we can use the expression 2 to create a new action $safe\_on(X, Y)$, with the following definition:

$$safe\_on(X, Y) \leftarrow achieve\_safety \otimes achieve\_on(X, Y) \otimes safe\_environ$$

Another anomaly that can be prevented via programming artifice is the destructive interaction between transactions. Analyzing the definition of action $achieve\_on(X, Y)$, we noticed that after clearing X, this action can put an object on X when trying to clear Y. To solve this problem we used the simple and efficient solution presented by Bonner and Kifer [3]. The idea is to protect a specific database atom P from being updated. This can be accomplished with the following rules:

$$lock(P) \leftarrow ins(locked(P)) \qquad unlock(P) \leftarrow del(locked(P))$$

Therefore, after achieving an intended action effect, we lock this effect. Next we present the new definition of action $achieve\_on(X, Y)$.

$$achieve\_on(X, Y) \leftarrow achieve\_clear(X) \otimes lock(clear(X)) \otimes$$
$$achieve\_clear(Y) \otimes move(X, Y)$$

We modify the respective elementary action preconditions in such a way that it will update the world state only if the database atom is not locked. Therefore, the new definition of action $pickup(X)$ is the following:

$$putdown(X, Y) \leftarrow clear(Y) \otimes unlocked(Y) \otimes X \neq Y \otimes$$
$$\neg \, rounded(Y) \otimes Y \neq duct \otimes$$
$$ins(on(X, Y)) \otimes del(clear(Y))$$

The following classical Horn rule is inserted in the knowledge domain:

$$unlocked(X) \leftarrow \neg locked(X)$$

4 Planning Problem Description

Essentially, a planner is a system which receives a planning problem description as input and produces a plan as output. In general, a planning problem description is a model that enables the representation of the following concepts:

- the initial world state;
- the goal;
- the domain knowledge, i.e., the non-mutable set of laws which rules the world;
- the actions which could be carry out in the world.

Note the close relation between this model and the action model presented in Section 3. Both represent the world state, the domain knowledge and the action operators. In the case of the planning problem description model, we have to represent another entity: the goal.

4.1 Representing goals

Considering these circumstances where we have in hand a first order language to describe planning problems, a goal is essentially characterized as a sentence of this language, which must be valid after the plan execution, i.e., at the final world state. In effect, one should expect that this language be sufficiently expressive so that it could represent with one sentence different kinds of goals.

Among the several sorts of goals that an agent can face in real situations [13], two are basic: queries that must be valid at the actual world state, e.g., $on(ball, book) \otimes on(book, floor)$, and the explicit invocation of high-level action abstractions (complex actions), e.g.:

$$safe\_on(X, tv) \otimes safe\_on(Y, box) \otimes color(X, blue) \otimes color(Y, blue) \qquad (3)$$

Since our approach adopts the *plans are programs* paradigm, the only way to provide an output plan for a planning problem description is using the goal to trigger the executional deduction process. It is evident that a query can not trigger this process, but as we can observe in Expression 3, it plays an important role in imposing constraints to the way the satisfaction of complex actions takes place. In this case, objects X and Y in Expression 3 must be both blue.

Another interesting property of $\mathcal{TR}$ is the capability to represent subgoals in a unordered way. In equation 3, if the order of putting an object on the television and an object on the book is not relevant, we can define this goal as follows:

$$[safe\_on(X, tv) \otimes safe\_on(Y, box) \lor safe\_on(X, box) \otimes safe\_on(Y, tv)] \otimes \\ color(X, blue) \otimes color(Y, blue) \qquad (4)$$

This kind of unordered subgoals can be represented in a more synthetic form using the shuffle connective, &, presented in [3]. Therefore, sentence 4 could be represented as follows:

$$(safe\_on(X, tv) \& safe\_on(Y, box)) \otimes color(X, blue) \otimes color(Y, blue)$$

We can also use the combination of queries and the invocation of complex actions in a goal formula as another artifice to eliminate the occurrence of destructive interaction between subgoals. For example, in $\mathcal{TR}$ we know that the atom $on(X, Y)$ is valid at the database state immediately after the execution of the complex action $achieve\_on(X, Y)$. If we invoke more than one $achieve\_on(X_i, Y_i)$ action (Expression 5), their respective $on(X_i, Y_i)$ must also be valid immediately after the accomplishment of the last complex action. Therefore, we can use this semantic property to force a backtracking in the goal satisfaction if some destructive interaction occurred during the executional deduction, as represented in the following goal:

$$[achieve\_d_1 \ \& \ achieve\_d_2 \ \& \cdots \ \& achieve\_d_n] \otimes d_1 \otimes d_2 \cdots d_n \qquad (5)$$

5 Discussion

Analyzing the essence of the $\mathcal{TR}$ semantic/syntactic characteristics presented in the previous sections, one could notice that the world state representation and the explicit formalization of updates applied to this state are inherent to the $\mathcal{TR}$'s paradigm. In the case of the *plans are programs* paradigm, inspecting the executional deduction of a logic program (skeletal plan) we can access points of the proof where the inference system invoked elementary actions. The resulting sequence of elementary actions is the output plan. During this executional deduction process, if some subgoal is not satisfied the resolution process backtracks, a new proof and a new action sequence is determined.

The central objective of our work was to present an approach to the *plans are programs* paradigm using $\mathcal{TR}$. Through this analysis we intended to show that even without considering the frame problem, $\mathcal{TR}$ can still be very useful to combine elementary and complex actions in a convenient way. The logic's deductive mechanism allows not only for the generation of plans but also for the symbolic execution of plans by generating data updates.

The logical framework can also be used as specification tool during all steps of the planning process, i.e., from the world modeling, the specification of an action system, the definition of a planning problem description, to the generation of plans for this problem.

We also showed that there is no gap between a formal planning speficification and its implementation in a computer. The user can still improve the planning problem description by using programming techniques to modify the action definitions with the objective of optimizing the backtracking process and avoiding destructive interaction between subgoals.

Another characteristic of our approach is that the user can combine the invocation of complex actions and queries when specifying a planning problem goal. With this artifice he can establish ordered and/or unordered strategies for subgoal satisfaction, among others.

6 Acknowledgments

Thanks are due to CAPES, the Brazilian Research Council, for the research grant, to Eric Harley for reviewing the text, and specially to Anthony Bonner for the important discussions on Transaction Logic.

References

1. S. Biundo. Present-day deductive planning. In *Current Trends in AI Planning – 2nd European WorkShop on Planning (EWSP-93)*, pages 1–5. IOS Press, 1994.
2. A.J. Bonner and M. Kifer. Representing complex actions in transaction logic. In preparation.
3. A.J. Bonner and M. Kifer. Transaction logic programming. Technical Report CSRI-323, Computer Systems Research Institute, University of Toronto, 1993.
4. M. V. T. dos Santos, P. E. Santos, F. S. Correa, and M. Rillo. Actions as prolog programs. In *IEEE Symposia on Intelligence in Automation and Robotics*, Nov 96.
5. M.V.T. dos Santos. On the formalization of actions using transaction logic. In *ECAI-96 Workshop on Cross-fertilization in Planning*, Aug 96.
6. R. E. Fikes and N. J. Nilsson. Strips: A new approach to theorem proving in problem solving. *Journal of Artificial Intelligence*, 2:189–208, 1971.
7. D. Harel. *First Order Dynamic Logic*. Springer LNCS 68, 1979.
8. R. Kowalski. *Logic for Problem Solving*. North-Holland Publishing Company, 1979.
9. H.J. Levesque, R. Reiter, Y. Lespérance, F. Lin, and R. B. Scherl. GOLOG: a logic programming language for dynamic domains. *Journal of Logic Programming*, 1997. To appear.
10. V. Lifschitz. On the semantics of strips. In M.P. Georgeff and L. Lansky A, editors, *Proc. 1986 Workshop Reasoning about Actions and Plans*, pages 1–9, 1987.
11. J. M. McCarthy and P. J. Hayes. Some philosophical problems from the standpoint of artificial intelligence. In B. Meltzer and D. Michie, editors, *Machine Intelligence*, pages 463–502. Edinburgh University Press, 1969.
12. M.L.Ginsberg and D.E.Smith. Reasoning about action i: A possible worlds approach. *Journal of Artificial Intelligence*, 35:165–195, 1988.
13. E.C. Schank and R.P. Abelson. *Scripts, Plans Goals and Understanding*. Freeman Publ. Co., 1975.
14. W. Stephan and S. Biundo. A new logical framework for deductive planning. In *Proceedings of the 13th International Joint Conference on Artificial Intelligence (IJCAI-93)*, pages 32–38. Morgan Kaufmann, 1993.

Event Calculus Planning Revisited

Murray Shanahan

Department of Computer Science,
Queen Mary and Westfield College,
Mile End Road, London E1 4NS,
England.
Email: mps@dcs.qmw.ac.uk

Abstract

In 1969 Cordell Green presented his seminal description of planning as theorem proving with the situation calculus. The most pleasing feature of Green's account was the negligible gap between high-level logical specification and practical implementation. This paper attempts to reinstate the ideal of planning via theorem proving in a modern guise. In particular, I will show that if we adopt the event calculus as our logical formalism and employ abductive logic programming as our theorem proving technique, then the computation performed mirrors closely that of a hand-coded partial order planning algorithm. Furthermore, if we extend the event calculus in a natural way to accommodate compound actions, then using exactly the same abductive theorem prover we obtain a hierarchical planner. All this is a striking vindication of Kowalski's slogan "Algorithm = Logic + Control".

Introduction

In 1969, Green offered a logical characterisation of planning couched in terms of the situation calculus, in addition to an implementation based on a resolution theorem prover. What makes Green's treatment so attractive is the close correspondence between implementation and specification. The very same axioms that feature in the formal description of the planning task form the basis of the representation deployed by the implemented planner, and each computation step performed by the planner is a step in the construction of a proof that a suitable plan exists.

However, Green's seminal work, though much admired, has had little impact on subsequent work in planning, owing to the widespread belief that a theorem prover cannot form the basis of a practical planning system. The following quote from [Russell & Norvig, 1995] exemplifies the widely held belief that planning via theorem proving is impractical.

> Unfortunately a good theoretical solution does not guarantee a good practical solution. . . . To make planning practical we need to do two things: (1) Restrict the language with which we define problems. . . . (2) Use a special purpose algorithm . . . rather than a general-purpose theorem prover to search for a solution. The two go hand in hand: every time we define a new problem-description language, we need a new planning algorithm to process the language. . . . The idea is that the algorithm can be designed to process the restricted language more efficiently than a resolution theorem prover. [Russell & Norvig, 1995, page 342]

The aim of the present paper is to demonstrate that a good theoretical solution can indeed co-exist with a good practical solution, through the provision of a logical account of partial order and hierarchical planning in the spirit of Green's work. However, where Green's account was based on the formalism of the situation calculus, the present paper adopts the event calculus [Kowalski & Sergot, 1986], [Shanahan, 1997]. Furthermore, while Green regarded planning as a deductive process, planning with the event calculus is most naturally considered as an abductive process. When event calculus formulae are submitted to a suitably tailored resolution based abductive theorem prover, the result is a purely logical planning system whose computations mirror closely those of a hand-coded planning algorithm.

1 A Circumscriptive Event Calculus

The formalism for reasoning about action used in this paper is derived originally from Kowalski and Sergot's event calculus [Kowalski & Sergot, 1986], but is based on many-sorted first-order predicate calculus augmented with circumscription [Shanahan, 1997]. This section presents the bare outlines of the formalism.[1] An example of the use of the formalism, which should make things clearer to those unfamiliar with it, appears in the next section. For a more thorough treatment, consult [Shanahan, 1997].

Formula	Meaning
$Initiates(\alpha,\beta,\tau)$	Fluent β holds after action α at time τ
$Terminates(\alpha,\beta,\tau)$	Fluent β does not hold after action α at time τ
$Releases(\alpha,\beta,\tau)$	Fluent β is not subject to the common sense law of inertia after action α at time τ
$Initially_P(\beta)$	Fluent β holds from time 0
$Initially_N(\beta)$	Fluent β does not hold from time 0
$Happens(\alpha,\tau_1,\tau_2)$	Action α starts at time τ_1 and ends at time τ_2
$HoldsAt(\beta,\tau)$	Fluent β holds at time τ

Table 1: The Language of the Event Calculus

Table 1 presents the essentials of the language of the calculus, which includes sorts for fluents, actions (events), and time points.

We have the following axioms, whose conjunction is denoted EC.[2]

$$HoldsAt(f,t) \leftarrow Initially_P(f) \wedge \neg\, Clipped(0,f,t) \tag{EC1}$$

$$HoldsAt(f,t3) \leftarrow \tag{EC2}$$
$$Happens(a,t1,t2) \wedge Initiates(a,f,t1) \wedge$$
$$t2 < t3 \wedge \neg\, Clipped(t1,f,t3)$$

$$Clipped(t1,f,t4) \leftrightarrow \tag{EC3}$$
$$\exists\, a,t2,t3\, [Happens(a,t2,t3) \wedge t1 < t3 \wedge t2 < t4 \wedge$$
$$[Terminates(a,f,t2) \vee Releases(a,f,t2)]]$$

$$\neg\, HoldsAt(f,t) \leftarrow Initially_N(f) \wedge \neg\, Declipped(0,f,t) \tag{EC4}$$

$$\neg\, HoldsAt(f,t3) \leftarrow \tag{EC5}$$
$$Happens(a,t1,t2) \wedge Terminates(a,f,t1) \wedge$$
$$t2 < t3 \wedge \neg\, Delipped(t1,f,t3)$$

---

[1] [Shanahan, 1997a] shows how the calculus can be used to handle domain constraints, continuous change, and non-deterministic effects. Indeed, the planner described in this paper can handle many types of domain constraint without further modification.

[2] Variables begin with lower-case letters, while function and predicate symbols begin with upper-case letters. All variables are universally quantified with maximum possible scope unless otherwise indicated.

Delipped(t1,f,t4) ↔   (EC6)
    ∃ a,t2,t3 [Happens(a,t2,t3) ∧ t1 < t3 ∧ t2 < t4 ∧
    [Terminates(f,t2) ∨ Releases(a,f,t2)]]

Happens(a,t1,t2) → t1 ≤ t2   (EC7)

A two-argument version of Happens is defined as follows.

Happens(a,t) ≡$_{def}$ Happens(a,t,t)

The frame problem is overcome through circumscription. Given a conjunction Σ of Initiates, Terminates, and Releases formulae describing the effects of actions (a *domain description*), a conjunction Δ of Initially, Happens and temporal ordering formulae describing a *narrative* of actions and events, and a conjunction Ω of uniqueness-of-names axioms for actions and fluents, we're interested in,

CIRC[Σ ; Initiates, Terminates, Releases] ∧ CIRC[Δ ; Happens] ∧ EC ∧ Ω.

By minimising Initiates, Terminates and Releases we assume that actions have no unexpected effects, and by minimising Happens we assume that there are no unexpected event occurrences. In all the cases we're interested in, Σ and Δ will be conjunctions of Horn clauses, and the circumscriptions will reduce to predicate completions. This result will come in handy when we come to implement the event calculus as a logic program.

2 Planning as Abduction

Planning can be thought of as the inverse operation to temporal projection, and temporal projection in the event calculus is naturally cast as a deductive task. Given Σ, Ω and Δ as above, we're interested in HoldsAt formulae Γ such that,

CIRC[Σ ; Initiates, Terminates, Releases] ∧ CIRC[Δ ; Happens] ∧ EC ∧ Ω ⊨ Γ.

Conversely, as first pointed out by Eshghi [1988], planning in the event calculus can be considered as an abductive task. Given a domain description Σ, a conjunction Γ of goals (HoldsAt formulae), and a conjunction Δ_0 of Initially formulae describing the initial situation, a *plan* is a consistent conjunction Δ of Happens and temporal ordering formulae such that,

CIRC[Σ ; Initiates, Terminates, Releases] ∧
    CIRC[Δ_0 ∧ Δ ; Happens] ∧ EC ∧ Ω ⊨ Γ.

As suggested by the title of Levesque's Green-inspired paper, "What is planning in the presence of sensing?" [Levesque, 1996], logical characterisations such as this aim to settle the question of the underlying nature of one or other type of planning. Levesque's answer, echoing Green's 1969 paper, is based on the situation calculus. In the situation calculus, a plan is expressed using the Result function, which maps an action and a situation onto a new situation. The Result function does not facilitate the representation of narratives of events whose order is incompletely known. By contrast, since the narrative of actions described by Δ above doesn't have to be totally ordered, the event calculus seems a natural candidate for answering the question "What is partial order planning?".

As an example, let's formalise the shopping trip domain from [Russell & Norvig, 1995]. The domain comprises just two actions and two fluents. The term Go(x) denotes the action of going to x, and the term Buy(x) denotes the action of buying x. The fluent At(x) holds if the agent is at location x, and the fluent Have(x) holds if the agent possesses item x. Let Σ be the conjunction of the following Initiates, Terminates and sundry formulae.

Initiates(Go(x),At(x),t)

Terminates(Go(x),At(y),t) ← x ≠ y

Initiates(Buy(x),Have(x),t) ← HoldsAt(At(y),t) ∧ Sells(y,x)

Sells(DIYShop,Drill)   Sells(Supermarket,Banana)

Sells(Supermarket,Milk)

Let Ω be the conjunction of the following uniqueness-of-names axioms.

UNA[Go, Buy]   UNA[At, Have]

Our desired goal state is to have a banana, some milk, and a drill. Let Γ be the following conjunction of HoldsAt formulae.

HoldsAt(Have(Banana),T) ∧ HoldsAt(Have(Milk),T) ∧ HoldsAt(Have(Drill),T)

Let Δ be the conjunction of the following Happens and temporal ordering formulae.

Happens(Go(Supermarket),T0)   Happens(Buy(Banana),T1)

Happens(Buy(Milk),T2)   Happens(Go(DIYShop),T3)

Happens(Buy(Drill),T4)

T0 < T1   T0 < T2

T1 < T3   T2 < T3

T3 < T4   T4 < T

Note that Δ is not committed to any particular ordering of the Buy(Banana) and Buy(Milk) actions. As we would expect, according to the definition above, Δ is indeed a plan for Γ. In other words,we have,

CIRC[Σ ; Initiates, Terminates, Releases] ∧ CIRC[Δ ; Happens] ∧ EC ∧ Ω ⊨ Γ.

The provision of a logical characterisation of the planning task is all very well. But for a complete picture, and to address the issues raised in the Russell and Norvig quote in the introduction, we need to look at computational matters. These are the focus of the sequel.

3 Partial Order Planning = Event Calculus + Abduction

The title of this section deliberately echoes Kowalski's slogan "Algorithm = Logic + Control" [Kowalski, 1974]. The aim of the section is to sketch the use of logic programming techniques to render the previous section's logical specification of partial order planning into a practical implementation. The basis of this implementation will be a resolution based abductive theorem prover, coded as a Prolog meta-interpreter. This theorem prover is tailored for the event calculus by compiling the event calculus axioms into the meta-level, resulting in an efficient implementation.

As pointed out by [Missiaen, et al., 1995], the event calculus axioms, in particular (EC1) to (EC6), can be likened to Chapman's "modal truth criterion" (but stripped of the modalities) [Chapman, 1987]. The logic programming approach to planning advocated in this paper can be thought of as *directly executing* the modal truth criterion. The event calculus Initiates, Terminates and Releases formulae that constitute a purely logical description of the effects of actions in a particular domain are used directly as the domain description in the implemented planner.

Many of the computational concepts central to the literature on partial order planning, such as threats, protected links, promotions and demotions [Chapman, 1987], [Penberthy & Weld, 1992], turn out to have direct counterparts in the theorem proving process. It's interesting to note that these features of the logic programming implementation weren't designed in. Rather, they are naturally arising features of the theorem prover's search for a proof. So our attempt to provide a mathematically respectable answer to the question "What is partial order planning?" inadvertantly offers similar answers to questions like "What are protected links?". To see all this we need to delve into the details of the meta-interpreter. In what follows, I will assume some knowledge of logic programming concepts and terminology.

3.1 An Abductive Meta-Interpreter for the Event Calculus

Meta-interpreters are a standard part of the logic programmer's toolkit. For example, the following "vanilla" meta-interpreter, when executed by Prolog, will mimic Prolog's own execution strategy.[3]

```
demo([]).
demo([G|Gs1]) :-
    axiom(G,Gs2), append(Gs2,Gs1,Gs3), demo(Gs3).
demo([not(G)|Gs]) :- not demo([G]), demo(Gs).
```

The formula demo(Gs) holds if Gs follows from the object-level program. If Π is a list of Prolog literals $[\lambda_1, \ldots, \lambda_n]$, then the formula axiom(λ_0,Π) holds if there is a clause of the following form in the object-level program.

$$\lambda_0 \ :- \ \lambda_1, \ \ldots, \ \lambda_n$$

One of the tricks we'll employ here is to compile object-level clauses into the meta-level. For example, the above clause can be compiled into the definition of demo through the addition of the following clause.

```
demo([λ0|Gs1]) :-
    axiom(λ1,Gs2), append(Gs2,[λ2, ..., λn|Gs1],Gs3),
    demo(Gs3).
```

The resulting behaviour is equivalent to that of the vanilla meta-interpreter with the object-level clause. Now consider the following object-level clause, which corresponds to Axiom (EC2) of Section 1.

```
holds_at(F,T3) :-
    happens(A,T1,T2), T2 < T3, initiates(A,F,T1), not
clipped(T1,F,T2).
```

This can be compiled into the following meta-level clause, in which the predicate before is used to represent temporal ordering.

```
demo([holds_at(F,T3)|Gs1]) :-
    axiom(initiates(A,F,T1),Gs2), axiom(happens(A,T1,T2),Gs3),
    axiom(before(T2,T3),[]), demo([not clipped(T1,F,T3)]),
    append(Gs3,Gs2,Gs4), append(Gs4,Gs1,Gs5), demo(Gs5).
```

To represent Axiom (EC5), which isn't in Horn clause form, we introduce the function neg. Throughout our logic program, we replace the classical predicate calculus formula $\neg$ HoldsAt(f,t) with holds_at(neg(F),T). So we obtain the following object-level clause.

```
holds_at(neg(F),T3) :-
    happens(A,T1,T2), T2 < T3, terminates(A,F,T1),
    not declipped(T1,F,T2).
```

This compiles into the following meta-level clause.

---

[3] Throughout the paper, I use standard Edinburgh syntax for Prolog. Variables begin with upper-case letters, while predicate and function symbols with lower-case letters, which is the opposite convention to that used for predicate calculus.

```
demo([holds_at(neg(F),T3)|Gs1]) :-
    axiom(terminates(A,F,T1),Gs2), axiom(happens(A,T1,T2),Gs3),
    axiom(before(T2,T3),[]), demo([not declipped(T1,F,T3)]),
    append(Gs3,Gs2,Gs4), append(Gs4,Gs1,Gs5), demo(Gs5).
```

The Prolog execution of these two meta-level clauses doesn't mimic precisely the Prolog execution of the corresponding object-level clause. This is because we have taken advantage of the extra degree of control available at the meta-level, and adjusted the order in which the sub-goals of holds_at are solved. For example, although we resolve on initiates immediately, we postpone further work on the sub-goals of initiates until after we've resolved on happens and before. This manoeuvre is required to prevent looping.

The job of an abductive meta-interpreter is to construct a *residue* of *abducible* literals that can't be proved from the object-level program. In the case of the event calculus, the abducibles will be happens and before literals. Here's a "vanilla" abductive meta-interpreter, without negation-as-failure.

```
abdemo([],R,R).
abdemo([G|Gs],R1,R2) :- abducible(G), abdemo(Gs,[G|R1],R2).
abdemo([G|Gs1],R1,R2) :-
    axiom(G,Gs2), append(Gs2,Gs1,Gs3), abdemo(Gs3,R1,R2).
```

The formula abdemo(Gs,R1,R2) holds if Gs follows from the conjunction of R2 with the object-level program. (R1 is the input residue and R2 is the output residue.) Abducible literals are declared via the abducible predicate. In top-level calls to abdemo, the second argument will usually be [].

Things start to get tricky when we incorporate negation-as-failure. The difficulty here is that when we add to the residue, previously proved negated goals may no longer be provable. So negated goals have to be recorded and re-checked each time the residue is modified. Here's a version of abdemo which handles negation-as-failure.

```
abdemo([],R,R,N).                                            (A1)
abdemo([G|Gs],R1,R3,N) :-                                     (A2)
    abducible(G), abdemo_nafs(N,[G|R1],R2), abdemo(Gs,R2,R3,N).
abdemo([G|Gs1],R1,R2,N) :-                                    (A3)
    axiom(G,Gs2), append(Gs2,Gs1,Gs3), abdemo(Gs3,R1,R2,N).
abdemo([not(G)|Gs],R1,R3,N) :-                                (A4)
    abdemo_naf([G],R1,R2), abdemo(Gs,R2,R3,[[G]|N]).
```

The last argument of the abdemo predicate is a list of negated goal lists, which is recorded for subsequent checking (in Clause (A2)). If $N = [\gamma_{1,1} \ldots \gamma_{1,n_1}] \ldots [\gamma_{m,1} \ldots \gamma_{m,n_m}]]$ is such a list, then its meaning, assuming a completion semantics for our object-level logic program, is,

$$\neg\,(\gamma_{1,1} \wedge ... \wedge \gamma_{1,n_1}) \wedge \neg\,(\gamma_{m,1} \wedge ... \wedge \gamma_{m,n_m}).$$

The formula abdemo_nafs(N,R1,R2) holds if the above formula is provable from the (completion of the) conjunction of R2 with the object-level program. (In the vanilla version, abdemo_nafs doesn't add to the residue. However, we will eventually require a version which does, as we'll see shortly.)

abdemo_nafs(N,R1,R2) applies abdemo_naf to each list of goals in N. abdemo_naf is defined in terms of Prolog's findall, as follows.

```
abdemo_naf([G|Gs1],R,R) :- not resolve(G,R,Gs2).
```

```
abdemo_naf([G1|Gs1],R1,R2) :-
  findall(Gs2,(resolve(G1,R1,Gs3),
    append(Gs3,Gs1,Gs2)),Gss),
  abdemo_nafs(Gss,R1,R2).
resolve(G,R,Gs) :- member(G,R).
resolve(G,R,Gs) :- axiom(G,Gs).
```

The logical justification for these clauses is as follows. In order to show, $\neg (\gamma_1 \wedge ... \wedge \gamma_n)$, we have to show that, for every object-level clause $\lambda :- \lambda_1 ... \lambda_m$ which resolves with γ_1, $\neg (\lambda_1 \wedge ... \wedge \lambda_m, \gamma_2 \wedge ... \wedge \gamma_n)$. If no clause resolves with γ_1 then, under a completion semantics, $\neg \gamma_1$ follows, and therefore so does $\neg (\gamma_1 \wedge ... \wedge \gamma_n)$.

However, in the context of incomplete information about a predicate we don't wish to assume that predicate's completion, and we cannot therefore legitimately use negation-as-failure to prove negated goals for that predicate.

The way around this is to trap negated goals for such predicates at the meta-level, and give them special treatment. In general, if we know $\neg \phi \leftarrow \psi$, then in order to prove $\neg \phi$, it's sufficient to prove ψ. Similarly, if we know $\neg \phi \leftrightarrow \psi$, then in order to prove $\neg \phi$, it's both necessary and sufficient to prove ψ.

In the present case, we have incomplete information about the before predicate. Accordingly, when the meta-interpreter encounters a goal of the form not before(X,Y), which it will when it comes to prove a negated clipped goal, it attempts to prove before(Y,X). One way to achieve this is to add before(Y,X) to the residue, first checking that the resulting residue is consistent.[4]

Similar considerations affect the treatment of the holds_at predicate, which inherits the incompleteness of before. When the meta-interpreter encounters a not holds_at(F,T) goal, where F is a ground term, it attempts to prove holds_at(neg(F),T), and conversely, when it encounters not holds_at(neg(F),T), it attempts to prove holds_at(F,T). In both cases, this can result in further additions to the residue. (The story is a little more complicated if F is a variable, but there isn't space to go into this issue here.)

Note that these techniques for dealing with negation in the context of incomplete information are general in scope. They're generic theorem proving techniques, and their use isn't confined to the event calculus. For further details of the implementation of abdemo_naf, the reader should consult the (electronic) appendix.

As with the demo predicate, we can compile the event calculus axioms into the definition of abdemo and abdemo_naf via the addition of some extra clauses, giving us a finer degree of control over the resolution process. Here's an example.

```
abdemo([holds_at(F,T3)|Gs1],R1,R4,N) :-                           (A5)
  axiom(initiates(A,F,T1),Gs2),
  abdemo_nafs(N,[happens(A,T1,T2),before(T2,T3)|R1],R2),
  abdemo_nafs([clipped(T1,F,T3)],R2,R3),
  append(Gs2,Gs1,Gs3), demo(Gs3,R3,R4,[clipped(T1,F,T3)|N]).
```

Now, to solve a planning problem, we simply describe the effects of actions directly as Prolog initiates, terminates and releases clauses, we present a list of holds_at goals to abdemo, and the returned residue, comprising happens and

---

[4] In [Shanahan, 1989] and [Missiaen, et al., 1995], this problem is tackled via the use of nested negations-as-failure at the object level. The approach of the present paper is more principled.

before literals, is a plan. Notice that, since the sub-goals of initiates are solved abductively, actions with context-dependent effects are handled correctly, unlike the implementation described in [Missiaen, *et al.*, 1995].

Further details of the implementation are relegated to the (electronic) appendix, which presents a full program listing. But with this sketch, we're already in a position to compare the behaviour of an abductive theorem prover applied to the event calculus to that of a hand-coded partial order planning algorithm.

3.2 Protected Links, Threats, Promotions and Demotions

The algorithm below, which is very similar to UCPOP [Penberthy & Weld, 1992], illustrates the style of algorithm commonly found in the literature on partial order planning. It constructs a partially ordered plan given a goal list. A goal list is a list of pairs $\langle F, T \rangle$ where F is a fluent and T is a time point. A plan is a list of pairs $\langle A, T \rangle$ where A is an action (more properly called an operator in planning terminology) and T is a time point.

The key idea in the algorithm is the maintenance of a list of *protected links*. This is a list of triples $\langle T1, F, T2 \rangle$, where T1 and T2 are time points and F is a fluent. The purpose of this list is to ensure that, once a goal has been achieved by the addition of a suitable action to the plan, that goal isn't "clobbered" by a subsequent addition to the plan. Accordingly, each addition to the plan is followed by a check to see whether it constitutes a *threat* to any protected link. An action $\langle A, T1 \rangle$ threatens a protected link $\langle T2, F, T3 \rangle$ if the ordering constraint T2 < T1 < T3 is consistent with the plan and one of the effects of A is to make F false. By *promoting* or *demoting* the new action, in other words by constraining its time of occurrence to fall either before T2 or after T3, we eliminate the threat.

```
1   while goal list non-empty
2       choose a goal <F1,T1> from goal list
3       choose an action <A,T2> whose effects include F1
4       for each precondition F2 of A add <F2,T2> to goal list
5       add <A,T2> to plan
6       add T2 < T1 to plan
7       add <T2,F1,T1> to protected links
8       for each <A,T3> in plan that threatens some <T4,F3,T5>
        in protected links
9           choose either
10              promotion: add T3 < T4 to plan
11              demotion: add T5 < T3
12      end for
13  end while
```

Since the algorithm is non-deterministic, it has to be combined with a suitable search strategy. With some minor modifications, the algorithm can be turned into UCPOP, which is both sound and complete, assuming a breadth-first or iterative deepening search strategy [Penberthy & Weld, 1992]. Unlike the above algorithm, but like the abductive meta-interpreter of the last section, UCPOP can also handle actions with context-dependent effects.

The close correspondence between the behaviour of this algorithm and that of the abductive theorem prover of the previous section can be established by inspection. In particular, consider Clause (A5). Line 3 of the algorithm (choosing an action) corresponds to the first sub-goal of (A5) (resolving on initiates). Line 4 (adding new preconditions to the goal list) corresponds to the fourth sub-goal. The effect of

Lines 5 and 6 (adding the new action to the plan) is achieved in (A5) by the second sub-goal. Line 7 (adding the new protected link) and the for loop of Lines 8 to 12 are matched by the third sub-goal of (A5), which adds a new `clipped` literal to the list of negations. Promotion and demotion (Lines 11 and 12) are achieved in the theorem prover by `abdemo_nafs` which, as explained in the previous section, will add further `before` literals to the residue if necessary.

Like the non-deterministic hand-coded algorithm, the search space defined by Clauses (A1) to (A5) can be explored with a variety of strategies. If executed by Prolog, a depth-first search strategy would result, but a breadth-first or iterative deepening strategy is also possible.

To summarise, the concepts of a protected link, of a threat, and of promotion and demotion, rather than being special to partial order planning, turn out to be instances of general concepts in theorem proving when applied to general purpose axioms for representing the effects of actions. In particular,

- A protected link is a negated `clipped` goal which, like any negated goal in abduction with negation-as-failure, is preserved for subsequent checking when new literals are added to the residue,

- A threat is an addition to the residue which, without further additions, would undermine the proof of a previously solved negated `clipped` goal.

- Promotion and demotion are additions to the residue which preserve the proof of a previously solved negated `clipped` goal.

4 Hierarchical Planning

It's a surprisingly straightforward matter to extend the foregoing logical treatment of partial order planning to planning via hierarchical decomposition. The representation of compound actions and events in the event calculus is very natural, and is best illustrated by example. The following formulae axiomatise a robot mail delivery domain.

First we formalise the effects of the primitive actions. The term Pickup(p) denotes the action of picking up package p, the term PutDown(p) denotes the action of putting down package p, and the term GoThrough(d) denotes the action of going through door d. The fluent Got(p) holds if the robot is carrying the package p, and the fluent In(x,r) holds if object x is in room r. The formula Connects(d,r1,r2) represents that door d connects rooms r1 and r2.

Initiates(Pickup(p),Got(p),t) ←
    $p \neq$ Robot $\wedge$ HoldsAt(In(Robot,r),t) $\wedge$ HoldsAt(In(p,r),t)

Releases(Pickup(p),In(p,r),t) ←
    $p \neq$ Robot $\wedge$ HoldsAt(In(Robot,r),t) $\wedge$ HoldsAt(In(p,r),t)

Initiates(PutDown(p),In(p,r),t) ←
    $p \neq$ Robot $\wedge$ HoldsAt(Got(p),t) $\wedge$ HoldsAt(In(Robot,r),t)

Initiates(GoThrough(d),In(Robot,r1),t) ←
    HoldsAt(In(Robot,r2),t) $\wedge$ Connects(d,r2,r1)

Terminates(GoThrough(d),In(Robot,r),t) ← HoldsAt(In(Robot,r),t)

Next we have our first example of a compound action definition. Compound actions have duration, while primitive actions will usually be represented as instantaneous. The term ShiftPack(p,r) denotes the action of retrieving and delivering package p to room r. It comprises a number of sub-actions: two GoToRoom actions, a Pickup action and a PutDown action. A GoToRoom action is itself a compound action, to be defined shortly.

Happens(ShiftPack(p,r1),t1,t6) ←
    HoldsAt(In(p,r2),t1) ∧ Happens(GoToRoom(r2),t1,t2) ∧ t2 < t3 ∧
        Happens(Pickup(p),t3) ∧ t3 < t4 ∧ Happens(GoToRoom(r1),t4,t5) ∧
           t5 < t6 ∧ Happens(PutDown(p),t6)

Initiates(ShiftPack(p,r),In(p,r),t)

The effects of compound actions should follow from the effects of their sub-actions, as can be verified in this case by inspection. Next we have the definition of a GoToRoom action.

Happens(GoToRoom(r),t,t) ← HoldsAt(In(Robot,r),t)

Happens(GoToRoom(r1),t1,t3) ←
    HoldsAt(In(Robot,r2),t1) ∧ Connects(d,r2,r3) ∧
        Happens(GoThrough(d),t1) ∧ t1 < t2 ∧ Happens(GoToRoom(r1),t2,t3)

Initiates(GoToRoom(r),In(Robot,r),t)

This illustrates both conditional decomposition and recursive decompostion: a compound action can decompose into different sequences of sub-actions depending on what conditions hold, and a compound action can be decomposed into a sequence of sub-actions that includes a compound action of the same type as itself. A consequence of this is that the event calculus with compound actions is formally as powerful as any programming language. In this respect, it can be used in the same way as GOLOG [Levesque, et al., 1997], a programming language built on a different logic-based action formalism, namely the situation calculus. Note, however, that we can freely mix direct programming with planning from first principles.

Once again, the effects of the compound action should follow from the effects of its components. This property is made more precise below.

Let Ω denote the conjunction of the following uniqueness-of-names axioms.

    UNA[Pickup, PutDown, GoThrough, ShiftPack, GoToRoom]

    UNA[Got, In]

The definition of the planning task from Section 2 is unaffected by the inclusion of compound events. However, it's convenient to distinguish *fully decomposed* plans, comprising only primitive actions, from those that include compound actions.

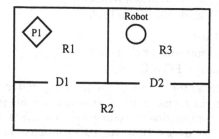

Figure 1: A Mail Delivery Domain

Now let's take a look at a particular mail delivery task. Let Σ_p be the conjunction of the above Initiates, Terminates and Releases formulae for primitive actions, and let Σ_c be the conjunction of the above Initiates formulae for compound actions. Let Δ_c be the conjunction of the above compound event definitions.

The conjunction Φ of the following Connects formulae represents the layout of rooms illustrated in Figure 1.

Connects(D1,R1,R2)   Connects(D1,R2,R1)

Connects(D2,R2,R3)   Connects(D2,R3,R2)

Let Δ_0 denote the conjunction of the following formulae representing the initial situation depicted in Figure 1.

Initially(In(Robot,R3))   Initially(In(P1,R1))

Let Γ denote the following HoldsAt formula, which is our goal state.

HoldsAt(In(P1,R2),T)

Consider the following narrative of actions Δ_p.

Happens(GoThrough(D2),T0)   Happens(GoThrough(D1),T1)

Happens(Pickup(P1),T2)   Happens(GoThrough(D1),T3)

Happens(PutDown(P1),T4)

T0 < T1   T1 < T2

T2 < T3   T3 < T4

T4 < T

Now we have, for example,

CIRC[$\Sigma_p \wedge \Sigma_c$; Initiates, Terminates, Releases] $\wedge$
    CIRC[$\Delta_0 \wedge \Delta_p \wedge \Delta_c$; Happens] $\wedge$ EC $\wedge$ Ω $\wedge$ Φ $\models$
        Happens(ShiftPack(P1,R2),T0,T4).

We also have,

CIRC[$\Sigma_p \wedge \Sigma_c$; Initiates, Terminates, Releases] $\wedge$
    CIRC[$\Delta_0 \wedge \Delta_p \wedge \Delta_c$; Happens] $\wedge$ EC $\wedge$ Ω $\wedge$ Φ $\models$ Γ.

So Δ_p constitutes a plan. Furthermore, we have,

CIRC[Σ_p ; Initiates, Terminates, Releases] $\wedge$
    CIRC[$\Delta_0 \wedge \Delta_p$; Happens] $\wedge$ EC $\wedge$ Ω $\wedge$ Φ $\models$ Γ.

So Δ_p constitutes a plan in the context of only the primitive actions. In general, if we let Δ_p be any narrative description comprising only primitive actions and Φ be any conjunction of Connects formulae, we have the following theorem. For any fluent β and time point τ, HoldsAt(β,τ) follows from,

CIRC[$\Sigma_p \wedge \Sigma_c$; Initiates, Terminates, Releases] $\wedge$
    CIRC[$\Delta_p \wedge \Delta_c$; Happens] $\wedge$ EC $\wedge$ Ω $\wedge$ Φ

if and only if it follows from,

CIRC[Σ_p ; Initiates, Terminates, Releases] $\wedge$
    CIRC[Δ_p ; Happens] $\wedge$ EC $\wedge$ Ω $\wedge$ Φ.

We should expect such a property to follow from any correctly formulated domain description involving compound actions, since the (chief) purpose of compound actions is to adjust the computation by cutting down on search, and not to increase the set of consequences of the theory. However, the inclusion of compound actions in the logical account gives meaning to partially decomposed plans, which are the intermediate steps in this computation. This is an example of a logical innovation which is highly suggestive of the form the computation should take.

In general we will require our planner to find fully decomposed plans, although it's extremely useful to be able to suspend the planning process before a fully decomposed plan has been found, and still to have a useful result in the form of a partially decomposed plan. The suspension of planning can be achieved in a logic programming implementation with a resource-bounded meta-interpreter such as that described by Kowalski [1995]. Furthermore, the use of hierarchical decomposition facilitiates the generation of plans in progression order (first action first), as opposed to the regression order (last action first) usually found in logic-based planners. The generation of plans in regression order would rule out the possibility of suspending planning in mid-execution and still receiving useful results.

This brings us to the issue of implementation. What modifications are required to the abductive meta-interpreter of Section 3 to enable it to perform hierarchical decomposition? The answer is remarkable. Almost none at all. When presented with compound event definitions of the above form, it automatically performs hierarchical decomposition. Whenever a happens goal is reached for a compound action, its resolution yields further happens sub-goals, and this process continues until primitive actions are reached, which are added to the residue.[5]

Section 3 was entitled "Partial Order Planning = Event Calculus + Abduction". Now we've arrived at another instantiation of Kowalski's equation. Hierarchical planning = event calculus with compound events + abduction. Using the methodology of this paper, all we have to do to obtain a hierarchical planner from a partial order planner is represent compound actions in the obvious way.

Concluding Remarks

This paper continues a line of work on event calculus planning begun in [Eshghi, 1988]. Eshghi's techniques were simplified (and applied to temporal explanation) in [Shanahan, 1989]. But neither of these papers described a practical planner. The first usable event calculus planner was developed in Belgium by Missiaen, et al. [1995]. Recently, another abductive event calculus planner has been developed at DFKI in Germany [Jung, et al., 1996]. All of these planners are based on similar ideas to those presented in this paper: all use abductive logic programming techniques to generate plans using a similar style of representation via initiates, terminates and happens predicates.

The present paper goes beyond the work of its predecessors in several ways. First, it tackles the issue of hierarchical planning. Second, the event calculus formalism used is not just a logic program, but is specified in first-order predicate calculus augmented with circumscription. Third, the paper exposes close correspondences with existing planning algorithms. Since the planner is simply the result of applying general purpose theorem proving techniques to a general purpose action formalism, it can be argued that this illuminates the nature of several commonly deployed concepts in the planning literature. Fourth, unlike the planners in [Missiaen, et al., 1995] and [Jung, et al., 1996], the planner of the present paper can handle actions with context-dependent effects. Finally, since it uses abduction to solve initiates and terminates goals, the planner is both sound and complete, and performs correctly on a number of potentially anomalous examples described in [Missiaen, et al., 1995].

---

[5] Furthermore, if we make Connects abducible in the mail delivery example instead of Happens, we can use exactly the same meta-interpreter to determine room connectivity given a narrative of actions and a conjunction of formulae of the form $HoldsAt(In(Robot,\rho),\tau)$. This further underlines the generic nature of the techniques being applied here.

Acknowledgments

Thanks to Rob Miller. This work was carried out as part of the EPSRC funded project GR/L20023 "Cognitive Robotics".

References

[Chapman, 1987] D.Chapman, Planning for Conjunctive Goals, *Artificial Intelligence*, vol. 32 (1987), pp. 333–377.

[Eshghi, 1988] K.Eshghi, Abductive Planning with Event Calculus, *Proceedings of the Fifth International Conference on Logic Programming* (1988), pp. 562–579.

[Green 1969] C.Green, Applications of Theorem Proving to Problem Solving, *Proceedings IJCAI 69*, pp. 219–240.

[Jung, *et al.*, 1996] C.G.Jung, K.Fischer and A.Burt, *Multi-Agent Planning Using an Abductive Event Calculus*, DFKI Report RR-96-04 (1996), DFKI, Germany.

[Kowalski, 1979] R.A.Kowalski, Algorithm = Logic + Control, Communications of the ACM, vol. 22, pp. 424–436.

[Kowalski, 1995] R.A.Kowalski, Using Meta-Logic to Reconcile Reactive with Rational Agents, in *Meta-Logics and Logic Programming*, ed. K.R.Apt and F.Turini, MIT Press (1995), pp. 227–242.

[Kowalski & Sergot, 1986] R.A.Kowalski and M.J.Sergot, A Logic-Based Calculus of Events, *New Generation Computing*, vol 4 (1986), pp. 67–95.

[Lespérance, *et al.*, 1994] Y.Lespérance, H.J.Levesque, F.Lin, D.Marcu, R.Reiter, and R.B.Scherl, A Logical Approach to High-Level Robot Programming: A Progress Report, in *Control of the Physical World by Intelligent Systems: Papers from the 1994 AAAI Fall Symposium*, ed. B.Kuipers, New Orleans (1994), pp. 79–85.

[Levesque, 1996] H.Levesque, What Is Planning in the Presence of Sensing? *Proceedings AAAI 96*, pp. 1139–1146.

[Levesque, *et al.*, 1997] H.Levesque, R.Reiter, Y.Lespérance, F.Lin and R.B.Scherl, GOLOG: A Logic Programming Language for Dynamic Domains, *The Journal of Logic Programming* (1997), to appear.

[Missiaen, *et al.*, 1995] L.Missiaen, M.Bruynooghe and M.Denecker, CHICA, A Planning System Based on Event Calculus, *The Journal of Logic and Computation*, vol. 5, no. 5 (1995), pp. 579–602.

[Penberthy & Weld, 1992] J.S.Penberthy and D.S.Weld, UCPOP: A Sound, Complete, Partial Order Planner for ADL, *Proceedings KR 92*, pp. 103–114.

[Russell & Norvig, 1995] S.Russell and P.Norvig, *Artificial Intelligence: A Modern Approach*, Prentice Hall International (1995).

[Shanahan, 1989] M.P.Shanahan, Prediction Is Deduction but Explanation Is Abduction, *Proceedings IJCAI 89*, pp. 1055–1060.

[Shanahan, 1997] M.P.Shanahan, *Solving the Frame Problem: A Mathematical Investigation of the Common Sense Law of Inertia*, MIT Press (1997).

Appendix

A fully commented program listing of the latest version of the planner is available electronically from http://www.dcs.qmw.ac.uk/~mps/planner.txt. The planner is written in LPA MacProlog 32, but should be easy to port to other Prolog systems. Stripped of comments, the current version of the planner is 300 lines long.

Constraint Based Reactive Rescheduling in a Stochastic Environment

J.E. Spragg,[1] G. Fozzard,[2] and D.J. Tyler[3]

[1] School of Information Technology, Mid Sweden University,
Mitthögskolan, Sundsvall, Sweden.
[2] School of Design and Manufacture, De Montfort University,
Leicester, United Kingdom.
[3] Department of Clothing Design and Technology,
Manchester Metropolitan University,
Manchester, United Kingdom.

Abstract. The problem of scheduling manufacturing systems where the capacity of a production resource is subject to stochastic change, is the subject of this paper. Resources which are dependent upon labour intensive processes provide typical examples. In the United Kingdom the manufacture of clothing garments is still dominated by the progressive bundle system. Garments are produced on a continuous-flow production line in which garment pieces are passed in succession through a network of workstations where skilled manual workers complete operations on garments using sewing machines. These production systems are subject to numerous perturbations caused by operator absenteeism and machine breakdown necessitating the need for reactive rescheduling to maintain line balance. In the approach described here, line balance is maintained via periodic schedule repair, based upon reassignment heuristics, supported by partial order backtracking.

1 Introduction

The problem of scheduling manufacturing systems, where the capacity of a production resource is subject to stochastic change, is the subject of this paper. Resources which are dependent upon labour intensive processes provide typical examples.

In many sectors of the industry, the manufacture of clothing garments is still dominated by the progressive bundle system (PBS)[1]. Garments are produced on a continuous-flow production line in which garment pieces are passed in succession through a network of workstations where skilled manual workers complete operations on garments using sewing machines. The workstations which comprise the flow line can be connected in either a serial or a parallel fashion depending upon the sequencing constraints which govern the order in which the garments are to be assembled. The rate of flow of work through each workstation is determined by the individual performance of each machinist.

The dominance of labour-intensive assembly systems relates to the difficulties of automating the assembly of garment pieces. The automation of handling a flimsy material like cloth alone has proved a major bottleneck in the adoption of Computer Integrated Manufacturing (CIM) practices.

Despite advances in automation in other sectors of manufacturing industry, it is clear that the requirement to successfully manage skilled manual labor will continue to be employed until appropriate technologies can be found. The PBS represents a serious scheduling problem for factory managers and line supervisors. This problem is not alleviated by the trend towards smaller contract sizes which reflect a fluid fashion market.

The determination of the optimum order in which sewing operations should be arranged is not a major scheduling problem. In fact, it is the classic sequencing problem, $n/m/P/Cmax$, discussed in French[2]. The real scheduling problem associated with a PBS arises from the constant need for reactive rescheduling to maintain line balance and to maximize productivity. The frequency of operator absenteeism, or machine breakdown, or unstable operator performance, requires constant reassignment of operators and operations. In such systems, reactive rescheduling becomes so frequent that it takes on the character of supervisory control. In the approach described here, line balance is maintained via periodic schedule repair, based upon reassignment heuristics, supported by partial order backtracking.

2 Line Balance

Schedule repair activity is triggered by monitoring the flow line. At the start of a new line, operators are allocated to operations by line supervisors and production managers. The number of operators required for each operation is calculated using the principles of load and capacity planning. In practice, the operators' skills and performance rarely fit the work content of the operations and potential bottlenecks become inherent in the line's design. Moreover, even if it were possible to achieve a perfect line balance, it would be impossible to maintain it over time due to line perturbations caused by machine breakdowns, operator absenteeism and fluctuations in operator performance. The schedule must be repaired to maintain *balance control*. Balance control is necessary because of the sectionalization of the line that leads to different operations being performed at different rates. To provide protection against variations in output over discrete periods of time, an agreed amount of work-in-progress is allowed to act as a buffer between individual operations. A requirement for supervisory control is to set the flow of work through each operation to be as similar as possible. The success of this behavior is reflected in the operational measures of line efficiency and productive performance. Therefore, the primary indicators of unbalanced work flow are idle workstations and declining or overloaded work-in-progress buffers.

The monitoring task is necessarily accompanied by analysis. The cause of problems must be identified. Calculations are required to identify which operations require additional resources and which operations can be alleviated of resources.

3 A Formal PBS Model

Formally, a PBS flow line can be viewed as a set of operations, O, where each operation, o, is a 2-tuple which consists of a set of operators, Op, and a set of machines, M^4, which have been assigned to the operation:

$$o(Op, M)$$

The scheduling problem consists of assigning operators, op, and machines, m, to an operation, o_1, until the calculated output from the operation is equal, or greater than the next operation, o_2, in the sequence.

$$o_1(\{op_1, op_2, \ldots, op_n\}, \{m_1, m_2, \ldots, m_n\})$$
$$\geq$$
$$o_2(\{op_1\prime, op_2\prime, \ldots, op_n\prime\}, \{m_1\prime, m_2\prime, \ldots, m_n\prime\})$$

The sequence constraint, $o_1 \prec o_2$, is determined by the technical necessity of having to perform operation o_1 before operation o_2.

Other constraints prohibit the operators and machines that can be assigned to an operation. An operation requires a particular skill from an operator, and a particular type of machine. For simplicity we can say that the assigned operator's skill must equal the type of the machine assigned:

$$skill(op) = type(m)$$

A typical operator has a set of skills, S (operations that she or he can perform), and a particular performance level, p.

The process time required for each operation is determined by the work content of the operation, measured by a standard minute value (SMV), which is often empirically determined by time and motion study, and the performance of the operators. The process time is calculated by dividing the standard minute value of the operation by an operator performance factor. Operator performance is, again, determined by time study practitioners. The industry recognizes that a '100' performer can perform a sewing operation with a 3 minute work value in 3 minutes (including rest and contingency allowances). Whereas a '50' performer would take 6 minutes (including allowances).

The maintenance of line balance requires that the process times (pt) for all operations are kept as close as possible to a mean value (which will be dependent on the particular set of operators working on the specific product). So that pt_1 and pt_2 of $o_1(pt_1) \prec o_2(pt_2)$ are either equal or within an acceptable range which can be absorbed by the work-in-progress buffers between the operations.

4 Initial Line Balance

The initial line balance is achieved by employing a greedy algorithm which assigns operators to machines and operations.

---

[4] Op and M have the same cardinality.

The greedy algorithm (*Init-Flow-Line*) that assigns the operators and machines to the operations takes two sets as arguments: the unordered set of operations, O, and an ordered set of skill holders, Sk. The members of the set Sk are constraint satisfaction *variables* which denote a skill. The *domain* of the *variables* is the set of operators, Op, with that skill. Both the variables Sk and their domains Op are ordered. The variables are ordered according to the cardinality of their domains. The variables with few domain members are processed first. The domains of each $sk_i \in Sk$ are ordered according to the cardinality of the skill set of the operators they represent, those operators with few skills are more constrained than those with multiple skills and are processed first. The algorithm also takes a variable, t, which denotes the target output of the line. The operations, **PUSH**, **POP**, **GET**, and **REMOVE**, are primitive procedures with obvious interpretations.

Greedy Algorithm

INIT-FLOW-LINE(O, Sk, t)
1   **while** $O \neq NIL$
2   **do** $sk \leftarrow \text{POP}(Sk)$
3        $o \leftarrow \text{GET}(o_{sk}, O)$
4   **repeat**
5            $op \leftarrow \text{POP}(Domain_{sk})$
6            $\text{PUSH}(op, Op_o)$
7   /* Remove op from future domains. */
8            $\text{FORWARD-CHECK}(op, Sk)$
9            $\text{PUSH}(\text{MACHINE}(o), M_o)$
10   /* Have we assigned enough operators to o? */
11
12   **until** ENOUGH-P(o, t) or $Domain_{sk} = NIL$
13   REMOVE(o, O)

If there are insufficient operators or machines to cover the tasks, it means that the daily output parameter, t, must be relaxed. It can be considered to be a soft constraint. The greedy algorithm ignores operator performance, p. Operator performance is considered to be a soft constraint which can be relaxed. (The buffers between operations can absorb the additional output of a '100' performer doing a '75' job.) The algorithm only attempts to assign correctly skilled operators to the various tasks. The added complexity of satisfying performance constraints would require an alternative search procedure, for example, a beam search. This is considered unnecessary because the impact that performance has on output is averaged out over an entire shift. *It is a constraint which can be satisfied over time.* Satisfying operator performance constraints is actually an optimization problem. At any one point in time, the partial satisfaction of the performance constraint is acceptable because the buffers between operations can absorb excess and feed down stream operations. The satisfaction of the operator performance constraint is achieved over the entire work shift and measured as a constraint which satisfies an objective function.

It is the function of schedule repair to maintain line balance by keeping the process times of operations as equal as possible. This is achieved by transferring, and exchanging, operators between operations. The identification of which operator or operators to transfer or exchange is determined by reassignment heuristics.

5   Schedule Repair

Schedule repair attempts to solve a dynamic constraint satisfaction problem, and is achieved by reassigning operators to other operations. This activity is supported by partial order backtracking which identifies the appropriate set of candidates.

Schedule repair is triggered by monitoring the flow line. The primary indicators of line unbalance is work-in-progress buffers. An empty (or rapidly emptying) work-in- progress buffer suggests that process times between operations have become unequal. This could be because of human factors, an operator's performance could have dropped because of boredom or illness. Alternatively, an operator could be absent, or a machine could have broken down. Whatever the reason, the analysis task must generate two sets, the set of those candidate operators, C, whose performance, p_{from}, can be transferred from its current operation, and the set of operations, T, which must have additional performance, p_{in}.

The members of set T are prioritized to identify the most desperate imbalance. Any operator from C whose performance, p_{from}, equals some p_{in} in T would be an ideal candidate for transfer.

Unfortunately, it is rare that such an ideal candidate can be identified. It is usual that a sequence of exchanges is necessary before a candidate can be freed to add additional performance to an operation.

For example, assume that analysis has identified an operation which requires an additional '75' performance from an overlock[5] operator. The set C of possible candidates does not contain such an operator. However, there is an operator in C with cross stitch skills that can be transferred to a cross stitch operation which allows a '75' performer, with both cross stitch and overlock skills, to be transferred to the priority operation in T[6]

---

[5] Overlock, lockstitch, bartack, cross stitch, and button hole are kinds of sewing operations.

[6] There is a limit on how recursive these exchanges can be: each time an operator is moved, her or his, performance declines and it takes some time before it returns to its previous level. A flow line which has been seriously perturbed by operator transfers will lose production efficiency. In practice it is better to nominate a small set of operators as floater candidates, and use these exclusively for exchanges (see Tyler, Tennent, and Lowe[3]).

The application of reassignment heuristics to rostering problems, and constraint satisfaction problems in general, is described in Smith[4].

6 Partial Order Backtracking: A discipline for reactive rescheduling

The mechanism which supports the selection of exchange candidates is partial order backtracking. Spragg and Kelleher[5] have described how partial order backtracking offers the rescheduler a framework for schedule repair, based upon a set of *nogoods*, which impose a systematic partial order on the set of activities to be repaired but allows non systematic techniques to be used within that framework.

Ginsberg and McAllester[6] have identified a hybrid search algorithm that combines the advantages of systematic and non systematic methods of solving constraint satisfaction problems. The systematic search method described by these authors, dynamic backtracking, employs a polynomial amount of justification information to guide problem solving. The non systematic methods, GSAT[7] and Min Conflict[8], offer the search algorithm freedom to explore the search space by abandoning the notion of extending a partial solution to a CSP and instead modelling the search space as a total, if inconsistent, assignment of values to variables. A hill climbing procedure is employed on this total set of assignments to try and minimize the number of constraints violated by the overall solution. Ginsberg and McAllester have called their hybrid algorithm *partial-order backtracking*.

Partial order backtracking replaces the fixed variable ordering which constrains dynamic backtracking with a partial order that is dynamically sorted during the search. When a new *nogood* is added to the *nogood* set, this partial ordering does not fix a static sequence on the choice of variable to appear in the *nogood*'s conclusion. As it turns out, there is considerable freedom as to the choice of the variable whose value is to be changed during backtracking, thereby allowing greater control in the directions that the procedures takes in exploring the search space.

However, there is not total freedom: *safety conditions* need to be maintained that model the partial orderings of the variables. It is necessary for variables in the antecedents of *nogoods* to precede the variables in their conclusion. This is because the antecedent variables are responsible for determining the current domains of such variables.

Partial order backtracking supplies a framework for reactive rescheduling. The management of a progressive bundle flow line system approaches scheduling as a problem of repair over time. From a constraint based scheduling perspective, rescheduling introduces an extra set of constraints which need to be addressed. These new constraints are related to the need to preserve the old assignments of operators to operations as far as possible to maintain stability. The old schedule represents an investment in planned resources, allocation of machines and people, which should not be disturbed any more than necessary.

7 Example

An example will illustrate our approach to reactive rescheduling in a stochastic environment . We can imagine a progressive bundle flow line with 4 operations:

$$o_1 \prec o_2 \prec o_3 \prec o_4$$

Where o_1 is an overlock (ol) operation with a standard minute value of 2; o_2 is a cross stitch (xs) operation with a standard minute value of 2; o_3 is a overlock operation with a standard minute value of 2; and o_4 is a lock stitch (ls) operation with a standard minute value of 0.5.

We also have a pool of skilled manual workers (operators) who can be assigned to these operations, $op(Skills, performance)$:

$op_1 (S = \{ol, xs, ls\}, p = 100)$
$op_2 (S = \{ol, xs, ls\}, p = 50)$
$op_3 (S = \{ls\}, p = 75)$
$op_4 (S = \{xs, ls\}, p = 100)$
$op_5 (S = \{xs, ls, ol, bt, bh\}, p = 100)$

We assume for simplicity that sewing machines are an unconstrained resource (i.e. when a sewing machine of a particular type is requested, it is always available).

Therefore, formulating this example as a constraint satisfaction problem gives the variables, o_1, o_2, o_3 and o_4, the following domains:

$o_4 = op_3, op_4, op_2, op_1, op_5$
$o_1 = op_1, op_2, op_5$
$o_3 = op_1, op_2, op_5$
$o_2 = op_4, op_1, op_2, op_5$

The initial solution to this CSP (using a version of the greedy algorithm already described), $o_{1.1} = op_1$, $o_{1.2} = op_2$, $o_2 = op_4$, $o_3 = op_5$, and $o_4 = op_3$, is supported by the following *nogoods*:

$o_4 = op_3$
$o_{1.1} = op_1 \wedge o_{1.2} = op_2 \longrightarrow o_3 \neq op_1 \wedge o_3 \neq op_2 \wedge o_2 \neq op_2$
$o_3 = op_5 \longrightarrow o_2 \neq op_5$
$o_2 = op_4$

Note, the operation o_1 is covered by two operators to increase output by reducing the process time. This initial configuration of the flow line gives the following line performance, measured in the process times (pt)[7] of each operation:

$$o_1(1.33) \prec o_2(2) \prec o_3(2) \prec o_4(0.6)$$

---

[7] $\dfrac{SMV}{\sum per f_{op}} \times 100 = pt$

Such a configuration would result in an estimated output of at least 252 garments a day (8 hour work shift).[8] With this current configuration, it is clear that o_4 can process garments about three times faster than o_3 can supply them, and o_1 can supply garments about one and half times faster than o_2 can process them.

An intuitive solution would be to allow either op_1 or op_2 to 'float' between o_1 and o_3 when necessary to maintain line balance. Such an intuitive, deterministic, solution disregards the problems of environmental uncertainty, machine breakdown, operator absenteeism, declining operator performance because of illness or boredom, and so forth. The line needs to be monitored, and if there are no perturbations to the work flow we can employ the default strategy of using op_1 or op_2 as 'floaters'.

The identification of either op_1 or op_2 as appropriate candidates for reassignment to o_3 is determined by examining the *nogoods* for o_1 (i.e. those *nogoods* which have o_1 as their antecedent); o_3 appears in the conclusion of the *nogood* identifying both op_1 and op_2 as suitable candidates for o_3. Which operator is chosen depends upon the analysis of the *performance-analyzer*, a knowledge source which calculates the amount of additional performance required by an operation, or the amount of performance that can be alleviated from an operation.

Let us assume that our analysis suggests that we reschedule the line by reassigning op_1 to o_3, what is the significance of this for the existing schedule, and what are the procedures necessary to discover this significance?

First, we must remove $o_1 = op_1$ from the set of *nogoods*. We also need to post safety conditions with the set of *nogoods* to identify those existing assignments that are now suspect because o_1's assignment of op_1 determined their 'live' domains at the time of their instantiation. These variables are recorded by the *nogoods*. In our example, o_3 appears in the conclusion of that *nogood* in which o_1 is the antecedent. The safety condition, $o_1 \prec o_3$, triggers consistency checks on the reordered variable o_3. We need to determine what affect the reassigning of o_1 will have on its 'future' variables, those variables whose instantiations were determined after o_1 was assigned. Consistency checks show that $o_3 = op_5$ is consistent with op_1 being assigned to o_3. Which is to be expected with a simple 'floater' transfer. Under such circumstances we simply need to reorder and adjust the set of *nogoods* to reflect the reassignment of op_1:

$$o_4 = op_3$$
$$o_{3.1} = op_5 \wedge o_{3.2} = op_1 \longrightarrow o_2 \neq op_5 \wedge o_1 \neq op_1 \wedge o_2 \neq op_1$$
$$o_1 op_2 \longrightarrow o_2 \neq op_2$$
$$o_2 = op_4$$

A more interesting situation arises when op_3 is absent. First, we must remove $o_4 = op_3$ from the set of assignments. Here, it is unnecessary to post *safety conditions*. The ordering heuristics which forced the assignment ensured that no *nogoods* were posted. An analysis of o_4's domain identifies the ordered set $\{op_3, op_4, op_2, op_1, op_5\}$ as possible candidates for the now unassigned operation.

---

[8] This is assuming that o_4 can be maintained with work.

If op_4 is chosen then a substitute for o_2 is also required. Likewise with op_2, a substitute would be required for o_1. Actually, the selection of a candidate operator would be decided, in part, by the *performance-analyzer*. With the current configuration of the line it seems likely this would be either op_1, or op_5. Alternatively, given the performance characteristics of the operators, a sequence of transfers might be recommended by the system:

$$op_2 \longrightarrow o_4, \textbf{ then } op_5 \longrightarrow o_1$$

However, before suggesting such a perturbation to the line, with possible consequences on production efficiency, a judgment would need to be made based on the costs and benefits of such an action. Operational matters concerning due dates and job priorities would need to be weighed. This is essentially a managerial judgment. Given that the system, and the human user, accepts that op_5 is the ideal candidate, what is the significance of this to the existing schedule, and what procedures are necessary to discover this significance? After removing $o_4 = op_3$ from the set of assignments we reassign op_5 to o_4:

$$o_4 = op_5 \longrightarrow o_3 \neq op_5 \land o_1 \neq op_5 \land o_2 \neq op_5$$
$$o_3 = op_1 \longrightarrow o_1 \neq op_1 \land o_2 \neq op_1$$
$$o_1 = op_2 \longrightarrow o_2 \neq op_2$$
$$o_2 = op_4$$

The growth in *nogood* information shows that perturbations to the line, caused for example by operator absenteeism, is mirrored in perturbations to the heuristic ordering of CSP variables and domains. Partial order backtracking allows intelligent reordering of 'past' (previously assigned) variables to allow reassignment heuristics to identify, via *nogood* sets, suitable candidates for reassignment. The management of a PBS represents a tension between the need for stability which is associated with line balance, and flexibility which demands a rapid response to line disruptions. The ordering heuristics employed by the assignment procedure ensure that operators, such as op_3, which offer little support for flexible response, are assigned first so that multi skilled operators can, if necessary, 'jump' back in the search space to provide a rapid response to disruptions. Therefore, the objective of a good reassignment move is to reduce the amount of *nogood* information; *nogoods* indicate bottlenecks in the choice of reassignment candidates.

The system which implements the ideas discussed in this paper is discussed, with experimental results, in Spragg, Tyler, and Fozzard[9]. The architecture is modeled on the *OPIS* system developed at the *Center for Integrated Manufacturing Decision Systems* at Carnegie Mellon University by Steven Smith.[10] The reactive rescheduling framework is a component of the simulation modelling environment described in Fozzard, Spragg, and Tyler[11] and Fozzard, Spragg and Tyler.[12]

8 Conclusion

There is considerable pressure on clothing manufacture in the United Kingdom to remain competitive in the face of competition from low labor cost countries. In addition, market forces and a trend of decreasing contract sizes have resulted in numerous practical difficulties with traditional flowline methods of manufacture.

Faced with these problems there are broadly two lines of action available to the industry: radical changes in the system of production or improvement of the existing systems . Flexible manufacturing concepts are being explored, but as yet they have not been realized. The improvement option provides the context for our research in reactive rescheduling techniques. Despite advances in automation, it has become clear that the requirement to successfully manage skilled manual labour will continue until alternative technologies are identified. Traditional flow line assembly systems continue to be used, not only on clothing production, but also in other manufacturing sectors.

9 Acknowledgments

This paper relates to research funded by the **ACME** Directorate of **SERC**, **GR./D 74246**: *The Simulation of Clothing Manufacture.*

We gratefully acknowledge the contribution of ideas from Matthew Ginsberg, Gerry Kelleher, Barbara Smith and Steven Smith.

References

1. Chuter, A.J.: An Introduction to Clothing Production Management, BSP Professional Books, Oxford, 1988.
2. French, S.: Sequencing and Scheduling, An introduction to the mathematics of the Job-Shop, Ellis Horwood Limited 1990.
3. Tyler, D., Tennent, L.F., and Lowe, T.J.: Simulation as a Training Medium for Industrial Supervisors, Journal of Clothing Technology and Management, (1994) 11(2), 31-44.
4. Smith, B.M.: Filling the Gaps: Reassignment Heuristics for Constraint Satisfaction Problems, Report 92.29, School of Computer Studies, University of Leeds, November 1992.
5. Spragg, J.E. and Kelleher, G.: A Discipline for Reactive Rescheduling, Proceedings of the 3rd International Conference on Artificial Intelligence Planning Systems, Edited Brian Drabble, The AAAI Press, (1996) 199-204.
6. Ginsberg, M.L. and McAllester, D.A.: GSAT and Dynamic Backtracking, Knowledge Representation and Reasoning Conference, 1994.
7. Selman, B., Levesque, H., and Mitchell, D.: A New Method for Solving Hard Satisfiability Problems, In Proceedings of the Tenth National Conference on Artificial Intelligence (1992) 440-446.
8. Minton, S., Johnston, M.D., Philips, A.B., and Laird, P.: Solving Large-Scale Constraint Satisfaction and Scheduling Problems Using a Heuristic Repair Method, In Proceedings of the Eighth National Conference on Artificial Intelligence (1990) 17-24.

9. Spragg, J.E., Tyler, D. and Fozzard, G.: FLEAS: flow line environment for automated supervision of simulated clothing manufacture. (forthcoming).

10. Smith, S.: Reactive Scheduling Systems, In Intelligent Scheduling Systems, (eds. D.E. Brown and W.T. Scherer), Kluwer Academic Publishers, Boston (1995) 155-192.

11. Fozzard, G., Spragg, J.E. and Tyler, D.: Simulation of Flow Lines in Clothing Manufacture, Part 1: model construction, International Journal of Clothing Science and Technology, **Vol 8**, No. 4, (1996) 17-27.

12. Fozzard, G., Spragg, J.E. and Tyler, D.: Simulation of Flow Lines in Clothing Manufacture, Part 2: credibility issues and experimentation, International Journal of Clothing Science and Technology, **Vol 8**, No. 5 (1996) 42-50.

Plan-Refinement Strategies and Search-Space Size[1]

Reiko Tsuneto
reiko@cs.umd.edu

Dana Nau
nau@cs.umd.edu

James Hendler
hendler@cs.umd.edu

Department of Computer Science
and Institute for Systems Research
University of Maryland
College Park, MD 20742
USA

Abstract

During the planning process, a planner may have many options for refinements to perform on the plan being developed. The planner's efficiency depends on how it chooses which refinement to do next. Recent studies have shown that several versions of the popular "least commitment" plan refinement strategy are often outperformed by a *fewest alternatives first* (FAF) strategy that chooses to refine the plan element that has the smallest number of alternative refinement options.

In this paper, we examine the FAF strategy in more detail, to try to gain a better understanding of how well it performs and why. We present the following results:

- A refinement planner's search space is an AND/OR graph, and the planner "serializes" this graph by mapping it into an equivalent state-space graph. Different plan refinement strategies produce different serializations of the AND/OR graph.

- The sizes of different serializations of the AND/OR graph can differ by an exponential amount. A planner whose refinement strategy produces a small serialization is likely to be more efficient than a planner whose refinement strategy produces a large serialization.

- The FAF heuristic can be computed in constant time, and in our experimental studies it usually produced an optimal or near-optimal serialization. This suggests that using FAF (or some similar heuristic) is preferable to trying to guarantee an optimal serialization (which we conjecture is a computationally intractible problem).

Keywords: planning and search; refinement strategies; commitment strategies

[1] This research was supported in part by grants from NSF (IRI-9306580 and EEC 94-02384), ONR (N00014-J-91-1451), AFOSR (F49620-93-1-0065), the ARPA/Rome Laboratory Planning Initiative (F30602-93-C-0039), the ARPA I3 Initiative (N00014-94-10907), the ARL (DAAH049610297), and ARPA contract DABT-95-C0037. Any opinions, findings, and conclusions or recommendations expressed in this material are those of the authors and do not necessarily reflect the view of the funders.

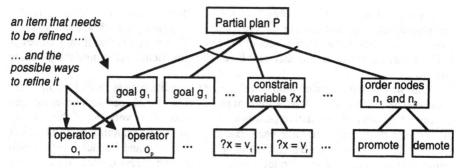

Figure 1. Possible refinement choices in planning.

1. Introduction

One characteristic of partial-order planners—regardless of whether they are Hierarchical Task Network (HTN) planners such as UMCP [Erol, 1995] and O-Plan [Currie and Tate, 1994], or planners that use STRIPS-style operators such as UCPOP [Penberthy and Weld, 1992]—is that they search a space in which the nodes are partially developed plans. The planner refines the plans into more and more specific plans, until either a completely developed solution is found or every plan is found incapable of solving the problem.

During this process, a planner may often have many different options for what kind of refinement to perform next, as illustrated in Figure 1. A planner that uses STRIPS-style operators may need to choose which unachieved goal to work on next, which operator to use to achieve a goal, or which technique to use (promotion, demotion, or variable separation) to resolve a goal conflict. An HTN planner usually has an even larger array of options: it may need to choose which unachieved task to work on next, which method to use to accomplish the task, or which constraint (from among a number of different possibilities) to impose on the plan. The planner's efficiency depends greatly on its *plan refinement strategy*, which is the way it goes about choosing among these options.

In the planning literature, the term "least commitment" generally refers to a refinement strategy in which the planner postpones making some particular kind of refinement until it is forced to do so. For example, if a planner uses a "least commitment to step orderings" strategy, then whenever more than one ordering is possible among the steps of a plan, the planner will avoid committing to a particular ordering unless it must do so in order to proceed with the rest of the planning. The "least commitment" idea was originally applied to step orderings [Sacerdoti, 1975], but it has also been applied to other kinds of refinements. For example, Stefik's MOLGEN program [Stefik, 1981] used a "least commitment to constraint posting" approach; and Tsuneto *et al.* [1996] have examined both a "least commitment to variable bindings" strategy and a "least commitment to task achievement" strategy for HTN planning.

One reason why least-commitment strategies are useful is that if the planner can avoid making refinements prematurely, this can reduce the number of alternative plans it might need to examine. However, it is not necessarily a good idea to apply the same least-commitment strategy throughout the entire planning process. In order to do planning at all, a planner has to refine *something*[2]—and thus, when a planner postpones refining one aspect of the plan it is generating, this may make it prematurely refine some other aspect of the plan. This suggests that it may be better to choose dynamically among different kinds of refinements throughout the planning process.

One way to choose what kind of refinement to make next is to look at all of the items that need to be refined in the current partial plan, and choose whichever one has the fewest number of alternative possible refinements. Two versions of this *"fewest alternatives first"* heuristic have been examined in the AI planning literature. For partial-order planning with STRIPS-style operators, Joslin and Pollack [1994; 1996] found that a version of this strategy outperformed the "least commitment to step orderings" strategy; and for HTN planning, Tsuneto *et al.* [1996] found that a version of this strategy outperformed both a "least commitment to variable bindings" strategy and a "least commitment to task achievement" strategy.

Although AI planning researchers have begun to investigate the FAF heuristic only recently, a similar heuristic has been known in the constraint satisfaction literature for more than 20 years: Bitner and Reingold [1975] used it as a search rearrangement method, and Purdom [1983] analyzed its application to SAT problems. One reason why it has taken so long for this heuristic to become known to AI planning researchers is that the relationship between control strategies for search algorithms and refinement strategies for AI planning is a rather complicated one, whose precise nature has not been clearly understood. In this paper, we examine that relationship in detail, and present the following results:

- The search process that is carried out by an AI planning system corresponds to taking an AND/OR graph and generating from it an equivalent state-space graph, one OR-branch at a time. This process we call *serializing* the AND/OR graph. Different plan refinement strategies produce different serializations of the AND/OR graph.

- Different serializations of the AND/OR graph contain different numbers of nodes, and the largest serialization can contain an exponentially greater number nodes than the smallest one. In the worst case, the planner may need to examine every node in the search space—so a planner whose search space is small is likely to be more efficient than a planner whose search space is large.

- The FAF strategy uses a greedy heuristic: each time it needs to decide which OR-branch to include next in the search space, it chooses the one that has the smallest number of branches. This heuristic does not always result in the smallest possible serialization—but it can be computed in constant time, and in our studies it usually resulted in a serialization that was either optimal or near-optimal.

- We conjecture that when the planner needs to decide which OR-branch to include next in the search space, the task of deciding which OR-branch is *optimal* (i.e., which OR-branch is in the smallest possible serialization) is an NP-hard problem. If this conjecture is correct, this suggests that any plan refinement strategy that is guaranteed to produce the smallest possible search space will incur an unacceptably high overhead—and thus it is better for AI planning systems to use

---

[2] Of course, this refinement need not necessarily be an irrevocable one. Most modern planning systems use a tentative control strategy such as backtracking, so that they can go back and undo decisions that do not work out.

a refinement strategy such as FAF which is quickly computable and gives good results most of the time.

2. Partial-Order Planning and AND/OR Graphs

As illustrated in Figure 1, the space searched by a partial-order planner may be thought of as an AND/OR graph in the following manner:

- In a partially developed plan, there may be several elements of the plan that need to be refined in one way or another. These may include both unachieved goals or tasks (which would be refined by finding ways to achieve them), and unsatisfied constraints (which might be satisfied by binding variables or specifying node orderings). All of these elements will sooner or later need to be refined—and thus the choice of which refinement to make next corresponds to an AND-branch in the planner's search space.

- For each element that needs refining, there may be more than one way to refine it (for example, several ways to instantiate a variable, or several operators or methods applicable to an unachieved goal or task), generating different partial plans. Any applicable refinement will be satisfactory provided that it produces a satisfactory plan—and thus the choice of how to reduce an element corresponds to an OR-branch in the planner's search space.

If the refinements performed on a plan were independent in their effects on the plan, a refinement planner could search the AND/OR graph directly, building up a solution to the planning problem straightforwardly by finding independent solutions to subproblems and composing them into solutions to higher-level problems. However, since the goals usually are not independent, refinement planners usually do not decompose the search space. Instead, when they refine some element of a plan, they keep track not only of the element that is being refined, but also of the entire rest of the plan. Thus, the planner searches a state-space graph that is a "serialization" of the AND/OR graph.

Although the concept of serializing an AND/OR graph is conceptually straightforward, the formal definition is rather complicated notationally. To keep the notation simple, in this paper we give a formal definition only for the special case where the AND/OR graph is binary (i.e., each non-leaf node has exactly two children). We trust that it will be obvious to the reader how to generalize this definition for the case where the AND/OR graph is not binary.

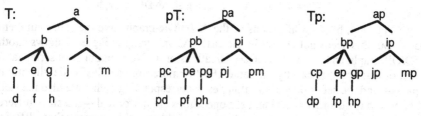

Figure 2. A tree T, and the trees pT and Tp (where p is a node not in T).

First, we will need the following notation (see Figure 2 for examples). Let T be a tree whose node set is N and whose edge set is E. If p is any node not in N, then:

- Tp is the tree with node set $\{np : n \in N\}$ and edge set $\{(mp,np) : (m,n) \in E\}$;

- pT is the tree with node set $\{pn : n \in N\}$ and edge set $\{(pm,pn) : (m,n) \in E\}$.

If G is a binary AND/OR graph, there are three possible cases for what its serializations are:

Case 1: G consists of a single node. Then the only serialization of G is G itself.

Case 2: G contains more than one node, and the branch at G's root node g is a binary OR-branch leading to two subgraphs H and I. If S and T are serializations of H and I, respectively, then as shown in Figure 3, the tree R whose root is g and whose subtrees are S and T is a serialization of G.

Case 3: G contains more than one node, and the branch at G's root g is a binary AND-branch leading to two subgraphs H and I. Let S and T be serializations of H and I, respectively. Let S's root be s and its leaf nodes be $s_1, s_2, ..., s_p$; and let T's root be t and its leaf nodes be $t_1, t_2, ..., t_q$. Then as shown in Figure 4, the following trees are serializations of G:

- the tree R_1 formed by taking the tree St, and attaching to its leaves $s_1t, s_2t, ..., s_pt$ the trees $s_1T, s_2T, ..., s_pT$, respectively;

- the tree R_2 formed by taking the tree sT, and attaching to its leaves $st_1, st_2, ..., st_q$ the trees $St_1, St_2, ..., St_q$, respectively.

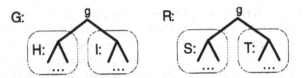

Figure 3. Case 2 of serializing an AND/OR graph.

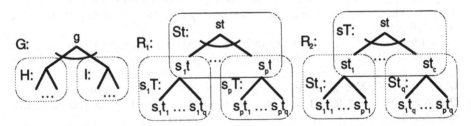

Figure 4. Case 3 of serializing an AND/OR graph.

In Figure 4, both serializations of the AND/OR graph have the same number of nodes—but this needs not always be the case. As an example, Figure 5 shows another AND/OR graph, and three possible serializations of it. Note that in each serialization, the set of leaf nodes is exactly the same. Furthermore, for each leaf node, the number of paths—and the set of operations along each corresponding path—are also the same. What differs is the order in which these operations are performed—and since different operations produce different numbers of children, this means that different serializations contain different numbers of nodes.

The idea of serializing an AND/OR graph occurs in a number of search procedures, although the first case we know of where such a technique was described explicitly was in the SSS* game-tree search procedure [Stockman, 1979]. One well known example is Prolog's search procedure (for example, see [Clocksin and Mellish, 1981], which serializes AND/OR graphs in a depth-first left-to-right manner. For example, in the graph G of Figure 5, suppose that each node corresponds to a logical atom, each AND-branch corresponds to a Horn clause, and each OR-branch corresponds to the different ways a literal might match the head of a Horn clause. Then Prolog would do a depth-first search of the tree S_1. In general, the number of possible serializations of an AND/OR graph can be combinatorially large; for example, there are ten possible serializations of the graph G of Figure 5. Which serialization will actually be used depends on the search procedure. For example, a procedure that achieves goals and subgoals in a depth-first left-to-right fashion (as Prolog does) would serialize G into S_1, but a procedure that achieves goals and subgoals in a depth-first right-to-left fashion would serialize G into S_3 instead.

Obviously, a planner will not necessarily examine every node in its serialized search tree. It may prune some of these nodes as infeasible, and it may find its desired solution before it examines all of the unpruned nodes. However, in the worst case, the planner will need to examine every one of the nodes in the serialized search tree. In such a case, a planner that searches the tree S_3 of Figure 5 will be more efficient than a planner that searches the trees S_1 or S_2.

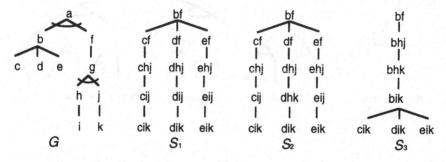

Figure 5. A simple AND/OR graph G, and three serializations S_1, S_2, and S_3.

4. Best and Worst Serializations

If we could find a serialization strategy that would always find the smallest serialization of an AND/OR graph, how much would this help? To get an idea of the answer, suppose we take the pattern shown in Figure 6a, and use it repeatedly to form an AND/OR tree $G_{b,k}$ of height $2k$, as shown in Figure 6b. In $G_{b,k}$, the number of occurrences of the pattern is

$$c_{b,k} = 1+(b+1)+(b+1)^2+\ldots+(b+1)^{k-1} = \Theta(b^k),$$

so the total number of nodes in $G_{b,k}$ is

$$n(G_{b,k}) = 1+(b+3)c_{b,k} = \Theta(b^k).$$

Let $T^-_{b,k}$ and $T^+_{b,k}$ be the serializations of $G_{b,k}$ that have the smallest and largest node counts, respectively. Both of these trees have the same height, which can be calculated recursively as follows:

$$h(T^-_{b,k}) = h(T^+_{b,k}) = \begin{cases} 2 & \text{if } k = 1, \\ 2h(T^+_{b,k-1}) + 2 & \text{otherwise} \end{cases}$$

$$= \sum_{i=1}^{k} 2^i = 2^{k+1} - 2.$$

$T^-_{b,k}$ and $T^+_{b,k}$ both consist of 2^k-1 levels of unary OR-branches interspersed with 2^k-1 levels of b-ary OR-branches. However, $T^-_{b,k}$ has its unary OR-branches as near the top as possible and its b-ary OR-branches as near the bottom as possible; and vice versa for $T^+_{b,k}$. As shown in Figure 6c, the branches at the top k levels of $T^-_{b,k}$ are all unary, and those at its bottom 2^{k-1} levels are all b-ary; the reverse is true for $T^+_{b,k}$.

Calculating the node counts for $T^-_{b,k}$ and $T^+_{b,k}$ is too complicated to do here, but in a forthcoming technical report we show that the numbers of nodes in these trees are $n(T^-_{b,k}) = \Theta(b^{2^k})$ and $n(T^+_{b,k}) = \Theta(2^k b^{2^k})$. Thus, the numbers of nodes in the worst possible serialization and the best possible serialization differ by a multiplicative factor of $\Theta(2^k)$.

(a) Basic pattern, with parameter b.

(b) AND/OR tree $G_{2,3}$ produced by the pattern if $b = 2$ and $k = 3$.

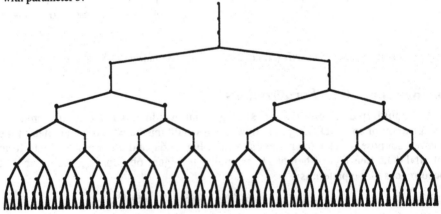

(c) The smallest possible serialization $T_{2,3}$ of $G_{2,3}$.

Figure 6. An AND/OR tree formed by repetitions of a pattern; and the smallest possible serialization of the AND/OR tree.

4. Fewest Alternatives First

During the course of its operation, an AI planning algorithm will generate a serialization of an AND/OR graph one OR-branch at a time. For example, starting from the node a in the AND/OR graph G shown in Figure 5, the first choice is whether to expand the OR-branch rooted at b or the OR-branch rooted at f. If we choose b then we will end up with a search space similar to S_1 or S_2; and if we choose f then we will end up with a search space similar to S_3. One way to choose which OR-branch to expand next is to use the "fewest alternatives first" (FAF) heuristic of Section 1. In many cases, this simple heuristic produces optimal results. For example, in Figure 5, this heuristic would choose to expand f, h, and j before expanding b, thereby producing the tree S_3.

FAF also is easy to compute. The cost of computing FAF at any node n is $O(c(n)+g(n))$, where $c(n)$ is the number of n's children, and $g(n)$ is the number of n's grandchildren. Thus, if one assumes (as is typical in analyses of AI search algorithms) that the branching factor of each node is bounded by some constant b, then the cost of computing FAF is $O(b + b^2) = O(1)$.

In empirical studies on various planning domains, adaptations of the FAF strategy have performed quite well in comparison with other popular refinement strategies. The "least cost flaw repair" strategy investigated by Joslin and Pollack [1994, 1996] uses the FAF heuristic to choose among all of the refinements available to a STRIPS-style planner; and the "DVCS" strategy investigated by Tsuneto *et al.* [1996] for HTN planning uses the FAF heuristic to choose among some (but not all) of the refinements available to an HTN planner. In these studies, least-cost flaw repair and DVCS outperformed a number of other strategies, including the well known "least commitment to step orderings" strategy.

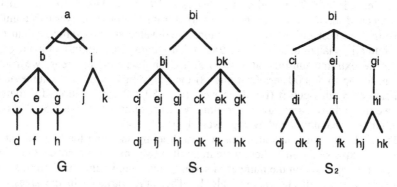

Figure 7. A situation where the FAF heuristic fails to produce the best serialization of an AND/OR graph. FAF chooses to expand i before b, thus producing S_1; but S_2 contains fewer nodes.

Despite its good empirical performance, FAF does not always produce optimal results. For example, consider the graph G of Figure 7. To serialize G, FAF would choose to expand i before expanding b, thus producing the tree S_1. However, if it had chosen to expand b first, it would have been able to produce the smaller tree S_2. This situation is reminiscent of what happens in a number of NP-hard optimization problems, in which the obvious greedy heuristics will make the best choice in a large number of situations, but will sometimes make choices that cause greater costs to be incurred later on. At least one example of this occurs in the AI planning literature, involving a greedy heuristic for the block-stacking problem [Gupta and Nau, 1992]

To formalize the notion of "optimal results" in the previous paragraph, first we define a *minimal serialization* of an AND/OR graph G to be a serialization T of G

such that no other serialization of G contains fewer nodes than T. Now, suppose we have an AND/OR graph G whose root branch is an AND branch. Let the children of the root node be $n_1, ..., n_k$. Then for $i = 1,...,k$, the node n_i is an *optimal candidate* for expansion if there is a minimal serialization T of G whose root branch is formed by expanding n_i. For example, f is the optimal candidate in Figure 5, and b is the optimal candidate in Figure 7. We conjecture that finding an optimal candidate for expansion is NP-hard.

5. Experimental Studies of FAF

As discussed above, FAF usually seems to do better than other popular heuristics, but can sometimes do poorly. This raises two important questions: how close FAF comes (on the average) to finding the best possible serialization, and how it compares (on the average) with the best, worst, and/or average serializations. We have begun an experimental exploration to try to answer these questions.

We have compared the performance of FAF with an average serialization performed on 50 different randomly generated AND/OR trees. The sample trees were generated using a tree generation algorithm based on [Luke, 1997]. These trees had 1 to 5 branches at each node, with a maximum depth of 8. All nodes at even depths were AND-nodes, while all nodes at odd depths were OR-nodes. Thus, leaves were only placed at even depths. The algorithm was set to generate 50 random trees with an average close to 30 and the average depth close to the maximum. In the population that was actually generated, the average tree size (number of nodes) is 32.32 and the average depth is 7.64. The smallest tree is of size 19 and the largest tree is of size 51. The number of serializations for the trees varied from 1 through to over half a million.

To find the best and worst serializations, we developed a program to exhaustively enumerate all serializations, keeping track of minimum, maximum and average size. Due to the extreme number of serializations for many of the trees, we ran this program for up to 50,000 serializations. If the first program had not enumerated all serializations by this cutoff (i.e. there were more 50,000 serializations for the given tree), we instead used a separate algorithm which randomly generated 50,000 trials.[3] The minimum, maximum and average were again collected.

The FAF algorithm was also run on each tree, by applying the heuristic at each AND-node expansion (when there were more than two smallest branches, the leftmost one was chosen). Data on the number of serializations, minimum, maximum, average, and FAF sizes are all shown in Table 1. The large variance in the sizes of the serializations makes comparison of the raw data difficult. It is easy to see, however, that in 32 of the 47 cases where there was more than a single serialization size, the FAF algorithm found the optimal solution.

To see how the algorithm performs overall, and to compare the algorithm to the averages, we needed a means to measure performance. In Figure 8—which shows the performance of FAF versus the average—we normalized the results, with 0 representing the best overall serialization and 1 representing the worst. In 46 of the 47 cases, FAF performed better than the average. 32 times the optimal was found, and 44 further times the algorithm performed better than half way between optimal and average. We believe these results are quite encouraging, showing that the FAF algorithm performs quite well in the average case.

---

[3] These 50,000 could not be guaranteed unique without prohibitive computational costs; however a very large sample population was probabilistically guaranteed.

Table 1. Experimental results.

Tree	Number of possible serializations	Size of smallest serialization	Size of largest serialization	Average serialization size	Size of serialization found by FAF
1	4228	38	64	43.6	39
2	4	33	34	33.2	33
3	>50000	156	275	185.0	154
4	352	64	73	66.3	64
5	>50000	123	204	143.6	121
6	>50000	71	126	86.0	71
7	7	18	25	20.0	18
8	56	19	30	22.1	19
9	>50000	259	321	277.6	259
10	17424	156	175	162.0	159
11	5284	61	67	62.9	61
12	>50000	1488	2170	1697.0	1450
13	>50000	267	340	292.7	267
14	>50000	253	463	331.0	255
15	>50000	229	274	246.8	235
16	>50000	158	254	196.6	158
17	>50000	744	861	791.5	746
18	16777	56	93	71.2	56
19	180	29	44	35.4	29
20	>50000	109	157	129.8	111
21	4	36	38	36.8	36
22	>50000	117	136	125.4	117
23	14	17	23	19.6	17
24	>50000	84	122	101.2	84
25	5792	49	56	52.1	49
26	>50000	334	434	374.0	322
27	146	40	49	44.2	40
28	100	106	115	110.2	108
29	8992	71	83	76.6	71
30	44	32	41	36.4	34
31	>50000	335	434	381.4	330
32	4	33	34	33.5	33
33	3	28	29	28.5	28
34	20	27	33	30.0	28
35	>50000	354	462	405.9	348
36	>50000	162	184	173.2	165
37	28	40	45	42.5	40
38	>50000	226	327	280.9	239
39	>50000	249	310	282.4	278
40	>50000	173	225	201.5	173
41	>50000	237	355	300.6	232
42	>50000	659	929	803.1	643
43	>50000	80	86	83.5	83
44	>50000	520	621	580.2	525
45	60	27	36	32.7	27
46	>50000	161	226	207.6	161
47	1014	70	82	79.6	82
48	1	15	15	15.0	15
49	2	17	17	17.0	17
50	4	24	24	24.0	24

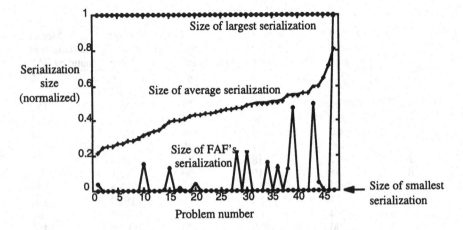

Figure 8. Sizes of FAF(◇) and average(+) serializations normalized with the smallest and largest serialization sizes.

There was, however, one case in which FAF produced the worst serialization (this is also the only case where FAF did worse than average). To see the cause of this, we analyzed the particular tree (shown in Figure 9). In this case, FAF could have produced the best serialization if it had chosen the right child of the root to expand first instead of the left child. Since our program simply chose leftmost in the case of the tie, FAF did poorly in our test. This does, however, show a potential weakness in implementations of FAF for planning, since it have an additional heuristic for use in this case. Examining what to do in this case could lead to further improvement of planning choice mechanisms, and this is a topic we are currently exploring.

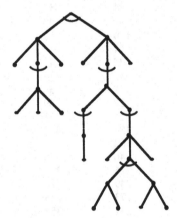

Figure 9. The one tree in which FAF produced the worst serialization.

6. Conclusions

In this paper, we have studied a plan refinement strategy, the "fewest alternatives first" (FAF) strategy, that chooses among various kinds of refinements depending on which one has the smallest number of alternative choices. In recent studies by Joslin and Pollack [1994, 1996] and Tsuneto et al. [1996], FAF usually outperformed several different "least commitment" refinement strategies. In this paper, we have examined the FAF strategy in more detail in an attempt to understand how well it performs and why.

We have shown that the search process that is carried out by an AI planning system corresponds to "serializing" an AND/OR graph—mapping it into an equivalent state-space graph. Different plan refinement strategies thus correspond to different ways to serialize the AND/OR graph representing the planning choice points.

Different serializations of an AND/OR graph have different sizes, and the smallest serialization can be exponentially smaller than the largest one. We have shown that a planner whose plan refinement strategy produces a small serialization of the AND/OR graph is likely to be more efficient than a planner whose plan refinement strategy produces a large serialization.

Like most greedy heuristics, FAF does not always produce optimal results—but in our studies it usually produced a serialization that was either optimal or near-optimal. If our conjecture is correct that any strategy that guaranteed the smallest possible serialization would be intractable to compute, then this suggests that it is better for AI planning systems to use a plan refinement strategy such as FAF, that is quickly computable and usually gives good results.

We believe these results explain why FAF performs well in the previous studies, and opens several interesting issues for exploration. First, as we have noted, better serializations produce smaller search spaces, thus potentially improving planning behavior. However, the exact relationship between a given planner and this search space is quite complex, and there may be cases where certain planners interact better with certain serializations. Second, while FAF performs quite well, it is clear that there is still plenty of room for improvement. This can include looking for algorithms that can better optimize search space (serialization) size, improvements on FAF (for example better tie-breaking rules), and identification of analytic techniques that could analyze the tree formed by the operators and better select or prune the search spaces.

Finally, we are beginning to explore other effects of search control on planning performance. Given the correspondence between these discussed in the paper, it seems that other ways of controlling search, particularly pruning unpromising branches, may also be successful. Gerevini and Schubert [1996] showed that various pruning strategies have beneficial properties for the UCPOP planner, and we plan to extend this work, examining how pruning can effect search in serializations of planning trees as discussed in the paper.

References

[Barret and Weld, 1994] Anthony Barret and Daniel Weld. Partial-order planning: Evaluating possible efficiency gains. *Artificial Intelligence* 67(1), pp. 71–112.

[Bitner and Reingold, 1975] James Bitner and Edward Reingold. Backtrack Programming Techniques. *CACM* 18(11), pp. 651–656.

[Clocksin and Mellish, 1981] W. Clocksin and C. Mellish. *Programming in PROLOG*. Springer-Verlag.

[Currie and Tate, 1991] Ken Currie and Austin Tate. O-plan: the open planning architecture. *Artificial Intelligence* 52, pp. 49–86.

[Erol, 1995] Kutluhan Erol. *HTN planning: Formalization, analysis, and implementation.* Ph.D. dissertation, Computer Science Dept., U. of Maryland.

[Gupta and Nau, 1992] Naresh Gupta and Dana Nau. On the complexity of blocks-world planning. *Artificial Intelligence* 56:2-3, pp. 223–254.

[Gerevini and Schubert, 1996] Alfonso Gerevini and Lenhart Schubert. Accelerating Partial-Order Planners: Some Techniques for Effective Search Control and Pruning. *Journal of Artificial Intelligence Research* 5, pp. 95– 137.

[Joslin and Pollack, 1994] David Joslin and Martha Pollack. Least-cost flaw repair: A plan refinement strategy for partial-order planning. In *Proceedings of the Twelfth National Conference on Artificial Intelligence*, pp. 1004– 1009.

[Joslin and Pollack, 1996] David Joslin and Martha Pollack. Is "early commitment" in plan generation ever a good idea? In *Proc. Thirteenth National Conference on Artificial Intelligence*, pp. 1188-1193.

[Kambhampati *et al.*, 1995] Subbarao Kambhampati, Craig Knoblock, and Qiang Yang. Planning as refinement search: A unified framework for evaluating design tradeoffs in partial-order planning. *Artificial Intelligence* 76, pp. 167–238.

[Kumar, 1992] Vipin Kumar. Algorithms for constraint -satisfaction problems: A survey. *AI Magazine*, pp. 32–44.

[Luke, 1997] Sean Luke. A Fast Probabilistic Tree Generation Algorithm. Unpublished manuscript.

[Penberthy and Weld, 1992] J. S. Penberthy and Daniel Weld. UCPOP: A sound, complete, partial order planner for ADL. *Proc. KR-92.*

[Purdom, 1983] Paul W. Purdom. Search Rearrangement Backtracking and Polynomial Average Time. *Artificial Intelligence* 21, pp. 117– 133.

[Purdom and Brown, 1983] Paul W. Purdom and Cynthia A. Brown. An Analysis of Backtracking with Search Rearrangement. *SIAM J. Computing* 12(4), pp.717– 733.

[Sacerdoti, 1977] Earl Sacerdoti. *A Structure for Plans and Behavior.* American Elsevier Publishing Company.

[Stefik, 1981] Mark Stefik. Planning with constraints (MOLGEN: part 1). *Artificial Intelligence* 16, pp. 111–140.

[Smith *et al.*, 1996] S. J. J. Smith, D. S. Nau, and T. A. Throop. Total-order multi-agent task-network planning for control bridge. *AAAI-96*, pp.108-113.

[Stockman, 1979] G. Stockman. A minimax algorithm better than alpha-beta? *Artificial Intelligence* 12(2), pp. 179–96.

[Tsuneto *et al.*, 1996] Reiko Tsuneto, Kutluhan Erol, James Hendler, and Dana Nau. Commitment strategies in hierarchical task network planning. In *Proc. Thirteenth National Conference on Artificial Intelligence*, pp. 536-542.

[Veloso and Stone, 1995] Manuela Veloso and Peter Stone. FLECS: Planning with a flexible commitment strategy. *JAIR* 3, pp. 25–52.

Replanning Using Hierarchical Task Network and Operator-Based Planning

Xuemei Wang* and Steve Chien

Jet Propulsion Laboratory, California Institute of Technology
4800 Oak Grove Drive, M/S 525-3660, Pasadena, CA 91109-8099

Abstract. To scale-up to real-world problems, planning systems must be able to replan in order to deal with changes in problem context. In this paper we describe hierarchical task network and operator-based replanning techniques which allow adaptation of a previous plan to account for problems associated with executing plans in real-world domains with uncertainty, concurrency, changing objectives. We focus on replanning which preserves elements of the original plan in order to use more reliable domain knowledge and to facilitate user understanding of produced plans. We present empirical results documenting the effectiveness of these techniques in a NASA antenna operations application. [2]

1 Introduction

As AI planning techniques move from the research environment to real-world applications, it is critical to address the needs that arise from their application environment. Specifically, many application domains are dynamic, uncertain, concurrent, and have changing objectives. Real domains may be dynamic because: the world can change independently of the plan being executed; the results of performing an action often cannot be predicted with certainty; actions and events may occur simultaneously; new goals can arise and old goals can become unimportant as time passes. To adapt to such context, planning systems must be able to replan, i.e., to appropriately adapt and modify the current plan to these unexpected changes in goal or state.

In this paper, we describe our replanning framework that addresses the above issues in real-world applications. This framework presumes a hybrid approach using both hierarchical task network (HTN) planning (as typified by [Erol et al 1994]) and operator-based (as typified by [Pemberthy and Weld 1992, Carbonell et al 1992]) methods. This is a common and powerful planning architecture (such as O-Plan [Currie and Tate 1991], DPLAN [Chien et al 1995], and [Kambhampati 1995]). We present our general framework as well as its application to a real application domain,

---

* Current address: Rockwell Science Center, 444 High St. Suite 400, Palo Alto, CA 94301, mei@rpal.rockwell.com
[2] This paper describes work performed by the Jet Propulsion Laboratory, California Institute of Technology, under contract with the National Aeronautics and Space Administration.

In our work, we focus on replanning which preserves elements of the original plan instead of planning from scratch from the current state for the following reasons:

- *Domain knowledge reliability.* Encoding of domain knowledge is imperfect — domain knowledge for nominal operations scenarios is most likely to be correct. Thus, by re-using as much of the nominal operations domain knowledge as possible, the risk of encountering faulty domain knowledge is reduced.
- *Operator understanding.* The users who actually carry out the plan executions are most familiar with nominal operations and small departures from nominal operations are far easier for them to understand than novel action sequences.

In this paper, we first briefly describe the DPLAN planning framework. We then give detailed descriptions for our replanning approach for unexpected state changes. We present application of the replanning approach to a real-world problem, namely the Deep Space Network (DSN) Antenna Operations domain. The empirical results demonstrate the effectiveness of our replanning algorithms. And finally we end this paper with discussions, related work, and conclusions.

2 Planning using hierarchical task network and operator-based planning

Our replanning approach presumes an integrated HTN/operator planning architecture as embodied in OPLAN ([Currie and Tate 1991]), [Kambhampati 1995] and DPLAN ([Chien et al 1995]). In this approach, a planner can use multiple planning methods and reason about both activity-goals and state-goals. Activity-goals correspond to operational or non-operational activities and are usually manipulated using HTN planning techniques. State-goals correspond to the preconditions and effects of activity-goals, and are achieved through operator-based planning. State-goals that have not yet been achieved are also considered non-operational. Figure 1 shows the procedures used for refining these two types of goals. As soon as a refinement strategy is applied to an activity-goal or state-goal, it is removed from the list of non-operational goals. Planning is complete when all activity goals are operational and all state goals have been achieved. Further details on integrating HTN and operator-based planning paradigms is described in [Chien et al 1995].

3 Replanning for unexpected state changes

This section describes our algorithm for replanning when the world changes independently of the plan being executed. The input to our algorithm consists of:

- the original plan being executed (*oplan*),
- a list of actions already executed (*executed-activities*), and

If g is an Activity-Goal,

1. Decompose: For each decomposition rule r in R which can decompose g, apply r to produce a new plan P', If all constraints in P' are consistent, then add P' to Q.
2. Simple Establishment: For each activity-goal g' in U that can be unified with g, simple establish g using g' and produce a new plan P'. If all constraints in P' are consistent, then add P' to Q.

If g is a State-Goal,

1. Step Addition: For each activity-goal effect that can unify with g, add that goal to P to produce a new plan P'. If the constraints in P' are consistent, then add P' to Q.
2. Simple Establishment: For each activity-goal g' in U that has an effect e that can be unified with g, simple establish g using e and produce a new plan P'. If all constraints in P' are consistent, then add P' to Q.

Fig. 1. Goal Refinement Strategies

— the current state (*current-state*) (in fact, it is not necessary to know the complete current state, as long as we have the ability to query whether a state-goal relevant to the original plan is true or false in the current state).

Our approach for replanning assumes that (1) there is a default value for each state-goal, (2) there are well-known methods (activities) for establishing the default value for each state-goal, (3) the original plan is applicable from a state where each relevant state-goal is at its default value. These assumptions are valid in most application domains. For example, in a manufacturing domain, (1) each device (e.g. robot, clamp) has a "home" position from which the original plan executes. The home position holds default values for state-goals relevant to the device; (2) there are methods to bring each device to its home position, thus establishing the default values for the relevant state-goals; (3) each device is always at its home position at the beginning of executing the original plan.

The replanning algorithm then re-uses as much of the original plan as possible while minimizing the amount of re-execution. The replanner returns a plan consisting of the activities that need to be re-executed and those not executed, as well as the ordering constraints.

Our replanning approach proceeds as shown in the following four steps. First, the algorithm creates an activity whose effects reflect the changes to the plan caused by the executed activities (Figure 3). Second, the algorithm determines the state-goals necessary for continuing execution of the plan, but are violated due to unexpected state changes; and then applies the "reset" activities to bring each state-goal to its default value (Figure 4). Finally, the planner determines which executed activities should be re-executed (Figure 5). This algorithm guarantees that the repaired plan re-executes all the activities that are necessary to successfully achieve the top-level goals.

The rest of this section gives detailed descriptions of our replanning paradigm. The descriptions employ a crucial concept, namely **violated state-goal**. A

Inputs: *oplan*, the original plan

     executed-activities, a list of activities already executed,

     current-state, the current state

Output: *repaired-plan*, repaired plan

1. *appliedGoal* ← executeActivities(*executed-activities, oplan*)
2. *ResetGoals* ← resetGoals (*oplan, current-state, executed-activities-list*)
3. *repaired-plan* ← replan(*oplan, resetGoals, appliedGoal*)

Fig. 2. Replanning for unexpected state changes

state-goal *sg* is **violated state-goal** given an original-plan (*oplan*) and a list of executed activities (*executed-activities-list*), if and only if there is a protection (protect *(not sg)*) from *g1* to *g2* in *oplan*, where *g1* is in the list of executed activities (*executed-activities-list*), while *g2* is not.

3.1 Executing activities

Figure 3 describes how the original plan is modified to reflect the changes in the plan by the executed activities. The algorithm creates an activity *appliedGoal* whose effects are the state changes caused by executing *executed-activities-list*. We assume that *executed-activities-list* is given in order of the completion of execution of each activity. In step 1, the effects and preconditions of *applied-Goal* are initialized to an empty set. In step 2, the effects of each activity in *executed-activities-list* are added to the effects of *appliedGoal* in order of their executions. An effect of an activity may overwrite the effect of a activity executed earlier. In step 3, all the activities in *executed-activities-list* are removed from the operational goal list of the plan, because in principle they should not have to be re-executed again. In step 4, all the **violated state-goals** are located and added back to the nonoperational goal list of the plan because they need to be re-achieved to ensure that the preconditions of the not executed activities are satisfied. In step 5, *appliedGoal* is promoted before all the activities that have not been executed yet.

3.2 Reset state-goals

Figure 4 describes how the original plan is modified to reflect the changes in the plan caused by resetting the violated state-goals. The algorithm creates an activity *ResetGoals* for resetting the state-goals, and adds this activity into the original plan. In step 1, we initialize *resetGoals* to an activity without preconditions or effects, and insert it to the original plan. In step 2, we compute all the **violated state-goals** due to unexpected state changes (*violatedGoals*), i.e., those that are true in the current state but not in the expected state of applying executed activities. In step 3, we update *resetGoals* to account for the activitites that establish the default values of *violatedGoals*. Since establishing the default values may result in further protection violation, in step 4 we locate all such violations and move them back to the nonoperational goals of *oplan* to reachieve them later. In step 5, *resetGoals* is promoted before all the activities that have not been executed.

Inputs: *executed-activities-list*, a list of activities already executed,
          oplan, original plan
Output: *appliedGoal*, an activity representing the effect of executing *executed-activities-list*

1. Initialize: $Effects(appliedGoal) \leftarrow \{\}$, $Preconds(appliedGoal) \leftarrow \{\}$
2. For each activity $a \in$ *executed-activities-list*, do:
     For each effect $e \in Effects(a)$, do:
       if $e \in Effect(appliedGoal)$, do nothing,
       else if *(not e)* $\in Effect(appliedGoal)$, do:
          $Effect(appliedGoal) \leftarrow (Effect(appliedGoal) \cup \{e\}) \backslash \{(not\ e)\}$
       else $Effect(appliedGoal) \leftarrow Effect(appliedGoal) \cup \{e\}$
3. $OperationalGoals(oplan) \leftarrow OperationalGoals(oplan) \backslash$ *executed-activities-list*.
4. For each effect $e \in Effects(appliedGoal)$ do:
     if *(not e)* is a **violated state-goal**, do:
        $NonOperationalGoals(oplan) \leftarrow NonOperationalGoals(oplan) \cup (not\ e)$
5. For every activity $a \in OperationalGoals(oplan)$, do: add a after *appliedGoal*

Fig. 3. Executing activities: creating an activity *appliedGoal* to reflect the changes to the plan caused by executing the activities.

Inputs: *current-state, executed-activities-list, oplan*
Output: *oplan* including *resetGoals*

1. Initialize *resetGoals* and insert it to *oplan*
2. *violatedGoals* $\leftarrow$ {state-goal g: $g \in$ *current-state*, $g \notin$ *expected-state*, and g is a **violated state-goal**}
3. For each $g \in ViolatedGoals$, do:
     $Effects(resetGoals) \leftarrow Effects(resetGoals) \cup$ *default-value* (g)
4. For each effect $e \in resetGoals$, do:
     if e is a **violated state-goal**, then
        $NonOperationalGoals(oplan) \leftarrow NonOperationalGoals(oplan) \cup (not\ e)$
5. For every activity $a \in OperationalGoals(oplan)$, do: a dd a after *resetGoals*

Fig. 4. Resetting goals: creating an activity *resetGoals* to reflect the changes to the plan caused by resetting the violated goals.

3.3   Replanning

Figure 5 describes how the replanner determines which activities need to be re-executed. The algorithm analyzes the protections in the original plan, re-executing activities that are necessary to re-establish the protections that are violated by the effects of *appliedGoal* or *resetGoals*. In this algorithm, the variable *re-execute-activities* is used to store the activities that need to be re-executed, or preconditions that need to be re-achieved. This variable is used to ensure that each precondition is re-achieved at most once so that the replanner does not go into an infinite loop. In essence, the replanning algorithm recursively determines which executed activities are used to achieve the protections that are violated by *appliedGoal* or *resetGoals*, re-executes these activities (i.e. adds them back to the operational goals of the plan) to ensure that the preconditions of the re-executed activities and not-executed activities are achieved. During replanning, the nonoperational goals of the plan are either the preconditions of a not executed activity that are undone by *appliedGoal* or *resetGoals*, or the activities that were used to achieve these preconditions in the original plan, or the regressed preconditions of these activities. The algorithm repeatedly chooses a goal, *currentGoal*, from the nonoperational goal list, and removes it from the list (steps 1 and 2). In step 3, if *currentGoal* is a precondition of an activity, then the activity *g* that was used to achieve *currentGoal* in the original plan is added to the operational (or nonoperational) goal list of *oplan*. In addition, for any protection from an executed activity to *g*, if the protection is violated by *resetOp* or *appliedGoal*, then the protected fact is added to the nonoperational goal list because it should be re-achieved. Furthermore, if the effects of *g* violate a protection from an executed activity to a not yet executed activity, then the violated protection is also added to the nonoperational goals so that it can be re-achieved. In step 4, if *currentGoal* is an activity goal, then the goals that *currentGoal* decomposed into in the original plan are added back to the (non)operational goal list of *oplan*. Finally, we ensure that *resetOp* is ordered before any other activities in the repaired plan. Activities in the operational goal list form the plan returned by the replanner.

The ordering constraints of the original plans are kept as they are. Since the only ordering constraints the replanner adds to the original plan are to add the *resetGoals* before any activities need to be re-executed and any activities not yet executed, the replanning algorithm does not add any inconsistency to the original plan. Analysis of the soundness and complexity can be found in Section 5.

For example, suppose the original plan is shown in Figure 6. The protections in the plan are: (1) P1: protect *q* from A to B, (where A achieves *q*), and (2) P2: protect *r* from B to D (where B achieves *r*). Suppose that when activities A, B, and C are executed, and activity D is not yet executed, an unexpected state change occurs that results in deleting *q* and *r* from the state. Then activity B needs to be re-executed because protection P2 is violated by the reset operator. Activity A also needs to be re-executed because P1 is violated by the reset operator and activity B needs to be re-executed. But activity C does not need to be re-executed. The repaired plan is shown in Figure 7.

4 Empirical Evaluation

Our replanning algorithm is a general approach which uses a domain-independent hybrid HTN/operator planning architecture. It has been tested in a real application, namely, the deep space network (DSN) antenna operation domain. This section describes the application domain, how the general replanning problem maps onto the real application domain, as well as empirical test results.

4.1 Planning for Deep Space Network Antenna Operations

The Deep Space Network is a set of world-wide antenna networks which is maintained by the Jet Propulsion Laboratory (JPL). Through these antennas, JPL

Inputs: *oplan*, plan with *appliedGoal* and *resetGoals* added in
Output: *repaired-plan*

- *re-execute-activities* ← *NonOperationalGoals(oplan)*;
- while *NonOperationalGoals(oplan)* is not empty, do:
  1. *currentGoal* ← choose a goal from *NonOperationalGoals(oplan)*;
  2. *NonOperationalGoals(oplan)* ← *NonOperationalGoals(oplan)* \ {*currentGoal*}
  3. if *currentGoal* is a precondition-goal, do:
     3.1. *g* ← locate the activity achieving *currentGoal*.
          if *g* ∈ *re-execute-activities*, goto 1.
     3.2. if *g* is an operational goal then:
          OperationalGoals(oplan) ← *OperationalGoals(oplan)* ∪ {*g*}
          else *NonOperationalGoals(oplan)* ← *NonOperationalGoals(oplan)* ∪ {*g*}
     3.3. for every protection (protect *p* from *g0* to *g*), do:
          if *p* is deleted by *resetGoals* or *appliedGoal*, and *g* ∉ *re-execute-activities*,
          then:
          NonOperationalGoals(oplan) ← *NonOperationalGoals(oplan)* ∪ {*p*},
          re-execute-activities ← *re-execute-activities* ∪ {*p*}
     3.4. for every protection (protect *p*) from *g1* to *g2*, and every effect *e* of *g*, such
          that *p* = *(not e)*, *g1* ∈ *executed-activities-list*, *g2* ∉ *executed-activities-list*,
          p ∉ *re-execute-activities*, do:
          NonOperationalGoals(oplan) ← *NonOperationalGoals(oplan)* ∪ {*p*}
          re-execute-activities ← *re-execute-activities* ∪ {*p*}
     3.5. *re-execute-activities* ← *re-execute-activities* ∪ {*g*}
  4. if *currentGoal* is an activity-goal, do:
     for every child *g* of *currentGoal*,
     If *g* ∉ *re-execute-activities*, then
     if *g* is an operational goal, then:
     OperationalGoals(oplan) ← *OperationalGoals(oplan)* ∪ {*g*}
     else *NonOperationalGoals(oplan)* ← *NonOperationalGoals(oplan)* ∪ {*g*}
- For every activity *a* ∈ *OperationalGoals(oplan)*, do: add *a* after *resetGoals*
- return *oplan*

Fig. 5. Replanning: determining which activities need to be re-executed.

is responsible for providing the communications link with a multitude of space-craft. Operations personnel are responsible for creating and maintaining this link by configuring the required antenna subsystems and performing test and calibration procedures. The task of creating the communications link is a manual and time-consuming process which requires operator input of over a hundred control directives and the constant monitoring of several dozen displays to determine the exact execution status of the system. Recently, a system called the Link Monitor and Control Operator Assistant (LMCOA), has been developed to improve operations efficiency and reduce precalibration time. The LMCOA provides semi-automated monitor and control functions to support operating DSN antennas. One of the main inputs to the LMCOA is a temporal dependency network (TDN). A TDN is a directed graph that incorporates temporal

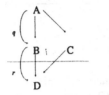

Fig. 6. An example of an original plan. Unexpected state changes occurs when activities A, B, and C are executed, but D is not executed.

Fig. 7. Repaired plan where activities A, B are re-executed upon an unexpected state change.

and behavioral knowledge. This graph represents the steps required to perform a communications link operation. In current operations, these TDNs are developed manually. DPLAN is an AI planning system designed to automatically generate these TDNs based on input information describing the antenna track type and the necessary equipment configuration. DPLAN integrates HTN planning and operator-based planning. Given a set of antenna tracking goals and equipment information, DPLAN then generates a list of antenna operation steps that will create a communications link with orbiting spacecraft.

4.2 Replanning Scenarios for the DSN domain

The DSN Antenna Operations domain is dynamic, uncertain, concurrent, and has changing objectives. This domain is dynamic because the current state may unexpectedly change due to external events such as equipment (subsystem) failures. It is uncertain because actions may not always achieve their desired effects. It is concurrent because actions pertaining to different subsystems may occur simultaneously. It has changing objectives because new goals may be added after the execution of the original plan has already begun. Our replanning system is able to replan in all these scenarios. In our empirical evaluation, we focus on the first scenario, i.e., replanning when the world changes independently of the plan being executed.

Note that one alternative to replanning would be to simply reset all of the subsystems in use and completely restart the plan from scratch, re-achieving all of the desired conditions. We name this approach *complete-reset* approach. In the general case this approach undesirable because of the *domain knowledge reliability* and *operator understanding* reasons described in Section 1. In the DSN antenna operations domain this approach is also too inefficient to be applicable for two reasons:

- *Complete-reset* approach is slow from an execution time standpoint. DSN antennas are a scarce over-subscribed resource. Completely restarting to recover from failures would reduce antenna availability for tracking purposes by increasing downtime due to time lost during recovery from changed goals, state changes, or failed actions. Additionally, delaying a track may result in lost data because it is generally infeasible to alter the spacecraft command sequence on short notice.

- *Complete-reset* approach involves resetting (powering off and then back on) all of the subsystems. This power cycling of the hardware introduces unnecessary wear on the expensive and scarce DSN subsystems.

Thus our replanning algorithm re-uses as much of the original plan as possible while minimizing the amount of re-execution by restoring the subsystem to a functioning state (generally through resetting the subsystem) and by re-achieving relevant states before continuing plan execution.

4.3 Empirical results

In Section 1, we stated that replanning by re-using the nominal plan was desirable because the domain knowledge for nominal operations is more reliable (for example, commonly there is an assumed execution context for an operator in nominal usage which is not explicitly represented in operator preconditions). To verify this claim, we tested our replanning algorithm on a series of replanning problems. In these experiments, our algorithm used knowledge developed for nominal operations to replan for 5 problems for each of the 3 types of replanning scenarios: subsystem failure, additional service request, and activity failure, to produce a total of 15 plans. A domain expert validated 6 plans randomly selected from the 15 repaired plans generated by our replanner. The limited size of the verified test set is due to the significant effort required to manually verify a TDN and the scarcity of the DSN domain experts. The domain expert considered all the 6 examined replans to be correct (i.e they would achieve the goals from the replan state). The results are summarized in Table 1.

# of plans	# of plans where $plan_{expert} = plan_{replanner}$	% correct repaired plans
6	6	100%

Table 1. Expert judged correctness of the repaired plan

The second criterion for evaluation is that it is critical to minimize execution time of the TDNs. From the replanning point of view, this means minimizing the number of activities that need to be re-executed. For this, we compared the number of activities that are re-executed in the repaired plan versus the corresponding number in the plans generated using complete brute force replanning (i.e. resetting everything and starting from scratch). In the 15 replanning cases, the average number of activities in the original TDN is 13.8, the average number of activities executed when the failure occurs is 8.07, and the average number of activities re-executed using our replanning algorithm is 1.13. We see that the proportion of re-executed activities using our replanning algorithm is only 14% (1.13/8.07) of those using brute force – resetting every subsystem and starting from scratch. This demonstrates that the repaired plans generated by our replanner are significantly more efficient than brute-force re-planning. Table 2 summarizes the empirical results for repaired plan efficiency.

# of plans	avg. # of re-executed activities		efficiency ratio
	in $plan_{replanner}$	in $plan_{from-scratch}$	
15	1.13	8.07	14%

Table 2. Efficiency of the repaired plan

5 Discussions

5.1 Termination and soundness

Our replanning algorithm for determining which activities require re-execution (described in Figure 5) will terminate because: (1) in the worst case when all the executed activities are added back to the operational goal list of the plan, the nonoperational goals of the plan will be empty; (2) when a violated precondition is added back to the nonoperational goal list, it takes a finite number of iterations to add the executed activity that achieves this precondition; and (3) every goal list is allowed to be added back to the (non)operational goal list at most once. Thus the complexity of the replanning algorithm is O(n) where n is the length of the original plan.

Our replanning algorithms are sound assuming that the domain knowledge is correct. The soundness proof follows from analyzing the algorithm in Figure 5 by showing: (1) every possible violation of the previously achieved state is identified in the algorithm; (2) every violated state is re-established by re-executing activities in the original plan that established these conditions. Since the original plan is sound, the replanning algorithm ensures that there are no violated protections in the repaired plan, and thus is sound.

5.2 Generality

Our replanning algorithm is based on protection analysis. The protections in our plans are derived from the the preconditions and effects of activities in the plan. Thus our replanning approach is applicable to all planners that maintain such protections, including [Pemberthy and Weld 1992, Carbonell et al 1992] and [Chien et al 1995].

We also learned that planners with only hierarchical decomposition capability are insufficient for replanning unless proper protections are specified. Most decompositional rules only specify how to decompose a high level activity to low level activities and the ordering constraints among them. Protections are not required to generate initial correct plans, although most HTN planners allow and encourage the specification of protections. In contrast, operator-based planning requires that preconditions and effects of each activity be encoded explicitly in order to function properly. Protections are generated by the planner automatically from the preconditions and effects. We believe that since protections are essential for replanning, operator-based planning is more natural for replanning purposes.

6 Related Work

One similar replanning system is the CHEF system [Hammond 1989]. In CHEF, failures are all due to unforseen goal interactions. The CHEF system classifies a failure, infers a missing goal, and applies a critic to repair the plan. This problem differs from our replanning problem - in our case the problem is not an unrecognized goal interaction but rather a change in the problem state or goals. Thus, in our replanning problem one (inefficient) alternative is to simply re-execute the entire plan. This would be unwise in the CHEF replanning context because it is assumed the plan would simply fail again. In our replanning context, the desired outcome is to recover so as to achieve the possibly altered goal set while retaining as much of the original plan as possible.

SIPE [Wilkins 1988] also performs replanning in response to unexpected external events that change the state. SIPE first classifies the failure type and then uses this classification to apply a critic to repair the plan. Again, our replanning problem is constrained such that resetting the subsystems and re-executing the entire plan is a viable alternative – the goal is to minimize unnecessary re-execution. In SIPE's replanning scenario arbitrary replanning may be required. Thus, SIPE uses specific information in the form of critics. In our replanning problem the emphasis is on replanning to re-use the original plan, thus our approach focusses on re-establishing conditions using portions of the original plan.

Other previous work in the case-based reasoning or analogy work concentrates on adapting a case for a similar problem to the new problem situation [Veloso 1992, Kambhampati 1990]. Their algorithms involve adding and deleting activities from the original plan based on an analysis of the applicability of the dependencies to the current problem context. This work differs from ours in two ways. First, in our approach, we handle situations where part of the plan is likely to have been executed when replanning occurs. Thus replanning must account for the altered initial state. Second, in our approach, minimizing the number of re-executed activities is desirable.

Previous work in the framework of integrating planning, executing, and replanning [Knoblock 1995, Drabble 1995] relies on the domain designer to provide repair methods for each type of failure. In the replanning problems we are addressing, it is impractical to specify a repair method for each specific class of failure. For example, in the DSN domain, there may be many different kinds of failures, failures may happen at almost any time during execution, there are tens of subsystems, etc. Hence, we have designed our algorithms to work from more general information (such as the execution status of activities). However, we still require certain specific information (e.g., the relevant subsystem to reset for an activity failure).

7 Future Work

This paper has presented a general framework for replanning required by changes in problem context. However, there are several areas for future work which are driven by operational requirements of our target application domain of DSN antenna operations. This paper represents a first step towards tackling this complex problem and there are numerous outstanding issues which remain to be addressed. We describe several of these issues below.

In the DSN, there is a tradeoff of the granularity of representing the activities. The activities are the lowest level primitives that the planner reasons about: each activity may contain tens of directives (commands). Sometimes during an execution failure, instead of re-executing a whole activity, it is possible to only re-execute a subset of all the directives in the activity, so that the total execution time may be shortened. To capture this plan repair knowledge, we can break an activity down to a number of activities, but then the planner must reason at a lower level of abstraction. This may result in a less maintainable knowledge base for the planner and degraded planner performance (planning speed). One area for future work is to better understand the tradeoffs and implications of selecting a particular level of abstraction for the planner.

In the DSN domain, actions take time. If the recovery actions take an extended amount of time, there may not be enough time to perform a planned equipment performance test as well as starting the acquisition of data at the required time. In this case, a tradeoff must be evaluated. For example, should the data be captured without doing the performance test? Or would the data be useless without the performance test? Endowing a planning system to reason about the utility of these differing courses of action to take the best overall course of action is a long-term goal.

In the DSN domain, during execution, some subsystems may be removed due to competing requests. Usually, these subsystems are not needed any more by the task, and are requested to be used by other tasks. What is the proper way to remove the equipment from the system? How do we unlink it with other subsystems? Enhancing the planning system to be able to reason about these types of temporal constraints and requests (using a more expressive temporal representation) is an area for future work.

Finally, in the DSN, the state of each of the subsystems is complex and contains a large amount of information. Although in principle, all relevant state information can be inferred by an expert operator, in practice this is quite difficult. How can the planning system recover from failures in a way so as to reduce the need for operators to perform complex, time-consuming and knowledge-intensive diagnoses?

8 Conclusions

To scale-up to real-world problems, planning systems must be able to replan in order to deal with changes in problem context. This paper has described hierarchical task network and operator-based re-planning techniques to adapt a previous plan to account for: state changes, added new goals, and failed actions. This approach attempts to preserve elements of the original plan in order to utilize more reliable nominal operations domain knowledge and to facilitate user understanding. In addition, the replanning methods attempt to avoid unnecessary re-achievement of goals. We have also presented empirical results documenting the effectiveness of these techniques in a NASA antenna operations application.

References

[Carbonell et al 1992] Carbonell, J.G.; Blythe, J.; Etzioni, O.; Gil, Y.; Joseph, R.; Kahn, D.; Knoblock, C.; Minton, S.; Pérez, M. A.; Reilly, S.; Veloso, M.; and Wang, X. PRODIGY 4.0: The Manual and Tutorial. *Technical report*, School of Computer Science, Carnegie Mellon University, 1992.

[Chien et al 1995] S. Chien, A. Govindjee, T. Estlin, X. Wang, and R. Hill Jr., Integrating Hierarchical Task Network and Operator-based Planning Techniques to Automate Operations of Communications Antennas, IEEE Expert, December 1996.

[Drabble 1995] B. Drabble. Replanning in the O(Plan) architecture. *Personal communication*, 1995.

[Erol et al 1994] K. Erol, J. Hendler, and D. Nau, UMCP:A Sound and Complete Procedure for Hierarchical Task Network Planning, *Proceedings of the Second International Conference on AI Planning Systems*, Chicago, IL, June 1994, pp. 249-254.

[Hammond 1989] K. Hammond. Case-Based Planning: Viewing planning as a memory task. 1989.

[Kambhampati 1990] S. Kambhampati. A theory of plan modification. In *Proceedings of the Eighth National Conference on Artificial Intelligence*, Boston, MA, 1990.

[Kambhampati 1995] S. Kambhampati. A Comparative analysis of Partial Order Planning and Task Reduction Planning In *ACM SIGART Bulletin*, Vol.6., No.1, 1995.

[Knoblock 1995] C. Knoblock. Planning, executing, sensing, and replanning for information gathering. In *Proceedings of IJCAI 95*, Montreal, CA, 1995.

[Pemberthy and Weld 1992] J. S. Pemberthy and D. S. Weld, UCPOP: A Sound Complete, Partial Order Planner for ADL, *Proceedings of the Third International Conference on Knowledge Representation and Reasoning*, October 1992.

[Currie and Tate 1991] K. Currie and A. Tate, The Open Planning Architecture, In *Artificial Intelligence, 51(1)*, 1991.

[Veloso 1992] M. Veloso. Learning by Analogical Reasoning in General Problem Solving. *PhD thesis*, School of Computer Science, Carnegie Mellon University, Pittsburgh, PA, 1992.

[Wilkins 1988] D. Wilkins. Practical Planning: Extending the Classical AI Planning Paradigm. Morgan Kaufmann, 1988.

BI-POMDP: Bounded, Incremental Partially-Observable Markov-Model Planning

Richard Washington

Caelum Research Corporation
NASA Ames Research Center
MS 269-1
Moffett Field, CA 94035-1000
rwashington@mail.arc.nasa.gov

Abstract. Given the problem of planning actions for situations with uncertainty about the action outcomes, Markov models can effectively model this uncertainty and offer optimal actions. When the information about the world state is itself uncertain, partially observable Markov models are an appropriate extension to the basic Markov model. However, finding optimal actions for partially observable Markov models is a computationally difficult problem that in practice borders on intractability. Approximate or heuristic approaches, on the other hand, lose any guarantee of optimality or even any indication of how far from optimal they might be.

In this paper, we present an incremental, search-based approximation for partially observable Markov models. The search is based on an incremental AND-OR search, using heuristic functions based on the underlying Markov model, which is more easily solved. In addition, the search provides a bound on the possible error of the approximation. We illustrate the method with results on problems taken from the related literature.

1 Introduction

Uncertainty abounds in real-world domains. Given the unpredictability of processes that act in the world and the complexity of agents and objects in the world, models of such domains necessarily rest uncertain. The uncertainty pervades models of actions as well as models of the state of the world.

Consider the problem of medical diagnosis and therapy. The state of the patient is only known indirectly through tests performed on the patient and sensors attached to the patient, from which one can induce in which states the patient might be. Based on this information, a therapeutic course of action is chosen that best addresses the possible problems, but the effects of this action on the patient are only imperfectly known. So the therapy must allow for multiple possible outcomes.

Markov models [1] are useful for representing and reasoning about uncertain domains. The process, whether it be a patient, robot, or chemical plant, is represented as a set of discrete states. At any moment in time, the process is in one of the states. When an action is taken, the state of the process changes, with the resulting state dependent on the action and predefined probabilities of transitions between states. The basic Markov model represents the uncertainty about action outcomes using the transition probabilities and offers optimal actions in the face of this uncertainty.

The basic Markov model can be extended to handle the case of partial observability, where the state of the process is not necessarily known. Instead, there are observations available that provide information about the state but may not fully identify it. So the choice of the optimal action must be made knowing only a probability distribution over states rather than the true state. This makes the problem of determining the optimal action much more difficult than for the fully observable case, and in fact is currently only possible for very small problems [4].

Approximations for partially-observable Markov models exist, but they tend to fall prey to a few problems. Either they themselves do not completely avoid the complexity problems [5], or they ignore aspects of the model that are necessary to ensure optimal actions [9,8].

In this paper, we present an incremental approach for partially observable Markov models that in the limit achieves the optimal action, and in the meantime provides an approximate solution that can be used when time is of the essence. In addition, the partial solution comes with a provable bound on its error (a best- and worst-case estimate), so that the underlying decision-making system can see the possible impact of taking the action at each moment. For example, in the medical example this would correspond to having an estimate of the optimistic and pessimistic estimates of the morbidity of a therapy (if that were the measure of utility), thus avoiding the problem of taking a therapy that looks good, only to find out that it in fact has a disastrous outcome in reality.

The organization of the paper is as follows. We present Markov models and the partially observable version thereof. Then we describe how to reason about partially observable Markov models as a search problem. Then we describe how this search can be performed incrementally, providing both optimistic and pessimistic bounds, which in turn can direct the search process. We present results on problems from the literature to illustrate the method and its effectiveness. Finally, we discuss the limitations of the method and current directions for research.

2 Partially Observable Markov Decision Processes

In this section we briefly review Markov processes, and in particular POMDPs. We will borrow the notation of [6], altering it only as required for the problem at hand; the reader can refer there for a more complete explanation of the framework.

We assume that the underlying process, the *core process*, is described by a finite-state, stationary Markov chain. The core process is captured by the following information:

- a finite set $\mathcal{N} \equiv \{1, \ldots, N\}$, representing the possible states of the process
- a variable $X_t \in \mathcal{N}$ representing the state of the core process at time t
- a finite set $\mathcal{A}$ of actions available
- a matrix $P = [p_{ij}], i, j \in \mathcal{N}$ specifying transition probabilities of the core process: $P(a) = [p_{ij}(a)]$ specifies the transition probabilities when action $a \in \mathcal{A}$ is chosen
- a reward matrix $R = [r_{ij}], i, j \in \mathcal{N}$ specifying the immediate rewards of the core process: $R(a) = [r_{ij}(a)]$ specifies the reward received when the action $a \in \mathcal{A}$ is executed. We will use the shorthand

$$\varrho_i(a) = \sum_{j \in \mathcal{N}} r_{ij}(a)p_{ij}(a)$$

to denote the reward of taking action a when in state i, and

$$\varrho(a) = \{\varrho_1(a), \ldots, \varrho_N(a)\}.$$

So at time t, the core process is in state $X_t = i$, and if an action $a \in \mathcal{A}$ is taken, the core process transitions to state $X_{t+1} = j$ with probability $p_{ij}(a)$, receiving immediate reward $r_{ij}(a)$.

Actions are chosen by a policy that maps states to actions. The optimal policy is the policy that maximizes the utility of each state. The value of a state under the optimal policy (given full observability) is defined as:

$$v(i) = \max_{a \in \mathcal{A}} \left\{ \varrho_i(a) + \beta \sum_{k \in \mathcal{N}} v(k)p_{ik}(a) \right\}$$

where $0 \leq \beta < 1$ is a discount factor (this ensures a bounded value function).

However, in a partially observable MDP, the progress of the core process is not known, but can only be inferred through a finite set of observations. The observations are captured with the following information:

- a finite set $\mathcal{M} \equiv \{1, \ldots, M\}$ representing the possible observations
- a variable $Y_t \in \mathcal{M}$ representing the observation at time t
- a matrix $Q = [q_{ij}], i \in \mathcal{N}, j \in \mathcal{M}$ specifying the probability of seeing observations in given states: $Q(a) = [q_{ij}(a)]$, where $q_{ij}(a)$ denotes the probability of observing j from state i when action $a \in \mathcal{A}$ has been taken
- a state distribution variable $\pi(t) = \{\pi_1(t), \ldots, \pi_N(t)\}$, where $\pi_i(t)$ is the probability of $X_t = i$ given the information about actions and observations
- an initial state distribution $\pi(0)$.

At time t, the observation of the core process will be Y_t. If action $a \in \mathcal{A}$ is taken, we can define a function to determine Y_{t+1}. In particular, we define

$$\gamma(j|\pi(t), a) = \sum_{i \in \mathcal{N}} q_{ij}(a) \sum_{k \in \mathcal{N}} p_{ki}(a)\pi_k(t) \tag{1}$$

as the probability that $Y_{t+1} = j$ given that action $a \in \mathcal{A}$ is taken at time t and the state distribution at that time is $\pi(t)$.

To determine the state distribution variable $\pi(t+1)$, we define the transformation T as follows:

$$\pi(t+1) = T(\pi(t)|j, a)$$
$$= \{T_1(\pi(t)|j, a), \ldots, T_N(\pi(t)|j, a)\}$$

where

$$T_i(\pi(t)|j, a) = \frac{q_{ij}(a) \sum_{k \in \mathcal{N}} p_{ki}(a) \pi_k(t)}{\sum_{l \in \mathcal{N}} q_{lj}(a) \sum_{k \in \mathcal{N}} p_{kl}(a) \pi_k(t)}, \qquad (2)$$

for $i \in \mathcal{N}$, and where $\pi(t)$ is the state distribution at time t, $a \in \mathcal{A}$ is the action taken at that time, resulting in observation $j \in \mathcal{M}$.

Actions are chosen by a decision rule (or plan) that maps state distributions to actions. The utility of a state distribution π under the optimal decision rule can be computed by the value function:

$$V_P(\pi) = \max_{a \in \mathcal{A}} \left\{ \pi \cdot \varrho(a) + \beta \sum_{j \in \mathcal{M}} V_P[T(\pi|j, a)] \gamma(j|\pi, a) \right\}. \qquad (3)$$

3 The problem with MDP-based solutions

It is better to make intelligent use of the time available rather than doing something that is always a bit wrong. This is one of the fundamental premises underlying the work presented here. The goal is to have something that converges towards the optimal solution. The simple use of an MDP-based solution method, albeit fast, is guaranteed not to work in certain cases.

To illustrate the importance of solving the POMDP rather than simply the underlying MDP, consider the problem shown in Figure 1. The agent starts in the center square, but without knowing which of 4 orientations it is in. The agent can only see the walls around it, and the walls have distinctive markings, so that once it is in a side area, it will know where it is. If we use a weighted MDP-based policy or some variant thereof [9], the action recommended will be to turn forever, since there will be two possible states with a recommendation to turn one direction, one possible state with a recommendation to turn the other direction, and one possible state with a recommendation to advance. In fact, the optimal action is to advance, read the wall if it isn't the goal, and then head toward the goal. This problem generalizes to any large open space.

4 Search-based POMDP Approximation

For an initial state distribution, there is a set of actions that may be taken. Each of these actions leads to a set of possible observations, each weighted by the probability of that observation occurring given the action and the preceding

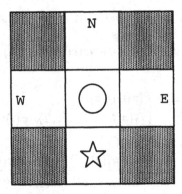

Fig. 1. Problem where an MDP-based model fails. The agent is in the center square, but in an unknown orientation. The goal is at the bottom.

state distribution. The end result of an action plus an observation is another state distribution. A POMDP policy specifies which action to take in each of the resulting state distributions. The optimal POMDP policy will choose the action with the highest value.

If the actions and observations are expanded in a search-tree form, they form an AND-OR tree. The nodes of the tree are state distributions. The actions form the OR branches, since the optimal action is a choice among the set of actions. The observations form the AND branches, since the utility of an action is a sum of the utility of the state distribution implied by each of the possible observations multiplied by the probability of that observation (see Equation 3).

If this tree were fully expanded to a depth d, the d-horizon POMDP value could be computed from this. The value of an OR node is the value of its child with maximum utility, weighted by the discount factor $\beta < 1$. The value of an AND node is the sum of the values of its children, each weighted by its probability. The subtree that corresponds to choosing the maximum utility child at each step is in fact the optimal policy for this horizon.

Since we want the optimal infinite-horizon policy, this technique is infeasible as stated. But we will work with a tree with estimated values at the fringe, which will give an estimated value for each branch of the tree. As the tree is expanded, the estimates will become more accurate (guaranteed by the discount factor β). The goal is to perform a search to find the policy with maximum utility.

If we invert the function so that the goal is to minimize disutility, we now have a classic search problem: given an AND-OR tree (the actions and observations) and an estimation function at the fringe, the goal is to find the path that minimizes the true function. Thus the AO* algorithm [7] can be used to expand the tree. Moreover, if the evaluation function is underestimating and monotonic, the algorithm is guaranteed not to return a non-optimal path as the goal. The AO* algorithm still involves a non-deterministic choice of which AND branch along the current best path to further expand (since that does not fall out directly from the evaluations, unlike in A*). We will discuss a strategy for choosing the fringe node to expand in the next section.

5 Bounded, Incremental Search for POMDPs

The AO* algorithm by itself is incremental, in that after every fringe node expansion the best path represents the best current policy or plan. However, the AO* algorithm is limited by the memory it uses. In earlier tests, we ran into memory limitations after a small number of iterations, as the tree size grew quickly and filled memory.

To remedy this problem, BI-POMDP uses an iterative AO* algorithm [11] that uses memory linear in the depth of the search. This allows searches that are for practical purposes unlimited, as long as the fringe-node expansion strategy avoids extremely deep searches along a single branch.

The AO* algorithm does not specify the order for expanding children of AND nodes. BI-POMDP uses a strategy that chooses the node that presents the greatest potential to change the estimated value of the overall path. Since this node is only known with certainty when the true values are known, we use instead a heuristic estimate, which is the weighted difference between an underestimate and an overestimate of the node value. This represents the maximum possible change to the overall path value based on expanding this node. To use this heuristic estimate, we need two heuristic functions, one that underestimates, and one that overestimates.

To get an underestimating, monotonic heuristic function, we solve the (much easier) underlying MDP model of the problem domain. The solution describes the optimal policy and state values for the case of full observation. Tractable solution methods exist for MDPs, and this computation can take place off-line. The MDP solution is then used to produce a value function that is the sum of the MDP value of each state, weighted by the probability of being in that state:

$$V_F(\pi) = \sum_{i \in \mathcal{N}} \pi_i v(i)$$

(this is the approach suggested in [4] and [9]). This is an optimistic function, guaranteed to overestimate the utility [10]. Since node values are disutilities, we are minimizing disutility, and this optimistic function can be seen as an underestimating heuristic estimate of the disutility. In addition, it is straightforward to show that the function is monotonic.

To get the corresponding overestimating heuristic function, we compute the worst-case MDP. In particular, instead of choosing the action at each state that maximizes the utility, we choose the action that minimizes the utility:

$$v(i) = \min_{a \in \mathcal{A}} \left\{ \varrho_i(a) + \beta \sum_{k \in \mathcal{N}} v(k) p_{ik}(a) \right\}$$

This then produces the strategy that is guaranteed to produce the worst possible action for each state. These are then used in a value function like before, with a weighted sum of the worst-case state values. This value function produces a pessimistic estimate that is guaranteed to be underestimate of the utility. So this function will produce an overestimate of the disutility, which is what we need. Note that this is a very crude bound, since in fact it produces a lower bound of the utility of the worst POMDP action, which is itself less than or equal to (usually significantly less than) the utility of the best POMDP action.

Note that by using a guaranteed optimistic and pessimistic estimate on the utility of a state distribution, we have not only an effective strategy for exploring useful parts of the search space, but we also have a bound on the possible utility of the current best action (see Figure 2). As the search proceeds, the upper and lower bounds narrow (since, after all, the search proceeds by expanding the branch with the largest gap). At the moment that the bounds meet, the policy is guaranteed to be optimal, since the optimal policy has a value between the upper and lower bounds. But earlier in the search it is possible to give a bound on the possible error of the value estimate: it is guaranteed to be in the range [lower bound, upper bound]. So this avoids the problem of following an action based on an overly optimistic estimate, only to find out that it was actually much worse.

6 Results

To test the BI-POMDP method, we have run it on a suite of problems from the POMDP literature. Here we present results from two of those problems, a one-trial version of the Tiger problem [4], and a robot navigation problem [10].

The Tiger problem is the choice between two doors, with a tiger behind one and money behind the other. A third action is to listen, gaining information but paying for the privilege. The one-trial version is simply that this choice is performed once, and then the process terminates (in a sink state). The listening may go on for an indefinite time, since conflicting information may be gathered from successive listens. The best case is that the money is chosen immediately. The worst case is that the tiger is chosen immediately. The optimal plan is to listen until enough certainty is accumulated, then choose. This is solvable by hand, although exact algorithms have difficulty with the one-trial version.

The robot navigation problem is a small corridor segment with alcoves. There is one alcove that is the goal, and the rest are highly penalized. The robot starts with ambiguity as to whether it is near the goal or another alcove. The best case is to move directly to the goal. The worst case is to move directly to another alcove. The optimal plan is to sense the world enough to determine whether it is near a goal or alcove, then move. This is small and reasonably obvious to the human eye, but unsolvable by current exact techniques.

For the Tiger problem, Figure 2(a) shows the bounds of the value estimate

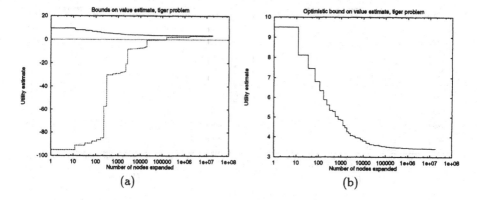

Fig. 2. Tiger problem. (a) Upper and lower bounds on the value of the best action, as a function of the number of nodes expanded[2]. (b) Optimistic bound on the value of the best action, as a function of the number of nodes expanded.

of the initial state distribution over time. As the search deepens, the bounds approach each other, reaching nearly provable optimality as they converge. To better show the evolution of the optimistic value estimate, which is fact the more accurate, Figure 2(b) isolates this. This in fact converges quickly towards the true value, but without an accurate pessimistic bound to help direct the search, it takes much longer for the bounds to converge.

For the robot navigation problem, Figure 3(a) shows the evolution of the bounds on the value estimate of the initial state distribution; Figure 3(b) shows the optimistic estimate. Note that in this case, the two bounds remain rather far apart, although the optimistic estimate is actually not far from the (hand-calculated) true value of about -116. Here the inaccurate overestimate proves to be a greater problem. In fact, the pessimistic bound is very bad in this case, since the worst possible action is to enter a highly-penalized alcove, of which there are plenty. A better pessimistic bound would help both the perceived value and the performance of the algorithm. Other problems in the suite of examples produce results varying between the two cases shown, with differences in rates of convergence.

Note that this is just one measure of plan quality, albeit an important one. Another important criterion, and perhaps the critical one, is the quality of the partial plan when it is executed. To test this, we constructed a version of the program that could be cut off after a given amount of time, after which the best known action would be executed, and the effects simulated stochastically. To test the quality of actions, this plan/execute cycle was repeated until the

---

[2] The plots are on a log scale in order to show the curve of convergence. This in fact makes the convergence look worse than it actually is—the bounds converge quickly at first and then asymptotically afterwards. When plotted on a linear scale, the graphs appear to show nearly immediate convergence followed by a straight line.

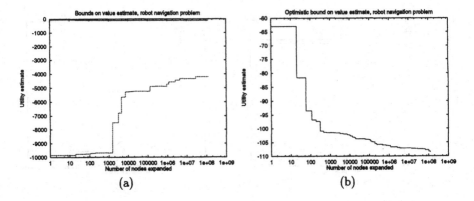

Fig. 3. Robot navigation problem. (a) Upper and lower bounds on the value of the best action, as a function of the number of nodes expanded. (b) Optimistic bound on the value of the best action, as a function of the number of nodes expanded.

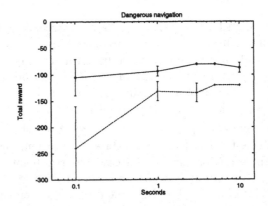

Fig. 4. Accumulated rewards from robot problem, as a function of the time cutoff. The two lines represent the cases where the robot starts near to or far from the goal.

process entered a stable state (sink or goal), and the total reward computed. We tested for a variety of time cutoffs, running 10 trials on each time cutoff.

The results for the robot navigation problem are shown in Figure 4. Note that when the robot is close to the goal, it does not improve much over time; this is because in fact it finds the optimal actions quickly (although more variation shows up with small time cutoffs). When the robot is far from the goal, the plan quality improves with the time allotted. In the Tiger problem, the plan quality remains flat because it is in fact too easy a problem and is solved nearly perfectly with minimal time expended. In both cases, the quality of the plan is somewhat hidden by the noise that exists from the stochastic simulation; for example, the reward may vary based on whether a robot motion succeeded or not.

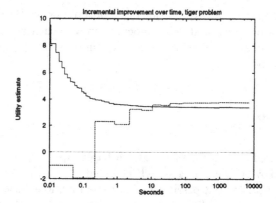

Fig. 5. Comparison of the convergence of BI-POMDP and Witness. Tiger problem. The curves cross due to small numerical inaccuracies accumulated by Witness and the underlying MDP estimate used by BI-POMDP.

7 Comparison to other POMDP approaches

Exact POMDP approaches are generally implemented as iterative algorithms that converge on the exact solution [4,6]. The algorithm generally regarded as the fastest is the Witness algorithm [2,4][3]. We compared the convergence of Witness and BI-POMDP on the two problems discussed here. Further comparisons are necessary (and planned) for other problems and also for the functional behavior of the approaches with respect to plan execution (what reward is actually received during execution of the incomplete plans).

For the Tiger problem, both the Witness and BI-POMDP approaches converge relatively quickly on the optimal value, as seen in Figure 5. In fact, the Witness algorithm did not converge to an exact solution after 2 hours of CPU time (Sun UltraSparc running Solaris).

For the robot navigation problem, the Witness algorithm terminated during the second iteration with a matrix inversion error. Monahan's algorithm warned of numerical instability during the second iteration, and then didn't finish the third iteration after more than two hours of CPU time[4]. Not surprisingly, the initial results of Witness and Monahan's algorithm are very inaccurate (-20 for Witness and -40 for Monahan, compared to the true value of approximately -116). In contrast, the BI-POMDP value converges to near the true value (starting at -63, -100 after 0.2 seconds), after which it converges more slowly. There remains some instability in the best action in the BI-POMDP case, since the bad

---

[3] A new algorithm by Zhang, Littman, and Cassandra has recently been released, but the program is still dependent on linear programming routines that are not public domain. A comparison to this new algorithm is forthcoming.

[4] This was using an implementation of Witness and Monahan's algorithms that relies on public-domain LP routines, which are more prone to numerical instability. The version of Witness described in published papers uses a superior, commercial LP product.

pessimistic bound forces the exploration of suboptimal search branches. However, the actions correspond to relatively innocuous moves, such as turning in place, instead of the optimal action of gathering more information to disambiguate the position of the robot.

8 Discussion

We have presented an incremental, search-based approximation for partially observable Markov models. The search is based on an incremental AND-OR search, using optimistic and pessimistic heuristic functions based on the underlying Markov model. In addition, the search provides a bound on the possible error of the approximation. In domains where a guarantee of safety is necessary, this bound is essential.

There remain limitations with this work. The current way of computing the pessimistic bound is very crude, and in fact the search strategy is hampered by the inaccuracy of this bound. A topic of current research is finding better pessimistic bounds, for instance using suboptimal policy graphs [3]. This will allow faster convergence and more useful information about the possible actions.

Partly because of the problem with pessimistic bounds, the search takes a long time to converge on a narrow bound. The policy itself may remain relatively stable, but the estimated value retains a wide bound.

The evaluation of the plan quality remains a problem. The ideal would be to compare the plan execution, as measured by accumulated reward, to the optimal plan execution. This however requires an optimal policy, and for those problems which would be most interesting to evaluate, an optimal policy remains out of reach.

Finally, other metrics for measuring the distance to optimal, such as policy similarity or functional behavior of partial policies, need to be investigated. In cases where the policy fluctuates, it is often due to nearly equivalent action choices, outweighed by the inaccuracies of the estimation functions. If the goal were to find a nearly optimal policy, eliminating those actions that are clearly worse, than perhaps a solution could be found more quickly with another metric.

9 Acknowledgements

Thanks to Michael Littman for supplying a suite of example problems and Tony Cassandra for the code for the exact POMDP methods. The work was started with support from a Veterans Affairs Medical Informatics fellowship, hosted jointly by the Philadelphia VAMC and the University of Pennsylvania; it was continued with a Chateaubriand Postdoctoral fellowship from the French government, hosted by the CRIN-CNRS & INRIA-Lorraine laboratory in Nancy, France.

References

1. R. Bellman. *Dynamic Programming.* Princeton University Press, 1957.
2. A. R. Cassandra, L. P. Kaelbling, and M. L. Littman. Acting optimally in partially observable stochastic domains. In *Proceedings of AAAI-94*, 1994.
3. M. L. Littman, 1996. Personal communication.
4. M. L. Littman, A. Cassandra, and L. P. Kaelbling. Learning policies for partially observable environments: Scaling up. In A. Prieditis and S. Russell, editors, *Proceedings of the Twelfth International Conference on Machine Learning*, pages 362–370, San Francisco, CA, 1995. Morgan Kaufmann.
5. W. S. Lovejoy. A survey of algorithmic methods for partially observed markov decision processes. *Annals of Operations Research*, 28:47–65, 1991.
6. G. E. Monahan. A survey of partially observable Markov decision processes: Theory, models, and algorithms. *Management Science*, 28(1):1–16, 1982.
7. N. J. Nilsson. *Principles of Artificial Intelligence.* Tioga Publishing Company, 1980.
8. R. Parr and S. Russell. Approximating optimal policies for partially observable stochastic domains. In *Proceedings of IJCAI-95*, 1995.
9. R. Simmons and S. Koenig. Probabilistic robot navigation in partially observable environments. In *Proceedings of IJCAI-95*, 1995.
10. R. Washington. Incremental Markov-model planning. In *Proceedings of TAI-96, Eighth IEEE International Conference on Tools With Artificial Intelligence*, 1996.
11. R. Washington. IDAO*: Incremental admissible AND-OR search. Draft paper, 1997.

Author Index

Springer
and the
environment

At Springer we firmly believe that an international science publisher has a special obligation to the environment, and our corporate policies consistently reflect this conviction.

We also expect our business partners – paper mills, printers, packaging manufacturers, etc. – to commit themselves to using materials and production processes that do not harm the environment. The paper in this book is made from low- or no-chlorine pulp and is acid free, in conformance with international standards for paper permanency.

Springer

Lecture Notes in Artificial Intelligence (LNAI)

Lecture Notes in Computer Science